LEARN EXCEL
FROM
MR EXCEL

277 Excel Mysteries Solved

Bill Jelen

Holy Macro! Books
13386 Judy Ave NW, Uniontown OH 44685

Learn Excel from Mr Excel

© 2005 by Bill Jelen

Printed in U.S.A.

First Printing: September 2005

Author: Bill Jelen

Editors: Linda DeLonais and Paragon Prepress Editorial Team

Production: Lisa Davis

Cover Design: Shannon Mattiza, 6Ft4 Productions

Cover Photo: Dallas Wallace, Paramount Photo

Interior Design: Paragon Prepress, Inc.

Published by: Holy Macro! Books, 13386 Judy Ave, Uniontown OH 44685

Distributed by Independent Publishers Group

ISBN 1-932802-12-6
Library of Congress Control Number: 2005929673

TABLE OF CONTENTS

ABOUT THE AUTHOR

In 1989, Bill Jelen took a job in a Finance department to maintain a very expensive reporting tool. When he discovered on day one that this new tool did not work, he began to learn how to use a $299 spreadsheet program in ways no sane person would ever think to use it. To the manager who hired him, he now wants to admit that all of the reports that allegedly came out of the $50K 4th GL reporting tool from 1989 through 1994 really were produced with Lotus 1-2-3 and, later, Excel.

Thinking he was the smartest spreadsheet guy he knew, Jelen launched MrExcel.com in 1998 and quickly learned that while he knew everything about taking 50,000 rows of mainframe data and turning them into a summary report, there were many people using Excel in many different ways. To all of the people who mailed in questions back in 1998 and 1999, Jelen thanks them for honing his spreadsheet skills. He now admits that he initially knew the answers to none of their questions, but secretly researched the answer before hitting Reply to their e-mails.

Today, MrExcel Consulting provides custom VBA solutions to hundreds of clients around the English speaking world. The MrExcel.com website continues to provide answers to 30,000 questions a year. In fact, with 135,000 answers archived, it is likely that the answer to nearly any Excel question has already been posted on the website's message board.

Jelen enjoys getting out to teach a Power Excel seminar. There are so many features in Excel, that Jelen has never taught a seminar without learning something new from someone in the audience who reveals some new technique or shortcut. Mostly, though, Jelen learns what is driving Excel users crazy. The questions in this book are the types of questions that Jelen hears over and over.

Jelen is the author of seven books on Excel and OneNote. You can see him regularly on TechTV Canada. In his spare time, you will find him promoting literacy causes as president of his local Rotary Club. He is the founder of the Fresh Writers Books program, encouraging high school students to pursue literary careers.

He lives outside of Akron, Ohio with his wife Mary Ellen, sons Josh and Zeke, and two dogs.

ACKNOWLEDGMENTS

This book was edited by a lot of people. Linda DeLonais provided the final technical editing. Along the way, Kat Chamberlin provided a great deal of feedback that ultimately led to this becoming a better book. During the spring of 2005, over 6,000 people took part in a free preview of the book and many readers sent in suggestions. Thanks to James Afflitto, Andres Alvear, Ron Binder, Alan Brady, Alan Brown, Phil Chamberlain, Richard Clapp, Dave Connors, Bryan Enos, Linda Foster, Margarita George, Odd Inge Halvorsen, Sue Hartman, G. Russell Hauf, Rich Herbert, Steve Hocking, Mike Howlett, David Komisar, Howard Krams, Ann Lasasso, Carl MacKinder, Al Marsella, Real Mayer, Wendy McCann, Henning Mikkelsen, Mark Miller, Mark Miller, E. Phillips, Dave Poling, Bill Robertson, Marty Ryerson, Ashokan Selliah, Don Smith, Bill Swearer, and Tim Wang for their suggestions. Suat Ozgur provided countless macros that helped me number or renumber or caption images. Freeda Roberts typed early sections of the book. Lisa Davis typed and proofed everything, including the illegible handwriting written on bumpy airplane flights. Shailander Malhotra and his team did a great job assembling the 277 topics into a meaningful book. Shannon Mattiza provided a great cover and publicity materials.

I always thank Dan Bricklin and Bob Frankston for inventing the spreadsheet in the first place. Without them, the computer industry would not be where it is today.

A good deal of this book was written on airplane flights from Cleveland to Toronto for appearances on TechTV. Thanks to the entire crew at Call For Help, including Leo LaPorte, Andy Walker, Amber MacArthur, Claudia Abate, Katya Diakow, Matt Harris, Steve Antal, Claudia Abate, Mike Lazazzera, Jenny Celly, Doug Robertson, Gregory Pilsworth, Basil Coward, Aaren Perrier, Lorraine Quirk, Hayden Mindell, Kelly Colasanti, and Malcolm Dunlop.

Tracy Syrstad managed MrExcel Consulting while I was writing this book. Wendy Kertesz handled publicity to make sure that you heard about the book. My sister Barb Jelen likely packed and shipped the book if you ordered it directly from MrExcel.com.

Thanks to Josh Jelen, Zeke Jelen, and Mary Ellen Jelen!

DEDICATION

Dedicated to every person who has ever asked
a question at one of my Excel seminars.

FOREWORD

I am a comic book superhero.

At least, I play one at work. As the mighty man of macro, I have the coolest job in town: playing MrExcel, the smartest guy in the world of spreadsheets.

Well, yes, that is a lot of hype. I am not really MrExcel. In fact, there are so many different ways to do the same thing in Excel that I am frequently shown up by one of my own students. Of course, I then appropriate that tip and use it as my own!

I have incorporated some of these discoveries in a pretty cool 45-minute seminar on Power Excel Tips. This is amazing stuff, like pivot tables, autofilters, and automatic subtotals. I love to be in front of a room full of accountants who use Excel 40+ hours a week and get oohs and ahhs within the first 90 seconds. I have to tell you, if you can make a room full of CPAs ooh and ahh, you know that you've got some good karma going. At that point, I know it will be a laugh-filled session and a great 45 minutes.

I also teach a much longer six-hour version of the Power Excel class at the University of Akron. This is a hands-on class where everyone gets to try each tip on his or her own computer.

One of these classes, which I was presenting at the Greater Akron Chamber, provided the Genesis moment for this book. One of the questions from the audience was about something fairly basic. As I went through the explanation, the room was silent as everyone sat in rapt attention. People were interested in this basic tip because it was something that affected their lives every day. It didn't involve anything cool. It was just basic Excel stuff. But, it was basic Excel stuff that a room full of pretty bright people had never figured out.

Think about how most of us learned Excel. We started a new job where they wanted us to use Excel. They showed us the basics of moving around a spreadsheet and sent us on our way. We were lucky to get five minutes of training on the world's most complex piece of software!

Here is the surprising part of this deal. With only five minutes of training, you CAN use Excel 40 hours a week and be productive. Isn't that cool? A tiny bit of training and you can do 80 percent of what you need to do in Excel.

The problem, though, is that there are lots of cool things you never learned about. Microsoft and Lotus were locked in a bitter battle for market share in the mid-90s. In an effort to slay one another, each succeeding version of Excel or Lotus 1-2-3 offered INCREDIBLY powerful new features. This stuff is still lurking in there, but you would never know to even look for it. My experience tells me that the average Excel user is still doing things the slow way. If you learn a just couple of these new tips, you could save two hours per week.

So, here is the plan. I have set out to write a book that talks about 277 of the most common and irritating problems in Excel. You will find each of these 277 items (which you have been stumbling over ever since your "five minutes of training") followed by the solution or solutions you need to solve that problem. A lot of these topics stem from the questions that were sent my way in seminars I've taught. They may not be the coolest tips in the whole world, but if you master even half of these concepts, you will be smarter than 95 percent of the Excel users in the world and will certainly save yourself several hours per week.

In each chapter, a problem and its solution will be discussed. There are plenty of books that go through all of Excel's menus in a serial fashion. The trouble with those books is that you have NO CLUE what to look up when you are having a problem. The last time I checked, no one at my dinner table ever used the word "CONCATENATION", so why would anyone ever think of looking up that word when they want to join a first name in column A with the last name in column B?

I expect this book will be a quick read. You can probably skim all 277 topics in a couple of hours to get a basic idea of what is in here. When you face a similar situation, find the case study, apply it to your own problem, and you should be all set.

This book takes a different approach than others I have tried to use. I am MrExcel, but I am hopelessly clueless with PhotoShop. Wow! This is an intimidating program. I own a ton of books on PhotoShop. There must be a bazillion toolbars in there. Most books that I pick up tell me to press the XYZ button on the ABC toolbar. I can't even begin to figure out where that toolbar is. I hate those books. So, my philosophy here is to explain the heck out of things. If you ever find yourself on a case study where I tell you to do something without explaining how to do it, please send me an e-mail to yell at me for not being clear.

Conventions Used in the Book

Each chapter will start with a problem and then a strategy for solving the problem. Various chapters may offer additional details, alternate strategies, results, gotchas, and other elements as is appropriate to the topic. Each chapter wraps up with a summary and a list of any Excel commands or functions used in the chapter.

I hate books where the text refers to a figure that is on the next two page spread. In the interest of readability, I've chosen to allow white space at the bottom of the right-hand page if it will allow the text and figure to remain together. This is a conscious decision. I'm not trying to pad the page count or increase the cost of paper in the book. I believe this layout will maximize the ease of use of the book.

PART 1

THE EXCEL ENVIRONMENT

SHOW FULL MENUS ALL THE TIME

Problem: You are trying to learn Excel. Microsoft only shows you the most common menu choices under each menu.

Fig. 1 shows a menu from one computer on my desk.

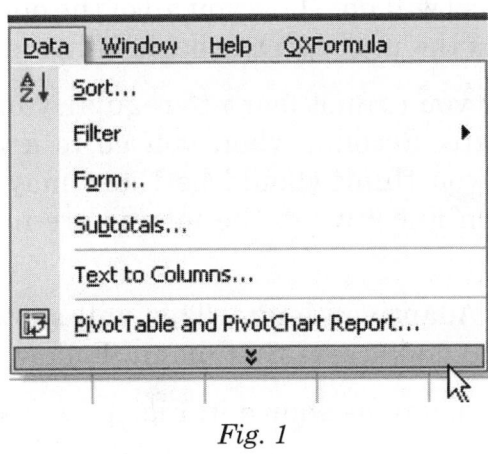

Fig. 1

Fig. 2 is a screenshot from another computer on my desk.

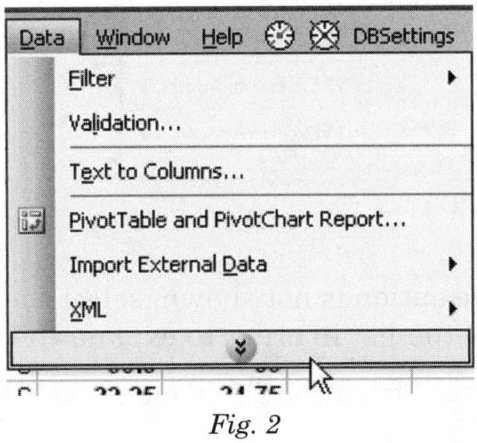

Fig. 2

A screenshot of the data menu of the third computer on my desk is seen here in Fig. 3.

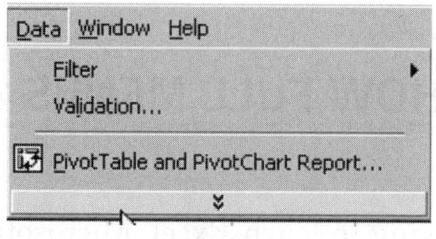

Fig. 3

This is maddening. How can you learn that there is a Sort option under the Data menu if Excel will not show you all of the options? Furthermore, Microsoft customizes the menu on the basis of items you use regularly.

First, this is insane; you cannot learn to regularly use something if you don't know it is there. Second, when you go to a new computer, one of the options that you think should be there may not show up. It is very difficult to learn Excel when the menus are not consistent across computers.

Strategy: Turn off Adaptive Menus. This will show you the complete menu every time that you access that menu. Follow these steps:

1)   Go to the Tools menu, as shown in Fig. 4.

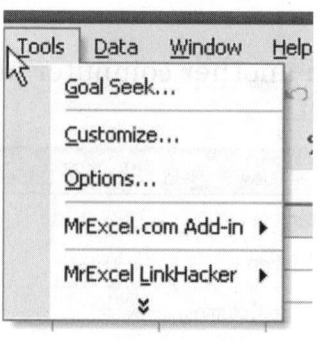

Fig. 4

2)   If the Customize option is not shown, select the double-down arrow at the bottom of the list in order to expand the menu.

3)   Select Customize... from the Tools menu, as shown in Fig. 5.

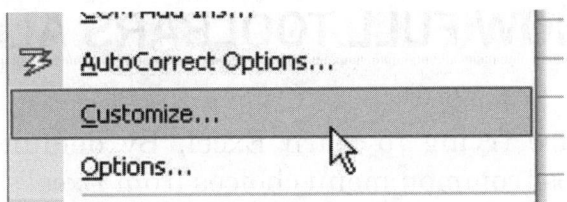

Fig. 5

4) As you will see in Fig. 6, there are three tabs across the top of the Customize dialog. Choose the Options tab and then choose the box for Always Show Full Menus.

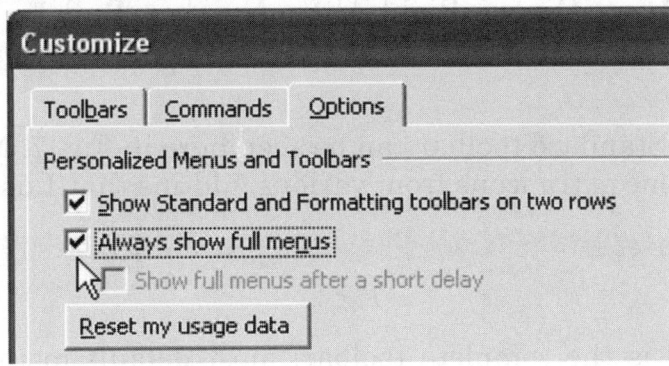

Fig. 6

Additional Details: If you are in the process of learning Excel, it also helps to choose the Show Standard and Formatting Toolbars on Two Rows option. This will enable you to see all of the icons on the important Standard and Formatting toolbars. In Excel 2000, this setting appears as Standard and Formatting Toolbars Share One Row. In that version, you will want to uncheck the option.

Gotcha: Changing this setting in Excel will also affect Word and other Office products. There is no way to have Excel show full menus while Word shows the abbreviated menus.

Summary: While learning Excel, use the Tools – Customize feature to show the complete list of commands on each menu.

Commands Discussed: Tools – Customize

Part
I

SHOW FULL TOOLBARS ALL THE TIME

Problem: You are trying to learn Excel. By default, Microsoft only shows you the most common menu choices from Excel's two most important toolbars: Standard and Formatting.

The Standard toolbar has icons for a New Workbook, Saving, Printing, Print Preview, Spell Check, Cut, Copy, Paste, Undo, and Redo. These are all fairly important items.

The Formatting toolbar has icons for Font, Font Size, Bold, Italic, Underline, Left Align, Center, Right Align, Number, Bullets, Indent, Outdent, Borders, Cell Color, and Font Color. These are also all fairly important items.

The complete Standard toolbar can be seen here in Fig. 7. Note that my toolbar has some extra icons from various add-ins that I use.

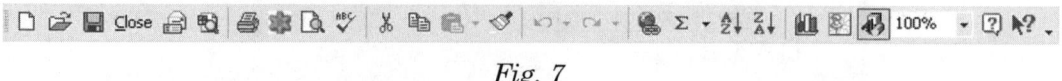

Fig. 7

Although this is the complete toolbar, most default installations will only show a subset of the icons on the toolbar. An example of the abbreviated toolbar follows in Fig. 8.

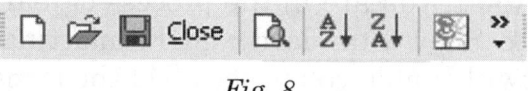

Fig. 8

In order to use any of the other icons on the Standard toolbar, you have to choose the double-right arrow on the toolbar, as shown in Fig. 9.

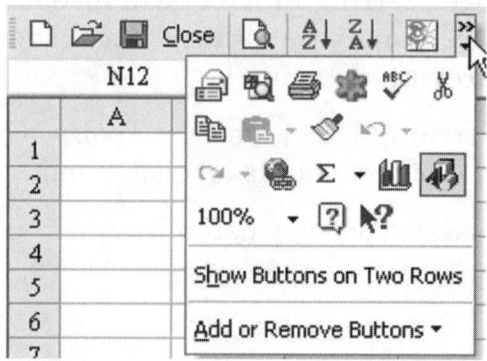

Fig. 9

The complete Formatting toolbar follows in Fig. 10.

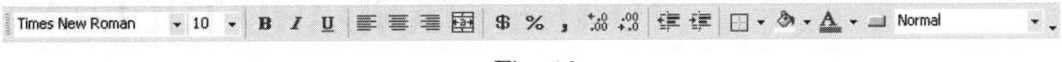

Fig. 10

Most users with a default installation will only see a portion of these icons and will have to use the double-right arrow on the toolbar to see all of the icons.

Microsoft does this in order to show you more rows of data in the spreadsheet. This may have been a problem in the days of VGA monitors. However, with today's high screen resolutions, you can afford to have the toolbars displayed on two rows and to see all of the available options at a glance.

Strategy: Display the toolbars on two rows. From the Tools menu, select Customize. On the Options tab, select the option for Show Standard and Formatting toolbars on two rows, as shown in Fig. 11.

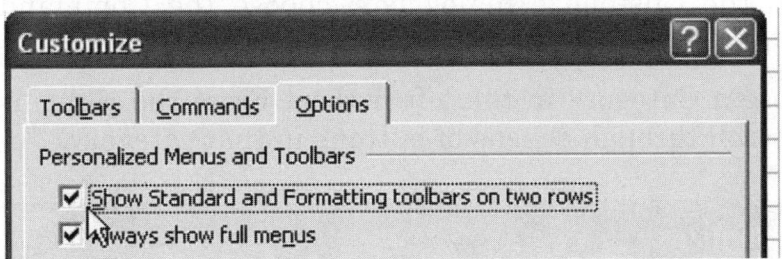

Fig. 11

Gotcha: In Excel 2000 and earlier, this option was called Display Standard and Formatting Toolbars on One Row.

Summary: While learning Excel, use the Tools – Customize feature to show the complete version of Standard and Formatting toolbars.

Commands Discussed: Tools – Customize

ADD A CLOSE BUTTON
TO THE STANDARD TOOLBAR

Problem: Your efficiency with Excel would increase if you had a one-click option for closing workbooks.

Strategy: Customize the Standard toolbar to include a Close option near the Save option. Follow these steps.

1) From the menu, select View – Toolbars – Customize. The Customize option is the final choice in the list of toolbars. This will display the Customize dialog box.

   While the Customize box is displayed, the toolbars are in a special state. You can take any toolbar button and drag it to a new location, to a new toolbar, or even drag it off the toolbar to delete it. Also, there are hundreds of new icons that you can add to your toolbars.

2) From the Customize dialog box, choose the Commands tab, as shown in Fig. 12.

3) Choose a Category in the left listbox. From the right listbox, you can scroll through dozens of buttons in that category.

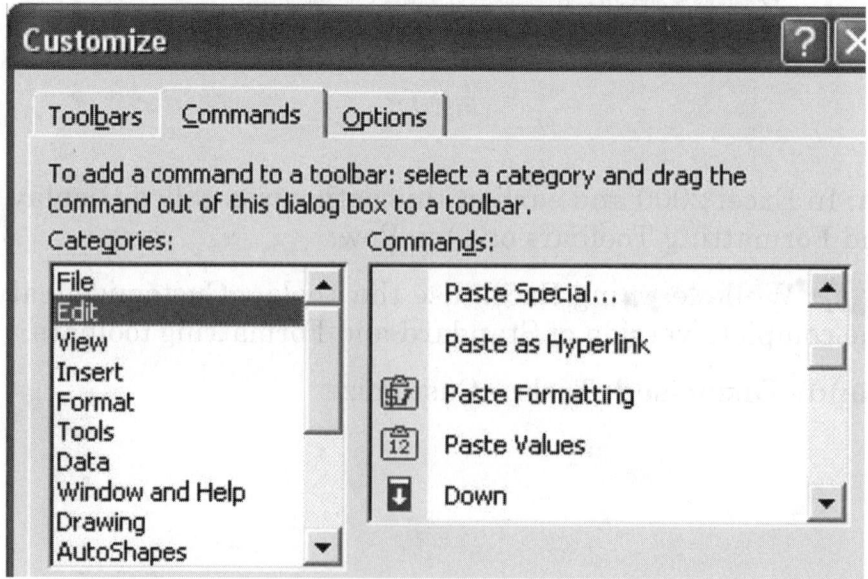

Fig. 12

4) The Close button is located in the File category. Choose File from the left listbox, as shown in Fig. 13.

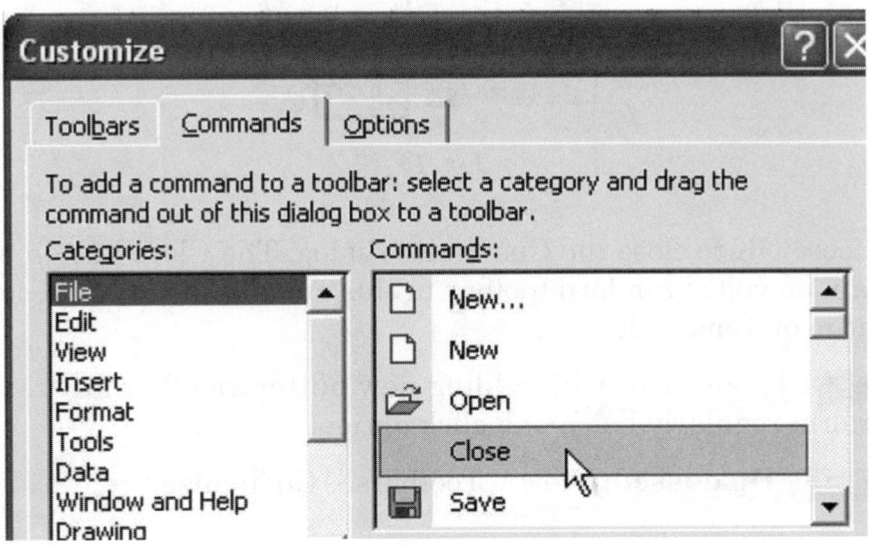

Fig. 13

5) Click on Close in the right listbox. Drag the item towards a toolbar. When you are on the toolbar, choose the desired location. Excel will display an I-Beam at the location where the button will be added, as shown in Fig. 14.

Fig. 14

6)   When the I-Beam is in the proper location, release the mouse button. The button is added to the toolbar, as shown in Fig. 15.

Fig. 15

7)   Choose OK to close the Customize dialog. The Close button will remain on your Standard toolbar in this and all future Excel sessions until you remove it.

Summary: Experiment with adding new buttons so that any task that you perform regularly has a one-click option.

Commands Discussed: View – Toolbars – Customize

CLOSE ALL OPEN WORKBOOKS

Problem: You have 22 Excel workbooks open. You want to keep Excel open but close all of the workbooks. Doing File – Close 22 times can get monotonous.

Strategy: Hold down the Shift key on the keyboard before selecting the File menu. This will allow you to see an alternate File menu with Close All in place of Close, as shown in Fig. 16.

Summary: Hold down the Shift key to access the timesaving Close All command.

Commands Discussed: File – Close All

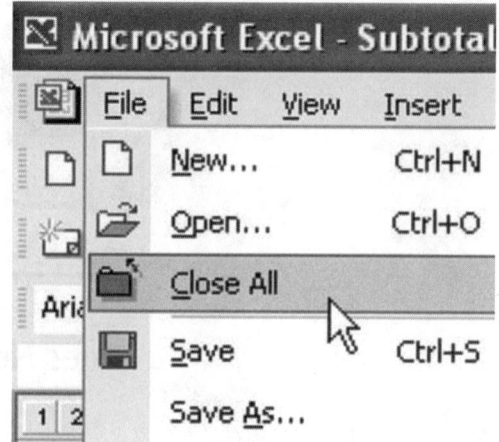

Fig. 16

DOUBLE THE VALUE
OF THE RECENTLY USED FILE LIST

Problem: You routinely open the same six workbooks. The File menu shows only the last four workbooks that you opened or saved. It sure would be nice if it showed at least the last six workbooks.

Strategy: Good news! You can increase the Recently Used File List (located at the bottom of the File menu) from four to nine workbooks. Go to Tools – Options – General. Use the spin button to dial the Recently Used File List from 4 to 9, as shown in Fig. 17.

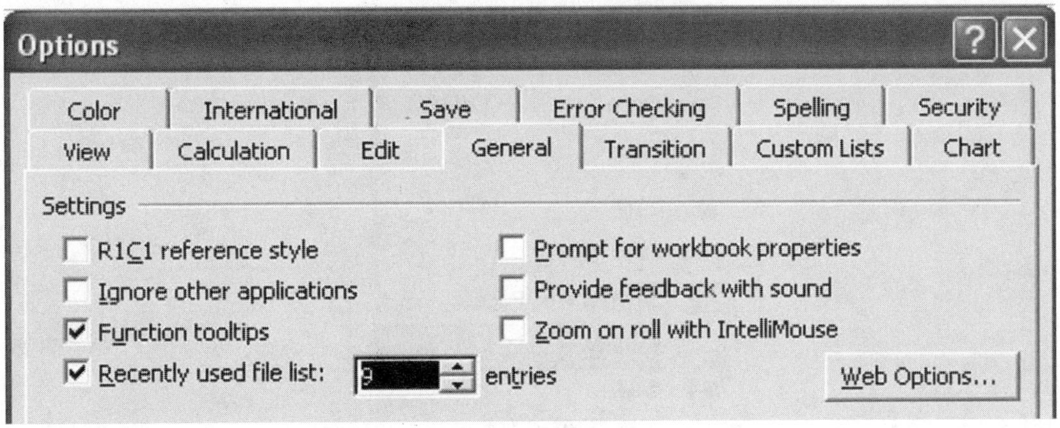

Part I

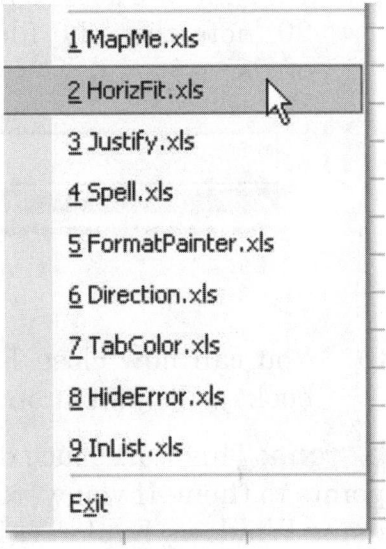

Fig. 17

Gotcha: Immediately after changing the value, your list may only show four files. You have to open and close additional files to expand the list, as shown in Fig. 18.

Summary: To have the File menu show more than the last four workbooks used, use Tools – Options – General and select the number of recently used files for it to show.

Commands Discussed: Tools – Options – General – Recently Used File List

Fig. 18

REMEMBER WORKBOOKS TO OPEN USING A WORKSPACE

Problem: You need to open seven files in order to prepare a weekly report. It is tedious to open all seven workbooks.

Strategy: Open the seven workbook files and save them as a workspace. Follow these steps.

1) Open the workbooks and then select File – Save Workspace, as shown in Fig. 19.

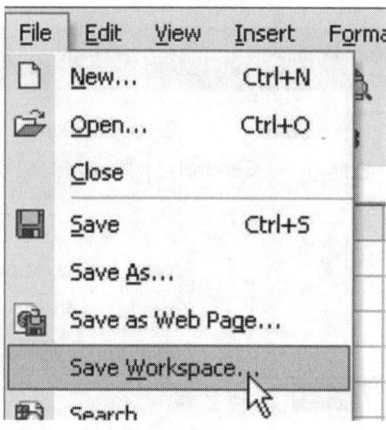

Fig. 19

2) Give the workspace file a name, such as MyFiles. As shown in Fig. 20, note that the file saved will have an .xlw extension instead of .xls.

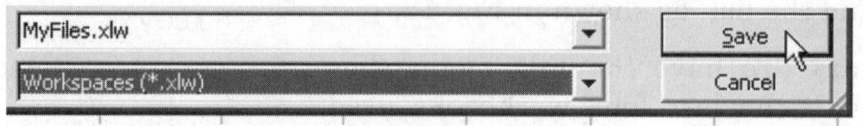

Fig. 20

3) You can now close Excel and open MyFiles.xlw. All seven workbooks will open at once.

Gotcha: This workspace does not actually store the seven files, but only points to them. If you were to move one of the seven files to a new folder using Windows Explorer, Excel would not be able to open that file.

Gotcha: Excel does not remember the arrangement of the workbooks in the workspace. Although your original workbooks may have been maximized, Excel might open them in a tiled arrangement. Choose the Maximize icon at the top of one workbook to return all workbooks to their original maximized state. This problem was worse in Excel 97, where Excel would frequently forget the zoom and frozen panes in the workspace.

Summary: To reduce the time in opening more than one workbook, use File – Save Workspace when opening workbooks, and then name the workspace.

Commands Discussed: File – Save Workspace

AUTOMATICALLY MOVE THE CELL POINTER IN A DIRECTION AFTER ENTERING A NUMBER

Problem: If you type a number and then press a direction arrow key, Excel will enter the number and move the cell pointer in the direction of the arrow key. However, if you are using the numeric keypad, it is much more convenient to use the Enter key on the numeric keypad rather than the arrow keys. By default, Excel will move the cell pointer down one cell when you type Enter. When entering data in a worksheet such as the one shown in Fig. 21, is there a way to have Excel automatically move the cell pointer to the next cell to the right after each entry?

	A	B	C	D	E	F	G	H
1	Region	Jan	Feb	Mar	Apr	May	Jun	Jul
2	City of London	432	754	136	302	91	194	89
3	Barking and Dagenham	95	238	183	713	601	772	559
4	Barnet	590	643	564	87	325	295	413
5	Bexley	454	657	455	354	542		
6	Brent							
7	Bromley							
8	Camden							
9	Croydon							
10	Ealing							
11	Enfield							

Fig. 21

Strategy: Go to Tools – Options. On the Edit tab, go to the Move Selection after Enter Direction dropdown. Choose Right, as shown in Fig. 22.

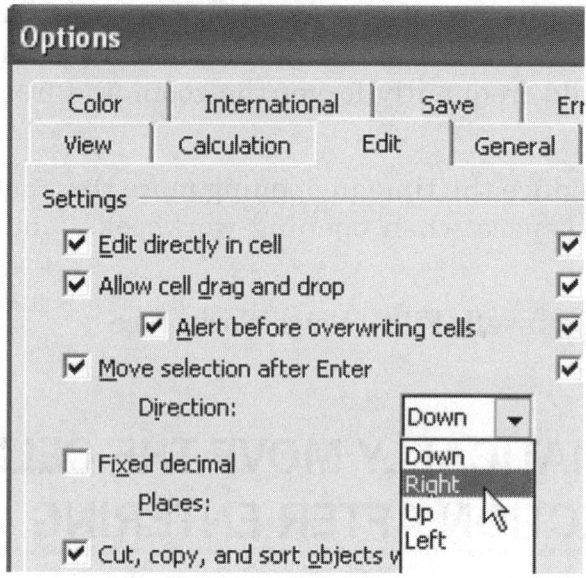

Fig. 22

Result: The cursor will automatically move one cell to the right every time you press the Enter key.

Summary: You can have the cell pointer move in any direction after using Enter by changing this setting on the Edit tab of the Options menu.

Commands Discussed: Tools – Options – Edit

HOW TO SEE HEADINGS AS YOU SCROLL AROUND A REPORT

Problem: You have a spreadsheet with headings at the top, as shown in Fig. 23. You want to be able to scroll through the data and always see the headings.

	A	B	C	D	E
1	Sales Report - 2006				
2					
3	Rep	Customer	Product	Sales	Revenue
4	Joe	RST Company	GHI	624	55536
5	Mary	EFG Pty Ltd	GHI	605	53845
6	Dan	TUV Company	DEF	733	65237
7	Dan	CDE GMbH	XYZ	634	56426
8	Bob	BCD Corporation	ABC	795	70755
9	Dan	CDE Pty Ltd	ABC	447	39783
10	Mary	NOP, LLC	ABC	627	55803
11	Bob	RST, Inc.	GHI	740	65860
12	Joe	LMN, Inc.	DEF	787	70043
13	Joe	JKL, Inc.	XYZ	626	55714
14	Dan	HIJ Company	GHI	587	52243
15	Bob	DEF & Sons	DEF	764	67996
16					

Fig. 23

Strategy: Use the Freeze Panes command on the Window menu. It is not obvious, but in order to make the Freeze Panes command work, you must place the cell pointer in the correct location before using the command.

Look at the spreadsheet shown in Fig. 23. It would be really handy to have rows 1 through 3 always visible while you scroll. Here's how to do that.

1) Place the cell pointer in cell A4, as shown in Fig. 24, before you select the Freeze Panes command. The Freeze Panes command will freeze all visible rows above the cell pointer and all visible columns to the left of the cell pointer. By placing the cell pointer in column A, you will not freeze any columns, only the rows.

	A	B	C	D	E
1	Sales Report - 2006				
2					
3	Rep	Customer	Product	Sales	Revenue
4	Joe	RST Company	GHI	624	55536
5	Mary	EFG Pty Ltd	GHI	605	53845
6	Dan	TUV Company	DEF	733	65237
7					

Fig. 24

2) With the cell pointer in cell A4, select Window – Freeze Panes. A solid horizontal line will be drawn between rows 3 and 4. As you scroll down past row 30, you will always be able to see the heading rows, as shown in Fig. 25.

	A	B	C	D	E
1	Sales Report - 2006				
2					
3	Rep	Customer	Product	Sales	Revenue
32	Dan	GHI GMbH	ABC	613	54557
33	Bob	UVW, Inc.	ABC	514	45746
34	Bob	JKL, Inc.	XYZ	691	61499

Fig. 25

Additional Details: To turn off this feature, go to the Window menu and select Unfreeze Panes. This menu item is only visible after you have frozen the panes.

If you want to maximize the number of rows visible, it is possible to freeze only row 3.

1) First, unfreeze the panes using Window – Unfreeze Panes. Place the cell pointer in the last visible row in the window. Hit the Down Arrow twice to force rows 1 and 2 to scroll above the window. Row 3 is now the first visible row, as shown in Fig. 26.

	A	B	C	D	E	
3	Rep	Customer	Product	Sales	Revenue	
4	Joe	RST Company	GHI	624	55536	
5	Mary	EFG Pty Ltd	GHI	605	53845	
6	Dan	TUV Company	DEF	733	65237	

Fig. 26

2) Place the cell pointer in cell A4 and invoke the Window – Freeze Panes command. You will now be able to scroll with only row 3 frozen at the top of the window, as shown in Fig. 27.

	A	B	C	D	E
3	Rep	Customer	Product	Sales	Revenue
64	Bob	VWX Pty Ltd	XYZ	645	57405
65	Mary	GHI GMbH	ABC	481	42809
66	Dan	RST Company	GHI	477	42453

Fig. 27

Summary: Use the Window – Freeze Panes command to keep certain rows visible at the top of the window as you scroll through the data.

Commands Discussed: Window – Freeze Panes; Window – Unfreeze Panes

Cross Reference: How to Print Titles at the Top of Each Page;

HOW TO SEE HEADINGS AND ROW LABELS AS YOU SCROLL AROUND A REPORT

Part
I

Problem: As shown in Fig. 28, you have a wide spreadsheet. There are headings at the top of the spreadsheet and there are several columns of labels at the left side of the spreadsheet. You also have monthly sales figures that extend far to the right. You need to be able to scroll through the sales figures while always seeing both the headings at the top and the labels at the left of the spreadsheet.

	A	B	C	D	E	F	G	H	I	J	K	L
1	OurCo LLC											
2	Sales Report by Month, Customer and Region											
3	12 Months Ending 12/31/2006											
4												
5	Country	Region	District	Sales Rep	Customer	Product	Jan	Feb	Mar	Q1	Apr	Ma
6	USA	West	No. California	Joe	RST Company	GHI	37	44	26	107	87	2
7	Australia	Australia	Australia	Mary	EFG Pty Ltd	GHI	40	92	72	204	33	2
8	USA	Central	Chicago	Dan	TUV Company	DEF	86	55	74	215	83	8
9	Germany	Germany	Germany	Dan	CDE GMbH	XYZ	73	20	5	98	58	5
10	USA	Central	Minneapolis	Bob	BCD Corporation	ABC	65	81	93	239	50	5
11	Australia	Australia	Australia	Dan	CDE Pty Ltd	ABC	55	26	23	104	1	
12	USA	East	MidAtlantic	Mary	NOP, LLC	ABC	86	87	33	206	74	2
13	USA	Central	Cleveland	Bob	RST, Inc.	GHI	98	10	90	198	33	5
14	USA	Central	Cleveland	Joe	LMN, Inc.	DEF	61	99	67	227	47	3
15	USA	East	New England	Joe	JKL, Inc.	XYZ	36	96	94	226	83	8
16	USA	Central	Chicago	Dan	HIJ Company	GHI	83	86	34	203	50	3
17	USA	East	Southeast	Bob	DEF & Sons	DEF	68	12	61	141	70	8
18	USA	Central	Cleveland	Bob	LMN, Inc.	ABC	18	90	52	160	59	5

Fig. 28

Strategy: Use the Freeze Panes command on the Window menu. Remember, to make the Freeze Panes command work, you must place the cell pointer in the correct location before using the command.

In the spreadsheet shown in Fig. 28, you might want row 5 and columns A through F visible at all times. You would then be able to scroll through the monthly figures, while always being able to see the customer information in the left columns and the month name information in row 5.

1) First, you want to scroll the worksheet so that cell A5 is in the upper left visible corner. You could try to do this with the scrollbars or the arrows, but this method will always work:

- Scroll A5 out of view by hitting PgDn a few times and the Tab key a few times.

- Hit the F5 key to bring up the Go To dialog.

- Enter A5 in the Reference box and hit Enter. Cell A5 will now be the first visible cell in the window.

2) Place the cell pointer in cell G6. Select Window – Freeze Panes. You will see a solid line between columns F and G and between rows 5 and 6.

Result: As shown in Fig. 29, you can scroll through any numeric data while being able to look at the row and column headings.

	A	B	C	D	E	F	S	T	U
5	Country	Region	District	Sales Rep	Customer	Product	Oct	Nov	Dec
97	USA	East	MidAtlantic	Mary	NOP, LLC	ABC	99	79	62
98	USA	East	New England	Dan	MNO Company	DEF	61	62	32
99	USA	Central	Chicago	Dan	IJK Company	DEF	82	2	47
100	England	England	England	Dan	UVW Ltd	ABC	81	16	20
101	USA	West	So. California	Bob	EFG, Inc.	ABC	7	43	62

Fig. 29

Gotcha: In Fig. 29, rows 1 through 4 cannot be accessed. You will have to unfreeze the panes to change those rows.

Gotcha: If you have many columns frozen at the left of the report and then make those columns wider, it is possible that the entire window will be filled with the frozen columns. You then have a situation where the arrow keys will move the cell pointer to other cells that you cannot see. The Address Bar and the Formula Bar will show you the active cell, but you cannot see it. You need to either make the frozen columns less wide, or use the Window – Unfreeze Panes command to unfreeze the panes.

Summary: Use the Window – Freeze Panes command to keep certain rows and columns visible at the top of the window as you scroll through the data. It is critical that you place the cell pointer in the first cell that is not to be frozen before invoking the command.

Commands Discussed: Window – Freeze Panes; Edit – Go To

Cross Reference: How to See Headings as You Scroll Around a Report

Part
I

HOW TO PRINT TITLES
AT THE TOP OF EACH PAGE

Problem: The report shown in Fig. 30 has 90 rows of data. You want to have the title rows print at the top of each printed page.

	A	B	C	D	E
1	XYZ Corporation				
2	Sales by Rep & Day				
3	January 2006				
4					
5	Sales Rep	Date	Quota	Sales	Over Quota
6	Joe	1/2/2006	800	666	0
7	Dan	1/2/2006	800	1290	490
8	Mary	1/2/2006	800	896	96
9	Joe	1/3/2006	800	559	0
10	Dan	1/3/2006	800	192	0
11	Mary	1/3/2006	800	703	0
12	Joe	1/4/2006	800	1131	331
13	Dan	1/4/2006	800	199	0
14	Mary	1/4/2006	800	320	0
15	Joe	1/5/2006	800	550	0
16	Dan	1/5/2006	800	552	0
17	Mary	1/5/2006	800	770	0
18	Joe	1/6/2006	800	615	0
19	Dan	1/6/2006	800	220	0

Fig. 30

Strategy: Printing options are controlled on the fourth tab of the Page Setup dialog box. In this case, you want rows 1 through 5 to print at the top of each page.

1) Select Page Setup from the File menu. The dialog box offers four tabs. Select the fourth tab, called Sheet. See Fig. 31.

2) Enter 1:5 in the box called Rows to Repeat at Top, as shown in Fig. 31, in order to have rows 1 through 5 repeated at the top of each printed page. Select Print Preview to ensure that the results are what you desire.

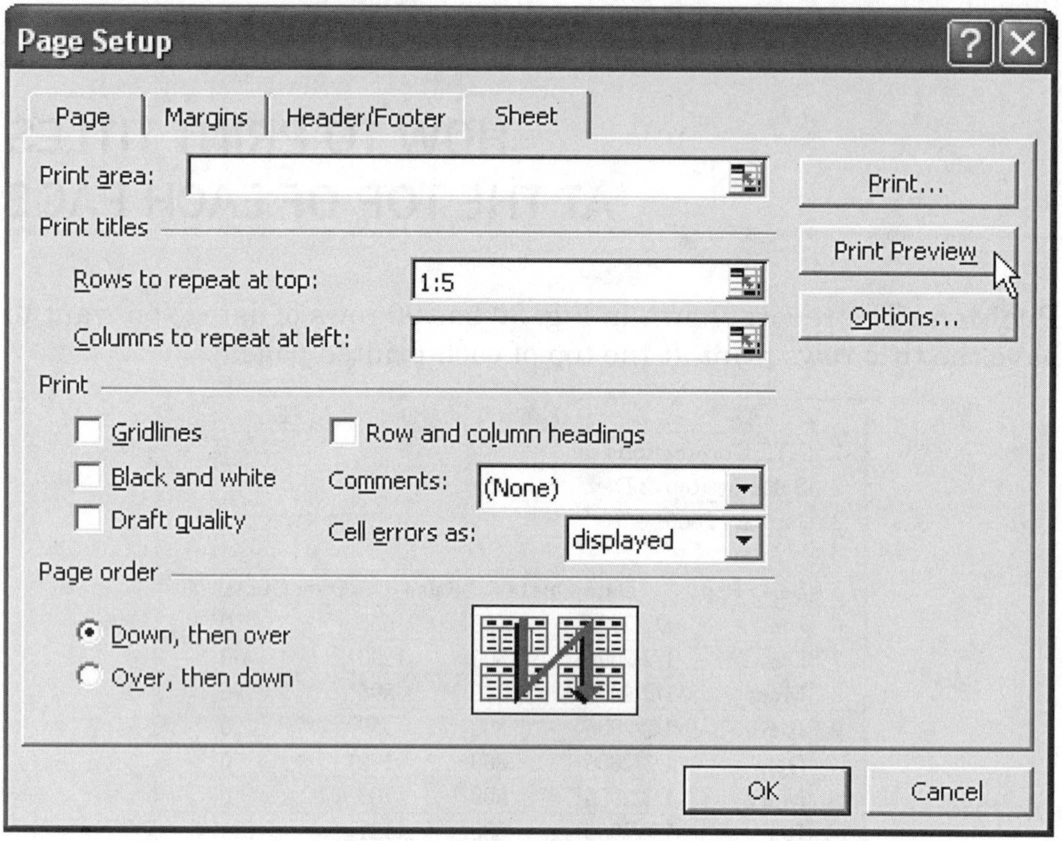

Fig. 31

Alternate Solution: Rather than typing 1:5 in the text box, you could click the reference icon on the right side of the box, as shown in Fig. 32.

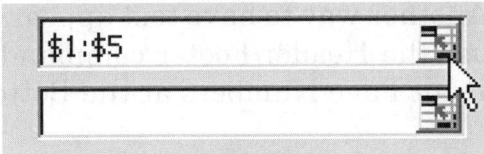

Fig. 32

This will shrink the Page Setup dialog box to just the Rows to Repeat at Top dialog. You can now use the mouse to select rows 1 through 5. Choose the icon at the right side of the text box to return to the Page Setup dialog box, as shown in Fig. 33.

Part I

	A	B	C	D	E	F	G	H
1	XYZ Corporation							
2	Sales by Rep & Day							
3	January 2006							
4								
5	Sales Rep	Date	Quota	Sales	Over Quota			

Page Setup - Rows to repeat at top: ? ✕

$1:$5

| 9 | Joe | 1/3/2006 | 800 | 559 | 0 | | | |
| 10 | Dan | 1/3/2006 | 800 | 192 | 0 | | | |

Fig. 33

Alternate Solution: If the rows you desire to repeat at the top are visible behind the dialog box, as shown in Fig. 34, use the mouse to highlight them while the cursor is in the Rows to repeat at top textbox.

	A	B	C	D	E
→	XYZ Corporatio	**Page Setup**			
2	Sales by Rep &				
3	January 2006	Page	Margins	Header/Footer	
4					
5	Sales Rep	Print area:			
6	Joe	1/2/	Print titles		
7	Dan	1/2/			
8	Mary	1/2/	Rows to repeat at top:		

Fig. 34

Summary: Use the Page Setup command on the File menu to have titles and headings appear at the top of every page.

Cross Reference: Another way to have text appear at the top or bottom of every page is to use the Header/Footer command on the Page Setup dialog. See How to Print Page Numbers at the Bottom of Each Page on Page 19.

Commands Discussed: File – Page Setup

PRINT A LETTER AT THE TOP OF PAGE 1 AND REPEAT HEADINGS AT THE TOP OF EACH SUBSEQUENT PAGE

Problem: As shown in Fig. 35, you are sending out a worksheet that contains instructions, followed by a lengthy report. You would like the headings to appear at the top of each page after the first page. You don't want the headings to appear at the top of the letter on page one.

	A	B	C	D	E	F	G	H	I	J	K	L	M	N	O
1	Welcome to the 2006-2007 Budget Process														
2															
3	Dear Manager,														
4															
5	This Excel workbook contains all of the worksheets that you need to complete in order														
6	to produce your forecast for our next fiscal year. The data below shows your actual sales														
7	by SKU for your region. You should build a sales forecast for the next year and then														
8	break the data out by month.														
9															
10	Your forecast should be sent to your regional VP for review no later than noon on														
11	March 12. Thank you for your attention to the forecast process.														
12															
13				Sincerely,											
14															
15				Joe Smith											
16				Director of Operations Analysis											
17				(330) 555-1212											
18															
19	SKU	Prior Sales	Planned Sales	Apr	May	Jun	Jul	Aug	Sep	Oct	Nov	Dec	Jan	Feb	Mar
20	S-001	562													
21	S-002	142													
22	S-003	451													
23	S-004	534													

Fig. 35

Strategy: Printing options are controlled on the fourth tab of the Page Setup dialog box. If you specify that a row in the middle of the print range should be repeated at the top of the pages, it will not begin repeating until the next page.

1) Select Page Setup from the File menu. The dialog box offers four tabs. Select the fourth tab, called Sheet. See Fig. 36.

2) Enter 19:19 in the box called Rows to Repeat at Top, as shown in Fig. 36, to have row 19 print at the top of each page after page 1.

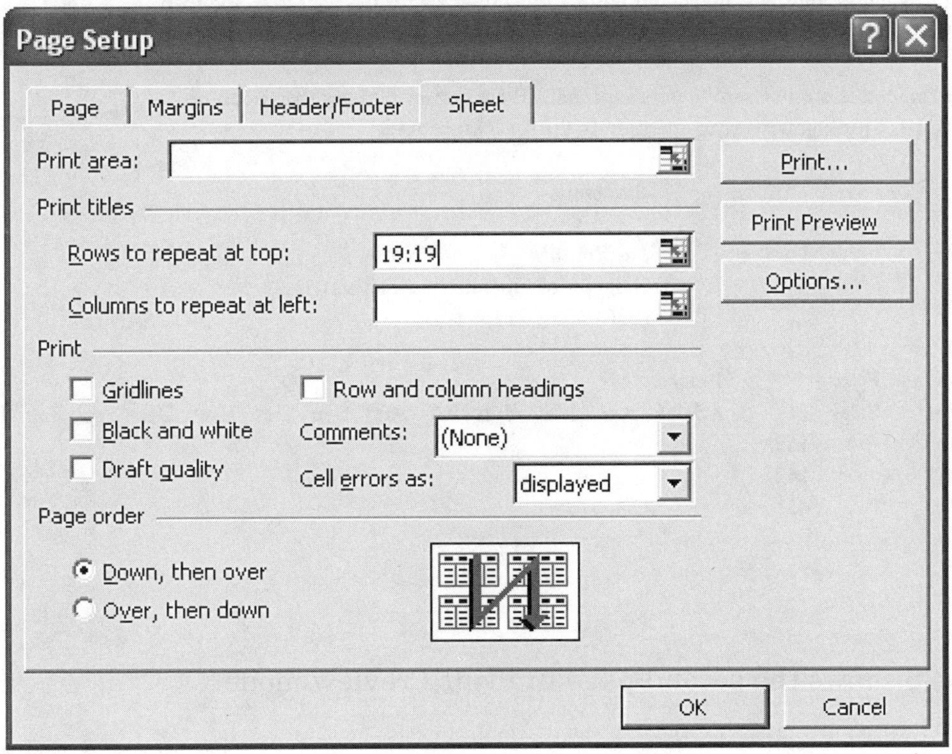

Part I

Fig. 36

Result: The headings do not print at the top of page 1, but at the top of pages 2 and beyond. Fig. 37 shows the first page in Print Preview mode.

Welcome to the 2006-2007 Budget Process

Dear Manager,

This Excel workbook contains all of the worksheets that you need to complete in order to produce your forecast for our next fiscal year. The data below shows your actual sales by SKU for your region. You should build a sales forecast for the next year and then break the data out by month.

Your forecast should be sent to your regional VP for review no later than noon on March 12. Thank you for your attention to the forecast process.

Sincerely,

Joe Smith
Director of Operations Analysis
(330) 555-1212

SKU	Prior Sales	Planned Sales	Apr	May	Jun	Jul	Aug	Sep	Oct	Nov	Dec	Jan	Feb	Mar
S-001	562													
S-002	142													
S-003	451													

Fig. 37

Fig. 38 shows the second page in Print Preview mode:

SKU	Prior Sales	Planned Sales	Apr	May	Jun	Jul	Aug	Sep	Oct	Nov	Dec	Jan	Feb	Mar
S-031	797													
S-032	465													
S-033	782													
S-034	667													
S-035	624													
S-036	503													

Fig. 38

Summary: The Rows to Repeat at Top figure does not have to be at the top of the print range. If your selection is in the middle of the print range, the headings will only print on subsequent pages.

Commands Discussed: File – Page Setup

HOW TO PRINT PAGE NUMBERS
AT THE BOTTOM OF EACH PAGE

Part
I

Problem: You are printing a lengthy report. You want the pages to be numbered.

Strategy: The Header and Footer options are controlled on the third tab of the Page Setup dialog box. There are a variety of formats that can be specified on this tab.

1) Select Page Setup from the File menu. The dialog box offers four tabs.

2) Select the third tab, called Header/Footer. There are a number of standard options in the Footer dropdown, as shown in Fig. 39.

3) Select the options called Page 1 of ?. This option will print a footer, such as Page 1 of 2, at the bottom center of each page.

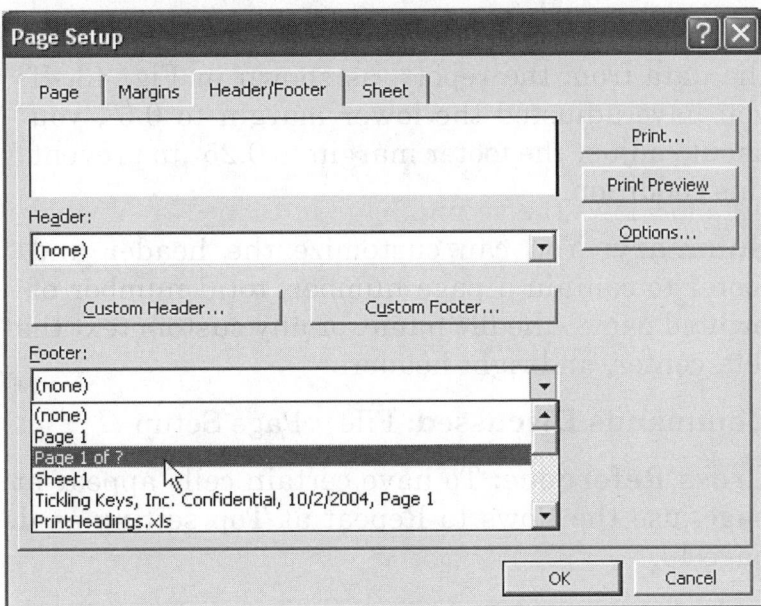

Fig. 39

Alternate Solution: It is possible to design a custom footer by selecting the Custom Footer... button. In a custom footer, you can build a footer for the left, center, and right sides of the page.

1) Select the Custom Footer... button.

2) Tab to the right section: Text box.

3) Type the word "Page" followed by a space.

4) Click the Page # icon (Fig. 40).

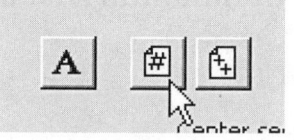

Fig. 40

5) Type a space, followed by the word "of", followed by another space.

6) Click the Total Pages icon (Fig. 41).

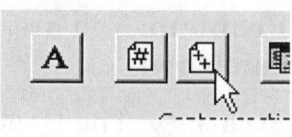

Fig. 41

Result: The custom footer text appears on the right side of the page, as shown in Fig. 42.

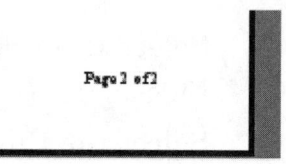

Additional Information: There are also left, center, and right headers that can be customized like the footers.

Fig. 42

Gotcha: Sometimes the footer text will crash into the data from the report, as shown in Fig. 43. If you have adjusted the lower margin to 0.5", you should adjust the footer margin to 0.25" to prevent this condition.

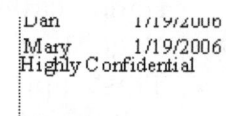

Fig. 43

Summary: You can customize the header and footer to contain a page number, total number of printed pages, the file name, or any custom text that you like. There are left, center, and right headers.

Commands Discussed: File – Page Setup

Cross Reference: To have certain cells appear at the top left of each page, use the Rows to Repeat at Top setting as described starting on page 14.

HOW TO MAKE A WIDE REPORT FIT TO ONE PAGE WIDE BY MANY PAGES TALL

Problem: After creating a wide report, it is printing four pages wide, as shown in Fig. 44. You want to make it fit one page wide.

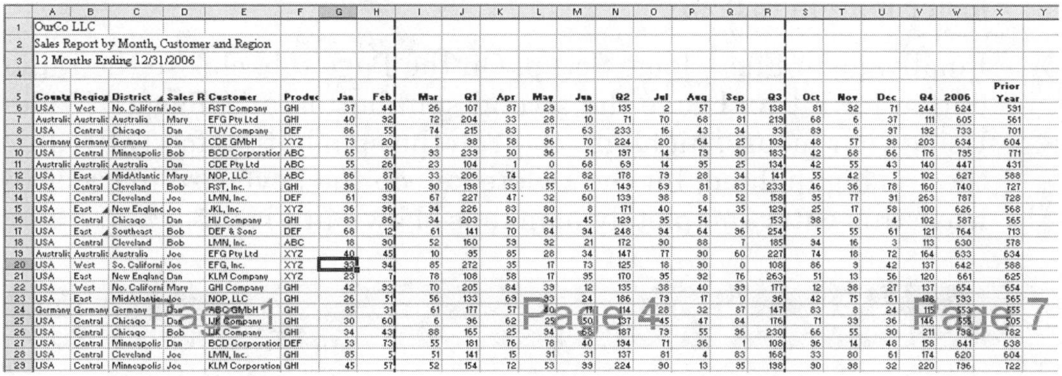

	A	B	C	D	E	F	G	H	I	J	K	L	M	N	O	P	Q	R	S	T	U	V	W	X
1	OurCo LLC																							
2	Sales Report by Month, Customer and Region																							
3	12 Months Ending 12/31/2006																							
4																								
5	Countr	Regior	District	Sales R	Customer	Produc	Jan	Feb	Mar	Q1	Apr	May	Jun	Q2	Jul	Aug	Sep	Q3	Oct	Nov	Dec	Q4	2006	Prior Year
6	USA	West	No. Californi	Joe	RST Company	GHI	37	44	26	107	87	29	19	135	2	57	79	138	81	92	71	244	624	591
7	Australi	Australi	Australia	Mary	EFG Pty Ltd	GHI	40	92	72	204	33	28	10	71	70	68	81	219	68	6	37	111	605	561
8	USA	Central	Chicago	Dan	TUV Company	DEF	86	55	74	215	83	87	63	233	16	43	34	93	89	6	97	192	733	701
9	Germany	Germany	Germany	Dan	CDE GMbH	XYZ	73	20	5	98	58	96	70	224	20	64	25	109	48	57	98	203	634	604
10	USA	Central	Minneapolis	Bob	BCD Corporatior	ABC	65	81	93	239	50	96	51	197	14	79	90	183	42	68	66	176	795	771
11	Australi	Australi	Australia	Dan	CDE Pty Ltd	ABC	55	26	23	104	1	0	68	69	14	95	25	134	42	55	43	140	447	431
12	USA	East	MidAtlantic	Mary	NOP, LLC	ABC	86	87	33	206	74	22	82	178	79	28	34	141	55	42	5	102	627	588
13	USA	Central	Cleveland	Bob	RST, Inc.	GHI	98	10	90	198	33	55	61	149	69	81	83	233	46	36	78	160	740	727
14	USA	Central	Cleveland	Joe	LMN, Inc.	DEF	61	99	67	227	47	32	60	139	98	8	52	158	95	77	91	263	787	728
15	USA	East	New Englanc	Joe	JKL, Inc.	XYZ	36	96	94	226	83	80	8	171	40	54	35	129	25	17	58	100	626	568
16	USA	Central	Chicago	Dan	HIJ Company	GHI	83	86	34	203	50	34	45	129	95	54	4	153	98	0	4	102	587	565
17	USA	East	Southeast	Bob	DEF & Sons	DEF	68	12	61	141	70	84	94	248	94	64	96	254	5	55	61	121	764	713
18	USA	Central	Cleveland	Bob	LMN, Inc.	ABC	18	90	52	160	59	92	21	172	90	88	7	185	94	16	3	113	630	578
19	Australi	Australi	Australia	Joe	EFG Pty Ltd	XYZ	40	45	10	95	85	28	34	147	77	90	60	227	74	18	72	164	633	634
20	USA	West	So. Californi	Joe	EFG, Inc.	XYZ	93	94	85	272	35	17	73	125	18	90	0	108	86	9	42	137	642	588
21	USA	East	New Englanc	Dan	KLM Company	XYZ	23	7	78	108	58	17	95	170	95	92	76	263	51	13	56	120	661	625
22	USA	West	No. Californi	Mary	GHI Company	GHI	42	93	70	205	84	39	12	135	38	40	99	177	12	98	27	137	654	654
23	USA	East	MidAtlantic	Joe	NOP, LLC	GHI	26	51	56	133	69	93	24	186	79	17	0	96	42	75	61	178	593	565
24	Germany	Germany	Germany	Dan	ABC GMbH	GHI	85	31	61	177	57	40	17	114	28	32	87	147	83	8	24	115	553	555
25	USA	Central	Chicago	Dan	IJK Company	GHI	30	60	6	96	62	25	50	137	45	47	84	176	71	39	36	146	555	505
26	USA	Central	Chicago	Bob	IJK Company	GHI	34	43	88	165	25	94	68	187	79	55	96	230	66	55	90	211	798	782
27	USA	Central	Minneapolis	Dan	BCD Corporatior	DEF	53	73	55	181	76	78	40	194	71	36	1	108	96	14	48	158	641	638
28	USA	Central	Cleveland	Joe	LMN, Inc.	GHI	85	5	51	141	15	91	31	137	81	4	83	168	33	80	61	174	620	604
29	USA	Central	Minneapolis	Joe	KLM Corporation	GHI	45	57	52	154	72	53	99	224	90	13	95	198	90	98	32	220	796	722

Fig. 44

Strategy: Ultimately, you will set the Page Setup to print to one page wide by <blank> pages tall. Before you can do that, you should follow these steps.

1) Eliminate extra columns from the print range.

   This worksheet has some lookup tables beyond column X that you do not want to print. Highlight columns A through X and select File – Print Area – Set Print Area.

2) Make the columns narrower.

   Select the data in A6:X130. From the menu, select Format – Column – AutoFit Selection.

3) Look for headings that could be on two lines.

   Sales Rep in cell D5 is an example of a heading that could be on two lines to save width in the column. Prior Year in X5 has already been split into two lines. (See Cross Reference.)

Part I

4)   Change the orientation to Landscape.

      From File – Page Setup, go to the Page tab and select Landscape in the orientation section.

5)   Adjust the margins.

      On the Margins tab of the File – Page Setup dialog, set the left and right margins at 0.25". Adjust the top and bottom to 0.5" and the footer margin to 0.25".

6)   Finally, go to File – Page Setup. On the Page tab, choose the radio button for Fit to. Leave the second spin button at 1 Page(s) Wide. Using your mouse, highlight the 1 in the spin button for Tall. After the 1 is highlighted, hit the Delete key on the keyboard in order to leave this entry completely blank, as shown in Fig. 45.

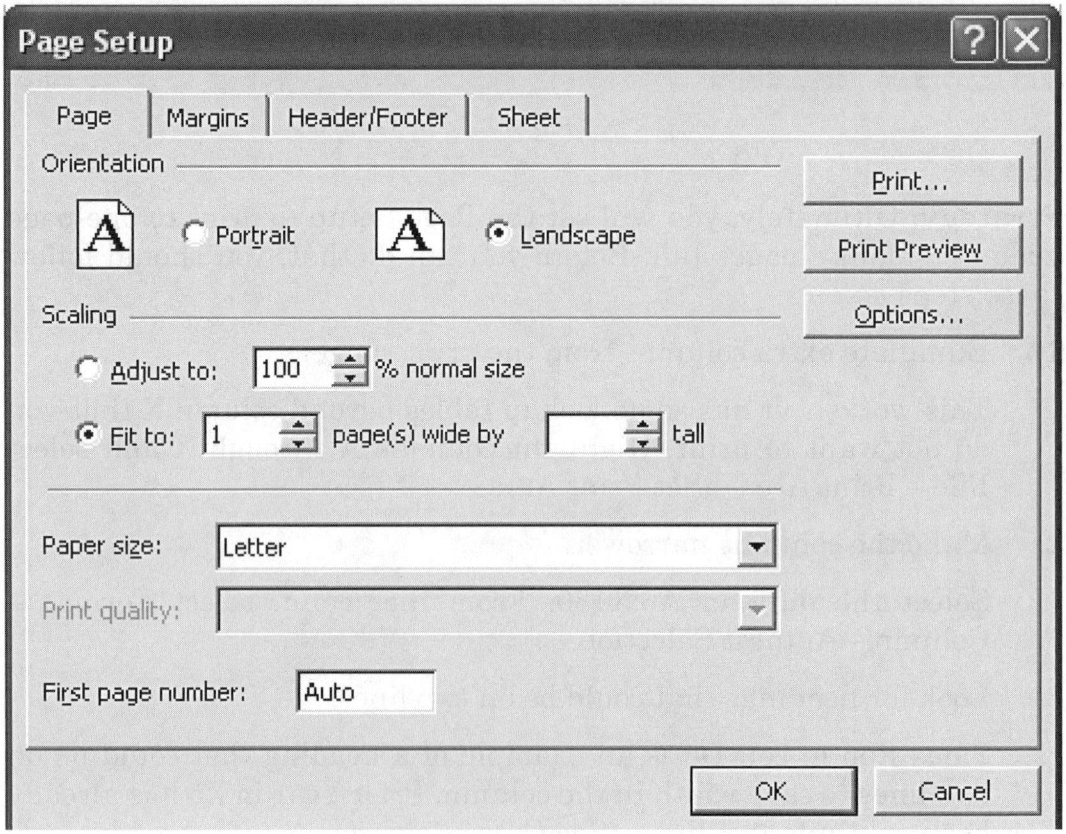

Fig. 45

Result: The report will fit on one page wide and three pages tall as shown in Fig. 46.

OurCo LLC
Sales Report by Month, Customer and Region
12 Months Ending 12/31/2006

Country	Region	District	Sales Rep	Customer	Product	Jan	Feb	Mar	Q1	Apr	May	Jun	Q2	Jul	Aug	Sep	Q3	Oct	Nov	Dec	Q4	2006	Prior Year
USA	West	No. California	Joe	RST Company	GHI	37	44	26	107	87	29	19	135	2	57	79	138	81	92	71	244	624	591
Australia	Australia	Australia	Mary	EFG Pty Ltd	GHI	40	92	72	204	33	28	10	71	70	68	81	219	68	6	37	111	605	561
USA	Central	Chicago	Dan	TUV Company	DEF	86	55	74	215	83	87	63	233	16	43	34	93	89	6	97	192	733	701
Germany	Germany	Germany	Dan	CDE GMbH	XYZ	73	20	5	98	58	96	70	224	20	64	25	109	48	57	98	203	634	604
USA	Central	Minneapolis	Bob	BCD Corporation	ABC	65	81	93	239	50	96	51	197	14	79	90	183	42	68	66	176	795	771
Australia	Australia	Australia	Dan	CDE Pty Ltd	ABC	55	26	23	104	1	0	68	69	14	95	25	134	42	55	43	140	447	431
USA	East	MidAtlantic	Mary	NOP, LLC	ABC	86	87	33	206	74	22	82	178	79	28	34	141	55	42	5	102	627	588
USA	Central	Cleveland	Bob	RST, Inc.	GHI	98	10	90	198	33	55	61	149	69	81	83	233	46	36	78	160	740	727
USA	Central	Cleveland	Joe	LMN, Inc.	DEF	61	99	67	227	47	32	60	139	98	8	52	158	95	77	91	263	787	728
USA	East	New England	Joe	JKL, Inc.	XYZ	36	96	94	226	83	80	8	171	40	54	35	129	25	17	58	100	626	568
USA	Central	Chicago	Dan	HIJ Company	GHI	83	86	34	203	50	34	45	129	95	54	4	153	98	0	4	102	587	565
USA	East	Southeast	Bob	DEF & Sons	DEF	68	12	61	141	70	84	94	248	94	64	96	254	5	55	61	121	764	713
USA	Central	Cleveland	Bob	LMN, Inc.	ABC	18	90	52	160	59	92	21	172	90	88	7	185	94	16	3	113	630	578
Australia	Australia	Australia	Dan	EFG Pty Ltd	XYZ	40	45	10	95	85	28	34	147	77	90	60	227	74	18	72	164	633	634
USA	West	So. California	Joe	EFG, Inc.	XYZ	93	94	85	272	35	17	73	125	18	90	0	108	86	9	42	137	642	588
USA	East	New England	Dan	KLM Company	XYZ	23	7	78	108	58	17	95	170	95	92	76	263	51	13	56	120	661	625
USA	West	No. California	Mary	GHI Company	GHI	42	93	70	205	84	39	12	135	38	40	99	177	12	98	27	137	654	654
USA	East	MidAtlantic	Joe	NOP, LLC	GHI	26	51	56	133	69	93	24	186	79	17	0	96	42	75	61	178	593	565
Germany	Germany	Germany	Dan	ABC GMbH	GHI	85	31	61	177	57	40	17	114	28	32	87	147	83	8	24	115	553	555
USA	Central	Chicago	Dan	UK Company	GHI	30	60	6	96	62	25	50	137	45	47	84	176	71	39	36	146	555	505
USA	Central	Chicago	Bob	UK Company	DEF	34	43	88	165	25	94	68	187	79	55	96	230	66	55	90	211	793	782
USA	Central	Minneapolis	Dan	BCD Corporation	DEF	53	73	55	181	76	78	40	194	71	36	1	108	96	14	48	158	641	638
USA	Central	Cleveland	Joe	LMN, Inc.	GHI	85	5	51	141	15	91	31	137	81	4	83	168	33	80	61	174	620	604
USA	Central	Minneapolis	Joe	KLM Corporation	GHI	45	57	52	154	72	53	99	224	90	13	95	198	90	98	32	220	796	722
USA	West	No. California	Bob	RST Company	GHI	97	13	73	183	77	97	16	190	6	44	50	100	81	42	51	174	647	626
USA	East	New England	Dan	OPQ, Inc.	XYZ	84	7	38	129	90	96	88	274	37	80	0	117	50	56	78	184	704	676
USA	East	New England	Mary	KLM Company	GHI	77	47	95	219	8	64	83	155	81	14	5	100	81	63	38	182	656	613
USA	East	Southeast	Bob	FGH & Sons	DEF	12	74	53	139	97	80	24	201	81	75	68	224	35	85	51	171	735	744
Germany	Germany	Germany	Dan	GHI GMbH	ABC	5	57	67	129	48	35	84	167	78	89	43	210	17	22	68	107	613	571
USA	Central	Cleveland	Bob	UVW, Inc.	ABC	99	5	24	128	35	68	8	111	94	53	13	160	78	30	7	115	514	493
USA	Central	Cleveland	Bob	JKL, Inc.	XYZ	19	76	55	150	13	34	27	74	65	93	61	219	93	81	74	248	691	638
USA	Central	Cleveland	Dan	WXY, Inc.	XYZ	65	29	64	158	81	45	22	148	59	68	73	200	81	22	72	175	681	638
USA	Central	Minneapolis	Dan	BCD Corporation	ABC	29	46	33	108	76	41	76	193	40	5	43	88	62	34	90	186	575	582
Germany	Germany	Germany	Bob	LMN GMbH	GHI	72	72	69	213	50	83	36	169	75	0	77	152	21	24	68	113	647	587
Germany	Germany	Germany	Dan	GHI GMbH	GHI	89	49	15	153	43	43	97	183	14	22	3	39	65	80	53	198	573	547
France	France	France	Dan	XYZ S.A.	GHI	91	79	40	210	74	14	79	167	86	96	0	182	79	90	33	202	761	755
Australia	Australia	Australia	Dan	TUV Pty Ltd	ABC	84	32	69	185	77	83	77	237	45	4	43	92	69	53	48	170	684	645
England	England	England	Joe	UVW Ltd	GHI	43	70	85	198	69	58	62	189	19	71	40	130	19	91	73	183	700	682
Australia	Australia	Australia	Dan	EFG Pty Ltd	GHI	25	95	40	160	81	36	30	147	34	0	71	105	25	4	83	112	524	486
France	France	France	Bob	QRS S.A.	GHI	39	86	3	128	77	35	23	135	58	30	28	116	53	58	47	158	537	502
Australia	Australia	Australia	Bob	VWX Pty Ltd	ABC	89	20	69	178	14	83	61	158	75	36	61	172	0	10	11	21	529	511
USA	East	New England	Bob	ABC Company	DEF	35	89	8	132	39	8	56	103	5	73	9	87	86	49	72	207	529	498
USA	West	No. California	Bob	XYZ Company	DEF	91	56	46	193	93	21	98	212	58	12	18	88	54	95	2	151	644	606
France	France	France	Dan	XYZ S.A.	GHI	34	98	63	195	67	79	55	201	7	5	32	44	85	56	92	233	673	608
Australia	Australia	Australia	Mary	CDE Pty Ltd	GHI	31	31	96	158	2	16	38	56	45	20	7	72	45	32	92	169	455	426
Germany	Germany	Germany	Bob	NOP GMbH	GHI	61	44	5	110	30	11	62	103	34	72	44	150	94	64	100	258	621	581
USA	Central	Chicago	Joe	UK Company	DEF	37	3	61	101	97	0	71	168	2	25	88	115	14	62	24	100	484	446
Germany	Germany	Germany	Dan	LMN GMbH	XYZ	66	57	31	154	36	21	76	133	79	37	27	143	86	78	52	216	646	639
USA	East	New England	Bob	OPQ, Inc.	XYZ	99	69	76	244	41	71	10	122	74	18	28	120	9	77	25	111	597	543

Highly Confidential   Page 1 of 3

Fig. 46

Summary: The secret to having the report constrained to one page wide and any number of pages tall is to use the Page Setup dialog and leave the entry for pages tall completely blank.

Commands Discussed: File – Page Setup – Page; File – Print Area – Set Print Area; Format – Column – AutoFit

Cross Reference: How to Fit a Multiline Heading into One Cell

Part
I

ARRANGE WINDOWS TO SEE
TWO OR MORE OPEN WORKBOOKS

Problem: You have two workbooks open. One workbook contains a listing of airport codes and their respective cities, as shown in Fig. 47. In the other workbook, you are building a list of recommended packing items for students going on seven-city tours. Currently, you are shifting back and forth between the workbooks, using Alt+Tab every time that you forget an airport code. It would be cool if you could see the airline codes at the same time you were working on the other workbook.

	A	B
1	Code	City
2	ABE	Allentown, PA
3	ABI	Abilene, TX
4	ABK	Kabri Dar, Ethiopia
5	ABL	Ambler, AK
6	ABM	Bamaga, Australia
7	ABQ	Albuquerque, NM
8	ABR	Aberdeen, SD
9	ACE	Lanzarote, Spain
10	ACV	Arcata, CA
11	ADB	Izmir, Turkey
12	ADK	Adak Island, AK
13	ADZ	San Andres Island, Colombia
14	AEP	Buenos Aires, Argentina - Jorge Newbery
15	AET	Allakaket, AK
16	AEX	Alexandria, LA

Fig. 47

Strategy: There are four Arrange options on the Window dialog, as shown in Fig. 48. Select Window – Arrange – Vertical to see both worksheets side by side.

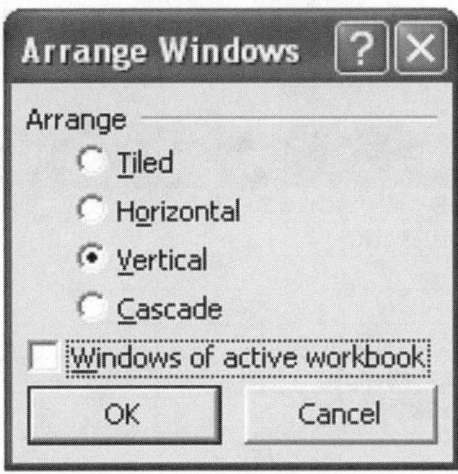

Fig. 48

Result: As shown in Fig. 49, you will see both windows, side by side. The window with the darker toolbar is the active window. Any data entry will occur in the active cell of that workbook.

StudentTours.xls				
	A	B	C	D
1	STUDENT TOURS, INC.			
2				
3				
4	School:	XYZ Local Schools		
5	Contact:	Mrs. Crabapple		
6	Departs:	June 28		
7	Tour:	CAK-ORD-SFO-BNA		

AirlineCodes.xls		
	A	B
1	**Code**	**City**
2	ABE	Allentown, PA
3	ABI	Abilene, TX
4	ABK	Kabri Dar, Ethiopia
5	ABL	Ambler, AK
6	ABM	Bamaga, Australia
7	ABQ	Albuquerque, NM

Fig. 49

You can resize the window widths, although this requires two moves.

1)   First, make the right window narrower by dragging the blue edge of the window to the right, as shown in Fig. 50.

StudentTours.xls				
	A	B	C	D
1	STUDENT TOURS, INC.			
2				
3				
4	School:	XYZ Local Schools		

AirlineCodes.xls		
	A	
1	**Code**	**City**
2	ABE	Allentown, PA
3	ABI	Abilene, TX
4	ABK	Kabri Dar, Ethiopia

Fig. 50

2) Next, drag the blue right edge of the left workbook to be wider, as shown in Fig. 51.

	A	B	C	D	E	
1	STUDENT TOURS, INC.					
2						
3						
4	School:	XYZ Local Schools				
5	Contact:	Mrs. Crabapple				
6	Departs:	June 28				

StudentTours.xls   AirlineCod

	A
1	Code
2	ABE
3	ABI
4	ABK
5	ABL
6	ABM

Fig. 51

3) To go back to full screen mode, as shown in Fig. 52, choose the Maximize icon at the top of each workbook.

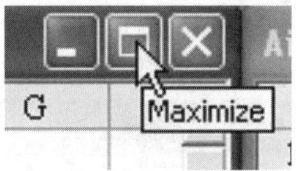

Fig. 52

Gotcha: If you have additional workbooks open, they will also appear side by side. The side-by-side display works fine for two or three workbooks, but may not work for ten open workbooks, as shown in Fig. 53.

	A	B		ice	Date			Sales	4	's Ice Crean		unt Codes	up		Inv	ion	Proc	City	DE
1	Acct	Inv																	
2	12345	1010		A4651 Ai	n-03	1(		5						1		XYZ	Aller		
3	23456	1011		533	31-N	b-03	1(		6	erature R		1010	QRS	1	ral	DEF	Abile		
4	34567	1012		559	19-	ar-03	(		7	64		1011	STU	1		ABC	Kabr	ol:	
5	45678	1013		756	24-/	r-03	11		8	95		1012	KLM	1	ral	XYZ	Amb	ac	
6	56789	1014																	
7	67890	1015																	

Fig. 53

Additional Information: In Excel 2003, a new option on the Window menu allows you to Compare Side by Side. If you have only two workbooks open, the menu option will name the other workbook, as shown in Fig. 54. If you have three or more workbooks open, you will have to select a workbook in a new dialog box. If there is only one workbook open, the option will be grayed out.

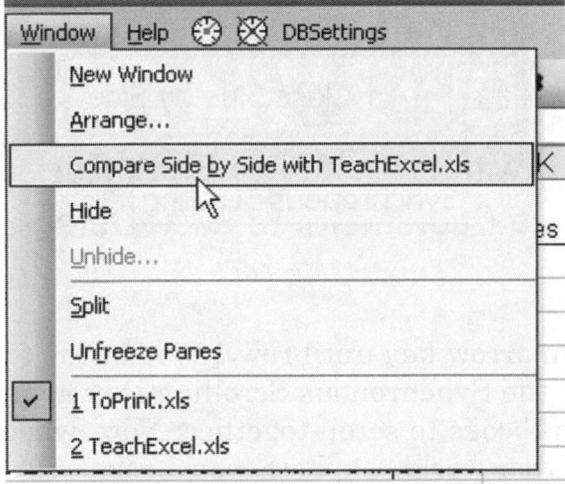

Fig. 54

As shown in Fig. 55, this will arrange two windows vertically and allow the scrolling action in the first workbook to cause the second workbook to scroll in a similar manner.

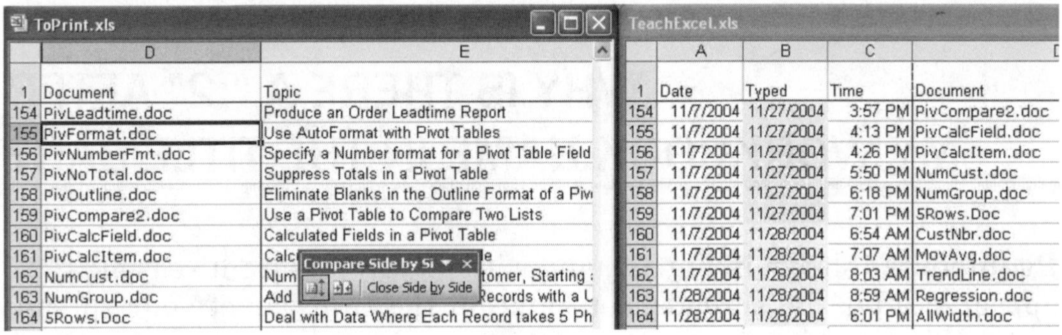

Fig. 55

Tip

*If you are comparing two workbooks that are supposed to be similar, it is likely that someone added some rows to one document or the other. In Fig. 55, the workbooks are synchronized so that when you see row 154 in one window, you see row 154 in the other window. In reality, row 159 of the left window matches row 154 in the right window and they will be scrolling out of synchronization. Follow these steps to correct the **problem**:*

1) In the Compare Side by Side toolbar, turn off synchronous scrolling, as shown in Fig. 56.

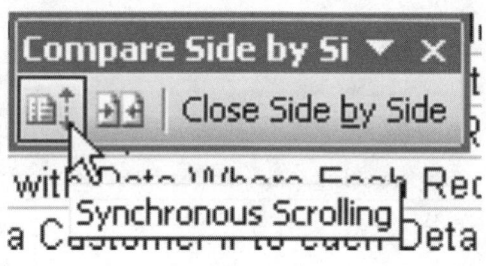

Fig. 56

2) Use the down arrow key until row 159 is at the top of the left window. Choose the Synchronous Scrolling icon again (see Fig. 56) to force the workbooks to scroll together. Now, when you move down 10 rows in either workbook, both workbooks will scroll together.

Summary: Arranging windows in a vertical fashion allows you to view two different workbooks at the same time.

Commands Discussed: Window – Arrange; Window – Compare Side by Side

WHY IS THERE A ":2" AFTER MY WORKBOOK NAME IN THE TITLE BAR?

Problem: As shown in Fig. 57, and without any apparent reason, a ":2" appeared after the spreadsheet name in the title bar of your spreadsheet. What is this and what caused it?

	A	B	C	D	E
1	111	111	111	111	1
2	111	111	111	111	1

Fig. 57

Strategy: This is an annoying thing. It got turned on when you accidentally chose Window – New Window from the menu. This setting applies to the workbook and persists from one usage of Excel to the next, so it is possible that the :2 showed up months ago and has been stuck there ever since. The other symptom is that you appear have two copies of the same workbook open in the Window menu as shown in Fig. 58.

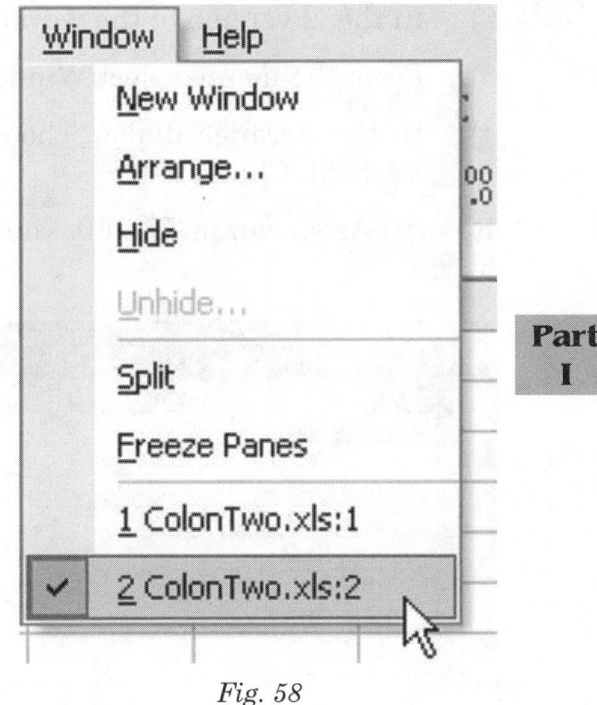

Part I

Fig. 58

To remove the :2, switch to the :2 version of the workbook. Use the black X to close that window, as shown in Fig. 59.

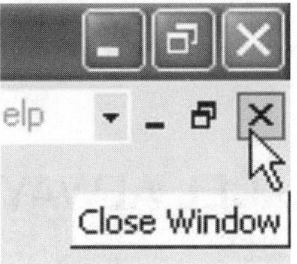

Fig. 59

This will close the second window of the workbook and both the :2 and :1 will be removed from the title bar.

Additional Information: Is there ever a time that you would want to use this feature? Is it useful to have two versions of the workbook? Yes. Let's say that you want to see both Sheet1 and Sheet2 of the workbook at the same time. Follow these steps:

1)   From the menu, select Window – New Window.

2)   In the :2 version of the workbook, switch to Sheet2.

3)   From the menu, select Window – Arrange.

4)   In the Arrange dialog, choose Windows of Active Workbook and Vertical. Choose OK.

Result: As shown in Fig. 60, you can see the two different sheets, side by side.

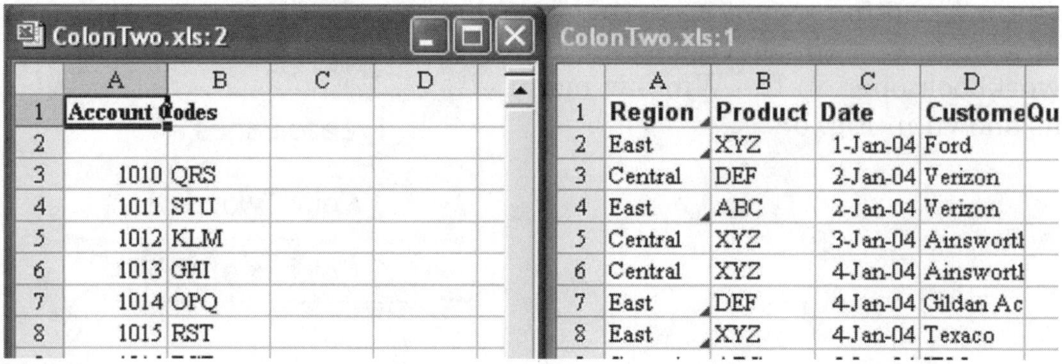

Fig. 60

Summary: The :2 usually happens when you accidentally choose Window – New Window. It can be removed. In certain instances it can also be useful.

Commands Discussed: Window – New Window; Window – Arrange

HAVE EXCEL ALWAYS OPEN CERTAIN WORKBOOK(S)

Problem: You always use Excel to work on a particular workbook. Every time that you open Excel, you want this workbook to open automatically.

Strategy: Place the file (or a shortcut to the file) in the XLStart folder. This folder can generally be found in the C:\Documents and Settings\ Username\Application Data\Microsoft\Excel\ folder. Anything in this folder will automatically start when Excel starts.

Alternate Strategy: You can specify one folder to act as an additional XLStart folder. Follow these steps.

1) Move the Excel workbook or workbooks to a new folder.

   Excel will try to open every file in this folder, so make sure that you do not have other files in it.

2) Open Excel. From the Tools menu, select Options.

3) In the Options dialog box, find the General tab.

There are five fields at the bottom of the General tab. As shown in Fig. 61, in Excel 2002 and later versions, the penultimate field is called At Startup, Open all Files in:. In Excel 2000 and earlier versions, this same field was called Alternate Startup File Location, as shown in Fig. 62. In either case, enter the path to the folder in this field.

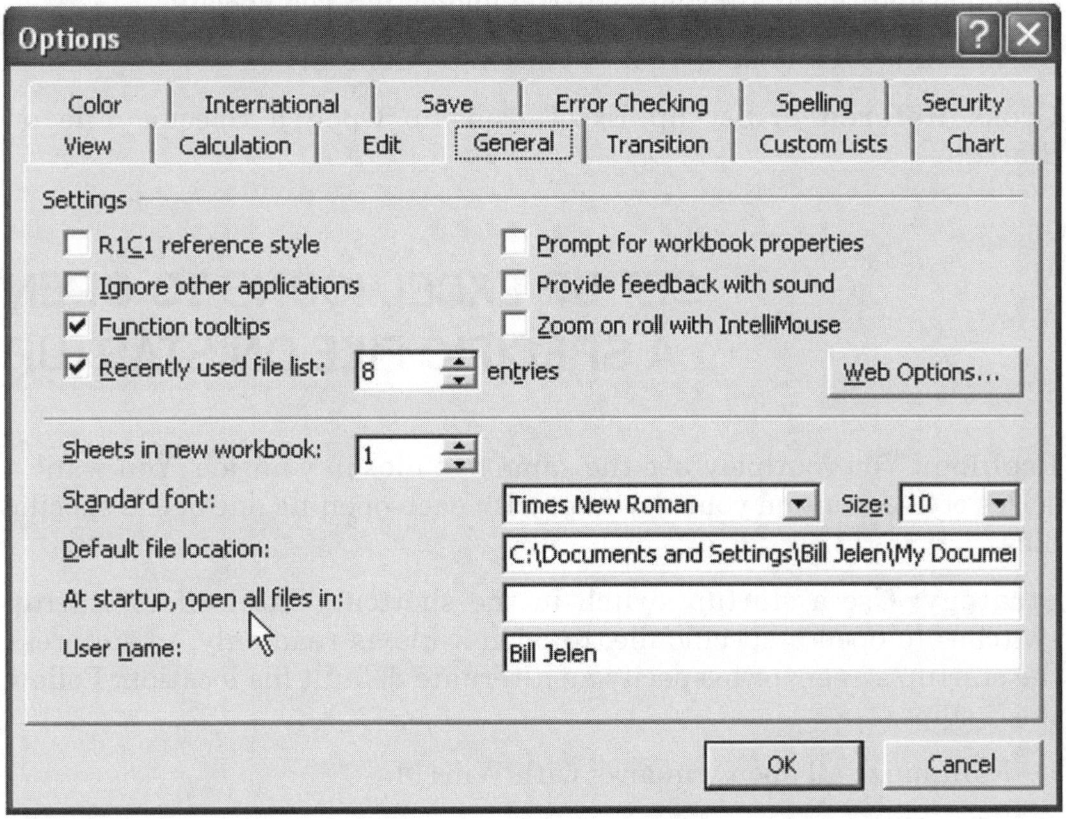

Fig. 61

Sheets in new workbook:	3
Standard font:	Arial	Size: 10
Default file location:	C:\Documents and Settings\a\My Documents
Alternate startup file location:	
User name:	Bill Jelen

Fig. 62

Alternate Strategy: A third strategy is to use a command line switch. This is discussed in the next topic.

Summary: Excel will automatically open all files in the XLStart folder or in one additional alternate startup folder that you specify.

Commands Discussed: Tools – Options – General

Cross Reference: Set up Excel Icons to Open a Specific File on Startup

SET UP EXCEL ICONS TO OPEN A SPECIFIC FILE ON STARTUP

Problem: You routinely use the same five files in your job. You want a series of five icons on your desktop, with each opening one of the specific files.

Strategy: Use a startup switch in the shortcut. Excel offers startup switches to open a specific file, to open a file as read-only, to suppress the startup screen, or to specify an alternate default file location. Follow these steps.

1)   Minimize all open windows with Win+M.

The Win key is usually located between the left Ctrl and left Alt keys. It has a picture of a flying Window icon, as shown in Fig. 63.

Fig. 63

2) Open Windows Explorer with Win+E.

3) Browse to one of these locations:

- For Excel 2003: \Program Files\Microsoft Office\Office11

- For Excel 2002: \Program Files\Microsoft Office\Office10

- For Excel 2000: \Program Files\Microsoft Office\Office

4) If Windows Explorer is in full screen mode, choose the Restore Down button in the upper right corner of the Window, as shown in Fig. 64.

Fig. 64

5) Using the mouse, grab the blue title bar of the Windows Explorer window and move it so that you can see part of the desktop.

6) Find the Excel icon in Windows Explorer. Right-click and drag the item to the desktop, as shown in Fig. 65.

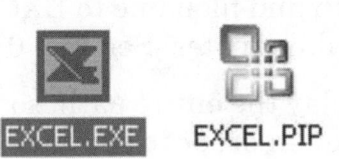

Fig. 65

7) When you release the right mouse button, a menu will appear, as shown in Fig. 66. Choose Create Shortcuts Here.

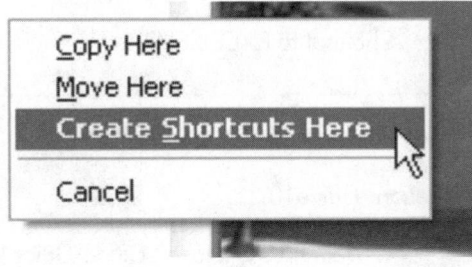

Fig. 66

8) Close Windows Explorer.

9) On the Desktop, right-click the new Shortcut to Excel icon and choose Properties.

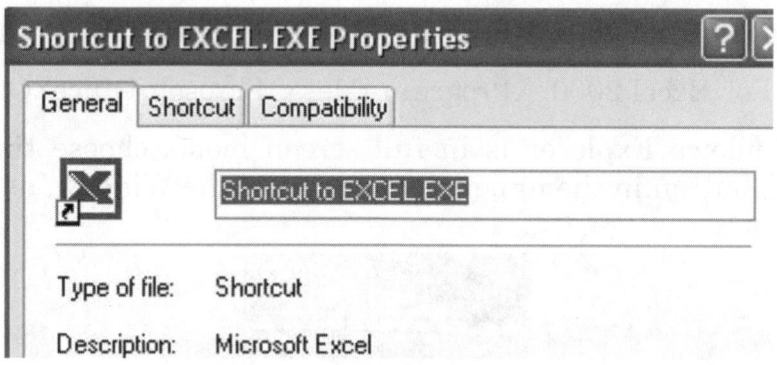

Fig. 67

10) There are three tabs in the Properties dialog, as shown in Fig. 67. Choose the General tab.

11) Change the name in the top textbox to something meaningful. If this icon will be used to open the Sales file, a short name like Sales would work.

12) On the Shortcut tab, locate the Target field.

This field contains the complete path and filename to EXCEL.EXE. The path and file name are wrapped in quotes. See Fig. 68.

13) The field is never big enough to display the entire path, so you must click in the field and hit the End key in order to see the end of the entry, as shown in Fig. 68.

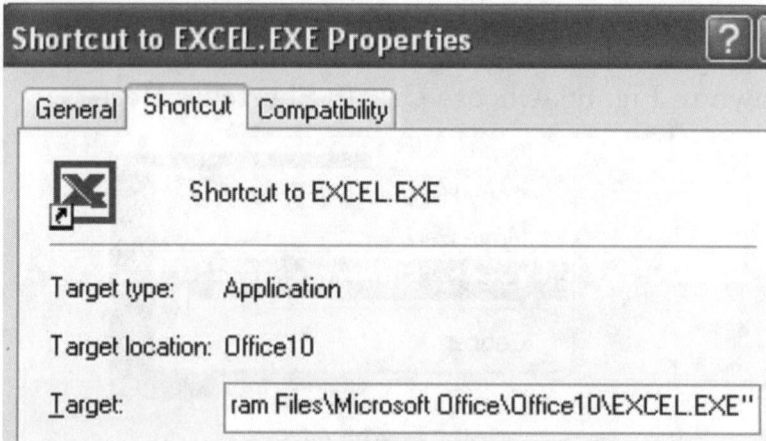

Fig. 68

14) The startup switch should be added after the final quotation mark. Type a space, and then the startup switch. If you use multiple startup switches, each must be separated by a space.

- To open a file in read-only mode, use the /R switch followed by the complete path and file name, as shown in Fig. 69.

> `,Office10\EXCEL.EXE" /R C:\Test2003.xls`

Fig. 69

- To open a file in normal mode, leave out the /R switch. Just have a space followed by the path and file name, as shown in Fig. 70.

> `\Office10\EXCEL.EXE" C:\Test2003.xls`

Fig. 70

Gotcha: If you start Excel normally, use File – Open and browse to the C:\ folder. All subsequent Open or Save As dialogs will start in the C:\ folder. Frustratingly, neither of the above switches will change the current path to the folder as the open file. In order to do that, use the /P switch with the same path as your file, as shown in Fig. 71.

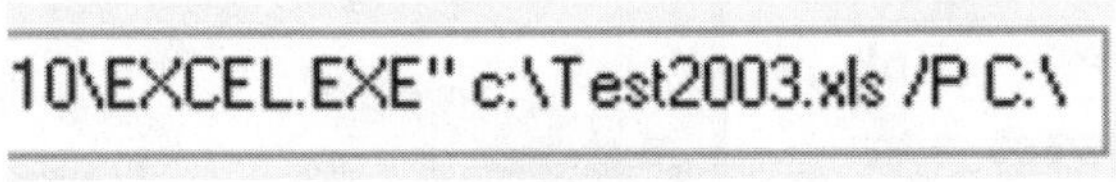

> `10\EXCEL.EXE" c:\Test2003.xls /P C:\`

Fig. 71

Additional Details: Try the /E switch to suppress the Excel splash screen as your file opens.

Summary: Customize your shortcut to Excel to open a specific file or to use a specific path as the current folder.

USE A MACRO TO FURTHER CUSTOMIZE STARTUP

Problem: Every time that you open a workbook, you would like to put the file in Data Form mode, as shown in Fig. 72, or to invoke any other Excel menu as the file opens.

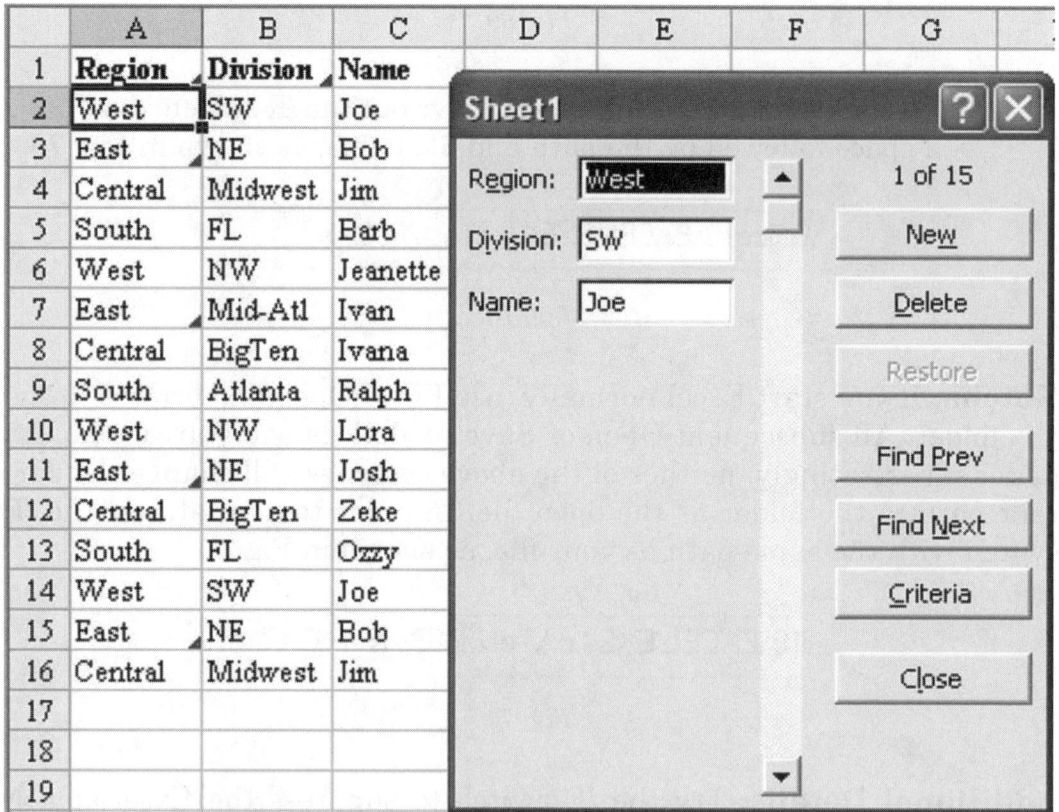

Fig. 72

Strategy: Startup switches can only do so many things. You will have to use a Workbook_Open macro in order to force Excel into Data Form mode. Follow these steps:

1) In Excel, go to Tools – Macro – Security. Set the security level to Medium or lower.

2) Open your workbook.

3) Hit Alt+F11 to open the VBA Editor. (**Caution:** The Microsoft Natural Multimedia keyboard does not support Alt+F keys. You might have to use Tools – Macros – Visual Basic Editor, instead.)

4) Hit Ctrl+R to show the Project Explorer in the upper left corner. You should see something that looks like VBAProject (Your Book-Name) in the Project Explorer, as shown in Fig. 73.

Fig. 73

5) If there is a + to the left of this entry, hit the + to expand it.

You will see a folder underneath, called Microsoft Excel Objects. If there is a + to the left of this entry, hit the + to expand it, also.

6) You will now see one entry for each worksheet, plus an entry called ThisWorkbook. Right-click on ThisWorkbook and choose View Code from the pop-up menu, as shown in Fig. 74.

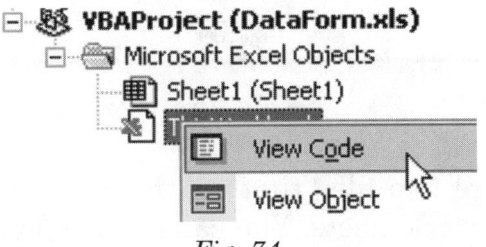

Fig. 74

7) Copy these three lines of code to the large white code window.

Private Sub Workbook_Open()

ActiveSheet.ShowDataForm

End Sub

8) Hit Alt+Q to return to Excel.

9) Save the file.

10) Open the file. The data form should open.

Additional Information: This simple macro invokes on Menu command. It is possible to build highly complex macros that would control literally anything. For a primer on macros, consult VBA & Macros for Microsoft Excel from QUE.

Summary: Customize your shortcut to Excel to open a specific file or to use a specific path as the current folder.

CONTROL SETTINGS FOR EVERY NEW WORKBOOK AND WORKSHEET

Problem: Every time that you start a new workbook or insert a new worksheet, you always make the same customizations. These may include setting print scaling to fit to one page wide, setting certain margins, adding a "Page 1 of n" footer to the worksheet, as shown in Fig. 75, making the heading row to be in bold text, and so forth.

Fig. 75

Strategy: There are two files that control the defaults for new workbooks and inserted worksheets. You can easily customize a blank workbook to contain your favorite settings and then save the file as book.xlt or sheet.xlt. Any time that you choose either the New Workbook icon, as shown in Fig. 76, or the Insert – Worksheet command, the new book or sheet will inherit the settings from these files.

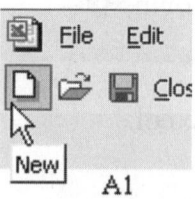

Fig. 76

Follow these steps to create book.xlt.

1)   In Excel, open a new blank workbook by using the New icon in the Standard toolbar.

2)   Customize the workbook.

     Feel free to make adjustments to any of the following:

     •   File – Page Setup

     •   File – Set Print Area

     •   Cell Styles

     •   Format – Cells

     •   Data – Validation settings

     •   Number and type of sheets in the workbook

     •   Window view options from the Tools – Options – View tab

3)   Decide where you want to save the file.

     This can be either in the XLStart folder (generally C:\Program Files\Microsoft Office\Officenn\XLStart) or in the Alternate Startup folder. (Find or setup an Alternate Startup folder on the Tools – Options – General dialog.)

4)   Select File – Save As. In the Save As dialog, Save as Type drop-down, choose Template, as shown in Fig. 77.

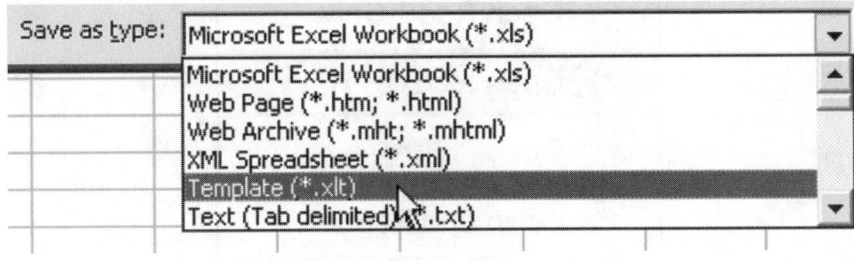

Fig. 77

5)   Browse to the XLStart folder (see Step 3).

6)   Save the file as Book.xlt

Result: All subsequent new workbooks will inherit the settings from this file.

Additional Information: You can also set up a workbook with one worksheet. Save this workbook as Sheet.XLT. All inserted worksheets will inherit the settings from this file.

Summary: Rather than constantly setting the same settings for all new workbooks, save your favorite settings in either book.xlt or sheet.xlt in the XLStart folder. All new workbooks will inherit these settings.

OPEN A COPY OF A WORKBOOK

Problem: You have an invoice.xls workbook. You want to keep the original file unchanged and save as a new workbook. Except, you tend to forget to use File – Save As.

Strategy: When using File – Open, you can specify that you want to open as a copy.

1) Instead of choosing the Open button, use the dropdown arrow next to the button. Choose Open as Copy, as shown in Fig. 78. The file that opens will be named "Copy (1) of invoice.xls".

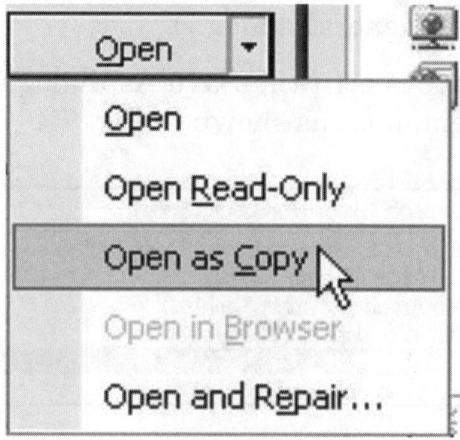

Fig. 78

2) Use File – Save As to save the file with a new name. However, even if you forget to use Save As, at least you will not overwrite the original invoice.xls.

Summary: To open a copy of a workbook, instead of choosing the Open button, use the dropdown arrow next to the button and choose Open as Copy.

Commands Discussed: File – Open as Copy; File – Save As

OPEN A SAVED FILE WHOSE NAME YOU CANNOT RECALL

Part I

Problem: You created and saved a file on last Wednesday. It is no longer in your recently used file list on the File menu and you cannot remember its name.

Strategy: Use the Details icon to find the files you saved last Wednesday.

1) Select File – Open. At the top of the open dialog, choose the Details icon, as shown in Fig. 79.

Fig. 79

2) You can now see file names and also dates and times of the last save. Sort by date by clicking on the Date Modified header, as shown in Fig. 80. The first click could sort either ascending or descending.

Size	Type	Date Modified ▲
73 KB	Microsoft...	11/14/2003 11:05 A
190 KB	Microsoft...	9/27/2004 9:02 AM
19 KB	Microsoft...	10/2/2004 5:34 PM
26 KB	Microsoft...	10/2/2004 5:57 PM
72 KB	Microsoft...	10/3/2004 7:04 AM
26 KB	Microsoft...	10/3/2004 9:14 AM
71 KB	Microsoft...	10/3/2004 9:36 AM

Fig. 80

3) Use the Scroll bar to go to the top of the list. If it does not contain recent files, click the date header again to sort descending. You can now scroll back to last Wednesday to find the file.

Summary: Use the Details mode of the Open dialog to sort files by date, time, or name.

Commands Discussed: File – Open

SUPPRESS THE UPDATE LINKS MESSAGE

Problem: You have a model that you send to others. When they open the model, they are always asked if they should update the links, as shown in Fig. 81. They need to answer Don't Update and the workbook will open fine. Is there any way to suppress the question in the first place?

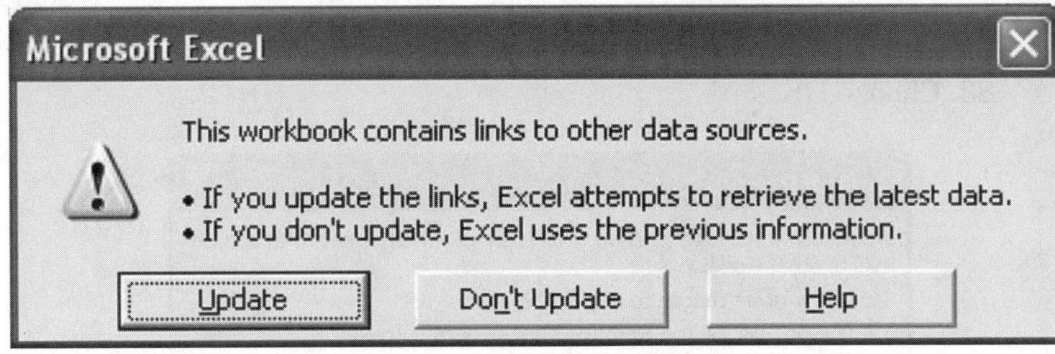

Fig. 81

Strategy: Control this message by using the Edit Links dialog box.

1) From the Excel menu, select Edit – Links to display the Edit Links dialog box. Choose the Startup Prompt button in the lower left corner of the dialog box, as shown in Fig. 82.

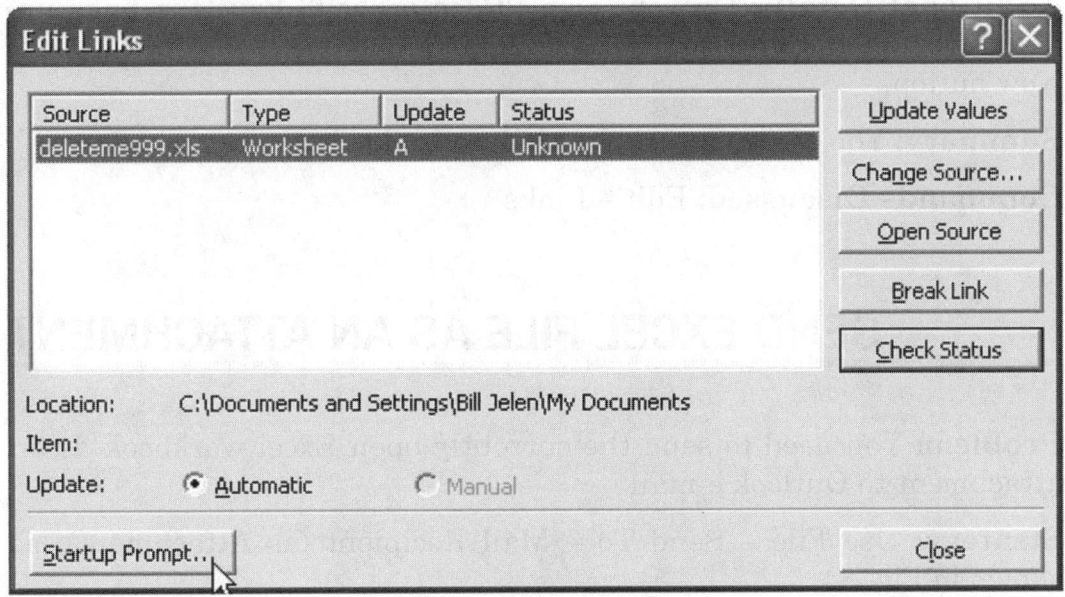

Fig. 82

2) In the Startup Prompt dialog, choose the second option, Don't Display the Alert and Don't Update Automatic Links, as shown in Fig. 83. Choose OK.

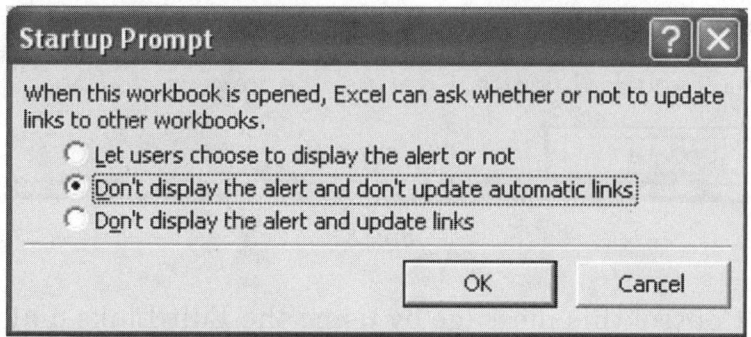

Fig. 83

This setting will only affect the current workbook.

Additional Details: On your own PC, in order to have the links updated, you should visit the Edit – Links dialog and choose the Update Now button.

Summary: You can suppress the Update Links dialog box.

Commands Discussed: Edit – Links

SEND EXCEL FILE AS AN ATTACHMENT

Problem: You need to send the currently open Excel workbook as an attachment to Outlook e-mail.

Strategy: Use File – Send To – Mail Recipient (as Attachment), as shown in Fig. 84.

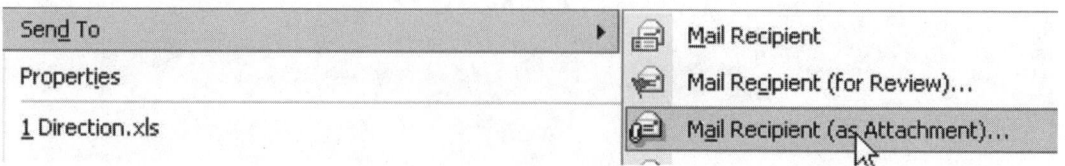

Fig. 84

This will open something that you will swear is the Outlook Send Mail dialog. Fill out the addressee list, a subject, and click send as shown in Fig. 85.

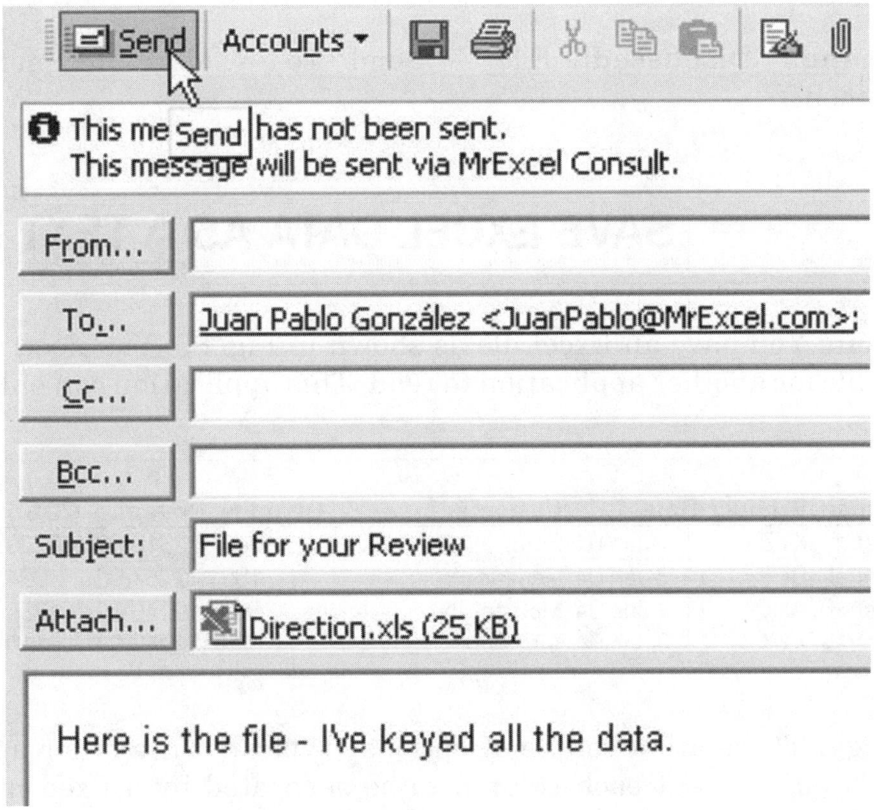

Fig. 85

Gotcha: Although this looks like Outlook, you are actually using an Excel version of the dialog. You will find that while this dialog is displayed, you cannot access other Outlook e-mails.

This is a problem. What if you receive a file from someone not in your address book, edit the file and then need to send it back? You will find that you need to access the original e-mail to get the sender's e-mail address, but you cannot switch to another e-mail message until you've sent this one.

The solution is to press the Save icon in the Standard toolbar of the e-mail dialog. Then use the Close X icon in the upper right corner of the window. This will save the unfinished e-mail from Excel to the Outlook inbox and return you to Excel. You can now safely switch back to the original Outlook e-mail to get the address.

Summary: To send an Excel file without leaving Excel, use File – Send To.

Commands Discussed: File – Send To – Mail Recipient (as Attachment)

SAVE EXCEL DATA AS A TEXT FILE

Problem: You have an Excel file as shown in Fig. 86. You need to produce a file for another application to read. This application can only read .txt files.

	A	B	C	D	E	F	G	H
1	Region	Product	Date	Customer	Quantity	Revenue	COGS	Profit
2	East	XYZ	1-Jan-04	Ford	1000	22810.00	10220	12590
3	Central	DEF	2-Jan-04	Verizon	100	2257.00	984	1273
4	East	ABC	2-Jan-04	Molson, Inc	500	10245.00	4235	6010
5	Central	XYZ	3-Jan-04	Ainsworth	500	11240.00	5110	6130

Fig. 86

Strategy: There are a couple of options. Typically, the other application will either want each column to be separated by a fixed number of spaces or separated by a comma. Files with columns separated by a comma are called Comma Separated Values, or CSV files. CSV files are easier to create than space-separated files.

Method 1: Create a CSV file.

1) Use File – Save As. In the Save as Type dropdown, choose CSV, as shown in Fig. 87.

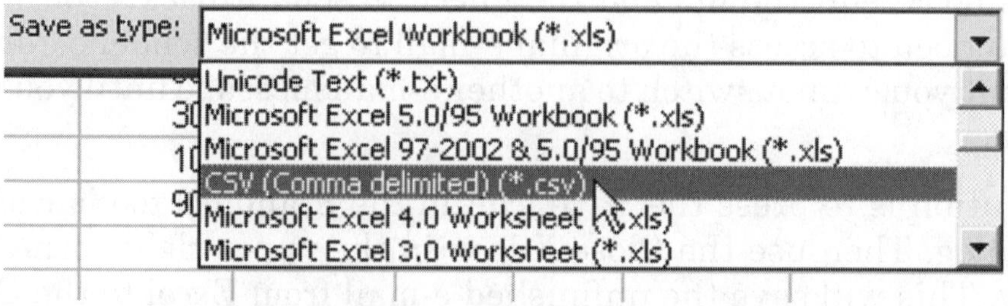

Save as type: Microsoft Excel Workbook (*.xls)
Unicode Text (*.txt)
Microsoft Excel 5.0/95 Workbook (*.xls)
Microsoft Excel 97-2002 & 5.0/95 Workbook (*.xls)
CSV (Comma delimited) (*.csv)
Microsoft Excel 4.0 Worksheet (*.xls)
Microsoft Excel 3.0 Worksheet (*.xls)

Fig. 87

2) Choose the Save button. *Important: Only the current worksheet is saved in the CSV file.* If you have multiple worksheets in the workbook, you will have to save each worksheet separately. Also, Excel will generally warn you that you are saving the file in a format that will leave out incompatible features, as shown in Fig. 88.

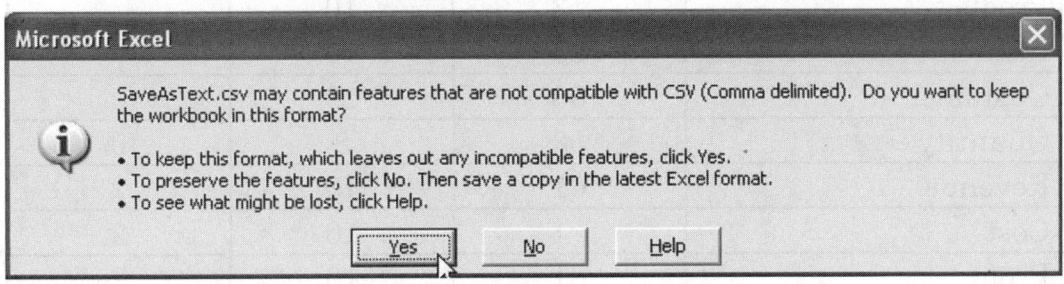

Fig. 88

Part I

3) You can generally keep two versions of each file. Save it as XLS and then save it as CSV.

Result: Fig. 89 shows the created file as it appears when edited with Notepad. Pay particular attention to the "Molson, Inc" entry. Because cell D4 already had a comma, Excel was smart enough to surround Molson, Inc with quotation marks, as shown in Fig. 89.

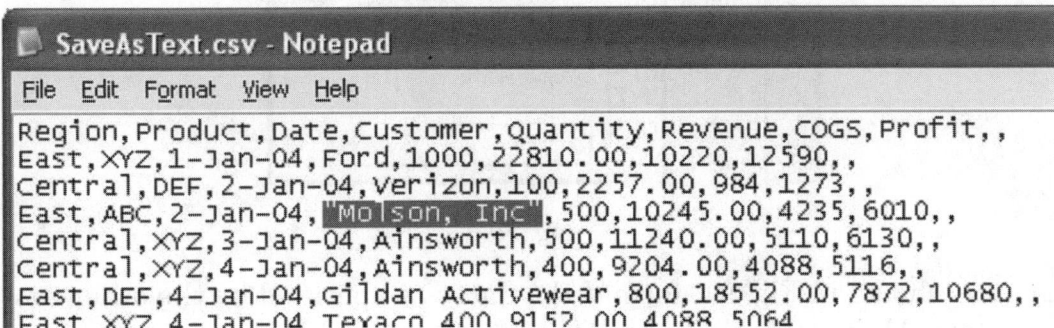

Fig. 89

Gotcha: The dates in column C are written to the file in the same format as they were shown on the worksheet. Most programs will not understand a date such as "1-Jan-04". You probably should format column C to appear as mm/dd/yyyy before exporting to CSV. Check the documentation of the program that will import the information.

Method 2: The second option is to create a file where each field is supposed to take a fixed number of characters. In this case, the other application will usually give you a file specification for you to follow. It might indicate:

Field Name	Start	Length	Decimals
Region	1	12	
Product	13	10	
Date	23	10	
Customer	33	20	
Quantity	53	8	0
Revenue	61	10	2
Cost	71	10	2
Profit	81	10	2

1) If this is the case, you will have to go through the columns in the worksheet, resetting the column width. If the other program expects the Region field to be 12 characters wide, select column A and use Format – Column – Width to change to 12, as shown in Fig. 90.

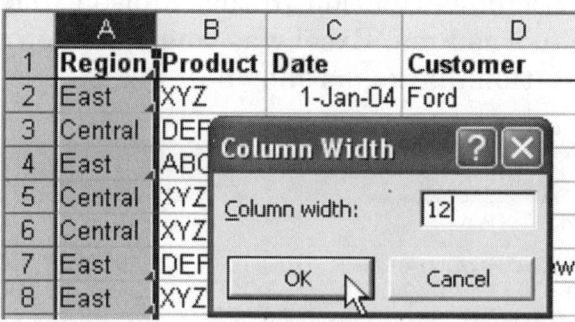

Fig. 90

2) As shown in Fig. 91, format the dates as specified by the other system. Make sure that the Revenue, Cost, and Profit columns show two decimal places. The other system probably will not want field headings. Delete row 1.

	A	B	C	D	E	F	G	H
1	East	XYZ	01/01/04	Ford	1000	22810.00	10220.00	12590.00
2	Central	DEF	01/02/04	Verizon	100	2257.00	984.00	1273.00
3	East	ABC	01/02/04	Molson, Inc	500	10245.00	4235.00	6010.00
4	Central	XYZ	01/03/04	Ainsworth	500	11240.00	5110.00	6130.00
5	Central	XYZ	01/04/04	Ainsworth	400	9204.00	4088.00	5116.00

Fig. 91

3)   Use File – Save As. In the Save as Type dropdown, select Format-
     ted Text (Space Delimited), as shown in Fig. 92.

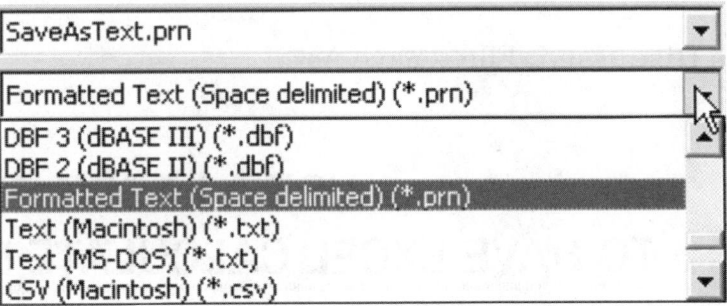

Fig. 92

> **Note:** *Excel changes the file name to have a .prn extension. Even if you try
> to change the extension to .txt here, Excel will still save the file as
> SaveAsText.Txt.Prn, as shown in Fig. 93. It is best to leave it as .prn
> and then rename in Windows Explorer.*

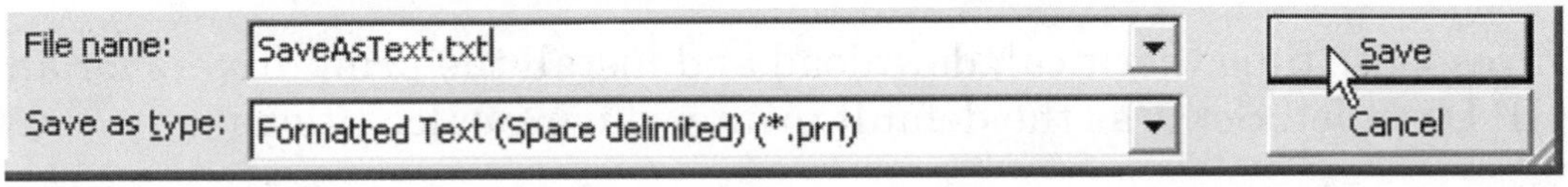

File name:	SaveAsText.txt	▼	Save
Save as type:	Formatted Text (Space delimited) (*.prn)	▼	Cancel

Fig. 93

4)   As shown in Fig. 94, Excel will warn you that you will lose features
     if you have multiple sheets. Choose OK.

Microsoft Excel

⚠ The selected file type does not support workbooks that contain multiple sheets.

• To save only the active sheet, click OK.
• To save all sheets, save them individually using a different file name for each, or choose a file type that supports multiple sheets.

[OK]   [Cancel]

Fig. 94

Fig. 95 shows the resulting file as viewed in Notepad:

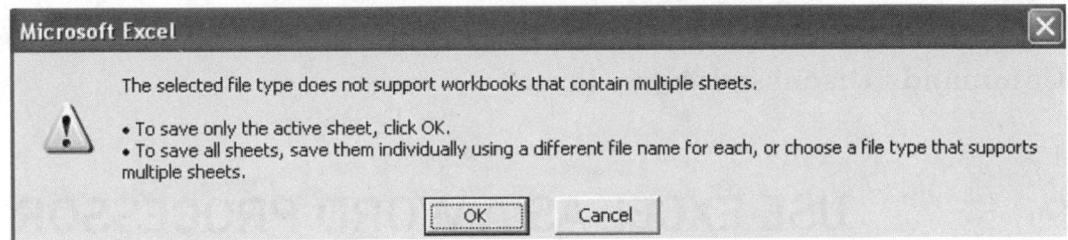

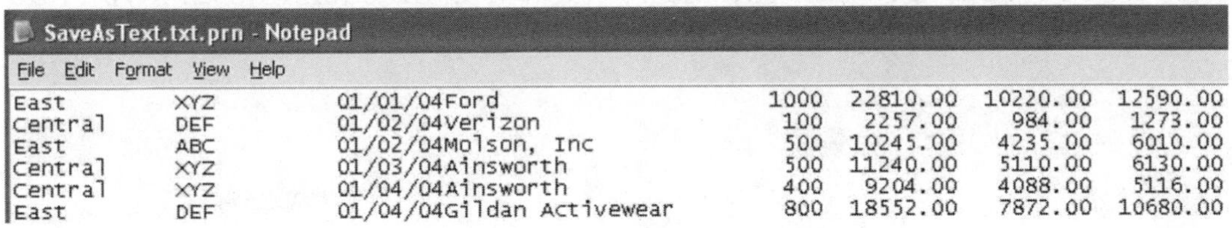

Fig. 95

Summary: Data in Excel can easily be exported to a text file. Determine if the receiving system needs CSV or text formatted by spaces before exporting.

Commands Discussed: File – Save As

USE A LASER PRINTER
TO HAVE EXCEL CALCULATE FASTER

Problem: Believe it or not, Excel uses your print driver to draw the screen.

Strategy: Having an HP LaserJet as your default printer can allow Excel operations to finish in one-fourth of the time it takes if you have a cheap inkjet driver as the default. We've tested this.

If response time is critical, download and install the print drivers for an HP LaserJet. Set it as the default printer during calculations.

Gotcha: If you don't actually have a LaserJet hooked to your printer, you will have to refrain from using the printer icon. You will always have to print with File – Print and choose a non-default printer.

Summary: Using an HP LaserJet driver during Excel calculations can speed up your Excel operations time.

Commands Discussed: File – Print

USE EXCEL AS A WORD PROCESSOR

Problem: You need to type some notes at the bottom of the report, as shown in Fig. 96. How can you make the words fill each line as if you had typed them in Word?

	A	B	C	D	E	F	G	H	I	J	K	L	M
21													
22													
23	This prospectus includes forward-looking statements.												
24	All statements other than statements of historical facts contained in this prospectus,												
25	including statements regarding our future financial position, business strategy and plans												
26	and objectives of management for future operations, are forward-looking statements.												
27	The words "believe," "may," "will," "estimate," "continue," "anticipate," "intend," "expect" and												
28	similar expressions are intended to identify forward-looking statements. We have based these												
29	forward-looking statements largely on our current expectations and projections about future events												
30	and financial trends that we believe may affect our financial condition, results of operations,												
31	business strategy, short term and long term business operations and objectives, and financial needs.												
32													

Fig. 96

Strategy: Use the Justify command on the Fill menu.

1)   If you want the words to fill columns A through K, then select a range such as A23:K35. Note that you are including a few blank rows in the selection, as shown in Fig. 97.

	A	B	C	D	E	F	G	H	I	J	K	L
21												
22												
23	This prospectus includes forward-looking statements.											
24	All statements other than statements of historical facts contained in this prospectus,											
25	including statements regarding our future financial position, business strategy and plans											
26	and objectives of management for future operations, are forward-looking statements.											
27	The words "believe", "may", "will", "estimate", "continue", "anticipate", "intend", "expect" and											
28	similar expressions are intended to identify forward-looking statements. We have based these											
29	forward-looking statements largely on our current expectations and projections about future eve											
30	and financial trends that we believe may affect our financial condition, results of operations											
31	business strategy, short term and long term business operations and objectives, and financial ne											
32												
33												
34												
35												
36												

Fig. 97

Part
I

2)   From the menu, select Edit – Fill – Justify, as shown in Fig. 98.

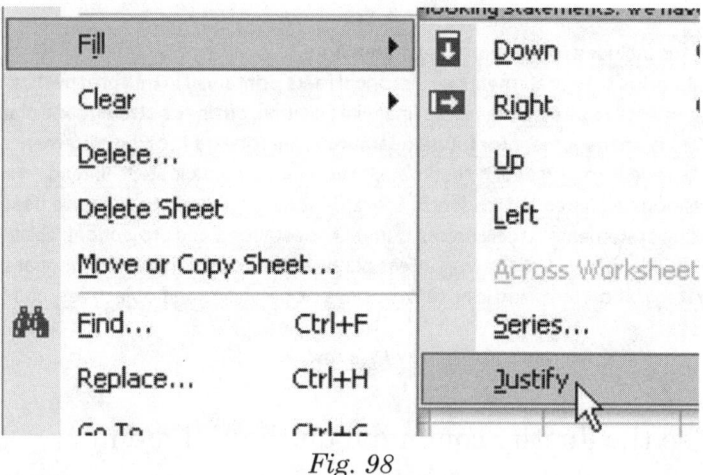

Fig. 98

Result: Excel will rearrange the text to fill each row, as shown in Fig. 99.

	A	B	C	D	E	F	G	H	I	J	K	L
21												
22												
23	This prospectus includes forward-looking statements. All statements other than											
24	statements of historical facts contained in this prospectus, including statements regarding											
25	our future financial position, business strategy and plans and objectives of management											
26	for future operations, are forward-looking statements. The words "believe", "may", "will",											
27	"estimate", "continue", "anticipate", "intend", "expect" and similar expressions are											
28	intended to identify forward-looking statements. We have based these forward-looking											
29	statements largely on our current expectations and projections about future events and											
30	financial trends that we believe may affect our financial condition, results of operations,											
31	business strategy, short term and long term business operations and objectives, and											
32	financial needs.											
33												
34												

Fig. 99

Gotcha: As shown in Fig. 100, if you have a few words in bold in one cell, this formatting will be lost.

| This prospectus includes *forward-looking statements* . All |
| statements of historical facts contained in this prospectus, incluc |
| our future financial position, business strategy and plans and obic |

Fig. 100

Alternate Strategy: Textboxes also solve this problem. Draw a textbox to fill columns A through K and paste your text into the textbox, as shown in Fig. 101.

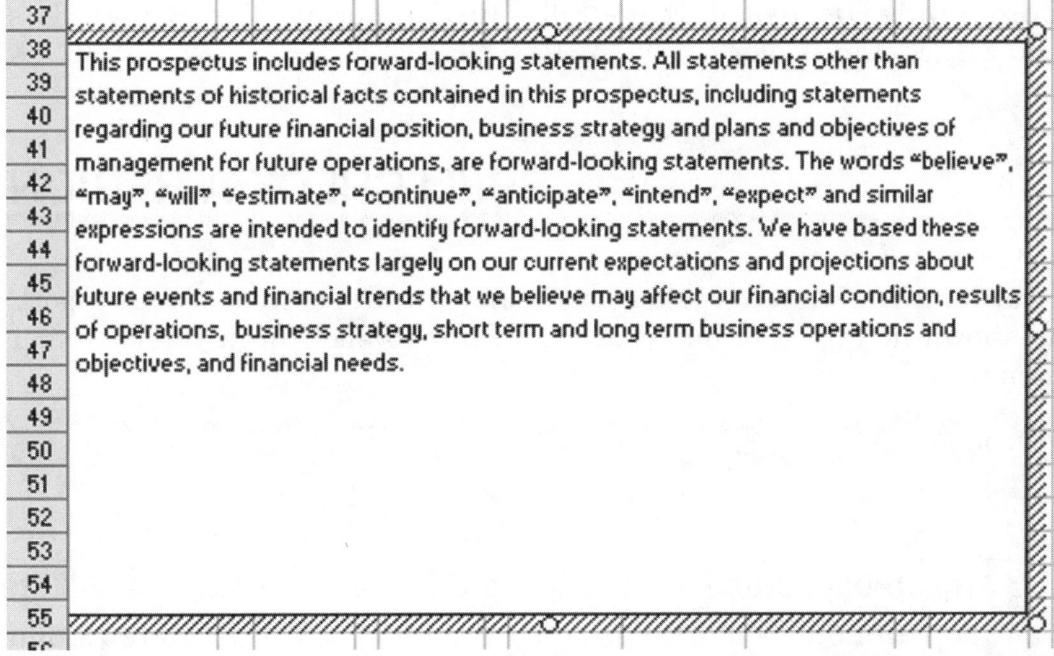

Fig. 101

You can format the textbox to hide its border. Ctrl+Right-click on the border of the text box and choose Format Textbox. On the Colors and Lines tab, choose No Line from the Line color dropdown, as shown in Fig. 102.

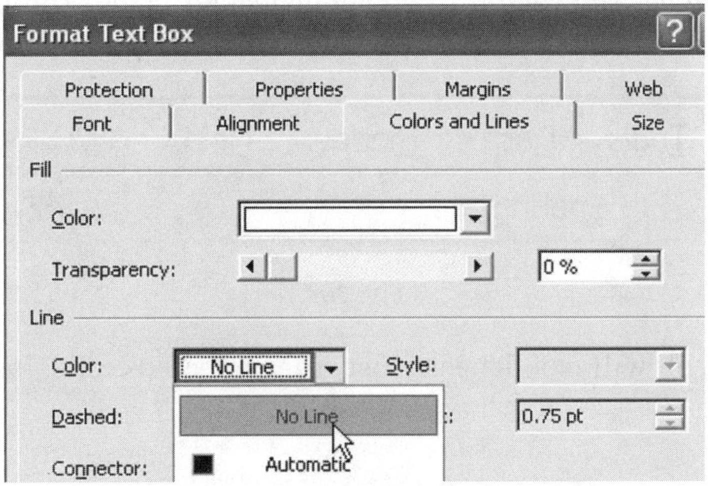

Fig. 102

Summary: When you need to add a bit of text to an Excel worksheet, the Justify command can make the range look as if it were created with a word processor.

Commands Discussed: Edit – Fill – Justify; Format Text Box – Colors and Lines – Line Color

SPELLCHECK A REGION

Problem: You want to spellcheck the notes at the bottom of your report, as shown in Fig. 103, but you don't want to spellcheck the customer names in the report.

	A	B	C	D	E	F	G	H
21								
22								
23	This prospectus includes forward-looking statements. All sta
24	contained in this prospectus, including statements regardin
25	and plans and objectives of management for future operatior
26	"believe", "may", "will", "estimate", "continue", "anticipate", "ir
27	intended to identify forward-looking statements. We have ba

Fig. 103

Strategy: Select the region to be spellchecked. From the menu, select Tools – Spelling or press the F7 key, as shown in Fig. 104.

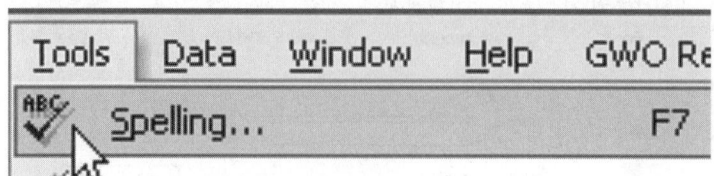

Fig. 104

Result: Excel will spellcheck just the selected cells, as shown in Fig. 105.

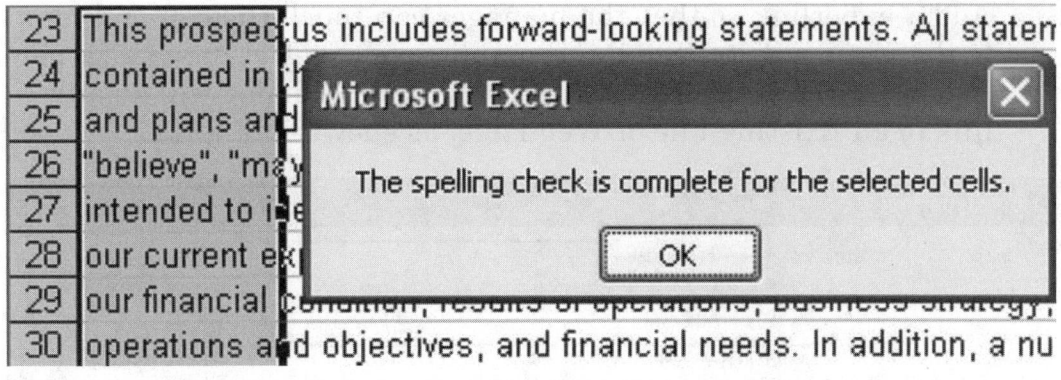

Fig. 105

Part I

Summary: To spellcheck only a part of your worksheet, select the area to be checked and then use Tools – Spelling or the F7 key.

Commands Discussed: Tools – Spelling; F7 key

USE HYPERLINKS TO CREATE AN OPENING MENU FOR YOUR WORKBOOK

Problem: You have designed a budget workbook. It has various worksheets. Managers throughout the company need to use it, but some of these managers are not entirely comfortable with Excel. A navigation tool would help them get through the worksheet.

Strategy: Make your first worksheet a menu with hyperlinks.

1) Insert an opening worksheet called Menu. Add an entry for each section of the workbook, as shown in Fig. 106.

	A	B	C	D	E
1	Welcome to the budget worksheet				
2					
3	Select an option below:				
4		Review Actuals			
5		Enter Forecast			
6		Submit to Corporate			
7					

Fig. 106

2)   Add a hyperlink so that the manager can touch the cell and jump to the section. Select cell B4. From the menu, select Insert – Hyperlink or Ctrl+K. Initially, the Insert Hyperlink dialog will default to link to an Existing File or Web Page, as shown in Fig. 107.

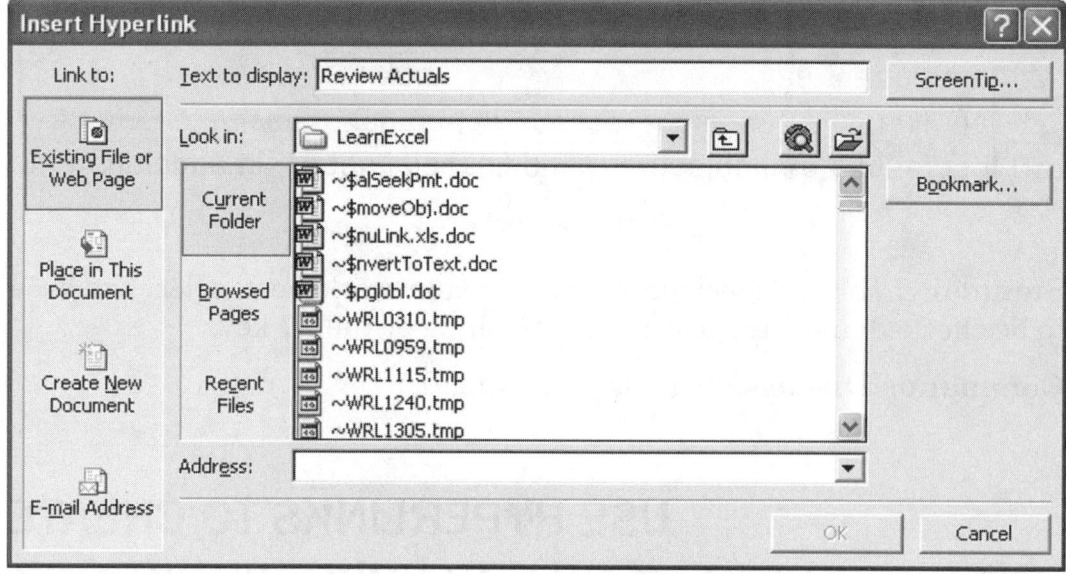

Fig. 107

3)   On the left side of the dialog, choose the second option, to link to a Place in This Document. The dialog changes to show you all of the worksheets in the document, as shown in Fig. 108.

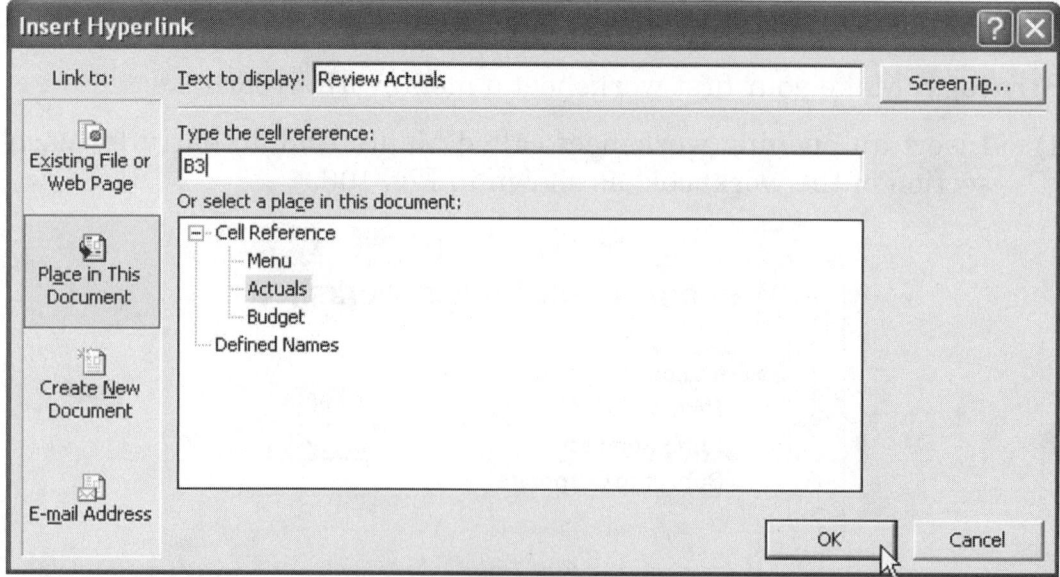

Fig. 108

4)   Choose a Worksheet. Choose a cell Address. Choose OK.

Result: The cell becomes a clickable hyperlink. Clicking on the link will take the manager to the Actuals worksheet. See Fig. 109.

	A	B	C	D	E
1	Welcome to the budget worksheet				
2					
3	Select an option below:				
4		Review Actuals			
5		Enter forecast			
6		Submit to Corporate			
7					

Fig. 109

Part I

Additional Information: Be sure to provide a hyperlink on the Actuals worksheet to take the manager back to the menu, as shown in Fig. 110.

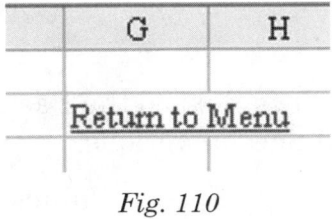

	G	H
	Return to Menu	

Fig. 110

Summary: Make Excel less intimidating for other people by adding hyperlinks to provide simple navigation around the workbook.

Commands Discussed: Insert – Hyperlink

GET QUICK ACCESS TO PASTE SPECIAL

Problem: After reading this book, you routinely find yourself using Edit – Paste Special – Values. It is fairly cumbersome to navigate to this command.

Strategy: Don't blame me just because you are using these cool features all the time! Relax – there is an even faster way you can go.

On the Standard toolbar, there is a Paste button. Next to the Paste button is a dropdown arrow, as shown in Fig. 111. From the arrow, you can choose to paste one of the six most common options: Paste Values, Paste Formats, No Border, Transpose, Paste Link, and Paste Special.

Fig. 111

Summary: Use the dropdown next to the Paste icon to get quick access to the most popular Paste Special options.

Commands Discussed: Paste Special Values

USE SHIFT KEY TO REVERSE POPULAR TOOLBAR ICONS

Problem: Your company makes you travel with an antique laptop that has only a low-resolution display. In order to see more than 10 rows in Excel, you accept Excel's default to display the Standard and Formatting toolbars on one line. This means that you can only see about 18 of the popular toolbar icons, as shown in Fig. 112.

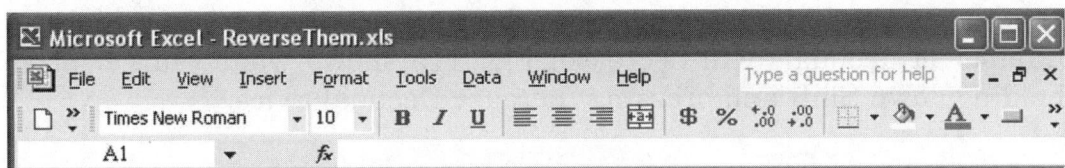

Fig. 112

If you use the >> icon to find a hidden icon, you will bring this icon back to the visible set and knock another icon off the toolbar.

Strategy: Many of Excel's icons are redundant. There is one icon to increase decimals and another one icon to decrease decimals, as shown in Fig. 113. These toolbar icons do the opposite action from each other. By holding down the Shift key while using either icon, you can cause Excel to do the reverse action.

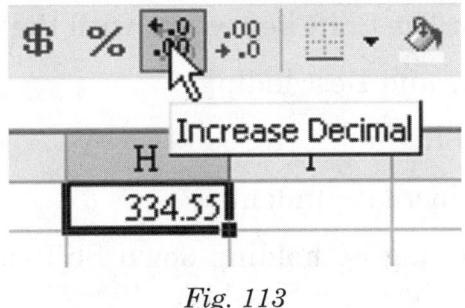

Fig. 113

Press the Increase Decimal icon and the number of decimal places shown will increase, as shown in Fig. 114.

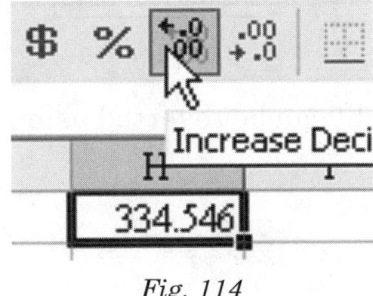

Fig. 114

Hold down the Shift key and press the Increase Decimal icon and the number of decimals will decrease! Fig. 115 shows what you get after holding down Shift and pressing Increase Decimal twice.

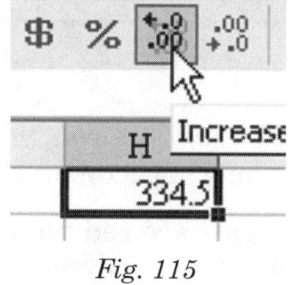

Fig. 115

Provided that you can remember the Shift key trick, you don't need the Decrease Decimal icon on the toolbar.

Additional Details: The Shift key works with the following icons:

- Sort Ascending and Descending
- Align Left and Right
- Decrease and Increase Indent

You can Sort Descending by holding down Shift while using the Sort Ascending button, as shown in Fig. 116.

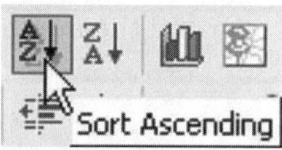

Fig. 116

Align Left and Align Right can be reversed using the Shift key, as shown in Fig. 117.

Fig. 117

Using the Shift key can also reverse the Decrease and Increase Indent, as shown in Fig. 118.

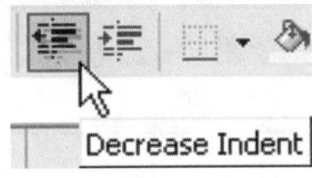

Fig. 118

Part I

Summary: Knowing which toolbar icons can be reversed will allow you to avoid hunting for the opposite icon in the infrequently used icon area. Or, you can customize your toolbars to remove one of each pair of redundant icons.

Commands Discussed: Increase and Decrease Decimal; Sort Ascending and Descending; Align Left and Right; Increase and Decrease Indent

CREATE A MENU OR A TOOLBAR OF YOUR FAVORITE ICONS

Problem: You rarely use half of the icons in the Standard or Formatting toolbar. Why not create a Steve-O toolbar with just your favorites?

Strategy:

1)   Choose View – Toolbars – Customize. From the Toolbars tab, select New..., as shown in Fig. 119.

Fig. 119

2)   Give the new toolbar a name, as shown in Fig. 120. You should probably only use Steve-O if your name is actually Steve.

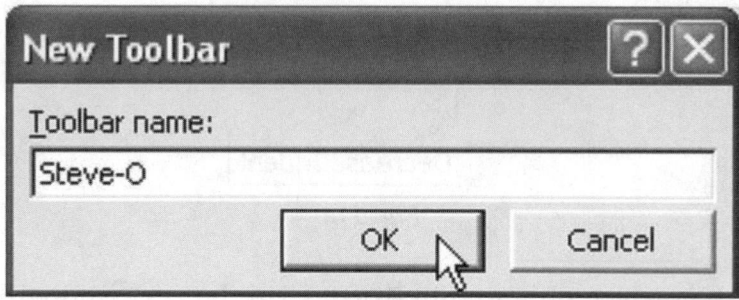

Fig. 120

3)   As shown in Fig. 121, a new toolbar will appear without any icons. In the Customize dialog, choose the Commands tab. Drag any icon(s) you use regularly from the Commands tab to the new bar.

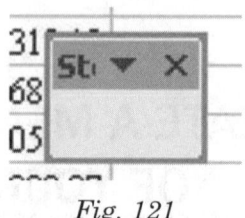

Fig. 121

Additional Information: Consider some of these unusual but useful icons:

If you routinely paste formulas as values, the Paste Values icon (located in the Edit category) will speed up the process for you. See Fig. 122 below.

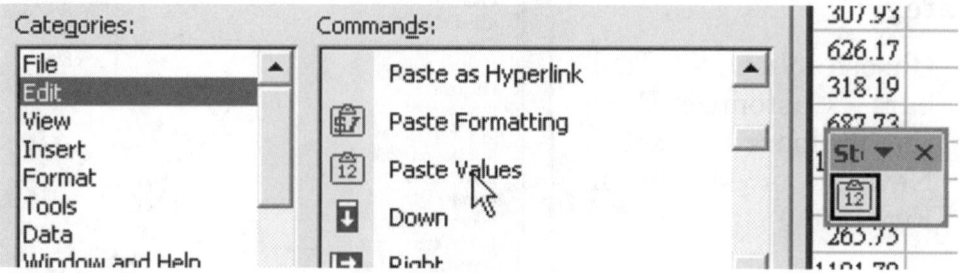

Fig. 122

The Select Visible Cells icon will gather just the total lines when your subtotals are in Group mode. This icon will save you from choosing Edit – Go To – Special – Visible Cells only. It is located near the end of the Edit category, as shown in Fig. 123.

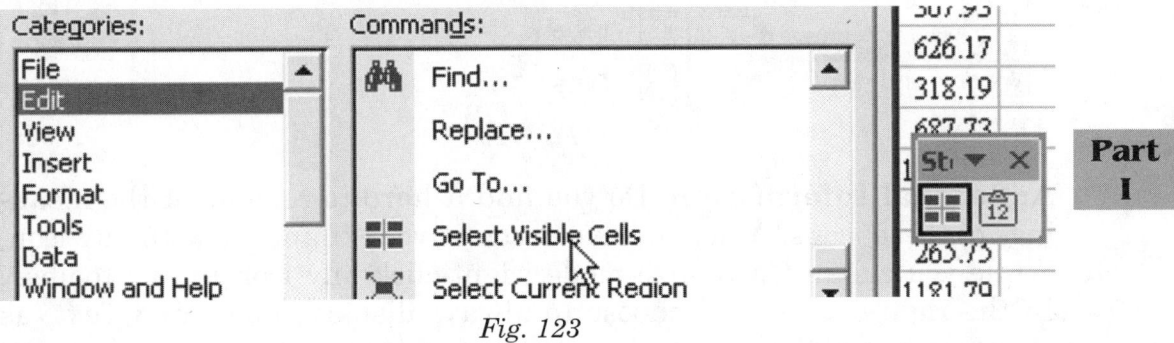

Fig. 123

Part I

As shown in Fig. 124, selecting the Cycle Font Color icon will change the font to a different color with each click. If you just need your cells to be different colors but don't want the burden of selecting the color, this is for you. This icon is located near the top of the Format category.

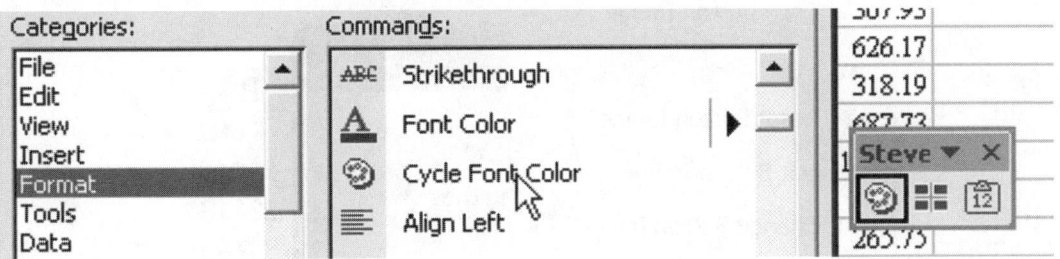

Fig. 124

Choose Symbol from the Insert category if you routinely have to use unusual symbols. The icon provides a shortcut to the Symbol dialog. See Fig. 125.

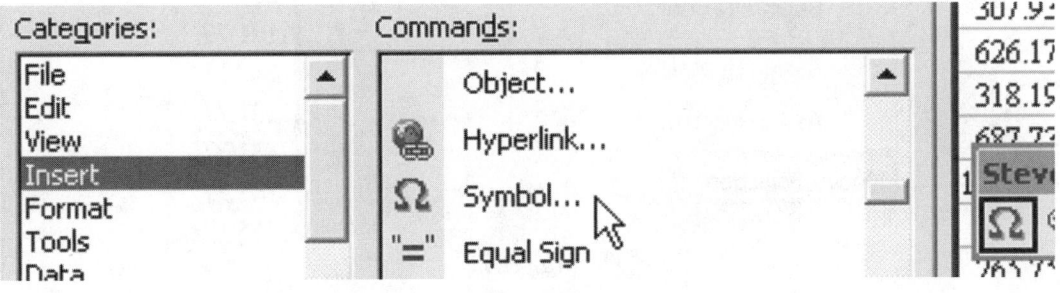

Fig. 125

As shown in Fig. 126, select Pivot Labels if you do a lot of pivot tables. This icon will select just the label areas of a pivot table for easy formatting. The icon is located halfway through the Data category.

Fig. 126

Additional Information: Do you find it hard to remember the meanings of these icons? You can have descriptive text appear with any icon. While you are in Customize mode, right-click any icon in any toolbar. In the right-click menu, choose to always display Image and Text, as shown in Fig. 127.

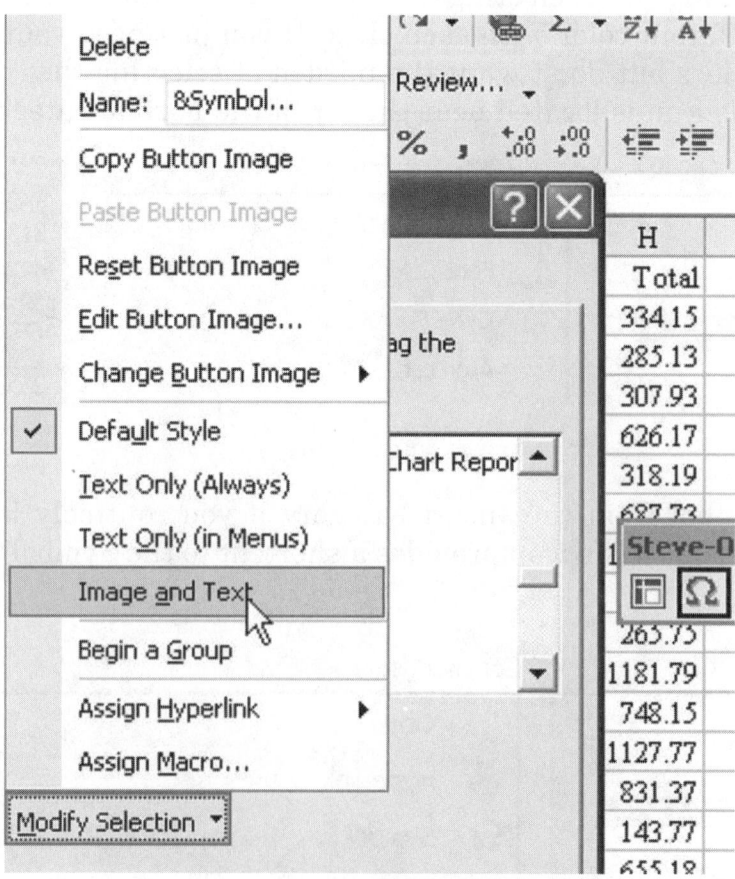

Fig. 127

The icon will appear with its text in the toolbar, as shown in Fig. 128. You can add text to any toolbar button using this method.

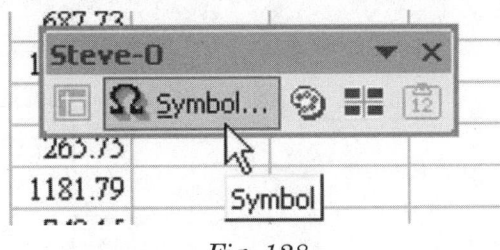

Fig. 128

Additional Details: If you would like to send your custom toolbar along with the workbook, you can attach it to the workbook. On the Customize dialog, choose the Toolbars tab. Select the Steve-O toolbar and choose the Attach button, as shown in Fig. 129.

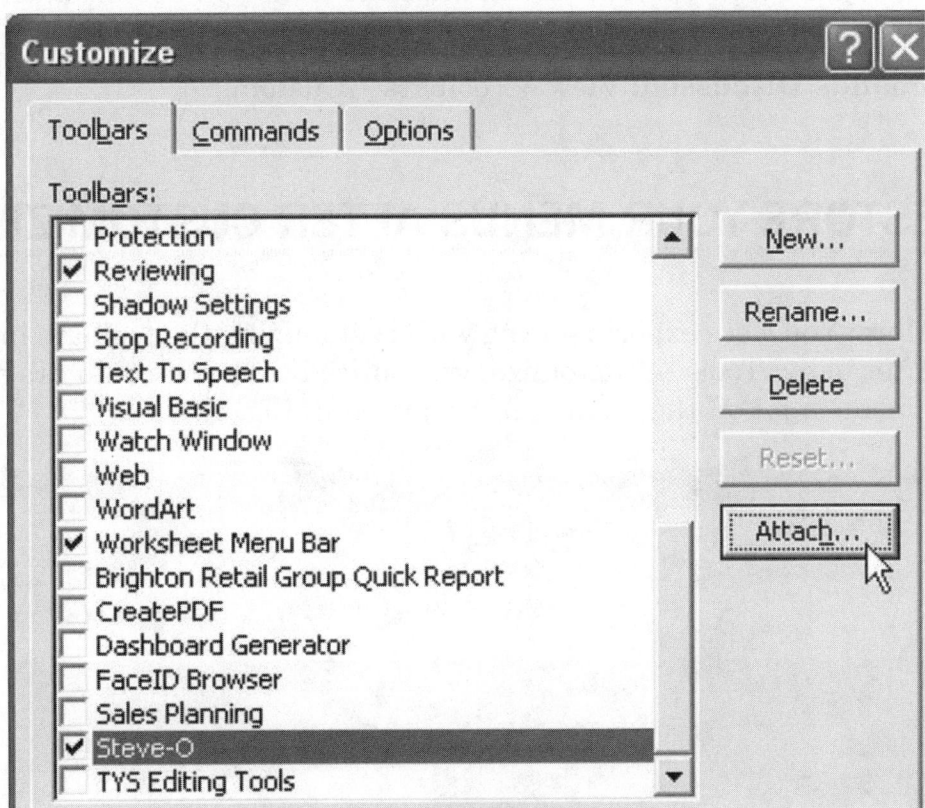

Fig. 129

You can choose which custom toolbars should be attached to this work-book, as shown in Fig. 130.

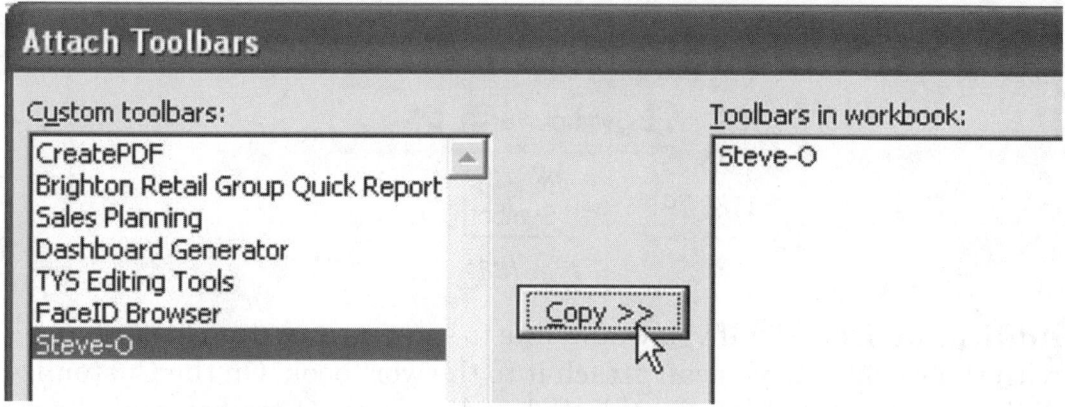

Fig. 130

Summary: To create a tool bar that has the icons you use most, choose View – Toolbars – Customize.

Commands Discussed: View – Toolbars – Customize

RESTORE YOUR MENUS AFTER CUSTOMIZING

Problem: You were experimenting with customizing the toolbars in Excel. After using Tools – Customize, you noticed that you could drag the Data menu right off the menu bar, as shown in Fig. 131.

Fig. 131

For some unknown reason, you then removed the remaining menu items from the toolbar, leaving only the File menu. You did this either because you were bored or perhaps as an April Fool's day prank on your manager. As shown in Fig. 132, it would be pretty startling to see this shortened menu in Excel.

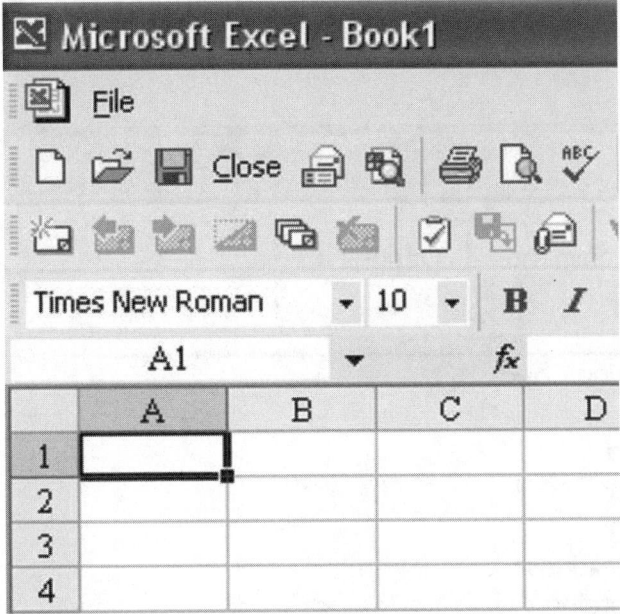

Fig. 132

All the while, you figured this was good fun, because you thought that you could simply quit Excel, restart Excel, and then have the menus back.

However, your gut wrenches as you re-open Excel only to learn that the changes to the menu bar are permanent, as shown in Fig. 133!

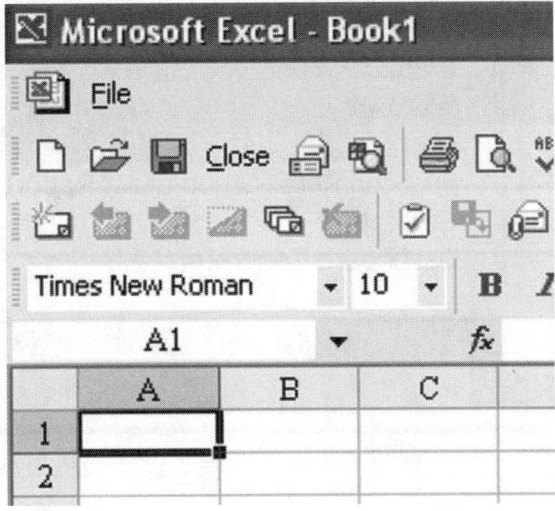

Fig. 133

You don't even have a Tools menu to select Customize from!

Strategy: Relax.

1)   Right-click the menu bar and select Customize.

2)   In the Customize dialog, go to the Toolbars tab. Scroll down to find the Worksheet Menu bar option. Highlight the Worksheet Menu Bar by clicking on that option, as shown in Fig. 134.

Fig. 134

3) As shown in Fig. 135, choose the Reset button along the right side of the dialog.

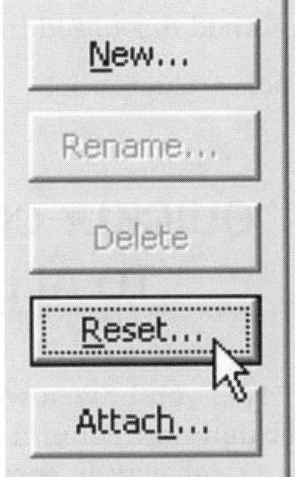

Fig. 135

4) Confirm that you really do want to reset the menu bar, as shown in Fig. 136.

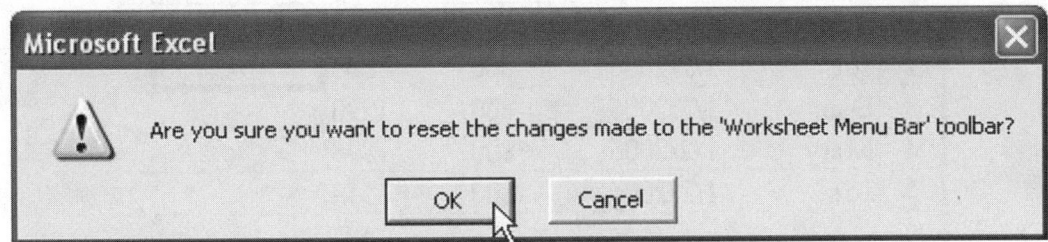

Fig. 136

The menu bar will return to its original state. See Fig. 137.

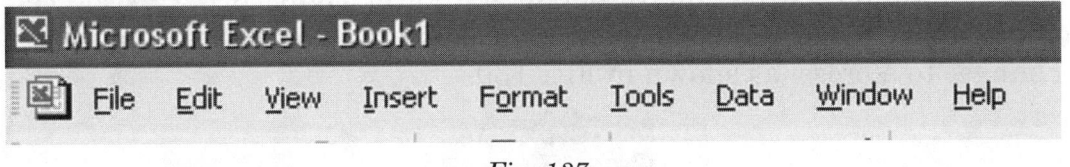

Fig. 137

Summary: Many Excel users have been scared away from customizing their toolbars when they accidentally deleted something important. There is nothing to be concerned about. You can always restore the factory defaults by using the method discussed in this chapter.

Commands Discussed: Tools – Customize

QUICKLY COPY A FORMULA TO ALL ROWS OF DATA

Problem: As shown in Fig. 138, you have a worksheet with 5,000 rows of data. You enter a formula in a new column and need to copy it down to all of the rows. Is there a faster way to copy the formula down to all rows?

	A	B	C	D	E
	E2		fx	=MAX(D2-C2,0)	
1	Salesrep	Date	Quota	Sales	Over Quota
2	Joe	1/2/2006	800	666	0
3	Dan	1/2/2006	800	1290	
4	Mary	1/2/2006	800	896	
5	Joe	1/3/2006	800	559	

Fig. 138

Strategy: Double-click the Fill handle. This shortcut will copy the formula down until Excel encounters a blank cell in column D or F.

The Fill handle is the square dot in the lower right corner of the cell pointer box. When you hover your mouse pointer over the Fill handle, it changes to a cross, as shown in Fig. 139.

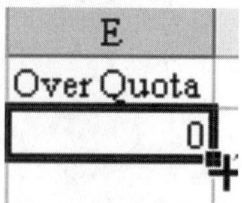

Fig. 139

If there is data in the cell to the left of E2, then Excel will copy the formula based on the first blank cell in column D. If there is no data in D2, but there is data in F2, then Excel will copy down to the first blank cell in column F.

Additional Information: The Fill handle can be used to extend a series. Select two cells that Excel can use to extrapolate the series. Double-click the Fill handle to extend the series down to all rows. In Fig. 140, the record numbers will continue in a 1, 2, 3, 4 sequence.

	A	B	C
1	Rec #	Salesrep	Date
2	1	Joe	1/2/2006
3	2	Dan	1/2/2006
4		Mary	1/2/2006
5		Joe	1/3/2006

Fig. 140

There are other Fill possibilities. One cool technique is to Fill Weekdays. Enter a starting date in one cell. Place the cell pointer in that cell. Right-click and drag the Fill handle down several cells. The tooltip will indicate that you are filling the series with daily dates. When you release the mouse button, you will have several options to choose from, as shown in Fig. 141. Select Fill Weekdays to fill in only Monday through Fridays.

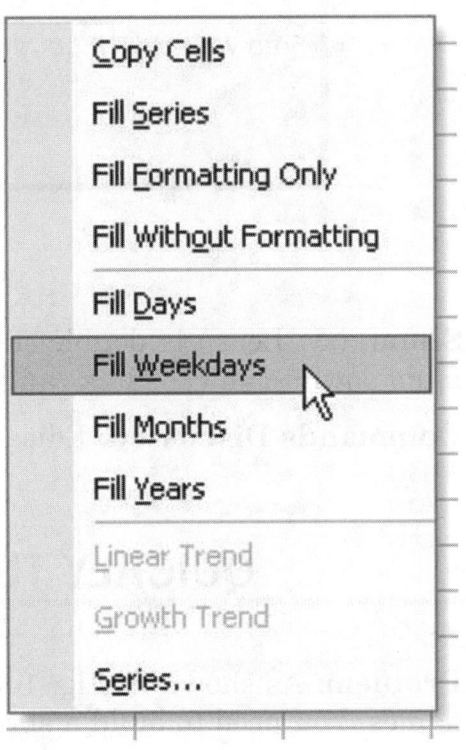

Fig. 141

Additional Information: The Fill handle is a shortcut to default settings in the Edit – Fill – Series command. Enter a cell, select that cell and choose Edit – Fill – Series to display a dialog where you can specify any type of series. As shown in Fig. 142, the dialog will fill the odd numbers from 1 to 99, down a column starting with the active cell.

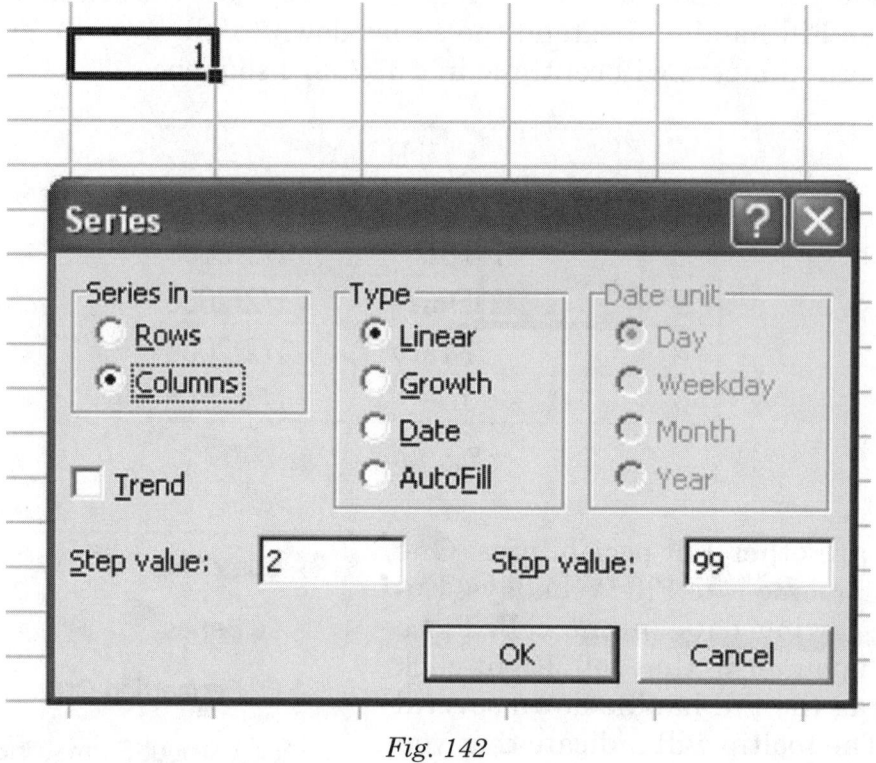

Fig. 142

Summary: Learn to double-click the Fill handle to quickly copy a formula down to all cells in a range of data.

Commands Discussed: Edit – Fill – Series

QUICKLY TURN A RANGE ON ITS SIDE

Problem: As shown in Fig. 143, you have a column of 20 department names. You need to build a spreadsheet with those names going across row 1.

	A
1	**Department**
2	Accounting
3	Finance
4	Marketing
5	Sales - East
6	Sales - Central
7	Sales - West
8	Inside Sales

Fig. 143

Strategy: Use the Paste Special – Transpose option to turn the range on its side.

1) Highlight the department names in column A.

2) From the menu, select Edit – Copy to copy the cells to the clipboard.

3) Move the cell pointer to a blank area of your worksheet. In this case, perhaps cell C1.

4) From the menu, select Edit – Paste Special. In the Paste Special dialog box, choose the Transpose option, as shown in Fig. 144. Choose OK.

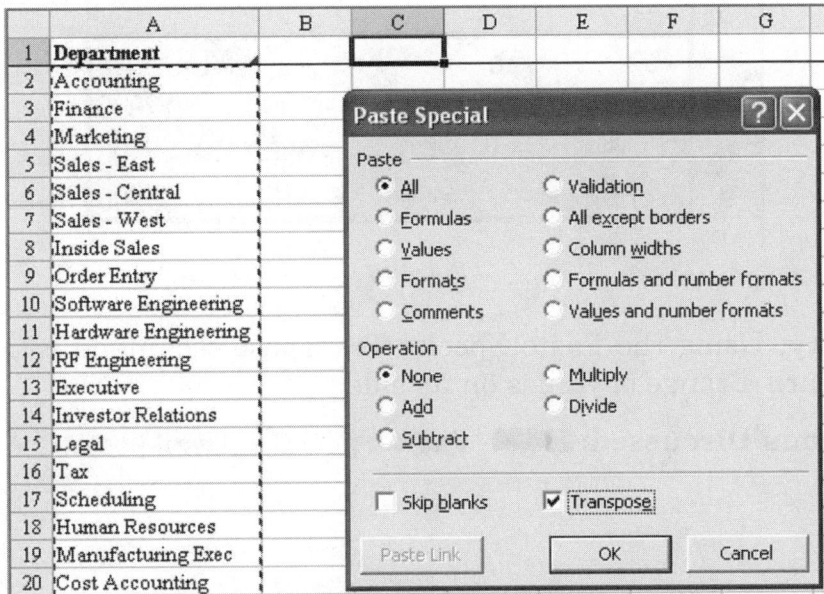

Fig. 144

Result: As shown in Fig. 145, the department numbers from column A are turned sideways and fill cells C1 to Z1.

C	D	E	F	G	H
Accountir	Finance	Marketing	Sales - Ea:	Sales - Ce:	Sales - W:

Fig. 145

Gotcha: The columns that you paste to will not automatically resize to fit the data. Select C1:Z1 and from the menu, choose Format – Columns – AutoFit Selection.

Additional Information: The Paste Special Transpose technique can also be used to convert a horizontal row of numbers into a column.

The technique can also be used to turn a rectangular range on its side. In Fig. 146, Range A1:D4 was transposed to Range A6:D9.

	A	B	C	D
1		Sales	COGS	Profit
2	Jan	10000	5400	4600
3	Feb	11000	5900	5100
4	Mar	12000	6500	5500
5				
6		Jan	Feb	Mar
7	Sales	10000	11000	12000
8	COGS	5400	5900	6500
9	Profit	4600	5100	5500
10				

Fig. 146

Summary: Using the Paste Special Transpose technique is useful to quickly turn a range of values on its side.

Commands Discussed: Edit – Paste Special – Transpose

STOP EXCEL FROM AUTOCORRECTING CERTAIN WORDS

Problem: Every time you type the name of your WYA Division, as shown in Fig. 147, Excel changes "WYA" to "WAY", as shown in Fig. 148. It is impossible to type WYA without entering it as a formula: ="W"&"Y"&"A.

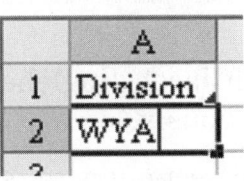

Fig. 147

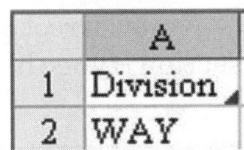

Fig. 148

Strategy: There is a large list of words that are automatically replaced as you type. Excel added this feature to correct common mistypings. This is a good feature, unless you routinely have to type one of the words that Excel thinks is wrong. Luckily, you can edit this list without turning it off.

From the Tools menu, select AutoCorrect options. On the AutoCorrect dialog, go to the AutoCorrect tab. Look in the Replace Text as You Type section. Scroll down to the list to find where it replaces WYA with WAY. Select that line and click Delete, as shown in Fig. 149.

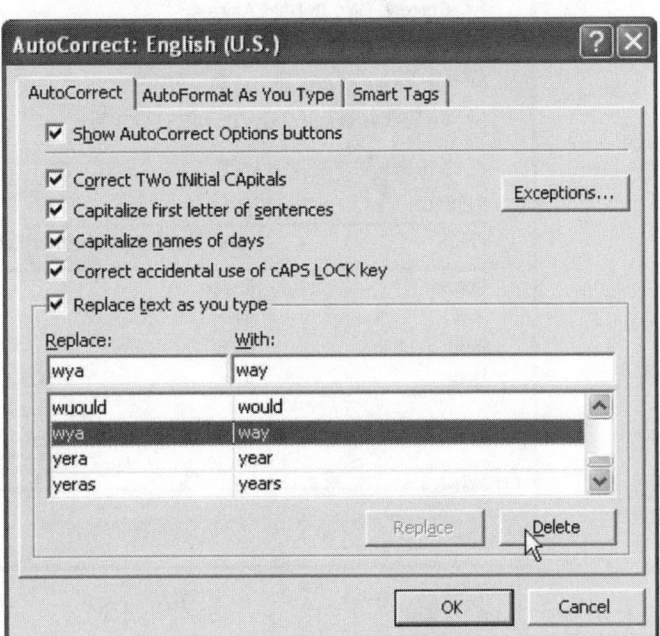

Fig. 149

Part I

Summary: You can edit how Excel will autocorrect words without turning off the feature by going to Tools – AutoCorrect – Options and removing the selected lines from the list.

Commands Discussed: Tools – AutoCorrect – Options

USE AUTOCORRECT TO ENABLE A SHORTCUT

Problem: You work for John Jacob Jingleheimer Schmidt. It is frustrating to type this name continuously.

Strategy: Set up an AutoCorrect entry to replace JJJS with John Jacob Jingleheimer Schmidt.

From the menu, select Tools – AutoCorrect options. In the Replace section, type JJJS. In the With section, type the complete name, click Add, as shown in Fig. 150.

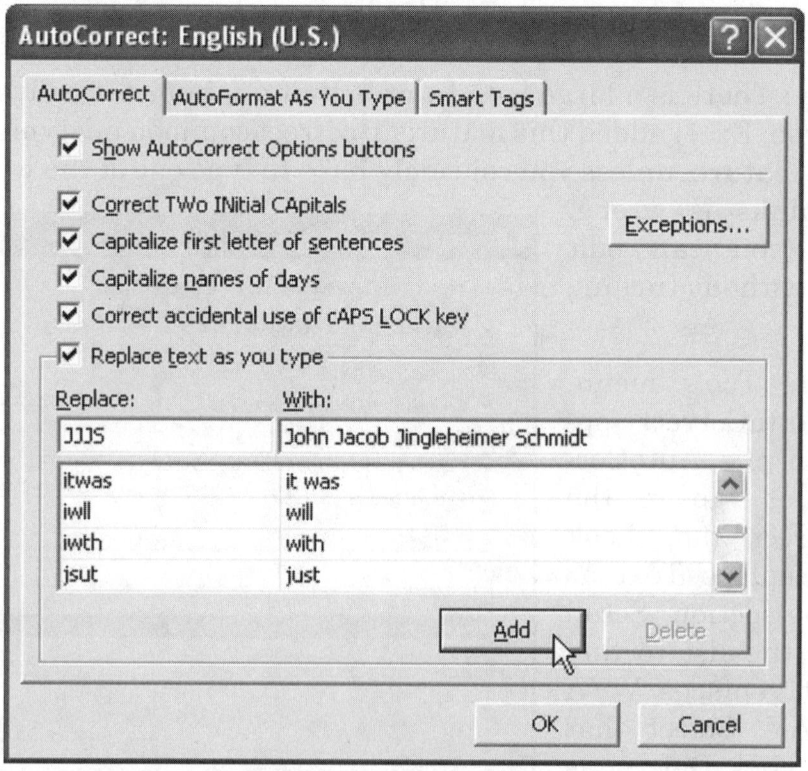

Fig. 150

Result: Typing "JJJS", as shown in Fig. 151, will cause the just the replacement word to appear.

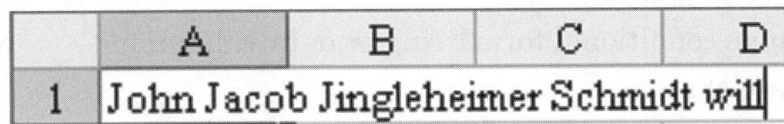

Fig. 151

After typing a Space or hitting Enter to finish the cell, "JJJS" will change to the complete name, as shown in Fig. 152.

	A	B	C	D
1	John Jacob Jingleheimer Schmidt will			

Fig. 152

Summary: Using Tools – AutoCorrect and adding a shortcut for a long or difficult word will cause AutoCorrect to fill it in for you.

Commands Discussed: Tools – AutoCorrect Options

WHY WON'T THE TRACK CHANGES FEATURE WORK IN EXCEL?

Problem: After using Tools – Track Changes, you cannot insert cells.

Strategy: Track Changes is a great feature in Word. However, when you turn on Track Changes in Excel, Microsoft automatically makes your workbook a shared workbook. If you select Tools – Track Changes, Excel will share your workbook, as shown in Fig. 153.

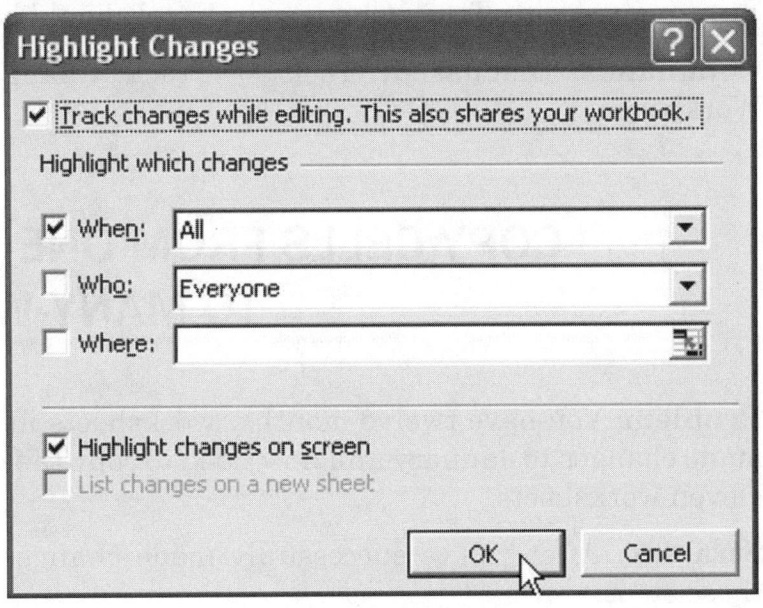

Fig. 153

The shared workbook function in Excel has so many limitations that it is nearly impossible to use. Once you share a workbook, you cannot do any of the following tasks:

- Insert blocks of cells
- Delete worksheets
- Merge or unmerge cells
- Change conditional formatting or data validation
- Create charts
- Insert drawing objects, hyperlinks, scenarios
- Use automatic subtotals
- Use pivot tables
- Record or edit macros
- Enter CSE or array formulas
- Use data tables

It is possible that a novice Excel user might never use the above features. It is even possible that before you bought this book, you never used those features. However, sharing a workbook makes it virtually unusable for an intermediate Excel user. There is no strategy for this. Unless your changes will only involve radically simple worksheet changes, avoid the Track Changes and Share Workbook options.

Summary: Using Track Changes in Excel should be avoided.

Commands Discussed: Tools – Track Changes; Tools – Share Workbooks

COPY CELLS FROM ONE WORKSHEET TO MANY WORKSHEETS

Problem: You have twelve monthly worksheets in a workbook. You've made changes to January and now need to copy the changes to the other eleven worksheets.

Strategy: After you've successfully made changes to January, follow these steps:

1)   Select the January worksheet. While holding down the Shift key, select the December worksheet. This will select all twelve worksheets and the January worksheet will be the active sheet.

> **Note:** *If your changes are in a middle sheet, such as April, then the process is different. First, click the April worksheet. Next, Shift+Click the December sheet, and then Ctrl+Click the January, February, March sheets.*

2)   Select the cells that you want to copy. If the cells are not adjacent, select the first range and then Ctrl+ select the remaining ranges.

3)   From the menu, select Edit – Fill – Fill Across Worksheets, as shown in Fig. 154.

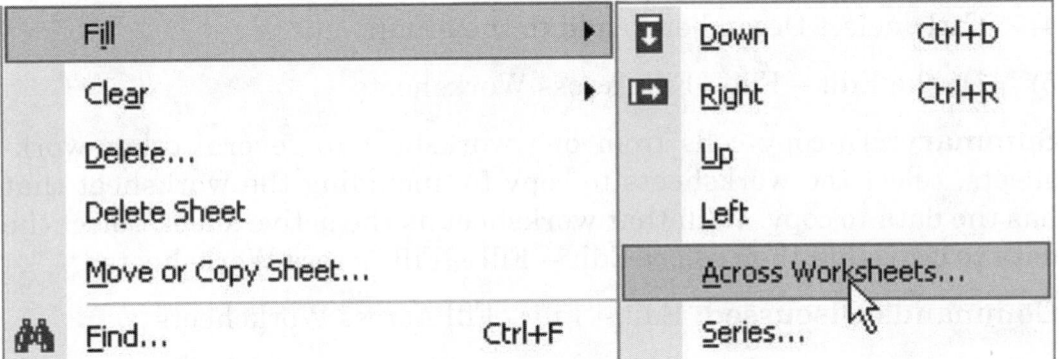

Fig. 154

4)   From the dialog, as shown in Fig. 155, select if you want to copy values, formats, or both.

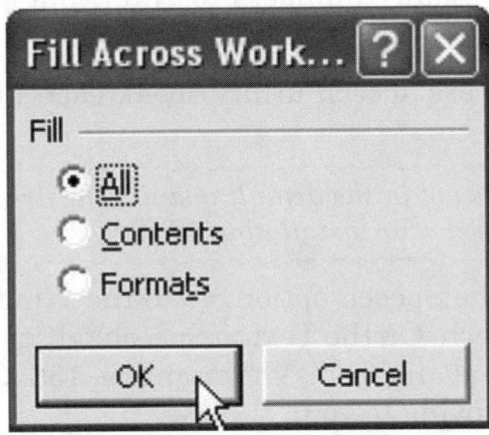

Fig. 155

Gotcha: After this, right-click any sheet tab and select Ungroup. If you fail to ungroup, any changes you make to the active worksheet will be made to all worksheets.

Additional Details: This command is fairly difficult to use. You have to be able to group sheets and then make the sheet with the changes to copy the active (top) sheet. The above steps are designed to help select all sheets. If you need to copy from March to only June, September, December, then you might do this:

1)   Select March to make it the active sheet.

2)   Ctrl+ select June to add to the group.

3)   Ctrl+ select September to add to the group.

4)   Ctrl+ select December to add to the group.

5)   Do the Edit – Fill – Fill Across Worksheets.

Summary: To copy cells from one worksheet to several other worksheets, select the worksheets to copy to, including the worksheet that has the data to copy. With that worksheet as the active sheet, select the data to copy, and then select Edit – Fill – Fill Across Worksheets.

Commands Discussed: Edit – Fill – Fill Across Worksheets

HAVE EXCEL TALK TO YOU

Problem: You have many numbers to enter, but you are notoriously bad at keying data.

Strategy: Have Excel's speech utility speak each number as you complete an entry.

> **Note:** *This feature is not in the default install. The first time you try to use it, you may need your installation CDs.*

1)   Before trying the Speech option, go to the Windows Control Panel and choose Speech. On the Text to Speech tab, there should be three different voices available, as shown in Fig. 156. Choose the one that is the least annoying to you.

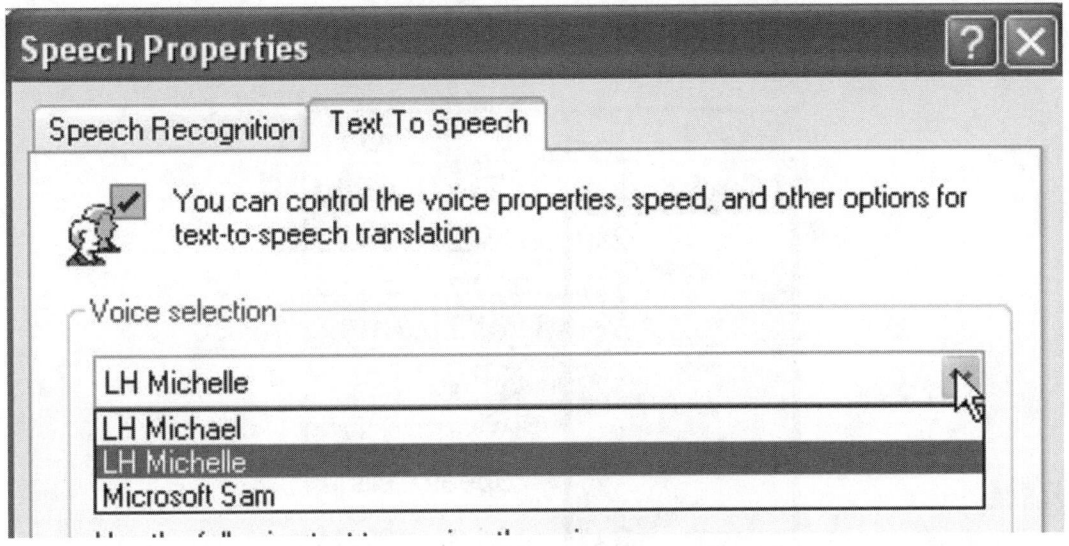

Fig. 156

2) Back in Excel, select Tools – Speech – Show Text to Speech toolbar from the menu, as shown in Fig. 157.

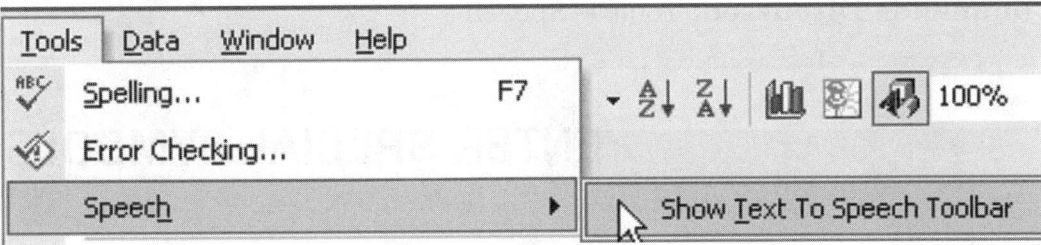

Fig. 157

3) Choose the Speak On Enter icon in the Text To Speech toolbar, as shown in Fig. 158. As you enter new cells, the computer voice will speak the entry, allowing you to audibly check the entries.

Fig. 158

Part
I

4)　You can also select a range of cells and, as shown in Fig. 159, press the Speak Cells button to have all of the cells read to you.

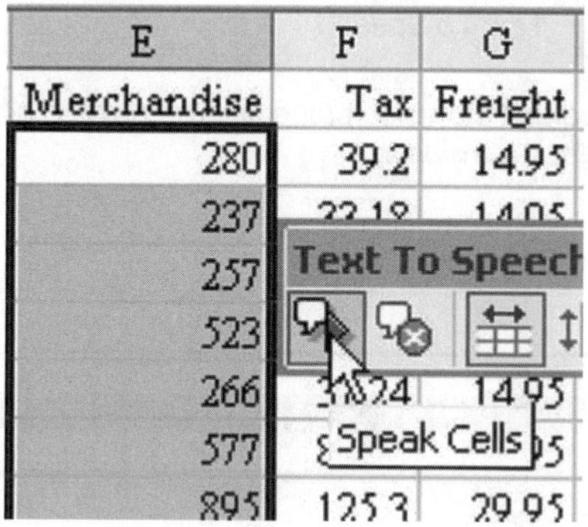

Fig. 159

Summary: Excel's text-to-speech tools can help you to verify your data entry.

Commands Discussed: Tools – Speech

ENTER SPECIAL SYMBOLS

Problem: You work in the music business. You routinely have to enter copyright symbols.

Strategy: Use (c) followed by a space as a shortcut for the © symbol. Use (r) as the shortcut for the registered trademark symbol, ®. For other special symbols, use Insert – Symbol to display the Symbol dialog, as shown in Fig. 160.

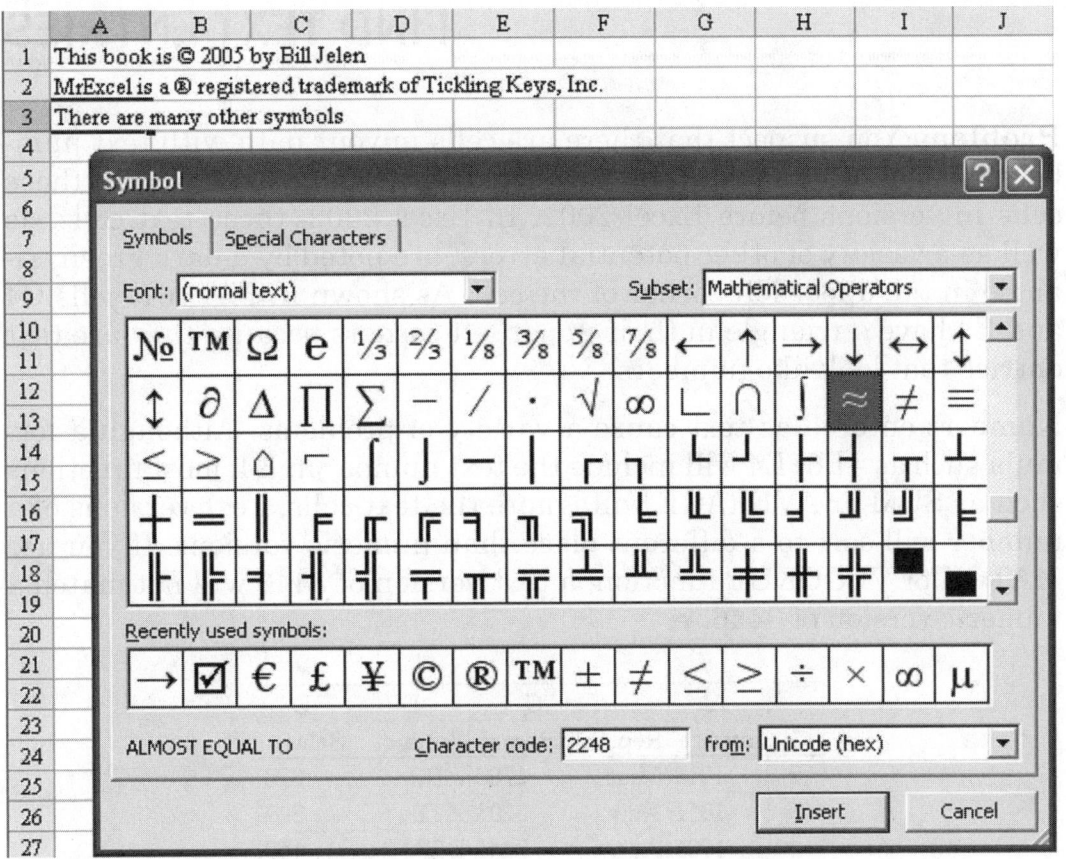

Fig. 160

Select any symbol from the dialog and choose Insert to type the symbol in the cell.

Summary: To insert symbols in your worksheet use Insert – Symbol.

Commands Discussed: Insert – Symbol

FIND TEXT ENTRIES

Problem: You suspect that there are cells in your data with text numbers instead of numbers. There is no easy way to visually locate these cells in versions before Excel 2002. In Excel 2002, these text cells, as well as a variety of other potential errors, are noted by a dark green triangle in the upper left corner of the cell. As shown in Fig. 161, cells C4 and E4 have a triangle in their upper left corners because they are text entries that look like numbers.

Numbers entered as text cause a variety of problems. Although a formula such as =E6+E4 will include the text number in E4, most functions such as SUM or AVERAGE will ignore the text cells. Text versions of a number will sort to a different place than numeric versions. If you use MATCH or VLOOKUP function, a text version of 3446 will not match a numeric version of 3446.

	A	B	C	D	E
1	Invoice	Rep	Customer	Product	Sales
2	1018	Chaz	1700	ABC	320
3	1051	Amy	3203	XYZ	309
4	1086	Amy	3446	DEF	150
5	1049	Chaz	4580	XYZ	228
6	1054	Chaz	6969	ABC	260
7	1034	Amy	7717	ABC	251
8	1077	Chaz	5387	ABC	228
9	1070	Amy	9484	XYZ	111
10	1082	Ben	3023	DEF	227

Fig. 161

Strategy: Locate all the text entries so you can convert them to numbers.

1) Select the entire range of data by selecting one cell and then hitting Ctrl+*.

2) From the menu, select Edit – Go To Special – Constants – Text.

   In order to select Text, as shown in Fig. 162, you will actually have to unselect the other three options: Numbers, Logicals, and Errors.

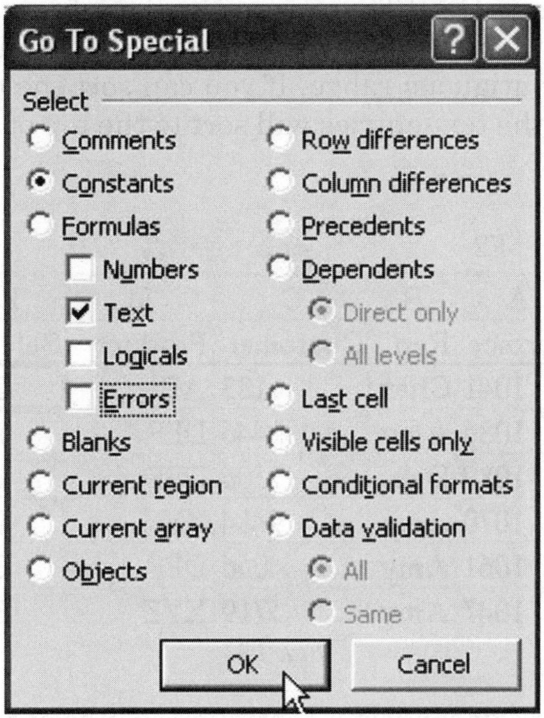

Fig. 162

Part
I

Result: All of the text entries will be highlighted, as shown in Fig. 163.

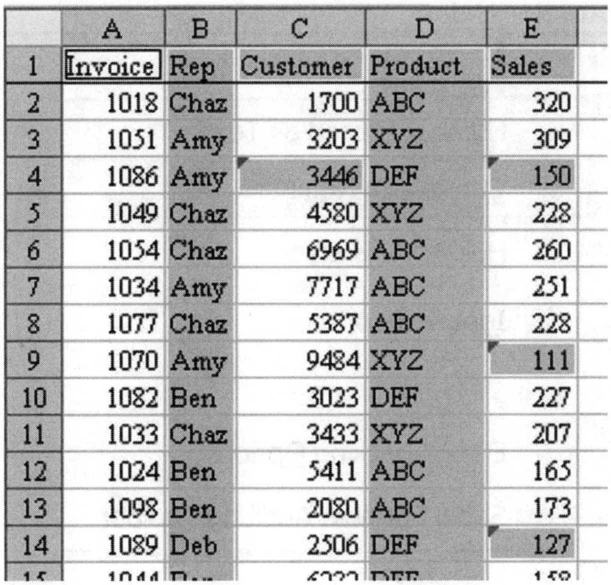

	A	B	C	D	E
1	Invoice	Rep	Customer	Product	Sales
2	1018	Chaz	1700	ABC	320
3	1051	Amy	3203	XYZ	309
4	1086	Amy	3446	DEF	150
5	1049	Chaz	4580	XYZ	228
6	1054	Chaz	6969	ABC	260
7	1034	Amy	7717	ABC	251
8	1077	Chaz	5387	ABC	228
9	1070	Amy	9484	XYZ	111
10	1082	Ben	3023	DEF	227
11	1033	Chaz	3433	XYZ	207
12	1024	Ben	5411	ABC	165
13	1098	Ben	2080	ABC	173
14	1089	Deb	2506	DEF	127
15	1044	Ben	6232	DEF	158

Fig. 163

Additional Information: There are a number of ways to convert these cells from text to numbers. The easiest way, though, is to get all of the text cells in one contiguous range. If you can sort the data by column E descending, all of the text entries will sort to the top of the list, as shown in Fig. 164.

	A	B	C	D	E
	E2		▼	*fx* '216	
1	Invoice	Rep	Customer	Product	Sales
2	1041	Chaz	1183	AB◊⟨!⟩	216
3	1086	Amy	3446	DEF	150
4	1089	Deb	2506	DEF	127
5	1070	Amy	9484	XYZ	111
6	1061	Amy	4056	DEF	349
7	1047	Amy	5719	XYZ	345

Fig. 164

In Excel 2002, you can convert a contiguous range of text numbers. Use the Exclamation dropdown and select Convert to Number, as shown in Fig. 165. This method only works if the top left cell in your selection contains a number stored as text.

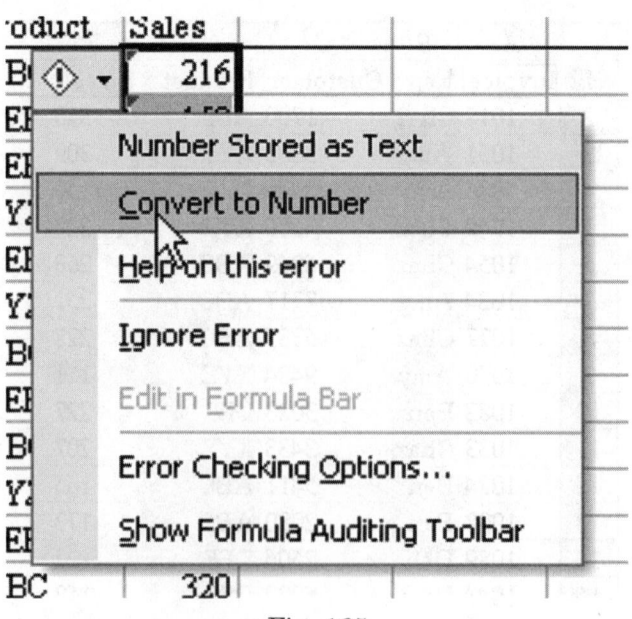

Fig. 165

For earlier versions of Excel, you can use this trick. Enter a zero in a blank cell. Copy the cell with the zero using Ctrl+C. Highlight the text cells. As shown in Fig. 166, from the menu, choose Edit – Paste Special – Values – Add – OK. By adding a zero to the text cells, they will be converted to real numbers.

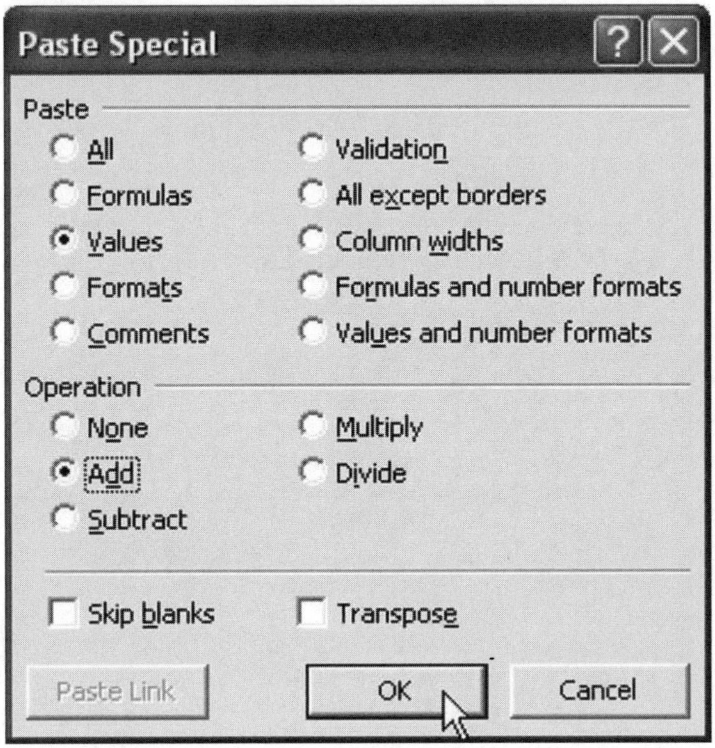

Part
I

Fig. 166

Summary: Text entries that look like numbers are one of the more confusing aspects of Excel. Formulas that directly refer to the cell will calculate correctly, yet common functions like SUM and AVERAGE will not work. This technique shows a way to locate text cells and a couple of strategies for correcting them.

Commands Discussed: Edit – Go To Special – Constants; Edit – Paste Special – Add

PART 2

CALCULATING
WITH EXCEL

COPY A FORMULA
THAT CONTAINS RELATIVE REFERENCES

Problem: You have 5,000 rows of data. After entering a formula to calculate Gross Profit Percent for the first row, as shown in Fig. 167, how do you copy the formula down to other rows?

G2		fx	=IF(E2>0,1-F2/E2,"NA")			
	A	B	C	D	E	F	G
1	Region	Product	Date	Quantity	Unit Price	Unit Cost	GP%
2	East	XYZ	1/1/04	10000	22.81	10.22	55.2%
3	Central	DEF	1/2/04	1000	22.57	9.84	
4	East	ABC	1/2/04	5000	20.49	8.47	
5	Central	XYZ	1/3/04	5000	22.48	10.22	
6	Central	XYZ	1/4/04	4000	23.01	10.22	

Fig. 167

Strategy: All of the cell references in the formula are known as relative references. The amazing thing about Excel is that when you copy a formula, all of the relative cell references are automatically adjusted. If you copy a formula from row 2 down to row 3, as shown in Fig. 168, then every reference pointing at row 2 will change to point at row 3.

G3		fx	=IF(E3>0,1-F3/E3,"NA")			
	A	B	C	D	E	F	G
1	Region	Product	Date	Quantity	Unit Price	Unit Cost	GP%
2	East	XYZ	1/1/04	10000	22.81	10.22	55.2%
3	Central	DEF	1/2/04	1000	22.57	9.84	56.4%
4	East	ABC	1/2/04	5000	20.49	8.47	

Fig. 168

So, the solution to the problem is simply to copy the formula down to all the other rows. A shortcut for doing this is to select the cell and then double-click the Fill handle to copy the formula down to all rows with values in the adjacent column.

Additional Details: Relative references will move in all four directions. In Fig. 169, if you copy the formula in cell F7 to E6, the referenced cell will change from D3 to C2.

	A	B	C	D	E	F
1						
2						
3				1		
4						
5						
6						
7						=D3
8						

Fig. 169

In Fig. 170, you can see how the formula copied from F7 to E6:G8 will change.

	A	B	C	D	E	F	G
1							
2							
3				1			
4							
5							
6					=C2	=D2	=E2
7					=C3	=D3	=E3
8					=C4	=D4	=E4

Fig. 170

| Hint | *Fig. 170 was shot in Show Formula mode. To enter Show Formula mode, hit Ctrl+~. To toggle back to regular mode, hit Ctrl+~ again.* |

Gotcha: It is possible to copy a formula so that it will point to a cell that does not exist. As shown in Fig. 171, what would happen if you copied C4 to B3?

	A	B	C
1	2		
2			
3			
4			=A1
5			

Fig. 171

Part II

The reference to A1 would have to point to the cell one row above and one column to the left of A1. This cell does not exist, so Excel will return a #REF error, as shown in Fig. 172.

	A	B	C
1	2		
2			
3		=#REF!	
4			=A1
5			

Fig. 172

Summary: The 'miracle' of Excel is that you can enter a formula in one place and copy it to many other places and it will still work. This is because a regular cell reference, such as B1, is a relative reference.

COPY A FORMULA
WHILE KEEPING ONE REFERENCE FIXED

Problem: You have 5,000 rows of data. As shown in Fig. 173, each row contains a quantity and the unit price. The sales tax rate for all orders is shown in cell C1. After entering a formula to calculate the total with sales tax in the first row, how do you copy the formula down to other rows?

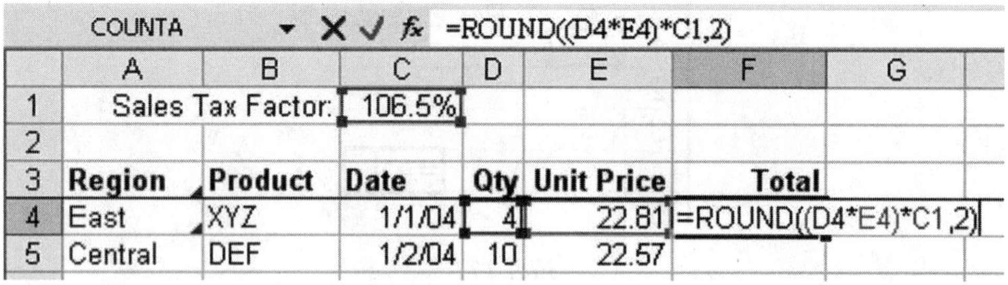

Fig. 173

If you copy the formula in F4 to F5, you get an invalid result, as shown in Fig. 174.

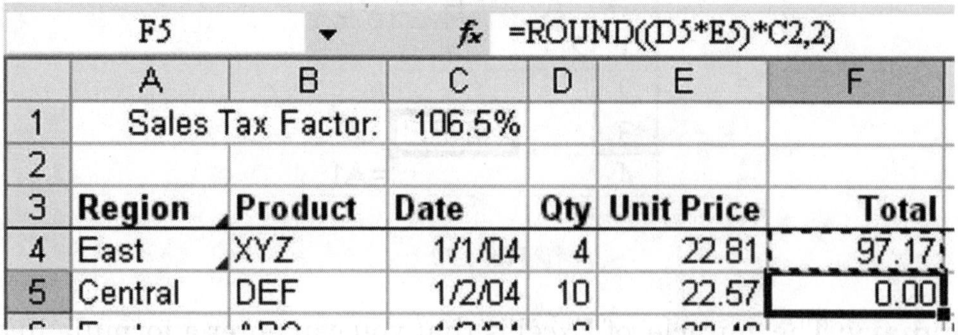

Fig. 174

Look at the formula in the formula bar in Fig. 174. As you copied the formula, the references to D4 and E4 changed as expected. However, the reference to C1 moved to C2. You need to find a way to copy this formula and always have the formula reference C1.

Frankly, this is the most important technique in the entire book. I once had a manager who would enter every formula by hand in the entire dataset. I didn't have the heart to tell him there was an easier way.

Strategy: You need to indicate to Excel that the reference to C1 in the formula is Absolute. Do this by inserting a dollar sign before the C and before the 1 in the formula. The formula in F4 would change to =ROUND((D4*E4)*$C$1,2).

As you copy this formula down to other rows in your dataset, the portion that refers to $C$1 will continue to point at $C$1, as shown in Fig. 175.

	A	B	C	D	E	F	G
1	Sales Tax Factor:		106.5%				
2							
3	**Region**	**Product**	**Date**	**Qty**	**Unit Price**	**Total**	
4	East	XYZ	1/1/04	4	22.81	97.17	
5	Central	DEF	1/2/04	10	22.57	240.37	
6	East	ABC	1/2/04	8	20.49	174.57	
7	Central	XYZ	1/3/04	8	22.48	191.53	
8	Central	XYZ	1/4/04	8	23.01	196.05	
9	East	DEF	1/4/04	7	23.19	=ROUND((D9*E9)*$C$1,2)	
10	East	XYZ	1/4/04	2	22.88	48.73	
11	Central	ABC	1/5/04	6	17.15	109.59	

Fig. 175

Additional Details: See the next chapter to understand the effect of using just one dollar sign in a reference instead of two. Read "Simplify Entry of Dollar Signs in Formulas" a few chapters after that to learn a cool shortcut for entering the dollar signs automatically.

Summary: Entering dollar signs in a reference will lock the reference and make it absolute. No matter where you copy the formula, it will continue to point to the original cell.

Functions Discussed: =ROUND()

Cross Reference: Create a Multiplication Table; Simplify Entry of Dollar Signs in Formulas

Part II

CREATE A MULTIPLICATION TABLE

Problem: Create a multiplication table to help your kids in school. In Fig. 176, you want to enter a single formula in cell B2 that can be copied to the entire table.

	A	B	C	D	E	F	G	H	I	J	K	L	M
1		1	2	3	4	5	6	7	8	9	10	11	12
2	1												
3	2												
4	3												
5	4												
6	5												
7	6												
8	7												
9	8												
10	9												
11	10												
12	11												
13	12												

Fig. 176

Strategy: In the last chapter, you learned how to use an absolute reference, such as $C$1, so that Excel would not change from column C or row 1 as it copied the formula. To create a multiplication table, you need to use a mixed reference. A mixed reference, such as $B1, will lock the formula to column B, while allowing the row to change. A mixed reference, such as B$1, will lock the row to row 1, while allowing the column to change.

The formula that you need for the multiplication table is a formula that will multiply whatever is in row 1 above the cell by whatever is in column A to the left of the cell.

To have a reference that always points to row 1, use something in the format of B$1. To have a reference that points to column A, use a reference in the format of $A2.

1) As shown in Fig. 177, the formula you want to enter in B2 is =$A2*B$1.

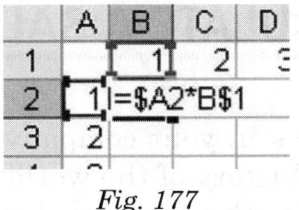

Fig. 177

2) Copy the formula in B2 to the entire range, and it will always properly multiply row 1 by column A as shown in Fig. 178.

M13					fx	=$A13*M$1						
	A	B	C	D	E	F	G	H	I	J	K	L	M
1		1	2	3	4	5	6	7	8	9	10	11	12
2	1	1	2	3	4	5	6	7	8	9	10	11	12
3	2	2	4	6	8	10	12	14	16	18	20	22	24
4	3	3	6	9	12	15	18	21	24	27	30	33	36
5	4	4	8	12	16	20	24	28	32	36	40	44	48
6	5	5	10	15	20	25	30	35	40	45	50	55	60
7	6	6	12	18	24	30	36	42	48	54	60	66	72
8	7	7	14	21	28	35	42	49	56	63	70	77	84
9	8	8	16	24	32	40	48	56	64	72	80	88	96
10	9	9	18	27	36	45	54	63	72	81	90	99	108
11	10	10	20	30	40	50	60	70	80	90	100	110	120
12	11	11	22	33	44	55	66	77	88	99	110	121	132
13	12	12	24	36	48	60	72	84	96	108	120	132	144

Fig. 178

Summary: Using a single dollar sign in a cell reference will create a mixed reference. Only the row or column will be fixed as you copy the formula.

Part II

CALCULATE A SALES COMMISSION

Problem: The VP of Sales in your company dreamt up the most convoluted sales plan in the history of the world. Rather than just pay the reps a straight commission, this plan involves a base rate of 2 percent, bonuses based on the product sold, and the monthly profit sharing bonuses. For the spreadsheet shown in Fig. 179, using Relative, Mixed, and Absolute formulas, create a formula that can be copied to all rows and all months.

	A	B	C	D	E	F	G	H	I	J
1	**Base Rate**	2%		**Bonus Factor:**	102%	100%	104%			
2										
3						SALES			COMMISSION	
4										
5	**Rep**	**Product**	**Prod Rate**	**Customer**	**Jan**	**Feb**	**Mar**	**Jan**	**Feb**	**Mar**
6	Jones	ABC	5%	General Motors	8132	25350	18904			
7	Jones	DEF	8%	Molson, Inc	17136	25140	17136			
8	Doe	DEF	8%	Verizon	2042	25140	19368			

Fig. 179

Strategy: This formula will contain all four reference types. While entering the first formula in H6, you will want to base the commission calculation on the January sales in E6. As you copy the formula from January to February, you will want the E6 reference to be able to change to F6. As you copy the formula down to other rows, you will want the E6 to change to E7, E8, etc. Thus, the E6 portion of the formula needs to be a relative reference and will have no dollar signs.

You will multiply the sales times the base rate in B1. As you copy the formula to other months and rows, it always needs to point to B1. Thus, you need to use dollar signs to before the B and before the 1: $B$1.

To incorporate the product bonus, you will need to multiply sales by the Product Rate in column C. All of the months in row 6 will have to refer to C6. All of the months in row 7 will have to refer to C7. Thus, you need a mixed reference where column C is locked. Use the address of $C6.

Finally, the VP of Sales added the monthly profit sharing bonus. The entire commission calculation is multiplied by the bonus factor shown in row 1. The January commission calculation uses the factor in E1. The February factor is in F1. The March factor is in G1. In this case, you need to allow the formula to point to different columns but always to row 1. This requires a mixed reference of E$1.

Now that you have the four components of the formula, you can enter this formula in E6, as shown in Fig. 180: =E6*($B$1+$C6)*E$1.

	A	B	C	D	E	F	G	H	I	J
1	Base Rate	2%		Bonus Factor:	102%	100%	104%			
2										
3						SALES			COMMISSION	
4										
5	Rep	Product	Prod Rate	Customer	Jan	Feb	Mar	Jan	Feb	Mar
6	Jones	ABC	5%	General Motors	8132	25350	18904	=E6*($B$1+$C6)*E$1		
7	Jones	DEF	0%	Molson, Inc	17136	25140	17136			

Fig. 180

Result: As shown in Fig. 181, you have created one single formula that can be copied to all columns and rows of your dataset.

J7	▼		f_x	=G7*($B$1+$C7)*G$1						
	A	B	C	D	E	F	G	H	I	J
1	Base Rate	2%		Bonus Factor:	102%	100%	104%			
2										
3						SALES			COMMISSION	
4										
5	Rep	Product	Prod Rate	Customer	Jan	Feb	Mar	Jan	Feb	Mar
6	Jones	ABC	5%	General Motors	8132	25350	18904	580.6	1775	1376
7	Jones	DEF	8%	Molson, Inc	17136	25140	17136	1748	2514	1782
8	Doo	DEF	8%	Verizon	3042	25140	10369	308.3	2514	2014

Fig. 181

Summary: The concept of relative, absolute, and mixed references is one of the most important concepts in Excel. Being able to use the right reference will allow you to create a single formula that can be copied everywhere.

Part II

SIMPLIFY ENTRY OF
DOLLAR SIGNS IN FORMULAS

Problem: It is a pain to type the dollar signs in complex formulas such as the formula shown in Fig. 182.

$$=E7*(\$B\$1+\$C7)*E\$1$$

Fig. 182

Strategy: Use the F4 key as you are entering the formula. The F4 key will toggle a reference through the four possible reference types.

As shown in Fig. 183, start to type the formula =E7*(B1.

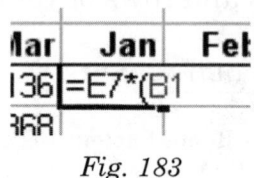

Fig. 183

Immediately after you type B1, hit the F4 key. Excel will insert both dollar signs in the B1 reference, as shown in Fig. 184.

Fig. 184

As an illustration, hit the F4 key again. Excel changes from an absolute reference to a mixed reference, with the row portion of the reference locked, as shown in Fig. 185.

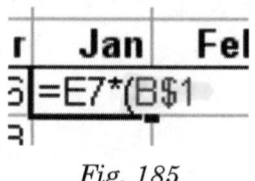

Fig. 185

Hit the F4 key again. Excel changes to a mixed reference, with the column portion of the reference locked, as shown in Fig. 186.

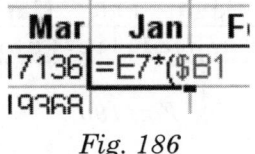

Fig. 186

Hit the F4 key once more. Excel changes back to a relative reference, as shown in Fig. 187.

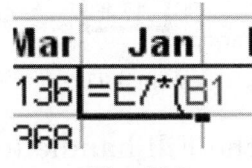

Fig. 187

Here are the steps for entering the complex formula shown in Fig. 182.

1) Type =E7*(B1.

2) Hit the F4 key once.

3) Type +C7.

4) Hit the F4 key 3 times. Your formula will now appear as shown in Fig. 188.

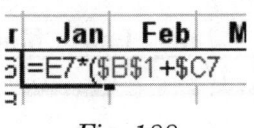

Fig. 188

5) Type the parentheses, an asterisk for multiplication, and E1, as shown in Fig. 189.

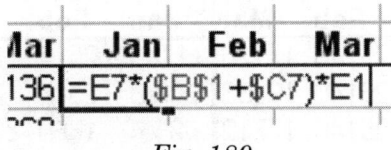

Fig. 189

6)   Hit the F4 key twice to change E1 to a reference with the row locked, as shown in Fig. 190.

ir	Jan	Feb	Mar
6	=E7*($B$1+$C7)*E$1		
8			

Fig. 190

7)   Hit Ctrl+Enter to accept the formula without moving the cell pointer to the next cell, as shown in Fig. 191.

Mar	Jan	F
7136	1748	
9368		

Fig. 191

8)   With the mouse, grab the Fill handle (the square dot in the lower right corner of the cell) and drag it to the right for two cells, as shown in Fig. 192.

Mar	Jan	Feb	Mar
136	1748		
368			+
712			

Fig. 192

This will copy the formula from January to the other two months, as shown in Fig. 193.

r	Jan	Feb	Mar
6	1748	2514	1782

Fig. 193

9)   Double-click the Fill handle. This will copy the three cells down to all of the rows with data, as shown in Fig. 194.

Jan	Feb	Mar	Jan	Feb	Mar
17136	25140	17136	1748	2514	1782
2042	25140	19368	208.3	2514	2014
11700	25140	17712	835.4	1760	1289
15856	25140	12690	1617	2514	1320
16008	25140	17160	1143	1760	1249
2157	25060	16696	220	2506	1736

Fig. 194

Additional Information: You might find mixed references confusing. As you work on building the first formula, you might know that you need to point to C7. Enter C7 in the formula and then use F4 to toggle between the various reference types. Say to yourself, "OK. There is a dollar sign before the C that will lock the column and let the row change – is that what I need?". As long as you say this to yourself without your lips moving, your officemates won't think any less of you.

Further Information: If you did not add the dollar signs as you typed the formula, you can still use the F4 trick later.

Using the mouse, highlight the proper reference in the formula bar, as shown in Fig. 195.

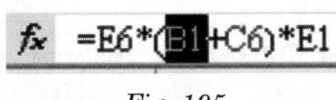

Fig. 195

After the reference is highlighted, you can hit the F4 key to toggle that particular reference through the four states, as shown in Fig. 196.

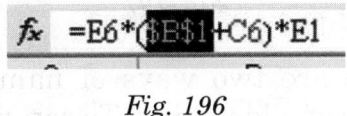

Fig. 196

Summary: Master the F4 key to easily add dollar signs to a reference in order to toggle it from relative to absolute to mixed to mixed.

LEARN R1C1 REFERENCING
TO UNDERSTAND FORMULA COPYING

Problem: All of a sudden, the column letters along the top of your spreadsheet have been replaced by numbers, as shown in Fig. 197. None of the formulas that you enter will work.

R6C4			▼		*fx*	=+R[-1]C+RC[-1]-RC[-2]	
	1	2	3	4	5	6
1	Loan	8,000		Term	24	
2	Rate	5%		Pmt	$350.97	
3						
4	#	Pmt Amt	Interest	Balance		
5				8,000		
6	1	$350.97	33.33333	$7,682.36		
7	2	$350.97	32.00984	$7,363.40		
8	3	$350.97	30.68084	$7,043.11		

Fig. 197

Strategy: Relax. There are two ways of naming cells. Someone has turned on the R1C1 style of addressing. To return to the normal A1 style of cell addressing, go to Tools – Options. On the General tab, uncheck the box for R1C1 Reference Style, as shown in Fig. 198.

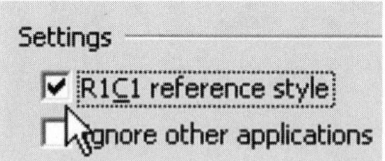

Fig. 198

But wait – while you are here, you can learn something fascinating about spreadsheets. In the topic "Copy a Formula That Contains Relative References", I suggested it was miraculous that Excel could automatically change a formula as you copied it. If you take two minutes to learn about this other method of cell addressing, you will understand that it may not be so amazing after all.

When Dan Bricklin and Bob Frankston invented VisiCalc, they used the A1 style of cell naming. When Mitch Kapor started selling Lotus 1-2-3, he used the same style. When Microsoft came out with their first spreadsheet product – Microsoft Multiplan – they used a very different method of cell addressing. This method is known as R1C1. In the Microsoft system, the rows are numbered just as in the A1 system. However, the columns are also numbered. Each cell is given a name, such as "R4C8". This name stands for the cell at Row 4, Column 8. This is the cell that you and I know as H4.

In the R1C1 style, the formulas are interesting. Look at this formula in cell D6, as shown in Fig. 199.

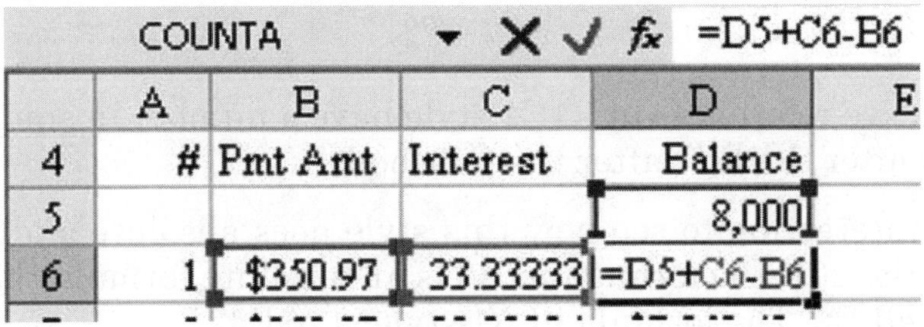

Fig. 199

The formula in the formula bar says =D5+C6–B6. But when you think about this formula in plain language, what it is really means is "Take the cell just above me, add the interest in the cell just to the left of me, and subtract the payment in the cell two cells to the left of me".

Formulas in R1C1 style are more like the plain language description above. If you want to enter a formula in D6 that points to the cell just above, it would be =R[–1]C. The number in square brackets after the R indicates to how many rows ahead or back you are referring. In our case, row 5 is one row above row 6, so you would put a –1 in the square brackets. There is no number after the C portion of the address, which means that you are referring to the same column as the cell that contains the formula.

If you want to refer to a cell that is two cells to the left of the cell with the formula, you would use =RC[–2].

Part II

As shown in Fig. 200, the formula from Fig. 199 can be restated in R1C1 style as follows:

=R[–1]C+RC[–1]–RC[–2]

COUNTA			▾ ✗ ✓ *fx* =R[-1]C+RC[-1]-RC[-2]		
	1	2	3	4	5	6
4		#	Pmt Amt	Interest	Balance	
5					8,000	
6		1	$350.97	33.33333	=R[-1]C+RC[-1]-RC[-2]	
7		2	$350.97	32.00984	$7,363.40	
8		3	$350.97	30.68084	$7,043.11	

Fig. 200

So, all relative references in R1C1 style have a number in square brackets, either after the R or after the C or both.

It is very interesting to see how this style does absolute addresses. As shown in Fig. 201, the formula in B6 is an absolute formula that always points to cell E2. The formula in A1 style is =$E$2.

COUNTA		▾ ✗ ✓ *fx* =$E$2		
	A	B	C	D	E
1	Loan	8,000		Term	24
2	Rate	5%		Pmt	$350.97
3					
4		#	Pmt Amt	Interest	Balance	
5					8,000
6	1	=$E$2		33.33333	$7,682.36
7	2	$350.97		32.00984	$7,363.40
8	3	$350.97	30.68084	$7,043.11

Fig. 201

To enter a similar absolute reference in R1C1 style, you do not include square brackets in the address. As shown in Fig. 202, a formula of =R2C5 will ALWAYS point to cell E2.

COUNTA		▼	✕ ✓	fx =R2C5	
	1	2	3	4	5
1	Loan	8,000		Term	24
2	Rate	5%		Pmt	$350.97
3					
4	#	Pmt Amt	Interest	Balance	
5				8,000	
6	1	=R2C5	33.33333	$7,682.36	
7	2	$350.97	32.00984	$7,363.40	

Fig. 202

It is also possible to have mixed references. Flip back to Fig. 177 in the multiplication table topic. Fig. 203 shows that formula in R1C1 style:

COUNTA		▼	✕ ✓	fx	=RC1*R1C		
	1	2	3	4	5	6	7
1		1	2	3	4	5	6
2	1	=RC1*R1C	2	3	4	5	6
3	2	2	4	6	8	10	12

Fig. 203

Additional Details: Now that you understand the basics of R1C1 style formulas, you can appreciate the amazing part. Remember that Microsoft invented this method for their Multiplan product. Lotus 1-2-3 was the dominant spreadsheet in the late 1980s and early 1990s. Microsoft was battling for market share. Everyone using spreadsheets was familiar with the A1 style. No one would want to learn the R1C1 style in order to switch to Microsoft. So, in their Microsoft Excel product, they developed an elaborate system to actually store the formulas in R1C1 style, but then to translate the R1C1 formulas to A1 style to make it easier for all the Lotus fans to understand.

By default, Microsoft starts with the A1 style addressing. However, you can remember from Fig. 198 that you are just one checkmark away from switching back to R1C1 style addressing.

Finally, here is the amazing part. Examine the amortization table example in Formula View mode. (Hit Ctrl+~ to toggle into Formula View mode.) The Formula View mode in A1 style can be seen in Fig. 204. Every formula in column D is different.

	A	B	C	D	E
1	Loan	8000		Term	24
2	Rate	0.05		Pmt	=-PMT(B2/12,E1,B1)
3					
4	#	Pmt Amt	Interest	Balance	
5				=B1	
6	1	=$E$2	=D5*$B$2/12	=D5+C6-B6	
7	=1+A6	=$E$2	=D6*$B$2/12	=D6+C7-B7	
8	=1+A7	=$E$2	=D7*$B$2/12	=D7+C8-B8	
9	=1+A8	=$E$2	=D8*$B$2/12	=D8+C9-B9	
10	=1+A9	=$E$2	=D9*$B$2/12	=D9+C10-B10	
11	=1+A10	=$E$2	=D10*$B$2/12	=D10+C11-B11	
12	=1+A11	=$E$2	=D11*$B$2/12	=D11+C12-B12	
13	=1+A12	=$E$2	=D12*$B$2/12	=D12+C13-B13	

Fig. 204

The Formula View Mode in R1C1 style can be seen in Fig. 205.

	1	2	3	4	5
1	Loan	8000		Term	24
2	Rate	0.05		Pmt	=-PMT(RC[-3]/12,R[-1]C,R[-1]C[-3])
3					
4	#	Pmt Amt	Interest	Balance	
5				=R[-4]C[-2]	
6	1	=R2C5	=R[-1]C[1]*R2C2/12	=R[-1]C+RC[-1]-RC[-2]	
7	=1+R[-1]C	=R2C5	=R[-1]C[1]*R2C2/12	=R[-1]C+RC[-1]-RC[-2]	
8	=1+R[-1]C	=R2C5	=R[-1]C[1]*R2C2/12	=R[-1]C+RC[-1]-RC[-2]	
9	=1+R[-1]C	=R2C5	=R[-1]C[1]*R2C2/12	=R[-1]C+RC[-1]-RC[-2]	
10	=1+R[-1]C	=R2C5	=R[-1]C[1]*R2C2/12	=R[-1]C+RC[-1]-RC[-2]	
11	=1+R[-1]C	=R2C5	=R[-1]C[1]*R2C2/12	=R[-1]C+RC[-1]-RC[-2]	
12	=1+R[-1]C	=R2C5	=R[-1]C[1]*R2C2/12	=R[-1]C+RC[-1]-RC[-2]	
13	=1+R[-1]C	=R2C5	=R[-1]C[1]*R2C2/12	=R[-1]C+RC[-1]-RC[-2]	
14	=1+R[-1]C	=R2C5	=R[-1]C[1]*R2C2/12	=R[-1]C+RC[-1]-RC[-2]	
15	=1+R[-1]C	=R2C5	=R[-1]C[1]*R2C2/12	=R[-1]C+RC[-1]-RC[-2]	

Fig. 205

In A1 style, it seems AMAZING that Excel can change a reference from D10 to D11 when the formula is copied down. However, look closely at the formulas in each row of rows 7 and higher in the R1C1 style shown in Fig. 205. Each formula in a column is identical to the formula located just above it!

While VisiCalc and Lotus 1-2-3 made the formula replication seem amazing because of their A1 reference style, if the Multiplan invention of R1C1 style had taken hold, it would not seem amazing at all because, in fact, every formula is exactly identical as you copy it down through the rows.

If you ever plan on writing VBA macros in Excel, it is important to understand the R1C1 style of formulas. For general use in Excel, you never really need to totally understand the R1C1 style, but it is interesting to see how Microsoft's R1C1 style is actually superior to A1 when copying formulas in a spreadsheet.

Part II

Summary: Learn R1C1 style formulas to better understand how formulas are replicated across a worksheet.

Commands Discussed: Tools – Options – General

CREATE EASIER-TO-UNDERSTAND FORMULAS WITH NAMED RANGES

Problem: As shown in Fig. 206, your worksheet contains several different formulas. It would be easier to understand the results if each component of every formula were named for what it represented and not just for the cell it came from.

B6	▼	f_x =B3-B4
	A	B
	Budget	
		FY 2005
	Gross Revenue	$91,500
	COGS	$33,640
	Gross Profit	$57,860
	Rent	$15,400
	Utilities	$1,800
	G&A	$3,100
	Expenses	$20,300
	Operating Income	$37,560

Fig. 206

Strategy: Use named ranges to make formulas easier to understand.

1)   Give cell B3 a name of Revenue.

Select cell B3. In the Name box (the area to the left of the formula bar), type Revenue and press Enter, as shown in Fig. 207.

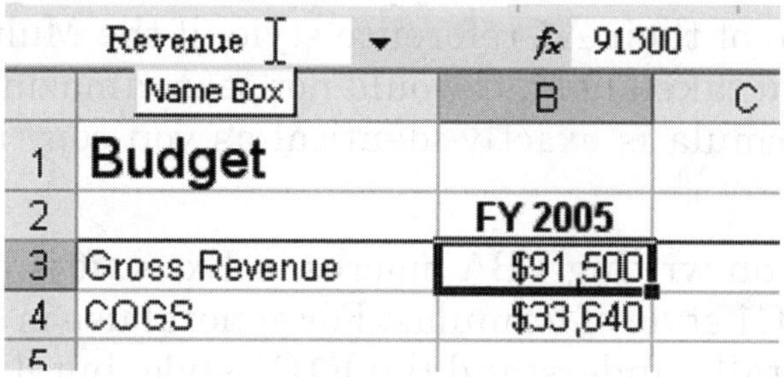

Fig. 207

2)   Give cell B4 a name of COGS.

Select cell B4. Click in the name box, type COGS and hit Enter.

3)   Clear the formula in B6. Re-enter the formula and use the mouse to select the cells. Type an Equal sign. Using the mouse, touch B3. Type a Minus sign. Using the mouse, touch B4. This will enter the formula as =Revenue–COGS, as shown in Fig. 208. This is easier to understand than a typical formula.

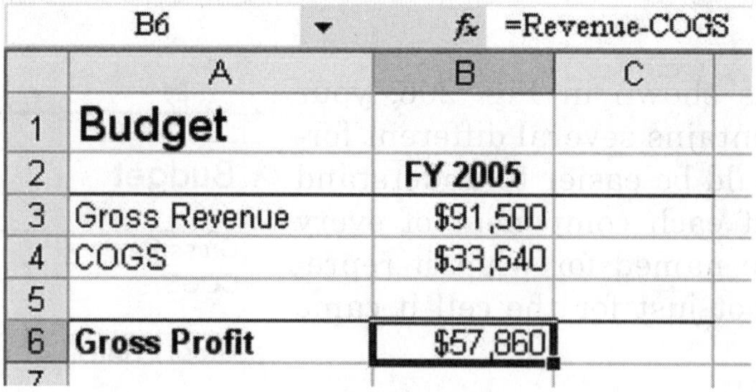

Fig. 208

Gotcha: You need a lot of foresight to use this technique. In order to have this work automatically, you are supposed to be smart enough to create the range names before you enter the formula. However, most people get the formula first and then decide to make the worksheet easier to understand.

1) If you want to assign names after the formulas are created, use Insert – Name – Apply to apply names to existing formulas, as shown in Fig. 209.

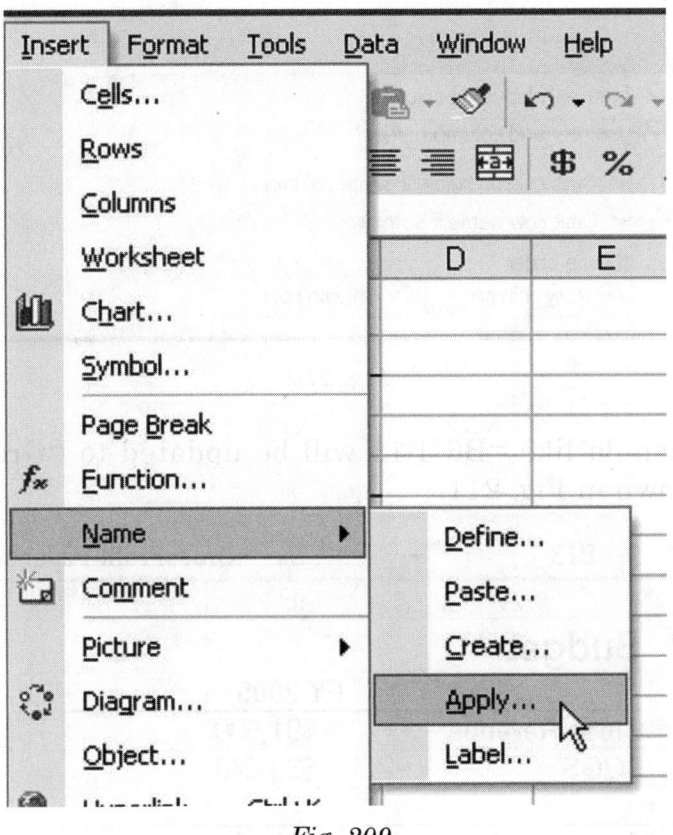

Fig. 209

2)   As shown in Fig. 210, select all of the names that you want to apply.

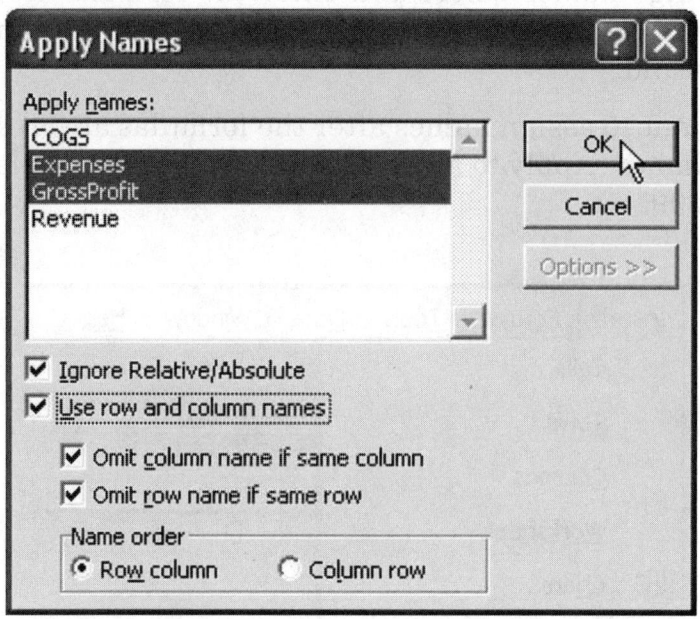

Fig. 210

Result: A formula like =B6–B11 will be updated to =GrossProfit–Expenses, as shown in Fig. 211.

	A	B	C	D
1	**Budget**			
2		**FY 2005**		
3	Gross Revenue	$91,500		
4	COGS	$33,640		
5				
6	**Gross Profit**	$57,860		
7				
8	Rent	$15,400		
9	Utilities	$1,800		
10	G&A	$3,100		
11	**Expenses**	$20,300		
12				
13	**Operating Income**	$37,560		

Fig. 211

Summary: To create plain language formulas, first assign a range name to each cell in your formula. Use the mouse when entering the formula. To assign range names to a formula after the fact, use Insert – Name – Apply.

Commands Discussed: Insert – Name – Apply

USE NAMED CONSTANTS TO STORE NUMBERS

Problem: You've seen how you can assign a name to a cell. It is also possible to assign a name to a constant. This could be useful if you have a number, such as a local sales tax rate, that changes once a year.

Strategy: From the menu, use Insert – Name – Define. Type a name like SalesTax. In the Refers to box, type =0.065 and click Add, as shown in Fig. 212.

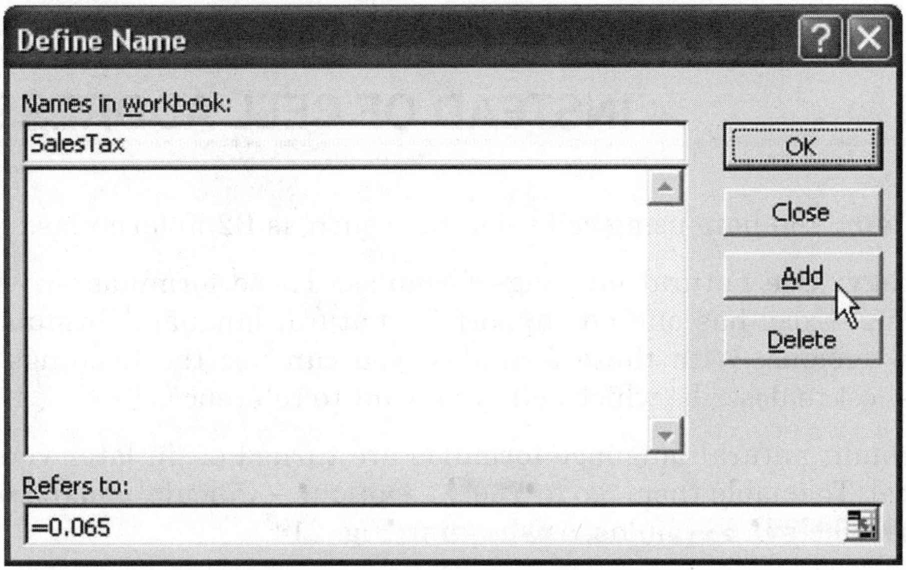

Fig. 212

In this workbook, you can now use a formula such as =SalesTax*D2, as shown in Fig. 213.

E2		▼		*fx* =SalesTax*D2
	A	B	C	D	E
1	Item	Qty	Price	Total	Tax
2	PR197	100	1.54	154	10.01

Fig. 213

If the tax rate changes later use Insert – Name – Define to change the constant assigned to the name.

Summary: To name a constant in a workbook use Insert – Name – Define, type in the name of the constant, and then define the constant in the Refers to: box.

Commands Discussed: Insert – Name – Define

BUILD A FORMULA USING LABELS INSTEAD OF CELL ADDRESSES

Problem: You hate using cell references such as B2 in formulas.

Strategy: Use natural language formulas. These formulas are fairly amazing. Excel has offered support for natural language formulas for many versions. With these formulas, you can use the headings in a worksheet to describe which cells you want to reference.

By default, natural language formulas are turned off in later versions of Excel. To enable them, go to Tools – Options – Calculation and select Accept Labels in Formulas, as shown in Fig. 214.

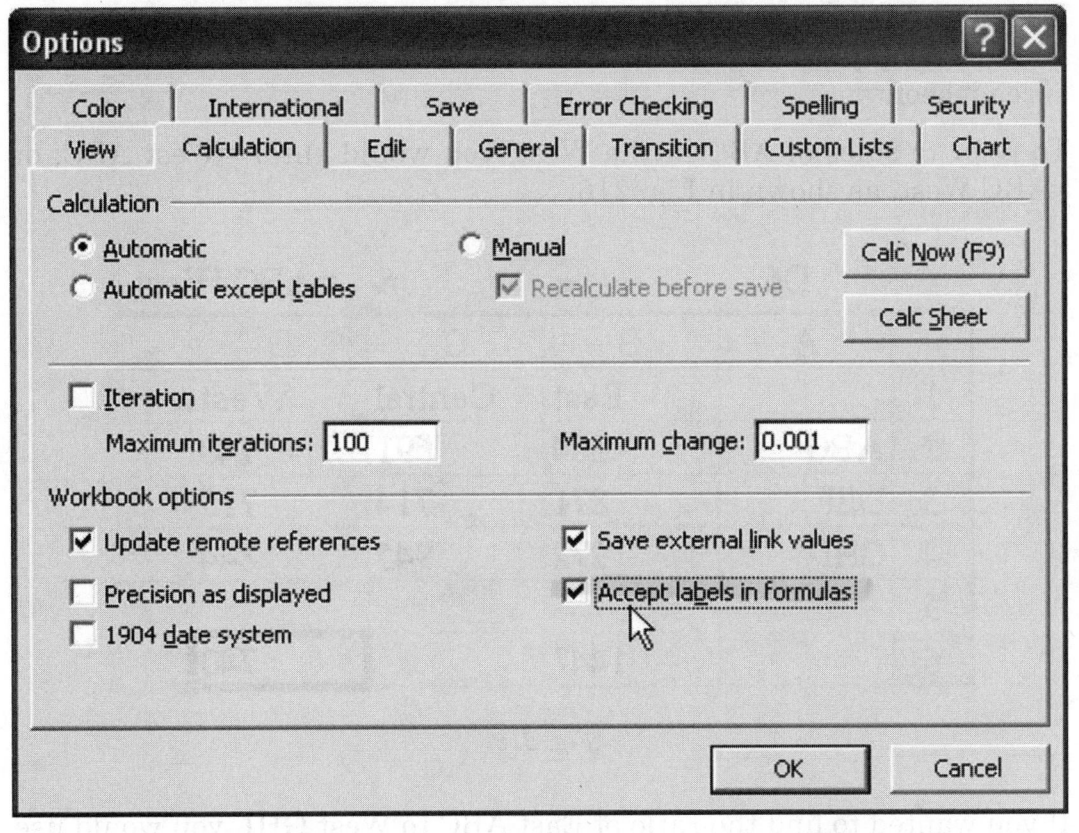

Fig. 214

As shown in Fig. 215, you can now enter formulas such as these: =SUM(East) and =SUM(ABC)

B6	▼	f_x =SUM(East)	
	A	B	C	D
1		East	Central	West
2	ABC	304	691	740
3	DEF	871	714	715
4	GHI	272	945	844
5				
6		1447		
7				

Fig. 215

It is important to note that *there are no named ranges in this worksheet!* Excel is simply looking at the labels in the first column and row of the spreadsheet.

To refer to sales of ABC in the West, you would enter =West ABC, or =ABC West, as shown in Fig. 216.

D6	▼		f_x =ABC West	
	A	B	C	D
1		East	Central	West
2	ABC	304	691	740
3	DEF	871	714	715
4	GHI	272	945	844
5				
6		1447		740

Fig. 216

If you wanted to find the ratio of East ABC to West GHI, you would use this formula =ABC East/GHI West, as shown in Fig. 217.

	f_x =ABC East/GHI West		
C	D	E	
Central	West		
691	740		
714	715		
945	844		
36.0%	740		

Fig. 217

Additional Information: Amazingly, these formulas can even handle labels with space in them. As shown in Fig. 218, the formula of =ABC Gross Profit will work.

	B6		fx	=ABC Gross Profit	
	A	B	C	D	E
1		Qty	Revenue	Cost	Gross Profit
2	ABC	100	150	67.5	82.5
3	DEF	150	337.5	151.875	185.625
4	GHI	200	400	180	220
5					
6		82.5			
7					

Fig. 218

Also, if you've ignored all of my pleas to have headings take up only a single row of cells, and have a spreadsheet with "Gross" in E1 and "Profit" in E2, you can still use the formula =Gross Profit ABC, as shown in Fig. 219. *Important:* You must refer to the headings in the order that they appear from top to bottom.

	C7		▼	fx	=Gross Profit ABC	
	A	B	C	D	E
1					Gross
2		Qty	Revenue	Cost	Profit
3	ABC	100	150	67.5	82.5
4	DEF	150	337.5	151.875	185.625
5	GHI	200	400	180	220
6					
7			82.5		
8					

Fig. 219

You can even figure out the Gross Profit on a Gross quantity, as shown in Fig. 220.

	B7		▼	fx	=Gross Gross Profit	
	A	B	C	D	E
1				Gross	
2		Price	Cost	Profit	
3	Unit	2	1	1	
4	Dozen	22	12	10	
5	Gross	242	144	98	
6					
7		98			
8					

Fig. 220

Part II

Gotcha: If your data set is missing labels, Excel may have trouble calculating formulas that are in cells that are not adjacent to your dataset.

Summary: Natural Language Formulas present an alternative to typical formulas in Excel. They might be great for your boss' boss who can't quite get the hang of using cell references in Excel.

Commands Discussed: Tools – Options – Calculation

USE NATURAL LANGUAGE FORMULAS TO REFER TO THE CURRENT ROW

Problem: In the previous example, a natural language formula referred specifically to one cell by indicating a row name and a column name. It is also possible to have natural language formulas that refer to a specific column in the current row.

Strategy: As shown in Fig. 221, you have a census of employees and their benefit selections.

	A	B	C	D
1	Name	DOB	Age	Dependants
2	Bill	2/17/1965	39	4
3	Bob	3/5/1955	49	2
4	Barb	11/22/1952	52	2
5	Robert	5/27/1922	82	2

Fig. 221

The company buys life insurance for anyone under the age of 65. The rate for life insurance is $4 per dependant. As shown in Fig. 222, you can write a natural language formula in E2: =IF(Age<65,Dependants*4,0).

E2			▼		*fx* =IF(Age<65,Dependants*4,0)	
	A	B	C	D	E	F
1	Name	DOB	Age	Dependants	Life Ins Cost	
2	Bill	2/17/1965	39	4	16	
3	Bob	3/5/1955	49	2	8	
4	Barb	11/22/1952	52	2	8	
5	Robert	5/27/1922	82	2	0	

Fig. 222

As you copy this formula down the column, Excel will properly calculate the formulas based on the age and dependents in the current row.

Summary: Again, natural language formulas allow non-technical people to write formulas in plain language.

Part II

ASSIGN A FORMULA TO A NAME

Problem: You have thousands of identical formulas on 20 worksheets, as shown in Fig. 223. Every time that you want to change the formula, you have to edit all 20 sheets. Is there a way to make a formula be variable and change it in just one place?

C2			▼		*fx* =COS(A2)/SIN(B2)
	A	B	C	D	E
1	X	Y	Formula		
2	0.639523	0.477897	1.744636		
3	0.966707	0.194101	2.944834		
4	0.238926	0.150594	6.47619		
5	0.703421	0.129919	5.886595		

Fig. 223

Strategy: Use a Name, but assign a formula to the name.

Think about what you do when you set up a named range. For instance, you could assign a name of MyData to cell D1, as shown in Fig. 224.

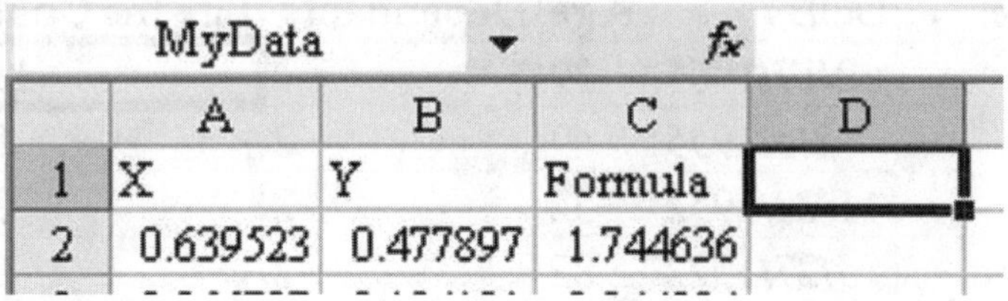

Fig. 224

However, when you look at this in the Define Name dialog (Insert – Name – Define), you will see that MyData is really equal to a formula called =Sheet1!$D$3, as shown in Fig. 225.

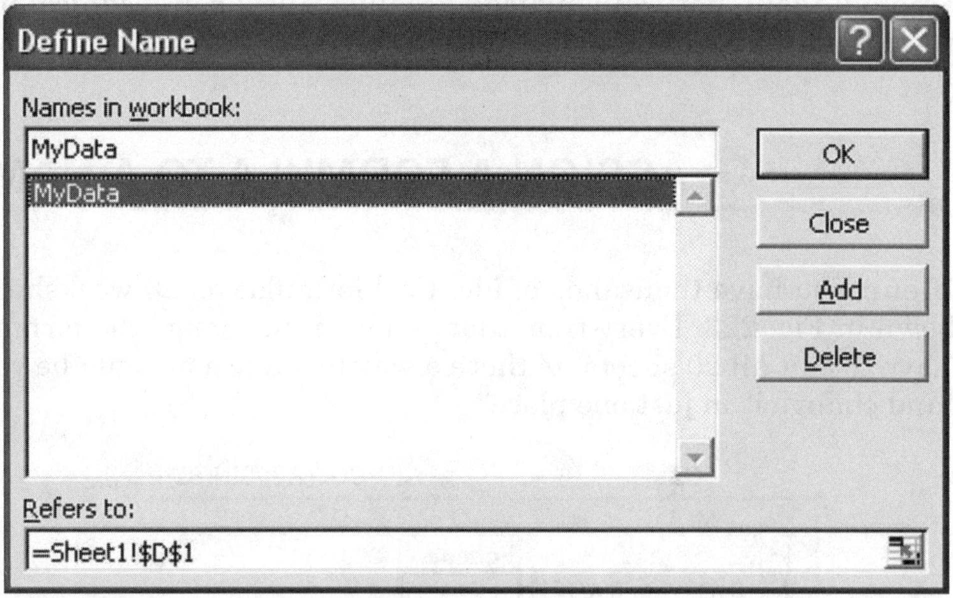

Fig. 225

If you understand this, then it is easy to make the leap that any formula can be assigned a name.

You could define a name called GlobalFormula. When you enter =GlobalFormula in the thousand cells on each of the 20 sheets, it will inherit the formula from GlobalFormula.

Gotcha: Do you remember the topic about R1C1 style addressing? If you were using R1C1 style addressing, then all of the formulas in column C would be identical, as shown in Fig. 226, and this would be an easy task.

R2C3	▼	*fx* =COS(RC[-2])/SIN(RC[-1])	
	1	2	3
1	X	Y	Formula
2	0.639522999675372	0.477897179105964	=COS(RC[-2])/SIN(RC[-1])
3	0.966706811830214	0.194101066101121	=COS(RC[-2])/SIN(RC[-1])
4	0.238925984531771	0.150593908366368	=COS(RC[-2])/SIN(RC[-1])
5	0.703421086521319	0.129919485480946	=COS(RC[-2])/SIN(RC[-1])
6	0.509817725872427	0.15557668185373	=COS(RC[-2])/SIN(RC[-1])
7	0.131212793105752	0.607468104030328	=COS(RC[-2])/SIN(RC[-1])
8	0.852168091593241	0.691925072915592	=COS(RC[-2])/SIN(RC[-1])
9	0.354154537215777	0.572903023935741	=COS(RC[-2])/SIN(RC[-1])
10	0.363036996146451	0.036489316365333	=COS(RC[-2])/SIN(RC[-1])
11	0.597666154295454	0.518157536128334	=COS(RC[-2])/SIN(RC[-1])
12	0.890628335658092	0.437970352360872	=COS(RC[-2])/SIN(RC[-1])
13	0.0722114981168067	0.72876760445498	=COS(RC[-2])/SIN(RC[-1])

Fig. 226

However, I realize that no one uses R1C1 style references, so you will have to build this formula the hard way. In A1 style references, each formula is different in each cell, as shown in Fig. 227.

	A	B	C
1	X	Y	Formula
2	0.639522999675372	0.477897179105964	=COS(A2)/SIN(B2)
3	0.966706811830214	0.194101066101121	=COS(A3)/SIN(B3)
4	0.238925984531771	0.150593908366368	=COS(A4)/SIN(B4)
5	0.703421086521319	0.129919485480946	=COS(A5)/SIN(B5)
6	0.509817725872427	0.15557668185373	=COS(A6)/SIN(B6)
7	0.131212793105752	0.607468104030328	=COS(A7)/SIN(B7)
8	0.852168091593241	0.691925072915592	=COS(A8)/SIN(B8)

Fig. 227

If you want GlobalFormula to =COS(A2), you cannot just write that. You need to develop a formula that takes the COS function of the cell two cells to the left of the current cell. This is possible, but it requires a whole bunch of new functions that you might never have used before.

First, look at the InDirect function. =INDIRECT("A2") will return the value that is in A2. When you try to use the results of an INDIRECT function in another calculation, it always helps to put the INDIRECT function inside of a SUM function, as shown below.

=SUM(INDIRECT("A2"))

So, if you wanted to take the COS of A2, you could use the following formula.

=COS(SUM(INDIRECT("A2")))

The next trick to figure out is how to return the text of A2 to refer to a cell. To do this, use the ADDRESS function. =ADDRESS(2,1) will return the text "A2" because A2 is in the 2nd row, first column. =ADDRESS(52,26) would return "Z52" because this is the fifty-second row, twenty-sixth column.

Is there a function that will return the row number of the cell containing the formula? Yes, the ROW function will return the row number of the cell that contains the formula, as shown in Fig. 228.

=ROW()		
	D	E
		1
5		2
3		3
5		4
4		5
5		6
3		7
4		8
1		9
4		10

Fig. 228

Similarly, =COLUMN() will return the column number of the cell containing the formula, as shown in Fig. 229.

	I1	▼		*fx*	=COLUMN()	
	F	G	H	I	J	
1		7	8	9	10	

Fig. 229

So, you could write a formula that returns the name of the cell, like this one shown in Fig. 230:

	E1	▼		*fx*	=ADDRESS(ROW(),COLUMN())	
	A	B	C	D	E	F
1	$A$1	$B$1	$C$1	$D$1	$E$1	$F$1
2	$A$2	$B$2	$C$2	$D$2	$E$2	$F$2
3	$A$3	$B$3	$C$3	$D$3	$E$3	$F$3
4	$A$4	$B$4	$C$4	$D$4	$E$4	$F$4
5	$A$5	$B$5	$C$5	$D$5	$E$5	$F$5
6	$A$6	$B$6	$C$6	$D$6	$E$6	$F$6

Fig. 230

Part II

To return the address of a cell two columns to the left of the current cell, add a "−2" after the COLUMN() function, as shown in Fig. 231.

	C1	▼		*fx*	=ADDRESS(ROW(),COLUMN()-2)	
	A	B	C	D	E	F	G
1			$A$1	$B$1	$C$1	$D$1	
2			$A$2	$B$2	$C$2	$D$2	
3			$A$3	$B$3	$C$3	$D$3	
4			$A$4	$B$4	$C$4	$D$4	

Fig. 231

Therefore, the formula that you need to take the COS of the cell two cells to the left of the cell containing the formula is:

=COS(SUM(INDIRECT(ADDRESS(ROW(),COLUMN()–2)))).

The actual current formula is =COS(A2)/SIN(A2). This is the formula that you would use:

=COS(SUM(INDIRECT(ADDRESS(ROW(),COLUMN()–2))))/ SIN(SUM(INDIRECT(ADDRESS(ROW(),COLUMN()–1))))

From the menu, choose Insert – Name – Define. As shown in Fig. 232, in the Define Name box, type a name, type the formula, and choose Add.

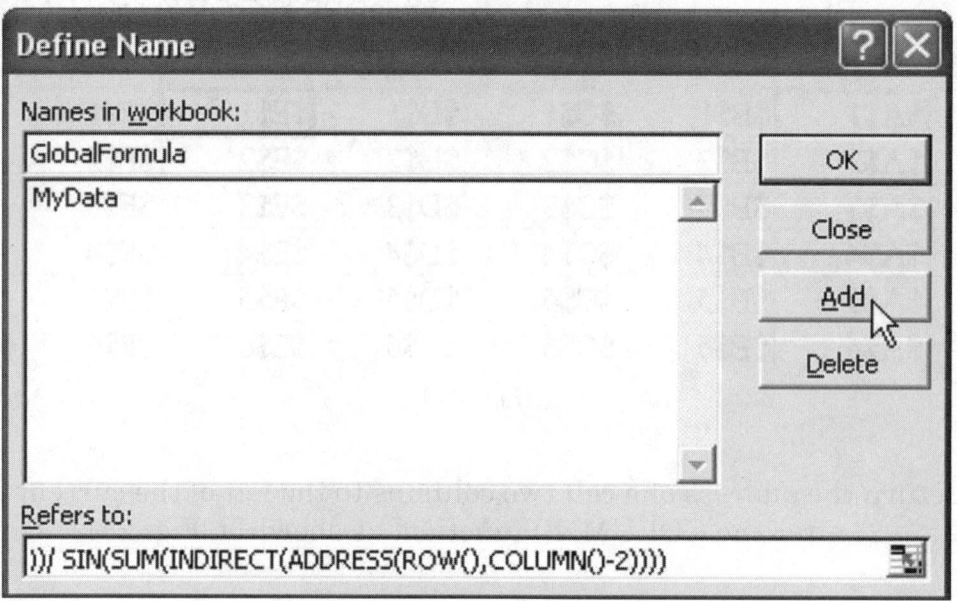

Fig. 232

Result: A name is added to the Workbook Names. The name is assigned your formula, as shown in Fig. 233.

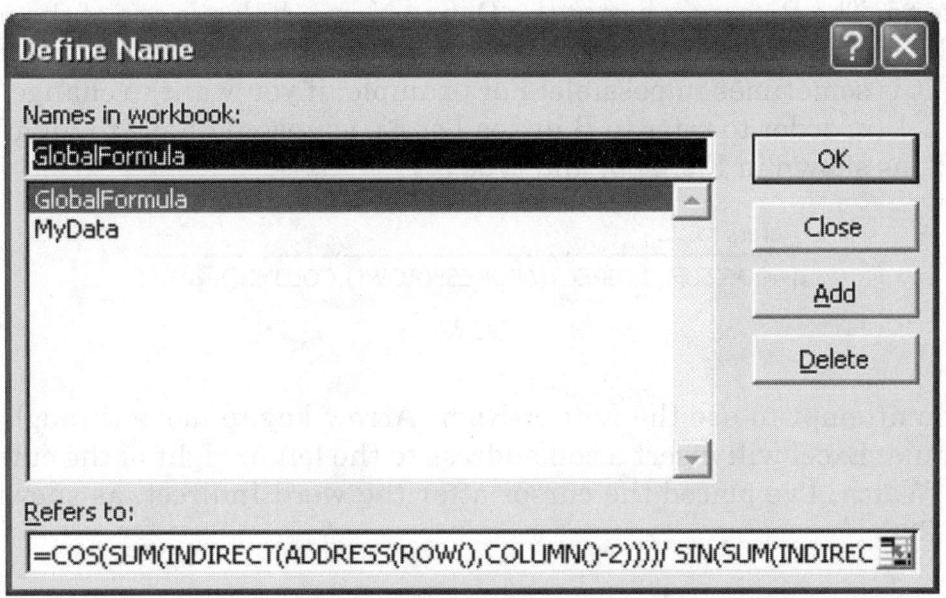

Fig. 233

Now, in any cell in the workbook, you can use the formula =GlobalFormula, as shown in Fig. 234.

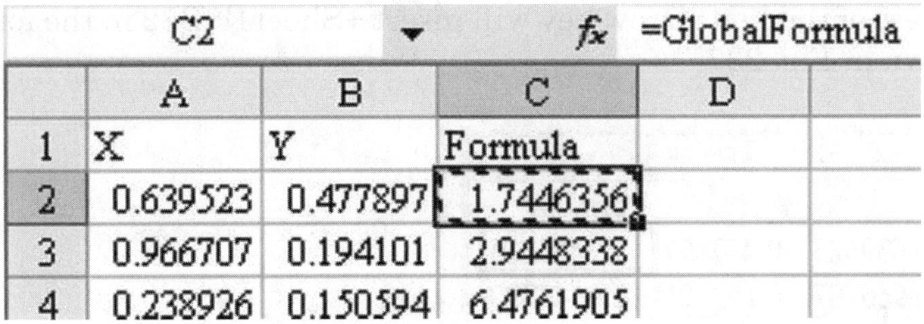

C2	▾	*fx* =GlobalFormula		
	A	B	C	D
1	X	Y	Formula	
2	0.639523	0.477897	1.7446356	
3	0.966707	0.194101	2.9448338	
4	0.238926	0.150594	6.4761905	

Fig. 234

Additional Details: Any time that you need to change the formula, simply redefine it in the Define Name box and choose Add.

Gotcha: The Refers to: box in the Define Name dialog is one of the most maddening things in all of Excel. If you want to edit a formula in that box, it is sometimes impossible. For example, if you want to change this 2 to a 1 (in order to refer to B instead of A), you would have to highlight the 2, as shown in Fig. 235, and type a 1.

Fig. 235

If you attempt to use the Left or Right Arrow key to move through the formula, Excel will insert a cell address to the left or right of the current cell. Watch, I've placed the cursor after the word Indirect, as shown in Fig. 236.

Fig. 236

One press of the Left Arrow key will insert +Sheet1!$B$2 in the formula, as shown in Fig. 237.

	A	B	C
1	X	Y	Formula
2	0.639523	0.477897	1.7446356
3	0.966707	0.194101	2.9448338
4	0.238926	0.150594	6.4761905
5	0.703421	0.129919	5.8865954
6	0.509818	0.155577	5.6330066

Refers to:

=COS(SUM(INDIRECT+Sheet1!$B$2(ADI

Fig. 237

The main problem with this is that sometimes the formula is so long that you cannot see the end of the formula in the Refers to box. When you try to click near the end of the field and hit the Right Arrow, you end up adding references to the formula.

The only solution that I have found is to click early in the formula and drag all of the way to the end. This will force Excel to scroll to the end of the formula, as shown in Fig. 238.

Fig. 238

You can then click and drag to isolate the portion of the formula that you need to change, as shown in Fig. 239.

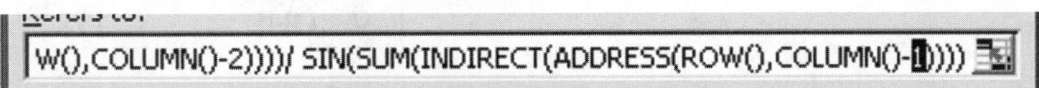

Fig. 239

Additional Details: I try to come up with reasonable examples for the case studies in this book. One day, as I was writing about the conditional sum wizard, the telephone rang and my friend Dave was on the line with this exact problem. So, with thanks to Dave, you have this incredibly complex solution to what anyone thought would be an easy problem.

Summary: Named Formulas can save the day, although they can be incredibly complex.

Commands Discussed: Insert – Name – Define

TOTAL WITHOUT USING A FORMULA

Problem: Your manager calls on the telephone and asks for the total sales of a particular product. You need to quickly find a total. Is there a faster way than entering a formula?

Part
II

Strategy: The QuickSum indicator in the status bar will show the total of the highlighted cells. With your manager on the phone, highlight the numbers in question, as shown in Fig. 240.

	A	B
1	Item	**Total**
2	ABC	288
3	ABC	122
4	ABC	281
5	DEF	213
6	DEF	204
7	DEF	274
8	GHI	256
9	GHI	178

Fig. 240

Result: As shown in Fig. 241, the QuickSum indicator in the status bar at the bottom of the screen will show that the total of those three cells is 691.

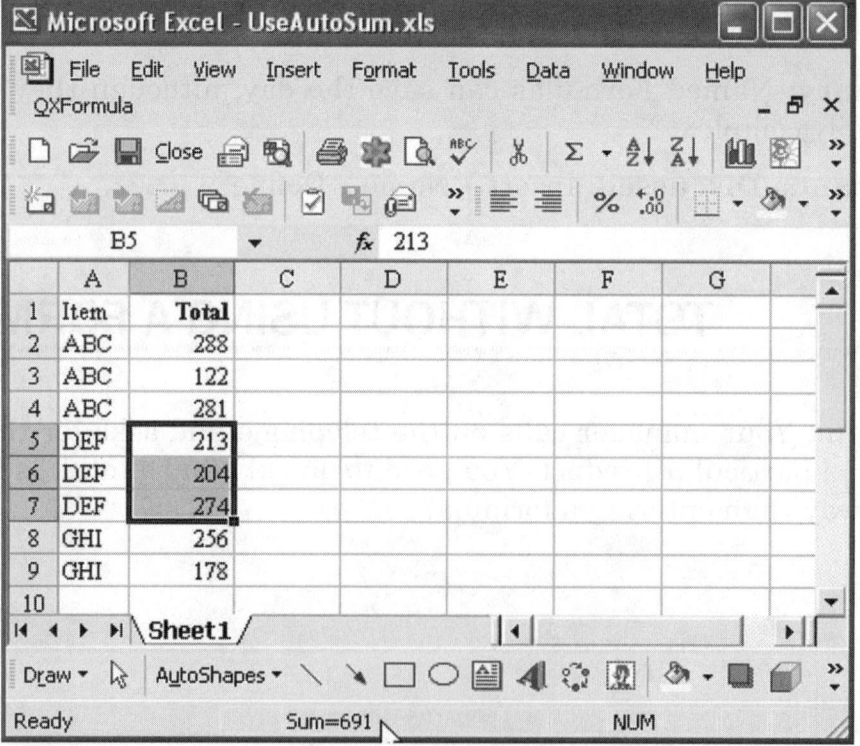

Fig. 241

Additional Information: It is possible that you have turned off the status bar. If the status bar is not visible at the bottom of your screen after selecting a range of numeric cells, select View – Status Bar from the menu, as shown in Fig. 242.

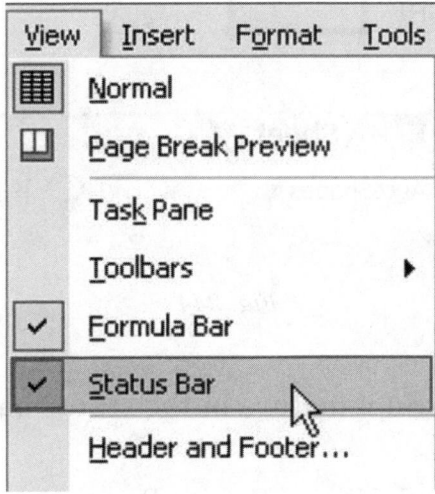

Fig. 242

Gotcha: If one of the values that you select is text, the status bar will show the total of just the numeric entries, as shown in Fig. 243.

	A	B	C
1	Item	**Total**	
2	ABC	288	
3	ABC	122	
4	ABC	281	
5	DEF	213	
6	DEF	204	
7	DEF	274	
8	GHI	256	
9	GHI	178	
10			
11			

Ready   Sum=691

Fig. 243

Part II

However, as shown in Fig. 244, if one of the highlighted cells is an error such as #N/A, then the status bar total will not appear.

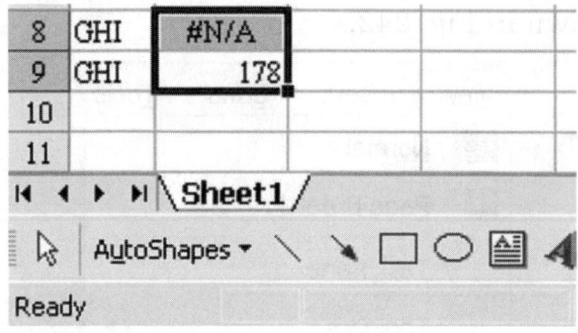

Fig. 244

Summary: The QuickSum feature in the status bar will show the total of selected cells.

Commands Discussed: View – Status Bar

COUNT, AVERAGE, ETC.
WITHOUT USING A FORMULA

Problem: Your manager calls on the telephone and asks for the average price of a particular product. You need to quickly find an average of the prices in Fig. 245. Is there a faster way than entering a formula?

	A	B	C
1	Item	Store	**Total**
2	Coke Case	Giant Eagle	5.99
3	Coke Case	Acme	5.99
4	Coke Case	Fishers	5.45
5	Coke Case	Marc's	4.99

Fig. 245

Strategy: The QuickSum feature in the status bar can be customized to show Average, Min, Max, Count, or Count Numbers. Highlight a range of numbers. Look for the QuickSum value in the status bar at the bottom of the window.

As shown in Fig. 246, right-click the QuickSum and a menu pops up allowing you to choose Average, Count, Count Numbers, Max, Min, or Sum. Select Average.

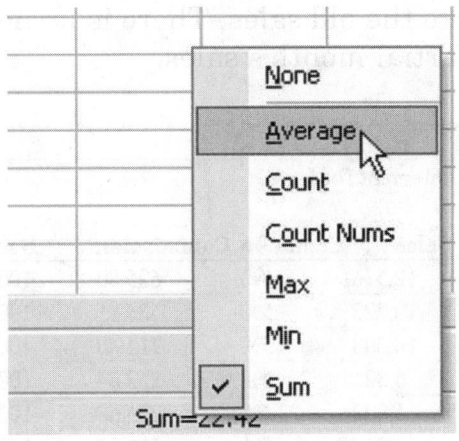

Fig. 246

Result: The QuickSum changes to show an average, as shown in Fig. 247.

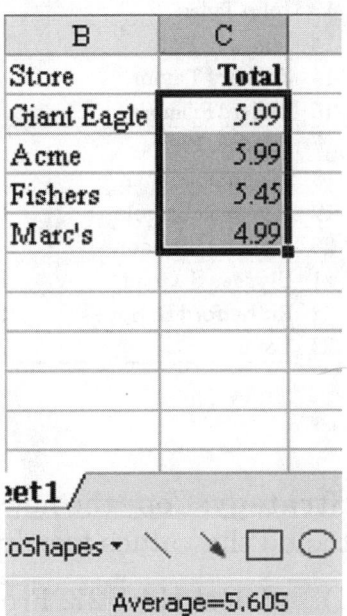

Additional Information: Excel will remember the setting of the QuickSum area from session to session. If you change from Sum to Average, it will continue to show averages of the selected cells until you change this back to a Sum.

Count will count all non-blank cells in the selection. Count Nums will only count cells that contain numeric or date values.

Summary: You can quickly find the average, count, min, or max of a range by using the right-click menu to customize the QuickSum information in the status bar.

Commands Discussed: Status Bar – QuickSum

Fig. 247

ADD TWO COLUMNS
WITHOUT USING FORMULAS

Problem: You prepared a summary of sales by rep for the month. Due to an accounting glitch, someone gave you a similar file with additional sales made on the last day of the month, as shown in Fig. 248. You need to add the new sales to the old sales. There is no need to keep the original two columns of partial month's sales.

	A	B	C	D	E	F	G	H
1	XYZ Co - Commission Statement for June							
2								
3	Sales Rep	Sales	Comm %	Commission	Base	Salary		New Sales
4	George Washington	12,516	5%	625.80	1000	1,625.80		609
5	John Adams	10,723	5%	536.15	1000	1,536.15		983
6	Thomas Jefferson	14,308	5%	715.40	1000	1,715.40		205
7	James Madison	6,321	4%	252.84	1000	1,252.84		536
8	James Monroe	5,892	4%	235.68	1000	1,235.68		355
9	John Quincy Adams	10,377	5%	518.85	1000	1,518.85		269
10	Andrew Jackson	7,845	4%	313.80	1000	1,313.80		795
11	Martin Van Buren	14,649	5%	732.45	1000	1,732.45		215
12	William Henry Harrison	13,429	5%	671.45	1000	1,671.45		676
13	John Tyler	9,510	4%	380.40	1000	1,380.40		877
14	James K. Polk	5,322	4%	212.88	1000	1,212.88		78
15	Zachary Taylor	5,166	4%	206.64	1000	1,206.64		214
16	Millard Fillmore	7,635	4%	305.40	1000	1,305.40		943
17	Franklin Pierce	7,173	4%	286.92	1000	1,286.92		60
18	James Buchanan	12,817	5%	640.85	1000	1,640.85		795
19	Abraham Lincoln	13,033	5%	651.65	1000	1,651.65		871
20	Andrew Johnson	5,074	4%	202.96	1000	1,202.96		10
21	Ulysses S. Grant	13,874	5%	693.70	1000	1,693.70		203
22	Rutherford B. Hayes	14,640	5%	732.00	1000	1,732.00		894
23	Total	190,304		8,915.82	19000	27,915.82		

Fig. 248

Strategy: Copy the new values in column H and use Paste Special – Add to add the values to column B. Follow these steps.

1)   Select H4:H22. From the menu, select Edit – Copy to copy the cells to the clipboard.

2)   Move the cell pointer to B4. From the menu, select Edit – Paste Special.

3)   As shown in Fig. 249, in the Paste Special dialog box, choose the Add option in the Operation section. Optionally, also choose Values in the Paste section in order to preserve the formatting in column B. Choose OK.

Sales	Comm %	Commission	Base	Salary	New Sales
12,516	5%	625.80	1000	1,625.80	609
10,723	5%	536.15	1000	1,536.15	983
14,308					205
6,32					536
5,89					355
10,37					269
7,84					795
14,649					215
13,429					676
9,510					877
5,32					78
5,166					214
7,63					943
7,17					60
12,817					795
13,03					871
5,074					10
13,874					203
14,640					894
190,304		8,915.82	19000	27,915.82	

Paste Special dialog box overlay:

Paste Special   [?][X]

Paste
- ○ All
- ○ Formulas
- ● Values
- ○ Formats
- ○ Comments
- ○ Validation
- ○ All except borders
- ○ Column widths
- ○ Formulas and number formats
- ○ Values and number formats

Operation
- ○ None
- ● Add
- ○ Subtract
- ○ Multiply
- ○ Divide

☐ Skip blanks   ☐ Transpose

[Paste Link]   [OK]   [Cancel]

Fig. 249

Result: As shown in Fig. 250, the new sales data from column H is added to the values in column B. You can safely delete column H.

Sales Rep	Sales	C
George Washington	13,125	
John Adams	11,706	
Thomas Jefferson	14,513	
James Madison	6,857	
I---- M-----	C 2.17	

Fig. 250

Gotcha: If column B is properly formatted and the temporary data in H is not formatted, the default option of Paste All will cause the formats in column B to be lost. This is why you should consider choosing both Values and Add in the Transpose dialog.

Additional Information: The Paste Special – Add technique has an interesting effect if you add cells to a range that contains a formula. Amazingly, Excel does handle this correctly. Cell D4 contains a formula, as shown in Fig. 251.

=+B4*C4

D
656.25
585.30

Fig. 251

If you Paste Special – Add a value to this formula, Excel changes the formula to add the value, as shown in Fig. 252.

=(+B4*C4)+609

D
1265.25

Fig. 252

Summary: Using the Paste Special Add technique is useful to add two columns of numbers without using a formula.

Commands Discussed: Edit – Paste Special – Add

HOW TO CALCULATE SALES OVER QUOTA

Problem: In the spreadsheet shown in Fig. 253, enter a formula to calculate the excess of sales over quota on a record-by-record basis.

	A	B	C	D	E
1	Salesrep	Date	Quota	Sales	Over Quota
2	Joe	1/2/2006	800	666	
3	Dan	1/2/2006	800	1290	
4	Mary	1/2/2006	800	896	
5	Joe	1/3/2006	800	559	
6	Dan	1/3/2006	800	192	
7	Mary	1/3/2006	800	703	
8	Joe	1/4/2006	800	1131	
9	Dan	1/4/2006	800	199	
10	Mary	1/4/2006	800	320	
11	Joe	1/5/2006	800	550	

Fig. 253

Part
II

Strategy: There are a couple of functions that would work in this situation. For instance, you could use an IF function. Give the IF function a logical test and specify one calculation if the test is true and one calculation if the test is false.

If the Sales value is greater than the Quota, the IF function would return Sales (D2) – Quota (C2). If the sales did not exceed quota, then the IF function would return 0.

The syntax for the IF function is =IF(logical test, value if true, value if false). Thus, as shown in Fig. 254, the formula would be:

=IF(D2>C2,D2–C2,0)

E2	▼	f_x	=IF(D2>C2,D2-C2,0)	

	A	B	C	D	E
1	Salesrep	Date	Quota	Sales	Over Quota
2	Joe	1/2/2006	800	666	0
3	Dan	1/2/2006	800	1290	490
4	Mary	1/2/2006	800	896	96
5	Joe	1/3/2006	800	559	0
6	Dan	1/3/2006	800	192	0
7	Mary	1/3/2006	800	703	0
8	Joe	1/4/2006	800	1131	331

Fig. 254

Alternate Solution: Use the MAX function. One parameter to the MAX function will be D2–C2. This number will be either positive or negative, as shown in column F in Fig. 255.

F2	▼	f_x	=+D2-C2		

	A	B	C	D	E	F
1	Salesrep	Date	Quota	Sales	Over Quota	Temp
2	Joe	1/2/2006	800	666		-134
3	Dan	1/2/2006	800	1290		490
4	Mary	1/2/2006	800	896		96
5	Joe	1/3/2006	800	559		-241
6	Dan	1/3/2006	800	192		-608
7	Mary	1/3/2006	800	703		-97
8	Joe	1/4/2006	800	1131		331
9	Dan	1/4/2006	800	199		-601
10	Mary	1/4/2006	800	320		-480
11	Joe	1/5/2006	800	550		-250
12	Dan	1/5/2006	800	552		-248

Fig. 255

You can ask Excel to calculate the larger of either the calculation in F or a zero. If you think about it, the Max of 0 and a positive number is the positive number. The Max of 0 and a negative number is 0. As shown in Fig. 256, using =MAX() is slightly shorter and quicker than entering the =IF() function.

	E2	▼		ƒₓ	=MAX(D2-C2,0)

	A	B	C	D	E
1	Salesrep	Date	Quota	Sales	Over Quota
2	Joe	1/2/2006	800	666	0
3	Dan	1/2/2006	800	1290	490
4	Mary	1/2/2006	800	896	96
5	Joe	1/3/2006	800	559	0
6	Dan	1/3/2006	800	192	0
7	Mary	1/3/2006	800	703	0
8	Joe	1/4/2006	800	1131	331
9	Dan	1/4/2006	800	199	0
10	Mary	1/4/2006	800	320	0

Fig. 256

Part II

Summary: To find only positive results of a calculation, you can use either the =IF() or =MAX(0,Calc) function. Either will work. The =MAX is slightly better. Use =MIN(0,Calc) to find only negative values.

Functions Discussed: =IF(); =MAX();=MIN()

HOW TO JOIN TWO TEXT COLUMNS

Problem: As shown in Fig. 257, you have data with First Name in column A and Last Name in column B. You want to merge these into one column.

	A	B
1	FIRST	LAST
2	BRITNEY	SPEARS
3	PAUL	MCCARTNEY
4	BILL	JELEN
5	JON	TESSMER
6	SUSAN	HALLORAN
7	AMY	MCMASTER
8	TAMMY	ROSSI
9	RANDOLF	COFFIN
10	FRANK	DOYLE
11	TOYA	WHITE

Fig. 257

Strategy: Use the ampersand (&) as a concatenation operator in a formula in column C. Change the formulas in column C to values before deleting columns A and B. Follow these steps.

1) In cell C2, enter the formula =A2&B2, as shown in Fig. 258.

C2		▼	f_x =A2&B2
	A	B	C
1	FIRST	LAST	Name
2	BRITNEY	SPEARS	BRITNEYSPEARS
3	PAUL	MCCARTNEY	

Fig. 258

2) You need to insert a space between the first name and last name. If you join cell A2, a space in quotes, and cell B2, the answer will look acceptable. The formula is =A2&" "&B2. Copy this formula down to all of the cells in your range, as shown in Fig. 259.

C2		▼	f_x =A2&" "&B2
	A	B	C
1	FIRST	LAST	Name
2	BRITNEY	SPEARS	BRITNEY SPEARS
3	PAUL	MCCARTNEY	PAUL MCCARTNEY
4	BILL	JELEN	BILL JELEN
5	JON	TESSMER	JON TESSMER
6	SUSAN	HALLORAN	SUSAN HALLORAN

Fig. 259

Additional Information: To convert BRITNEY SPEARS to Britney Spears, use the PROPER function. =PROPER(A2&" "&B2) will convert the names to Proper Case, as shown in Fig. 260. This will work for all of your names except names with an interior capital such as "Paul McCartney" or "Dave VanHorn". After using the PROPER function, you will have to manually fix any names with an interior capital letter.

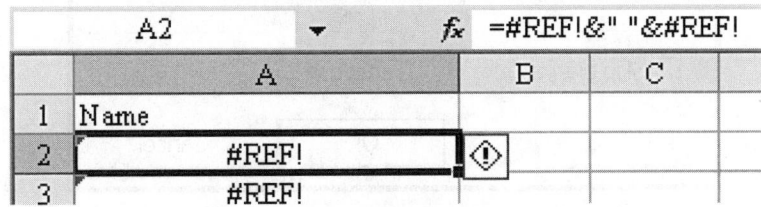

	A	B	C
			C2 ▾ *fx* =PROPER(A2&" "&B2)
1	FIRST	LAST	Name
2	BRITNEY	SPEARS	Britney Spears
3	PAUL	MCCARTNEY	Paul Mccartney
4	BILL	JELEN	Bill Jelen

Fig. 260

Gotcha: If you delete columns A and B while column C still contains formulas, then all of the formulas will change to #REF! errors, as shown in Fig. 261. This tells you that you have a formula that points to cells(s) that are no longer there. Immediately hit Ctrl+Z to undo the delete.

Part II

	A	B	C
	A2 ▾ *fx* =#REF!&" "&#REF!		
1	Name		
2	#REF!		
3	#REF!		

Fig. 261

To work around this situation, first convert all of the formulas in column C to values. Follow these steps:

1)   Select the data in column C.

2)   Select Ctrl+C to copy the data to the clipboard.

3)   Without changing the selection, select Edit – Paste Special....

4) In the Paste Special dialog box, choose Values and then OK, as shown in Fig. 262.

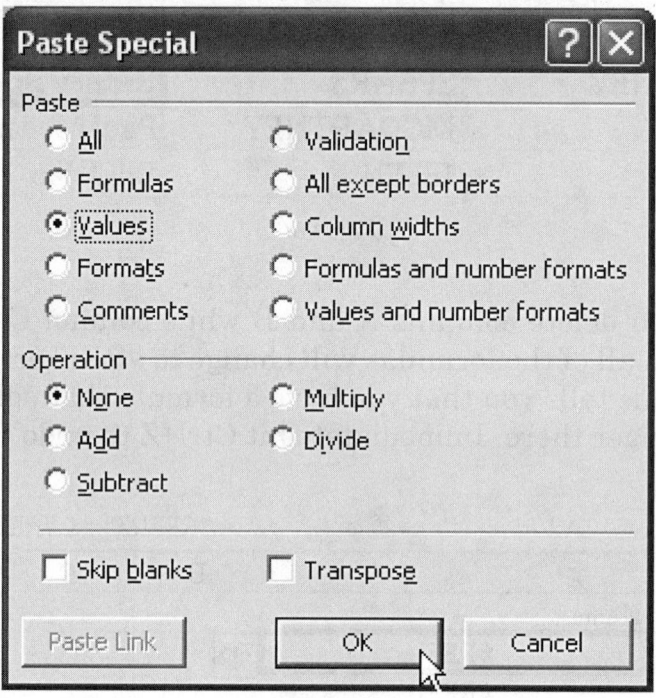

Fig. 262

5) This converts column C from live formulas to static values. You can now delete columns A and B.

Summary: The ampersand (&) is the concatenation character used to join text cells with other text cells or with literal values in a formula.

Commands Discussed: Edit – Paste Special

Functions Discussed: =PROPER()

HOW TO SORT ON
ONE SEGMENT OF AN ACCOUNT ID

Problem: Your company assigns an account ID to every customer. One segment of the account ID contains useful information, such as a parent company code. You want to be able to sort on the basis of a portion of the account ID. In Fig. 263, the first three digits of the account are used to identify an office.

	A	B	C	D	E	F
1	Account	Product	Jan	Feb	Mar	Q1
2	4010	XYZ	37	82	12	131
3	4021	ABC	89	20	69	178
4	4030	XYZ	73	90	62	225
5	4030	ABC	55	26	23	104
6	4030	GHI	33	0	25	58
7	4030	GHI	25	95	40	160
8	4030	XYZ	20	50	97	167
9	4030	DEF	50	21	74	145

Fig. 263

Strategy: Insert a new column and use the LEFT function to isolate the necessary digits from the account field.

1) In the blank column, enter a heading such as the word "Key". In cell G2, enter the formula =LEFT(A2,3), as shown in Fig. 264. This indicates that the new field should contain just the three characters leftmost of the ID field.

f_x	=LEFT(A2,3)	
E	F	G
Mar	Q1	Key
12	131	401
69	178	
62	225	
23	104	

Fig. 264

Part
II

2)   Double-click the Fill handle in cell G2 to copy the formula down to all of the rows in your dataset. The Fill handle is the black square dot in the lower right corner of the cell pointer.

3)   Change the formulas in column G to values.

Highlight all of the cells in column G. Use Ctrl+C to copy. As shown in Fig. 265, from the menu, select Edit – Paste Special – Values – OK.

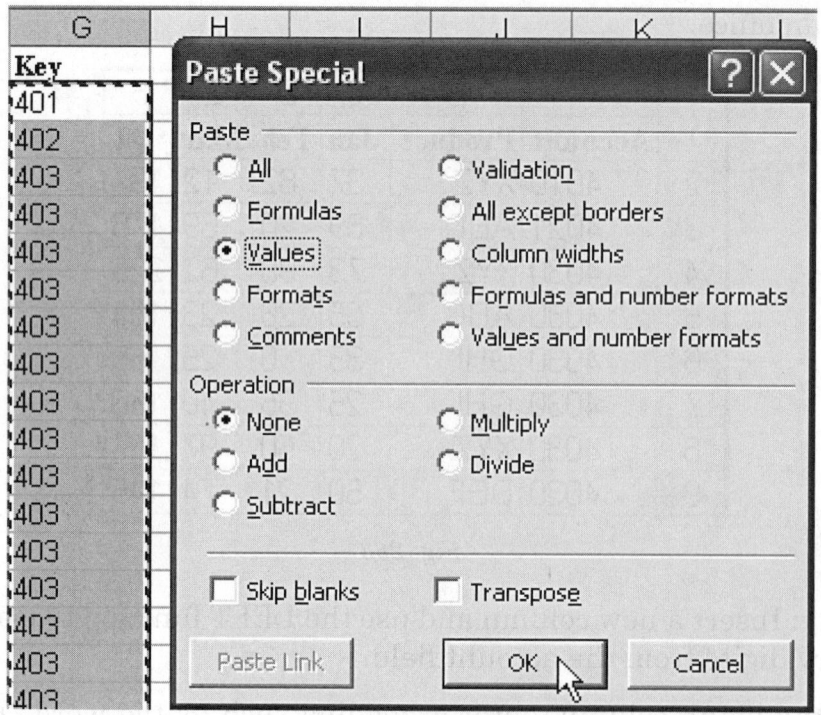

Fig. 265

Result: A certain portion of the Account field is now available in a new column. You can now use data tools, such as Sort, Filter, or Subtotal, to isolate certain offices.

Summary: When you need to isolate a portion of the characters in another column, creating a temporary column is the solution.

Commands Discussed: Edit – Paste Special

Functions Discussed: =LEFT()

HOW TO ISOLATE
THE CENTER PORTION OF AN ACCOUNT ID

Problem: Your company assigns an account ID in the format of SSS-XX-YYYY as shown in Fig. 266. You need to isolate the XX portion of the account ID in order to subtotal or sort the data.

	A	B	C	D	E	F
1	**Account**	**Product**	**Jan**	**Feb**	**Mar**	**Q1**
2	668-50-3295	XYZ	93	94	85	272
3	126-70-6950	DEF	99	79	87	265
4	620-60-3797	GHI	79	67	98	244
5	844-50-3736	XYZ	99	69	76	244
6	546-60-1875	ABC	65	81	93	239
7	417-70-3488	DEF	63	95	80	238
8	516-70-6693	ABC	68	62	99	229
9	221-60-1082	DEF	61	99	67	227
10	672-50-8695	XYZ	36	96	94	226

Fig. 266

Strategy: Insert a new column and use the MID function to isolate the necessary digits from the account field.

The MID function takes three arguments. The first argument is a cell containing a text value. The second argument is the character number where you want the result to start. The final argument is the length of the result.

In a well-formed account number, like 123-45-6789, you can predict that the start of the second segment will always be in the fifth character position. The length of the second segment is always two characters.

Part
II

In a blank column, enter a heading, such as the word "Key". In cell G2, enter the formula =MID(A2,5,2). Copy the formula down to all rows, as shown in Fig. 267.

	G2	▼				f_x	=MID(A2,5,2)	
	A	B	C	D	E	F	G	
1	Account	Product	Jan	Feb	Mar	Q1	Key	
2	668-50-3295	XYZ	93	94	85	272	50	
3	126-70-6950	DEF	99	79	87	265	70	
4	620-60-3797	GHI	79	67	98	244	60	
5	844-50-3736	XYZ	99	69	76	244	50	

Fig. 267

Additional Details: In order to capture the final four digits of the account number, you could either use the =MID(A2,8,4) or the =RIGHT(A2,4) function to isolate the final four digits of the account number.

Result: You can now sort by the new column and add subtotals by this field.

Summary: When you need to isolate a portion of the characters in another column, creating a temporary column is the solution.

Functions Discussed: =MID(); =RIGHT()

Cross Reference: How to Sort on One Segment of an Account ID

HOW TO ISOLATE EVERYTHING BEFORE A DASH IN A COLUMN BY USING FUNCTIONS

Problem: A vendor provides an Excel worksheet. As shown in Fig. 268, one field has a manufacturer code, a dash, and a part number. The manufacturer codes are not always the same length. You need to isolate the manufacturer code in a new column.

	A	B	C	D	E
1	**Item**	**Jan**	**Feb**	**Mar**	**Q1**
2	KO-4679855	93	94	85	272
3	CISCO-85590	99	69	76	244
4	TLXN-859	36	96	94	226
5	KO-9694625	80	66	70	216
6	KO-3664228	86	55	74	215
7	MSFT-4904	59	76	76	211
8	KO-5013563	91	70	45	206
9	A-54306	40	92	72	204
10	A-40674	68	43	93	204
11	MSFT-7791	43	70	85	198
12	TLXN-762	34	98	63	195
13	KO-8515183	60	88	39	187

Fig. 268

Part II

Strategy: Use the FIND function to locate the dash in the item number. The FIND function will return the character position of the dash. You can then use that result minus one in the LEFT function to isolate the manufacturer code.

The FIND function requires two arguments. The first argument is the text that you are trying to locate. In this case, you are trying to locate a dash, so you should include the dash in quotes. The second argument is the location of the cell containing the text to search.

1) Enter =FIND("-",A2) in cell F2. Copy down to all of the other cells, as shown in Fig. 269.

F2	▼			*fx*	=FIND("-",A2)	
	A	B	C	D	E	F	G
1	**Item**	**Jan**	**Feb**	**Mar**	**Q1**	**Find**	
2	KO-4679855	93	94	85	272	3	
3	CISCO-85590	99	69	76	244	6	
4	TLXN-859	36	96	94	226	5	

Fig. 269

The 3 in cell F2 indicates that the dash is located in the third character position of cell A2. The 6 in cell F3 indicates that the dash is in the sixth position of cell A3. If you want to isolate the manufacturer code, you will want to grab one less than this number from the left of the code.

2)   In cell G2, enter the formula =LEFT(A2,F2–1), as shown in Fig. 270. Double-click the Fill handle to copy this formula down to all cells.

	G2	▼			f_x	=LEFT(A2,F2-1)	
	A	B	C	D	E	F	G
1	Item	Jan	Feb	Mar	Q1	Find	Manufacturer
2	KO-4679855	93	94	85	272	3	KO
3	CISCO-85590	99	69	76	244	6	CISCO
4	TLXN-859	36	96	94	226	5	TLXN
5	KO-9694625	80	66	70	216	3	KO

Fig. 270

Alternate Strategy: You do not need to enter the formulas in two different columns. You could easily have used this formula in cell F2:

=LEFT(A2,FIND("-",A2)–1)

Additional Details: Once the formula has isolated the manufacturer code, change the formulas to values. See the Cross Reference.

Result: You can now sort by the new column and add subtotals by this field.

Summary: When you need to isolate a portion of the characters in another column, creating a temporary column is the solution.

Functions Discussed: =FIND(); =LEFT()

Cross Reference: How to Sort on One Segment of an Account ID

HOW TO USE FUNCTIONS TO ISOLATE EVERYTHING AFTER A DASH IN A COLUMN

Problem: A vendor provides an Excel worksheet. One field has a manufacturer code, a dash, and a part number, as shown in Fig. 271. The manufacturer codes are not always the same length. You need to isolate the part number in a new column.

	A	B	C	D	E
1	Item	Jan	Feb	Mar	Q1
2	KO-4679855	93	94	85	272
3	CISCO-85590	99	69	76	244
4	TLXN-859	36	96	94	226
5	KO-9694625	80	66	70	216
6	KO-3664228	86	55	74	215
7	MSFT-4904	59	76	76	211
8	KO-5013563	91	70	45	206
9	A-54306	40	92	72	204
10	A-40674	68	43	93	204
11	MSFT-7791	43	70	85	198
12	TLXN-762	34	98	63	195
13	KO-8515183	60	88	39	187

Fig. 271

Part II

Strategy: Use the MID function to extract a portion of text from the middle of the text. The MID function requires three arguments: =MID(Cell with Text, Character Number to Start, Number of Characters). You can use the FIND function to locate the dash in the item number and start at one character to the right. You can use the LEN function to figure out how long the text is.

The FIND function requires two arguments. The first argument is the text that you are trying to locate. In this case, you are trying to locate a dash, so you should include the dash in quotes. The second argument is the location of the cell containing the text to search.

1) Enter =FIND("-",A2) in cell F2. Copy down to all of the other cells, as shown in Fig. 272.

F2					f_x	=FIND("-",A2)	
	A	B	C	D	E	F	G
1	Item	Jan	Feb	Mar	Q1	Find	
2	KO-4679855	93	94	85	272	3	
3	CISCO-85590	99	69	76	244	6	
4	TLXN-859	36	96	94	226	5	

Fig. 272

The 3 in cell F2 indicates that the dash is located in the third character position of cell A2. If you want to isolate the part number, you will want to start one character to the right of this position. So, you know the start of your formula will be =MID(A2,F2+1. The hard part is figuring out how many characters there are in the part number.

2)　In cell G2, enter the formula =LEN(A2). Copy this formula down to all rows, as shown in Fig. 273.

	G2		▼			*fx* =LEN(A2)	
	A	B	C	D	E	F	G
1	Item	Jan	Feb	Mar	Q1	Find	Length
2	KO-4679855	93	94	85	272	3	10
3	CISCO-85590	99	69	76	244	6	11
4	TLXN-859	36	96	94	226	5	8
5	KO-9694625	80	66	70	216	3	10
6	KO-3664228	86	55	74	215	3	10

Fig. 273

The LEN function will tell you the total number of characters in cell A2. Cell G2 tells you that there are 10 characters in A2. If the dash is in the third position, then you want to grab (G2–F2) characters or (10–3). This will give you seven characters.

3)　In cell H2, enter the formula =MID(A2,F2+1,G2–F2), as shown in Fig. 274. In plain language, this tells Excel to extract characters from A2. Excel should start at the character after the result in F2 and continue for a length of (G2–F2) characters.

	H2		▼			*fx* =MID(A2,F2+1,G2-F2)		
	A	B	C	D	E	F	G	H
1	Item	Jan	Feb	Mar	Q1	Find	Length	Item
2	KO-4679855	93	94	85	272	3	10	4679855
3	CISCO-85590	99	69	76	244	6	11	85590
4	TLXN-859	36	96	94	226	5	8	859
5	KO-9694625	80	66	70	216	3	10	9694625

Fig. 274

In this case, it is much harder to enter the formula in one column instead of three columns. This is because the result of the FIND function is used twice in the H2 formula. In order to build a single formula, you will be entering the FIND function twice in that formula. As shown in Fig. 275, you could have entered the following formula in H2: =MID(A2,FIND ("-",A2)+1,LEN(A2)–FIND("-",A2)).

| H2 | ▼ | fx | =MID(A2,FIND("-",A2)+1,LEN(A2)-FIND("-",A2)) |

	A	B	C	D	E	F	G	H	I
1	Item	Jan	Feb	Mar	Q1	Find	Length	Item	
2	KO-4679855	93	94	85	272	3	10	4679855	
3	CISCO-85590	99	69	76	244	6	11	85590	

Fig. 275

Alternate Strategy: You might be tempted to use a formula such as =MID(A2,F2+1,50). The third parameter, 50, will ensure that it can grab a part number of any conceivable length. This approach will work, but the resulting answer will have forty-four blanks appended to the end of the part number. This makes it impossible to use successfully in a VLOOKUP formula as it stands. However, you can use =TRIM(MID(A2,F2+1,50)) to remove the trailing spaces.

Part II

Summary: Use a combination of LEN and FIND functions as an aide to help you locate the proper start or end position for the LEFT, MID, and RIGHT functions.

Functions Discussed: =FIND(); =MID(); =LEN(); =TRIM()

HOW TO USE FUNCTIONS TO ISOLATE EVERYTHING AFTER THE SECOND DASH IN A COLUMN

Problem: A vendor file contains a three-segment part number, as shown in Fig. 276. Each segment is separated by a dash. The length of each segment could be any number of characters. Find the second or third segment.

	A	B	C	D	E
1	Item	Jan	Feb	Mar	Q1
2	KO-4679855-A34	93	94	85	272
3	CISCO-85590-B7	99	69	76	244
4	TLXN-859-A3	36	96	94	226
5	KO-9694625-B95	80	66	70	216
6	KO-3664228-A52	86	55	74	215

Fig. 276

Strategy: There is an optional third argument in the FIND function. This tells Excel to start looking after a certain character position in the text. In this case, to find the second dash, you want Excel to start looking after the location of the first dash.

1)   As in the prior examples, use =FIND("-",A2) in cell F2 to locate the first dash.

2)   Enter =FIND("-",A2,F2+1) in cell G2, as shown in Fig. 277. The F2+1 parameter tells Excel that you want to find a dash starting in the fourth character position of cell A2.

G2		▼			*fx*	=FIND("-",A2,F2+1)	
	A	B	C	D	E	F	G
1	Item	Jan	Feb	Mar	Q1	Dash1	Dash2
2	KO-4679855-A34	93	94	85	272	3	11
3	CISCO-85590-B7	99	69	76	244	6	12
4	TLXN-859-A3	36	96	94	226	5	9
5	KO-9694625-B95	80	66	70	216	3	11

Fig. 277

3)   Enter =LEFT(A2,F2–1) in H2. The formula in H2 locates the first segment of the part number.

4)   Enter =MID(A2,F2+1,G2–F2) in I2. The formula in I2 locates the middle segment of the part number.

5)   To get the right segment of the part number, you can use the RIGHT function. Just like the LEFT function, the RIGHT function requires a cell and the number of characters from the right side of the item number. To find the number of characters, use =LEN(A2)–G2.

Enter the resulting formula, =RIGHT(A2,LEN(A2)–G2), in J2. See Fig. 278.

	J2		▼			f_x	=RIGHT(A2,LEN(A2)-G2)			

	A	B	C	D	E	F	G	H	I	J
1	Item	Jan	Feb	Mar	Q1	Dash1	Dash2	Item1	Item2	Item3
2	KO-4679855-A34	93	94	85	272	3	11	KO	4679855	A34
3	CISCO-85590-B7	99	69	76	244	6	12	CISCO	85590	B7
4	TLXN-859-A3	36	96	94	226	5	9	TLXN	859	A3
5	KO-9694625-B95	80	66	70	216	3	11	KO	9694625	B95

Fig. 278

Gotcha: All of these formulas are trusting that the vendor always included two dashes in the item number. If an item number exists without a second dash, the second FIND function would return a #VALUE! error, leading to errors in the calculation for the second and third items. Before converting formulas to values and deleting the original part number, sort the data by column F and then sort descending by column G. As shown in Fig. 279, any #VALUE! errors will sort to the top of the dataset, where you can locate and correct the errors in the part number.

Part II

	A	B	C	D	E	F	G	H	I	J
1	Item	Jan	Feb	Mar	Q1	Dash1	Dash2	Item1	Item2	Item3
2	KO-4679855A34	93	94	85	272	3	#VALUE!	KO	#VALUE!	#VALUE!
3	CISCO-85590-B7	99	69	76	244	6	12	CISCO	85590	B7
4	TLXN-859-A3	36	96	94	226	5	9	TLXN	859	A3

Fig. 279

Summary: Using combinations of FIND, LEN, MID, LEFT, and RIGHT, it is possible to parse nearly any data imaginable.

Functions Discussed: =FIND(); =LEN(); =MID(); =LEFT(); =RIGHT()

HOW TO SEPARATE A PART NUMBER INTO THREE COLUMNS

Problem: A vendor file contains a three-segment item number, as shown in Fig. 280. Each segment is separated by a dash. The FIND function makes your head hurt. Break the Part Number into three columns.

	A	B	C	D	E
1	Item	Jan	Feb	Mar	Q1
2	KO-4679855-A34	93	94	85	272
3	CISCO-85590-B7	99	69	76	244
4	TLXN-859-A3	36	96	94	226
5	KO-9694625-B95	80	66	70	216
6	KO-3664228-A52	86	55	74	215

Fig. 280

Strategy: Use the Text to Columns command on the Data menu to parse the item number. Follow these steps.

1) Copy the item number to the right side of your data in column F. The Text To Columns command will fill several columns to the right of the original column. Make sure you have plenty of blank columns.

2) Select the entire range of data in column G. Place the cell pointer in G2. Hit the End key. While holding down the Shift key, hit the Down Arrow key to select the entire range.

3) From the menu, select Data – Text to Columns. The Wizard will work on either data that is delimited or on data that has a fixed width to each segment. Our data is delimited by a dash. As shown in Fig. 281, in Step 1, leave the radio button on the Delimited setting. Click Next.

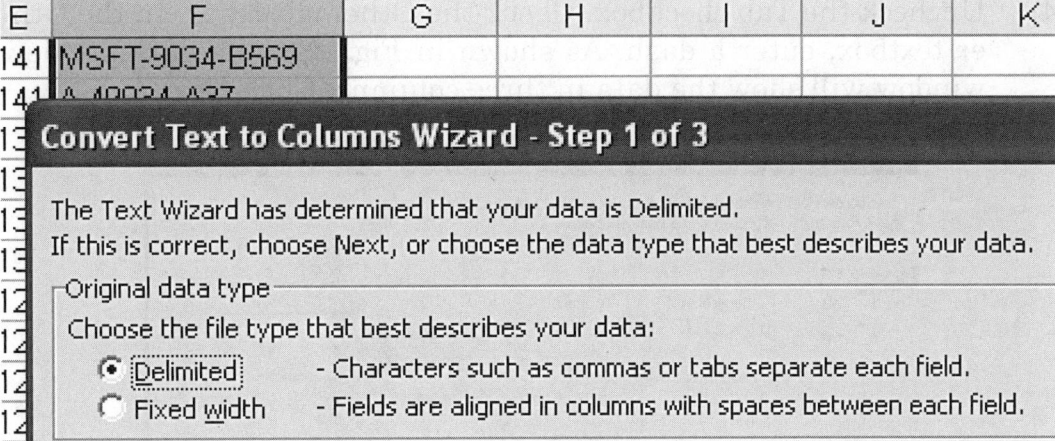

Fig. 281

Part
II

By default, Step 2 assumes that the data is delimited by a tab. As shown in Fig. 282, other choices are commas, spaces, and semicolons. Note that dash is not in the list.

Convert Text to Columns Wizard - Step 2 o

This screen lets you set the delimiters your data cont.
how your text is affected in the preview below.

Delimiters
☑ Tab   ☐ Semicolon   ☐ Comma
☐ Space ☐ Other: [   ]

Fig. 282

4) Uncheck the Tab checkbox. Check the Other checkbox. In the Other textbox, enter a dash. As shown in Fig. 283, the data preview window will show the data in three columns. Click Next.

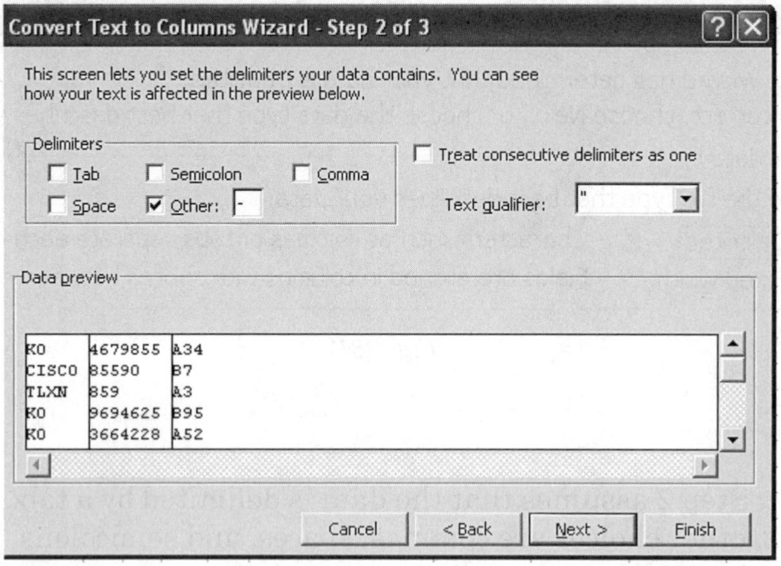

Fig. 283

5) In Step 3, you can optionally specify the data type of the columns. Unless you have dates, the General type is OK. Note that if you want to preserve the leading zeroes in the second segment of the item number, you should choose the heading of that field and change from General to Text, as shown in Fig. 284. Click Finish.

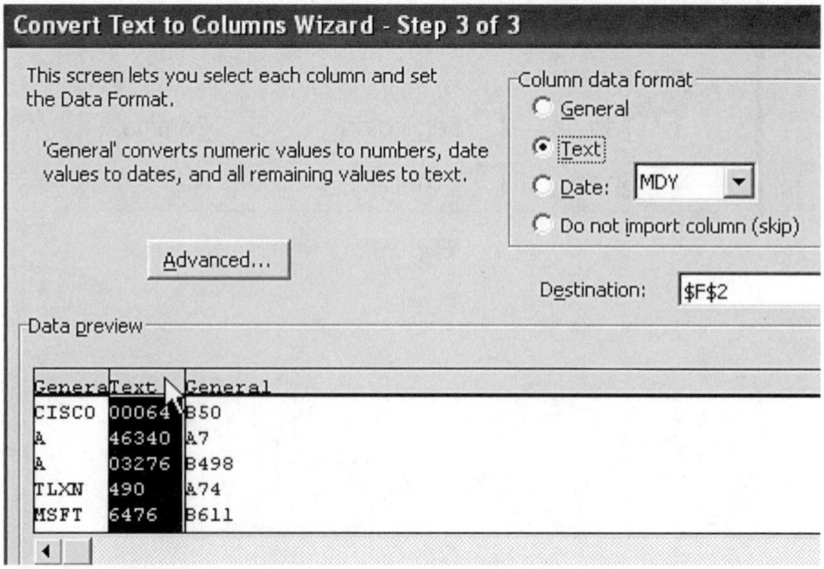

Fig. 284

Result: The original column F has been overwritten with the first portion of the result. New columns G and H contain the second and third segments of the item number, as shown in Fig. 285.

F	G	H
Item		
KO	4679855	A34
CISCO	85590	B7
TLXN	859	A3
KO	9694625	B95
KO	3664228	A52
MSFT	4904	B636
KO	5013563	A910
A	54306	B28

Fig. 285

Part
II

Gotcha: A very strange anomaly will appear for the remainder of this Excel session. If you later open a Notepad file, copy data that contains dashes, and attempt to paste to Excel, Excel will automatically split the data into columns where the dash is located, as shown in Fig. 286 and Fig. 287. This can be a very handy feature if you are expecting it, or a very puzzling situation if you are not.

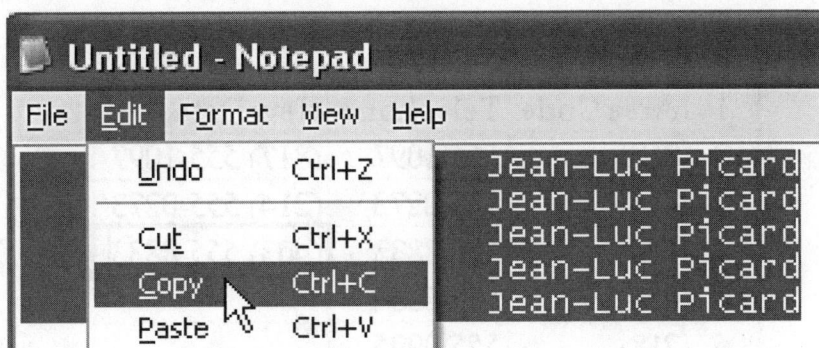

Fig. 286

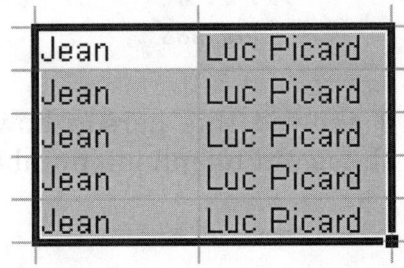

Fig. 287

Summary: If your data is set up with consistent delimiters, the Text to Columns Wizard is a fast way to parse data.

Commands Discussed: Data – Text to Columns...

AVOID #REF! ERRORS
WHEN DELETING COLUMNS

Problem: Excel is great at computing results. Sometimes, you only need to keep the results of a formula and you want to erase the columns that the calculation was based upon. If you delete a column used in the formula, the formula result changes to #REF!. How can you prevent the #REF! Error?

Here is a true story. When I was working at my last day job, someone in our marketing department was given a list of leads from a trade show. The Excel file had the area codes in one column and the telephone numbers in another column. There were several thousand leads. Someone in Marketing was retyping all of the telephone numbers in order to get the area code and phone number in one cell, as shown in Fig. 288.

	H	I	J
1	Area Code	Telephone	New Data
2	817	555-1097	(817) 555-1097
3	214	555-0273	(214) 555-0273
4	403	555-8833	(403) 555-8833
5	416	555-8364	
6	218	555-0995	
7	405	555-7888	
	204	555-6649	

Fig. 288

As shown in Fig. 289, I showed this person how to use a formula to quickly convert all five thousand telephone numbers to the format that she wanted.

J5	▼		f_x	="("&H5&") "&I5

	H	I	J	K
1	Area Code	Telephone	New Data	
5	416	555-8364	(416) 555-8364	
6	218	555-0995	(218) 555-0995	
7	405	555-7888	(405) 555-7888	

Fig. 289

I started to walk away, whistling a little tune because I had just saved someone a whole lot of typing. I had just about reached the door of the marketing department when I heard a scream. Since column J contained the information that she needed, she had deleted columns H and I. However, since column J was still a live formula, Excel no longer knew how to calculate the results in J. And, because cells referenced in the formula had been deleted, all of the telephone numbers that were in column J now showed the #REF! error, as shown in Fig. 290.

="("&#REF!&") "&#REF!	
H	**I**
New Data	
#REF!	
#REF!	
#REF!	

Fig. 290

Strategy: Immediately hit Ctrl+Z to undo the delete and get the source columns back. Next, you will copy the formulas and use Paste Special to paste the cells as values instead of formulas.

1) With the cell pointer in cell J2, hold down the Shift key while you tap the End key and then the Down Arrow key. This will select the entire contiguous range of cells in column J.

2) From the menu, select Edit – Copy to copy the cells to the clipboard.

3)   Without changing the selection, select Edit – Paste Special from the menu. In the Paste Special dialog box, choose the Values option, as shown in Fig. 291. Choose OK.

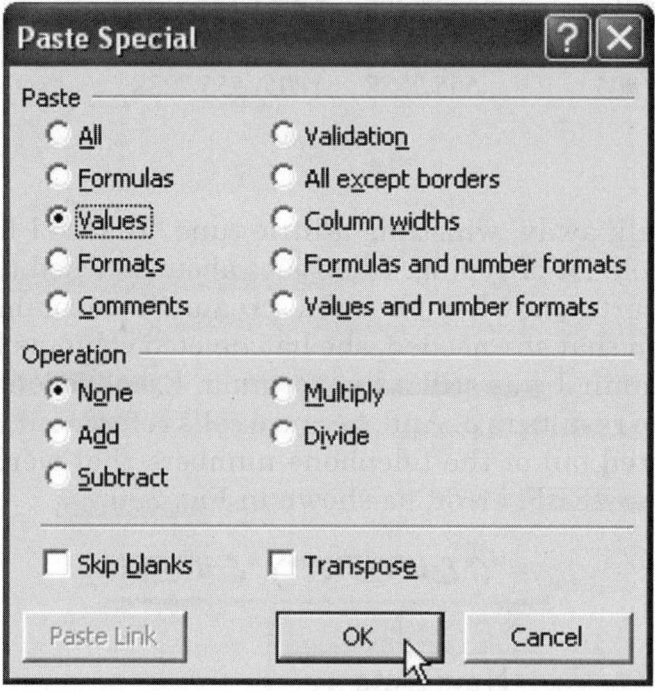

Fig. 291

Result: The telephone numbers in column J are converted from formulas to the results of those formulas, as shown in Fig. 292.

	fx	'(804) 555-6649	
H	**I**	**J**
Area Code	Telephone	New Data
804	555-6649	(804) 555-6649
313	555-1162	(313) 555-1162
307	555-3180	(307) 555-3180
313	555-3780	(313) 555-3780
804	555-0159	(804) 555-0159

Fig. 292

You can now safely delete columns H and I and the telephone numbers in column J will not change to #REF! errors.

Summary: Using the Paste Special Values technique is essential to becoming proficient in Excel. It will convert a range of formulas to the current value of the formula. You can then safely delete the source columns.

Commands Discussed: Edit – Copy; Edit – Paste Special; Undo

CREATE RANDOM NUMBERS

Problem: You want to create a range of random numbers in order to illustrate a concept in a class. As shown in Fig. 293, you want to fill in random numbers in columns C through E.

	A	B	C	D	E
1	Account	Product	Jan	Feb	Mar
2	4010	XYZ			
3	4021	ABC			
4	4030	XYZ			
5	4030	ABC			
6	4030	GHI			
7	4030	GHI			
8	4030	XYZ			
9	4030	DEF			
10	4030	XYZ			
11	4030	DEF			

Fig. 293

Strategy: Use the RAND function. This function will return a random number between 0 and 0.99999.

You will often need to create random numbers between a range of digits. In Fig. 294, you might want sales between 1 and 100 for each cell. Use a formula such as =RAND()*100 to return figures between 0 and 99.999.

99.95165
89.86699
77.50628
67.09817
54.39128
42.62482
33.7236
25.8575
15.16122
0.01162

Fig. 294

To return just integers, use the INT function to return the integer portion. =INT(RAND()*100) will return numbers such as these shown in Fig. 295.

99
89
77
67
54
42
33
25
15
0

Fig. 295

Note that the formula is returning values from 0 to 99. If you really want values from 1 to 100, then use =INT(RAND()*100)+1. See Fig. 296.

f_x	=INT(RAND()*100)+1			
C	D	E	F	G
Account	Product	Jan	Feb	Mar
4010	XYZ	77	69	65
4021	ABC	23	69	81
4030	XYZ	32	35	20
4030	ABC	26	99	39
4030	GHI	77	13	58
4030	GHI	32	68	51
4030	XYZ	8	30	33
4030	DEF	34	40	57
4030	XYZ	92	50	75
4030	DEF	18	65	38
4030	ABC	23	62	71

Fig. 296

Part II

Additional Information: Every time that you hit F9 or enter a new value in the worksheet, the random numbers will change. You might want to change the formulas to values to freeze the random numbers. Select the range of random numbers. Use Edit – Copy, and then use Edit – Paste Special – Values to convert formulas to numbers.

Summary: The RAND function can be used to return random numbers.

Commands Discussed: Edit – Paste Special – Values

Functions Discussed: =INT(); =RAND()

CREATE RANDOM NUMBERS
TO SEQUENCE A CLASS OF STUDENTS

Problem: The students in your class must present an oral book report. Rather than have them go alphabetically, as shown in Fig. 297, you want to randomly sequence them.

	A
1	**Student**
2	Adam
3	Alex
4	Andrew
5	Ashley
6	Athena
7	Brandon
8	D. J.
9	Danielle
10	Davis
11	Gabby
12	Jeremy
13	Josh W
14	Madeline
15	Mattie
16	Megan
17	Nick G
18	Nick M
19	Robbie
20	Rowen
21	Tyler M
22	Zeke

Fig. 297

Strategy: Use the RAND function in column B and then sort by column B. Follow these steps.

1)   Enter a heading of Rand in B1.

2)   Select cells B2:B22. Enter =RAND() and press Ctrl+Enter. Each student will be assigned a random decimal between 0 and 1, as shown in Fig. 298.

	A	B
1	**Student**	Rand
2	Adam	0.804538
3	Alex	0.580895
4	Andrew	0.185482
5	Ashley	0.831056
6	Athena	0.011357
7	Brandon	0.746444

Fig. 298

3)   Select a single cell in column B and choose the AZ button on the Standard toolbar. The list will be sorted in a random sequence.

Gotcha: The data is sorted and then column B is recalculated. It will appear that the new figures in column B are not in ascending order, as shown in Fig. 299. This is because the sort was based on the previous values in column B.

	A	B
1	**Student**	Rand
2	Athena	0.24198
3	D. J.	0.314784
4	Nick G	0.335703
5	Andrew	0.788417
6	Madeline	0.889228
7	Zeke	0.582238

Fig. 299

4)   You can now delete column B.

Additional Information: If you want to fill column B with sequential numbers, then enter 1 in B2 and 2 in B3. Highlight these two cells and double-click the Fill handle to extend the series to your entire dataset.

Summary: The RAND function can be used to provide a column of data to fairly and randomly sort a list of students.

Commands Discussed: Edit – Paste Special – Values

Functions Discussed: =RAND()

PLAY DICE GAMES WITH EXCEL

Problem: Your Monopoly set is missing the dice. Create a spreadsheet that will simulate randomly rolling two dice.

Strategy: Use the RAND function and clever spreadsheet formatting to simulate two or more dice. Follow these steps.

1) Select cell A2. From the menu, select Format – Row – Height. Set the row height to 41, as shown in Fig. 300.

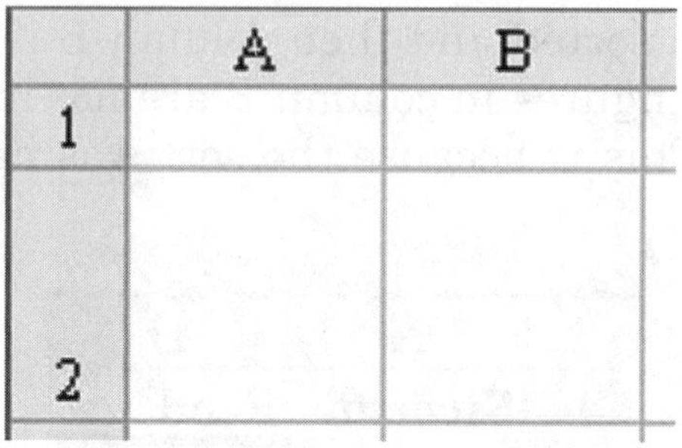

Fig. 300

2) In cell B2, enter the formula =INT(RAND()*6)+1, as shown in Fig. 301.

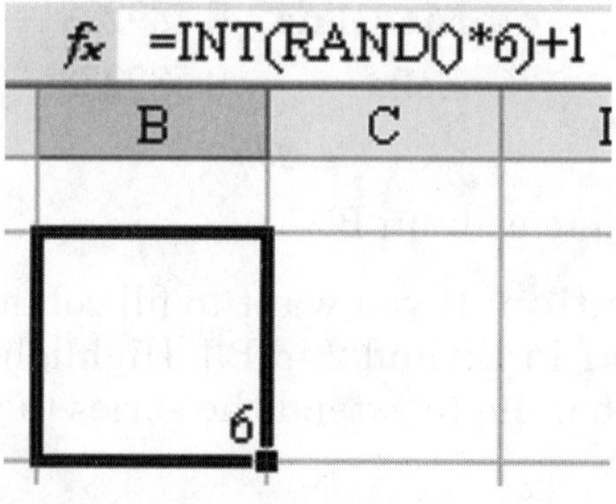

Fig. 301

3) With cell B1 selected, hit Ctrl+1 to open the Format Cells dialog. On the Alignment tab, change both Text Alignment fields to Center, as shown in Fig. 302.

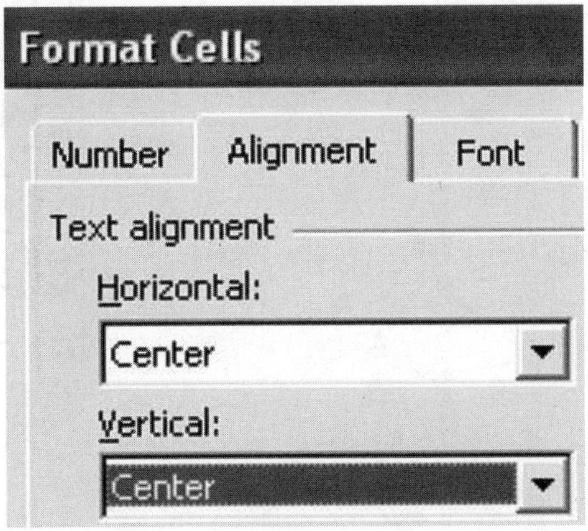

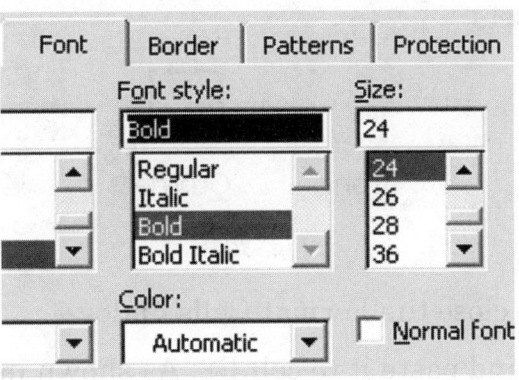

Fig. 302

4) On the Font tab, choose Bold and 24 point, as shown in Fig. 303.

Fig. 303

5) On the Border tab, first choose the thick border style on the right side of the dialog, as shown in Fig. 304.

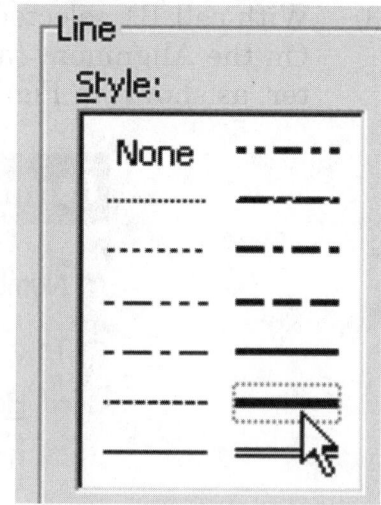

Fig. 304

6) Next, select the Outline Preset in the top of the dialog, as shown in Fig. 305.

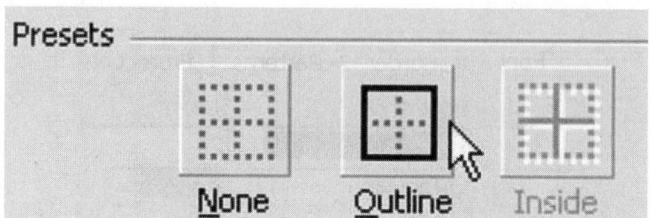

Fig. 305

7) Choose OK to close the Format Cells dialog.

8) Copy cell B2 and paste it to cell D2. As shown in Fig. 306, you will have the two dice required for Monopoly.

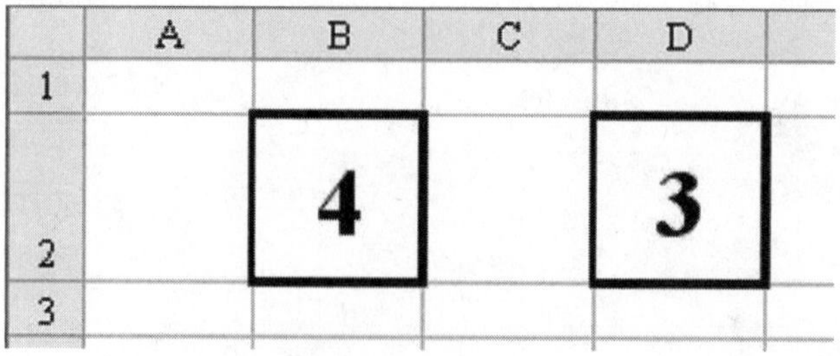

	A	B	C	D	
1					
2		**4**		**3**	
3					

Fig. 306

Results: You will have one die in cell B2 and another in cell D2. Every time that you hit the F9 key, you will have a new roll of the dice.

Summary: Use the RAND function and worksheet formatting to create a dice simulation.

Commands Discussed: Format Cells

Functions Discussed: =RAND()

PLAY BUNCO WITH EXCEL

Problem: Your kids are bored waiting somewhere. Pull out your laptop and build a quick Bunco game to keep them occupied.

Strategy: Without using macros, you will have to use the manual calculation mode and a single iteration mode to allow the worksheet to keep track of scoring. Follow these steps.

1)   From the menu, select Tools – Options – Calculation.

2)   In the Calculation section, choose Manual. Uncheck the option to Recalculate Before Save. In the Iteration section, choose the Iteration checkbox. Change both parameters to 1, as shown in Fig. 307.

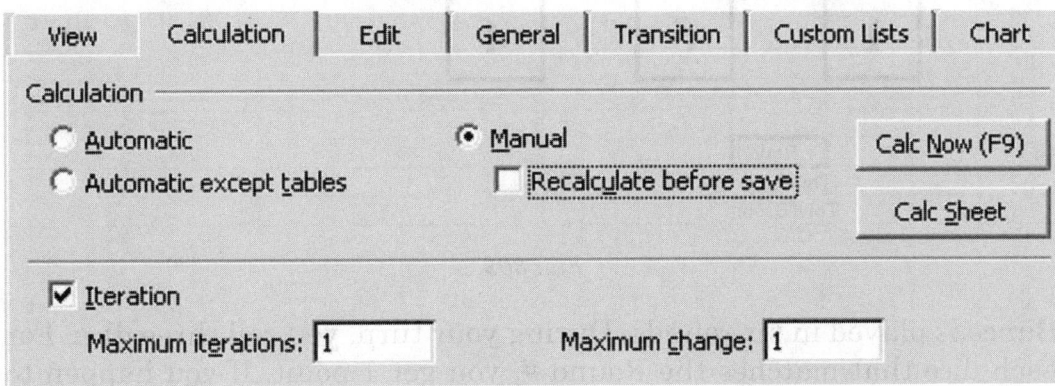

Fig. 307

Manual calculation with iteration will allow spreadsheets with circular references to actually work. Every time that you hit the F9 key to calculate the worksheet, the cell with a circular reference will recalculate on the basis of the previous value of the cell.

3)   Follow the steps in the previous chapter, Play Dice Games with Excel, to build three dice in B2, D2, and E2, as shown in Fig. 308.

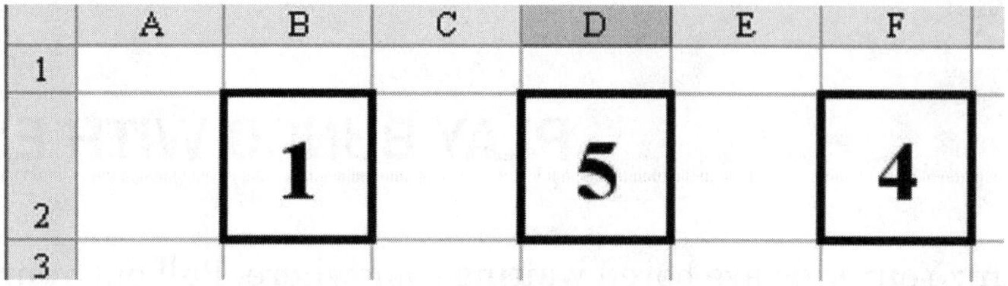

Fig. 308

4)   In cell C5 enter the label "Round". In cell C6, enter the label "This Score". In cell C7, enter the label "Total Score". Right-justify each label using the button on the Standard toolbar, as shown in Fig. 309.

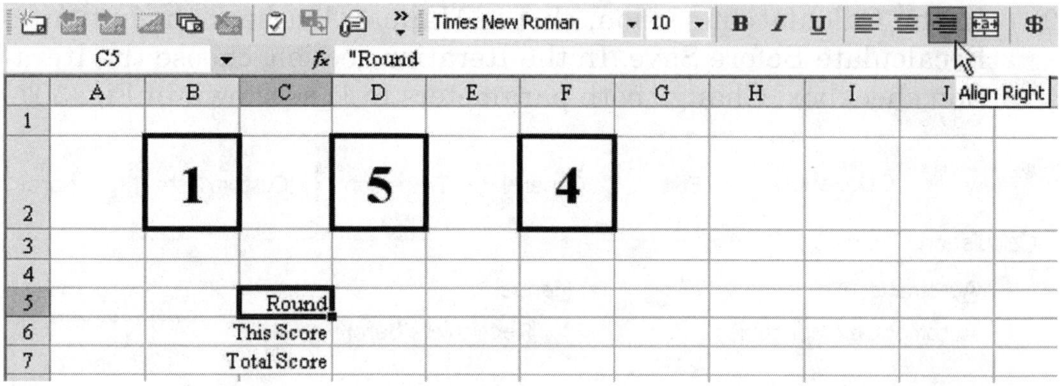

Fig. 309

Bunco is played in six rounds. During your turn, you roll three dice. For each dice that matches the Round #, you get 1 point. If you happen to roll three matching dice that do not match the round number, you get 5 points. If you roll three dice that match the round number, you get 21 points. On any turn where you get no points, you then advance to the next round.

5) For now, enter the number 1 in D5.

The formula for the score in D6 is fairly complex. You can break down the rules as follows:

- If B2, D2, and F2 all match, and they match the round number in D5, then you get 21 points.

- Otherwise, if B2, D2, and F2 all match then you get 5 points.

- Otherwise, add one point if B2 matches D5. Add one point if D2 matches D5. Add one point if F2 matches D5.

You will have to nest a couple of IF functions. The syntax of the IF function is: =IF(Some Test, Value if True, Value if False).

If the test portions of the IF statements have several conditions that must be met, then you should include all of the conditions as arguments of the AND function.

Our first scoring rule is "If B2, D2, F2, and D5 all match, then 21 points". The AND statement for this is =AND(B2=D2,D2=F2,F2=D5). The IF statement to give 21 points would be =IF(AND(B2=D2,D2=F2,F2=D5),21,___).

The next scoring rule replaces the ___ in the third parameter of the IF function. This scoring rule says that if B2, D2, and F2 match, then you get 5 points. The AND statement would be AND(B2=D2,D2=F2). This portion of the IF statement would be =IF(AND(B2=D2,D2=F2), 5,___).

The final scoring rule says that for any of the dice that match the round number, you get 1 point. This actually requires three new IF functions, added together: IF(B2=D5,1,0)+IF(D2=D5,1,0)+IF(F2=D5,1,0).

6) Nesting all of these together, you get the following formula. Enter it in cell D6.

=IF(AND(B2=D2,D2=F2,B2=D5),21,IF(AND(B2=D2,D2=F2),5,IF(B2=D5,1,0)+IF(D2=D5,1,0)+IF(F2=D5,1,0)))

Part
II

7) Hit the F9 key until you get three dice that match, as shown in Fig. 310. Check that the scoring for This Score works as planned.

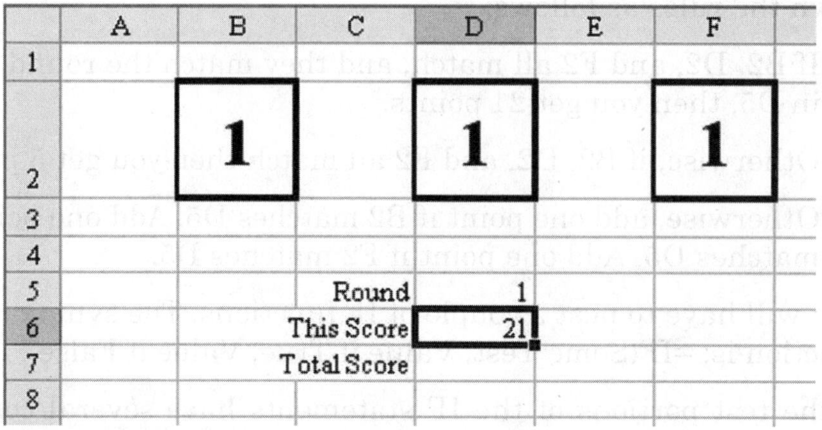

	A	B	C	D	E	F
1						
2		**1**		**1**		**1**
3						
4						
5			Round	1		
6			This Score	21		
7			Total Score			
8						

Fig. 310

8) Hit F9 again until you have a setting where This Score is 0.

This is the tricky part. Before you can enter the circular reference formula, you need to enter the initial value for the cells in the worksheet.

9) In cell D5, enter a –1.

10) In cell D7, enter the number 0, as shown in Fig. 311.

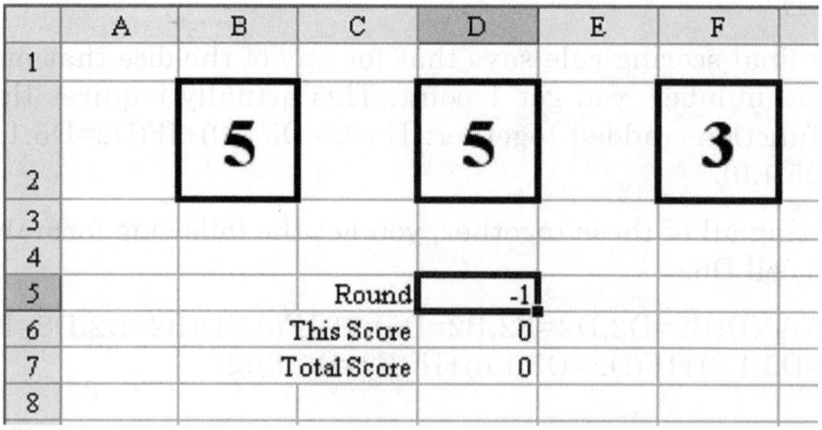

	A	B	C	D	E	F
1						
2		**5**		**5**		**3**
3						
4						
5			Round	-1		
6			This Score	0		
7			Total Score	0		
8						

Fig. 311

11) In cell D7, enter the formula =D6+D7. This formula will add the score from This Score to the Total Score.

12) In cell D5, enter the formula =IF(D6=0,1+D5,D5). This gives you a formula that will increment the round number any time that the dice produce zero points. When you enter this formula, because D6 is initially 0, the −1 will change to a 0.

13) Immediately Save and Close the game after entering these formulae. It is important that Excel NOT CALCULATE before saving. That is why you unchecked the Calculate Before Save option in Fig. 307.

Result: To play a round of Bunco, hit the F9 key to roll the three dice, as shown in Fig. 312. When the game is complete, close the worksheet WITHOUT SAVING. Open the worksheet to start a new game.

	A	B	C	D	E	F
1						
2		**3**		**4**		**4**
3						
4						
5			Round	6		
6			This Score	0		
7			Total Score	2		
8						
9						

Fig. 312

Gotcha: Before entering the numbers in D5, make sure that the dice do not all match.

Summary: Using manual calculation mode, you can create simple dice games.

Commands Discussed: Manual Calculation

Functions Discussed: =RAND(); =IF(); =AND()

PLAY CRAPS WITH EXCEL

Problem: How can you play a Craps simulation in Excel?

Strategy: Craps is a game played with two dice. On your first roll, if you roll a 7 or 11, you win. If you roll a 2, 3, or 12, you lose. If you roll a 4, 5, 6, 8, 9, or 10, then this number becomes your point. On subsequent rolls, you must roll your point number again before you roll a 7. If you roll your point, then you win. If you roll anything else, then you lose.

Set up a worksheet with manual calculation and one iteration. The worksheet will require several circular references. Use the Random Dice example to generate two dice in cells B2 and D3. Use a series of IF formulas to keep track if you win or lose.

1)   In columns B and C, enter the text values shown in Fig. 313.

	A	B	C
5			Start Game
6			Which Roll?
7			Total Rolled:
8			
9		Come-Out Roll	
10		Craps: 2, 3, 12 Loses	
11		7 or 11 Wins	
12		Point	
13			
14		Subsequent Rolls	
15		7 Loses	
16		Point Wins	
17			
18		Game Over	
19		Game Result	
20			
21		Number of Wins	
22		Number of Losses	

Fig. 313

2) In cell D5, enter the value TRUE until the rest of the formulas are set up. In the rest of column D, enter the formulas as shown in Fig. 314.

	D
6	=IF(D5,1,D6+1)
7	=D2+B2
8	
9	
10	=AND(D6=1,OR(D7=2,D7=3,D7=12))
11	=AND(D6=1,OR(D7=7,D7=11))
12	=IF(D6=1,D7,D12)
13	
14	
15	=AND(D6>1,D7=7)
16	=AND(D6>1,D7=D12)
17	
18	=OR(D15:D16,D10:D11)
19	=IF(D18,IF(OR(D11,D16),"Win","Lose"),"")
20	
21	=IF(D19="Win",D21+1,D21)
22	=IF(D19="Lose",D22+1,D22)

Fig. 314

3) Finally, in cell D5, enter the circular reference =D18, as shown in Fig. 315.

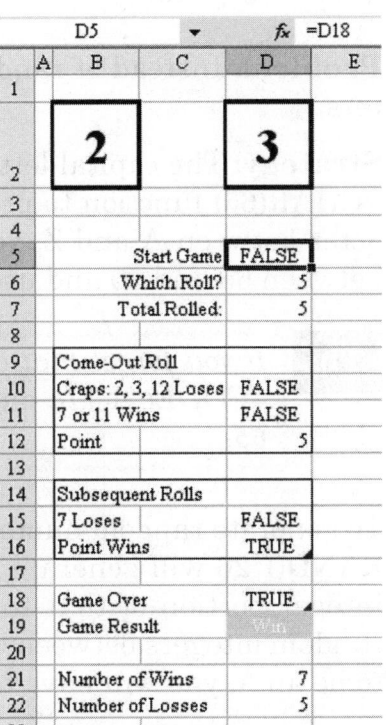

Fig. 315

Part
II

Cell D5 is a circular reference that keeps track of whether this is the first roll in each game. If the value in D5 is True, then the rules in D10 and D11 will determine if you win or lose on the first roll of the game.

The circular reference in D6 will keep track of the roll number. Once this cell is above 1, then the rules in D15 and D16 will keep watch to see if you roll a 7 or your point.

Rows 18 and 19 keep track if this dice roll ended the current game and the result of that game. Two circular formulas in D21 and D22 will keep track of your lifetime wins and losses in the game.

To play, press the F9 key to roll the dice.

Summary: Using intentional circular references, you can design simple games like Craps.

Commands Discussed: Tools – Options – Calculation – Manual

Functions Discussed: =IF()

CREATE RANDOM LETTERS

Problem: Instead of random numbers, you need to create random letters.

Strategy: The capital letter A is character number 65. You can use the =CHAR(65) function to produce an A. Thus, to produce a random character between A and Z, you would want to produce a random number between 65 and 90 and use it as the argument to the CHAR function.

> **Tip** *If you forget that an "A" is character 65, you can always enter =CODE("A") in any cell to learn that the letter "A" is character 65.*

To generate random numbers between 65 and 90, follow this logic. First, RAND()*26 will generate numbers between 0 and 25.9999. Taking the integer portion of that function with =INT(RAND()*26) will generate random integers between 0 and 25. Because you want the first character to be an A, you will have to add 65 to the preceding formula.

As shown in Fig. 316, the formula to use is =CHAR(INT(RAND()*26)+ 65).

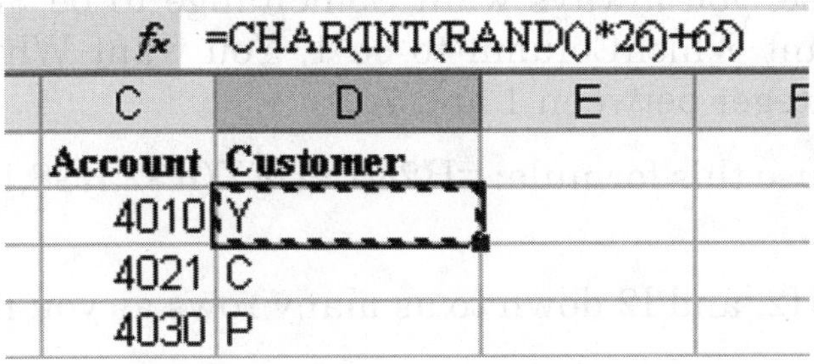

f_x	=CHAR(INT(RAND()*26)+65)		
C	**D**	**E**	**F**
Account	**Customer**		
4010	Y		
4021	C		
4030	P		

Fig. 316

Additional Details: In many places in this book, I use customers in the form of ABC, Inc. In order to generate these names, I start with a random letter between A and X. Follow these steps.

1) In cell G2, enter the formula: =INT(RAND()*24)+65.

2) In cell H2, enter the formula: =CHAR(G2)&CHAR(G2+1)&CHAR(G2+2).

3) In a blank area of the worksheet, enter a table with some different company name suffixes.

   My table is in K2:K8. Note that each suffix either begins with a comma or a space, as shown in Fig. 317.

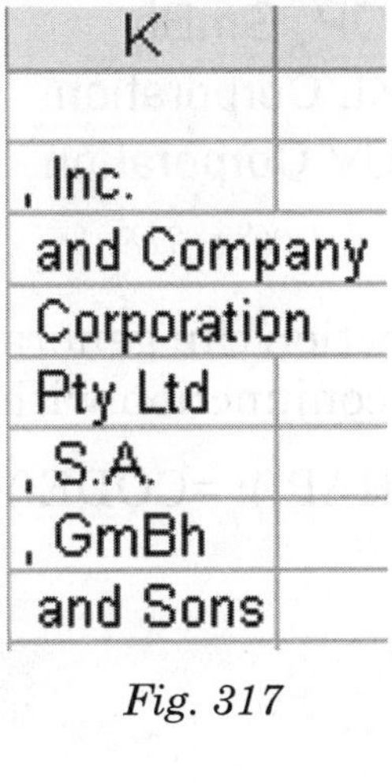

K	
, Inc.	
and Company	
Corporation	
Pty Ltd	
, S.A.	
, GmBh	
and Sons	

Fig. 317

There is a function called INDEX, which has three parameters. You might say: =INDEX(SomeRange, WhichRow, WhichColumn). In this case, you always want SomeRange to be $K$2:$K$8. You always want WhichColumn to be 1. You want WhichRow to be a random integer between 1 and 7.

4) In cell I2, use this formula: =H2&INDEX(K$2:K$8,INT(RAND()*7) +1,1).

5) Copy G2, H2, and I2 down to as many rows as you need data.

Result: As shown in Fig. 318, you have a column of random company names. You can safely use these in a book without infringing any trademarks.

=+H2&INDEX(K$2:K$8,INT(RAND()*7)+1,1)

F	G	H	I	J	K	L
	80	PQR	PQR Corporation		, Inc.	
	84	TUV	TUV and Company		and Company	
	74	JKL	JKL and Sons		Corporation	
	68	DEF	DEF, GmBh		Pty Ltd	
	65	ABC	ABC, S.A.		, S.A.	
	78	NOP	NOP, Inc.		, GmBh	
	75	KLM	KLM, S.A.		and Sons	
	78	NOP	NOP, GmBh			
	74	JKL	JKL Corporation			
	84	TUV	TUV Corporation			

Fig. 318

Summary: The RAND() function can generate random letters as well as numbers when it is used in conjunction with the CHAR function.

Functions Discussed: =CHAR(); =CODE(); =INDEX(); =RAND()

CONVERT NUMBERS TO TEXT

Problem: You have a field that may contain numbers or text. You need the numeric entries to sort with the text entries. Instead, Excel always sorts the numeric entries to the top of the list, followed by the text entries, as shown in Fig. 319.

	A
1	**Style**
2	5500
3	6000
4	7000
5	5500A
6	6000B
7	7000A

Fig. 319

Strategy: This is a rare case where you need to convert numeric entries to text entries.

If you were building this spreadsheet from scratch, you could have selected column A, and from the Format – Cells dialog, you could have formatted the column as Text, as shown in Fig. 320. This would allow all future entries to automatically be converted to text. However, converting cells to have a text format does NOT retroactively convert numbers to text.

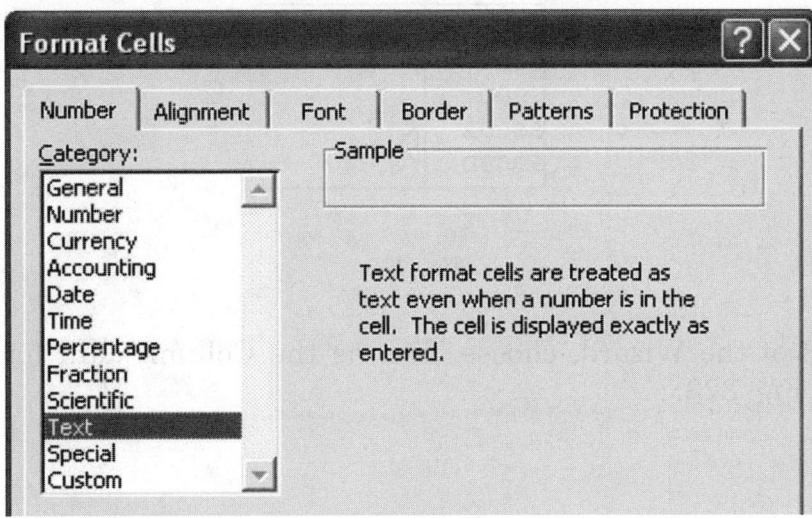

Fig. 320

Another option would be to edit each cell that contains a number. Select the cell. Hit F2 to edit the cell. Hit Home to move to the beginning of the cell. Type an apostrophe. Hit Enter (or the Down Arrow) to move to the next cell. This could get very tedious if you have more than a few cells to change.

The good news is, there are two easy methods for converting all of the entries in a column to text.

Method 1: Select all of the data in a column. From the menu, select Data – Text to Columns. In Step 1 of the Wizard, indicate that your data is fixed width, as shown in Fig. 321.

Fig. 321

In Step 2 of the Wizard, you may or may not have any vertical lines drawn in the Data Preview section, as shown in Fig. 322. If you do, double-click to remove them.

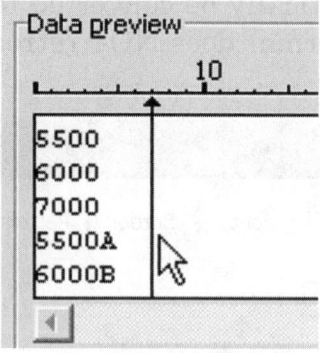

Fig. 322

In Step 3 of the Wizard, choose Text as the Column data format, as shown in Fig. 323.

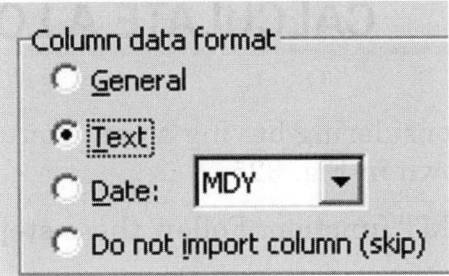

Fig. 323

After you choose Finish, the column will be converted to text.

Gotcha: You cannot sort using the AZ button in this case. You must select Sort from the Data menu. After you choose OK to sort, you will get the Sort Warning dialog shown in Fig. 324. Choose to Sort Numbers and Numbers Stored as Text Separately.

Part II

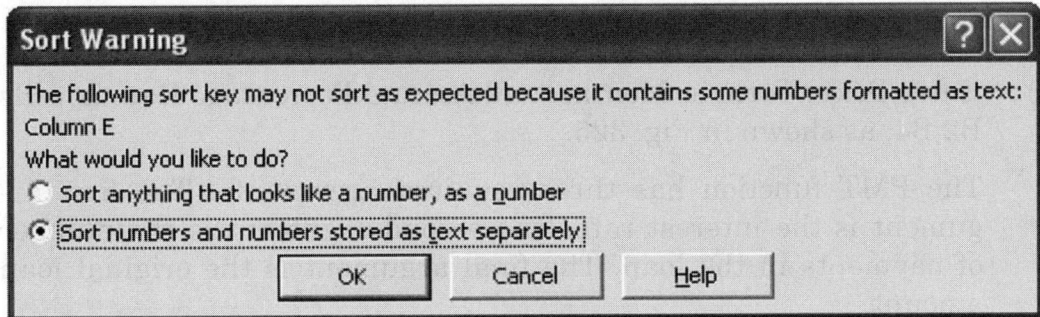

Fig. 324

Alternate Strategy: You could also insert a temporary column with the following formula: =TEXT(A2,"@").

Summary: Use Data – Text to Columns to convert a column to text.

Commands Discussed: Data – Text to Columns; Data – Sort

CALCULATE A LOAN PAYMENT

Problem: You are considering buying a car. You want to calculate the loan payment, as shown in Fig. 325.

Strategy: Use the PMT function. Follow these steps.

	A	B
1		
2	Price	25000
3	Term	60
4	Rate	5%
5		
6	Pmt	
7		

Fig. 325

1) Enter Price, Term in Months, and Annual Percentage Rate in cells B2:B4, as shown in Fig. 325.

   The PMT function has three required arguments. The first argument is the interest rate. The second argument is the number of payments in the loan. The final argument is the original loan amount.

Gotcha: The interest rate must be entered as a percentage. If you are planning on monthly payments (which is normal), then you have to divide the annual percentage rate by twelve.

Gotcha: In financial terms, the bank is loaning you $25,000 – a positive amount coming to you. Thus, the payments that you make to the bank are really a negative amount – it is money leaving your wallet. For this reason, the result of the PMT function will be negative. However, you can precede the PMT function with a minus sign in order to return a positive payment amount.

2)   Enter this formula in cell B6: =–PMT(B4/12,B3,B2). See Fig. 326.

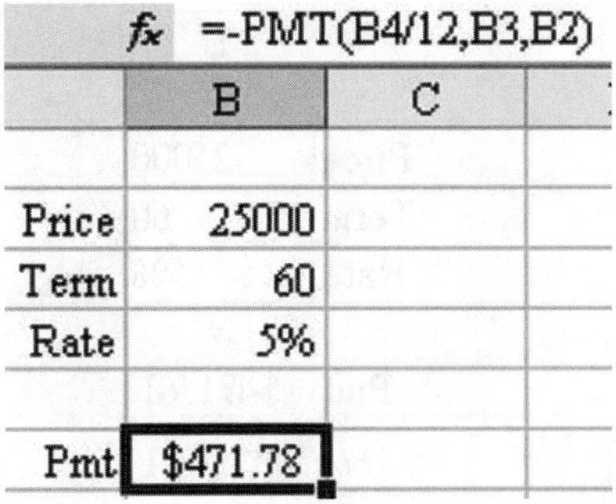

Fig. 326

Summary: The PMT function is great at calculating house or car loans.

Functions Discussed: =PMT()

CALCULATE MANY SCENARIOS FOR LOAN PAYMENTS

Problem: You are considering buying a car. You used the previous tip to calculate a loan payment, as shown in Fig. 326. You want to do some "what-if" scenarios in order to see various options of increasing or decreasing the term or price.

Strategy: Follow the same setup that you used for the previous tip, as shown in Fig. 327.

1)   Enter Price, Term in Months, and Annual Percentage Rate in cells B2:B4. See Fig. 327.

2)   Enter this formula in cell B6: =–PMT(B4/12,B3,B2). See Fig. 327.

	B
Price	25000
Term	60
Rate	5%
Pmt	$471.78

Fig. 327

3)   Copy cells B2:B6 over for several columns. Plug in different numbers for the price and/or term, as shown in Fig. 328.

	B	C	D	E	F	G	H
Price	25000	25000	25000	29000	29000	29000	21000
Term	60	48	54	60	66	72	60
Rate	5%	5%	5%	5%	5%	5%	5%
Pmt	$471.78	$575.73	$517.96	$547.27	$503.49	$467.04	$396.30

Fig. 328

Summary: This is where Excel shines. After you have entered the formulas for one loan model, you can easily copy and create many more loan models.

Functions Discussed: =PMT()

Cross Reference: Calculate a Loan Payment

GET HELP ON ANY FUNCTION
WHILE ENTERING A FORMULA

Problem: There are hundreds of functions available in Excel. You might remember that you need to use a particular function, but you cannot remember the sequence of the arguments in the function.

Strategy: In Excel 2002 and later, type the function and the opening parenthesis. A tooltip will appear to remind you of the order of the arguments. Any arguments in square brackets are optional. As shown in Fig. 329, the argument in bold is the argument that you need to type now.

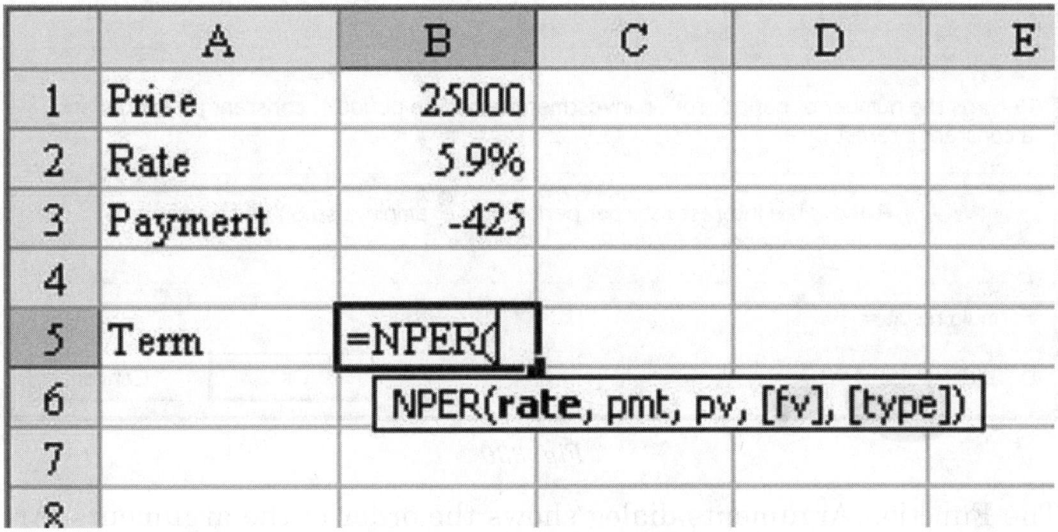

Part II

	A	B	C	D	E
1	Price	25000			
2	Rate	5.9%			
3	Payment	-425			
4					
5	Term	=NPER(			
6		NPER(**rate**, pmt, pv, [fv], [type])			
7					
8					

Fig. 329

Alternate Strategy: If you are using Excel 2000 or if you need more help than the abbreviations of "pmt" and "pv", then use the Function Arguments dialog. Type the function name and the opening parenthesis. Hit Ctrl+A to display the Function Arguments dialog, as shown in Fig. 330.

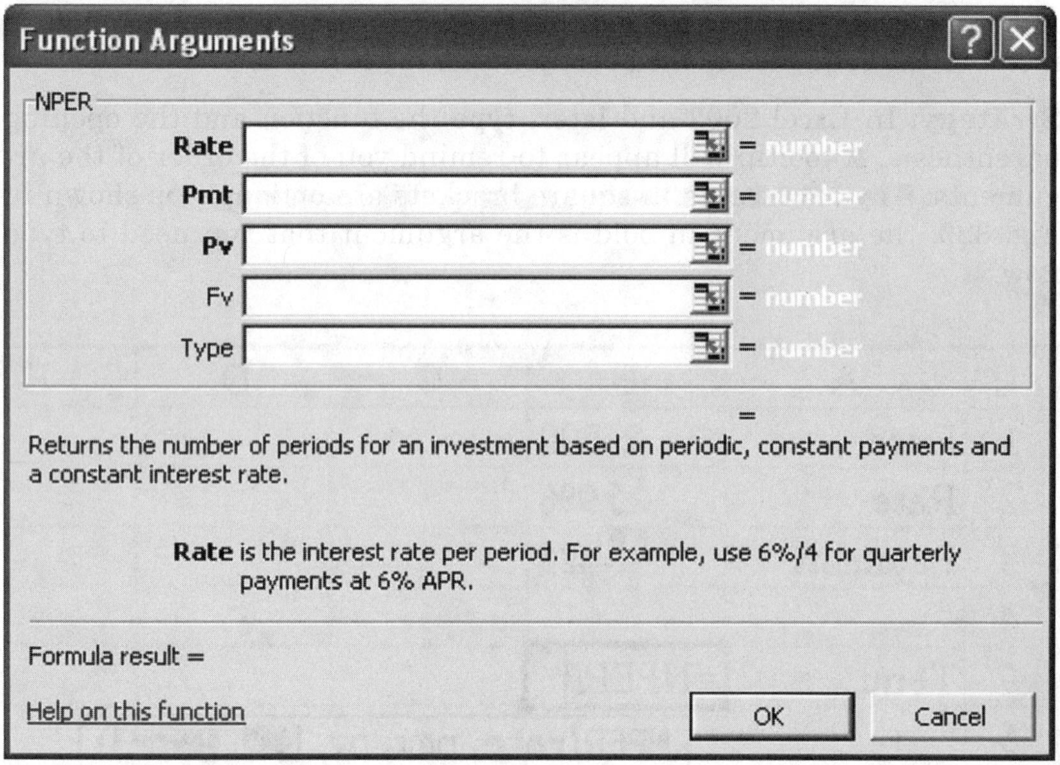

Fig. 330

The Function Arguments dialog shows the order of the arguments. Arguments in bold are required. The other arguments are optional. As you click into each text box in the dialog, the text at the bottom describes that argument in detail.

If you still need more help, there is a hyperlink to the complete help topic for this function.

As you enter the value for each argument, the Function Arguments dialog will calculate the numeric results of that argument. After you have entered all of the required arguments, the Function Wizard will display the result of the function, as shown in Fig. 331. You can consider whether this result is a reasonable number before accepting the formula.

In Fig. 331, the formula result indicates that if you want to pay $425 a month for a $25,000 car, you will be paying for 69.6 months. This seems about right, so choose OK.

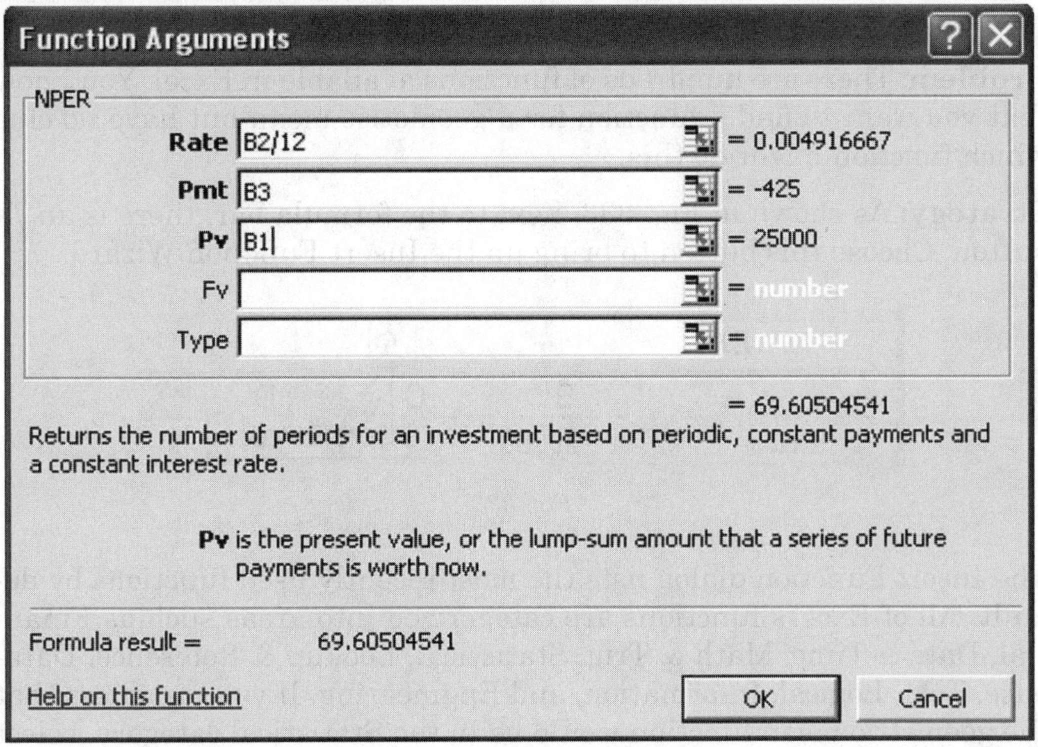

Function Arguments	?	X

NPER

Rate	B2/12	= 0.004916667
Pmt	B3	= -425
Pv	B1	= 25000
Fv		= number
Type		= number

= 69.60504541

Returns the number of periods for an investment based on periodic, constant payments and a constant interest rate.

   Pv is the present value, or the lump-sum amount that a series of future
      payments is worth now.

Formula result =   69.60504541

Help on this function   OK   Cancel

Part
II

Fig. 331

Result: As shown in Fig. 332, you've entered a fairly complex function without having to remember its details.

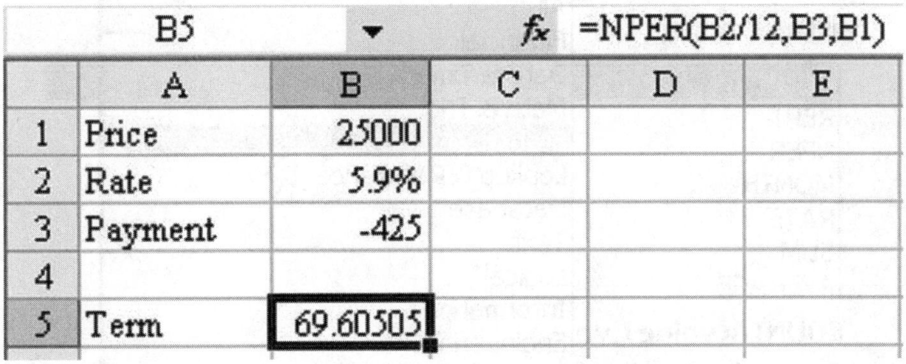

B5	▼	f_x =NPER(B2/12,B3,B1)		
	A	B	C	D	E
1	Price	25000			
2	Rate	5.9%			
3	Payment	-425			
4					
5	Term	69.60505			

Fig. 332

Summary: Use Ctrl+A shortcut after entering the opening parenthesis of a function to display the Function Arguments dialog box.

DISCOVER NEW FUNCTIONS USING THE *fx* BUTTON

Problem: There are hundreds of functions available in Excel. You know that you want to find a function for a geometric mean but have no clue which function might do this.

Strategy: As shown in Fig. 333, next to the formula bar, there is an *fx* button. Choose this button to bring up the Insert Function Wizard.

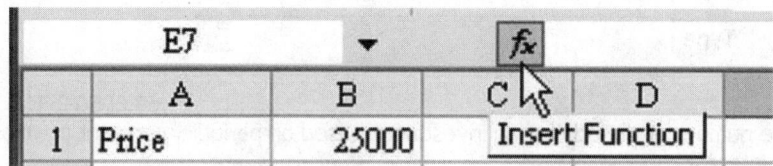

Fig. 333

The Insert Function dialog lists the most recently used functions by default. All of Excel's functions are categorized into areas such as Financial, Date & Time, Math & Trig, Statistical, Lookup & Reference, Database, Text, Logical, Information, and Engineering. If you can guess that the geometric mean function would be in the Statistical category, select this category from the dropdown, as shown in Fig. 334.

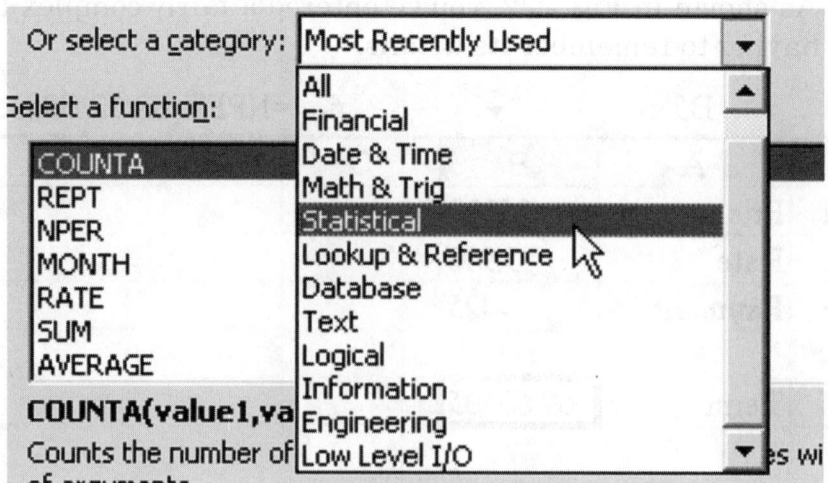

Fig. 334

Additional Information: Selecting Statistical provides you with over 100 choices. To narrow the choices down, type geometric mean in the search box and choose Go. This will result in one possible choice, as shown in Fig. 335.

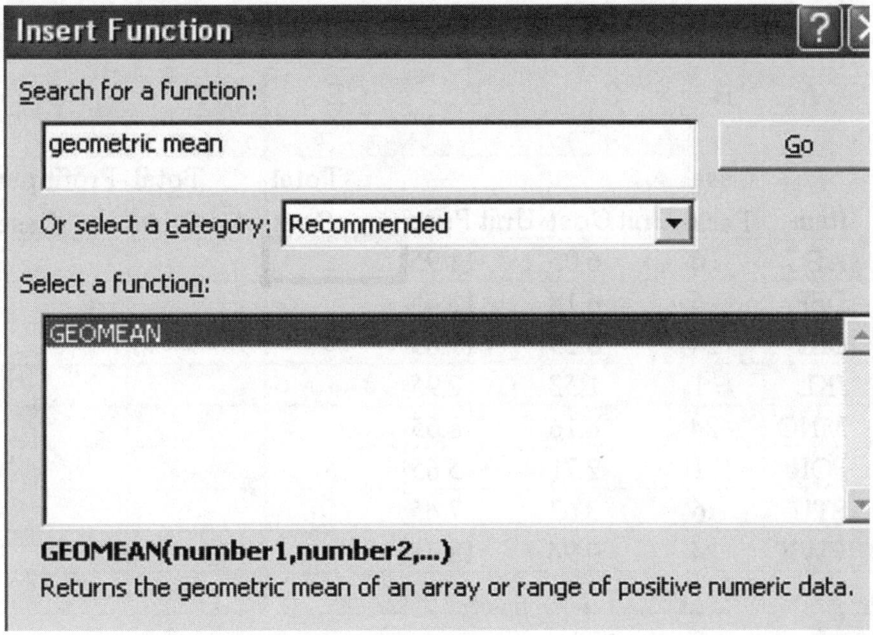

Fig. 335

Summary: Use the ƒx button to help find a function.

THREE METHODS OF ENTERING FORMULAS

Problem: There are three basic ways of entering simple calculations in Excel. Knowing all three ways will allow you to enter formulas faster, according to the situation. Consider the worksheet shown in Fig. 336.

	A	B	C	D	E	F	G
1							
2	Item	Case Pack	Unit Cost	Unit Price	Total Cost	Total Price	Profit per Case
3	ABC	6	6.06	11.95			
4	DEF	6	6.18	13.45			
5	GHI	24	8.35	17.65			
6	JKL	1	1.53	2.95			
7	MNO	24	4.16	8.65			
8	PQR	1	2.71	5.65			
9	STU	6	3.67	7.45			
10	VWX	24	9.94	18.75			
11							

Fig. 336

In Fig. 336, you want to calculate total cost in E3 as the Case Quantity in B3 times the Unit Cost in C3.

Strategy: You can simply type the formula.

1) Put the cell pointer in E3 and type =b3*c3, as shown in Fig. 337, and then hit Enter.

	A	B	C	D	E
1					
2	Item	Case Pack	Unit Cost	Unit Price	Total Cost
3	ABC	6	6.06	11.95	=b3*c3
4	DEF	6	6.18	13.45	

Fig. 337

2)   The formula will calculate. You will see the original formula in the formula bar above E1. The worksheet itself will show the result of the calculation, as shown in Fig. 338.

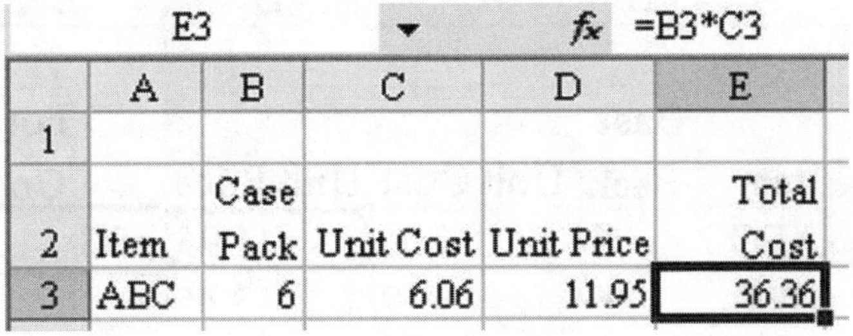

E3			fx	=B3*C3
	A	B	C	D	E
1					
2	Item	Case Pack	Unit Cost	Unit Price	Total Cost
3	ABC	6	6.06	11.95	36.36

Fig. 338

Advantage: If you are a good typist, you only need to type seven keystrokes.

Part II

Disadvantage: This method gets complicated when you are dealing with complex formulas.

Alternate Strategy: Use the arrow keys. Anyone who was using spreadsheets in the days of Lotus 1-2-3 often used this method. Once you have mastered this method, it is very fast and very intuitive.

1)   Move the cell pointer to E3. As shown in Fig. 339, type an Equal sign to let Excel know that you are about to enter a formula.

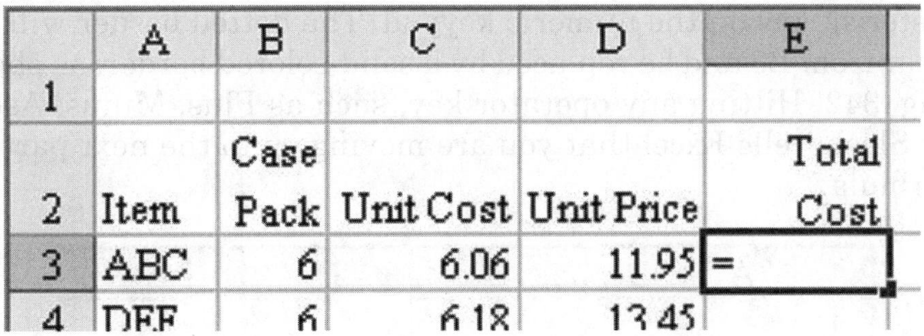

	A	B	C	D	E
1					
2	Item	Case Pack	Unit Cost	Unit Price	Total Cost
3	ABC	6	6.06	11.95	=
4	DEF	6	6.18	13.45	

Fig. 339

2)   Hit the Left Arrow. As shown in Fig. 340, a dotted border surrounds the cell to the left of E3. Excel starts to build a formula of =D3.

	A	B	C	D	E
1					
2	Item	Case Pack	Unit Cost	Unit Price	Total Cost
3	ABC	6	6.06	11.95	=D3
4	DEF	6	6.18	13.45	

Fig. 340

3)   Hit the Left Arrow key two more times. Your provisional formula is now =B3, as shown in Fig. 341.

	A	B	C	D	E
1					
2	Item	Case Pack	Unit Cost	Unit Price	Total Cost
3	ABC	6	6.06	11.95	=B3
4	DEF	6	6.18	13.45	

Fig. 341

4)   On the keyboard, hit the * key. You can either hit Shift+8 or use the Asterisk key on the numeric keypad. The dotted border will disappear from B3 and be replaced by a solid-colored border, as shown in Fig. 342. Hitting any operator key, such as Plus, Minus, Asterisk, or Slash, tells Excel that you are moving on to the next part of the formula.

	A	B	C	D	E
1					
2	Item	Case Pack	Unit Cost	Unit Price	Total Cost
3	ABC	6	6.06	11.95	=B3*
4	DEF	6	6.19	13.45	

Fig. 342

5) Next, hit the Left Arrow key. The dotted border reappears. You now have a provisional formula of =B3*D3, as shown in Fig. 343. This isn't quite right, yet, but you're getting close.

	A	B	C	D	E
1					
2	Item	Case Pack	Unit Cost	Unit Price	Total Cost
3	ABC	6	6.06	11.95	=B3*D3

Fig. 343

6) Hit the Left Arrow key one more time. As shown in Fig. 344, the provisional formula is now correct.

	A	B	C	D	E
1					
2	Item	Case Pack	Unit Cost	Unit Price	Total Cost
3	ABC	6	6.06	11.95	=B3*C3
4	DEF	6	6.18	13.45	

Fig. 344

7) Next, hit Enter. The formula will calculate. You will see the original formula in the formula bar above E1. The worksheet itself will show the result of the calculation.

Advantage: You never have to type cell references with this method. You merely point to them, using the arrow keys. If you are building formulas that are based on cells near the formula cell, formulas can be entered very quickly with this method.

Alternate Strategy: Use the mouse. Follow these steps.

1)   As shown in Fig. 345, type an Equal sign. This tells Excel that you are about to enter a formula.

	A	B	C	D	E
1					
2	Item	Case Pack	Unit Cost	Unit Price	Total Cost
3	ABC	6	6.06	11.95	=
4	DEF	6	6.18	13.45	

Fig. 345

2)   Using the mouse, touch cell B3. Excel starts to build your formula, as shown in Fig. 346.

	A	B	C	D	E
1					
2	Item	Case Pack	Unit Cost	Unit Price	Total Cost
3	ABC	6	6.06	11.95	=B3
4	DEF	6	6.18	13.45	

Fig. 346

3)   Using the keyboard, hit the Asterisk key on the numeric keypad or the Shift+8 keys. See Fig. 347.

	A	B	C	D	E
1					
2	Item	Case Pack	Unit Cost	Unit Price	Total Cost
3	ABC	6	6.06	11.95	=B3*
4	DEF	6	6.18	13.45	

Fig. 347

4)   Using the mouse, touch cell C3. The provisional formula now looks correct, as shown in Fig. 348.

	A	B	C	D	E
1					
2	Item	Case Pack	Unit Cost	Unit Price	Total Cost
3	ABC	6	6.06	11.95	=B3*C3
4	DEF	6	6.18	13.45	

Fig. 348

5)   Hit the Enter key. The formula will calculate. You will see the original formula in the formula bar above E1. The worksheet itself will show the result of the calculation.

Advantages of the Mouse: It is easy to use the mouse to directly touch the cells you need in the formula.

Disadvantage of the Mouse: It takes a long time to move your hands back and forth from the keyboard to the mouse. To enter the above formula, you have to hit a key, use the mouse, hit a key, use the mouse, and hit a key again. That is four movements back and forth from the keyboard to the mouse and back.

Summary: There are three basic methods for entering formulas in Excel. Using the right method for the situation can radically improve your efficiency.

Part
II

USE AUTOSUM TO QUICKLY ENTER A TOTAL FORMULA

Problem: You have data in Excel, as shown in Fig. 349. You need to total the rows quickly.

	A	B	C	D	E	F
1	Item	Q1	Q2	Q3	Q4	Total
2	ABC	91	92	22	83	
3	DEF	31	41	17	33	
4	GHI	72	63	82	64	
5	JKL	21	98	4	90	
6	MNO	36	81	52	35	
7	PQR	22	90	87	75	
8	STU	65	85	72	34	
9	VWX	91	40	41	6	
10	Total					

Fig. 349

Strategy: Use the AutoSum button on the Standard toolbar. The Auto-Sum button looks like the Greek letter sigma, as shown in Fig. 350.

Fig. 350

1)   Place the cell pointer in cell B10. Touch the AutoSum button, as shown in Fig. 351.

	A	B	C	D
1	Item	Q1	Q2	Q3
2	ABC	91	92	22
3	DEF	31	41	17
4	GHI	72	63	82
5	JKL	21	98	4
6	MNO	36	81	52
7	PQR	22	90	87
8	STU	65	85	72
9	VWX	91	40	41
10	Total	=SUM(B2:B9)		
11		SUM(**number1**, [number2], ...)		
12				

Fig. 351

2)   Excel analyzes your data and predicts that you want to total the range of numbers above the cell pointer. As shown in Fig. 352, Excel enters a provisional formula of =SUM(B2:B9). Hit Enter to accept this formula.

B10   ▼   *fx* =SUM(B2:B9)

	A	B	C	D	E
1	Item	Q1	Q2	Q3	Q4
2	ABC	91	92	22	83
3	DEF	31	41	17	33
4	GHI	72	63	82	64
5	JKL	21	98	4	90
6	MNO	36	81	52	35
7	PQR	22	90	87	75
8	STU	65	85	72	34
9	VWX	91	40	41	6
10	Total	429			

Fig. 352

3) The square dot in the lower right corner of the cell pointer is the AutoFill handle. With the mouse, drag the Fill handle to the right to include cells C10 through F10. Release the mouse button and the formula will be copied to all five columns.

Summary: The AutoSum button on the Standard toolbar is a powerful tool for quickly entering a total formula.

Functions Discussed: =SUM()

AUTOSUM DOESN'T ALWAYS PREDICT
MY DATA CORRECTLY

Problem: When using the AutoSum button, Excel sometimes predicts the wrong range of data to total. In Fig. 353, the AutoSum worked fine in F2 and F3, but in cell F4, Excel gets fooled into thinking that you want to total the rows above F4.

	A	B	C	D	E	F	G	H
1	Item	Q1	Q2	Q3	Q4	Total		
2	ABC	91	92	22	83	288		
3	DEF	31	41	17	33	122		
4	GHI	72	63	82	64	=SUM(F2:F3)		
5	JKL	21	98	4	90	SUM(**number1**, [number2], ...)		
6	MNO	36	81	52	35			
7	PQR	22	90	87	75			
8	STU	65	85	72	34			
9	VWX	91	40	41	6			
10	Total	429	590	377	420			

Fig. 353

Strategy: After hitting the AutoSum button, the provisional range address is highlighted in the provisional formula. Using your mouse, highlight the right range.

As shown in Fig. 353, AutoSum will work correctly in B2 and B3. It will predict that you want to sum the data in that row. However, in cell B4 Excel has a choice: do you want to sum the two cells in that column or the four cells in the row? Excel always chooses to sum the two cells above in this situation.

After hitting the AutoSum button, note that F2:F3 is highlighted in the formula. This allows you to enter the correct range. There are three methods:

1)   With the mouse, highlight B4:E4 and hit Enter.

2)   With the keyboard, type B4:E4.

3)   Using the arrow keys, hit the Left Arrow to move to E2. Hit the Down Arrow twice to move to E4. While holding down the Shift key, hit the Left Arrow three times to highlight B4:E4, as shown in Fig. 354.

4)

	A	B	C	D	E	F	G	H
1	Item	Q1	Q2	Q3	Q4	Total		
2	ABC	91	92	22	83	288		
3	DEF	31	41	17	33	122		
4	GHI	72	63	82	64	=SUM(B4:E4)		
	1R x 4C	21	98	4	90	SUM(**number1**, [number2], ...)		
6	KJNI	36	91	52	35			

Fig. 354

Additional Details: The problem described in this section will always happen in the third and fourth rows of the data. When you try using the AutoSum button in F6 and beyond, Excel will correctly sum all the data in that row.

AutoSum can also fail when one number in your range contains a SUM formula. The provisional formula will offer to sum a formula extending up to but not including the previous SUM formula.

Alternate Strategy: You can choose to enter all of the totals at one time by using the AutoSum button. This is faster and will eliminate the problem described above. Follow these steps.

1) Highlight the entire range that needs a SUM formula as shown in
    Fig. 355.

	A	B	C	D	E	F
1	Item	Q1	Q2	Q3	Q4	Total
2	ABC	91	92	22	83	
3	DEF	31	41	17	33	
4	GHI	72	63	82	64	
5	JKL	21	98	4	90	
6	MNO	36	81	52	35	
7	PQR	22	90	87	75	
8	STU	65	85	72	34	
9	VWX	91	40	41	6	
10	Total	429	590	377	420	

Fig. 355

Part II

2) Hit the AutoSum button. Excel makes a prediction and fills in the
    total formulas automatically, as shown in Fig. 356. Excel does not
    show the provisional formula. So, check one formula to see that it
    is correct.

	A	B	C	D	E	F
1	Item	Q1	Q2	Q3	Q4	Total
2	ABC	91	92	22	83	288
3	DEF	31	41	17	33	122
4	GHI	72	63	82	64	281
5	JKL	21	98	4	90	213
6	MNO	36	81	52	35	204
7	PQR	22	90	87	75	274
8	STU	65	85	72	34	256
9	VWX	91	40	41	6	178
10	Total	429	590	377	420	1816

Fig. 356

Summary: The AutoSum function does not always correctly predict the range to be totaled. It is easy to use the mouse or keyboard to show Excel the correct range.

Functions Discussed: =SUM()

USE AUTOSUM BUTTON TO ENTER AVERAGES, MIN, MAX, AND COUNT

Problem: Instead of totals, you need to enter an Average formula quickly, as shown in Fig. 357.

	A	B
4	Time	Reading
5	1:00 AM	86.2
6	1:05 AM	86.22
7	1:10 AM	86.21
8	1:15 AM	86.26
9	1:20 AM	86.24
10	1:25 AM	86.31
11	1:30 AM	86.33
12	1:35 AM	86.33
13	1:40 AM	86.43
14	1:45 AM	86.61
15	1:50 AM	86.88
16	1:55 AM	87.18
17	Average	

Fig. 357

Strategy: Use the dropdown arrow located next to the AutoSum button, as shown in Fig. 358. Instead of selecting Sum, use the Average option.

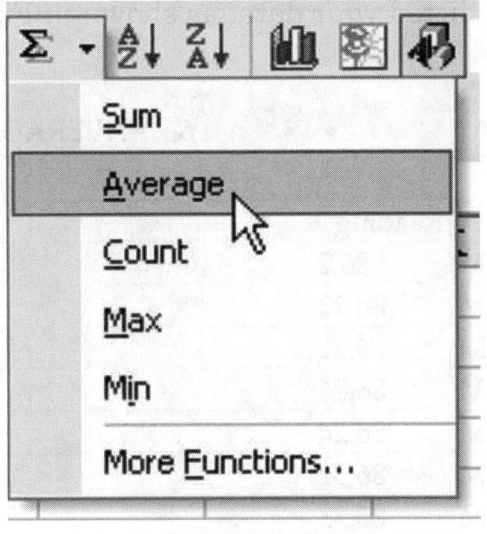

Fig. 358

Excel enters a provisional Average formula, as shown in Fig. 359.

	A	B	C	D	E
4	Time	Reading			
5	1:00 AM	86.2			
6	1:05 AM	86.22			
7	1:10 AM	86.21			
8	1:15 AM	86.26			
9	1:20 AM	86.24			
10	1:25 AM	86.31			
11	1:30 AM	86.33			
12	1:35 AM	86.33			
13	1:40 AM	86.43			
14	1:45 AM	86.61			
15	1:50 AM	86.88			
16	1:55 AM	87.18			
17	Average	=AVERAGE(B5:B16)			
18		AVERAGE(**number1**, [number2], ...)			
19					

Fig. 359

If Excel correctly predicted your data, as shown in Fig. 360, hit Enter to accept the formula.

	A	B	C	D	E
	B17	▼		*fx* =AVERAGE(B5:B16)	
4	Time	Reading			
5	1:00 AM	86.2			
6	1:05 AM	86.22			
7	1:10 AM	86.21			
8	1:15 AM	86.26			
9	1:20 AM	86.24			
10	1:25 AM	86.31			
11	1:30 AM	86.33			
12	1:35 AM	86.33			
13	1:40 AM	86.43			
14	1:45 AM	86.61			
15	1:50 AM	86.88			
16	1:55 AM	87.18			
17	Average	86.43333			

Fig. 360

Additional Details: Excel does NOT remember the last setting of the AutoSum button. If you do an Average and then use just the AutoSum button, it will return to using a SUM formula.

Additional Details: The Max option will use the MAX function to find the largest numeric value. The Min option will use the MIN function to return the smallest numeric value. The Count option will count the number of numeric entries in the list using the COUNT function.

Summary: The dropdown arrow next to the AutoSum function offers access to finding the Average, Min, Max, or Count of a range.

Functions Discussed: =AVERAGE(); =MIN(); =MAX(); =COUNT()

THE COUNT OPTION OF THE AUTOSUM DOESN'T APPEAR TO WORK

Problem: You are using the Count option from the dropdown next to the AutoSum button on the toolbar. It does not appear to provide consistent results. In Fig. 361, cells B11 and C11 both contain a count of the cells in rows 2 through 10 of each column. One function indicates that there are nine entries; the other function indicates there are only two. Clearly, both columns have nine entries.

B11	▼	f_x =COUNT(B2:B10)

	A	B	C	D	
1		Purchase Order	Amount		
2		A12345	878.31		
3		05J123	566.41		
4		WMJ987	165.91		
5		9878	115.97		
6		KJHK98	788.5		
7		87-9878	890.7		
8		34H8987	665.17		
9		87888	161.94		
10		H12354	681.09		
11	Count:	2	9		

Fig. 361

Part II

Strategy: The COUNT function will only count numeric entries. If you need to count all entries, you have to use the COUNTA function. One solution is to edit the formula in B2 and add an A after the T in COUNT. The other method is to enter the formula correctly in the first place.

1) Put the cell pointer in B11. Choose the dropdown arrow next to the AutoSum button. From the list, select More Functions..., as shown in Fig. 362.

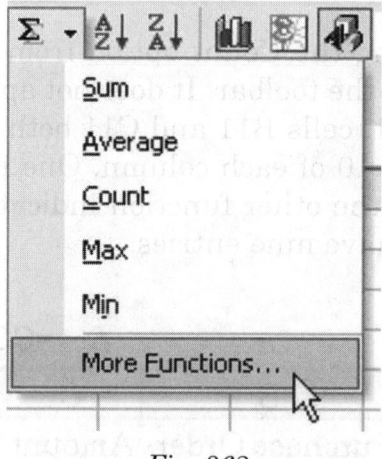

Fig. 362

2) There are hundreds of functions available. You can never remember if COUNTA is in the Math & Trig section or somewhere else. Type the word "count" in the search box and choose Go, as shown in Fig. 363.

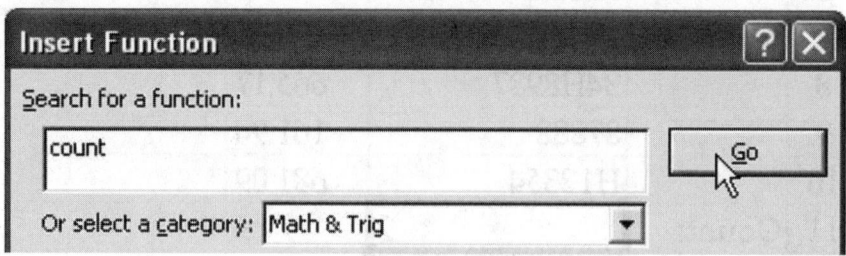

Fig. 363

Excel will return a list of all functions related to the COUNT function. A description of the selected function appears below the list, as shown in Fig. 364.

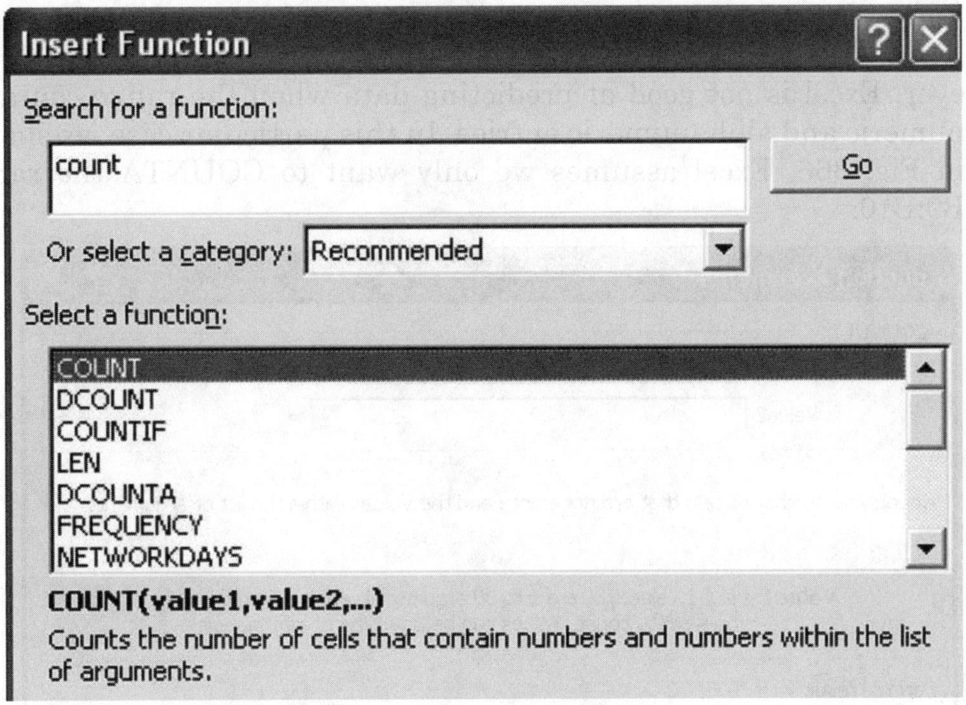

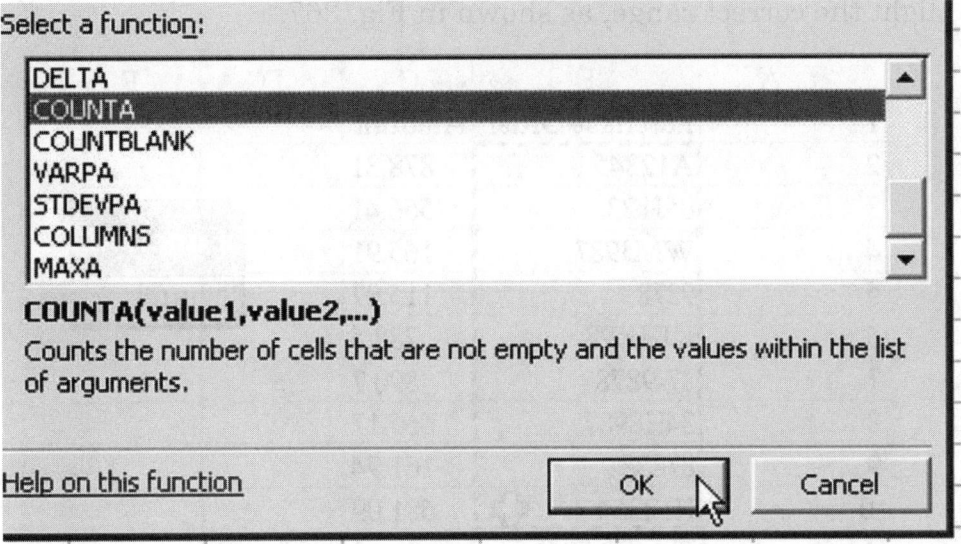

Fig. 364

3)   You might need to scroll through the list to find the COUNTA function. As shown in Fig. 365, when you find COUNTA, choose OK.

Fig. 365

You will now see the Function Arguments dialog box. Excel has analyzed your data and predicted the range that you want to use. However, Excel is not good at predicting data when the range contains numeric and alphanumeric entries. In this particular case, as shown in Fig. 366, Excel assumes we only want to COUNTA the range B9:B10.

Function Arguments		**?** **✕**
COUNTA		
Value1	39:B10	= {87888;"H12354"}
Value2		= number
	= 2	
Counts the number of cells that are not empty and the values within the list of arguments.		
	Value1: value1,value2,... are 1 to 30 arguments representing the values and cells you want to count. Values can be any type of information.	
Formula result =	2	
Help on this function		OK　Cancel

Fig. 366

4)　If you can see the data on the worksheet, use the mouse and highlight the correct range, as shown in Fig. 367.

	A	B	C	D	E
1		Purchase Order	Amount		
2		A12345	878.31		
3		05J123	566.41		
4		WMJ987	165.91		**Function**
5		9878	115.97		B2:B10
6		KJHK98	788.5		
7		87-9878	890.7		
8		34H8987	665.17		
9		87888	161.94		
10		H12354	681.09		
11	Count:	TA(B2:B10)	9R x 1C		
12					

Fig. 367

5)   Release the mouse. Choose OK in the function arguments dialog to accept the formula.

Result: As shown in Fig. 368, the COUNTA function returns the proper value.

	A	B	C	D	E
1		Purchase Order	Amount		
2		A12345	878.31		
3		05J123	566.41		
4		WMJ987	165.91		
5		9878	115.97		
6		KJHK98	788.5		
7		87-9878	890.7		
8		34H8987	665.17		
9		87888	161.94		
10		H12354	681.09		
11	Count:	9	9		

B11   =COUNTA(B2:B10)

Fig. 368

Summary: The COUNT function does not count text entries in a list. Use the COUNTA function instead.

Functions Discussed: =COUNT(); =COUNTA()

AUTOMATICALLY NUMBER A LIST OF EMPLOYEES

Problem: You work in Human Resources. You have a list of employees separated by department. As shown in Fig. 369, you have a numerical sequence in column A and the employees' names in column B. Every time that you hire or fire an employee, you have to manually renumber all of the employees.

	A	B	C	D
1	**Marketing Department**			
2	1	George Washington		
3	2	John Adams		
4	3	Thomas Jefferson		
5	4	James Madison		
6	5	James Monroe		
7				
8	**Human Resources**			
9	6	John Quincy Adams		
10	7	Andrew Jackson		
11	8	Martin Van Buren		
12	9	William Henry Harrison		
13				
14	**Manufacturing**			
15	10	John Tyler		
16	11	James K. Polk		
17	12	Zachary Taylor		
18	13	Millard Fillmore		
19	14	Franklin Pierce		
20	15	James Buchanan		
21	16	Abraham Lincoln		
22	17	Andrew Johnson		
23	18	Ulysses S. Grant		
24	19	Rutherford B. Hayes		

Fig. 369

Strategy: Replace the numbers in column A with a formula that will count the entries in column B. The formula should count from the current row all the way up to row 1.

The COUNT function will not work, because it only counts numeric entries. You need to use the COUNTA function.

· The range that should be counted should extend from B1 to the current row.

· The notation to always use B1 is B$1.

1) As shown in Fig. 370, enter this formula in cell A2: =COUNTA(B$1:B2).

	A	B	C	D	E	F
	A2		▼		*fx* =COUNTA(B$1:B2)	
1	Marketing Department					
2	1	George Washington				
3		John Adams				
4		Thomas Jefferson				
5		James Madison				
6		James Monroe				

Fig. 370

When you copy this formula down a row, the range that is counted will extend from B1 to B3, as shown in Fig. 371. This is because the B2 portion of the above formula is a relative reference that is allowed to change as the formula is copied. The dollar sign in the B$1 reference tells Excel that no matter where you copy the formula, it should always refer to cell 1.

	A	B	C	D	E	F
	A3		▼		*fx* =COUNTA(B$1:B3)	
1	Marketing Department					
2	1	George Washington				
3	2	John Adams				
4		mas Jefferson				
5		James Madison				
6		James Monroe				

Fig. 371

2)   Copy the formula down to all of the names in your list. They will be numbered 1 through 19, just as when you typed the names in manually.

When an employee leaves the company, you can simply delete the row, All of the other numbers will change to indicate that you now have a total of 18 employees, as shown in Fig. 372.

	A23		▼		f_x =COUNTA(B$1:B23)	
	A	B	C	D	E	F
1	**Marketing Department**					
2	1	George Washington				
3	2	Thomas Jefferson				
4	3	James Madison				
5	4	James Monroe				
6						
7	**Human Resources**					
8	5	John Quincy Adams				
9	6	Andrew Jackson				
10	7	Martin Van Buren				
11	8	William Henry Harrison				
12						
13	**Manufacturing**					
14	9	John Tyler				
15	10	James K. Polk				
16	11	Zachary Taylor				
17	12	Millard Fillmore				
18	13	Franklin Pierce				
19	14	James Buchanan				
20	15	Abraham Lincoln				
21	16	Andrew Johnson				
22	17	Ulysses S. Grant				
23	18	Rutherford B. Hayes				

Fig. 372

When you hire a new marketing person, insert a blank row, enter his or her name, and then copy any formula from A to the new row.

As shown in Fig. 373, all of the subsequent employees will be renumbered.

	A	B	C	D	E	F
	A5			f_x =COUNTA(B$1:B5)		
1	**Marketing Department**					
2	1	George Washington				
3	2	Thomas Jefferson				
4	3	James Madison				
5	4	Ronald Reagan				
6	5	es Monroe				

Fig. 373

Summary: While this is a specific example, the concept of using a range as an argument where only one portion of the range contains an absolute reference is a common solution to keeping a running total of all cells above the current row.

Functions Discussed: =COUNT(); =COUNTA()

RANK SCORES

Problem: You have four writers working on a project. Each week, you report how many pages they have written towards their goal, as shown in Fig. 374. You wish to have a formula that ranks them in high-to-low order.

	G	H
22		Pages
23	Tessa	145.6137
24	Josh	247.9678
25	Ashley	86.63641
26	Lee	96.58829

Fig. 374

Strategy: If you are not concerned about ties, then use the RANK function. The function requires two arguments. In plain language, you are asking the function to assign a rank to the value in H23 amongst all values in H23:H26.

As shown in Fig. 375, in cell F23, use =RANK(H23,$H$23:$H$26). Note that the H23:H26 range in the second parameter is in absolute reference style due to the dollar signs. This allows the formula to be easily copied to each name in the list.

fx	=RANK(H23,H$23:H$26)	
F	**G**	**H**
Rank		Pages
2	Tessa	145.6137
1	Josh	247.9678
4	Ashley	86.63641
3	Lee	96.58829

Fig. 375

Additional Details: The above version of the function will rank the values in high-to-low order. Sometimes you might need to rank in a low-to-high fashion. Golf is one such instance. You can specify an optional third parameter to specify the order. Using a third parameter of 1 will force the rank results to be reported in low-to-high order, as shown in Fig. 376.

=RANK(H23,H$23:H$26,1)		
F	**G**	**H**
Rank		Pages
3	Tessa	145.6137
4	Josh	247.9678
1	Ashley	86.63641
2	Lee	96.58829

Fig. 376

Summary: The RANK function is useful for producing a ranking by using formulas.

Functions Discussed: =RANK()

Cross Reference: Rank a List Without Ties; Sorting with a Formula

SORTING WITH A FORMULA

Problem: In the previous example, you used the RANK function to find the relative rank order of four writers, as shown in Fig. 377. Now you want to use a formula to produce a sorted list of the writers in high-to-low sequence.

	F	G	H
22	Rank		Pages
23	2	Tessa	145.6137
24	1	Josh	247.9678
25	4	Ashley	86.63641
26	3	Lee	96.58829
27			
28	1		
29	2		
30	3		
31	4		

Fig. 377

Strategy: In cells F28 through F31, enter the numbers 1 through 4. Use the VLOOKUP function to return the name in column G and the pages in column H. Here is how this function works.

VLOOKUP stands for vertical lookup. There are four parameters to the VLOOKUP function. In plain language, you are asking Excel to look for the value in F28 in the first column of F23:H26. When Excel finds an exact matching value, it returns the name in the second column of the lookup range.

The first parameter is the value that you are trying to match. In the case of cell G28, you would be looking for the value in F28. Write this as

$F28 so that you can copy the formula to column H without rewriting that parameter.

The second parameter is the database range containing rows and columns of data. The key value that you are looking up must be in the first column of the range. In this case, it would be $F$23:$H$26. Note that you use dollar signs before both the column letters and row numbers in order to keep the database range absolute as you copy the formula.

The third parameter tells Excel the column from which you want to return the answer. For the name in column G, it is column 2 of the range F23:H26. For the page count in column H, it is column 3 of the range F23:H26.

The fourth parameter tells Excel if you will allow a close match. If your original data is not sorted, you are required to specify an exact match. For the fourth parameter, use TRUE for a close match and FALSE for an exact match.

Follow these steps:

1)   As shown in Fig. 378, enter the following formula in G28: =VLOOK UP($F28,$F$23:$H$26,2,FALSE).

	D	E	F	G	H	I	J	K	L
				G28	▼	*fx* =VLOOKUP($F28,$F$23:$H$26,2,FALSE)			
22			Rank		Pages				
23			2	Tessa	145.6137				
24			1	Josh	247.9678				
25			4	Ashley	86.63641				
26			3	Lee	96.58829				
27									
28			1	Josh					
29			2						
30			3						
31			4						
32									

Fig. 378

2)   Copy cell G28 to H28. The result in H28 will also be Josh, as shown in Fig. 379.

	D	E	F	G	H	I	J	K	L
H28					fx =VLOOKUP($F28,$F$23:$H$26,2,FALSE)				
22			Rank		Pages				
23			2	Tessa	145.6137				
24			1	Josh	247.9678				
25			4	Ashley	86.63641				
26			3	Lee	96.58829				
27									
28			1	Josh	Josh				
29			2						
30			3						
31			4						

Fig. 379

3)   Edit the formula in the formula bar to change the third parameter from column 2 to column 3, as shown in Fig. 380.

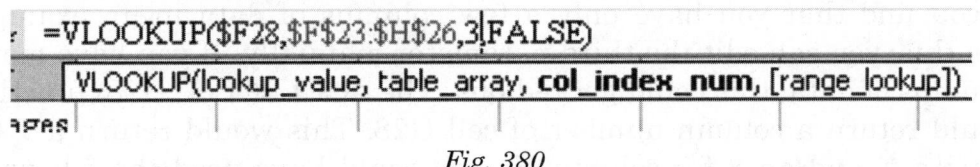

=VLOOKUP($F28,$F$23:$H$26,3,FALSE)

VLOOKUP(lookup_value, table_array, **col_index_num**, [range_lookup])

Fig. 380

The result in H28 will now contain the number of pages written by Josh, as shown in Fig. 381.

	D	E	F	G	H	I	J	K	L
H28					fx =VLOOKUP($F28,$F$23:$H$26,3,FALSE)				
22			Rank		Pages				
23			2	Tessa	145.6137				
24			1	Josh	247.9678				
25			4	Ashley	86.63641				
26			3	Lee	96.58829				
27									
28			1	Josh	247.9678				
29			2						

Fig. 381

Part
II

4)   Copy G28:H28 down to the next three rows. You will now have a sorted list of the data, as shown in Fig. 382.

F	G	H
1	Josh	247.9678
2	Tessa	145.6137
3	Lee	96.58829
4	Ashley	86.63641

Fig. 382

Additional Details: Your goal is to always enter one formula that you can copy to the entire data range. In this case, your formula in G28 could be copied to anywhere in column G, but when you copied it to column H, the third parameter had to be manually edited. You needed to plan ahead to use the proper combination of dollar signs in the references in order to ensure that three of the four parameters were correct when you copied the formula to column H.

If you find that you have only a few columns of data in an example like this, you can edit the third parameter manually. If you have many columns of data, this could get tedious. The =CELL("Col",G28) function would return a column number of cell G28. This would return a 7 for column G and an 8 for column H. You could have used the following formula in G28:

=VLOOKUP($F28,$F$23:$H$26,CELL("Col",G28)–5,FALSE)

If you enter this formula in G28, you can copy it to all rows and columns of your results table.

Summary: After using a RANK function to assign rank values to a list, use a second table with the numbers 1 through n and a series of VLOOKUP formulas in order to return a sorted list of the data.

Functions Discussed: =VLOOKUP(); =CELL(); =RANK()

Cross Reference: Rank Scores

RANK A LIST WITHOUT TIES

Problem: The RANK function behaves strangely when there are ties. It is possible to have a list where two people are ranked second and no one is ranked third. In Fig. 383, Dora and Jerry are ranked second with 90 units produced. Next is Harry with 86 units. Harry will receive a rank of 4.

This behavior is by design. However, if you are later going to use VLOOKUPs to sort the employees by productivity, having two people ranked as #2 and no one ranked as #3 is not a good situation.

	C4		▼		fx	=RANK(B4,$B$4:$B$13)
	A	B	C	D	E	F
1	Widget Production					
2						
3	Name	Total	Rank			
4	Ashley	80	6			
5	Bill	80	6			
6	Carl	92	1			
7	Dora	90	2			
8	Ed	79	8			
9	Fred	78	9			
10	Gary	84	5			
11	Harry	86	4			
12	Inez	70	10			
13	Jerry	90	2			

Fig. 383

Part
II

In the formulas in columns F and G, the spreadsheet designer counted on there being one employee at each rank from 1 to 10. Since Excel did not assign anyone to a rank of #3 or #7, Jerry and Bill do not show up in the list, as shown in Fig. 384.

	A	B	C	D	E	F	G	H	I	J
	F4				fx	=INDEX($A$4:$A$13,MATCH($E4,$C$4:$C$13,FALSE),1)				
1	Widget Production				Widget Production					
2										
3	Name	Total	Rank		Rank	Name	Total			
4	Ashley	80	6		1	Carl	92			
5	Bill	80	6		2	Dora	90			
6	Carl	92	1		3	#N/A	#N/A			
7	Dora	90	2		4	Harry	86			
8	Ed	79	8		5	Gary	84			
9	Fred	78	9		6	Ashley	80			
10	Gary	84	5		7	#N/A	#N/A			
11	Harry	86	4		8	Ed	79			
12	Inez	70	10		9	Fred	78			
13	Jerry	90	2		10	Inez	70			

Fig. 384

Strategy: In this case, you absolutely want the list in A4:A13 to be ranked without ties. The generally accepted solution may seem rather convoluted, but it works. In plain language, the formula in column C will say, "Give me the RANK of this value, plus 1 for every row above me that has an identical score." As shown in Fig. 385, this can be accomplished with the following formula:

=RANK(B4,$B$4:$B$13)+COUNTIF(B$3:B3,B4)

	C4		▼		f_x	=RANK(B4,$B$4:$B$13)+COUNTIF(B$3:B3,B4)		
	A	**B**	**C**	**D**	**E**	**F**	**G**	**H**	**I**
1	Widget Production				Widget Production				
2									
3	Name	Total	Rank		Rank	Name	Total		
4	Ashley	80	6		1	Carl	92		
5	Bill	80	7		2	Dora	90		
6	Carl	92	1		3	Jerry	90		
7	Dora	90	2		4	Harry	86		
8	Ed	79	8		5	Gary	84		
9	Fred	78	9		6	Ashley	80		
10	Gary	84	5		7	Bill	80		
11	Harry	86	4		8	Ed	79		
12	Inez	70	10		9	Fred	78		
13	Jerry	90	3		10	Inez	70		

Fig. 385

As you copy this formula down, the first parameter of COUNTIF will expand to include B3 down to the row above the current row. Thus, in cell C13, the formula will be as follows:

=RANK(B13,$B$4:$B$13)+COUNTIF(B$4:B12,B13)

The COUNTIF portion of the formula counts how many rows above the current row have an identical score. For each row above that is a tie, 1 gets added to the current row. This causes Bill to be ranked seventh instead of sixth. It may not be fair that Ashley appears before Bill, but in the summary report, anyone can notice that they have a tie.

Summary: Add a COUNTIF function to the RANK function in order to prevent ties.

Functions Discussed: =RANK(); =COUNTIF()

Part
II

ADD COMMENTS TO A FORMULA

Problem: You spent a great deal of time perfecting a formula, as shown in Fig. 386. You would like to leave yourself notes about it.

C4			▼		f_x	=RANK(B4,$B$4:$B$13)+COUNTIF(B$3:B3,B4)			
	A	B	C	D	E	F	G	H	I
1	Widget Production				Widget Production				
2									
3	Name	Total	Rank		Rank	Name	Total		
4	Ashley	80	6		1	Carl	92		
5	Bill	80	7		2	Dora	90		

Fig. 386

Strategy: There is an old Lotus 1-2-3 function that is still in Excel. This function is the N function. It turns out that N of a number is the number and N of any text is zero. Thus, you can add several N functions to a formula without changing the result, provided that they contain text.

Thus, if you have figured out some obscure formula, you can leave yourself notes about the formula, as shown in Fig. 387.

C4			▼		f_x	=RANK(B4,$B$4:$B$13)+N("The first part
	A	B	C	D		of the formula returns a rank, but ties are
1	Widget Production					given the same value")+COUNTIF(B$3:B3,
2						B4)+N("The CountIf finds any cells in the
3	Name	Total	Rank			rows above this row that match this row.
4	Ashley	80	6			For each row that matches, 1 is added to
5	Bill	80	7			the rank. This ensures that the second
6	Carl	92	1			occurence of a tie is given a one-higher
7	Dora	90	2			ranking.")+N("For more details, see page
8	Ed	79	8			232 of the MrExcel book")

Fig. 387

Summary: For particularly complicated formulas, leave yourself detailed comments right in the formula.

Functions Discussed: =N()

CALCULATE A MOVING AVERAGE

Problem: You have 36 months of sales data, as shown in Fig. 388. In order to create a prediction of sales, you want to calculate a three-month moving average. You will then later create a trendline from the moving average.

Strategy: You need two months of history before you can begin calculating a three-month moving average.

1) In cell C4, use the formula =AVERAGE(B2: B4).

Note that when you enter this formula, Excel will be concerned because your formula ignores similar data in cell B5. In this case, you are smarter than Excel, so you can use the dropdown on the Exclamation sign to tell Excel to ignore the error, as shown in Fig. 389.

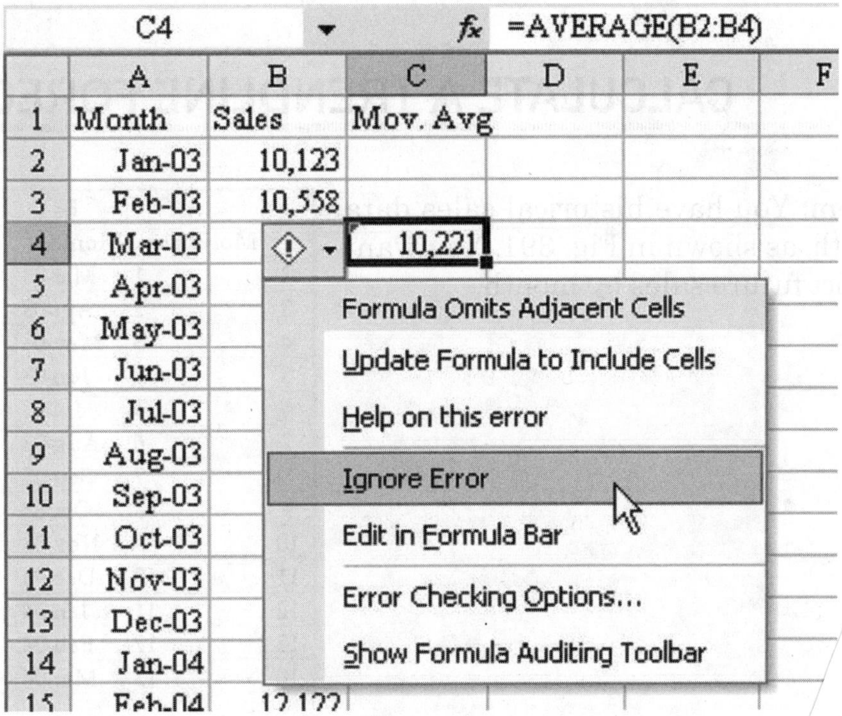

	A	B
1	Month	Sales
2	Jan-03	10,123
3	Feb-03	10,558
4	Mar-03	9,982
5	Apr-03	11,547
6	May-03	11,090
7	Jun-03	11,607
8	Jul-03	11,988
9	Aug-03	12,059
10	Sep-03	12,531
11	Oct-03	12,442
12	Nov-03	12,850
13	Dec-03	12,214
14	Jan-04	12,092

Fig. 388

Fig. 389

2) Double-click the Fill handle in C4 to copy the formula down to the rest of your dataset.

Result: Moving averages are good if your underlying data has spikes in the sales. It is hard for an automatic system to predict spikes. The moving average smoothes these spikes out of the system, as shown in Fig. 390. A forecast based on the moving average line may be more accurate than a forecast based on the original data.

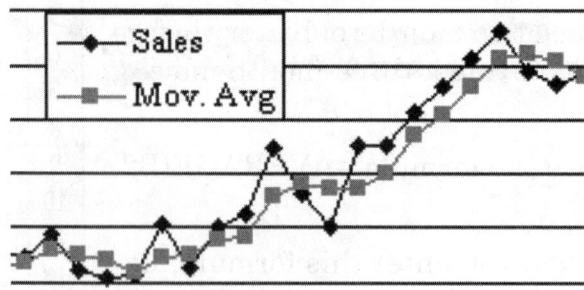

Fig. 390

Summary: Use the AVERAGE function to create a three-month moving average to be used for forecasting.

Functions Discussed: =AVERAGE()

CALCULATE A TRENDLINE FORECAST

Problem: You have historical sales data by month, as shown in Fig. 391. You want to predict future sales by month.

	A	B	C
1	MoNumber	Month	Sales
2	1	Mar-03	10,221
3	2	Apr-03	10,696
4	3	May-03	10,873
5	4	Jun-03	11,415
6	5	Jul-03	11,562
7	6	Aug-03	11,885
8	7	Sep-03	12,193
9	8	Oct-03	12,344
10	9	Nov-03	12,608
11	10	Dec-03	12,502
12	11	Jan-04	12,385
13	12	Feb-04	12,143
14	13	Mar-04	12,427

Fig. 391

Strategy: You want to use the least-squares method to fit the sales data to a trendline. Excel offers a function called LINEST that will calculate the formula for the trendline.

You might remember from math that a trendline is represented by this formula:

$y = mx + b$.

Y is the revenue for the month, M is the slope of the line, X is the month number, and B is the y intercept. If you were to look at the data, you might guess that the prediction for a given month is $10,000 + the month number times $400. In this case, the value for b would be 10000 and the value for m would be 400. This is just my wild guess – Excel can calculate the number exactly.

However, LINEST is a very special function. Instead of returning one number, it actually returns two (or more) numbers as the result.

Fig. 392, shows the wrong way to enter the LINEST function. If you select a single cell and enter =LINEST(C2:C35), it will return a single number.

	A	B	C	D	E	F	G	H	I	J	K	L
1	MoNumber	Month	Sales									
2	1	Mar-03	10,221		=LINEST(C2:C35)							
3	2	Apr-03	10,696									
4	3	May-03	10,873									
5	4	Jun-03	11,415									
6	5	Jul-03	11,562									
7	6	Aug-03	11,885									
8	7	Sep-03	12,193									
9	8	Oct-03	12,344									
10	9	Nov-03	12,608									
11	10	Dec-03	12,502									
12	11	Jan-04	12,385									
13	12	Feb-04	12,143									
14	13	Mar-04	12,427									
15	14	Apr-04	12,487									
16	15	May-04	12,777									
17	16	Jun-04	12,840									
18	17	Jul-04	13,579									
19	18	Aug-04	13,795									
20	19	Sep-04	13,709									
21	20	Oct-04	13,725									
22	21	Nov-04	14,018									
23	22	Dec-04	14,725									

Function Arguments   ? X

LINEST

Known_y's   C2:C35   = {10221;10695.6666⋯

Known_x's   = reference

Const   = logical

Stats   = logical

                                       = {204.813292589763,102

Returns statistics that describe a linear trend matching known data points, by fitting a straight line using the least squares method.

Known_x's is an optional set of x-values that you may already know in the relationship y = mx + b.

Formula result =   204.8132926

Help on this function   OK   Cancel

Fig. 392

Entering the formula the wrong way returns a single answer of 204.8133, as shown in Fig. 393. The first time that you do this, you might wonder how the number 204.81 could describe a line.

	E2		▼		*fx* =LINEST(C2:C35)	
	A	B	C	D	E
1	MoNumber	Month	Sales		
2	1	Mar-03	10,221		204.8133
3	2	Apr-03	10,696		

Fig. 393

It turns out that Excel really wants to return two numbers from the function. The trick is to first select two cells that are side-by-side.

1)   Begin to enter the function in the first cell, as shown in Fig. 394.

	COUNTA	▼ ✕ ✓	*fx* =LINEST(C2:C35)			
	A	B	C	D	E	F
1	MoNumber	Month	Sales			
2	1	Mar-03	10,221		=LINEST(C2:C35)	
3	2	Apr-03	10,696			
4	3	May-03	10,872			

Fig. 394

2)   After you type the closing parenthesis, hold down Ctrl+Shift while you hit Enter. Excel returns both the slope and the y-intercept, as shown in Fig. 395.

	E2		▼		*fx* {=LINEST(C2:C35)}	
	A	B	C	D	E	F
1	MoNumber	Month	Sales			
2	1	Mar-03	10,221		204.8133	10248.74
3	2	Apr-03	10,696			

Fig. 395

3)   Fill in headings, as shown in Fig. 396. In column D, enter a formula
       to calculate the predicted sales trendline.

D2			f_x =$F$2+$E$2*A2			
	A	B	C	D	E	F
1	MoNumber	Month	Sales	Prediction	Slope	Y-Intercept
2	1	Mar-03	10,221	10,454	204.8133	10248.74
3	2	Apr-03	10,696	10,658		
4	3	May-03	10,873	10,863		
5	4	Jun-03	11,415	11,068		
6	5	Jul-03	11,562	11,273		
7	6	Aug-03	11,885	11,478		
8	7	Sep-03	12,193	11,682		
9	8	Oct-03	12,344	11,887		

Fig. 396

You can then graph columns B:D to show how well the prediction matches the historical actuals.

Tip *When data along the x-axis of your chart contains dates, it is
best to delete the upper left corner cell of your dataset before
creating the chart.*

4)   Clear cell B1. Select B1:D47 and select Insert – Chart. Select a line
       chart and hit Finish.

As shown in Fig. 397, the resulting chart shows that the predicted trend-line comes fairly close to the actuals. You can also see that the formula predicts that you will be selling almost $20K a month one year from now.

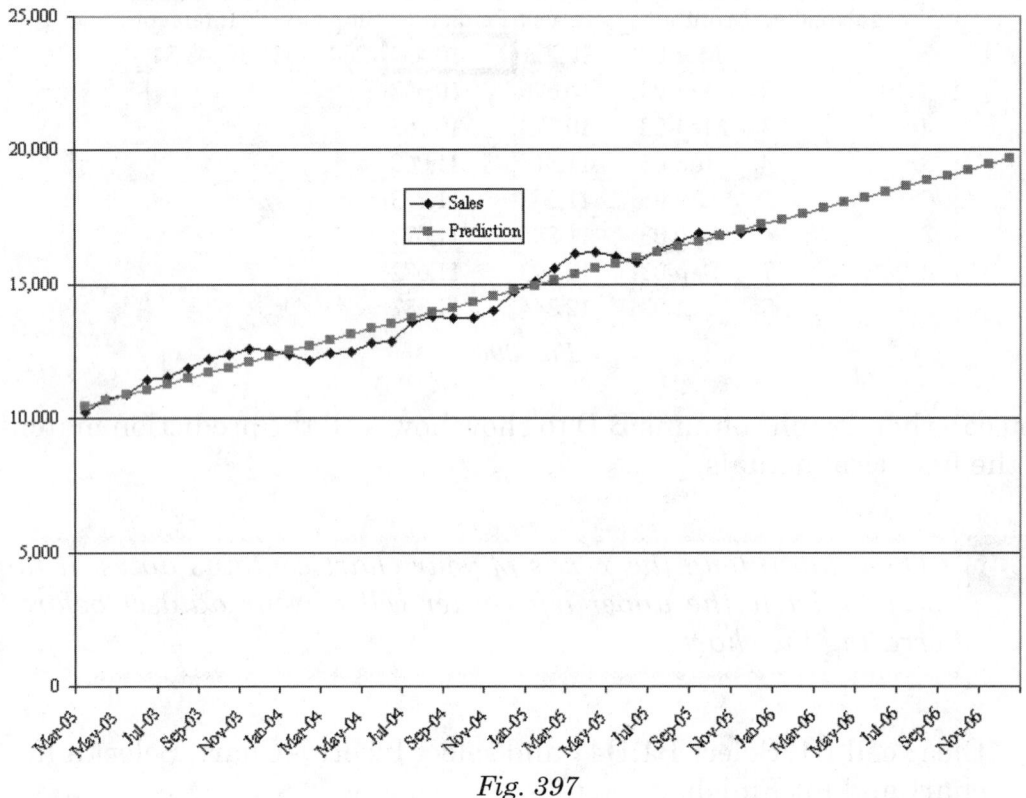

Fig. 397

Gotcha: When you select two cells for the LINEST function, they must be side by side. If you try to select two cells that are one above the other, you will just get two copies of the slope.

Alternate Strategy: A different method is to use the INDEX function to pluck a specific answer from the array.

=INDEX(LINEST(C2:C35),1,1) will return the first element from the array, as shown in Fig. 398. This is the slope.

=INDEX(LINEST(C2:C35),1,2) will return the second element from the array. This is the y-intercept.

=INDEX(LINEST(C2:C35),1,1)

	D	E	F	G
.5	11,068			
52	11,273		Slope	204.8133
35	11,478		Y-Intercept	10248.74
)3	11,682			
1/4	11 887			

Fig. 398

Summary: The LINEST function will automate the process of performing a least-squares method to fit a line to a series of actual sales. Because the function returns multiple values, you have to use care when entering. Either enter it in multiple cells with the Ctrl+Shift+Enter key combination or use the INDEX function to extract values.

Functions Discussed: =LINEST(); =INDEX()

BUILD A MODEL TO PREDICT SALES BASED ON MULTIPLE REGRESSION

Problem: You run an ice cream stand. After 10 days of sales, you discover that you either make a lot of money or nearly go broke. As you analyze sales, you feel that temperature and rain might be two important determining factors. On rainy or cool days, fewer people buy ice cream.

As shown in Fig. 399, you set up this table showing sales, temperature, and whether or not it rained.

	A	B	C
1	Sally's Ice Cream Stand		
2			
3	Temperature	Rain	Sales
4	64	1	$28
5	95	0	$270
6	74	1	$48
7	84	1	$68
8	94	1	$88
9	75	0	$150
10	56	0	$36
11	85	0	$210
12	65	0	$90
13	55	1	$10
14			

Fig. 399

You want to determine the relationship between sales, temperature, and rainfall.

Strategy: You need to do a multiple regression. After a multiple regression, you will have a formula that predicts sales like this:

$Y = m1x1 + m2x2 + b$

Sales = Temperature x M1 + Rain x M2 + b

The LINEST function can return the values M1, M2, and b that best describe your sales model.

1)   LINEST is going to return three values. Select a range of three cells that are side by side, as shown in Fig. 400. The first argument is the range of known sales figures. The second argument is the range of temperatures and rainfall.

	A	B	C	D	E	F	G
1	Sally's Ice Cream Stand						
2							
3	Temperature	Rain	Sales		Rain	Temperature	Constant
4	64	1	$28		=LINEST(C4:C13,A4:B13)		
5	95	0	$270				
6	74	1	$48				
7	84	1	$68				
8	94	1	$88				
9	75	0	$150				
10	56	0	$36				
11	85	0	$210				
12	65	0	$90				
13	55	1	$10				
14							

Fig. 400

2)   Hit Ctrl+Shift+Enter to calculate the array formula. As shown in Fig. 401, enter a prediction formula in column D to see how well the formula describes sales.

	D4	▼		*fx*	=$H$4+($G$4*A4)+($F$4*B4)		
	A	B	C	D	E	F	G	H
1	Sally's Ice Cream Stand							
2						Slope	Slope	Y Intercept
3	Temperature	Rain	Sales	Prediction		Rain	Temperature	Constant
4	64	1	$28	$8	Slope	-98.8	4	-149.6
5	95	0	$270	$230				
6	74	1	$48	$48				
7	84	1	$68	$88				
8	94	1	$88	$128				
9	75	0	$150	$150				
10	56	0	$36	$74				
11	85	0	$210	$190				
12	65	0	$90	$110				
13	55	1	$10	-$28				

Fig. 401

The results are so-so. The prediction in D6 is right on the mark. The predictions in D11 and D12 are off by $20 each – an error of 10 percent.

3)   The LINEST function can return additional statistics that will tell you how well the results match reality. To get the statistics, add a fourth argument of TRUE. Enter the function in a five-row range, as shown in Fig. 402.

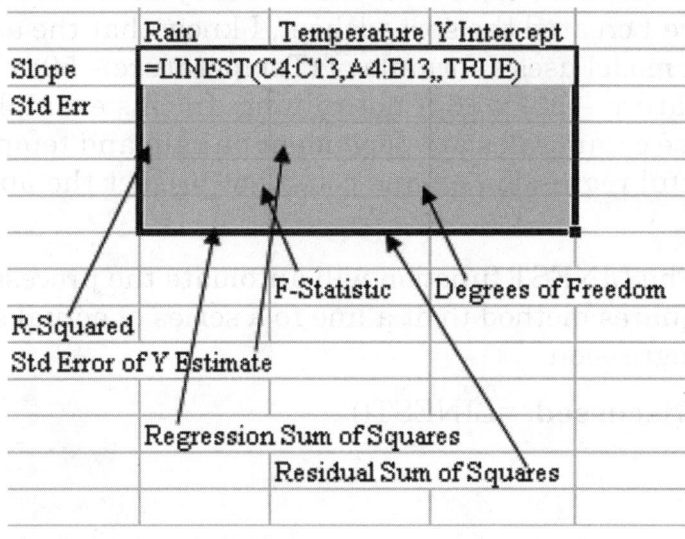

Fig. 402

4)   As shown in Fig. 403, after hitting Ctrl+Enter, you get the results.

	Rain	Temperature	Y Intercept	
Slope	-98.8	4	-149.6	
Std Err	20.971273	0.755928946	58.7457476	
	0.8814771	33.13694529	#N/A	
	26.030157	7	#N/A	
	57165.2	7686.4	#N/A	
		F-Statistic	Degrees of Freedom	
R-Squared				
Std Error of Y Estimate				
	Regression Sum of Squares			
		Residual Sum of Squares		

Fig. 403

Personally, I only somewhat paid attention in statistics class. One of the key indicators that I look at is the R-Squared value. This ranges from 0 to 1, where 1 is a perfect match and 0 is a horrible match. The 0.88 value here confirms that the prediction model is pretty good, but not perfect.

Additional Details: Regression models try to force actual results into a straight-line formula. The fact is that life may not fit in a straight-line formula. Since I created the spreadsheet, I know that the actual data in the ice cream model uses a formula of (Temperature – 50) x $2 if raining and (Temperature – 50) x $6 if not raining. In this example, Sally was correct that ice cream sales are dependent on rain and temperature, but even a powerful regression engine could not predict the absolutely correct formula.

Summary: The LINEST function will automate the process of performing a least-squares method to fit a line to a series of actual sales using a multifactor regression.

Functions Discussed: =LINEST()

USE F9 IN FORMULA BAR
TO TEST A FORMULA

Problem: You have a complex formula that does not appear to be providing the correct result. As shown in Fig. 404, the formula has multiple terms and you are not sure which part is not working correctly.

	C25		▼	*fx* =($C$9-$C$20)*G4*1.5		
	A	B	C	D	E	F
22		New Mix	240	99360000	9820800	10
23						
24	Cost of Closing Stores					
25		Labor	787320			
26		Lost Rent	388800			

Fig. 404

Strategy: Select the cell, press F2 to put the cell in edit mode, as shown in Fig. 405.

	COUNTA		▼ X ✓ *fx*	=($C$9-$C$20)*G4*1.5			
	A	B	C	D	E	F	G
1	Section 1: Historical Trends (Per Month)						
2							
3		Store Type	Size	Rent	Sales	Profit	Labor
4		Regular	1200	2400	12456	6228	6480
5		BigBox	2600	5200	34500	17250	8640
6							
7	Section 2: Number of Stores						
8							
9		Regular	81				
10		BigBox	184				
11							
12	Section 3: Analysis of Profitability of Current Store Mix						
13			Sales	Net Profit	NP%		
14		Total Chain	88283232	4951536	5.6%		
15		Regular	12107232	-2577744	-21.3%		
16		Big Box	76176000	7529280	9.9%		
17							
18	Section 4: Profit Projections with a New Mix of Stores						
19				Sales	Profit	NP%	
20		Regular	0	0	0		
21		BigBox	240	99360000	9820800		
22		New Mix	240	99360000	9820800	10%	
23							
24	Cost of Closing Stores						
25		Labor	=($C$9-$C$20)*G4*1.5				
26		Lost Rent	388800				

Fig. 405

Part II

> **Tip** *Remember to press the Esc key to change back to the original formula after using this technique.*

In edit mode, the various cells are color-keyed. You can selectively calculate just a portion of the formula. As shown in Fig. 406, using the mouse, highlight a portion of the formula.

Fig. 406

Hit the F9 key. As shown in Fig. 407, that portion of the formula will be replaced with the current result of the formula.

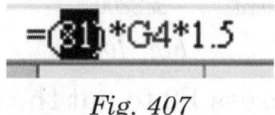

Fig. 407

Additional information: If you hit F9 without selecting anything, it will calculate the entire formula and replace it in the result, as shown in Fig. 408.

Fig. 408

Summary: Placing a cell containing a formula in edit mode, selecting part of the formula, and hitting the F9 key will verify that the selected part of the formula is correct.

Commands Discussed: F2 with a selected cell; F9 in the edit mode.

QUICK CALCULATOR

Problem: You need to find a quick answer to a mathematical problem and you don't have a calculator.

Strategy: Follow these steps:

1) Go to a blank cell.

2)   Type an Equal sign.

3)   Enter a calculation, as shown in Fig. 409.

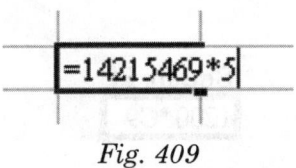

Fig. 409

4)   Hit F9 key. Note the result, as shown in Fig. 410.

Fig. 410

5)   Hit the Esc key to clear the cell.

Summary: Excel can provide a quick calculator in a blank cell by typing the Equal sign, typing in the problem, and then hitting F9.

Commands Discussed: F9 key

WHEN ENTERING A FORMULA, YOU GET THE FORMULA INSTEAD OF THE RESULT

Problem: When entering a formula, you get the formula instead of the result, as shown in Fig. 411.

	A	B	C	D
1	Section 1: Historical Trends (Per Month)			
2				
3		Store Type	Size	Rent
4		Regular	1200	2400
5		BigBox	2600	5200
6				
7	Section 2: Number of Stores			
8				
9		Regular	81	=C9/(C9+C10)
10		BigBox	184	

Fig. 411

Strategy: There are three possibilities.

Possibility 1: As shown in Fig. 412, you forgot to start the formula with the Equal sign.

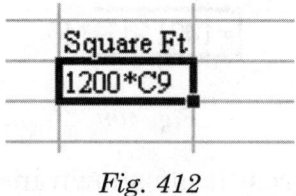

Fig. 412

1)   Select the cell, hit F2 to edit the cell, as shown in Fig. 413.

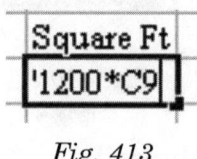

Fig. 413

2)   Hit home to move cursor to start of formula, as shown in Fig. 414.

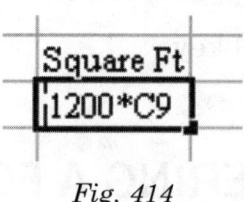

Fig. 414

3)   Hit Delete key to delete the leading apostrophe. Type the = sign, as shown in Fig. 415.

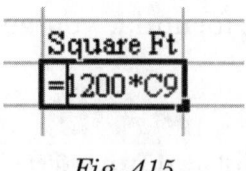

Fig. 415

4)   Hit Enter to enter the formula, as shown in Fig. 416.

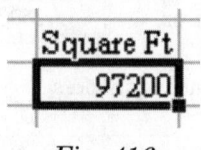

Fig. 416

Gotcha: Typically, in a cell with general formatting, Excel will right-align numbers and left-align text. Because you forgot to hit the Equal sign, Excel thinks you have a text cell and even after converting to a valid formula, the result might be left-aligned. Hit the Align Right icon in the Formatting toolbar, as shown in Fig. 417.

Fig. 417

Possibility 2: The cell might have been assigned a numeric format of "@", which is the code for a text cell. The maddening part is that this format can get set even without you knowing it. A column can inherit a text format if you import a text file and use the text setting for the import.

Part II

1) Here's how to fix this. Select the cell. Hit Ctrl+1 to show the Format Cells dialog. Confirm that the cell has a Text format assigned, as shown in Fig. 418.

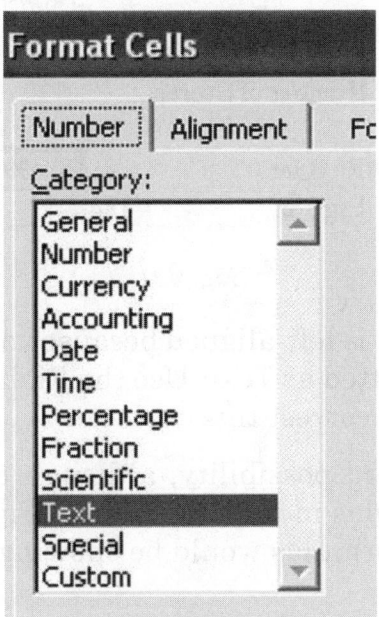

Fig. 418

2)   As shown in Fig. 419, change to a numeric format.

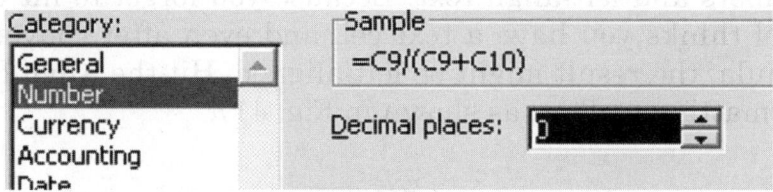

Fig. 419

3)   This does not fix the formula! You can now edit the cell using the F2 key. As shown in Fig. 420, note that Excel added an apostrophe before the formula.

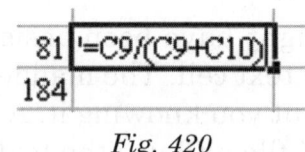

Fig. 420

4)   Hit the Home key to move to the beginning of the formula and the Delete key to delete the apostrophe. Hit Enter to accept the formula, as shown in Fig. 421.

	A	B	C	D
7	Section 2: Number of Stores			
8				
9		Regular	81	30.6%
10		BigBox	184	

D9 — fx =C9/(C9+C10)

Fig. 421

5)   The cell alignment is left-aligned because you entered a value while the cell was formatted as Text. Use the Right-Align icon on the Formatting toolbar to correct this.

Possibility 3: The third possibility, although the least likely, is that you are in Show Formulas mode, as shown in Fig. 422. In this mode, all of the cells that have formulas would be showing their formulas.

	A	B	C	D	E	F
7	Section 2: Number of					
8						Square Ft
9		Regular	81	=C9/(C9+C10)		=1200*C9
10		BigBox	184			
11						
12	Section 3: Analysis					
13			Sales	Net Profit	NP%	
14		Total Chain	=+C15+C16	=+D15+D16	=+D14/C14	
15		Regular	=(C9*E4)*12	=(C9*H4)*12	=+D15/C15	
16		Big Box	=(C10*E5)*12	=(C10*H5)*12	=+D16/C16	
17						

Fig. 422

1) Hit CTRL+~ to toggle in and out of Show Formulas mode.

Summary: The three possible options to fix a formula that shows when you actually want the results to show in a cell are: (1) check to make sure you started the formula with an Equal (=) sign, (2) make sure the cell is formatted for numeric and, lastly, (3) make sure the worksheet is not in Show Formula mode.

Commands Discussed: F2 to enter edit mode; CTRL+~ for Show Formula mode

CALCULATE A PERCENTAGE OF TOTAL

Problem: Your spreadsheet lists a number of customers with revenue, as shown in Fig. 423. There is a total at the bottom. You want to express each customer as a percentage of the total.

	A	B
1	Customer	Revenue
2	Ainsworth	2,308,900
3	Exxon	2,907,800
4	Ford	2,522,600
5	General Motors	3,145,200
6	IBM	1,693,000
7	Lucent	265,100
8	Molson, Inc	2,519,100
9	Nortel Networks	1,564,200
10	P&G	245,100
11	SBC Communications	290,100
12	Sears Canada	240,500
13	Shell Canada	292,500
14	Sun Life Financial	1,994,200
15	Verizon	1,636,700
16	Wal-Mart	3,490,000
17	Total	25,115,000
18		

Fig. 423

Part II

Strategy: Follow these steps:

1) Select a cell next to the first revenue cell.

2) Type an Equal sign. Hit the Left Arrow.

3) Type the Forward Slash (/) sign. Hit the Left Arrow. Type the End key. Hit the Down Arrow. Your cell pointer should now be on the total cell. Type the F4 key. The formula bar should now show B2/$B$17, as shown in Fig. 424.

COUNTA		▾ X ✓ ƒx	=B2/$B$17	
	A	B	C	
1	Customer	Revenue		
2	Ainsworth	2,308,900	=B2/$B$17	
3	Exxon	2,907,800		

Fig. 424

4) Hit Ctrl+Enter to enter the formula and stay in the current cell. Format the calculation as a percentage using the % icon, as shown in Fig. 425.

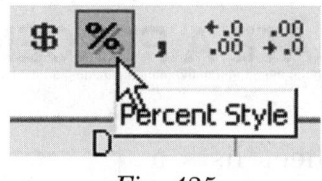

Fig. 425

5) If you wish to use a format of 9.2 percent instead of 9 percent, then choose the Increase Decimal button, as shown in Fig. 426.

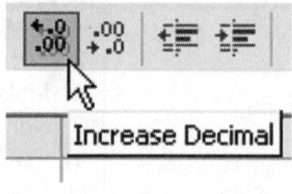

Fig. 426

6) In cell C2, double-click the Fill handle to copy the formula down to the other rows.

7) Add a heading for "% of Total".

Additional Details: The key element of this procedure is hitting the F4 key to add dollar signs to the reference for the total row. As you copy the formula from C2 to C16, the formula is always going to compare the revenue in the current row to the total revenue in row 17, as shown in Fig. 427.

	C16	▼	*fx* =B16/$B$17

	A	B	C
1	Customer	Revenue	% of Total
2	Ainsworth	2,308,900	9.2%
3	Exxon	2,907,800	11.6%
4	Ford	2,522,600	10.0%
5	General Motors	3,145,200	12.5%
6	IBM	1,693,000	6.7%
7	Lucent	265,100	1.1%
8	Molson, Inc	2,519,100	10.0%
9	Nortel Networks	1,564,200	6.2%
10	P&G	245,100	1.0%
11	SBC Communications	290,100	1.2%
12	Sears Canada	240,500	1.0%
13	Shell Canada	292,500	1.2%
14	Sun Life Financial	1,994,200	7.9%
15	Verizon	1,636,700	6.5%
16	Wal-Mart	3,490,000	13.9%
17	Total	25,115,000	100.0%

Fig. 427

Summary: Creating a Percentage of Total is a common task in Excel. Being able to quickly enter an initial formula that can be copied to all cells is a good technique to have in your skill set.

Part
II

CALCULATE A RUNNING PERCENTAGE
OF TOTAL

Problem: You have a report of revenue by customer, sorted in descending order, as shown in Fig. 428. Management consultants will often argue that you should concentrate your best team on the 20 percent of the customers who provide 80 percent of your revenue. How can you calculate a cumulative running percentage of the total?

	A	B	C
1	Customer	Revenue	Running % Tot
2	Wal-Mart	3,490,000	
3	General Motors	3,145,200	
4	Exxon	2,907,800	
5	Ford	2,522,600	
6	Molson, Inc	2,519,100	
7	Ainsworth	2,308,900	
8	Sun Life Financial	1,994,200	
9	IBM	1,693,000	
10	Verizon	1,636,700	
11	Nortel Networks	1,564,200	
12	Shell Canada	292,500	
13	SBC Communications	290,100	
14	Lucent	265,100	
15	P&G	245,100	
16	Sears Canada	240,500	
17			
18	Total	25,115,000	

Fig. 428

Strategy: I hate solutions that require two different formulas, but this is one of them. You will need one formula for cell C2 and a different formula for cells C3 and below.

1)   In cell C2, enter a formula of =B2/$B$18. Format the result as a percentage with one decimal place, as shown in Fig. 429.

C2		▾	*fx* =B2/$B$18	
	A		B	C
1	Customer		Revenue	Running % Tot
2	Wal-Mart		3,490,000	13.9%
3	General Motors		3,145,200	

Fig. 429

2)   Copy C2 to just the next cell, as shown in Fig. 430. If you want, you can drag the Fill handle down one cell to copy the formula. Or, use Ctrl+C and then Ctrl+V.

	A	B	C
1	Customer	Revenue	Running % Tot
2	Wal-Mart	3,490,000	13.9%
3	General Motors	3,145,200	12.5%

Fig. 430

3)   Hit F2 to edit the cell, as shown in Fig. 431.

	A	B	C
1	Customer	Revenue	Running % Tot
2	Wal-Mart	3,490,000	13.9%
3	General Motors	3,145,200	=B3/$B$18

Fig. 431

4)   As shown in Fig. 432, type a Plus sign and touch cell C2. Hit Enter.

C3		▾	*fx* =B3/$B$18+C2	
	A		B	C
1	Customer		Revenue	Running % Tot
2	Wal-Mart		3,490,000	13.9%
3	General Motors		3,145,200	26.4%
4	Exxon		2,907,800	

Fig. 432

5)   Double-click the Fill handle in C3 to copy this formula down to all of the other cells.

Note that you do not want this formula to be added to your total row. As shown in Fig. 433, the dataset was purposely set up with the total row and the data separated by a blank row in order to prevent this formula from copying to the total row.

	A	B	C
1	Customer	Revenue	Running % Tot
2	Wal-Mart	3,490,000	13.9%
3	General Motors	3,145,200	26.4%
4	Exxon	2,907,800	38.0%
5	Ford	2,522,600	48.0%
6	Molson, Inc	2,519,100	58.1%
7	Ainsworth	2,308,900	67.3%
8	Sun Life Financial	1,994,200	75.2%
9	IBM	1,693,000	81.9%
10	Verizon	1,636,700	88.5%
11	Nortel Networks	1,564,200	94.7%
12	Shell Canada	292,500	95.9%
13	SBC Communications	290,100	97.0%
14	Lucent	265,100	98.1%
15	P&G	245,100	99.0%
16	Sears Canada	240,500	100.0%
17			
18	Total	25,115,000	
19			

Fig. 433

Additional Information: If you absolutely want to produce this total with a single formula, you could use this formula in C2 and copy it down, as shown in Fig. 434: =SUM(B2:B$2)/B$18. This works because the range B2:B$2 is an interesting reference. It says to add up everything from the current row to the top row. This formula seems a bit less intuitive, so you might prefer the method shown earlier.

f_x	=SUM(B2:B$2)/B$18
B	C
Revenue	Running % Tot
3,490,000	13.9%
3,145,200	26.4%

Fig. 434

Summary: The formula for a running percentage of the total is another common analysis tool. This technique offers two different options for calculating the formula.

USE ^ SIGN FOR EXPONENT

Problem: You have a room that is 10 feet x 10 feet x 10 feet. What is the volume of the cube?

Strategy: The formula for volume is width x length x height. In this case, it is 10 x 10 x 10, or ten to the third power. In Excel, the carat symbol (also known as "the little hat", or "the symbol when you press Shift 6") is used to calculate exponents. In cell B2, enter 10; in cell B3, enter the formula =B2^3. The result will be 1000 cubic feet of volume in the room, as shown in Fig. 435.

Part II

	C2		▼	f_x	=B2^3
	A	B	C	D	
1					
2		10	1000		
3					
4					

Fig. 435

Summary: Use a carat to calculate exponents.

RAISE A NUMBER TO A FRACTION TO FIND THE SQUARE OR THIRD ROOT

Problem: Excel offers a SQRT function to find the square root of a number. What if you need to figure out the third root or the fourth root?

Strategy: You can raise a number to a fraction to find a root. To find the square root of a number, you can raise the number to (1/2). To find the cube root of a number, you can raise the number to (1/3). To find the eighth root of a number, you can raise the number to (1/8).

Here are several examples.

If you need to find the square root, you can use the SQRT function, as shown in Fig. 436.

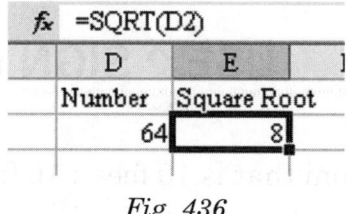

Fig. 436

As shown in Fig. 437, you can also raise the number to the one-half (1/2) power.

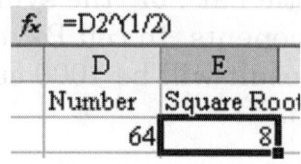

Fig. 437

Or, you can raise the number to 0.5, as shown in Fig. 438.

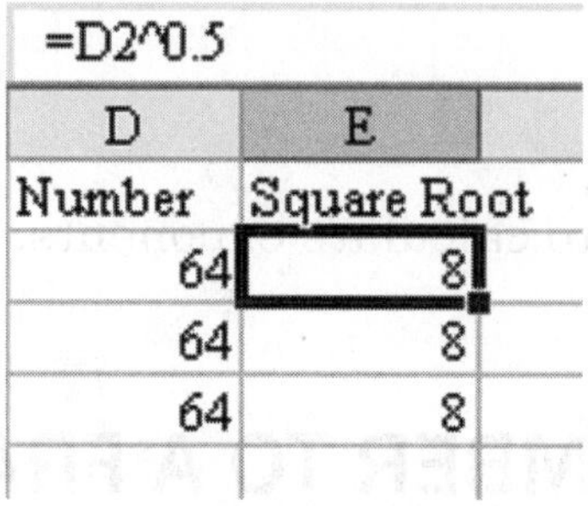

=D2^0.5		
D	E	
Number	Square Root	
64	8	
64	8	
64	8	

Fig. 438

To find the cube root of a number, you can raise the number to the one-third (1/3) power, as shown in Fig. 439.

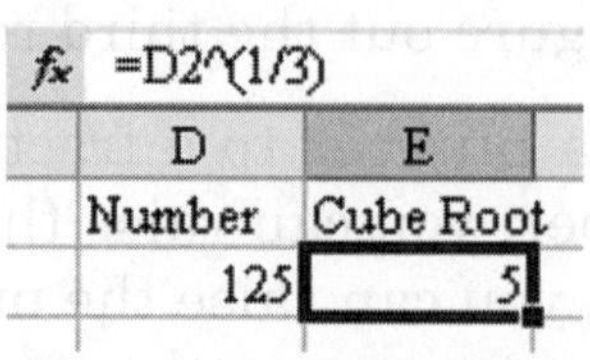

f_x =D2^(1/3)		
D	E	
Number	Cube Root	
125	5	

Fig. 439

To find the fourth root of a number, raise the number to either one-forth (1/4) or 0.25 power, as shown in Fig. 440 and Fig. 441, respectively.

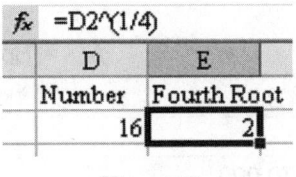

Fig. 440

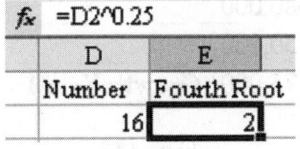

Fig. 441

To find the seventeenth root of a number, raise it to the one-seventeenth (1/17) power, as shown in Fig. 442.

f_x	=D2^(1/17)	
	D	E
	Number	17th Root
	1197964098	3.42

Fig. 442

Summary: Although Excel only offers a function for a square root, you can use the technique of raising to a fractional power in order to determine any root of a number.

Commands Discussed: Exponent operator

Functions Discussed: =SQRT()

CALCULATE A GROWTH RATE

Problem: You work for a fast growing company. In the first year, they had $970,000.00 in sales. In the fifth year, they had $6,175,000.00 in sales. What was the compounded annual growth rate?

Strategy: Sales in the fifth year are 6175/970 higher than the first year. The formula for growth is (year 5/year 1) – 100 percent. So, as shown in Fig. 443, the growth rate is 537 percent.

	A	B	C	D
	D6		fx =(B6/B2)-1	
1				
2	Year 1	970,000		
3	Year 2	2,250,000		
4	Year 3	4,580,000		
5	Year 4	5,850,000		
6	Year 5	6,175,000	Growth Year 1 - Year 5	537%

Fig. 443

However, a compounded growth rate is a number, x, that will calculate out like this: Year 1 * (100% + x) *(100% + x) *(100% + x) * (100% + x)= Year 5

This is the same as:

Year 1 * (100% + x)^4 = Year 5

So, in order to calculate x, you have to be able to find the fourth root of (Year5/Year1). The formula to find the fourth root is to raise the number to the (1/4) power. Thus, as shown in Fig. 444, the formula to calculate the compounded growth rate is:

(Year 5/Year 1)^(1/4)–100% = x

	A	B	C	D
	D6		fx =(B6/B2)^(1/4)-100%	
1				
2	Year 1	970,000		
3	Year 2	2,250,000		
4	Year 3	4,580,000		
5	Year 4	5,850,000	Growth Year 1 - Year 5	537%
6	Year 5	6,175,000	Compounded Growth	59%
7				

Fig. 444

The compounded growth rate is 59 percent.

Summary: Compounded growth rates are common calculations that require you to raise a number to a fractional power.

FIND THE AREA OF A CIRCLE

Problem: You need to order pizza for the department staff meeting. The pizza joint has two deals. You can buy three Medium (12") pizzas for $15 or two Large (16") pizzas for $16. Which is the better deal?

Strategy: You will have to figure out the area of a 12" pizza vs. the area of a 16" pizza. The formula for the area of a circle is Pi times the square of the radius.

Part II

The radius of a pizza is one-half the diameter. If you enter the diameter of the pizza in B2, the radius is =B2/2.

Pi is a Greek letter that represents 3.141592654. Excel offers the PI function to return this number, as shown in Fig. 445. It is a lot easier to remember =PI() instead of 3.141592654.

	A	B	C	D
A1			f_x =PI()	
	A	**B**	**C**	**C**
1	3.141592654			

Fig. 445

1) Set up a worksheet. In cell B2, enter the diameter of the pizza.

2) In cell C2, calculate the radius as =B2/2, as shown in Fig. 446.

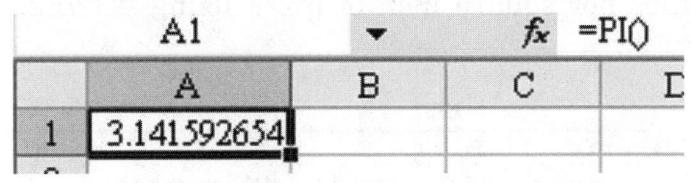

C2			f_x =B2/2
	A	**B**	**C**
1	Pizza Size	Diameter	Radius
2	Medium	12	6
3	Large	16	8

Fig. 446

3)   In cell D2, calculate the area of the pizza in square inches, using =PI()*C2^2, as shown in Fig. 447.

	D2		▼	*fx* =PI()*C2^2	
	A	B	C	D	
1	Pizza Size	Diameter	Radius	Area	
2	Medium	12	6	113.0973	
3	Large	16	8	201.0619	

Fig. 447

4)   In column E, enter the quantity of pizzas.

5)   Calculate the total square inches in column F using =E2*D2, as shown in Fig. 448.

	F2			▼	*fx* =E2*D2	
	A	B	C	D	E	F
1	Pizza Size	Diameter	Radius	Area	Quantity	Total Square Inches
2	Medium	12	6	113.0973	3	339.2920066
3	Large	16	8	201.0619	2	402.1238597

Fig. 448

6)   Enter the cost for the special in column G. In column H, calculate the pennies per square inch of pizza using =G2/F2, as shown in Fig. 449.

	H2			▼	*fx* =G2/F2			
	A	B	C	D	E	F	G	H
1	Pizza Size	Diameter	Radius	Area	Quantity	Total Square Inches	Cost	Cost/Sq Inch
2	Medium	12	6	113.0973	3	339.2920066	$15.00	$0.0442
3	Large	16	8	201.0619	2	402.1238597	$16.00	$0.0398

Fig. 449

Result: From a purely mathematical point of view, the special with two large pizzas is a slightly better deal, pricing the pizza at 3.98 cents per square inch.

Additional Information: My seventh grade math teacher, Mr. Irwin, would like me to mention, for the sake of completeness, that the circumference of the pizza is Pi times the diameter. That would be =PI()*B2, as shown in Fig. 450.

J2		▼	*fx* =PI()*B2	
	A	B	J	K
1	Pizza Size	Diameter	Circumference	
2	Medium	12	37.70	
3	Large	16	50.27	
4				

Fig. 450

Summary: To calculate the area of a circle, use the PI function times the radius squared.

Functions Discussed: =PI()

FIGURE OUT LOTTERY PROBABILITY

Problem: The Super Lotto jackpot is $8 million this week. Should you play?

Strategy: It depends on how many numbers are in the game. You need to figure out the number of possible combinations there are in the game.

You can use the COMBIN function to figure out the number of combinations by selecting six numbers out of a group of 40.

1) Set up a spreadsheet with the number of balls in your lotto game in cell C2.

2) Identify how many numbers you need to select correctly in cell D2.

3) Enter the formula =COMBIN(C2,D2) in cell E2, as shown in Fig. 451.

	▼	*fx* =COMBIN(C2,D2)
C	D	E
Range 1 to	# to Win	Combinations
40	6	3,838,380
44	6	7,059,052
48	6	12,271,512
54	6	25,827,165

Fig. 451

If your state lottery game requires you to select six numbers out of 40, then the odds against you winning are 3.83 million to one. For a $1 bet and an $8 million payout, the odds are in your favor.

For a game with 44 numbers, the odds are 7 million to one. This payoff is only slightly in your favor.

For games with 48 or 54 numbers, the payout is not worth the long odds of the game.

Additional Information: COMBIN figures combinations. Here, the sequence in which the balls are drawn in is not relevant. If you had a game where you had to match both the numbers and the order in which they were drawn, then you would want to use the PERMUT function to find the number of permutations of drawing six numbers in sequence out of 40.

Summary: Use the COMBIN or PERMUT functions for figuring the number of combinations or permutations.

Functions Discussed: =COMBIN(); =PERMUT()

HELP YOUR KIDS WITH THEIR MATH

Problem: Your kids have math homework. You want to check their answers. They are doing least common multiples, greatest common denominators, roman numerals, and factorials.

> **Caution:** *These functions require the Analysis Toolpack to be installed. From the menu, select Tools – Add-Ins, and select the Analysis Toolpack.*

Strategy: All of these problems are now solvable with Excel.

Least Common Multiples: When you have to add fractions with different denominators, one of the first steps is to find the least common multiple of the two denominators. The math homework asks them to add 3/4 + 3/26. You want to figure out the least common multiple of 4 and 26. Enter 4 in one cell and 26 in another cell. The formula to find LCM is =LCM(C2:D2), as shown in Fig. 452.

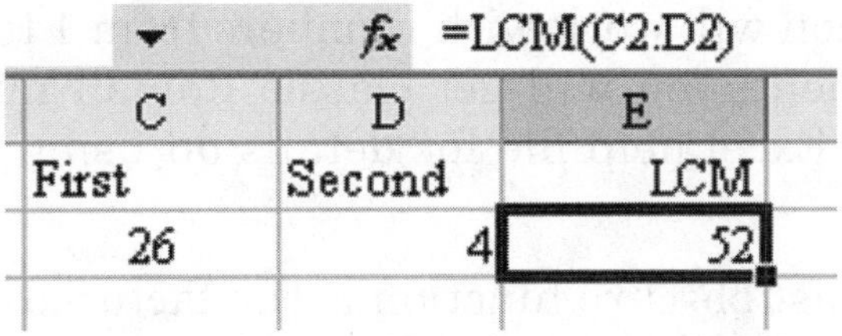

Fig. 452

You can now have your kids change 3/4 to 39/52 and 3/26 to 6/52. Expressing the problem as 39/52 + 6/52 makes it easy to see that the answer is 45/52.

Note: *The LCM function can accept up to 29 numbers.*

Part II

Greatest Common Denominators: This time the problem is 2/4 + 2/9. The LCM of 9 and 4 is 36. You can change 2/4 to 18/36. Change 2/9 to 8/36. The problem then becomes 18/36 + 8/36. The answer is 26/36. However, can the fraction 26/36 be further reduced? You need to find the greatest common denominator of 26 and 36. Use the =GCD(26,36) function, as shown in Fig. 453. As the answer is greater than 1, your 26/36 answer can be reduced by dividing both the numerator and denominator by 2. 26/36 is the same as 13/18.

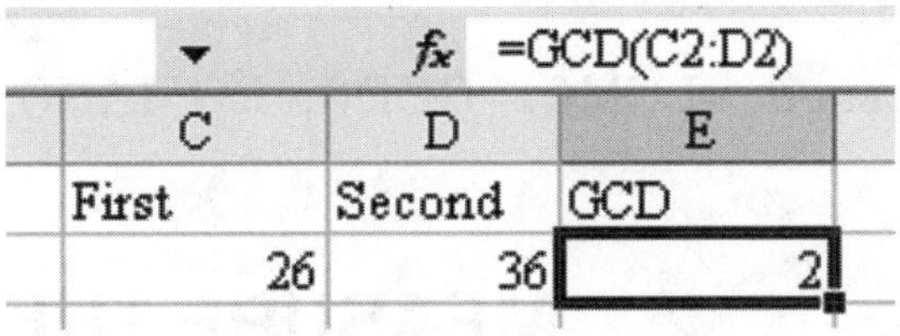

Fig. 453

Roman Numerals: The student is supposed to express the year that everyone in the family was born in Roman numerals. Use the =ROMAN function, as shown in Fig. 454.

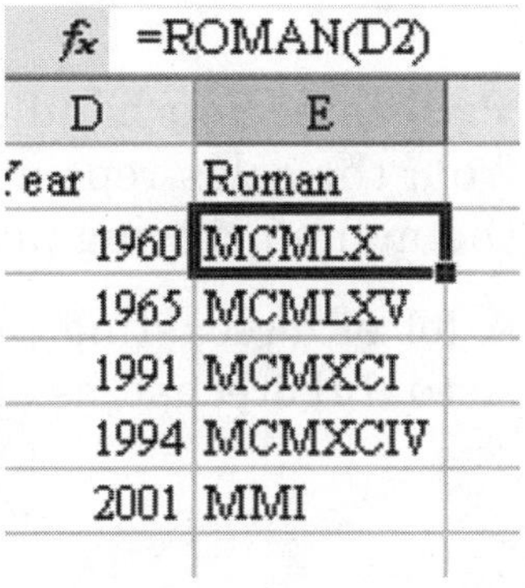

Fig. 454

The Roman function will work with numbers from 1 to 3999. If you omit the second argument, you will get classic Roman numerals as shown above. Check the Excel help file for details on using simplified Roman Numerals.

Factorials: The last obscure function is the factorial function. To write 5 factorial, you use the number 5 followed by an exclamation mark: 5!. To calculate a factorial, you multiply the number by every number between itself and 1. So, 5! is 5x4x3x2x1, or 120.

Use the FACT function to calculate factorials, as shown in Fig. 455.

			=FACT(D2)

D	E
Number	Fact
5	120
7	5040
8	40320
10	3628800

Fig. 455

Summary: If you had Excel in seventh grade, math would have been a lot easier.

Functions Discussed: =LCM(); =GCD();=ROMAN();=FACT()

MEASURE THE ACCURACY OF A SALES FORECAST

Problem: You handle forecasting for a company. You collect forecasts from the sales reps and attempt to turn this into a production plan for the manufacturing plant.

A lot of forecasting professionals measure forecast error as (Forecast–Actual)/Forecast, as shown in Fig. 456.

E2		▼	f_x	=(C2-D2)/C2	
	A	B	C	D	E
1	Product	Customer	Forecast	Actual	Error
2	DEF	Wal-Mart	300	270	10%
3	XYZ	Molson, Inc	100	130	-30%
4	XYZ	Ainsworth	400	0	100%
5	ABC	Ainsworth	0	400	#DIV/0!
6	ABC	General Motors	100	100	0%
7	DEF	Wal-Mart	800	800	0%

Fig. 456

When I had to measure forecast error, I did not agree with this method. You have to understand that there are two kinds of problems in forecasting. If you forecast 400 units and the order does not show up, then the manufacturing plant has 400 sets of material on hand and nowhere to send them to. Inventory goes up. This is bad. On the other side, if you forecast no units and an order for 400 shows up, the plant has to scramble and start buying material on the gray market. This means the product cost could double and your profits go away. This is also bad.

My formula for forecast accuracy treats both of these situations as equally bad. I take the absolute value of (Forecast–Actual) and divide by the larger of the forecasts or actuals.

My forecast accuracy calculation follows these steps.

1) First, calculate the absolute error on a product-by-product basis. Whether the forecast was high or low, the error is always a positive number. The ABS function returns the Absolute Value of a number, as shown in Fig. 457.

F2		▼	f_x	=ABS(C2-D2)
	C	D	E	F
1	Forecast	Actual	FC Err %	Error
2	300	270	10%	30
3	100	130	-30%	30
4	400	0	100%	400

Fig. 457

2) Then, calculate the divisor. This is what I call the "Size of the opportunity to screw up". If you miss a 1000 unit sale, it is much worse than missing a 2 unit sale. As shown in Fig. 458, for column G, use the MAX function to find whichever is larger, forecast or actuals.

	G2	▼		*fx* =MAX(C2:D2)	
	C	D	E	F	G
1	Forecast	Actual	FC Err %	Error	Divisor
2	300	270	10%	30	300
3	100	130	-30%	30	130
4	400	0	100%	400	400
5	0	400	#DIV/0!	400	400

Fig. 458

3) Finally, calculate the error percentage by dividing F2/G2, as shown in Fig. 459.

	H2	▼		*fx* =F2/G2		
	C	D	E	F	G	H
1	Forecast	Actual	FC Err %	Error	Divisor	Error %
2	300	270	10%	30	300	10%
3	100	130	-30%	30	130	23%
4	400	0	100%	400	400	100%

Fig. 459

As shown in Fig. 460, the traditional forecast error calculation is in E. My forecast error calculation is in H. Sometimes they are the same. Overall, though, because my calculation takes into account the negative effect of an unforecasted order showing up, my error percentage will be higher (and, I feel, more meaningful).

	A	B	C	D	E	F	G	H
1	Product	Customer	Forecast	Actual	FC Err %	Error	Divisor	Error %
2	DEF	Wal-Mart	300	270	10%	30	300	10%
3	XYZ	Molson, Inc	100	130	-30%	30	130	23%
4	XYZ	Ainsworth	400	0	100%	400	400	100%
5	ABC	Ainsworth	0	400	#DIV/0!	400	400	100%
6	ABC	General Motors	100	100	0%	0	100	0%
7	DEF	Wal-Mart	800	800	0%	0	800	0%
8	XYZ	Wal-Mart	500	1000	-100%	500	1000	50%
9	DEF	Molson, Inc	700	870	-24%	170	870	20%
10	XYZ	Exxon	400	500	-25%	100	500	20%
11	ABC	Ford	200	100	50%	100	200	50%
12	DEF	Sun Life Financial	600	589	2%	11	600	2%
13	ABC	SBC Communicatic	800	802	0%	2	802	0%
14	ABC	IBM	100	122	-22%	22	122	18%
15	XYZ	General Motors	900	922	-2%	22	922	2%
16	DEF	Ford	800	850	-6%	50	850	6%
17	XYZ	Texaco	400	450	-13%	50	450	11%
18			7100	7905	-11%	1887	8446	22%

Fig. 460

Summary: This started out as a tutorial on using ABS and MAX functions, but turned into a sermon on the best way to calculate forecast accuracy. Note that I am currently the only guy I know who calculates accuracy this way. When I bounce it off the pros at forecasting conventions, they reject this method. So, if you are doing forecasting, feel free to use this method at your own risk.

Functions Discussed: =ABS(); =MAX()

ROUND PRICES TO NEXT HIGHEST $5

Problem: You handle pricing for a company. You have a spreadsheet showing your cost per SKU, as shown in Fig. 461. Your manager tells you to take the current manufacturing cost for each item, multiply by 2, add $3, and then round up to the next highest multiple of 5.

	A	B
1	SKU	Mfg Cost
2	A409	209.03
3	A322	157.98
4	A356	18.97
5	A460	88.38
6	A976	165.08
7	A764	134.16
8	A865	71.02

Fig. 461

Part II

Strategy: The first portion of this calculation is fairly easy. The formula in C2 shows the manufacturing cost multiplied by 2 with an additional $3, as shown in Fig. 462.

C2		fx	=B2*2+3

	A	B	C
1	SKU	Mfg Cost	List Price
2	A409	209.03	421.06
3	A322	157.98	318.96
4	A356	18.97	40.94
5	A460	88.38	179.76
6	A976	165.08	333.16

Fig. 462

How do you round up to the nearest $5? You can use the CEILING function. This function takes one number and the number to round up to. =CEILING(421,5) will result in a 425, as shown in Fig. 463. The answer is always higher than the original number.

D2		fx	=CEILING(C2,5)

	A	B	C	D
1	SKU	Mfg Cost	Part 1	List Price
2	A409	209.03	421.06	425
3	A322	157.98	318.96	320
4	A356	18.97	40.94	45
5	A460	88.38	179.76	180
6	A976	165.08	333.16	335
7	A764	134.16	271.32	275
8	A865	71.02	145.04	150
9	A628	94.52	192.04	195
10	A196	190.05	383.1	385

Fig. 463

Additional Information: There is also a FLOOR function. With the FLOOR function, the number would be rounded down to the nearest multiple of 5.

Gotcha: Both CEILING and FLOOR require the Analysis toolpack to be installed.

Summary: The Ceiling function will round a number up to the nearest increment.

Functions Discussed: =CEILING(); =FLOOR()

WHY IS THIS PRICE SHOWING $27.85000001 CENTS?

Problem: You have a worksheet in which you expect the cells to show dollars and cents. For some reason, a price in the formula bar is showing a few millionths of a dollar, as shown in Fig. 464.

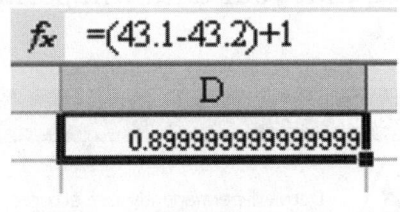

Fig. 464

Strategy: These stray values can happen due to something called floating-point arithmetic. Although you think in tens, computers actually calculate with twos, fours, eights, and sixteens. Excel has to convert your prices to sixteens, do the math, and then present it to you in tenths. A simple number like 0.1 in a base-10 system is actually a repeating number in binary.

Sometimes these seemingly bizarre rounding errors creep in. There is one quick solution, but you have to be careful when using it.

1) Format your prices to have two decimal places, as shown in Fig. 465.

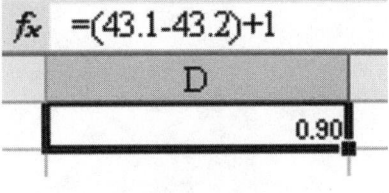

Fig. 465

2)   As shown in Fig. 466, from the menu, select Tools – Options –
      Calculate – Precision as Displayed. Excel will immediately trun-
      cate all values to only the number of decimals shown.

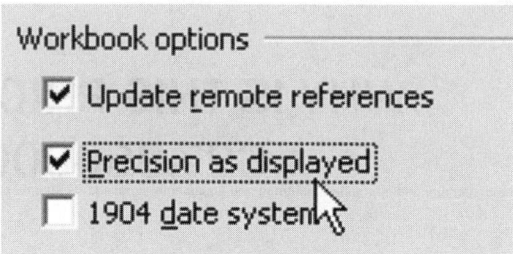

Fig. 466

Gotcha: There is neither Undo nor any way to regain those last numbers. Excel will warn you that your data will permanently lose accuracy,
as shown in Fig. 467.

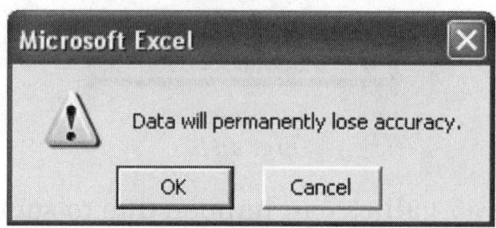

Fig. 467

Summary: If you have annoying floating-point errors in your data, you
can turn on Precision as Displayed. You should exercise caution when
using this option because it will permanently change the values of all
numbers in your workbook.

Commands Discussed: Tools – Options – Calculate – Precision as
Displayed

YOU CHANGE A CELL IN EXCEL
BUT THE FORMULAS DO NOT CALCULATE

Problem: You change a cell in Excel but the formulas do not calculate. As shown in Fig. 468, cell D2 indicates that two plus two is not four.

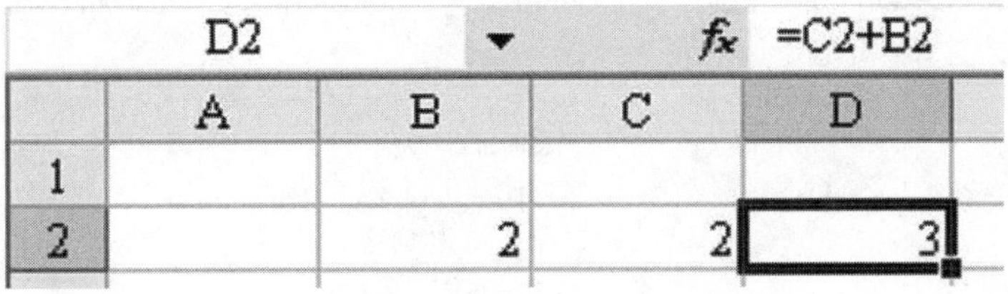

Fig. 468

Part II

Strategy: Someone put the worksheet in manual calculation mode. Try hitting F9 to calculate, as shown in Fig. 469.

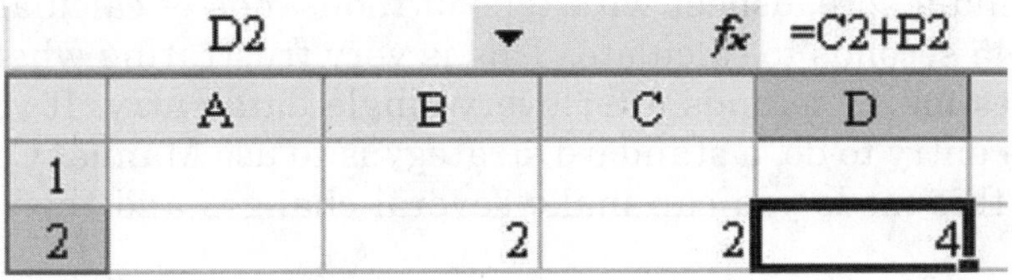

Fig. 469

- Pressing F9 will recalculate all cells that have changed since the last calculation, plus all formulas dependent on those cells in all open workbooks.

- For quicker calculation, use Shift+F9. This will limit the calculation to the current worksheet.

- For thorough calculation, use Ctrl+Alt+F9. This calculates all formulas in all open workbooks, whether Excel thinks they have changed or not.

- Finally, there is the Ctrl+Shift+Alt+F9. This will rebuild the list of dependent formulas and then do a thorough calculation.

Additional Details: Manual Calculation mode can be changed for a workbook. Go to Tools – Options – Calculation to see the various calculation options, as shown in Fig. 470.

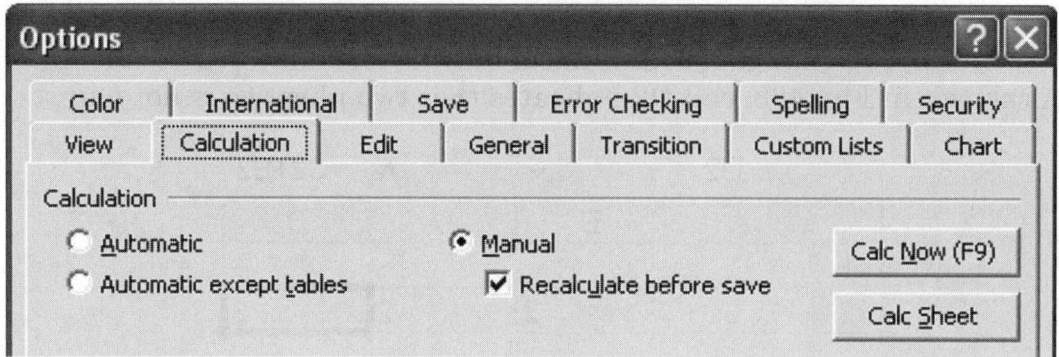

Fig. 470

Gotcha: Before you go back to Automatic mode, ask the person who created the worksheet why it is in Manual Calculation mode. Sometimes you will find a spreadsheet with tens of thousands of calculations that takes 30-45 seconds to calculate. This is very frustrating when the system pauses for 45 seconds after every single data entry. If you have a lot of data entry to do, a standard strategy is to use Manual Calculation mode. In this mode you can make several changes and then hit F9 to calculate.

Summary: Be aware that Excel offers a manual calculation mode. If you have a spreadsheet that takes too long to calculate after every data entry, you might consider using Manual Calculation mode temporarily, doing the data entry, and then switching back to Automatic Calculation mode.

Commands Discussed: F9 to calculate; Tools – Options – Calculate

USE PARENTHESES TO CONTROL
ORDER OF CALCULATIONS

Problem: In what order does Excel perform calculations? Is 2+3*4 equal to 20 or 14?

Strategy: Understand the default Excel order of calculations. If you do not use parentheses, the order is as follows:

1. Unary minus operation

2. Exponents

3. Multiply and divide left to right

4. Add and subtract left to right

Thus, if you had the formula =5+4*–5T3/6, Excel would do the following:

1. Figure unary minus on –5.

2. Raise –5 to the third power (–5*–5*–5 = –125).

3. Do division and multiplication from left to right (4*–125 is –500. Then –500/6 is –83.3).

4. Add 5 (–83.3 + 5 is –78.3).

The answer will be –78.3.

You can control the order of operations by using parentheses. For example, the formula =(5+4)*–(5T(1/2)) will give an answer of –20.1246, as shown in Fig. 471.

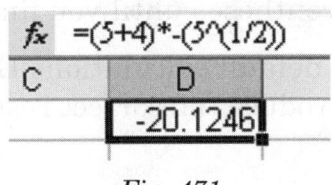

Fig. 471

Additional Details: In math class, you may have been taught that if you need to nest parentheses, start from the inside out using normal parenthesis, then square brackets, and then curly braces. In math class, you might have written:

{(5+4)*[–5*(3/6)]}+3

Forget all of that. In Excel, you use regular parentheses throughout.

((5+4)*(–5*(3/6)))+3

When I get the formula error message, as shown in Fig. 472, it is almost always because I've missed a closing parenthesis somewhere.

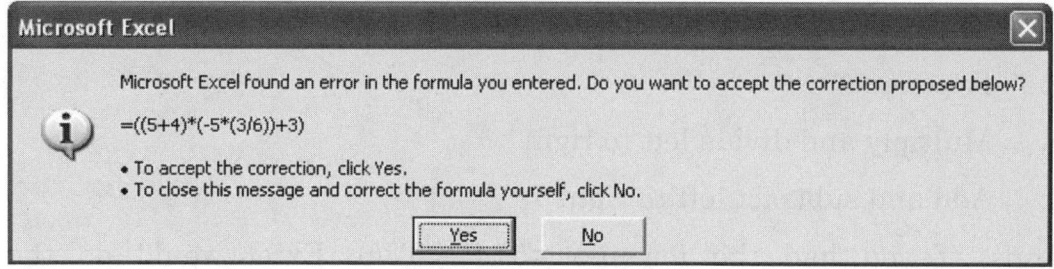

Fig. 472

In theory, as you enter or edit the formula, when you type a closing parenthesis, Excel bolds the corresponding opening parenthesis. However, this bolded condition lasts for only a moment and disappears before you can figure out what is going on. Fig. 473 was taken during the fleeting moment when the first and eighth parentheses were in bold.

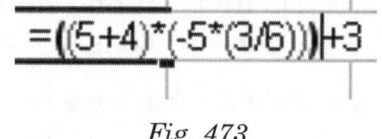

Fig. 473

Alternate Strategy: For a very confusing formula with many sets of parentheses, use this technique. Highlight the formula in the formula bar. Use Ctrl+C to copy the formula. Paste it to a blank Notepad or Wordpad window and print. Use different colored highlighters to match up the various sets of parentheses until you find the extra parentheses.

Summary: Based on the default calculations Excel uses, placing parenthesis in a formula will produce the correct results.

BEFORE DELETING A CELL, FIND OUT IF OTHER CELLS RELY ON IT

Problem: You are about to delete a section of the worksheet that you believe is no longer being used. However, you know that if you delete the cell and some other far-off range relies on the cell, the far-off range will change to the dreaded #REF! error. How can you determine if any other range refers to this cell?

Strategy: Select the cell that you are considering for deletion. From the menu, select Tools – Formula Auditing – Trace Dependents as shown in Fig. 474. Dependents are other cells that rely on the current cell for calculation.

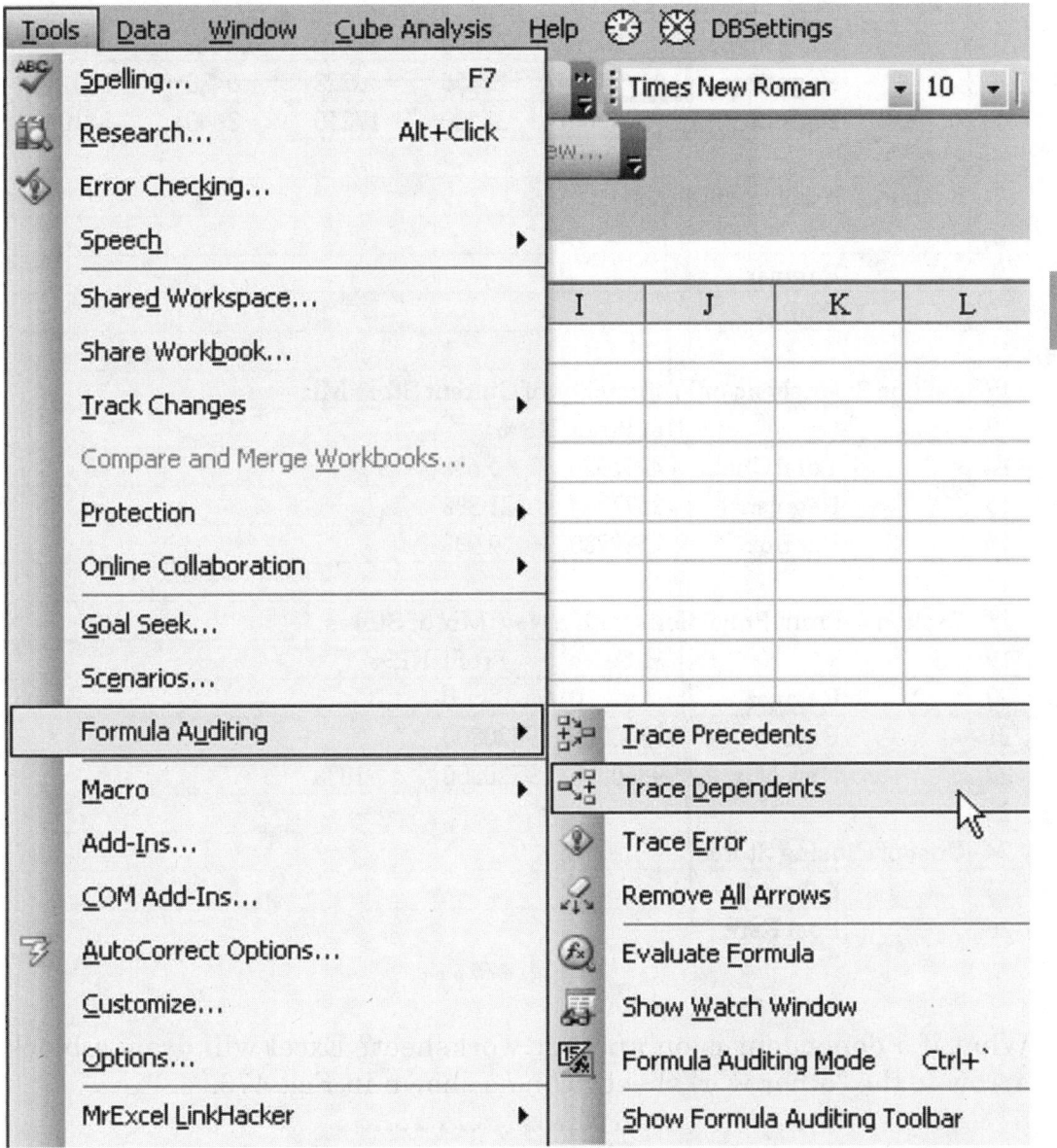

Fig. 474

Blue arrows will draw from the active cell out to any dependents. In Fig. 475, cell D4 is used to calculate H4, and also a hidden cell in C26.

	A	B	D	E	F	G	H
1	Section 1: Historical Trends (Per Month)						
2							
3		Store Type	Rent	Sales	Profit	Labor	Net
4		Regular	2400	12456	6228	6480	-2652
5		BigBox	5200	34500	17250	8640	3410
6							
7	Section 2: Number of Stores						
8							
9		Regular					
10		BigBox					
11							
12	Section 3: Analysis of Profitability of Current Store Mix						
13			Net Profit	NP%			
14		Total Chain	4951536	5.6%			
15		Regular	-2577744	-21.3%			
16		Big Box	7529280	9.9%			
17							
18	Section 4: Profit Projections with a New Mix of Stores						
19			Sales	Profit	NP%		
20		Regular	0	0			
21		BigBox	99360000	9820800			
22		New Mix	99360000	9820800	10%		
23							
24	Cost of Closing Stores						
25		Labor					
26		Lost Rent					

Fig. 475

What if a dependent is on another worksheet? Excel will draw a black arrow to the "other worksheet" icon as shown in Fig. 476.

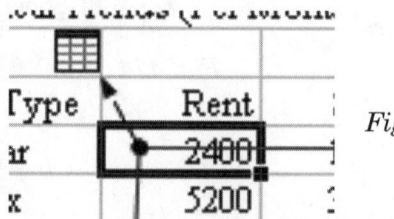

Fig. 476

Gotcha: Of course, it does not tell you *which* other worksheet has a dependent.

Additional Details: If you immediately invoke Tools – Formula Auditing – Trace Dependents, Excel will draw arrows from each of the dependent cells to their dependent cells. In Fig. 477, D4 is used to calculate H4. H4 is then used to calculate D15 and H20.

	A	B	D	E	F	G	H	I
1	Section 1: Historical Trends (Per Month)							
2								
3		Store Type	Rent	Sales	Profit	Labor	Net	
4		Regular	2400	12456	6228	6480	-2652	
5		BigBox	5200	34500	17250	8640	3410	
6								
7	Section 2: Number of Stores							
8								
9		Regular						
10		BigBox						
11								
12	Section 3: Analysis of Profitability of Current Store Mix							
13			Net Profit	NP%				
14		Total Chain	4951536	5.6%				
15		Regular	-2577744	-21.3%				
16		Big Box	7529280	9.9%				
17								
18	Section 4: Profit Projections with a New Mix of Stores							
19			Sales	Profit	NP%			
20		Regular	0	0				
21		BigBox	99360000	9820800				
22		New Mix	99360000	9820800	10%			
23								
24	Cost of Closing Stores							
25		Labor						
26		Lost Rent						
27				Year 1	Year 2	Year 3	Year 4	Yea
28	Increased Profit from New Stores			4869264	4869264	4869264	4869264	48692
29	Costs in year 1		1176120	0	0	0		

Fig. 477

Part II

If you immediately ask to Trace Dependents several times in a row, you will see all of the formulas that would change to #REF! if you delete cell C4.

You also have a big mess on your spreadsheet! To get rid of all arrows, choose Tools – Formula Auditing – Remove All Arrows.

Additional Information: If you think that there are no cells that use the current cell and you are right, then Excel will give you thes message shown in Fig. 478.

	A	B	C	D	E	F	G	H	I
1	Section 1: Historical Trends (Per Month)								
2									
3		Store Type	Size	Rent	Sales	Profit	Labor	Net	
4		Regular	1200	2400	12456	6228	6480	-2652	
5		BigBox	2600	5200	34500	17250	8640	3410	
6									
7	Section								
8									
9									
10									
11									
12	Section								
13									

Microsoft Excel

The Trace Dependents command found no formulas that refer to the active cell.

OK

Fig. 478

Summary: To determine if a cell can be deleted without affecting any other formulas, select the cell, and then select Tools – Formula Auditing – Trace Dependents.

Commands Discussed: Tools – Formula Auditing – Trace Dependents

NAVIGATE TO EACH PRECEDENT

Problem: A tip of the hat to Howard Krams in New York for this tip. Howard uses huge massive spreadsheets with formulas that have a dozen precedents. He discovered an obscure way to navigate to each precedent on the current worksheet.

Strategy: The trick only works if you turn off the "in-cell editing" feature. As shown in Fig. 479, this is on Tools – Options – Edit, the top item on the left side.

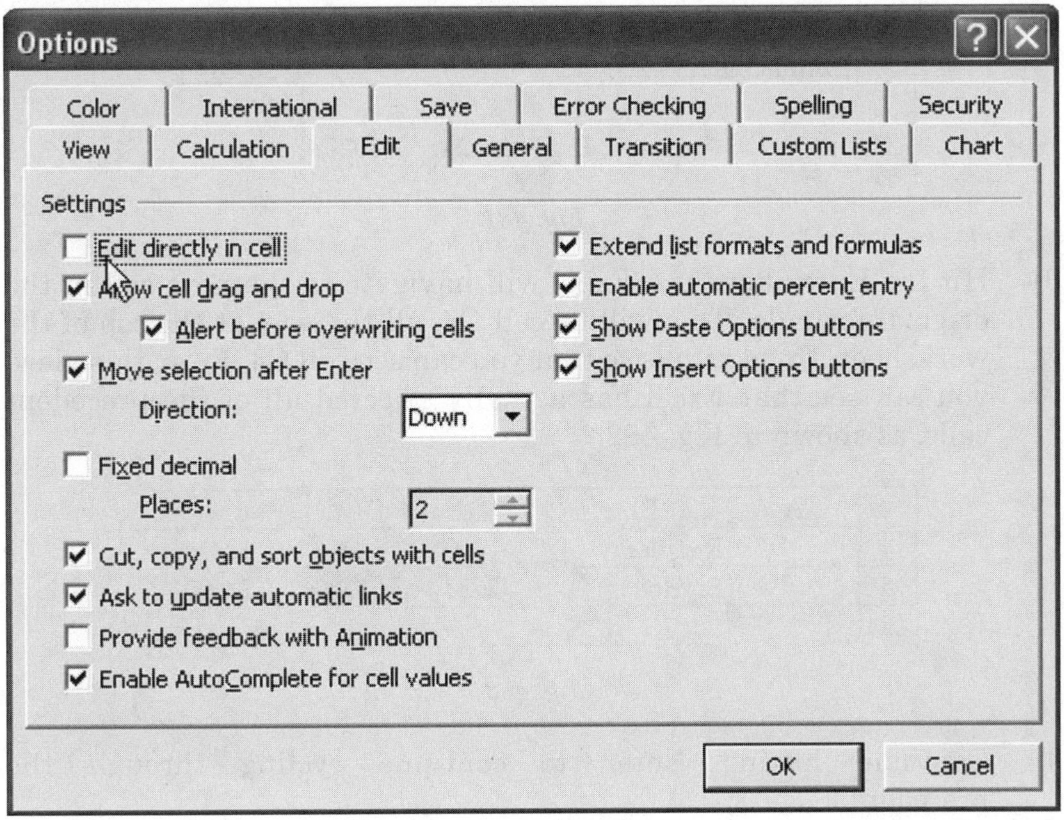

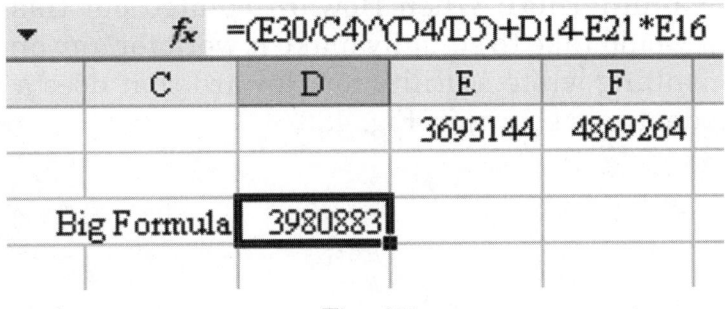

Fig. 479

Part
II

1)   Turn off the Edit Directly in Cell option. You can then go to any cell with a formula, as shown in Fig. 480.

	f_x	=(E30/C4)^(D4/D5)+D14-E21*E16		
	C	D	E	F
			3693144	4869264
	Big Formula	3980883		

Fig. 480

2) Double-click the cell with the mouse. Excel moves to the first cell in the original formula. In this case, as shown in Fig. 481, that is cell E30, just a couple of rows up.

	A	B	C	D	E
30	Bottom Line				3693144
31					
32			Big Formula	3980883	
33					

Fig. 481

3) Hit the Enter key, and Excel will navigate to the next cell in the original formula. This will be cell C4, all the way at the top of the worksheet. Excel scrolls so that you can see cell C4. From this view, you can see that Excel has actually selected all of the precedent cells, as shown in Fig. 482.

	A	B	C	D	E
4		Regular	1200	2400	12456
5		BigBox	2600	5200	34500
6					

Fig. 482

4) Continue hitting Enter to continue cycling through the precedents.

Gotcha: This feature was added to Excel back in Excel version 4. This was the last Excel version with only one worksheet in a workbook. They never dreamt of supporting precedents on other worksheets. So – this technique will not navigate to precedents on other sheets.

Shameless Commercial: When Howard pointed out this feature, he asked what it would take to actually make it work for any and all sheets. MrExcel Consulting wrote a utility for Howard that does a great job of tracing precedents, as shown in Fig. 483.

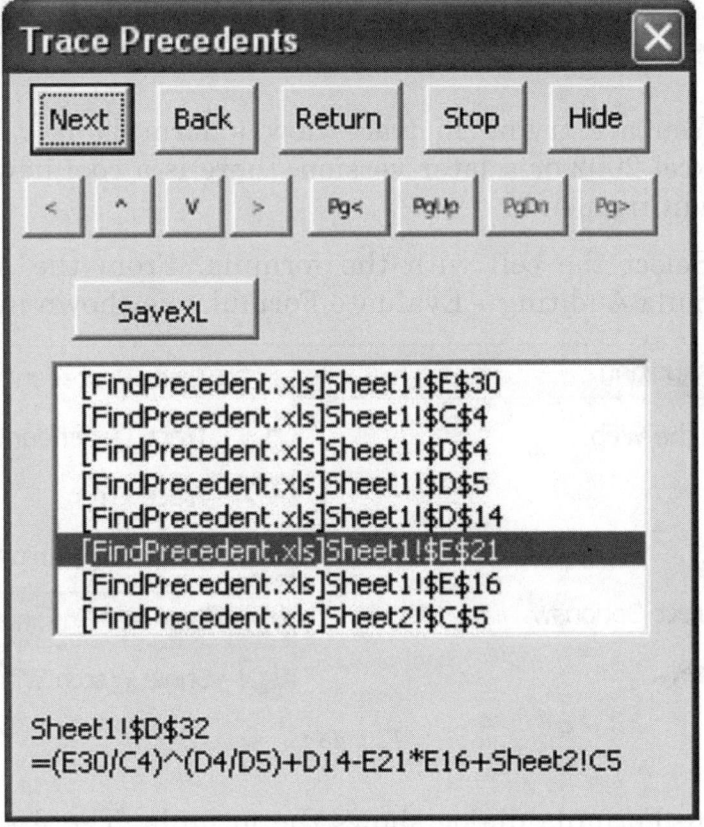

Fig. 483

It lists all of the precedents, even precedents on other worksheets or in other open workbooks. You can use Next/Prev to move that particular precedent to the middle of the screen. If you are someone who needs to be able to track precedents, write to MrExcel Consulting to buy this utility.

Summary: There is an obscure feature in Excel that lets you navigate to all precedents of a formula. It works fairly well for precedents on the current worksheet.

Commands Discussed: Tools – Options – Edit – Edit In Cell

FORMULA AUDITING

Problem: You are trying to trace how a formula is calculating. If you have Excel 2002 or a later version, there is a cool new tool on the Formula Auditing menu.

Strategy: Select the cell with the formula. From the menu, select Tools – Formula Auditing – Evaluate Formula, as shown in Fig. 484.

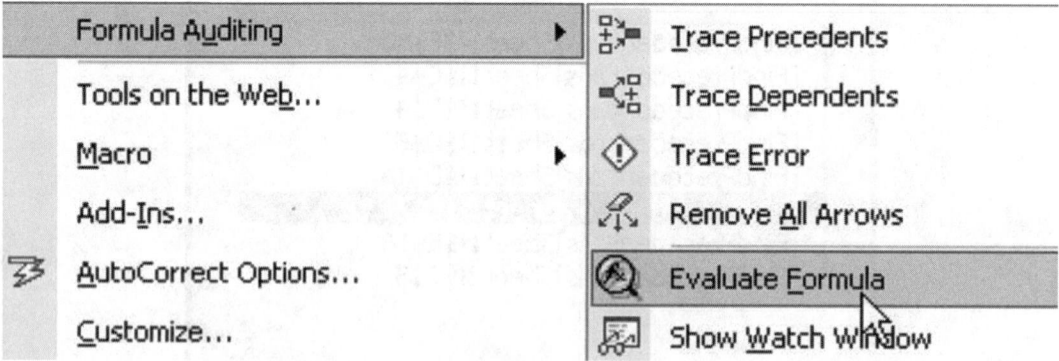

Fig. 484

The Evaluate Formula dialog shows the formula. The first item to be calculated is underlined, as shown in Fig. 485. Click Evaluate to calculate the underlined portion of the formula.

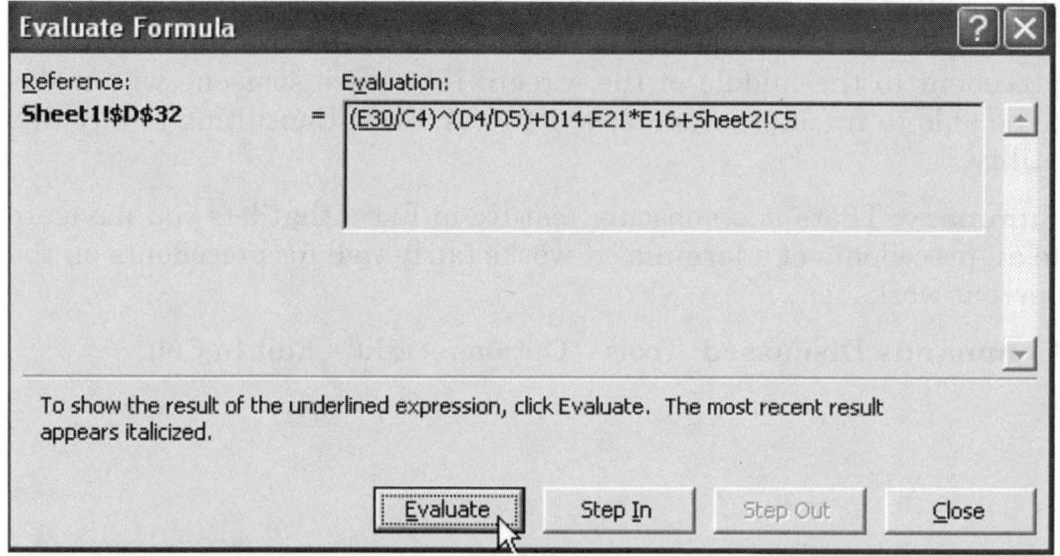

Fig. 485

With each click of Evaluate, Excel will calculate the underlined portion and show the results in italics. It will underline the next step in the calculation. Fig. 486 is after the second Evaluate. Excel just revealed that C4 is 1200 (in italics). It is about to calculate the first division in parentheses.

Fig. 486

Additional Information: Any time that the next term to be calculated is a cell reference, you can choose the Step In button to evaluate the formula in that cell. In Fig. 487, choosing Step In will evaluate D14.

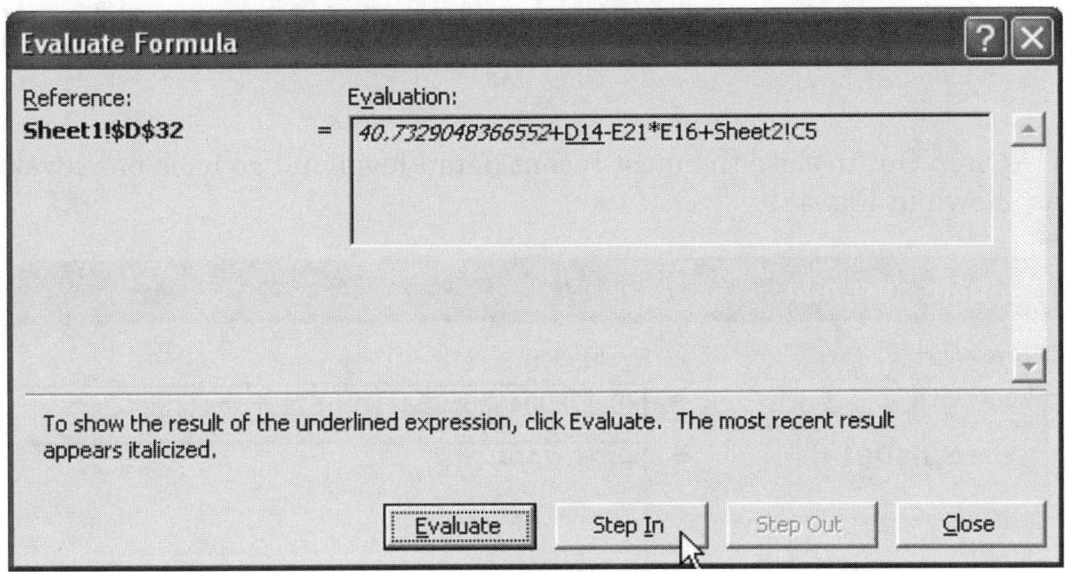

Fig. 487

As shown in Fig. 488, it is possible to Step In several levels. After seeing the formula for D14, you can choose to Step In to see the formula for D15.

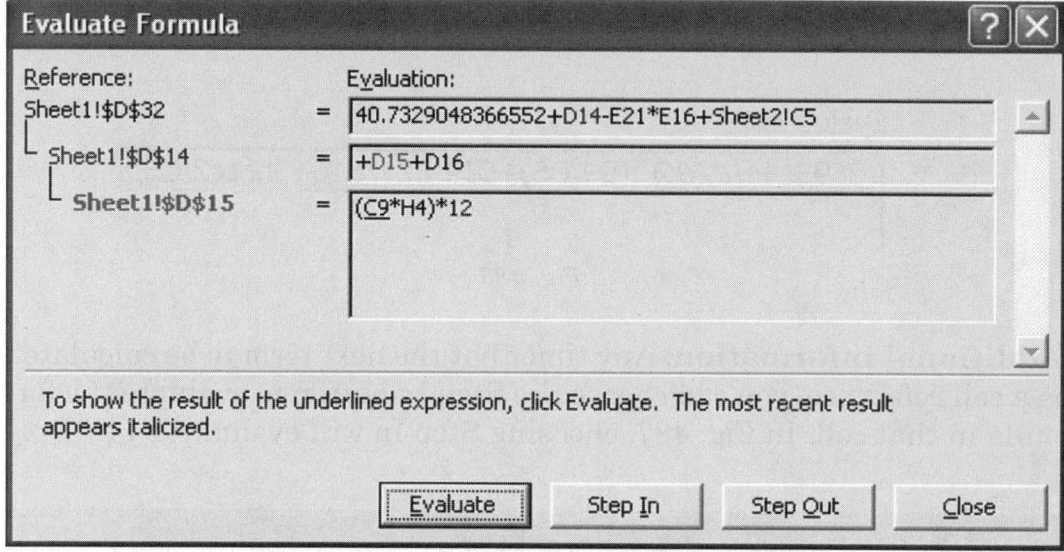

Fig. 488

Use Step Out to close the most recent detail level and go back one level, as shown in Fig. 489.

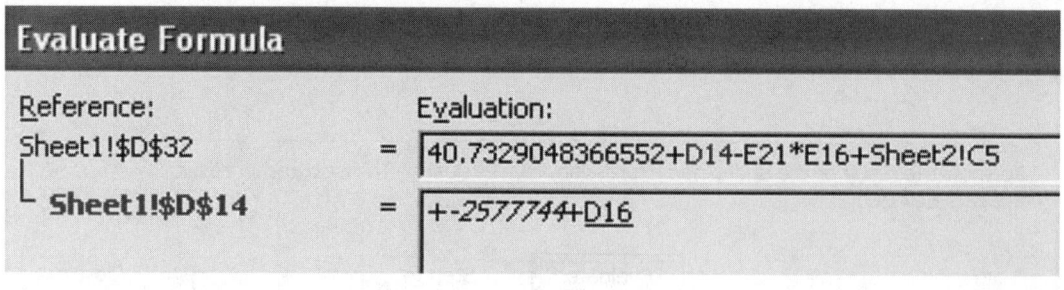

Fig. 489

Summary: This feature is a great tool. It basically gives you a great appreciation of just how much work Excel does every time you enter a formula, because it allows you to watch the calculation happen in slow motion.

Commands Discussed: Tools – Formula Auditing – Evaluate Formula

HOW IS THIS CELL CALCULATED?

Problem: You have a large formula. You would like to visually see how the cell is calculated.

Strategy: There are a few options.

Option 1: Select the cell. Hit F2 to edit the cell, as shown in Fig. 490.

COUNTA	▼ ✕ ✓ *fx* =(E30/C4)^(D4/D5)+D14-E21*E16+Sheet2!C5

	A	B	C	D	E	F	G	H
12		Section 3: Analysis of Profitability of Current Store Mix						
13			Sales	Net Profit	NP%			
14		Total Chain	88283232	4951536	5.6%			
15		Regular	12107232	-2577744	-21.3%			
16		Big Box	76176000	7529280	9.9%			
17								
18		Section 4: Profit Projections with a New Mix of Stores						
19				Sales	Profit	NP%		
20		Regular	0	0	0			
21		BigBox	240	99360000	9820800			
22		New Mix	240	99360000	9820800	10%		
23								
24		Cost of Closing Stores						
25		Labor	787320					
26		Lost Rent	388800					
27					Year 1	Year 2	Year 3	Year 4
28		Increased Profit from New Stores			4869264	4869264	4869264	4869264
29		Costs in year 1			1176120	0	0	0
30		Bottom Line			3693144	4869264	4869264	4869264
31								
32			Big Formula	Sheet2!C5				

Fig. 490

As shown in Fig. 490, all of the references in the formula bar will light up with different colors. If the precedent cell is in the visible portion of the window, the cell will be surrounded by a box of the same color as the formula. You can't tell from this black and white book but, in the formula bar, cell E30 is a bright blue. The box around cell E30 is a matching blue. Cell C4 is a dark green. You cannot see C4 in the visible worksheet, so there is no matching dark green cell. Cell D14 is a light green in the formula bar. The box around D14 is a matching green. The final term of the formula points to an off-sheet reference. This term appears black in the formula bar.

Additional Information: If you need something more permanent than this, you can use Formula Auditing to draw the blue arrows to all of the precedent cells. Select cell D32. From the menu, choose Tools – Formula Auditing – Trace Precedents. Blue arrows draw to all the cells that are referenced in the D32 formula. As shown near the bottom left of Fig. 491, the arrow to the sheet icon indicates that at least one reference is on another worksheet.

B	C	D	E
Type	Size	Rent	Sales
.ar	1200	2400	12456
)x	2600	5200	34500
2: Number of Stores			
.ar	81		
)x	184		
3: Analysis of Profitability of Current St			
	Sales	Net Profit	NP%
Chain	88283232	4951536	5.6%
.ar	12107232	-2577744	-21.3%
ox	76176000	7529280	9.9%
4: Profit Projections with a New Mix of S			
		Sales	Profit
.ar	0	0	0
)x	240	99360000	9820800
Mix	240	99360000	9820800
Closing Stores			
.	787320		
Rent	388800		
			Year 1
d Profit from New Stores			4869264
year 1			1176120
Line			3693144
Big Formula	3980883		

Fig. 491

If you immediately Trace Precedents enough times, Excel will trace the precedents of all the arrowed cells. After a few iterations of the command, you will see all of the cells that factor in to the calculation, as shown in Fig. 492.

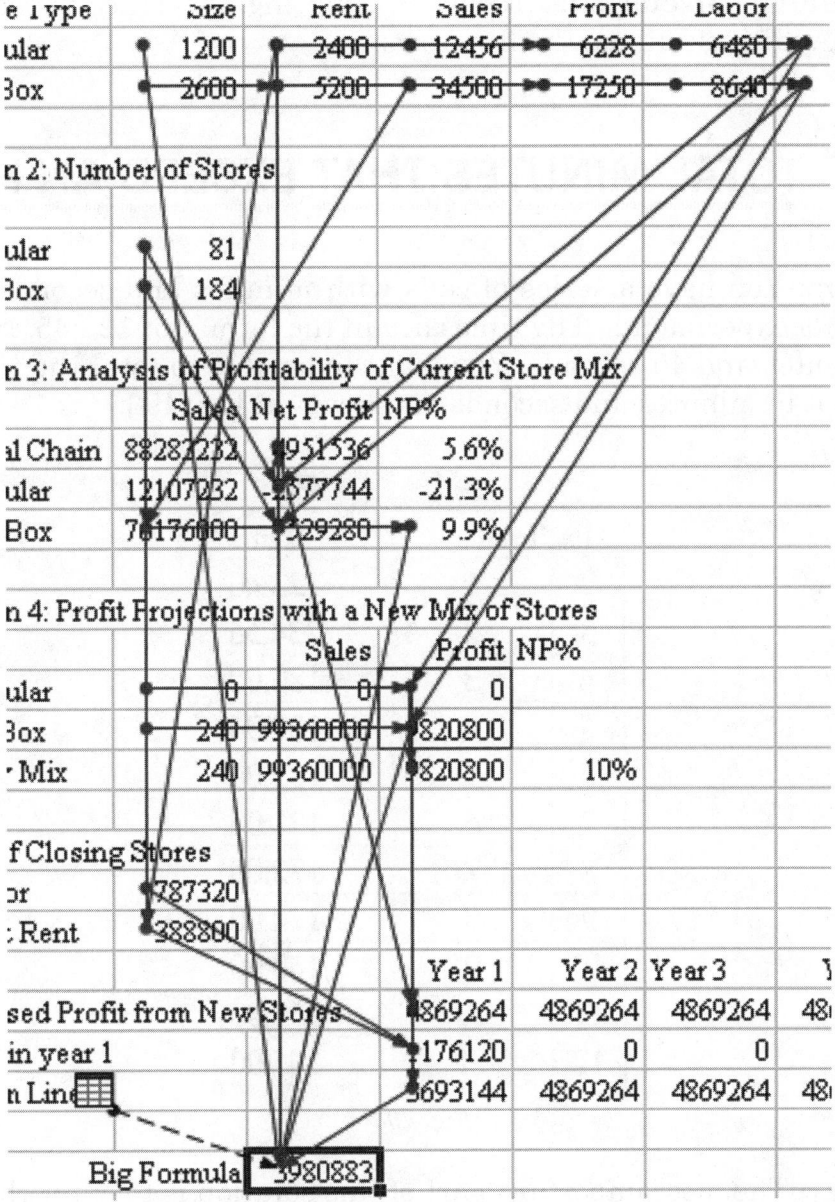

Fig. 492

To remove all of the arrows, choose Tools – Formula Auditing – Remove All Arrows.

Summary: Tracing Precedents gives you a quick visual view of all the cells that are used to calculate a formula.

Commands Discussed: Tools – Auditing – Trace Precedents; Tools – Auditing – Remove All Arrows

TOTAL MINUTES THAT EXCEED AN HOUR

Problem: You have a series of cells with minutes and seconds from a number of experiments. The times are in the format of 123:45, meaning 123 minutes and 45 seconds. You want to be able to total the time and express it in minutes and seconds, as shown in Fig. 493.

	A	B
1	Trial	Time
2	1	123:40
3	2	234:56
4	3	180:02
5	4	129:04
6	5	132:00
7	6	131:00
8	7	172:00
9	8	174:00
10	9	140:00
11	10	153:00
12	11	145:00

Fig. 493

Strategy: The most important part of this solution is to enter the times correctly. In order to have Excel understand that these are minutes and seconds, time should be entered with a leading zero for hours.

1) Enter 0:123:40, as shown in Fig. 494.

	A	B
1	Trial	Time
2	1	0:123:40
3	2	

Fig. 494

2) When you press Enter to accept the cell, Excel will change the value to a decimal portion of a day, as shown in Fig. 495.

	A	B
1	Trial	Time
2	1	0.08588

Fig. 495

3) Select the cell and from the menu, choose Format – Cells. On the Number tab, click the Custom Number format, as shown in Fig. 496.

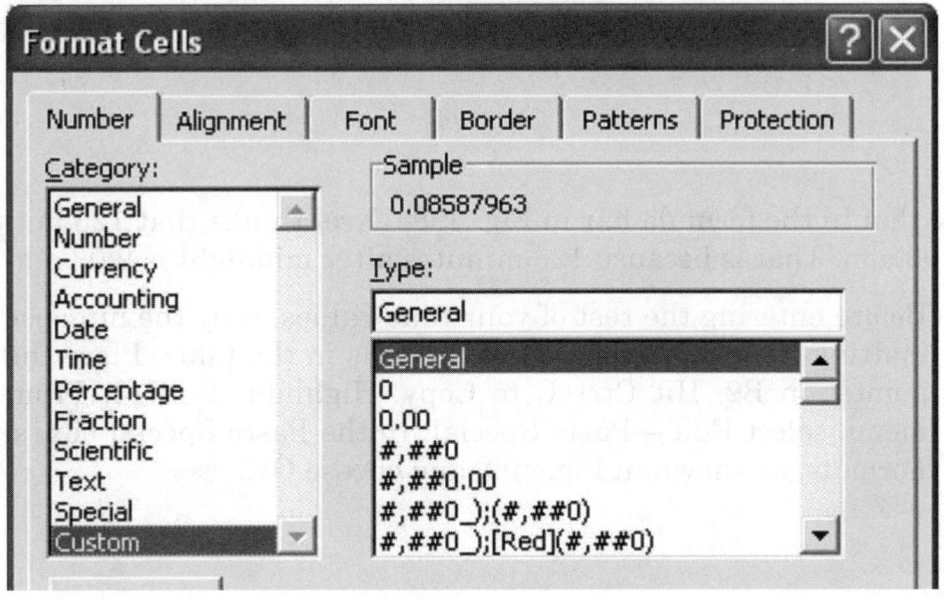

Fig. 496

4) In the Type box, change the Custom Number format from General to [m]:ss, as shown in Fig. 497. You will see in the Sample box that the entry is now formatted with just minutes and seconds. The square brackets tell Excel to display minutes in excess of an hour.

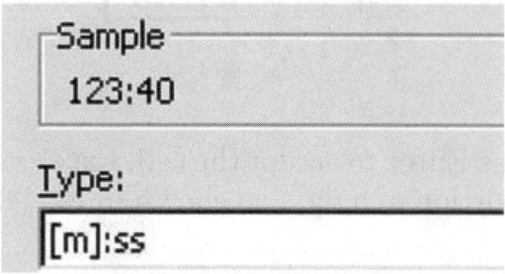

Fig. 497

5) Choose OK to close the Format Cells box. Your entry in B2 will appear correctly, as shown in Fig. 498.

	A	B	C	D	
1	Trial	Time			
2	1	123:40			
3	2				

B2   ▼   *fx*   2:03:40 AM

Fig. 498

Note that in the formula bar in Fig. 498, Excel thinks that 123 minutes is 2:03 a.m. That is because 123 minutes after midnight is 2:03 a.m.

6) Before entering the rest of your time values, copy the numeric formatting from B2 to the rest of the cells in the table. Place the cell pointer in B2. Hit Ctrl+C to Copy. Highlight B3:B14. From the menu, select Edit – Paste Special. In the Paste Special box, select Formats, as shown in Fig. 499, and choose OK.

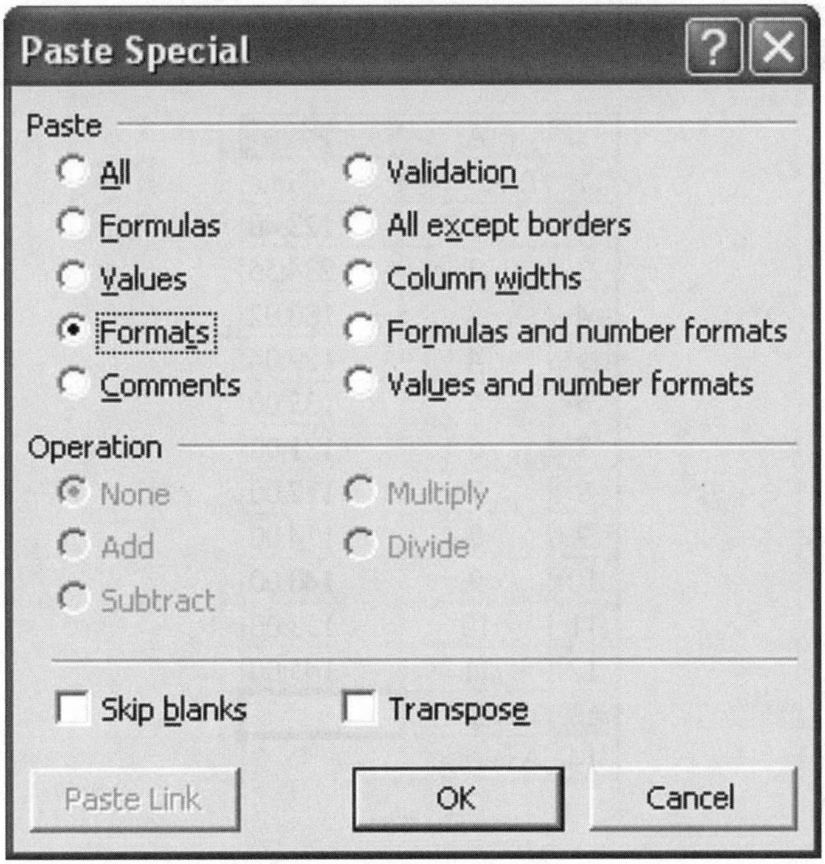

Fig. 499

Part
II

7)   You can now enter the remaining times, using the 0:234:56 format as you type, as shown in Fig. 500.

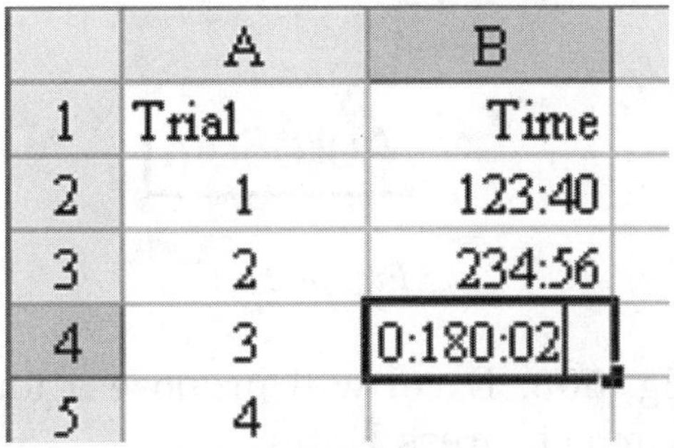

Fig. 500

8) After entering all of the time entries, place the cell pointer in the Total row, as shown in Fig. 501.

	A	B
1	Trial	Time
2	1	123:40
3	2	234:56
4	3	180:02
5	4	129:04
6	5	132:00
7	6	131:00
8	7	172:00
9	8	174:00
10	9	140:00
11	10	153:00
12	11	145:00
13	Total	
14	Average	

Fig. 501

9) In the Standard toolbar, click the AutoSum button, as shown in Fig. 502.

Fig. 502

10) As shown in Fig. 503, Excel will propose a formula of =SUM(B2: B12). If this is correct, press Enter.

	A	B	C	D
1	Trial	Time		
2	1	123:40		
3	2	234:56		
4	3	180:02		
5	4	129:04		
6	5	132:00		
7	6	131:00		
8	7	172:00		
9	8	174:00		
10	9	140:00		
11	10	153:00		
12	11	145:00		
13	Total	=SUM(B2:B12)		
14	Average	SUM(**number1**, [number2], …)		
15				

Fig. 503

11) Verify that the correct total appears, as shown in Fig. 504.

	A	B
1	Trial	Time
2	1	123:40
3	2	234:56
4	3	180:02
5	4	129:04
6	5	132:00
7	6	131:00
8	7	172:00
9	8	174:00
10	9	140:00
11	10	153:00
12	11	145:00
13	Total	1714:42

Fig. 504

Gotcha: Be very careful that the total cell is formatted with the square brackets around the M. If the square brackets are not around the M, Excel will show you only the minutes in excess of whole hours. In the case above, 1714 minutes is 28 hours and 34 minutes. With the wrong number format, you would see only 34 minutes and 42 seconds.

As shown in Fig. 505, the formula for an average time in B14 is:

=AVERAGE(B2:B12)

	B14	▼	*fx*	=AVERAGE(B2:B12)	
	A	B	C	D	E
1	Trial	Time			
2	1	123:40			
3	2	234:56			
4	3	180:02			
5	4	129:04			
6	5	132:00			
7	6	131:00			
8	7	172:00			
9	8	174:00			
10	9	140:00			
11	10	153:00			
12	11	145:00			
13	Total	1714:42			
14	Average	155:53			

Fig. 505

Summary: The formula to total a column of time entries is intuitive. However, using the proper numeric formats to allow the formula to work is very complex. The key is to use a custom number format with square brackets around the M. Also, you need to enter the times using 0 for the hours.

Commands Discussed: Format – Cells – Numeric

Functions Discussed: =SUM(); =AVERAGE()

CONVERT TEXT TO MINUTES AND SECONDS

Problem: Someone in another department set up a spreadsheet with hundreds of time values. However, instead of using Excel time formats, they entered each cell as text, as shown in Fig. 506. How can you convert the text entries to real Excel times?

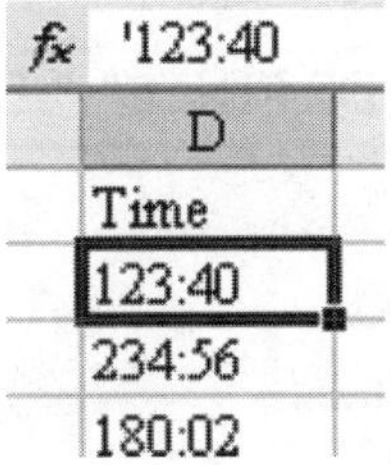

Fig. 506

Strategy: Use the TIME function. This function requires three arguments: hours, minutes, and seconds. The function will handle normal times, such as =TIME(1,23,40), which will return 1:23 a.m. with 40 seconds. It will also handle strange times, such as =TIME(0,123,40), to represent the 123 minutes and 40 seconds, as shown in the first cell above.

You will enter the TIME function in a temporary column next to your data. If there is already data in column E, insert a new column E.

Select the cells in the new column and format them with the proper custom number format. In this case, you need the [m]:ss format discussed in the preceding chapter, "Total Minutes that Exceed an Hour".

The challenge is then to create a formula that will parse the minutes and seconds from the text entry. You will use a series of nested functions.

- =FIND(":",D2) will find and tell you the location of the colon in the text entry. This function, less 1, can be used as the second parameter of the =LEFT function in the next step.

- =LEFT(D2,FIND(":",D2)–1) will return just the minutes portion of the entry in D2. This function can be used for the minutes parameter of the TIME function.

• =RIGHT(D2,2) will return just the seconds portion of the entry in D2. This parameter can be used as the seconds parameter of the TIME function.

1) As shown in Fig. 507, enter the following formula in cell E2: =TIME(0,LEFT(D2,FIND(":",D2)–1),RIGHT(D2,2)). This will have Excel return a time with 0 hours, and the proper number of minutes and seconds from the text entry.

f_x	=TIME(0,LEFT(D2,FIND(":",D2)-1),RIGHT(D2,2))				
	D	E	F	G	H
	Time				
	123:40	123:40			
	234:56				
	180:02				

Fig. 507

2) Double-click the Fill handle in cell E2 to copy the formula down to all of the rows with data in column D, as shown in Fig. 508. The Fill handle is the black square dot in the lower right corner of the cell pointer.

D	E
Time	
123:40	123:40
234:56	234:56
180:02	180:02
129:04	129:04

Fig. 508

Additional Details: Before you can delete column D, you need to change the times in column E from formulas to values. Highlight the cells in column E. Use Ctrl+C to Copy. Without changing the selection, use Edit – Paste Special to display the Paste Special dialog, as shown in Fig. 509. Choose Values and then OK.

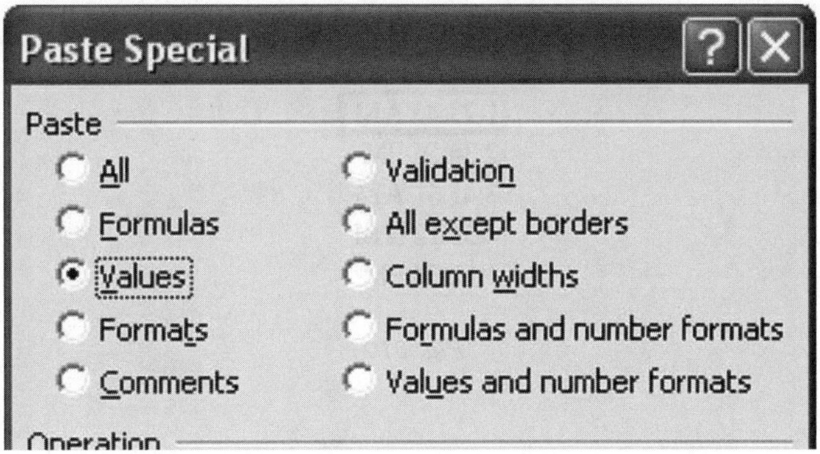

Fig. 509

Summary: The TIME(Hours,Minutes,Seconds) function is very useful in converting text entries to real times. It is critical to have times and dates entered as real Excel times and dates instead of text if you want to do any math with the entries.

Commands Discussed: Format – Cells – Numeric; Edit – Paste Special

Functions Discussed: =TIME(); =LEFT(); =RIGHT()

CONVERT TEXT TO HOURS, MINUTES, AND SECONDS

Problem: Someone in yet another department set up a spreadsheet with hundreds of time values (maybe your company should buy all of these people this book...). However, instead of using Excel time formats, they entered each cell as text with hours, minutes, seconds, and AM or PM, as shown in Fig. 510. How can you convert the text entries to real Excel times?

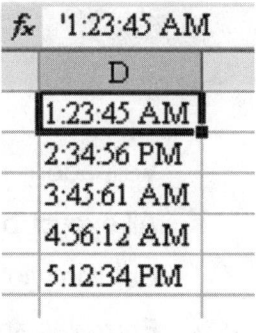

Fig. 510

Strategy:

1) Use the =TIMEVALUE() function. As shown in Fig. 511, this function requires one argument – a text value that looks like a valid time.

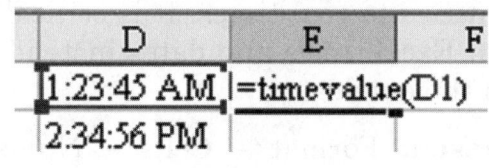

Fig. 511

2) Do not be alarmed when you hit Enter to accept the formula. Excel will normally display the result as the decimal portion of one day, as shown in Fig. 512.

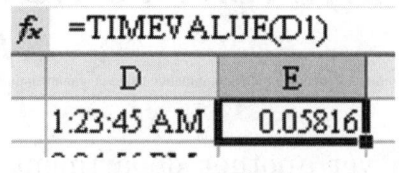

Fig. 512

3) Select the cell. Hit Ctrl+1 to display the Format Cells dialog box. As shown in Fig. 513, on the Number tab, choose an appropriate format from the time section.

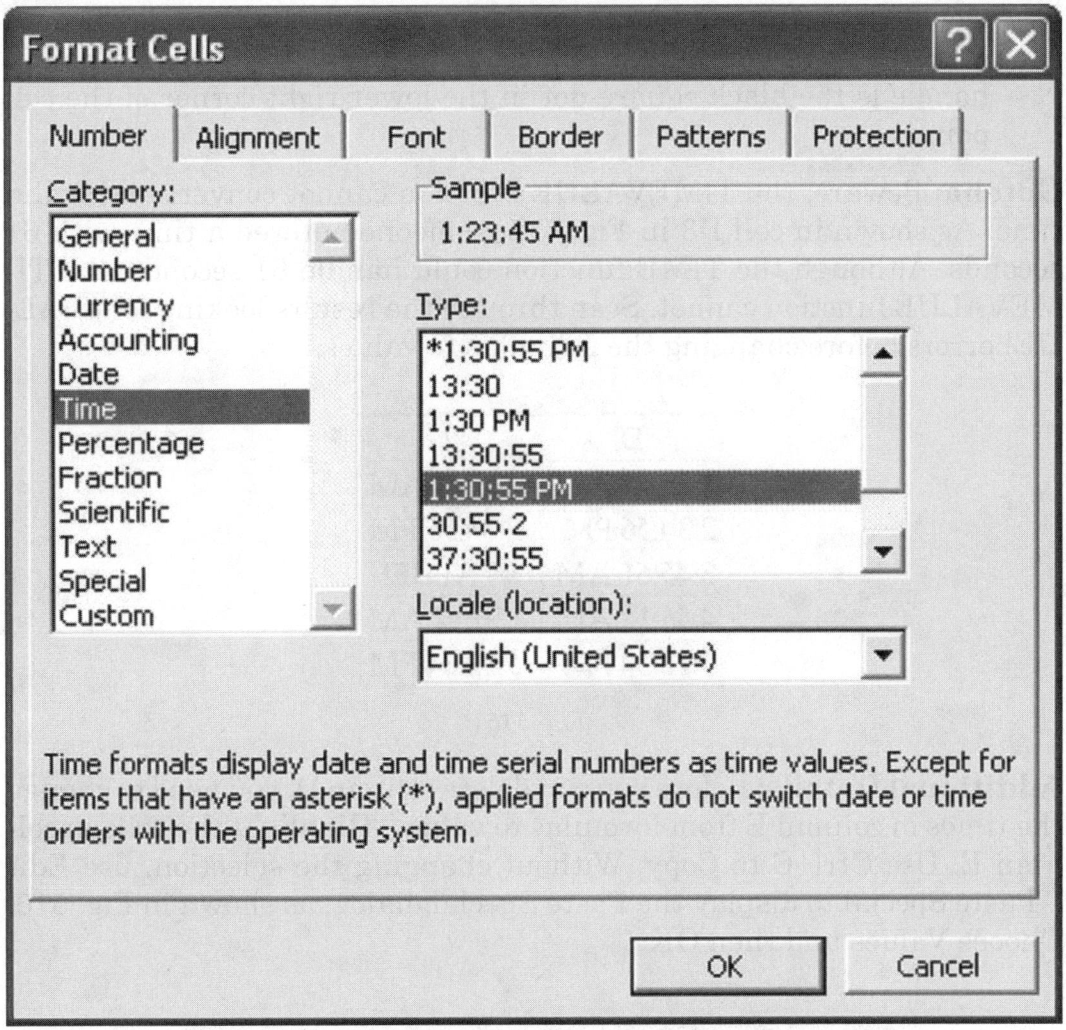

Fig. 513

As shown in Fig. 514, the result of the formula will now look like a real
time.

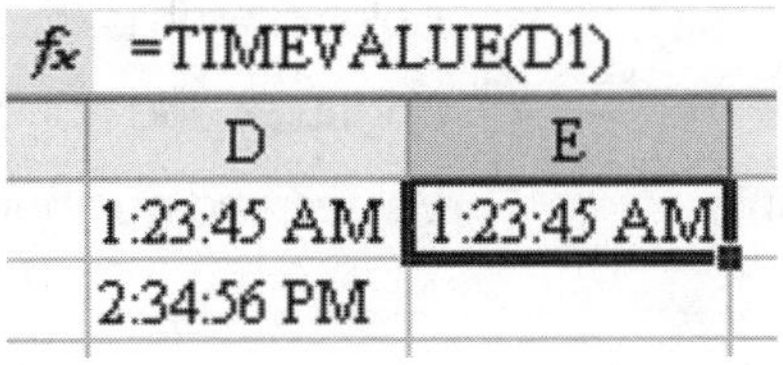

Fig. 514

4)   Double-click the Fill handle in cell E1 to copy the formula down to all of the rows with data in column D, as shown in Fig. 515. The Fill handle is the black square dot in the lower right corner of the cell pointer.

Gotcha: Beware; the TIMEVALUE function cannot convert an invalid time. As shown in cell D3 in Fig. 515, someone entered a time with 61 seconds. Although the TIME function could handle 61 seconds, the TIMEVALUE function cannot. Scan through the results looking for #VALUE! errors before changing the formulas to values.

D	E
1:23:45 AM	1:23:45 AM
2:34:56 PM	2:34:56 PM
3:45:61 AM	#VALUE!
4:56:12 AM	4:56:12 AM
5:12:34 PM	5:12:34 PM

Fig. 515

Additional Details: Before you can delete column D, you need to change the times in column E from formulas to values. Highlight the cells in column E. Use Ctrl+C to Copy. Without changing the selection, use Edit – Paste Special to display the Paste Special dialog, as shown in Fig. 516. Choose Values and then OK.

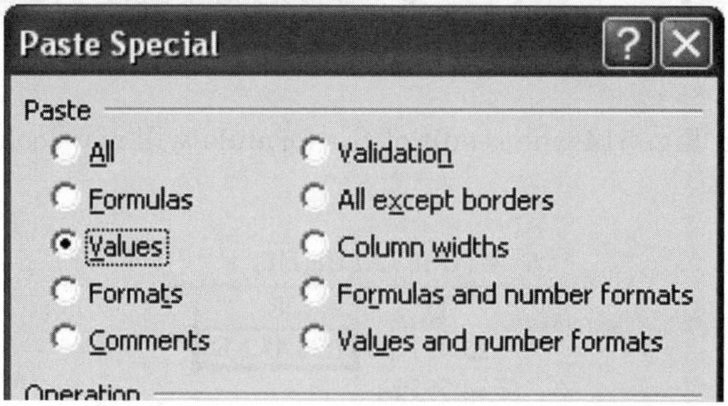

Fig. 516

Summary: The TimeValue function can convert text entries to real times. It is critical to have times and dates entered as real Excel times and dates instead of text if you want to do any math with the entries.

Commands Discussed: Format – Cells – Number; Edit – Paste Special

Functions Discussed: =TIMEVALUE()

CONVERT TIMES FROM H:MM TO M:SS

Problem: You entered the results of a running challenge for the students in your gym class. The results ranged from 2 minutes 35 seconds to 3 minutes and 15 seconds. When you total the times, something is clearly wrong. If you have eleven students at around 3 minutes each, you would expect an answer around 33 minutes. Instead, Excel gives you a total of 7:42, as shown in Fig. 517.

Part II

	A	B
1	Runner	Time
2	Andy	2:35
3	Bob	3:01
4	Carol	2:41
5	David	2:56
6	Ed	3:15
7	Frank	2:56
8	Gerry	2:32
9	Hank	3:04
10	Isabel	2:51
11	John	2:49
12	Kevin	3:02
13	Total	7:42
14		

Fig. 517

Although you thought that you were entering 2 minutes and 35 seconds, if you place the cell pointer in B2, and examine the formula bar, you will notice that Excel thought that you meant 2 hours and 35 minutes, as shown in Fig. 518.

	A	B	C	D
1	Runner	Time		
2	Andy	2:35		
3	Bob	3:01		

B2 f_x 2:35:00 AM

Fig. 518

Strategy: One solution is to re-enter all of the formulas, using 0:02:35 as the format. This is probably the fastest method for 11 entries, but if you had hundreds of entries, there is a better way. You can use a series of nested functions to extract the Hour and Minute from the incorrect entry and then use the results in the TIME function.

1) As shown in Fig. 519, in column D, use the =HOUR(B2) function to return the portion of the time before the colon.

D2 f_x =HOUR(B2)

	A	B	C	D	E
1	Runner	Time			
2	Andy	2:35		2	
3	Bob	3:01			
4	Carol	2:41			

Fig. 519

2) In cell E2, use the =MINUTE(B2) to return the portion of the time after the colon, as shown in Fig. 520.

f_x =MINUTE(B2)

B	C	D	E
Time			
2:35		2	35

Fig. 520

3)   You will use the =TIME function in cell C2, as shown in Fig. 521. This function requires an hour, a minute, and a second. The hour will be 0. The minute will be the result of the HOUR function in D2. The second will be the result of the MINUTE function in E2. The complete formula is =TIME(0,D2,E2).

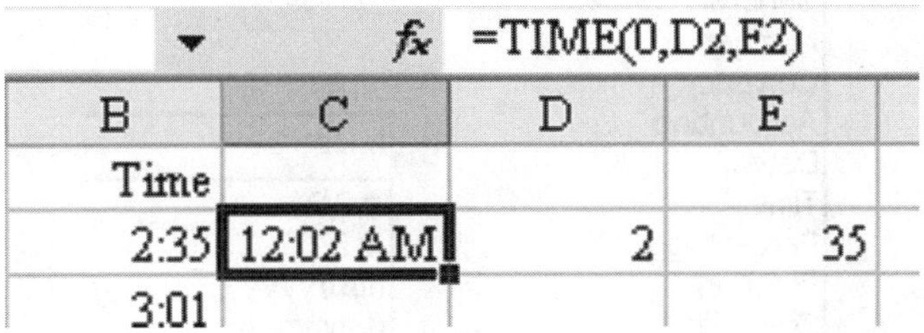

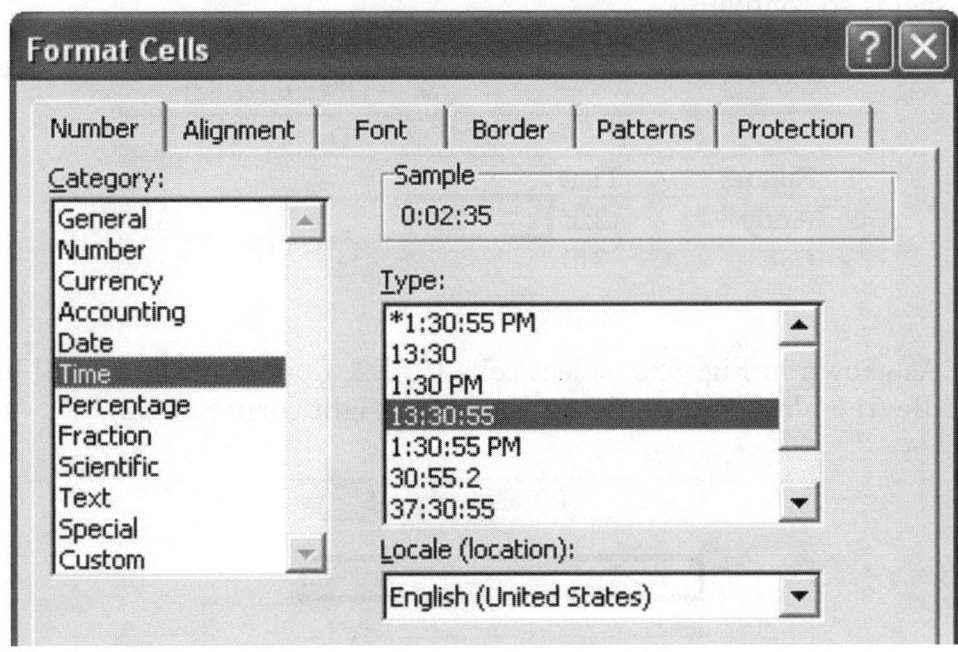

Fig. 521

4)   As usual, don't be immediately alarmed that the result of the formula is not what you expected. Select the cell. Hit Ctrl+1 to display the Format Cells dialog. On the Number tab, select a time format such as 13:30:55, as shown in Fig. 522.

Fig. 522

5)   Alternatively, select the Custom category and type a custom number format of M:SS, as shown in Fig. 523.

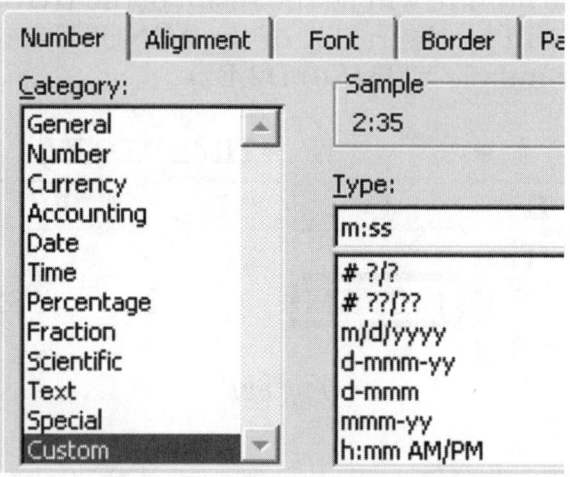

Fig. 523

It always seems funny that you've gone through all of the work in this chapter in order to get cell C2 to look exactly like the original cell in B2, as shown in Fig. 524. This is one of the reasons that working with times in Excel is so confusing.

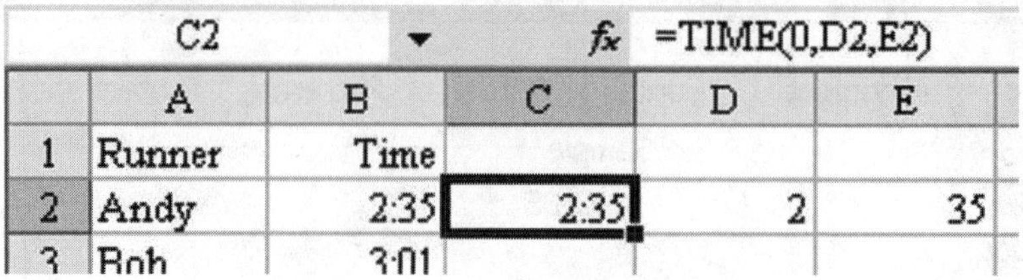

C2		▼	*fx* =TIME(0,D2,E2)	
	A	B	C	D	E
1	Runner	Time			
2	Andy	2:35	2:35	2	35
3	Bob	3:01			

Fig. 524

6)   As shown in Fig. 525, select cells C2:E2. Double-click the Fill handle (the black square dot in the lower right corner of E2).

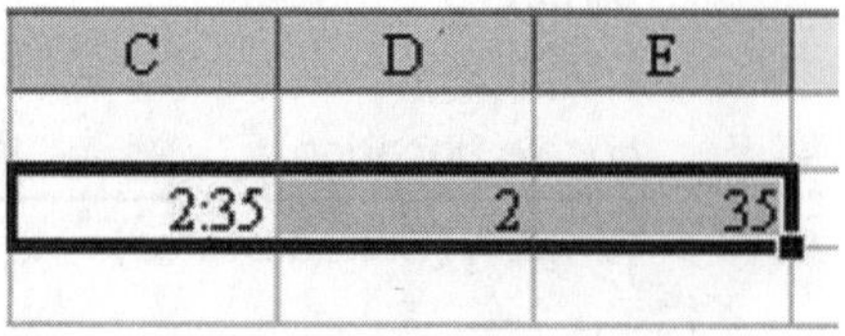

C	D	E
2:35	2	35

Fig. 525

7) Using the Fill handle trick will copy the formulas down to all rows with data in the adjacent column B. This will copy the formulas down to the total row, which is not what you want. Delete the formulas from C13:E13.

8) Copy the total formula from B13 to C13. As shown in Fig. 526, you will see that it now returns 31 minutes, a number that is about right.

	A	B	C
1	Runner	Time	
2	Andy	2:35	2:35
3	Bob	3:01	3:01
4	Carol	2:41	2:41
5	David	2:56	2:56
6	Ed	3:15	3:15
7	Frank	2:56	2:56
8	Gerry	2:32	2:32
9	Hank	3:04	3:04
10	Isabel	2:51	2:51
11	John	2:49	2:49
12	Kevin	3:02	3:02
13	Total	7:42	0:31

Fig. 526

To correct the format in C13, there are two options. If you had foresight, rather than doing a Copy and Paste from B13 to C13, you could have done Edit – Paste Special – Formulas to copy the formula, but not the number format. It is hard to have such foresight!

9) To fix the format in Fig. 526, select cell C12. Ctrl+C to Copy. Select cell C13, as shown in Fig. 527. Do Edit – Paste Special – Formats – OK.

11	John	2:49	2:49
12	Kevin	3:02	3:02
13	Total	7:42	31:42
14			

Fig. 527

10) The Paste Special Format command will wipe out the bold formatting in C13, so hit Ctrl+B to bold the cell again.

Additional Details: Before you can delete columns B, D, and E, you need to change the times in column C from formulas to values. Highlight the cells in C2:C12. Use Ctrl+C to Copy. Without changing the selection, use Edit – Paste Special to display the Paste Special dialog. Choose Values and then OK.

Just out of curiosity, what about that value in B13? Even if Excel thought we had 31 hours, why is it showing only 7 hours and 42 minutes? Select the cell. Hit F2 to edit the formula. Hit F9 to calculate the formula. You will see that Excel thinks this total is 1.320833, as shown in Fig. 528. This means that 31 hours is about 1.3 days. The default numeric format in B13 was causing Excel to only show the portion of hours in excess of whole days.

	A	B	C
1	Runner	Time	
2	Andy	2:35	2:35
3	Bob	3:01	3:01
4	Carol	2:41	2:41
5	David	2:56	2:56
6	Ed	3:15	3:15
7	Frank	2:56	2:56
8	Gerry	2:32	2:32
9	Hank	3:04	3:04
10	Isabel	2:51	2:51
11	John	2:49	2:49
12	Kevin	3:02	3:02
13	Total	1.32083333333333	

Fig. 528

After hitting F9 to see the result of the formula, hit the Esc key to return to the formula.

Summary: Beware – some entries can be ambiguous. What may seem like three minutes to you might be interpreted as three hours by Excel. Always select the cell and look in the formula bar to see if Excel is using hours or minutes.

Commands Discussed: Edit – Paste Special – Formats

Functions Discussed: =HOUR(); =MINUTE(); =TIME()

DISPLAY DATES AS MONTHS

Problem: Your dataset shows the actual date for each invoice, as shown in Fig. 529. When you print the invoice register, you would like to print this date as the month.

	A	B	C	D
1	**Month**	**Customer**	**Invoice**	**Revenue**
2	1/5/05	Ainsworth	1101	20,992
3	1/14/05	Air Canada	1102	72,030
4	1/16/05	Chevron	1103	13,438
5	1/22/05	Sun Life Financial	1104	58,901
6	1/23/05	Verizon	1105	4,937
7	2/3/05	Sears Canada	1106	74,173
8	2/5/05	Bell Canada	1107	43,097
9	2/12/05	Exxon	1108	25,991
10	2/17/05	Texaco	1109	47,662
11	3/3/05	Compaq	1110	42,172
12	3/6/05	SBC Communications	1111	6,475
13	3/9/05	Compton Petroleum	1112	72,587
14	3/21/05	Shell Canada	1113	69,013
15	3/29/05	Ford	1114	18,244
16	3/31/05	Sears	1115	46,756

Fig. 529

Part II

Strategy: You can use a numeric format to force dates to display the month instead of the actual date.

1)   Select the range of dates. If you have thousands of rows of data, here is one shortcut. Put the cell pointer in A2. Hit the End key. Hold down Shift while you hit the Down Arrow.

2)   From the menu, select Format – Cells (or hit Ctrl+1). In the Format Cells dialog, choose the Number tab.

3)   In the Category list box, choose Date.

4) In the Type list box, scroll through and find the format for either "Mar-01" or "March-01". Select the desired format and choose OK, as shown in Fig. 530.

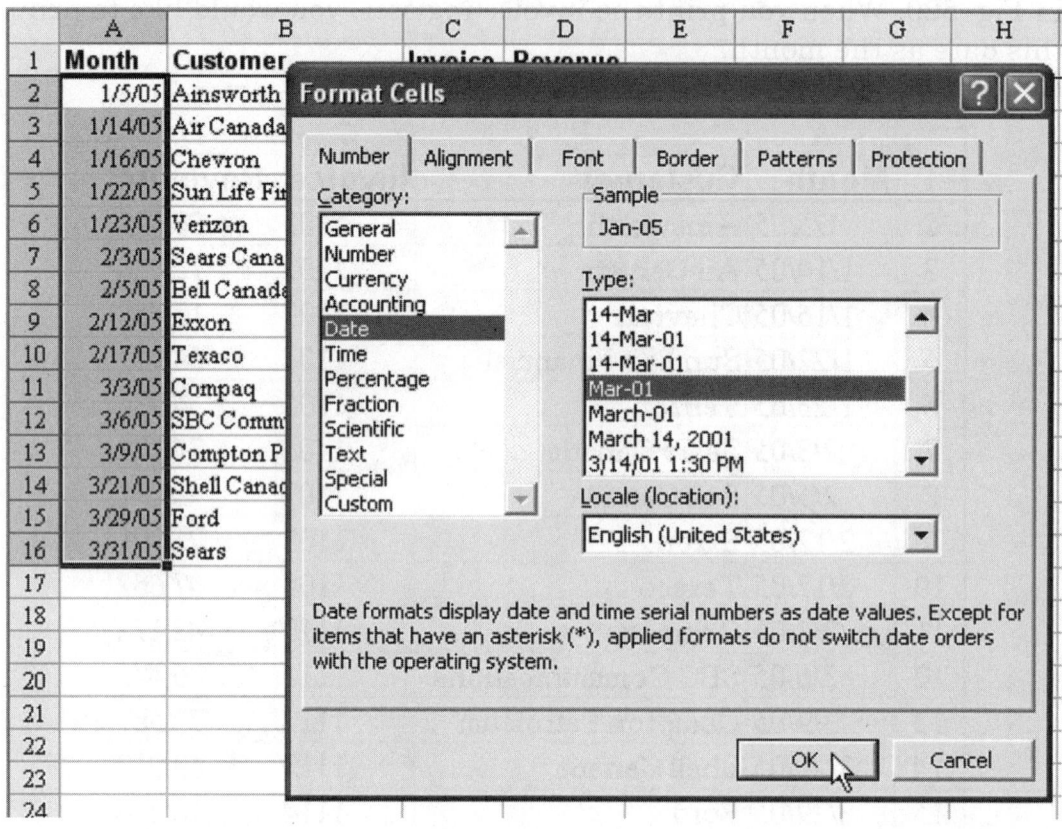

Fig. 530

Result: The daily dates will appear as monthly dates, as shown in Fig. 531.

	A	B	C	D
1	**Month**	**Customer**	**Invoice**	**Revenue**
2	Jan-05	Ainsworth	1101	20,992
3	Jan-05	Air Canada	1102	72,030
4	Jan-05	Chevron	1103	13,438
5	Jan-05	Sun Life Financial	1104	58,901
6	Jan-05	Verizon	1105	4,937
7	Feb-05	Sears Canada	1106	74,173
8	Feb-05	Bell Canada	1107	43,097
9	Feb-05	Exxon	1108	25,991
10	Feb-05	Texaco	1109	47,662
11	Mar-05	Compaq	1110	42,172
12	Mar-05	SBC Communications	1111	6,475
13	Mar-05	Compton Petroleum	1112	72,587
14	Mar-05	Shell Canada	1113	69,013
15	Mar-05	Ford	1114	18,244
16	Mar-05	Sears	1115	46,756

Fig. 531

Part II

This tip is fine for printing and even for doing automatic subtotals. It will not work for sorting, formulas, or pivot tables. See the next tip for more details if you need to actually transform the column into months.

Additional Details: If you need to display the month with a four-digit date, you will have to use a custom number format. In the Format Cells dialog, use the Custom category, as shown in Fig. 532. In the type box, use one of these formats:

- mmm yyyy for a format like "Mar 2005"

- mmmm yyyy for a format like "March 2005"

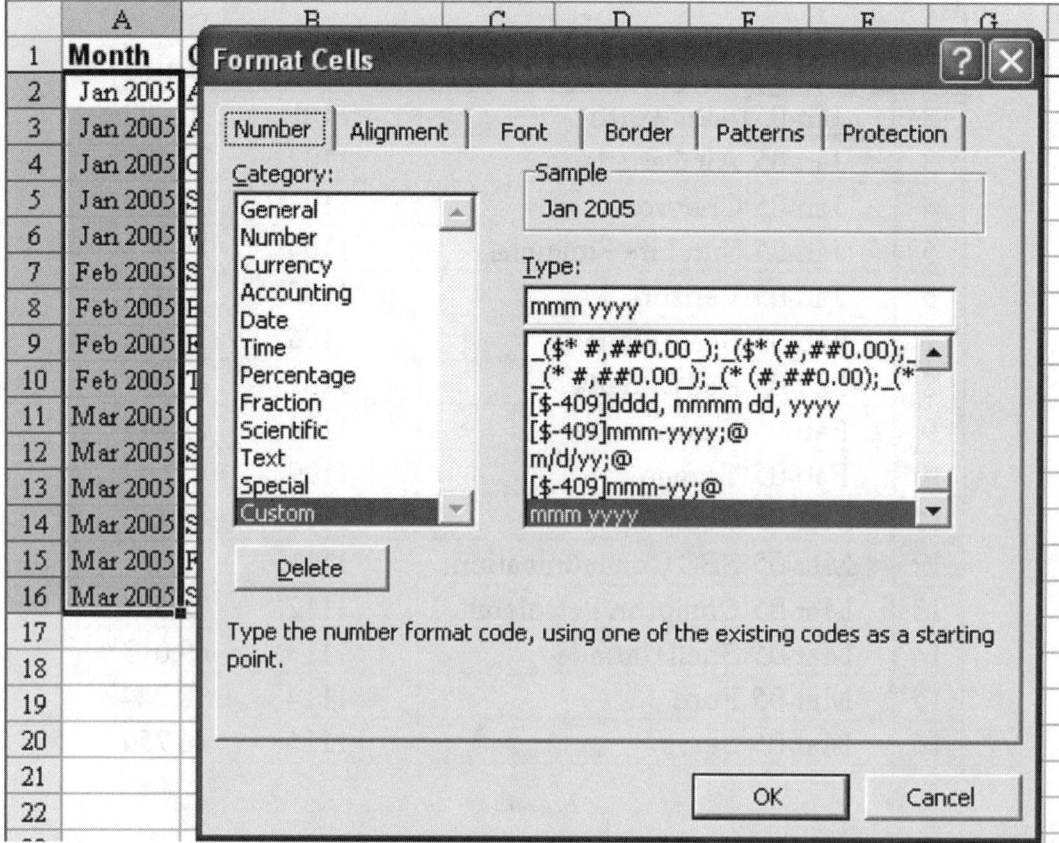

Fig. 532

Summary: Use a custom number format to make daily dates appear as monthly dates if you are printing or doing automatic subtotals. Do not use it if you want to sort or use the dates in formulas.

Commands Discussed: Format – Cells – Number

GROUP DATES BY MONTH

Problem: Your data has a series of invoice dates. You need to group the data by month. In the previous chapter, you learned how to format a date to look like a month. However, when you format a date to look like a month, the underlying value is still really the fifth of the month. You can see that it is the 5th by selecting the cell and looking at the value in the formula bar, as shown in Fig. 533. Some data analyses will not produce the desired result of one subtotal per month.

| | A2 | ▼ | fx | 1/5/2005 |

	A	B	C	D
1	**Date**	**Customer**	**Invoice**	**Revenue**
2	Jan-2005	Bell Canada	1101	20,992
3	Jan-2005	Compton Petroleum	1102	72,030
4	Jan-2005	Exxon	1103	13,438
5	Jan-2005	Sears	1104	58,901
6	Jan-2005	Texaco	1105	4,937
7	Feb-2005	Verizon	1106	74,173
8	Feb-2005	Air Canada	1107	43,097
9	Feb-2005	Compaq	1108	25,991
10	Feb-2005	Ford	1109	47,662
11	Mar-2005	Sun Life Financial	1110	42,172
12	Mar-2005	Ainsworth	1111	6,475
13	Mar-2005	Chevron	1112	72,587
14	Mar-2005	Sears Canada	1113	69,013
15	Mar-2005	SBC Communications	1114	18,244
16	Mar-2005	Shell Canada	1115	46,756

Fig. 533

Part II

Strategy: For some tasks, simply formatting the dates to look like months will work. As shown in Fig. 534, if you create automatic subtotals by the Date field, you will get the desired results.

1 2 3		A	B	C	D
	1	**Date**	**Customer**	**Invoice**	**Revenue**
	2	Jan-2005	Bell Canada	1101	20,992
	3	Jan-2005	Compton Petroleum	1102	72,030
	4	Jan-2005	Exxon	1103	13,438
	5	Jan-2005	Sears	1104	58,901
	6	Jan-2005	Texaco	1105	4,937
	7	**Jan-2005 Total**			170,298
	8	Feb-2005	Verizon	1106	74,173
	9	Feb-2005	Air Canada	1107	43,097
	10	Feb-2005	Compaq	1108	25,991
	11	Feb-2005	Ford	1109	47,662
	12	**Feb-2005 Total**			190,923
	13	Mar-2005	Sun Life Financial	1110	42,172
	14	Mar-2005	Ainsworth	1111	6,475
	15	Mar-2005	Chevron	1112	72,587
	16	Mar-2005	Sears Canada	1113	69,013
	17	Mar-2005	SBC Communications	1114	18,244
	18	Mar-2005	Shell Canada	1115	46,756
	19	**Mar-2005 Total**			255,247
	20	**Grand Total**			616,468
	21				

Fig. 534

However, if you attempt to test which fields are equal, it will not work. As shown in Fig. 535, the formula to detect a new month fails.

	E2	▼		*fx*	=IF(A2<>A1,"Yes","No")	
	A	B	C	D	E	F
1	Date	Customer	Invoice	Revenue	New Month?	
2	Jan-2005	Bell Canada	1101	20,992	Yes	
3	Jan-2005	Compton Petroleum	1102	72,030	Yes	
4	Jan-2005	Exxon	1103	13,438	Yes	
5	Jan-2005	Sears	1104	58,901	Yes	
6	Jan-2005	Texaco	1105	4,937	Yes	
7	Feb-2005	Verizon	1106	74,173	Yes	

Fig. 535

Similarly, a COUNTIF formula will not work, as shown in Fig. 536.

	D1	▼		*fx*	=COUNTIF(A4:A18,A1)
	A	B	C	D	
1	Jan-2005			0	
2					
3	Date	Customer	Invoice	Revenue	
4	Jan-2005	Bell Canada	1101	20,992	
5	Jan-2005	Compton Petroleum	1102	72,030	
6	Jan-2005	Exxon	1103	13,438	

Fig. 536

Even pivot tables will not work, as shown in Fig. 537.

	A	B
1	Drop Page Fields Here	
2		
3	Sum of Revenue	
4	Date ▼	Total
5	Jan-2005	20992
6	Jan-2005	72030
7	Jan-2005	13438
8	Jan-2005	58901
9	Jan-2005	4937
10	Feb-2005	74173
11	Feb-2005	43097
12	Feb-2005	25991
13	Feb-2005	47662
14	Mar-2005	42172
15	Mar-2005	6475
16	Mar-2005	72587
17	Mar-2005	69013
18	Mar-2005	18244
19	Mar-2005	46756
20	Grand Total	616468
21		

Fig. 537

Part II

If you want to sort by customer alphabetically within a month, you will not get the desired results. As shown in Fig. 538, Verizon on February 3 will appear before Air Canada on February 5.

A9		▼	fx	2/3/2005
	A	B		C
1	Jan-2005			
2				
3	**Date**	**Customer**		**Invoice**
8	Jan-2005	Texaco		1105
9	Feb-2005	Verizon		1106
10	Feb-2005	Air Canada		1107
11	Feb-2005	Compaq		1108

Fig. 538

So, although the special case of creating subtotals does work, in almost every other case you will need to use a formula to transform the dates in column A to a real month.

1)   Insert a new column A with a heading of Month. Format the date column with an m/d/yy format. As shown in Fig. 539, the formula for the new month column is =B2–Day(B2)+1.

2)   Copy that formula down and format the column as months.

A2	▼	f_x =B2-DAY(B2)+1		
	A	B	C	D	E
1	**Month**	**Date**	**Customer**	**Invoice**	**Revenue**
2	Jan-05	1/5/05	Bell Canada	1101	20,992
3	Jan-05	1/14/05	Compton Petroleum	1102	72,030
4	Jan-05	1/16/05	Exxon	1103	13,438
5	Jan-05	1/22/05	Sears	1104	58,901

Fig. 539

Here is why this works. The DAY(1/5/2005) function will return the number 5 because the date is the fifth of the month. January 5 minus 5 days will give you December 31. Add 1 to get back to the first day of this month.

Alternate Strategy: You will prefer the above formula because it is shorter and faster. You could also have used a formula like =DATE (Year(B2),Month(B2),1). However, this formula requires three function calls instead of one.

Summary: Use the DAY function in a formula to convert a date to the first of the month.

Commands Discussed: Subtotal; Pivot Table; Sort

Functions Discussed: =DAY(); =DATE(); =YEAR(); =MONTH(); =COUNTIF()

CALCULATE LAST DAY OF MONTH

Problem: Your dataset shows the actual date for each invoice, as shown in Fig. 540. You want a formula to convert this to the last day of the month.

	A	B	C	D
1	**Date**	**Customer**	**Invoice**	**Revenue**
2	1/5/2005	Ainsworth	1101	20,992
3	1/14/2005	Air Canada	1102	72,030
4	1/16/2005	Chevron	1103	13,438
5	1/22/2005	Sun Life Financial	1104	58,901
6	1/23/2005	Verizon	1105	4,937
7	2/3/2005	Sears Canada	1106	74,173
8	2/5/2005	Bell Canada	1107	43,097
9	2/12/2005	Exxon	1108	25,991
10	2/17/2005	Texaco	1109	47,662
11	3/3/2005	Compaq	1110	42,172
12	3/6/2005	SBC Communications	1111	6,475
13	3/9/2005	Compton Petroleum	1112	72,587
14	3/21/2005	Shell Canada	1113	69,013
15	3/29/2005	Ford	1114	18,244
16	3/31/2005	Sears	1115	46,756

Fig. 540

Part II

Strategy: Finding the last day of the month is trickier than finding the first day of the month. For the first day, you are always looking for a day of 1. For the last day, you might be looking for 31, 30, 28, or even 29 in February during leap years. Excellers have tried many different tricks for this problem. Many first attempts involve testing to see if the MONTH(A2) is equal to 1, 3, 4, 7, 8, 10, or 12 to assign a final date of 31. As you can imagine, this nested IF statement gets rather large.

One day this was being discussed on the MrExcel board and Aladin Aky-urek chimed in with his elegant solution. Aladin pointed out that it is easy to figure out the first date of the next month. After you have figured this out, you can simply subtract one from the first of next month to get the date for the last of this month. Here is a table showing this logic.

Invoice Date	First of Next Month	Less 1 Day
2/17/2003	3/1/2003	2/28/2003
2/17/2004	3/1/2004	2/29/2004
3/17/2004	4/1/2004	3/31/2004
4/17/2004	5/1/2004	4/30/2004

To figure out the first of the next month, you will use the DATE function. This function requires three arguments, the Year, the Month, and the Day. You know that the Day will be 1. The Month should be the month of the date + 1. The year should be the year of the date. It is obvious this will work in the first row of our example, as shown in Fig. 541.

E2	▼		f_x =DATE(YEAR(A2),MONTH(A2)+1,1)-1		
	A	B	C	D	E
1	Date	Customer	Invoice	Revenue	Last of Month
2	1/5/2005	Ainsworth	1101	20,992	1/31/2005
3	1/14/2005	Air Canada	1102	72,030	

Fig. 541

=YEAR(A2) is 2005.

=Month(A2) is 1. =Month(A2)+1 is 2.

=DATE(2005,2,1) will return February 1, 2005.

=DATE(2005,2,1)–1 will return January 31, 2005.

However, it is not so obvious that this formula would work if the Date in A2 were December 5, 2005. In this case, you would have:

=YEAR(A2) is 2005.

=Month(A2) is 12.

=Month(A2)+1 is 13.

Thus, you are asking for a date of =DATE(2005,13,1). It would seem like this would not work! What is the first day of the thirteenth month of 2005? Amazingly, Excel handles this with ease. As shown in Fig. 542, Excel returns a value of January 1, 2006.

f_x =DATE(2005,13,1)	
D	E
1/1/2006	

Fig. 542

Then, subtract 1 from the result. =DATE(Year(A2),Month(A2)+1,1)–1 will return 12/31/2005, which is the correct last day of the month, as shown in Fig. 543.

E2		▼	f_x =DATE(YEAR(A2),MONTH(A2)+1,1)-1		
	A	B	C	D	E
1	Date	Customer	Invoice	Revenue	Last of Month
2	12/5/2005	Ainsworth	1101	20,992	12/31/2005
3	1/14/2005	Air Canada	1102	72,030	

Fig. 543

I've said it before, but the fact that Microsoft allows the DATE function to correctly return the forty-seventh day of the eighteenth month of 2005 is miraculous and incredibly useful. See the result in Fig. 544.

	f_x =DATE(2005,18,47)	
	D	E
	17-Jul-06	

Fig. 544

So, the formula used in cell E2 in Fig. 545 can be copied down to all rows of the dataset. Your new column E now calculates the last day of the month for each date.

E2		▼	f_x =DATE(YEAR(A2),MONTH(A2)+1,1)-1		
	A	B	C	D	E
1	Date	Customer	Invoice	Revenue	Last of Month
2	1/5/2005	Ainsworth	1101	20,992	1/31/2005
3	1/14/2005	Air Canada	1102	72,030	1/31/2005
4	1/16/2005	Chevron	1103	13,438	1/31/2005
5	1/22/2005	Sun Life Financial	1104	58,901	1/31/2005
6	1/23/2005	Verizon	1105	4,937	1/31/2005
7	2/3/2005	Sears Canada	1106	74,173	2/28/2005
8	2/5/2005	Bell Canada	1107	43,097	2/28/2005
9	2/12/2005	Exxon	1108	25,991	2/28/2005
10	2/17/2005	Texaco	1109	47,662	2/28/2005
11	3/3/2005	Compaq	1110	42,172	3/31/2005
12	3/6/2005	SBC Communications	1111	6,475	3/31/2005
13	3/9/2005	Compton Petroleum	1112	72,587	3/31/2005
14	3/21/2005	Shell Canada	1113	69,013	3/31/2005
15	3/29/2005	Ford	1114	18,244	3/31/2005
16	3/31/2005	Sears	1115	46,756	3/31/2005

Fig. 545

Part II

Summary: To find the last day of a month, use the DATE() function to calculate the first of the next month and then subtract one day. This sure-fire method will find the last day, even if it falls on the 31st, 30th, 28th, or 29th.

Functions Discussed: =DATE(); =YEAR(); =MONTH()

CREATE A TIMESHEET THAT CAN TOTAL OVER 24 HOURS

Problem: You set up the timesheet shown below. Cell D2 contains a formula of C2–B2. Cell D2 is formatted with a time format of h:mm. Everything works fine for this part-time employee, as shown in Fig. 546.

	D9	▼		*fx* =SUM(D2:D8)	
	A	B	C	D	E
1	Day	Start	End	Hours	
2	Mon	8:00 AM	11:00 AM	3:00	
3	Tue	8:00 AM	11:00 AM	3:00	
4	Wed	8:00 AM	11:00 AM	3:00	
5	Thu	8:00 AM	11:00 AM	3:00	
6	Fri	9:00 AM	12:00 PM	3:00	
7	Sat			0:00	
8	Sun			0:00	
9	Total For the Week			15:00	
10					

Fig. 546

However, when you attempt to use the timesheet for someone who works full time, the total does not work. This person worked eight hours each day plus an extra three hours on Saturday. Their total should be 43 hours, yet the worksheet is reporting that they worked only 19 hours, as shown in Fig. 547.

	A	B	C	D
1	Day	Start	End	Hours
2	Mon	8:00 AM	4:00 PM	8:00
3	Tue	8:00 AM	4:00 PM	8:00
4	Wed	8:00 AM	4:00 PM	8:00
5	Thu	8:00 AM	4:00 PM	8:00
6	Fri	9:00 AM	5:00 PM	8:00
7	Sat	8:00 AM	11:00 AM	3:00
8	Sun			0:00
9	Total For the Week			19:00
10				

Fig. 547

Strategy: Remember that Excel stores dates as the number of days elapsed since January 1, 1900. Excel stores times as a portion of a day. 6 a.m. is stored as 0.25 because 25 percent of the day is elapsed by 6 a.m.

In the above scenario, Excel knows that the total is 43 hours. However, it thinks that 43 hours after midnight on January 1, 1900 is 7 p.m. on January 2, 1900. That cell really wants to report that it is 7 p.m. on January 2. This makes no sense in the current context. When you use a custom number format of h:mm, you are basically telling Excel to ignore the date and only report the time.

The solution is to use the non-intuitive custom number format of [h]:mm. The square brackets around the h allow Excel to report times in excess of 24 hours.

1) Select cell D9. Hit Ctrl+1 to display the Format Cells dialog. Select the Number tab. In the Category list, choose Custom. The type box will show the current numeric format for the cell, as shown in Fig. 548.

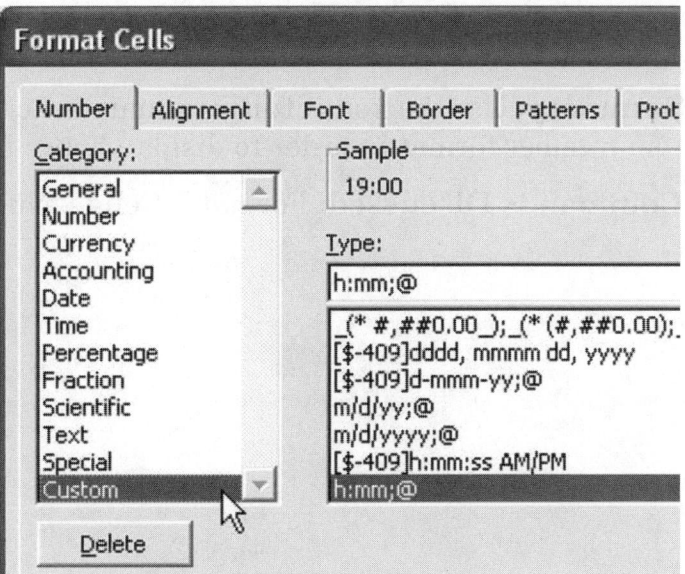

Fig. 548

2)   Click in the Type box and add square brackets around the h. As shown in Fig. 549, you will see in the Sample area that the cell is now reporting 43 hours.

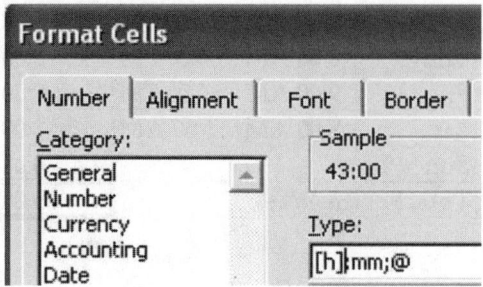

Fig. 549

Result: The time sheet reports the correct total, as shown in Fig. 550.

	A	B	C	D
1	Day	Start	End	Hours
2	Mon	8:00 AM	4:00 PM	8:00
3	Tue	8:00 AM	4:00 PM	8:00
4	Wed	8:00 AM	4:00 PM	8:00
5	Thu	8:00 AM	4:00 PM	8:00
6	Fri	9:00 AM	5:00 PM	8:00
7	Sat	8:00 AM	11:00 AM	3:00
8	Sun			0:00
9	Total For the Week			43:00
10				

Fig. 550

Summary: Use the non-intuitive square brackets around the h in a custom number format in order to display hours in excess of 24.

Commands Discussed: Format – Cells – Numeric

FIND WHICH CUSTOMERS ARE
IN AN EXISTING LIST

Problem: You have a list of month to date sales by customer, as shown in Fig. 551. Your co-worker sends you a list of sales for yesterday. Figure out which customers are new so that they can be added to the list.

	A	B	C	D	E
1	XYZ Co				
2	Month to Date Sales				
3	Through 06/20/2005			Sales for 6/21/05	
4					
5	**Customer**	**Revenue MTD**		**Customer**	**Revenue**
6	Exxon	68,200		Lucent	3137
7	Lucent	62,744		Nortel Networks	2355
8	Ainsworth	60,461		Molson, Inc	2273
9	P&G	60,299		Gildan Activewea	2116
10	HP	55,251		Compaq	1963
11	General Motors	54,569		Compton Petrole	1568
12	Chevron	54,048		Air Canada	1551
13	Bell Canada	51,240		IBM	1377
14	Shell Canada	47,521		Wal-Mart	1327
15	Nortel Networks	47,104		Sun Life Financi:	1028
16	Kroger	46,717		Ford	2629
17	Molson, Inc	45,460			
18	Gildan Activewear	42,316			
19	Compaq	39,250			
20	Verizon	35,367			
21	Compton Petroleum	31,369			
22	Air Canada	31,021			
23	IBM	27,533			
24	Wal-Mart	26,535			
25	Sun Life Financial	20,550			
26					

Fig. 551

Part

II

Strategy: Add a column to the new list. In this column, use the MATCH function. Any customers in the new list without a match in the existing list will be assigned a value of #N/A. The #N/A values can then be sorted to the bottom of the list.

The MATCH function requires three arguments. The first argument is the customer name to be looked up. The second argument is the range of existing customers. You will want to make the range an absolute address, with dollar signs in the reference. This way, the formula can be easily copied. The third argument is a zero to indicate that you are looking for an exact match.

1)   Enter this formula in cell F6 =MATCH(D6,$A$6:$A$25,0). Copy the formula down to the other cells in your new list, as shown in Fig. 552.

=MATCH(D6,$A$6:$A$25,0)

B	C	D	E	F
		Sales for 6/21/05		
ue MTD		Customer	Revenue	There?
68,200		Air Canada	1551	17
62,744		Compaq	1963	14
60,461		Compton Petrole	1568	16
60,299		Ford	2629	#N/A
55,251		Gildan Activewea	2116	13
54,569		IBM	1377	18
54,048		Lucent	3137	2
51,240		Molson, Inc	2273	12
47,521		Nortel Networks	2355	10
47,104		Sun Life Financi	1028	20
46,717		Wal-Mart	1327	19

Fig. 552

The MATCH formula is going to return an integer that represents the relative row number where the match is found. In the present case, we don't really care about the answer, unless a match is not found. If Excel cannot find a match, the answer will be the #N/A error. The #N/A errors will always sort to the end of a list.

2) Sort your new list ascending by column F and the new customers will sort into one spot. You can then copy and paste the new customers to the end of your existing list.

Summary: Use the MATCH function to find customers who are not in an existing list.

Functions Discussed: =MATCH()

USE VLOOKUP TO FIND WHICH CUSTOMERS ARE IN AN EXISTING LIST

Problem: Your co-worker uses VLOOKUP instead of MATCH to find which values are in an existing list, as shown in Fig. 553. This is different from the advice given in the previous chapter. Which is right?

	F6	fx	=VLOOKUP(D6,$A$6:$A$25,1,FALSE)			
	A	B	C	D	E	F	G
1	XYZ Co					
2	Month to Data Sales					
3	Through 06/20/2005			Sales for 6/21/05		
4						
5	Customer	Revenue MTD		Customer	Revenue	There?
6	Exxon	68,200		Air Canada	1551	Air Canada
7	Lucent	62,744		Compaq	1963	Compaq
8	Ainsworth	60,461		Compton Petrole	1568	Compton Petroleum
9	P&G	60,299		Ford	2629	#N/A
10	HP	55,251		Gildan Activewe:	2116	Gildan Activewear
11	General Motors	54,569		IBM	1377	IBM
12	Chevron	54,048		Lucent	3137	Lucent
13	Bell Canada	51,240		Molson, Inc	2273	Molson, Inc
14	Shell Canada	47,521		Nortel Networks	2355	Nortel Networks
15	Nortel Networks	47,104		Sun Life Financi:	1028	Sun Life Financial
16	Kroger	46,717		Wal-Mart	1327	Wal-Mart

Fig. 553

Strategy: Both are right. In the next chapter, you and your co-worker will use VLOOKUP to get the new day's sales for each existing customer. Most people seem to master the VLOOKUP function first, so it is common to see people using the VLOOKUP function to solve this step as well. Both work fine. Again, with VLOOKUP, you are interested in the #N/A errors. You have to type an additional parameter for VLOOKUP.

The VLOOKUP function requires four arguments. The first argument is the customer name to be looked up. The second argument is a rectangular range with existing customer numbers in the left column of the range. You will want to make the range an absolute address with dollar signs in the reference. This way, the formula can be easily copied. The third argument is the relative column number within the existing range that you want returned. In this case, you don't care which column is returned, you are merely looking for the #N/A values. So, you can use "1". The fourth argument is a FALSE to indicate that you are looking for an exact match.

1)   The formula for cell F6 is =VLOOKUP(D6,$A$6:$A$25,1,FALSE). Copy the formula down to the other cells in your new list.

      The VLOOKUP formula is going to return the customer name if it is in the existing list. If Excel cannot find a match, the answer will be the #N/A error. The #N/A errors will always sort to the end of a list.

2)   Sort your new list ascending by column F and the new customers will sort into one spot. You can then copy and paste the new customers to the end of your existing list.

Summary: You can use a VLOOKUP function to find customers who are not in an existing list.

Functions Discussed: VLOOKUP

MATCH CUSTOMERS USING VLOOKUP

Problem: You have a list of month-to-date sales by customer. You have a second list with new sales from today, as shown in Fig. 554. How can you add the sales from the new list to the old list?

	A	B	C	D	E	F	G
1	XYZ Co						
2	Month to Data Sales						
3	Through 06/20/2005					Sales for 6/21/05	
4							
5	**Customer**	**Revenue MTD**				**Customer**	**Revenue**
6	Exxon	68,200				Air Canada	1551
7	Lucent	62,744				Compaq	1963
8	Ainsworth	60,461				Compton Petrole	1568
9	P&G	60,299				Ford	2629
10	HP	55,251				Gildan Activewe	2116
11	General Motors	54,569				IBM	1377
12	Chevron	54,048				Lucent	3137
13	Bell Canada	51,240				Molson, Inc	2273
14	Shell Canada	47,521				Nortel Networks	2355
15	Nortel Networks	47,104				Sun Life Financi	1028
16	Kroger	46,717				Wal-Mart	1327
17	Molson, Inc	45,460					
18	Gildan Activewear	42,316					
19	Compaq	39,250					
20	Verizon	35,367					
21	Compton Petroleum	31,369					
22	Air Canada	31,021					
23	IBM	27,533					
24	Wal-Mart	26,535					
25	Sun Life Financial	20,550					
26	Ford	0					

Fig. 554

Strategy: Add a new column to the first list. Use the VLOOKUP function in the new column to grab the sales from the new list.

The VLOOKUP function requires four arguments. The first argument is the customer name to be looked up. The second argument is a rectangular range with new customer numbers in the left column of the range. In the example above, this is F4:G16. You will want to make the range an absolute address, with dollar signs in the reference: $F$4:$G$16. This way, the formula can be easily copied. The third argument is the relative column number within the existing range that you want returned. Since the sales are in column G, and G is the second column in the range

F4:G16, the third argument will be 2. The fourth argument is a FALSE to indicate that you are looking for an exact match.

The formula for cell C6 is =VLOOKUP(A6,$F$6:$G$16,2,FALSE), as shown in Fig. 555. Copy the formula down to the other cells in your new list.

C6	▼	fx	=VLOOKUP(A6,$F$6:$G$16,2,FALSE)					
	A	B	C	D	E	F	G
1	XYZ Co						
2	Month to Data Sales						
3	Through 06/20/2005					Sales for 6/21/05	
4							
5	**Customer**	**Revenue MTD**	New			**Customer**	**Revenue**
6	Ford	0	2629			Air Canada	1551
7	Sun Life Financial	20,550	1028			Compaq	1963
8	Wal-Mart	26,535	1327			Compton Petrole	1568
9	IBM	27,533	1377			Ford	2629
10	Air Canada	31,021	1551			Gildan Activewea	2116
11	Compton Petroleum	31,369	1568			IBM	1377
12	Verizon	35,367	#N/A			Lucent	3137
13	Compaq	39,250	1963			Molson, Inc	2273
14	Gildan Activewear	42,316	2116			Nortel Networks	2355
15	Molson, Inc	45,460	2273			Sun Life Financi	1028
16	Kroger	46,717	#N/A			Wal-Mart	1327
17	Nortel Networks	47,104	2355				
18	Shell Canada	47,521	#N/A				

Fig. 555

Look at row 12 in Fig. 556. Since we did not sell anything to this customer today, the result is #N/A. While the #N/As were useful in a previous chapter, they are fairly annoying here. The rule for calculation says that anything plus #N/A will return #N/A. When you add a new column to total column B & C, the #N/As will cause problems.

	D12	▼		*fx*	=C12+B12	
	A		**B**	**C**	**D**	
1	XYZ Co					
2	Month to Data Sales					
3	Through 06/20/2005					
4						
5	**Customer**		**Revenue MTD**	New	New Total	
6	Ford		0	2629	2,629	
7	Sun Life Financial		20,550	1028	21,578	
8	Wal-Mart		26,535	1327	27,862	
9	IBM		27,533	1377	28,910	
10	Air Canada		31,021	1551	32,572	
11	Compton Petroleum		31,369	1568	32,937	
12	Verizon		35,367	#N/A	#N/A	
13	Compaq		39,250	1963	41,213	
14	Gildan Activewear		42,316	2116	44,432	
15	Molson, Inc		45,460	2273	47,733	
16	Kroger		46,717	#N/A	#N/A	
17	Nortel Networks		47,104	2355	49,459	

Fig. 556

There are several methods for dealing with the #N/A cells. If you can sort your original list, simply sort by column C. All of the #N/A cells will sort to the bottom. Use the formula in column D only for the customers with sales today. In Fig. 557, you would copy D6:D16 and Paste Special Values into range C6.

	D6	▼		*fx*	=C6+B6	
	A		**B**	**C**	**D**	
1	XYZ Co					
2	Month to Data Sales					
3	Through 06/20/2005					
4						
5	**Customer**		**Revenue MTD**	New	New Total	
6	Sun Life Financial		20,550	1028	21,578	
7	Wal-Mart		26,535	1327	27,862	
8	IBM		27,533	1377	28,910	
9	Air Canada		31,021	1551	32,572	
10	Compton Petroleum		31,369	1568	32,937	
11	Compaq		39,250	1963	41,213	
12	Gildan Activewear		42,316	2116	44,432	
13	Molson, Inc		45,460	2273	47,733	
14	Nortel Networks		47,104	2355	49,459	
15	Ford		0	2629	2,629	
16	Lucent		62,744	3137	65,881	
17	Verizon		35,367	#N/A		
18	Kroger		46,717	#N/A		

Fig. 557

Additional Details: You could also use the ISNA function to deal with VLOOKUP results that return #N/A. The ISNA function will return a TRUE if the result of a formula is #N/A. You can then use the ISNA function as the first part of an IF function. One solution is to use ISNA and IF in the calculation of the new total. As shown in Fig. 558, the new total is the previous MTD number in B6 plus C6 if it is not #N/A.

D6	▼	f_x =B6+IF(ISNA(C6),0,C6)	
	A	B	C	D
1	XYZ Co			
2	Month to Data Sales			
3	Through 06/20/2005			
4				
5	**Customer**	**Revenue MTD**	New	New Total
6	Ainsworth	60,461	#N/A	60,461
7	Air Canada	31,021	1551	32,572
8	Bell Canada	51,240	#N/A	51,240

Fig. 558

The other solution is to use the ISNA function in the original VLOOKUP formula. This is the solution that I use most, even though it requires Excel to calculate the VLOOKUP twice. The formula becomes long:

=IF(ISNA(VLOOKUP(A6,$F$6:$G$16,2,FALSE)),0,VLOOKUP(A6,$F$6:$G$16,2,FALSE))

Summary: You can use a VLOOKUP function to match customers in two lists.

Functions Discussed: =VLOOKUP(); =ISNA(); =IF()

WATCH FOR DUPLICATES WHEN USING VLOOKUP

Problem: In previous chapters, you've used the VLOOKUP function to get sales from a second list into an original list. You need to be aware of how VLOOKUP handles duplicates in the lookup list.

Here is a scenario where duplicates can cause a problem. You receive the next day's sales in a file. When you add the MATCH function to find new customers, there is one new customer: Sun Life Finc'l, as shown in Fig. 559.

	A	B	C	D	E	F	G	H
1	XYZ Co							
2	Month to Data Sales							
3	Through 06/21/2005					Sales for 6/22/05		
4								
5	**Customer**	**Revenue MTD**				**Customer**	**Revenue**	There?
6	Ainsworth	60,461				Sun Life Finc'l	1,295	#N/A
7	Air Canada	32,572				Wal-Mart	1,950	21
8	Bell Canada	51,240				Verizon	2,476	20
9	Chevron	54,048				Sun Life Financi:	2,510	19
10	Compaq	41,213				Compaq	2,885	5
11	Compton Petroleum	32,937				Kroger	3,270	13
12	Exxon	68,200				Bell Canada	3,587	3
13	Ford	2,629				Chevron	3,783	4
14	General Motors	54,569				General Motors	3,820	9
15	Gildan Activewear	44,432				Ainsworth	4,232	1
16	HP	55,251						

Fig. 559

You realize that this is not really a new customer at all. Someone in the order entry department created a new customer instead of using the existing customer named "Sun Life Financial". As a quick fix, you copy cell F9 and paste it in cell F6. This seems like a fine solution and resolves the #N/A error in H6.

However, this will cause problems down the line. When you enter the VLOOKUP formula in column C to get the current day's sales, there are two rows that match Sun Life Financial. The VLOOKUP function is not capable of handling this. When two rows match a VLOOKUP, the function will return the sales from the first row in the list. As shown in Fig. 560, in cell C8, the $1295 in sales is coming from cell G6 only instead of cells G6 and G8.

C8			fx =IF(ISNA(VLOOKUP(A8,$F$6:$G$15,2,FALSE)),0,VLOOKUP(A8,$F$6:$G$15,2,FALSE))							
	A	B	C	D	E	F	G	H	I	J
1	XYZ Co									
2	Month to Data Sales									
3	Through 06/21/2005					Sales for 6/22/05				
4										
5	**Customer**	**Revenue MTD**	New			**Customer**	**Revenue**	There?		
6	Wal-Mart	27,862	1,950			Sun Life Financi:	1,295	3		
7	Verizon	35,367	2,476			Wal-Mart	1,950	1		
8	Sun Life Financial	21,578	1,295			Verizon	2,476	2		
9	Shell Canada	47,521	0			Sun Life Financi:	2,510	3		
10	P&G	60,299	0			Compaq	2,885	17		

Fig. 560

Part II

If you are not absolutely sure that the customers in the lookup table are unique, you should not use VLOOKUP. Instead, you would use a SUMIF formula, as shown in Fig. 561. Functions such as COUNTIF and SUMIF are explained in the next five topics.

	C8	▼	*fx*	=SUMIF($F$6:$F$15,A8,$G$6:$G$15)		
	A	B	C	D E	F	G
1	XYZ Co					
2	Month to Data Sales					
3	Through 06/21/2005				Sales for 6/22/05	
4						
5	Customer	Revenue MTD	New		Customer	Revenue
6	Wal-Mart	27,862	1,950		Sun Life Financi	1,295
7	Verizon	35,367	2,476		Wal-Mart	1,950
8	Sun Life Financial	21,578	3,805		Verizon	2,476

Fig. 561

Summary: The VLOOKUP function is excellent, but you need to be aware of the unintended problems that could be caused by having duplicates in the list.

Functions Discussed: =VLOOKUP(); =SUMIF()

COUNT RECORDS THAT MATCH A CRITERIA

Problem: You have a large dataset, as shown in Fig. 562. You want to count the number of records that meet a certain criteria.

	A	B	C	D
1	Name	Gender	DOB	Age
2	Robert	M	5/27/1922	82
3	Xavier	M	12/19/1939	64
4	Paul	M	8/21/1940	64
5	Ophelia	F	9/7/1941	63
6	Allen	M	10/21/1941	63
7	Raul	m	5/18/1942	62
8	Marc	M	3/27/1943	61

Fig. 562

Strategy: Use the COUNTIF function. This function requires two arguments. The first is a range of cells that you want to test. The second is a test. To count the records where the gender is "M", use =COUNTIF(B2: B57, "M"), as shown in Fig. 563.

| | | fx =COUNTIF($B$2:$B$57,"M") | | | | | |
| G2 | ▾ | | | | | | |

	A	B	C	D	E	F	G
1	Name	Gender	DOB	Age			Count
2	Robert	M	5/27/1922	82		Male	28
3	Xavier	M	12/19/1939	64		Female	
4	Paul	M	8/21/1940	64			

Fig. 563

Note that the second argument of "M" indicates tells Excel to count records that are equal to M. Since this function is not case sensitive, the function will count cells with M or m.

If you want to count the records where the age is a specific number, as shown in Fig. 564, then you can write the formula either with or without quotes around the number:

=COUNTIF(C2:C999,32)

=COUNTIF(C2:C999,"32")

| | | fx =COUNTIF($D$2:$D$57,"32") | | | | | |
| G5 | ▾ | | | | | | |

	A	B	C	D	E	F	G
1	Name	Gender	DOB	Age			Count
2	Zoe	F	3/2/1979	25		Male	28
3	Zeke	M	11/3/1949	55		Female	28
4	Zack	M	2/4/1944	60			
5	Xavier	M	12/19/1939	64		32	1
6	William	M	7/10/1951	53			
7	Wendy	F	10/15/1972	32			
8	Victor	M	10/25/1944	60			

Fig. 564

The criteria can look for items that are below or above a certain number:

=COUNTIF(C2:C999,"<40")

=COUNTIF(C2:C999,">21")

Summary: To count how many cells contain certain criteria, use the COUNTIF function by entering the two criteria it needs, which cells to count, and what to count.

Functions Discussed: =COUNTIF()

BUILD A TABLE THAT WILL COUNT BY CRITERIA

Problem: You need to build a summary table using COUNTIF functions. How can you enter one formula that can be copied?

Strategy: It is possible to use a cell reference as the second argument in the COUNTIF function. Set up a table below your data. Place all of the possible values for a column, such as department, in column A, as shown in Fig. 565.

	A	B	C	D
1	Name	Gender	DOB	Ag
53	William	M	7/10/1951	5
54	Xavier	M	12/19/1939	6
55	Zack	M	2/4/1944	6
56	Zeke	M	11/3/1949	5
57	Zoe	F	3/2/1979	2
58				
59	Employees by Department			
60				
61	Accounting			
62	Engineering			
63	Marketing			
64	Mfg			
65	Sales			

Fig. 565

1)   In column B of the first row, enter =COUNTIF($B$2=$B$56, A61), as shown in Fig. 566. Note that you should use the F4 key to make the B2:B56 range absolute. This will allow you to copy B61 to cells B62:B65.

B61   ▼   *fx* =COUNTIF($E$2:$E$57,A61)

	A	B	C	D	E	F
1	Name	Gender	DOB	Age	Department	
57	Zoe	F	3/2/1979	25	Engineering	
58						
59	Employees by Department					
60						
61	Accounting	7				
62	Engineering					
63	Marketing					
64	Mfg					
65	Sales					

Fig. 566

2)   Double-click the Fill handle to copy the formula down to B62:B65.

Result: As shown in Fig. 567, the table shown below provides a summary of your dataset.

B65   ▼   *fx* =COUNTIF($E$2:$E$57,A65)

	A	B	C	D	E	F
1	Name	Gender	DOB	Age	Department	
57	Zoe	F	3/2/1979	25	Engineering	
58						
59	Employees by Department					
60						
61	Accounting	7				
62	Engineering	11				
63	Marketing	9				
64	Mfg	22				
65	Sales	7				

Fig. 567

Summary: Using COUNTIF with a cell reference as the second argument allows you to set up various tables to summarize your data by department, gender, or any field.

Functions Discussed: =COUNTIF()

BUILD A SUMMARY TABLE TO PLACE EMPLOYEES IN AGE BANDS

Problem: How can you build a table that will group the employees in age ranges? The COUNTIF criteria cannot handle an argument that combines two conditions.

Strategy: This problem is more difficult.

1)   In column A, enter a variety of age ranges, such as ">=75", ">=65", ">=55", ">=45", etc. In column B, enter a formula =COUNTIF($D$2:$D$57,A61), as shown in Fig. 568.

	B61	▼		f_x =COUNTIF($D$2:$D$57,A61)		
	A	B	C	D	E	F
1	Name	Gender	DOB	Age	Department	
57	Zoe	F	3/2/1979	25	Engineering	
58						
59	Employees by Age					
60						
61	>=65	1				
62	>=55	17				
63	>=45	31				
64	>=35	41				
65	>=21	56				
66						

Fig. 568

However, the results of this formula are cumulative. The 17 employees in the over-55 category include the one employee in the over-65 category. The 41 employees in the over-35 category include all of the people in the over-45, -55, and -65 categories.

To get the real answer for any age band, you need to subtract all of the previous age bands. Look at this table:

Row 62: need to subtract row 61

Row 63: need to subtract rows 61 & 62

Row 64: need to subtract rows 61:63

Row 65: need to subtract rows 61:64

The rule, then, is that you need to subtract from row $61 to the row above the current cell.

2) Edit the formula in row 62. As shown in Fig. 569, add –SUM(B$61: B61) to the formula. Adding this new part to the formula will subtract the sum of B$61:B61. It is important that you have a dollar sign only before the first 61.

| | B62 | ▾ | f_x =COUNTIF($D$2:$D$57,A62)-SUM(B$61:B61) |

	A	B	C	D	E	F	G	H
1	Name	Gender	DOB	Age	Department			
57	Zoe	F	3/2/1979	25	Engineering			
58								
59	Employees by Age							
60								
61	>=65	1						
62	>=55	16						

Fig. 569

3) Copy the formula down to the other rows.

The single dollar sign in just one portion of the reference allows the formula to be copied down. As you copy this formula down to the other rows, the portion subtracted will expand. As you look at Fig. 570, note that in row 65 the formula is subtracting Rows 61 through 64.

| | B65 | ▾ | f_x =COUNTIF($D$2:$D$57,A65)-SUM(B$61:B64) |

	A	B	C	D	E	F	G	H
1	Name	Gender	DOB	Age	Department			
57	Zoe	F	3/2/1979	25	Engineering			
58								
59	Employees by Age							
60								
61	>=65	1						
62	>=55	16						
63	>=45	14						
64	>=35	10						
65	>=21	15						

Fig. 570

Additional Information: The solution above required two different formulas, one formula in 61 and a different formula in 62 through 65. Personally, I hate using two formulas. One workaround would have been to subtract from row $60:60. By having the anchor row be the row above the first row in the table, you could have used the same formula in all cells of the table.

Gotcha: At this point, the labels in column A are not technically correct. One solution would be to cut the formulas in column B and paste to column C, as shown in Fig. 571. It is important to use Cut and Paste instead of Copy and Paste so that the references keep pointing to column A. You can then type correct labels in column B and hide the information in column A by making the font white.

	A62	▼	fx	'>=55	
	A	B	C	D	
1	Name	Gender	DOB	Age	I
57	Zoe	F	3/2/1979	25	E
58					
59		Employees by Age			
60					
61		Over 65	1		
62		55-64	16		
63		45-54	14		
64		35-44	10		
65		21-34	15		

Fig. 571

Summary: This particular use of COUNTIF is tricky. You almost need two conditions, which COUNTIF cannot handle. Luckily, the criteria were adjacent to each other, so you could subtract the results of the previous formulas to get the result for a particular age band.

Functions Discussed: =COUNTIF(); =SUM()

TOTAL REVENUE FROM ROWS
THAT MATCH A CRITERION

Problem: Say that you want to total the sales made by Ben in the dataset shown in Fig. 572.

	A	B	C	D	E
1	Invoice	Rep	Customer	Product	Sales
2	1010	Deb	D6287	ABC	186
3	1011	Chaz	J4769	ABC	108
4	1012	Ben	O5956	ABC	157
5	1013	Amy	H1139	DEF	166
6	1014	Ben	W6177	XYZ	157

Fig. 572

Strategy: Excel offers the SUMIF function, which is somewhat similar to the COUNTIF function. To count records for Ben you would use: =COUNTIF(B2: B99,"Ben"), as shown in Fig. 573.

C101			▼	*fx* =COUNTIF(B2:B99,"Ben")		
	A	B	C	D	E	F	G
1	Invoice	Rep	Customer	Product	Sales		
97	1105	Chaz	N8977	ABC	202		
98	1106	Ben	K5508	ABC	116		
99	1107	Ben	W9236	ABC	188		
100							
101			25				

Fig. 573

To use SUMIF, the first two arguments are the same. The final argument is the range to be summed. This must be the same shape as the first argument: =SUMIF(B2:B99,"Ben",E2:E99). Instead of including "Ben" as a constant in the formula, you could enter Ben in a nearby cell and refer to the cell instead. Fig. 574 shows a table of sales by rep. The formula in E101 is copied down to E102:E104.

E101			▼	*fx* =SUMIF($B$2:$B$99,D101,$E$2:$E$99)			
	A	B	C	D	E	F	G	H
1	Invoice	Rep	Customer	Product	Sales			
97	1105	Chaz	N8977	ABC	202			
98	1106	Ben	K5508	ABC	116			
99	1107	Ben	W9236	ABC	188			
100								
101				Ben	5208			
102				Chaz	4684			
103				Amy	5408			
104				Deb	5157			
105								

Fig. 574

Additional Information: If for some reason the first and third arguments are the same range, you are allowed to drop the third argument. One example of this is if you need to sum all sales where sales are greater than 200, then you can use:

=SUMIF(E2:E99,">200")

Summary: Use SUMIF when you need to total certain rows from a dataset on the basis of one condition.

Functions Discussed: =SUMIF()

USE CONDITIONAL SUM WIZARD TO HELP WITH SUMIF

Problem: Conditional Formulas such as SUMIF and COUNTIF might be hard to figure out at first. CSE formulas needed to sum on the basis of two conditions are definitely hard to figure out. Is there an easier way?

Strategy: Excel offers a wizard that can walk you through building the formula. To install the wizard, Select Tools – Addins – Conditional Sum Wizard, as shown in Fig. 575.

Fig. 575

Caution: *This is no longer in the default install. You may need your installation CDs.*

As shown in Fig. 576, the Add-In adds a new item to the bottom of the Tools menu called "Conditional Sum".

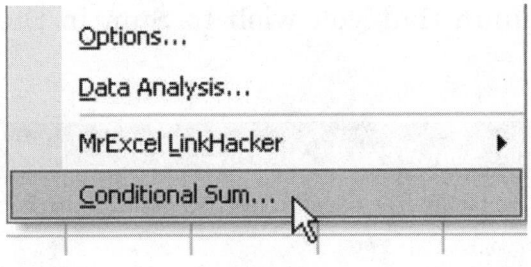

Fig. 576

1) Identify the range of your dataset in the Conditional Sum Wizard
   – Step 1 of 4, as shown in Fig. 577.

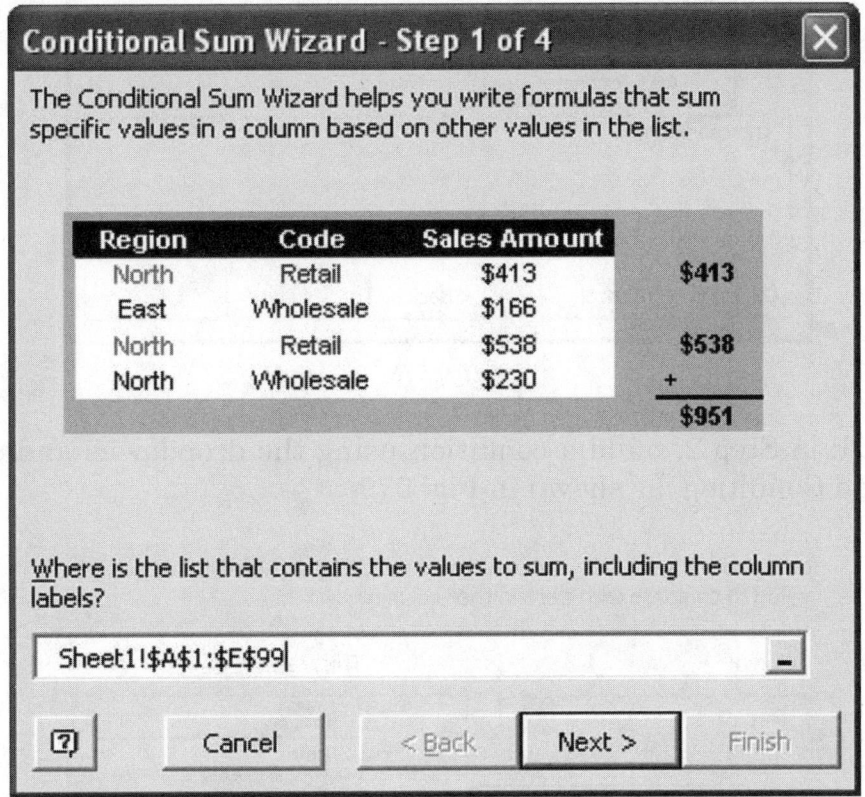

Fig. 577

**Part
II**

2)   Select the column that you wish to Sum in Step 2, as shown in
     Fig. 578.

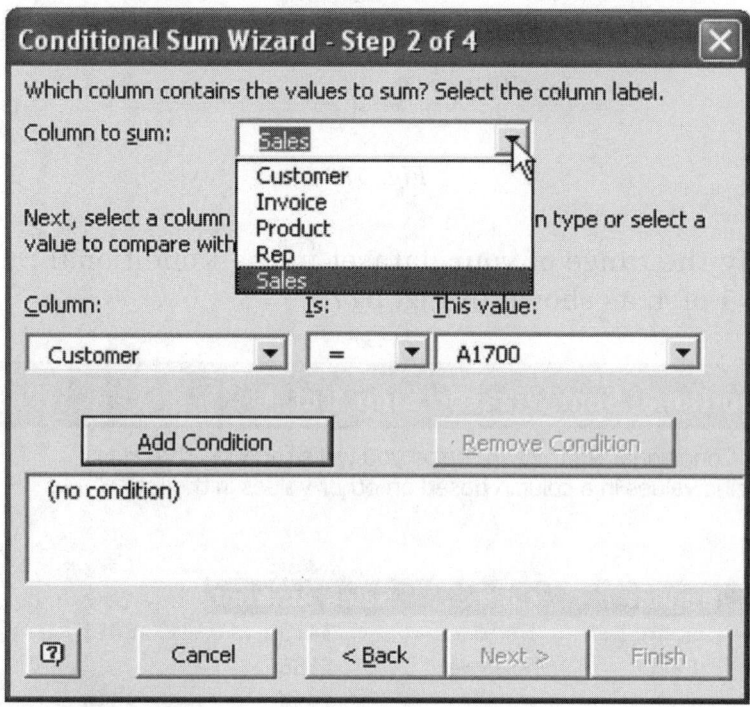

Fig. 578

3)   Still in Step 2, build a condition using the dropdowns and choose
     Add Condition, as shown in Fig. 579.

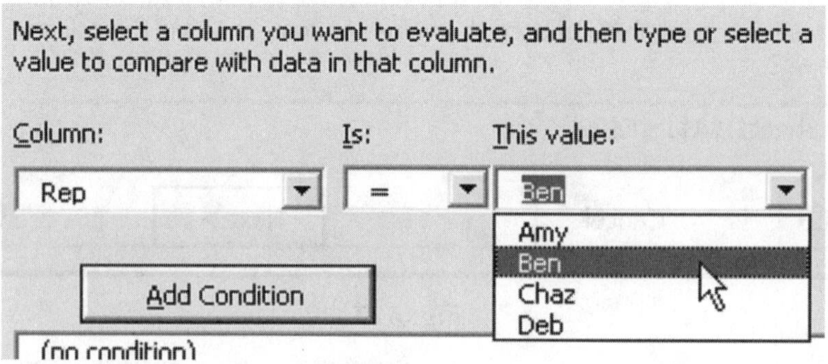

Fig. 579

You can even add multiple conditions, as shown in Fig. 580.

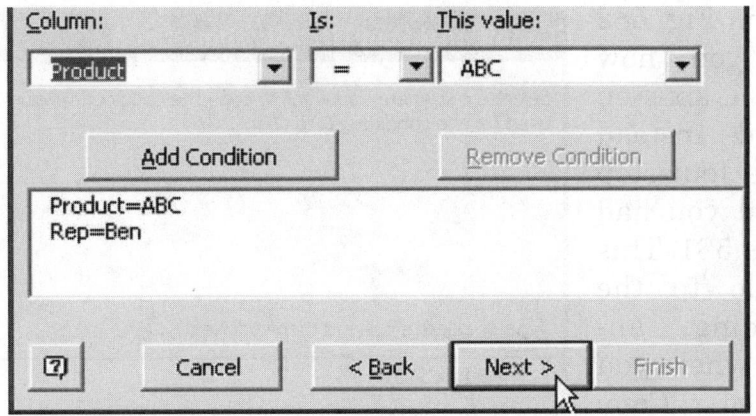

Fig. 580

4)   As shown in Step 3 in Fig. 581, you can either create a single cell
     with the answer or you can set up a range of cells with rep name,
     product name, and the formula for the answer. Choose the second
     option. This will allow you to change Ben to Amy and have the for-
     mula update.

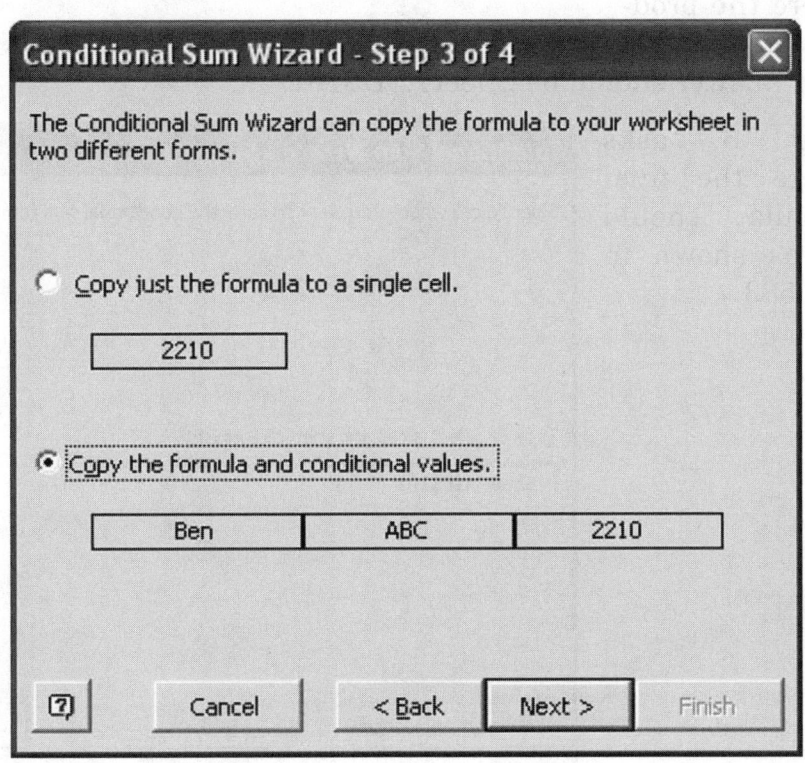

Fig. 581

5) Note in Fig. 582 that you now have a six-step wizard instead of the four-step wizard you had in Fig. 581. This is due to the preceding answer, where you selected "Copy the formula and conditional values". In Step 4 of 6, you choose where to put the first field.

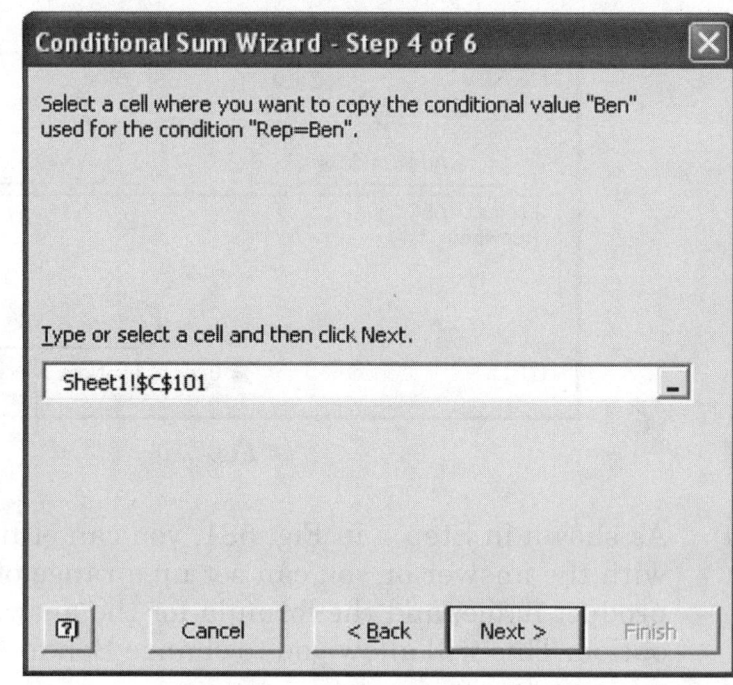

Fig. 582

6) Step 5 asks where the product should go. Your answer should be Sheet1!$D$101.

7) Step 6 asks where the final formula should go, as shown in Fig. 583.

Fig. 583

Result: The wizard has allowed you to build an incredibly complex CSE formula, as shown in Fig. 584.

	E101		▼		*fx* {=SUM(IF($B$2:$B$99=C101,IF($D$2:$D$99=D101,$E$2:$E$99,0),0))}					
	A	B	C	D	E	F	G	H	I	J	K
1	Invoice	Rep	Customer	Product	Sales						
98	1106	Ben	K5508	ABC	116						
99	1107	Ben	W9236	ABC	188						
100											
101			Ben	ABC	2210						
102											

Fig. 584

After the wizard has built the first formula, you can enter a table of reps and products and copy the formula down to the other rows, as shown in Fig. 585.

Part II

	A	B	C	D	E	F
1	Invoice	Rep	Customer	Product	Sales	
98	1106	Ben	K5508	ABC	116	
99	1107	Ben	W9236	ABC	188	
100						
101			Ben	ABC	2210	
102			Amy	ABC	998	
103			Chaz	ABC	2456	
104			Deb	ABC	1181	
105			Ben	DEF	1551	
106			Amy	DEF	2687	
107			Chaz	DEF	839	
108			Deb	DEF	1870	
109			Ben	XYZ	1447	
110			Amy	XYZ	1723	
111			Chaz	XYZ	1389	
112			Deb	XYZ	2106	

Fig. 585

Gotcha: When you copy cell E101, be sure that your paste range starts in E102. Normally, you could paste in E101:E112, but there is a limitation on CSE or Array formulas. If you attempt to paste E101 on top of itself, you will get the following error, as shown in Fig. 586: "You cannot change part of an array."

Fig. 586

To get around this, copy E101 and paste to E102:E112.

Additional Information: If you edit the result of the Conditional Sum Wizard, you cannot complete the edit by using Enter. You have to hold down Ctrl+Shift while hitting Enter.

Summary: The Conditional Sum Wizard is a fantastic tool for building complex formulas based on one or more conditions.

Commands Discussed: Tools – AddIns; Tools – Conditional Sum

CREATE A CSE FORMULA TO BUILD A SUPER FORMULA

Problem: Your dataset has a column with quantity sold and another column with unit prices, as shown in Fig. 587. You want one formula to figure out the total of quantity times unit price.

	A	B	C	D	E	F
1	Region	Product	Date	Customer	Quantity	Unit Price
553	West	XYZ	23-Dec-04	Verizon	900	95
554	East	ABC	24-Dec-04	Verizon	100	87
555	West	DEF	24-Dec-04	Ainsworth	500	78
556	Central	XYZ	24-Dec-04	Wal-Mart	200	95
557	Central	ABC	26-Dec-04	Ainsworth	100	87
558	West	DEF	26-Dec-04	Wal-Mart	700	78
559	East	XYZ	26-Dec-04	Exxon	600	95
560	West	XYZ	26-Dec-04	SBC Communicatic	500	95
561	Central	ABC	27-Dec-04	Sun Life Financial	500	87
562	Central	ABC	28-Dec-04	General Motors	600	87
563	Central	ABC	28-Dec-04	General Motors	600	87
564	Central	ABC	28-Dec-04	General Motors	900	87

Fig. 587

Part II

Strategy: The typical strategy is to add a new column with price times quantity and add that up. However, this is not necessary if you use a type of super formula that I call the CSE formula.

=SUM(E2:E564*F2:F564)

If you've been using Excel for a while, you will think that this looks like it will not work. In fact, if you enter the formula, you will get a #VALUE! error, confirming that it does not work, as shown in Fig. 588.

	F566	▼	*fx*	=SUM(E2:E564*F2:F564)	
	D	E	F	G	H
1	Customer	Quantity	Unit Price		
563	General Motors	600	87		
564	General Motors	900	87		
565					
566		◇	#VALUE!		
567					
568					

Fig. 588

However, if you know the secret you can still make the formula work. Edit the formula by hitting F2. Instead of using Enter to finish the formula, hold down Ctrl+Shift and then hit Enter.

CSE=Ctrl+Shift+Enter

As shown in Fig. 589, miraculously, Excel does 563 multiplications and then adds them up to give you a result.

	F566	▼	f_x {=SUM(E2:E564*F2:F564)}		
	D	E	F	G	H
1	Customer	Quantity	Unit Price		
563	General Motors	600	87		
564	General Motors	900	87		
565					
566			27,263,600		
567					

Fig. 589

In the formula bar above, you will note that there are curly braces around the formula. You do not enter these braces. Excel adds them when you use Ctrl+Shift+Enter.

Additional Details: Most people will only have an occasion to use this formula once a month. I found that I could never remember the keystroke combination, so I renamed these formulas "CSE" to help me to remember Ctrl+Shift+Enter. If you need to search Microsoft Help on the subject, check under the name "Array Formulas".

Summary: One single CSE formula can replace hundreds or even thousands of intermediate formulas.

Commands Discussed: Control+Shift+Enter

LEARN TO USE
BOOLEAN LOGIC FACTS TO SIMPLIFY LOGIC

Problem: If you have to enter multiple IF conditions, having a good understanding of logical operators will help you to simplify the formula.

Strategy: When you are dealing with conditions, the language is full of And, Or, Not, Nor, True, and False. All of these words have mathematical equivalents. Understanding them will enable you to build complex two-condition formulas.

A Boolean formula returns either TRUE or FALSE. In Fig. 590, the formula =A2>100 will return TRUE.

	A	B	C
	B2		f_x =A2>100
1	Sales	Sales>100?	
2	105	TRUE	
3	92	FALSE	
4	85	FALSE	
5	100	FALSE	
6	101	TRUE	

Fig. 590

Part
II

You can have many such tests. As shown in Fig. 591, this dataset has columns to test if the product is a particular product line or if the region is a particular region.

	A	B	C	D	E	F
	E2			f_x =B2="ABC"		
1	Sales	Product	Region	Sales>100?	Prod=ABC?	Region=East?
2	105	ABC	East	TRUE	TRUE	TRUE
3	92	ABC	West	FALSE	TRUE	FALSE
4	85	ABC	East	FALSE	TRUE	TRUE
5	100	DEF	West	FALSE	FALSE	FALSE
6	101	DEF	East	TRUE	FALSE	TRUE

Fig. 591

You can build a calculation from the results of multiple Boolean formulas. One popular operator in Boolean logic is the AND operator. If you want to know if D2 AND E2 is TRUE, you can state this as a formula.

In Boolean Logic,

- Think of each TRUE as the number 1.
- Think of each FALSE as the number 0.

- Think of each AND as a Multiplication Operator
- Think of each OR as an Addition Operator

If the result of the calculation is 0, then the answer is FALSE. If the result of the calculation is non-zero then the answer is TRUE.

Here is an example, as shown in Fig. 592:

Plain language: The bonus is paid if the sale is >100 and the product is ABC.

Excel: =(A2>100)*(B2="ABC")

A=105 B=ABC:	TRUE * TRUE=	1*1=1=TRUE
A=92 B=ABC:	FALSE * TRUE=	0*1=0=FALSE
A=85 B=DEF:	FALSE * FALSE=	0*0=0=FALSE
A=101 B=DEF:	TRUE * FALSE=	1*0=0=FALSE

	A	B	C	D	E	F	G
1	Sales	Product	Region	Sales>100?	Prod=ABC?	Region=East?	Bonus?
2	105	ABC	East	TRUE	TRUE	TRUE	1
3	92	ABC	West	FALSE	TRUE	FALSE	0
4	85	DEF	East	FALSE	FALSE	TRUE	0
5	101	DEF	West	TRUE	FALSE	FALSE	0

Fig. 592

Here are the logic rules for AND operators and OR operators.

AND	**OR**
TRUE*TRUE=TRUE	TRUE+TRUE=TRUE
TRUE*FALSE=FALSE	TRUE+FALSE=TRUE
FALSE*TRUE=FALSE	FALSE+TRUE=TRUE
FALSE*FALSE=FALSE	FALSE+FALSE=FALSE

Here is another example to work through.

Plain language: Bonus is paid for selling any item over $100.00 or for sales of DEF product.

Excel: =(A2>100)+(B2="DEF"), as shown in Fig. 593.

Sales	Product	Sales>100	Item=DEF	Bonus Calculation
80	DEF	FALSE	TRUE	=0+1=1=TRUE
105	DEF	TRUE	TRUE	=1+1=2=TRUE
90	ABC	FALSE	FALSE	=0+0=0=FALSE
110	ABC	TRUE	FALSE	=1+0=1=TRUE

F2			fx =(A2>100)+(B2="DEF")		
	A	B	C	D	E	F
1	Sales	Product	Region	Sales>100?	Prod=DEF?	Bonus?
2	80	DEF	East	FALSE	TRUE	1
3	105	DEF	West	TRUE	TRUE	2
4	90	ABC	East	FALSE	FALSE	0
5	110	ABC	West	TRUE	FALSE	1

Fig. 593

Using the above rules, you can write complex sets of Boolean logic. The formula in Fig. 594 would pay a $25 bonus for all West region sales of jackets at any price or caps above $50.

D2			fx =IF(((B2="Jacket")+((B2="Cap")*(A2>50)))*(C2="West"),25,0)					
	A	B	C	D	E	F	G	H	I
1	Price	Product	Region	Bonus?					
2	225	Jacket	East	0					
3	250	Jacket	West	25					
4	35	Cap	East	0					
5	55	Cap	West	25					
6	175	Jacket	East	0					
7	200	Jacket	West	25					
8	55	Cap	East	0					
9	35	Cap	West	0					

Fig. 594

Summary: Excel does offer the AND and OR functions. However, being able to use Boolean terms as the first parameter of an IF statement allows for more complex calculations.

Functions Discussed: =IF(); =AND(); =OR()

REPLACE IF FUNCTION WITH BOOLEAN LOGIC

Problem: As shown in Fig. 595, you need to calculate a 10 percent bonus on sales greater than $1000.00.

	A	B	C	D	E	F
1	Invoice	Product	Price	Qty	Total	Bonus
2	2010	Jacket	225	14	3150	
3	2011	Jacket	225	8	1800	
4	2012	Jacket	225	11	2475	
5	2013	Cap	25	6	150	
6	2014	Jacket	225	17	3825	

Fig. 595

Strategy: You can use the Boolean logic facts to do this calculation without an IF function. Remember that a Boolean test that results in a TRUE is treated as a 1 and a FALSE statement is treated as a 0. Thus, you could multiply the calculation E2*0.1 by the Boolean test (E2>1000), as shown in Fig. 596.

F2			f_x =(E2*0.1)*(E2>1000)			
	A	B	C	D	E	F
1	Invoice	Product	Price	Qty	Total	Bonus
2	2010	Jacket	225	14	3150	315
3	2011	Jacket	225	8	1800	180
4	2012	Jacket	225	11	2475	247.5
5	2013	Cap	25	6	150	0
6	2014	Jacket	225	17	3825	382.5
7	2015	Jacket	225	3	675	0
8	2016	Jacket	225	2	450	0

Fig. 596

Summary: This formula combines a math calculation with a Boolean test to produce a valid result. Using these types of calculations is one key to using conditional sums with two conditions. You will learn about these in the next chapter.

Functions Discussed: =IF()

TEST FOR TWO CONDITIONS IN A SUM

Problem: You need to sum a dataset based on two conditions. The SUMIF function can only handle one condition. As shown in Fig. 597, you want to write a formula that will total all sales by Amy of product ABC.

	A	B	C	D	E	F
1	Invoice	Rep	Customer	Product	Sales	
91	1099	Deb	L3917	XYZ	244	
92	1100	Deb	F8477	XYZ	198	
93	1101	Ben	Q7142	ABC	345	
94	1102	Chaz	D8695	DEF	342	
95	1103	Amy	J9467	ABC	245	
96	1104	Amy	M8580	XYZ	163	
97	1105	Chaz	N8977	ABC	202	
98	1106	Ben	K5508	ABC	116	
99	1107	Ben	W9236	ABC	188	
100						
101			ABC	DEF	XYZ	
102		Amy	=SUMIF(			
103		Ben	SUMIF(**range**, criteria, [sum_range])			
104		Chaz				
105		Deb				

Fig. 597

Strategy: You have to use a CSE formula to do this. This question comes up a lot at the MrExcel.com site. It is a definite collision point in Excel – it is a very common problem, but a very difficult solution.

The SUMIF Function will not do this for you. You have to use Boolean logic and a CSE formula. You want to test to see if each cell in B2:B99 is equal to B102. This would be represented by the following formula:

=($B$2:$B$99=$B102)

You also want to test to see if each cell in D2:D99 is equal to C101. This would be represented by the following formula:

=($D$2:$D$99=C$101)

If you multiply those two terms together, you will end up with a 1 wherever both conditions are True and a 0 wherever one condition is not True.

=($B$2:$B$99=$B102)*($D$2:$D$99=C$101)

As shown in Fig. 598, pretend that you actually entered these formulas in columns F, G, and H. After you have the 1 or 0 in column H, you have to multiply that result times Sales in column E and then sum up column I.

		I2		fx	=+H2*E2			
	A	B	C	D	E	F	G	H	I
1	Invoice	Rep	Customer	Product	Sales	Amy?	ABC?	F*G	Result
2	1018	Chaz	A1700	ABC	320	FALSE	TRUE	0	0
3	1051	Amy	A3203	XYZ	309	TRUE	FALSE	0	0
4	1086	Amy	A3446	DEF	150	TRUE	FALSE	0	0
5	1049	Chaz	A4580	XYZ	228	FALSE	FALSE	0	0
6	1054	Chaz	A6969	ABC	260	FALSE	TRUE	0	0
7	1034	Amy	A7717	ABC	251	TRUE	TRUE	1	251
8	1077	Chaz	B5387	ABC	228	FALSE	TRUE	0	0

Fig. 598

To multiply the Boolean terms by Sales, use:

=($B$2:$B$99=$B102)*($D$2:$D$99=C$101)*($E$2:$E$99)

To sum the result, use:

=SUM(($B$2:$B$99=$B102)*($D$2:$D$99=C$101)*($E$2:$E$99))

Enter this formula in C102. Instead of using Enter after typing the formula, use Ctrl+Shift+Enter. Excel will evaluate the formula as an array and produce the correct result, as shown in Fig. 599.

		C102		fx	{=SUM(($B$2:$B$99=$B102)*($D$2:$D$99=C$101)*($E$2:$E$99))}				
	A	B	C	D	E	F	G	H	I	J
1	Invoice	Rep	Customer	Product	Sales					
98	1020	Deb	Z2412	ABC	233					
99	1069	Amy	Z9822	DEF	278					
100										
101			ABC	DEF	XYZ					
102		Amy	998							
103		Ben								
104		Chaz								
105		Deb								

Fig. 599

> **Note:** *You do NOT type the curly braces around the formula. Excel will add those when you use Ctrl+Shift+Enter.*

Due to the careful use of the dollar signs in each reference, you've made a formula that can be copied to the rest of the table. Normally, you would copy C102 and paste it to C102:E105, but because of the limitation of CSE formulas, you cannot do this. You first have to copy C102 to C103: C105, as shown in Fig. 600.

	A	B	C	
1	Invoice	Rep	Customer	Pro
98	1020	Deb	Z2412	AB(
99	1069	Amy	Z9822	DEF
100				
101			ABC	DEF
102		Amy	998	
103		Ben	2210	
104		Chaz	2456	
105		Deb	1181	

Fig. 600

Then, copy C102:C105 and paste it to D102:E105, as shown in Fig. 601.

	A	B	C	D	E
1	Invoice	Rep	Customer	Product	Sales
98	1020	Deb	Z2412	ABC	233
99	1069	Amy	Z9822	DEF	278
100					
101			ABC	DEF	XYZ
102		Amy	998	2687	1723
103		Ben	2210	1551	1447
104		Chaz	2456	839	1389
105		Deb	1181	1870	2106

Fig. 601

Gotcha: CSE or array formulas are very powerful. They are also very memory intensive. Don't go overboard with them. I once tried to build a report of 800 CSE formulas with each one totaling a 50,000-row dataset using three conditions. If I hadn't rebooted the computer, it would still be trying to calculate the formula.

Alternate Strategy: Aladin Akyurek has written an excellent article about this topic at http://www.mrexcel.com/wwwboard/messages/8961. html. Aladin notes that this problem can be solved without using a CSE formula by using the SUMPRODUCT function. The equivalent formula for cell C102 would be as follows:

=SUMPRODUCT(($B$2:$B$99=$B102)*($D$2:$D$99=C$101)*($E$2:$E$99))

Summary: Using CSE formulas and Boolean logic, you can solve a problem where you need to sum on the basis of two conditions. This is not just a powerful extension of SUMIF. Using these types of formulas, you can write just about any conditional calculation that you can imagine.

CAN THE RESULTS OF A FORMULA BE USED IN COUNTIF?

Problem: You need to count the number of students who are above average. The student grades are arranged from B2:B26, as shown in Fig. 602.

	A	B
1	Name	Score
2	Allen	92
3	Barb	72
4	Bob	60
5	Carla	82
6	Charley	72
7	Ed	64
8	Gail	72
9	Katia	82

Fig. 602

Strategy: The second parameter of the COUNTIF can be a calculation. As shown in Fig. 603, you can concatenate a text operator with a calculation, such as the one that follows.

=COUNTIF(B2:B26,">"&AVERAGE(B2:B26))

D2		▼		*fx*	=COUNTIF(B2:B26,">"&AVERAGE(B2:B26))			
	A	B	C	D	E	F	G	
1	Name	Score						
2	Allen	92		13				
3	Barb	72						
4	Bob	60						

Fig. 603

Part II

Summary: Using the result of a calculation as the criteria argument for the COUNTIF opens up a wide possibility of measurements using COUNTIF and SUMIF.

Functions Discussed: =SUMIF(); =COUNTIF()

BACK INTO AN ANSWER USING GOAL SEEK

Problem: You've determined that you want to obtain a 48-month loan for a car. The interest rate is 5 percent. You want to find out what loan amount would result in a $490 monthly payment. As shown in Fig. 604, the sticker price of the car results in a $575 payment.

	A	B
1		
2	Price	25000
3	Term	48
4	Rate	5%
5		
6	Pmt	$575.73
7		

Fig. 604

Strategy: Although there is a financial function to determine the Present Value (PV), it is easier to use the Goal Seek command on the Tools menu.

1) From the Tools menu, select Goal Seek. This will bring up the dialog shown in Fig. 605.

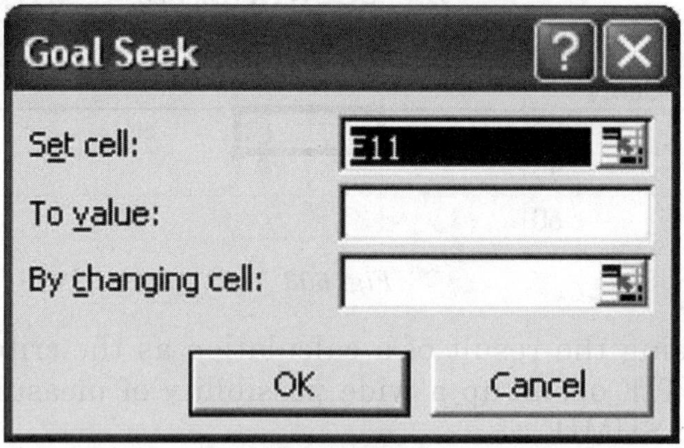

Fig. 605

2) In Fig. 604, you want to set cell B6 to $490 by changing cell B2. Enter these values and choose OK, as shown in Fig. 606.

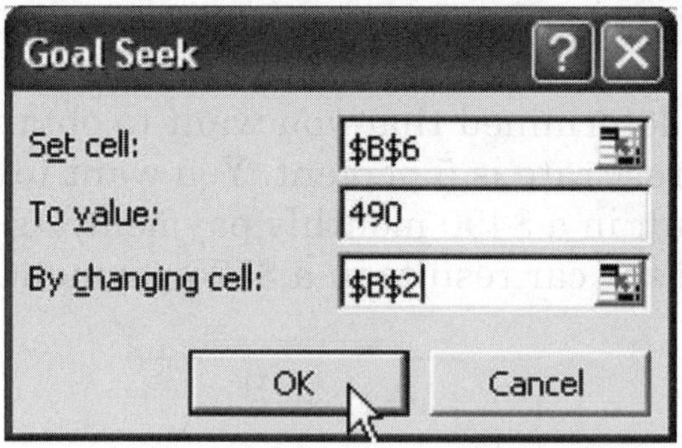

Fig. 606

In a simple case like this one, Goal Seek will almost always succeed. It will report back that it found a solution, as shown in Fig. 607.

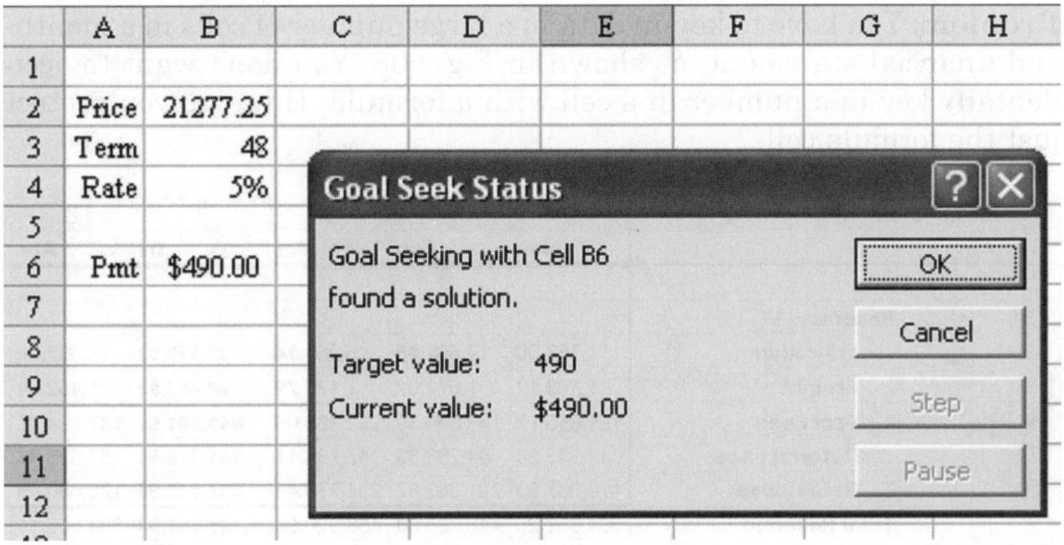

	A	B	C	D	E	F	G	H
1								
2	Price	21277.25						
3	Term	48						
4	Rate	5%						
5								
6	Pmt	$490.00						
7								
8								
9								
10								
11								
12								

Goal Seek Status

Goal Seeking with Cell B6 found a solution.

Target value: 490
Current value: $490.00

OK
Cancel
Step
Pause

Fig. 607

3)   To accept the solution, choose OK. To revert to the original value, select Cancel.

Result: You can afford to borrow $21,277.25.

Summary: The Goal Seek command on the tools menu is great for solving certain equations backwards.

PROTECT CELLS WITH FORMULAS

Problem: You have to key-in data in a large number of cells in a month-end financial statement, as shown in Fig. 608. You don't want to accidentally key-in a number in a cell with a formula. How can you protect just the formula cells?

	A	B	C	D	E	F	G	H	I	J	K
1							Jan	Feb	Mar	Q1	Apr
2			Income								
3				Revenue							
4					Education		11,767.30	12,551.48	15,261.14	39,579.92	15,857.08
5					Freight		1,609.12	1,672.02	1,176.79	4,457.92	1,452.94
6					Prof Fees		151,655.17	148,880.39	159,366.05	459,901.61	137,394.75
7					Referral Fees		43,343.06	64,238.33	47,738.11	155,319.50	57,320.46
8					Retail Sales		176,287.63	221,382.87	234,778.49	632,448.99	172,630.89
9				Total Revenue			384,662.28	448,725.08	458,320.58	1,291,707.94	384,656.11
10			Total Income				384,662.28	448,725.08	458,320.58	1,291,707.94	384,656.11
11			Cost of Goods Sold								
12				Cost of Goods Sold			48,067.54	44,100.56	30,651.39	122,819.49	31,099.77
13				Cost of Sales			20.48	26.89	24.83	72.20	19.96
14			Total COGS				48,088.03	44,127.44	30,676.22	122,891.69	31,119.73
15		Gross Profit					336,574.25	404,597.64	427,644.36	1,168,816.25	353,536.38
16			Expense								
17				Research			83.80	88.27	59.24	231.31	57.50
18				Agent Fees			438.30	312.61	388.65	1,139.55	421.66

Fig. 608

Strategy: After unlocking all cells, use the Edit – Go To – Special dialog to select only the cells with formulas and lock just those cells.

By default, all cells in the worksheet start with their Locked property set to TRUE. You don't realize this until you turn on protection for the first time. The first step is to unlock all of the cells.

1)   Select all cells with Ctrl+A. From the menu, select Format – Cells. Click on the Protection tab. As shown in Fig. 609, you will see that the Locked option is chosen.

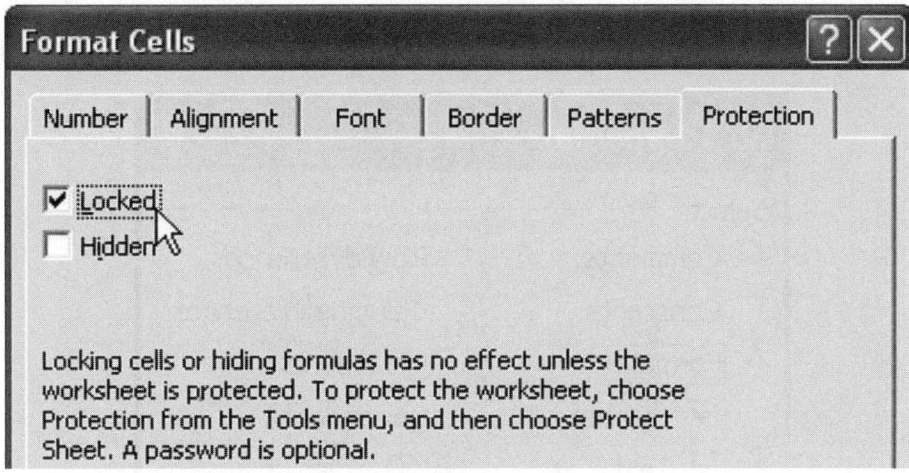

Fig. 609

2)   Uncheck the Locked box. Choose OK to dismiss the Format Cells
      dialog.

3)   You should still have all of the cells highlighted. From the menu,
      select Edit – Go To. On the Go To dialog, choose the Special button
      in the lower left corner, as shown in Fig. 610.

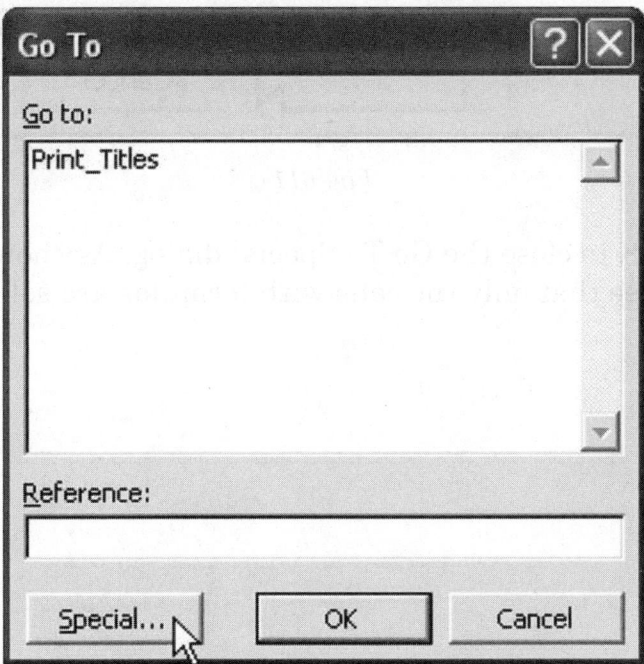

Fig. 610

4) On the Go To Special dialog box, choose the option button for For-
    mulas, as shown in Fig. 611.

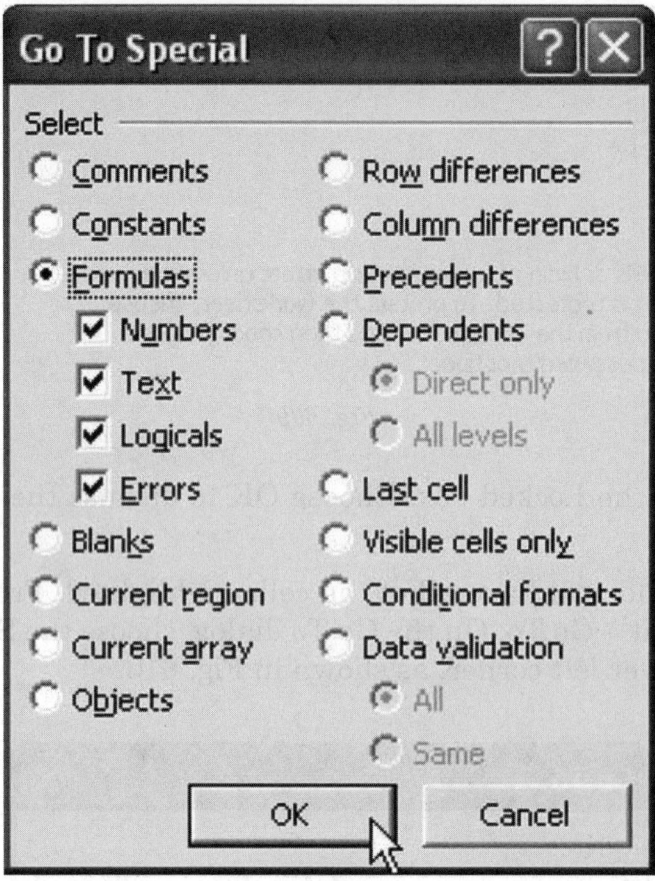

Fig. 611

5) Choose OK to close the Go To Special dialog. As shown in Fig. 612,
    you will see that only the cells with formulas are selected.

	A	B	C	D	E	F	G	H	I	J	K
1							Jan	Feb	Mar	Q1	A
2		Income									
3			Revenue								
4				Education			11,767.30	12,551.48	15,261.14	39,579.92	15,857.
5				Freight			1,609.12	1,672.02	1,176.79	4,457.92	1,452.
6				Prof Fees			151,655.17	148,880.39	159,366.05	459,901.61	137,394.
7				Referral Fees			43,343.06	64,238.33	47,738.11	155,319.50	57,320.
8				Retail Sales			176,287.63	221,382.87	234,778.49	632,448.99	172,630.
9			Total Revenue				384,662.28	448,725.08	458,320.58	1,291,707.94	384,656.
10		Total Income					384,662.28	448,725.08	458,320.58	1,291,707.94	384,656.
11		Cost of Goods Sold									
12			Cost of Goods Sold				48,067.54	44,100.56	30,651.39	122,819.49	31,099.
13			Cost of Sales				20.48	26.89	24.83	72.20	19.
14		Total COGS					48,088.03	44,127.44	30,676.22	122,891.69	31,119.
15		Gross Profit					336,574.25	404,597.64	427,644.36	1,168,816.25	353,536.

Fig. 612

6) From the menu, select Format – Cells. On the Protection tab, choose the Locked checkbox. This will lock only the selected cells, which are the formula cells.

7) The final important step is to enable protection for the sheet. If you miss this final step, you can still accidentally overwrite your formulas. From the menu, select Tools – Protection – Protect Sheet to display the Protect Sheet dialog, as shown in Fig. 613.

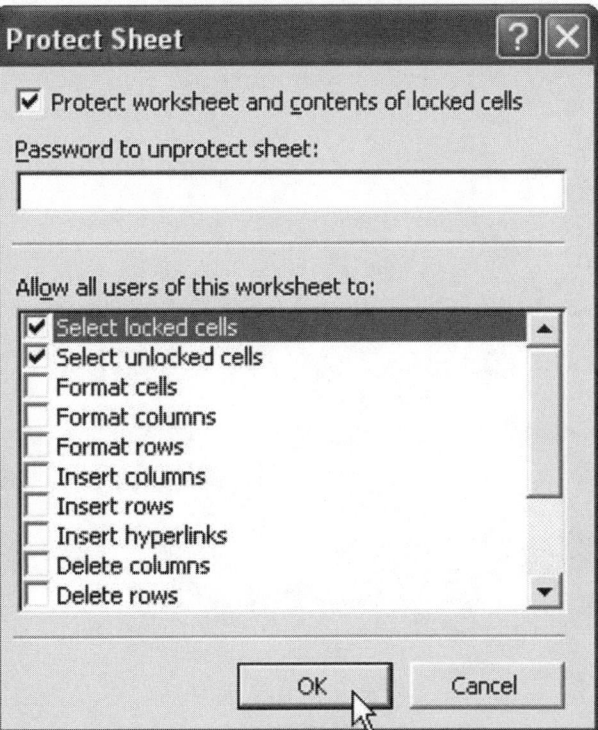

Fig. 613

Part II

Now, if you accidentally try to enter something in a formula cell, Excel will warn you, as shown in Fig. 614.

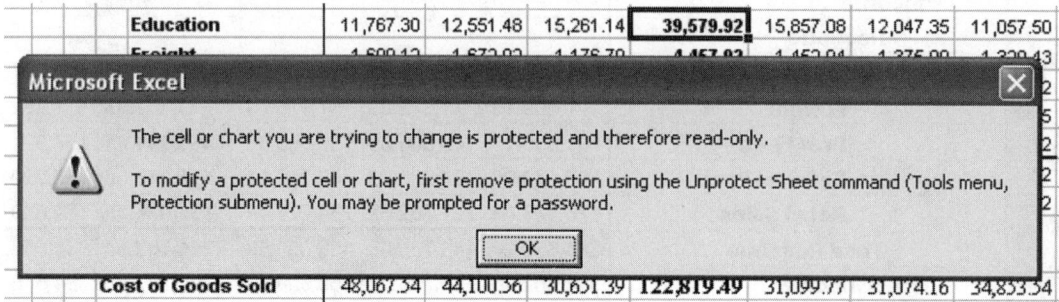

Fig. 614

Summary: Use the Go To Special dialog to select only the formula cells to protect just those cells. Remember to protect the sheet from overwriting.

Commands Discussed: Format – Cells – Protection; Edit – Go To Special

PART 3

WRANGLING DATA

HOW TO SET UP YOUR DATA
FOR EASY SORTING AND SUBTOTALS

Problem: You want to be able to use the powerful data commands in a spreadsheet, as shown in Fig. 615 — commands such as Sort, AutoFilter, Subtotals, Consolidate, and PivotTable. You can save yourself a lot of aggravation by properly setting up the data to begin with.

	A	B	C	D	E
1	OurCo Corporation				
2	Sales Report				
3	Fiscal Year 2006				
4					
5	Sales Rep	Customer	Product	Sales	Revenue
6	Joe	RST Company	GHI	624	55536
7	Mary	EFG Pty Ltd	GHI	605	53845
8	Dan	TUV Company	DEF	733	65237
9	Dan	CDE GMbH	XYZ	634	56426
10	Bob	BCD Corporation	ABC	795	70755
11	Dan	CDE Pty Ltd	ABC	447	39783
12	Mary	NOP, LLC	ABC	627	55803
13	Bob	RST, Inc.	GHI	740	65860

Fig. 615

Strategy: Follow all of the rules to keep your data in List Format. The rules are described below.

Rule 1: There should be a single row of headings above your data.

If you need to have a two-row heading, set it up as a single cell with two lines in the row, as shown in cell A5 (see next topic).

Rule 2: Never leave one heading cell blank.

You will find that you do this if you add a temporary column. If you forget to add a heading before you sort, this will completely throw off the intellisense and Excel will sort the headings down into the data.

Rule 3: There should be no entirely blank rows or blank columns in the middle of your data.

It is OK to have an occasional blank cell, but you should have no entirely blank columns.

Rule 4: If your heading row is not in row 1, be sure to have a blank row between your headings and any other filled cells.

In Fig. 615, you would want to have a blank row 4 between the titles in cells A1:A3 and the headings in row 5.

Rule 5: Formatting the heading cells in Bold will help the Excel intellisense module to understand that these are headings.

Gotcha: List Format won't help at all if your data is only two columns wide.

Result: Excel's intellisense will allow all of the Data commands to work flawlessly.

Additional Details: In Excel 2003, you can select your list and hit Ctrl+L to specify that a range is a list.

Summary: Follow the five rules presented here to set up your data before trying any of the commands on the Data menu.

Cross Reference: How to Fit a Multiline Heading into One Cell

HOW TO FIT A MULTILINE HEADING INTO ONE CELL

Problem: The problem on List Format indicated that your headings should occupy only one row to allow for easy sorting. Your manager requires that you format a report to have the heading "Prior Year" split with "Prior" in one row and "Year" in a second row, as shown in Fig. 616.

	S	T	U	V	W	X
1						
2						
3						
4						Prior
5	Oct	Nov	Dec	Q4	2006	Year
6	81	92	71	244	624	591
7	68	6	37	111	605	561
8	89	6	97	192	733	701
9	48	57	98	203	634	604
10	42	68	66	176	795	771
11	42	55	43	140	447	431
12	55	42	5	102	627	588

Fig. 616

This is a very real problem, where form meets function. The right thing to do in Excel is to have "Prior Year" in one cell. But, I've also worked for obsessive managers who absolutely, positively want the formatting to be exactly as they specify. Luckily, there is a strategy that makes it possible to make the manager happy and to have the dataset set up correctly in Excel, too.

Strategy: As shown in Fig. 617, in cell X5, type the word Prior. Hold down Alt while hitting Enter and type the word Year. The Alt+Enter combination adds a line feed character in the cell.

Delete the heading in X4 by moving the cell pointer there and hitting the Delete key.

	S	T	U	V	W	X
1						
2						
3						
4						Prior
						Prior
5	Oct	Nov	Dec	Q4	2006	Year
6	81	92	71	244	624	591
7	68	6	37	111	605	561

Fig. 617

Result: As shown in Fig. 618, you have a single cell that contains two lines of text. The cell will work as a heading in pivot tables, subtotals, and sorting, etc.

	S	T	U	V	W	X
						Prior
5	Oct	Nov	Dec	Q4	2006	Year
6	81	92	71	244	624	591
7	68	6	37	111	605	561
8	89	6	97	192	733	701

Fig. 618

Part
III

Additional Details: Using Alt+Enter automatically turns on the Wrap Text option for the cell. As shown in Fig. 619, you could also turn on the Wrap Text option by choosing Cells from the Format menu and then using the Alignment tab.

Turning on Wrap Text in this manner will probably work for a heading like "Prior Year". However, if you want to have control over a long heading, such as "Prior Year Results (Adjusted for Spin-off of the Widget Division)", then it is better to use Alt+Enter. Fig. 620 below shows the somewhat random

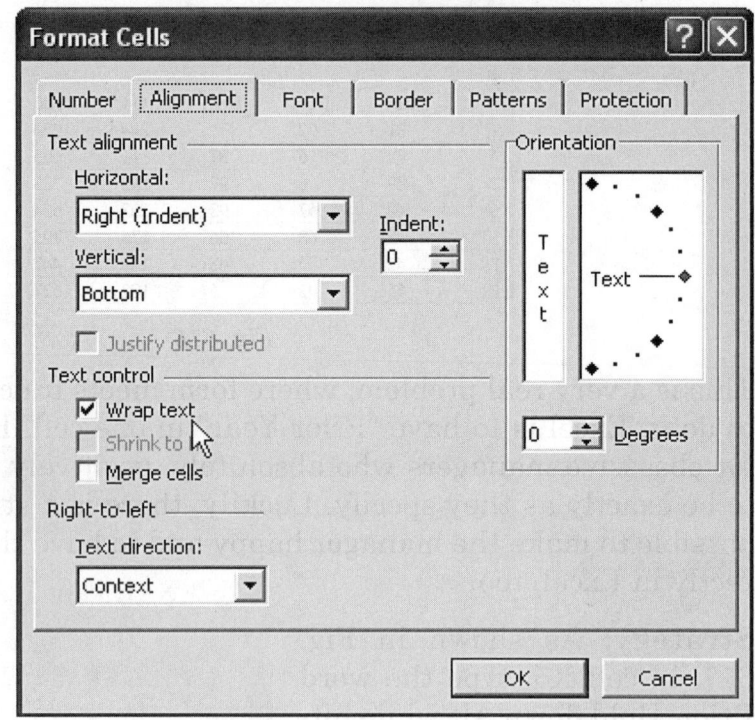

Fig. 619

splitting used by just turning on Wrap Text. As you make this column wider, you can get the results shown in Fig. 621 and Fig. 622.

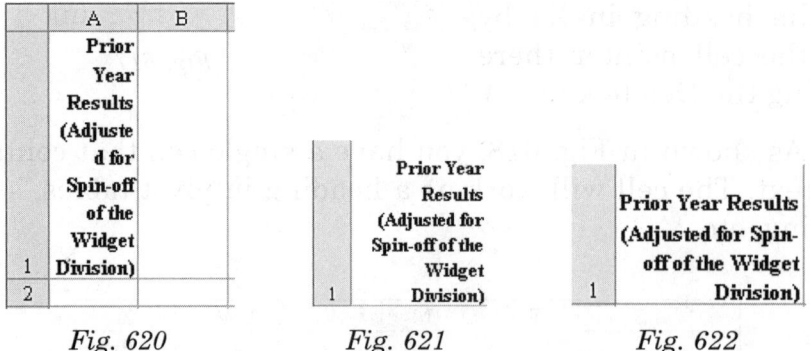

Fig. 620   Fig. 621   Fig. 622

Instead, if you use Alt+Enter, you can have absolute control over where the heading breaks. Fig. 623 shows a cell where you typed Prior Year R esultsAlt+Enter(Adjusted for theAlt+EnterSpin-off of theAltEnterWidgetDivision). Make the column wider and center it for the perfect-looking cell shown in Fig. 624.

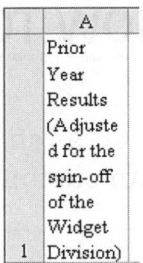
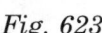
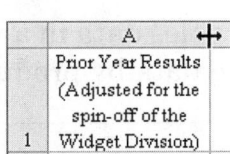

Fig. 623   Fig. 624

Gotcha: If you set up a cell that looks like Fig. 620 and resize the column to look like Fig. 622, the row height will stay tall enough to accommodate Fig. 620. To correct, select the cell and from the menu, choose Format – Row – Autofit.

Gotcha: Sometimes you will paste some cells and frustratingly find that many cells have Wrap Text. If you select all cells in the worksheet and globally turn off Wrap Text, the linefeeds where you hit Alt+Enter will show up as squares in the cell, as shown in Fig. 625.

W	X
2006	**Prior☐Year**
624	591
605	561

Fig. 625

Reselect these cells, hit Ctrl+1 to display the Format Cells dialog, go to Alignment and turn on the Wrap Text feature. Then select the cell and choose Format – Row – AutoFit to see both lines of the cell again.

Summary: Use Alt+Enter to make single cells that contain several rows of headings. This enables all of the commands on the Data menu to work properly.

Commands Discussed: Format – Cells; Format – Row – AutoFit

Part
III

HOW TO SORT DATA

Problem: You have sales data in a worksheet, as shown in Fig. 626. You would like to sort the data by product within customer.

	A	B	C	D	E
1	OurCo Corporation				
2	Sales Report				
3	Fiscal Year 2006				
4					
5	Sales Rep	Customer	Product	Sales	Revenue
6	Joe	RST Company	GHI	624	55536
7	Mary	EFG Pty Ltd	GHI	605	53845
8	Dan	TUV Company	DEF	733	65237
9	Dan	CDE GMbH	XYZ	634	56426
10	Bob	BCD Corporation	ABC	795	70755
11	Dan	CDE Pty Ltd	ABC	447	39783
12	Mary	NOP, LLC	ABC	627	55803
13	Bob	RST, Inc.	GHI	740	65860

Fig. 626

Strategy:

1) Select one cell within your data. The one cell can be in the heading row or any data row. From the menu, select Data – Sort.

2) In the Sort dialog, choose up to three fields to sort by. For each field, choose if the results should be presented in alphabetical order (ascending) or in high-to-low order (descending). If your data is set up correctly as outlined in the List Format topic, Excel will properly guess that your list has a header row, as shown in Fig. 627.

Fig. 627

3)   Choose OK to sort. Because Customer was the first sort key, all
       of the records for "ABC Company" will sort to the top. Records for
       "ABC GMbH" will appear next, as shown in Fig. 628.

Sales Rep	Customer	Product	Sales	Revenue
Bob	ABC Company	DEF	529	47081
Dan	ABC Company	DEF	430	38270
Bob	ABC GMbH	ABC	702	62478
Dan	ABC GMbH	ABC	512	45568
Joe	ABC GMbH	DEF	505	44945
Dan	ABC GMbH	GHI	553	49217
Joe	BCD Company	DEF	399	35511
Bob	BCD Corporation	ABC	795	70755
Dan	BCD Corporation	ABC	575	51175
Dan	BCD Corporation	ABC	734	65326
Dan	BCD Corporation	DEF	641	57049

Fig. 628

Additional Detail: When there is a tie – such as the four records for
"ABC GMbH" – those records will be sorted in ascending order by the
product field. For instance, the ABC product record appears before the
DEF product field.

If there is still a tie, the records remain in their original sequence from
before the sort.

Alternate Strategy: If your data is properly set up in list format, you
can select a single cell in the data and choose the Sort Ascending button
in the Standard toolbar, as shown in Fig. 629.

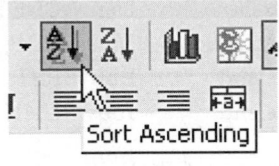

Fig. 629

This will sort the data by the column in which the cell pointer is currently located. Because Excel resolves ties by leaving the previous sequence
in place, you can duplicate the sort shown above. First, select a cell in
the product field and choose AZ to sort by product. Next, select a cell in
the Customer field and choose AZ to sort by Customer. The data will be
sorted by customer, with ties sorted by product.

The ZA button next to Sort Ascending can be used to Sort Descending.

Gotcha: Before trying any sort operation, you must either select the entire range or a single cell in that range. If you mistakenly choose two cells in a range, Excel will sort just those selected cells, resulting in a few cells of your data being sorted into new records – a disastrous result.

Summary: Sorting data is easy using either the Sort menu or the Sort buttons on the Standard toolbar.

Commands Discussed: Data – Sort

HOW TO SPECIFY MORE THAN THREE COLUMNS IN A SORT

Problem: As shown in Fig. 630, you want to sort by product within Customer, Rep, District, Region, and Country. The Sort dialog only offers three columns by which to sort.

	A	B	C	D	E	F	G
5	Country	Region	District	Sales Rep	Customer	Product	Jan
6	USA	West	No. California	Joe	RST Company	GHI	37
7	Australia	Australia	Australia	Mary	EFG Pty Ltd	GHI	40
8	USA	Central	Chicago	Dan	TUV Company	DEF	86
9	Germany	Germany	Germany	Dan	CDE GMbH	XYZ	73
10	USA	Central	Minneapolis	Bob	BCD Corporation	ABC	65
11	Australia	Australia	Australia	Dan	CDE Pty Ltd	ABC	55
12	USA	East	MidAtlantic	Mary	NOP, LLC	ABC	86
13	USA	Central	Cleveland	Bob	RST, Inc.	GHI	98
14	USA	Central	Cleveland	Joe	LMN, Inc.	DEF	61

Fig. 630

Strategy: Use two calls to the Sort menu. The first sort will get the minor sort criteria of Sales Rep, Customer, and Product. The next sort will sort by Country, Region, and District.

1)   Select a SINGLE CELL within your list and choose Sort from the Data menu. In the Sort dialog box, choose the last three fields in

your list, as shown in Fig. 631. Choose OK to complete the first sort.

Fig. 631

2)   Again select Sort from the Data menu. This time, select to sort by Country, Region, and District, as shown in Fig. 632. For all records where there is a tie between these three fields, the sequence of the first sort will be used as the tiebreaker.

Fig. 632

Result: The data is sorted by the six fields, as shown in Fig. 633.

	A	B	C	D	E	F	G
5	Country	Region	District	Sales Rep	Customer	Product	Jan
6	Australia	Australia	Australia	Bob	EFG Pty Ltd	XYZ	37
7	Australia	Australia	Australia	Bob	VWX Pty Ltd	ABC	89
8	Australia	Australia	Australia	Bob	VWX Pty Ltd	XYZ	73
9	Australia	Australia	Australia	Dan	CDE Pty Ltd	ABC	55
10	Australia	Australia	Australia	Dan	CDE Pty Ltd	GHI	33
11	Australia	Australia	Australia	Dan	EFG Pty Ltd	GHI	25
12	Australia	Australia	Australia	Dan	EFG Pty Ltd	XYZ	20
13	Australia	Australia	Australia	Dan	TUV Pty Ltd	DEF	50
14	Australia	Australia	Australia	Joe	EFG Pty Ltd	XYZ	40
15	Australia	Australia	Australia	Joe	OPQ Pty Ltd	DEF	23
16	Australia	Australia	Australia	Joe	TUV Pty Ltd	ABC	84
17	Australia	Australia	Australia	Mary	CDE Pty Ltd	GHI	31
18	Australia	Australia	Australia	Mary	EFG Pty Ltd	GHI	40
19	Australia	Australia	Australia	Mary	TUV Pty Ltd	DEF	18
20	Australia	Australia	Australia	Mary	VWX Pty Ltd	GHI	36
21	England	England	England	Bob	UVW Ltd	ABC	16
22	England	England	England	Dan	UVW Ltd	ABC	61
23	England	England	England	Joe	QRS Ltd	DEF	63
24	England	England	England	Joe	UVW Ltd	GHI	43
25	France	France	France	Bob	QRS S.A.	GHI	39

Fig. 633

Alternate Strategy: Use the AZ button on the Standard toolbar. Select one cell in the Product column and choose the AZ button on the toolbar. Next, select one cell in the Customer column and choose the AZ button. Continue selecting single cells in each prior column and choosing the AZ button.

Summary: When there is a tie among the three columns in a sort, Excel retains the prior order of the records. Thus, it is possible to sort six columns by using two calls to the Sort command, provided that you sort the least important fields first.

HOW TO SORT A REPORT INTO A CUSTOM SEQUENCE

Problem: Your manager wants you to sort a report geographically. As shown in Fig. 634, your annual report typically lists results from the USA first, then Europe, and then Australia. You need to sort so that the countries appear as USA, England, France, Germany, and Australia. Within the USA, you want the regions within the USA to appear in East, Central, West sequence.

	A	B	C	D	E	F	G
5	Country	Region	District	Sales Rep	Customer	Product	Jan
6	USA	West	No. California	Joe	RST Company	GHI	37
7	Australia	Australia	Australia	Mary	EFG Pty Ltd	GHI	40
8	USA	Central	Chicago	Dan	TUV Company	DEF	86
9	Germany	Germany	Germany	Dan	CDE GMbH	XYZ	73
10	USA	Central	Minneapolis	Bob	BCD Corporation	ABC	65
11	Australia	Australia	Australia	Dan	CDE Pty Ltd	ABC	55
12	USA	East	MidAtlantic	Mary	NOP, LLC	ABC	86
13	USA	Central	Cleveland	Bob	RST, Inc.	GHI	98
14	USA	Central	Cleveland	Joe	LMN, Inc.	DEF	61

Fig. 634

Part III

Strategy: Use a custom list. Follow the steps below.

1) Go to a blank section of the worksheet. As shown in Fig. 635, type the countries in the order you wish them to appear in a column.

	A
1	USA
2	England
3	France
4	Germany
5	Australia

Fig. 635

2)   From the menu, select Tools – Options. On the options dialog, se-
     lect the tab for Custom Lists.

3)   At the bottom of the Custom Lists tab, select the range containing
     your list and choose the Import button, as shown in Fig. 636.

Fig. 636

4)   The custom list is added to the Custom Lists box, as shown in Fig.
     637. Choose OK to close the Options dialog box.

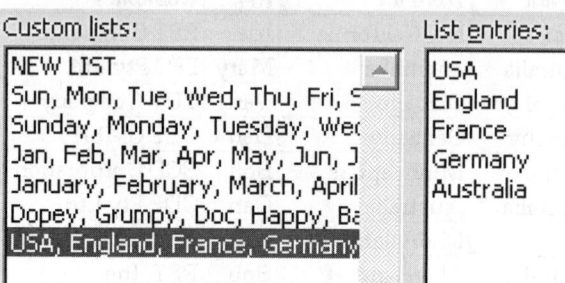

Fig. 637

5)   Select Sort from the Data menu. Specify that you want to sort by
     Country. In the lower left corner of the Sort dialog, choose the Op-
     tions... button. See Fig. 638.

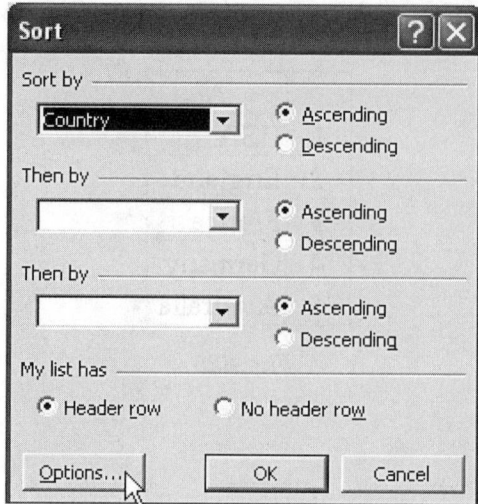

Fig. 638

6)   On the Sort Options dialog, use the dropdown to select a new value from First key sort order. As shown in Fig. 639, select the USA, England entry.

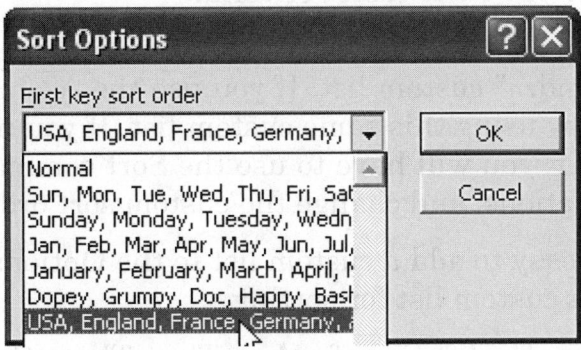

Fig. 639

7)   Choose OK to close Sort Options. Choose OK to perform the sort.

Result: As shown in Fig. 640, the data is sorted by country in the order that you specified.

A		
5	**Country**	**Reg**
90	USA	We
91	England	Eng
92	England	Eng
93	England	Eng
94	England	Eng
95	France	Frat
96	France	Frat
97	France	Frat
98	France	Frat
99	France	Frat
100	Germany	Gen

Fig. 640

Additional Information: If there is a value in the column that is not in your custom list, it is sorted alphabetically after the entries in the list. If you sort in descending order, these unlisted entries will come first, in Z-A order.

Gotcha: There is no way to specify that the second sort criteria should use different custom sort criteria. In this case, you will have to sort Region first, using a custom sort criteria and then Country in a separate sort, using a different custom sort criteria.

Gotcha: Excel remembers that the column was most recently sorted by the "USA, England..." custom list. If you use the AZ button, it will automatically sort by using this same custom list. If you need to return to alphabetical order, you will have to use the Sort command on the Data menu, reselect Options, and change the custom sort order to None.

Summary: It is easy to add a custom list to the Options dialog of Excel and then use this custom list for sorting.

Cross Reference: How to Specify More Than Three Columns in a Sort

QUICKLY FILTER A LIST TO CERTAIN RECORDS

Problem: You have 10,000 records, as shown in Fig. 641; you need to be able to quickly find records that match a criterion, such as all East ABC records.

	A	B	C	D	E	F
1	Region	Product	Date	Customer	Quantity	Revenue
2	East	XYZ	Jul-04	Nortel Networks	1000	25350
3	West	XYZ	May-04	Sun Life Financial	1000	25310
4	Central	XYZ	Feb-04	Wal-Mart	1000	25140
5	West	XYZ	Feb-04	General Motors	1000	25080
6	East	XYZ	Apr-04	Ford	1000	25060

Fig. 641

Strategy: Use the AutoFilter feature.

1) Make sure your data has a heading row. From the menu, select Data – Filter – AutoFilter. You will have a dropdown on each heading, as shown in Fig. 642.

	A	B	C	D	E	F
1	Regic ▼	Produ ▼	Date ▼	Customer ▼	Quant ▼	Reven ▼
2	East	XYZ	Jul-04	Nortel Networks	1000	25350
3	West	XYZ	May-04	Sun Life Financial	1000	25310
4	Central	XYZ	Feb-04	Wal-Mart	1000	25140

Fig. 642

2) As shown in Fig. 643, use the dropdown to select East from the region dropdown.

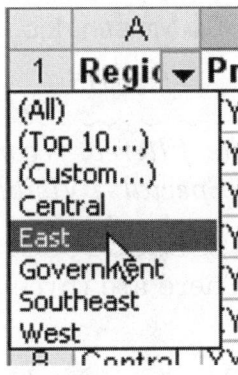

Fig. 643

3) As shown in Fig. 644, select ABC from the Product dropdown.

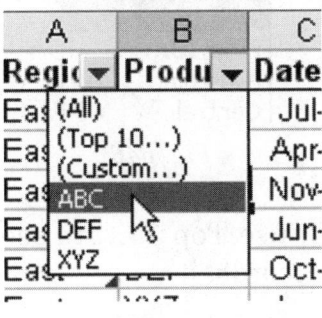

Fig. 644

Part
III

Result: You will see only sales of product ABC in the East region, as shown in Fig. 645. All of the other rows will be hidden.

	A	B	C	D	E	F
1	Regi▼	Produ▼	Date ▼	Customer ▼	Quant ▼	Reven ▼
65	East	ABC	Apr-04	Sun Life Financial	1000	20310
74	East	ABC	Jun-04	Verizon	1000	19630
101	East	ABC	Jul-04	Wal-Mart	1000	18660
102	East	ABC	Oct-04	Nortel Networks	900	18576
114	East	ABC	Dec-04	Wal-Mart	900	18243
117	East	ABC	Jun-04	Molson, Inc	900	18072

Fig. 645

Caution: *To copy just the filtered records, you will have to use Edit – Go To – Special – Visible Cells Only to select only the visible cells on the sheet.*

Additional Information: There are three special choices at the top of each column.

1) Use (All) to "cancel" a filter on one column, as shown in Fig. 646.

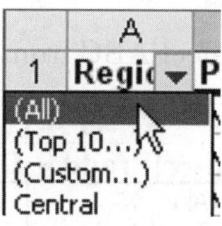

Fig. 646

2) As shown in Fig. 647, use Top 10... to see the top N records or the top n percent of the records.

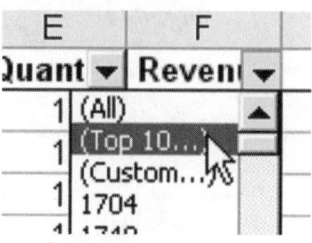

Fig. 647

3) After you select Top 10, the Top 10 AutoFilter dialog appears, as shown in Fig. 648. You can choose if you want the top 10 percent or the top 10 items, and also change the "10" to "5" or to any other number. This can also be used to show the bottom 10 records.

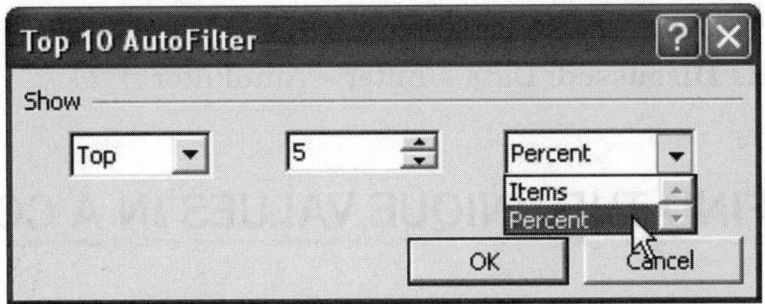

Fig. 648

4) As shown in Fig. 649, use Custom to build a criteria joined by AND or OR.

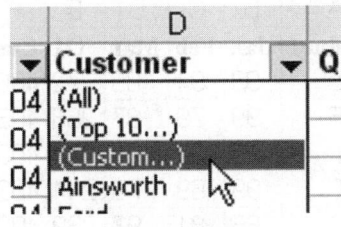

Fig. 649

5) In the Custom AutoFilter dialog box, you can choose two values and specify whether they should be joined by AND or OR, as shown in Fig. 650.

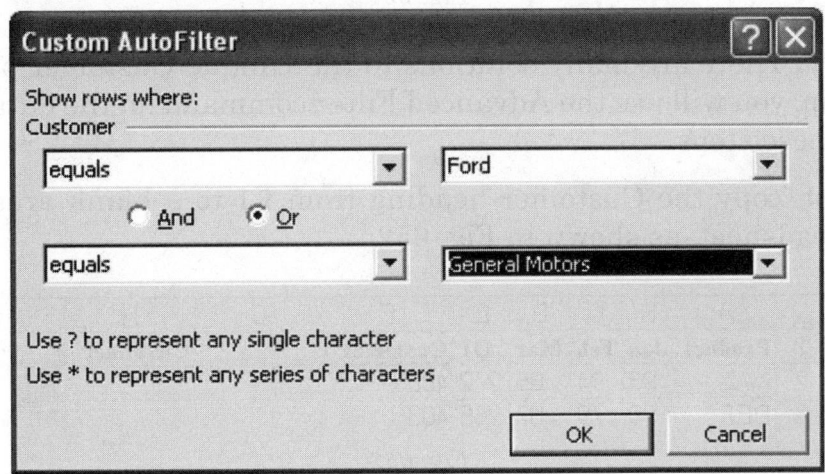

Fig. 650

6)   To remove the AutoFilter dropdowns and show all records, go to the Data menu again and re-select AutoFilter. This will toggle the AutoFilter off.

Summary: Use Data – Filter – AutoFilter to have Excel show you data matching certain criteria in a column.

Commands Discussed: Data – Filter – AutoFilter

FIND THE UNIQUE VALUES IN A COLUMN

Problem: You have a large database, as shown in Fig. 651. Before you can produce a report for each customer, you need to identify the complete list of unique customers.

	A	B	C	D	E	F
1	**Product**	**Jan**	**Feb**	**Mar**	**Q1**	**Customer**
2	XYZ	93	94	85	272	406
3	DEF	99	79	87	265	403
4	GHI	79	67	98	244	403
5	XYZ	99	69	76	244	403
6	ABC	65	81	93	239	403
7	DEF	63	95	80	238	403
8	ABC	68	62	99	229	405
9	DEF	61	99	67	227	403
10	XYZ	36	96	94	226	403

Fig. 651

Strategy: There are many solutions to the Unique Customer problem. In this tip, you will use the Advanced Filter command on the data menu. Follow these steps.

1)   First, copy the Customer heading from F1 to a blank area of the spreadsheet, as shown in Fig. 652.

	A	B	C	D	E	F	G	H	
1	**Product**	**Jan**	**Feb**	**Mar**	**Q1**	**Customer**		**Customer**	
2	XYZ	93	94	85	272	406			
3	DEF	99	79	87	265	403			

Fig. 652

2) Select a single cell in your data range. From the menu, select Data–Filter – Advanced Filter. The Advanced Filter dialog contains many powerful options. By default, it will look as shown in Fig. 653.

Fig. 653

Part
III

3) As shown in Fig. 654, choose the Unique Records Only checkbox. Change the Action section to Copy to Another Location. Selecting this action enables the Copy To range. Place the cursor in the Copy To dialog box and highlight the out-of-the-way copy of the Customer heading.

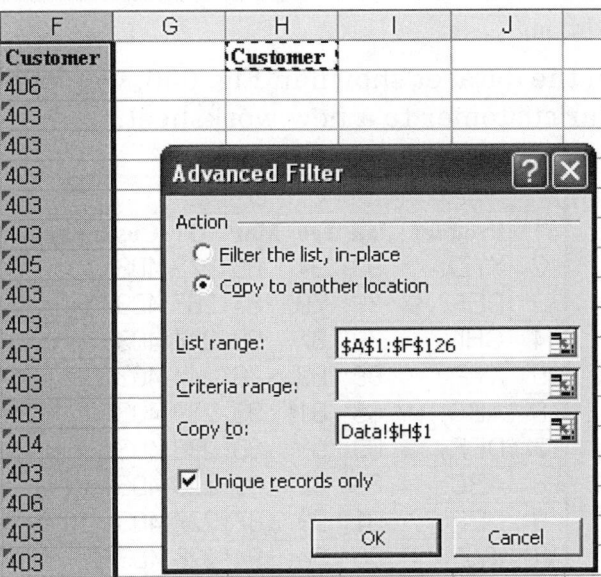

Fig. 654

4)   Choose OK. Excel will find the unique customer numbers and copy
       them to the range you specified, as shown in Fig. 655.

H
Customer
406
403
405
404
402
401

Fig. 655

Gotcha: Any subsequent use of the Advanced Filter command during
this Excel session will remember the List Range specified in the prior
Advanced Filter.

Summary: One use of the Advanced Filter command is to generate a
unique list of one particular field in a dataset.

Commands Discussed: Data – Advanced Filter

COPY MATCHING RECORDS
TO A NEW WORKSHEET

Problem: From the dataset shown in Fig. 656, you want to copy records
for one particular customer to a new worksheet.

	A	B	C	D	E	F
1	**Product**	**Jan**	**Feb**	**Mar**	**Q1**	**Customer**
2	XYZ	93	94	85	272	406
3	DEF	99	79	87	265	403
4	GHI	79	67	98	244	403
5	XYZ	99	69	76	244	403
6	ABC	65	81	93	239	403
7	DEF	63	95	80	238	403
8	ABC	68	62	99	229	405
9	DEF	61	99	67	227	403
10	XYZ	36	96	94	226	403

Fig. 656

Strategy: Use the Advanced Filter command with a Criteria range. Follow these steps.

1) First, copy the Customer heading from F1 to a blank area of the spreadsheet, as shown in Fig. 657. In this case, H1:H2 will be the criteria range for the filter.

	A	B	C	D	E	F	G	H
1	Product	Jan	Feb	Mar	Q1	Customer		Customer
2	XYZ	93	94	85	272	406		
3	DEF	99	79	87	265	403		

Fig. 657

2) In cell H2, enter the customer number that you want to extract. Make sure to use the same format in which the data exists in the database. In this case, 406 in F2 is a text value. If you want customer 406, copy cell F2 to H2 to ensure that they are in the same format.

3) Select a single cell in your data range. From the menu, select Data–Filter – Advanced Filter to display the Advanced Filter dialog, as shown in Fig. 658.

Fig. 658

4) The Action setting should remain as Filter the List, In-Place. Move the cursor to the Criteria Range column and highlight the criteria range of H1:H2 with the mouse. Click OK to perform the Advanced Filter.

Part
III

Result: As shown in Fig. 659, Excel will hide all of the rows that do not match the criteria.

	A	B	C	D	E	F
1	**Product**	**Jan**	**Feb**	**Mar**	**Q1**	**Customer**
2	XYZ	93	94	85	272	406
16	GHI	79	80	55	214	406
21	GHI	49	74	84	207	406
36	XYZ	99	50	44	193	406
37	ABC	60	88	39	187	406
118	DEF	17	9	59	85	406
127						

Fig. 659

In order to copy these cells to a new worksheet, you must select the visible cells only.

1)   Highlight the range A1:F118. From the menu, select Edit – Go To. In the lower left corner of the Go To dialog, choose the Special button. On the Go To Special dialog box, in the right column, select Visible cells only, as shown in Fig. 660.

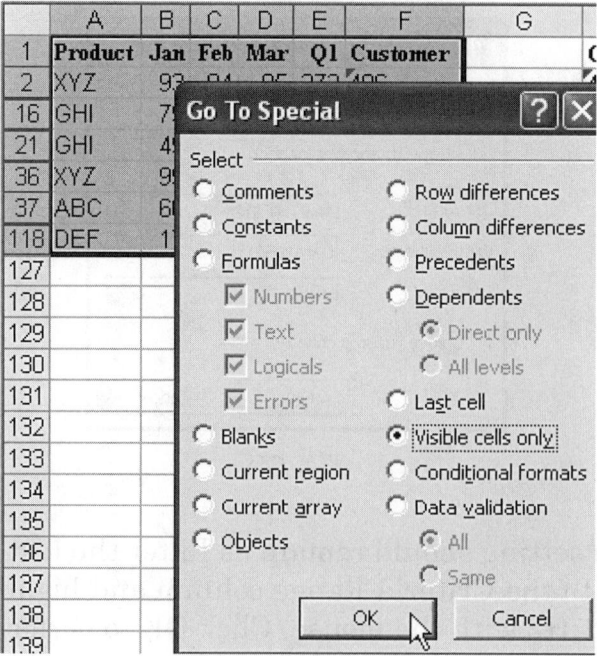

Fig. 660

2)   When you click OK, the display barely changes. As shown in Fig. 661, you will notice bands of white in between the rows. Excel is indicating to you that there are hidden rows that are not included in the selection.

	A	B	C	D	E	F
1	Product	Jan	Feb	Mar	Q1	Customer
2	XYZ	93	94	85	272	406
16	GHI	79	80	55	214	406
21	GHI	49	74	84	207	406
36	XYZ	99	50	44	193	406
37	ABC	60	88	39	187	406
118	DEF	17	9	59	85	406

Fig. 661

3)   You can now copy those rows with Ctrl+C and paste to a new worksheet.

Result: Only the matching rows are copied, as shown in Fig. 662.

	A	B	C	D	E	F
1	Product	Jan	Feb	Mar	Q1	Customer
2	XYZ	93	94	85	272	406
3	GHI	79	80	55	214	406
4	GHI	49	74	84	207	406
5	XYZ	99	50	44	193	406
6	ABC	60	88	39	187	406
7	DEF	17	9	59	85	406

Fig. 662

Additional Details: On the original sheet, to clear the Advanced Filter and show all of the rows again, choose Data – Filter – Show All, as shown in Fig. 663.

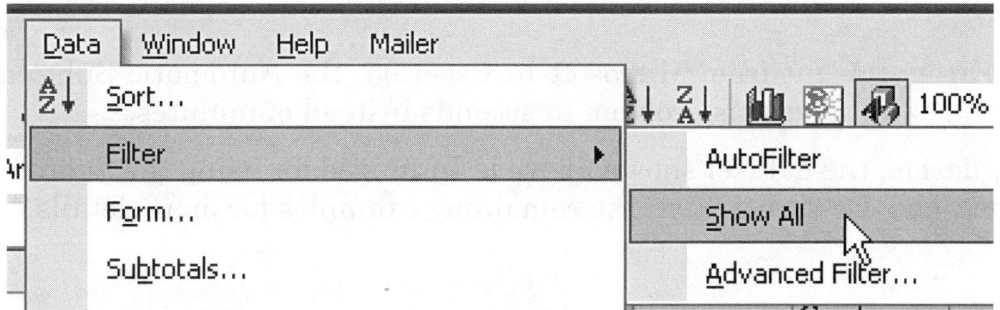

Fig. 663

Part III

Summary: One use of the Advanced Filter command is to extract a certain customer from a dataset.

Commands Discussed: Data – Filter – Advanced Filter; Edit – Go To – Special – Visible Cells Only; Data – Filter – Show All

ADD SUBTOTALS TO A DATASET

Problem: You have a lengthy report with invoice detail by customer, as shown in Fig. 664. You need to add a subtotal at each change in customer.

	A	B	C	D
1	**Acct**	**Customer**	**Invoice**	**Revenue**
2	A4368	Ainsworth	1014	10,445
3	A4368	Ainsworth	1015	15,544
4	A4368	Ainsworth	1030	3,922
5	A4368	Ainsworth	1054	12,838
6	A4368	Ainsworth	1091	17,712
7	A3108	Air Canada	1057	5,859
8	A3108	Air Canada	1061	2,358
9	A3108	Air Canada	1090	17,856
10	A3108	Air Canada	1108	4,948
11	B4504	Bell Canada	1013	15,104
12	B4504	Bell Canada	1069	18,072
13	B4504	Bell Canada	1074	14,004
14	B4504	Bell Canada	1077	4,060
15	C9651	Chevron	1018	8,116
16	C9651	Chevron	1071	7,032

Fig. 664

Strategy: A gift from Microsoft in Excel 95, the Automatic Subtotals feature will solve this problem in seconds instead of minutes.

By design, the dataset shown above is optimized for using the Subtotals command. Be sure to read the remaining examples for more details.

1) Start with data in list format. Select a single cell in the dataset. From the menu, select Data – Subtotals, as shown in Fig. 665.

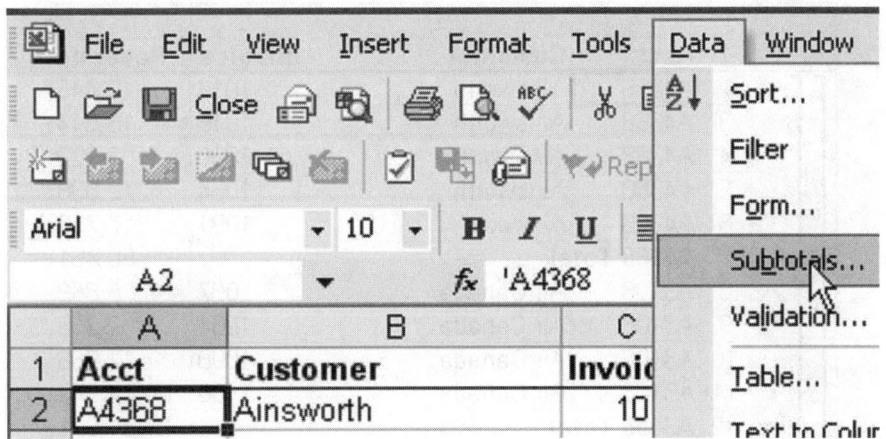

Fig. 665

2) The Subtotals dialog assumes that you want to subtotal by the field in the leftmost column of your data. It also assumes that you want to total the rightmost field. In the present example, shown in Fig. 666, this is correct, so you can choose OK.

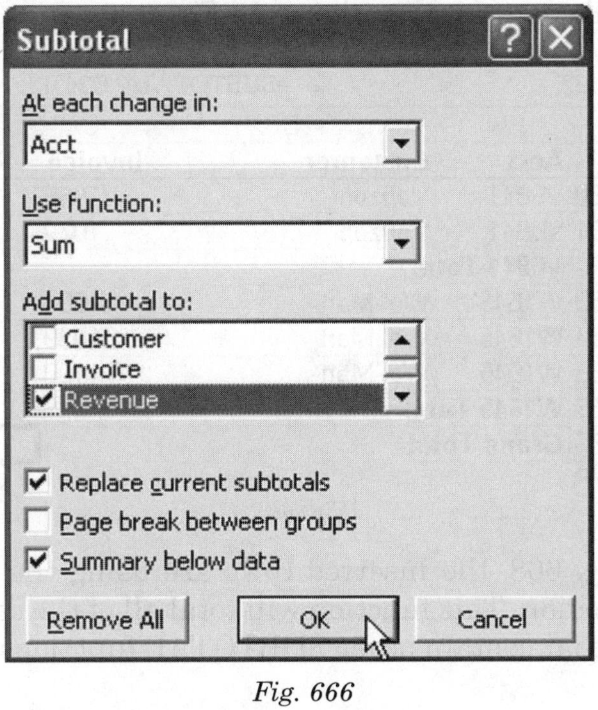

Fig. 666

In 1-2 seconds, subtotals will be inserted at each change in customer, as shown in Fig. 667.

			A	B	C	D
		1	**Acct**	**Customer**	**Invoice**	**Revenue**
	•	2	A4368	Ainsworth	1014	10,445
	•	3	A4368	Ainsworth	1015	15,544
	•	4	A4368	Ainsworth	1030	3,922
	•	5	A4368	Ainsworth	1054	12,838
	•	6	A4368	Ainsworth	1091	17,712
	−	7	**A4368 Total**			60,461
	•	8	A3108	Air Canada	1057	5,859
	•	9	A3108	Air Canada	1061	2,358
	•	10	A3108	Air Canada	1090	17,856
	•	11	A3108	Air Canada	1108	4,948
	−	12	**A3108 Total**			31,021
	•	13	B4504	Bell Canada	1013	15,104
	•	14	B4504	Bell Canada	1069	18,072
	•	15	B4504	Bell Canada	1074	14,004
	•	16	B4504	Bell Canada	1077	4,060
	−	17	**B4504 Total**			51,240

Fig. 667

If you scroll to the end of the dataset, you will notice that Excel added a grand total of all customers, as shown in Fig. 668.

D137   ▼   *fx* =SUBTOTAL(9,D2:D135)

			A	B	C	D
		1	**Acct**	**Customer**	**Invoice**	**Revenue**
	•	130	V6841	Verizon	1058	6,309
	•	131	V6841	Verizon	1072	11,922
	−	132	**V6841 Total**			35,367
	•	133	W1645	Wal-Mart	1004	7,180
	•	134	W1645	Wal-Mart	1039	10,385
	•	135	W1645	Wal-Mart	1100	8,970
	−	136	**W1645 Total**			26,535
	−	137	**Grand Total**			1,235,966
		138				

Fig. 668

As shown in Fig. 668, the inserted rows are using the somewhat new SUBTOTAL function. This function will total all of the cells in the range except for cells that contain other SUBTOTAL functions.

Additional Details: In order to remove subtotals, select a cell in the dataset. From the menu, select Data – Subtotals. In the Subtotals dialog, choose the Remove All button, as shown in Fig. 669.

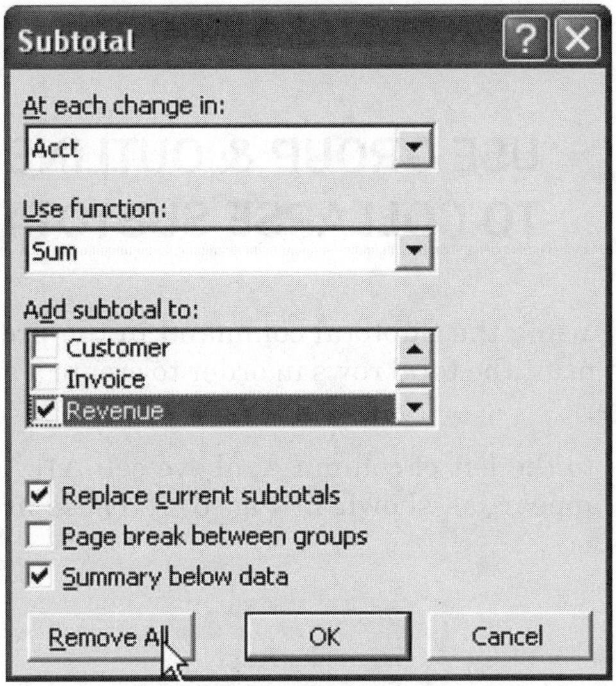

Fig. 669

Gotcha: This example worked because the data was sorted by Account Number. If the data had been sorted by Invoice Number instead, the result would have been fairly meaningless, as shown in Fig. 670.

Fig. 670

Summary: The Subtotals command on the data menu quickly automates the monotonous job of adding subtotals.

Commands Discussed: Data – Subtotals

Functions Discussed: =Subtotal()

USE GROUP & OUTLINE BUTTONS
TO COLLAPSE SUBTOTALED DATA

Problem: After using the Subtotal command in the previous example, you want to just print the total rows in order to create a summary report for your manager.

Strategy: Look to the left of column A, above cell A1. A series of three small numbers appear, as shown in Fig. 671. These are the Group & Outline buttons.

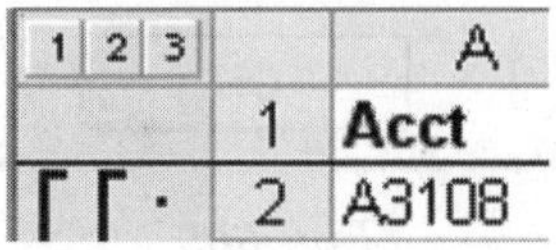

Fig. 671

Using the mouse, choose the small 2 button. You will see just the customer totals, as shown in Fig. 672.

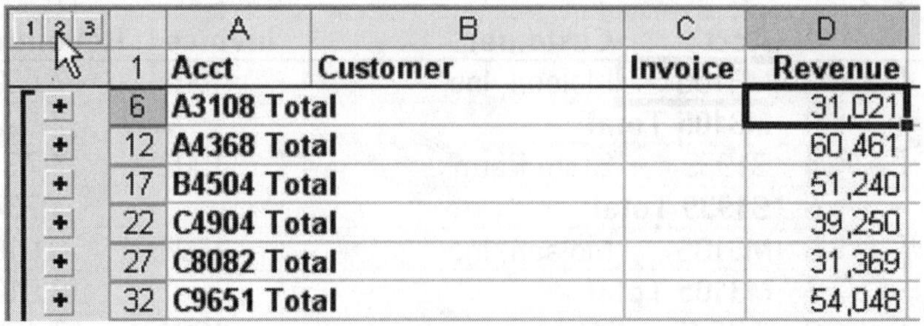

1 2 3		A	B	C	D
	1	Acct	Customer	Invoice	Revenue
+	6	A3108 Total			31,021
+	12	A4368 Total			60,461
+	17	B4504 Total			51,240
+	22	C4904 Total			39,250
+	27	C8082 Total			31,369
+	32	C9651 Total			54,048

Fig. 672

As shown in Fig. 673, choose the small 1 button to see just the grand total (which seems a bit pointless).

1 2 3		A	B	C	D
	1	Acct	Customer	Invoice	Revenue
+	137	Grand Total			1,235,966
	139				

Fig. 673

Choose the 3 button to go back to the detail view, with all records, as shown in Fig. 674.

1 2 3		A	B	C	D
	1	Acct	Customer	Invoice	Revenue
•	2	A3108	Air Canada	1057	5,859
•	3	A3108	Air Canada	1061	2,358
•	4	A3108	Air Canada	1090	17,856
•	5	A3108	Air Canada	1108	4,948
−	6	A3108 Total			31,021
•	7	A4368	Ainsworth	1014	10,445
•	8	A4368	Ainsworth	1015	15,544

Fig. 674

Part III

Additional Details: In the 2 button view, you can explode a single customer's detail records by clicking the + next to the customer total, as shown in Fig. 675.

+	27	C8082 Total			31,369
	28	C9651	Chevron	1018	8,116
•	29	C9651	Chevron	1071	7,032
•	30	C9651	Chevron	1084	18,290
•	31	C9651	Chevron	1098	20,610
−	32	C9651 Total			54,048
+	38	E9872 Total			68,200

Fig. 675

Use the minus sign next to A32, as shown in Fig. 675, to collapse the detail again. Or, select the 2 button to collapse all.

Summary: After using the Subtotals command, the Group & Outline buttons allow you to create multiple views of the data.

Commands Discussed: Data – Subtotals; Group & Outline

COPY JUST TOTALS FROM SUBTOTALED DATA

Problem: Your manager wants just the total rows sent to him in a file. You've added subtotals and then chosen the #2 Group & Outline button to see just the data that you want, as shown in Fig. 676.

	A	B	C	D
1	Acct	Customer	Invoice	Revenue
6	A3108 Total			31,021
12	A4368 Total			60,461
17	B4504 Total			51,240
22	C4904 Total			39,250

Fig. 676

However, when you copy this view and paste to a new workbook, all of the detail rows come along as well, as shown in Fig. 677.

	A	B	C	D
1	Acct	Custome	Invoice	Revenue
2	A3108	Air Canad	1057	5,859
3	A3108	Air Canad	1061	2,358
4	A3108	Air Canad	1090	17,856
5	A3108	Air Canad	1108	4,948
6	A3108 Total			31,021
7	A4368	Ainsworth	1014	10,445
8	A4368	Ainsworth	1015	15,544
9	A4368	Ainsworth	1030	3,922
10	A4368	Ainsworth	1054	12,838
11	A4368	Ainsworth	1091	17,712
12	A4368 Total			60,461
13	B4504	Bell Canad	1013	15,104

Fig. 677

Strategy: There is an obscure command on the Go To Special dialog box to assist with this task. Follow these steps.

1) Choose the #2 Group & Outline button to put the data in subtotal view.

2) Select everything from the headings to the grand total by selecting one cell with data and hitting Ctrl+* (you can use the * key on the numeric keypad).

3) Bring up the Go To dialog by choosing Edit – Go To or by hitting the F5 key on the keyboard. As shown in Fig. 678, choose the Special button in the lower left corner of the Go To dialog.

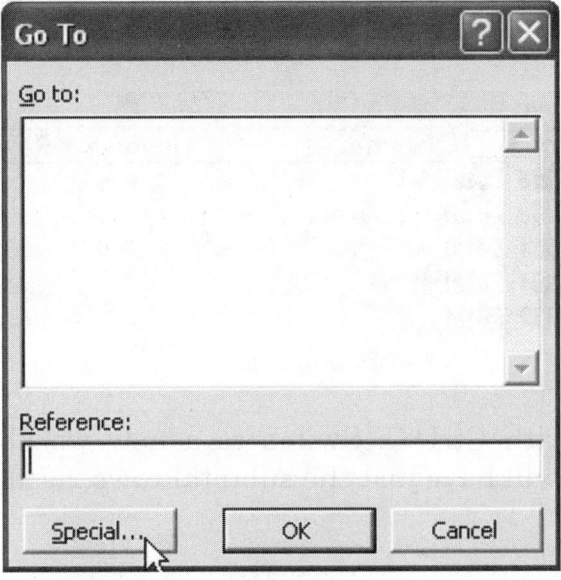

Fig. 678

4) In the Go To Special dialog, select Visible Cells Only and choose OK, as shown in Fig. 679.

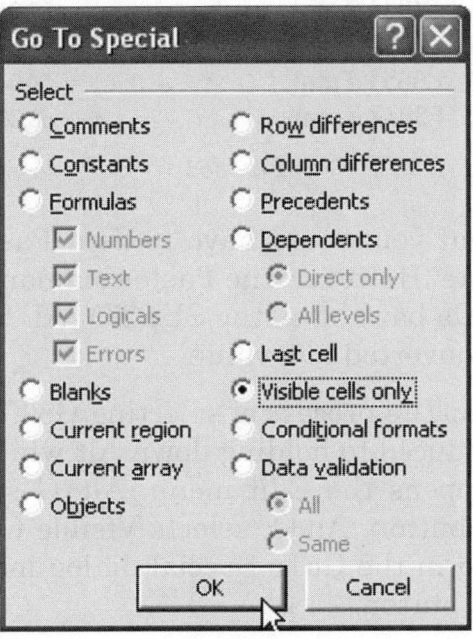

Fig. 679

The change will be almost imperceptible and may not even be noticeable in the printed resolution of this book. Amongst the blue highlighting, you will see fine white lines above and below each subtotal, as shown in Fig. 680. This is Excel's way of saying, "Hey – there are hidden rows back there which are not part of the selection."

	A	B	C	D
1	Acct	Customer	Invoice	Revenue
6	A3108 Total			31,021
12	A4368 Total			60,461
17	B4504 Total			51,240
22	C4904 Total			39,250
27	C8082 Total			31,369

Fig. 680

5)   Next, copy with Ctrl+C. Switch to a new workbook. Paste with Ctrl+V. You will have just the subtotal rows, as shown in Fig. 681.

D2			f_x	31021
	A	B	C	D
1	Acct	Customer	Invoice	Revenue
2	A3108 Total			31,021
3	A4368 Total			60,461
4	B4504 Total			51,240
5	C4904 Total			39,250
6	C8082 Total			31,369
7	C9651 Total			54,048
8	E9872 Total			68,200

Fig. 681

You might think that you would have to do a Paste Special – Values instead of just a paste. However, the Paste command works OK. As you can see in the formula bar above, the SUBTOTAL function, which used to be in the cell, is converted to a value.

Additional Details: The process of selecting Go To – Special – Visible Cells Only can be reduced to holding down Alt while hitting EGSY and then Enter. Alt+E opens the Edit menu. Alt+G selects Go To. Alt+S presses the Special button. Alt+Y selects Visible Cells Only (note that the "y" is underlined in the GoTo Special dialog in Fig. 679). Enter selects the default OK button.

Summary: This is a fairly obscure trick. I think it is more obscure because no one in his or her right mind uses the Go To dialog. If you are at cell A10 and need to go to cell A100, it is pretty easy to just hit PgDn a few times. Considering how seemingly useless the Go To dialog is, the fact that it houses the Special button is ironic.

Commands Discussed: Edit – Go To – Special – Visible Cells Only

ENTER A GRAND TOTAL OF DATA MANUALLY SUBTOTALED

Problem: Your manager doesn't know the trick for doing automatic subtotals. In the example below, he manually entered blank lines between each customer and entered SUM formulas for each customer, as shown in Fig. 682. How can you produce a grand total of all customers?

	A	B	C	D
1	Acct	Customer	Invoice	Revenue
2	A4368	Ainsworth	1014	10,445
3	A4368	Ainsworth	1015	15,544
4	A4368	Ainsworth	1030	3,922
5	A4368	Ainsworth	1054	12,838
6	A4368	Ainsworth	1091	17,712
7		Total Ainsworth		60,461
8				
9	A3108	Air Canada	1057	5,859
10	A3108	Air Canada	1061	2,358
11	A3108	Air Canada	1090	17,856
12	A3108	Air Canada	1108	4,948
13		Total Air Canada		31,021
14				
15	B4504	Bell Canada	1013	15,104
16	B4504	Bell Canada	1069	18,072
17	B4504	Bell Canada	1074	14,004
18	B4504	Bell Canada	1077	4,060
19		Total Bell Canada		51,240
20				
21	Grand Total			

Fig. 682

Strategy: Think about this dataset. Every sale is actually in there twice. As shown in Fig. 683, the $4,060 for invoice 1077 is in cell D18 and also totaled into D19. Thus, the formula to enter in D21 is =SUM(D2: D19)/2.

	D21 ▼		f_x =SUM(D2:D20)/2	
	A	B	C	D
1	**Acct**	**Customer**	**Invoice**	**Revenue**
2	A4368	Ainsworth	1014	10,445
3	A4368	Ainsworth	1015	15,544
4	A4368	Ainsworth	1030	3,922
5	A4368	Ainsworth	1054	12,838
6	A4368	Ainsworth	1091	17,712
7		Total Ainsworth		60,461
8				
9	A3108	Air Canada	1057	5,859
10	A3108	Air Canada	1061	2,358
11	A3108	Air Canada	1090	17,856
12	A3108	Air Canada	1108	4,948
13		Total Air Canada		31,021
14				
15	B4504	Bell Canada	1013	15,104
16	B4504	Bell Canada	1069	18,072
17	B4504	Bell Canada	1074	14,004
18	B4504	Bell Canada	1077	4,060
19		Total Bell Canada		51,240
20				
21	Grand Total			142,722

Fig. 683

This method works! It is one of those old accounting tricks (taught to me by an old accountant). It is not intuitive, especially if you hated algebra. Try it for yourself a few times, comparing the results to the method of =D19+D13+D7. You will see that you get the same result.

Gotcha: This method only works if every customer is totaled. A manager who doesn't know how to use subtotals might be the kind of manager who doesn't total the customers with only one detail line. In Fig. 684, line 9 will cause the total to not work.

	A	B	C	D
	D23	▼	f_x	=SUM(D2:D22)/2
1	**Acct**	**Customer**	**Invoice**	**Revenue**
2	A4368	Ainsworth	1014	10,445
3	A4368	Ainsworth	1015	15,544
4	A4368	Ainsworth	1030	3,922
5	A4368	Ainsworth	1054	12,838
6	A4368	Ainsworth	1091	17,712
7		Total Ainsworth		60,461
8				
9	A9875	Aironet	1040	17,250
10				
11	A3108	Air Canada	1057	5,859
12	A3108	Air Canada	1061	2,358
13	A3108	Air Canada	1090	17,856
14	A3108	Air Canada	1108	4,948
15		Total Air Canada		31,021
16				
17	B4504	Bell Canada	1013	15,104
18	B4504	Bell Canada	1069	18,072
19	B4504	Bell Canada	1074	14,004
20	B4504	Bell Canada	1077	4,060
21		Total Bell Canada		51,240
22				
23	Grand Total			151,347

Part III

Fig. 684

Tip *If you work for a manager who doesn't know this trick, giving him a copy of this book would be a great idea for Boss' Day! This falls on October 16 in the USA.*

Summary: =SUM()/2 is a great method for quickly determining the totals of a dataset with "manual" subtotals.

Functions Discussed: =SUM()

WHY DO SUBTOTALS COME OUT AS COUNTS?

Problem: You added automatic subtotals to this dataset. As shown in Fig. 685, the subtotals of four for Air Canada and five for Ainsworth are clearly not correct. What went wrong?

1 2 3		A	B	C	D	E
	1	**Acct**	**Customer**	**Invoice**	**Revenue**	**Rep**
	2	A3108	Air Canada	1057	5,859	Joe
	3	A3108	Air Canada	1061	2,358	Joe
	4	A3108	Air Canada	1090	17,856	Joe
	5	A3108	Air Canada	1108	4,948	Joe
	6	**A3108 Count**			4	
	7	A4368	Ainsworth	1014	10,445	Mary
	8	A4368	Ainsworth	1015	15,544	Mary
	9	A4368	Ainsworth	1030	3,922	Mary
	10	A4368	Ainsworth	1054	12,838	Mary
	11	A4368	Ainsworth	1091	17,712	Mary
	12	**A4368 Count**			5	

Fig. 685

Strategy: The first time that you subtotal a dataset, Excel assumes that you want to subtotal the final column in the dataset. If this column contains text data, then the subtotals dialog will default to a Count instead of a Sum, as shown in Fig. 686.

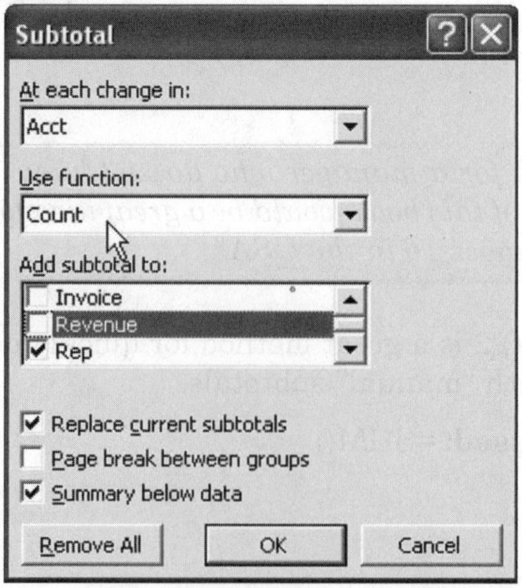

Fig. 686

Gotcha: This problem will also happen even if your final column contains mostly numbers but includes one blank cell.

To correct the problem once it appears, open the Subtotals dialog again. As shown in Fig. 687, change the Use Function dropdown from Count to Sum. Choose OK.

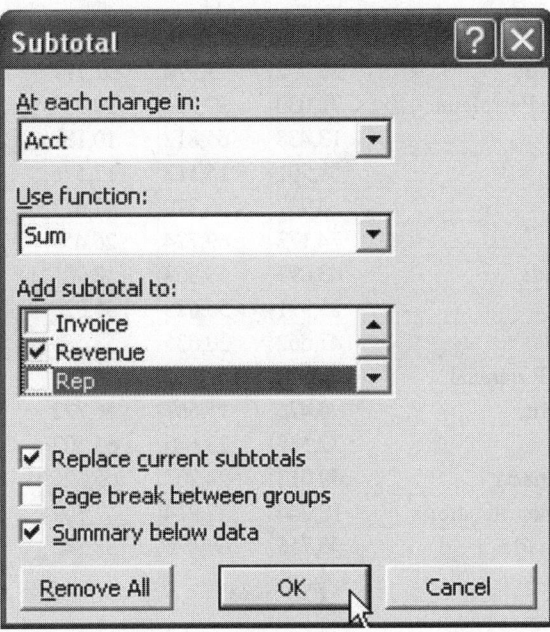

Fig. 687

To avoid the problem in the first place, remember to double-check the Use Function field in the Subtotals dialog, particularly if your data has text in the rightmost column.

Summary: Excel's Intellisense often gives you the correct choices, so you may get lulled into the habit of rarely paying attention to the Use Function field in the Subtotals dialog. When you see Counts instead of Sums, you will know how to correct it.

Commands Discussed: Subtotals

SUBTOTAL MANY COLUMNS AT ONCE

Problem: As shown in Fig. 688, you have data with 12 months going across the columns. You need to add subtotals to all 12 columns.

	A	B	C	D	E	F	G	H
1	**Rep**	**Customer**	**Jan**	**Feb**	**Mar**	**Apr**	**May**	
2	Bob	Bell Canada	20,992	9,970	57,797	49,839	35,534	22,!
3	Bob	Compton Petroleum	72,030	27,714	22,737	48,059	31,816	31,
4	Bob	Exxon	13,438	65,812	10,137	52,216	57,301	49,:
5	Bob	Sears	58,901	15,112	12,576	2,960	67,967	19,!
6	Bob	Texaco	4,937	56,399	42,673	8,706	18,554	64,
7	Bob	Verizon	74,173	69,724	26,459	2,303	66,832	51,
8	Joe	Air Canada	43,097	53,369	58,981	52,386	695	21,
9	Joe	Compaq	25,991	56,623	65,028	32,723	16,112	9,
10	Joe	Ford	47,662	30,635	58,536	29,054	63,375	1,
11	Joe	Sun Life Financial	42,172	43,469	30,493	17,100	39,140	42,:
12	Mary	Ainsworth	6,475	15,567	56,722	59,764	16,030	30,
13	Mary	Chevron	72,587	23,640	65,507	15,028	11,530	2,
14	Mary	Sears Canada	69,013	24,207	5,525	61,329	9,321	61,
15	Mary	SBC Communications	18,244	22,914	57,609	1,887	31,241	9,!
16	Mary	Shell Canada	46,756	60,476	32,342	21,848	19,619	25,

Fig. 688

Strategy: You can subtotal all of the columns at once.

1) In the Subtotal dialog, use the scroll bar to scroll through all fields. You can only display three fields at a time. Checkmark the last three fields, as shown in Fig. 689.

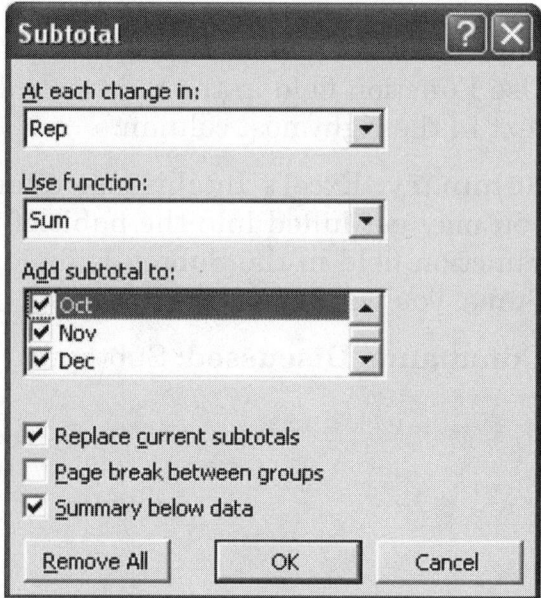

Fig. 689

2) Scroll up to show the previous three fields, as shown in Fig. 690.

3) Checkmark those three fields. Continue this routine, scrolling to reveal three fields, then checkmarking three fields. It gets particularly tedious when you have 36 months' data, but it is still infinitely faster than doing subtotals manually.

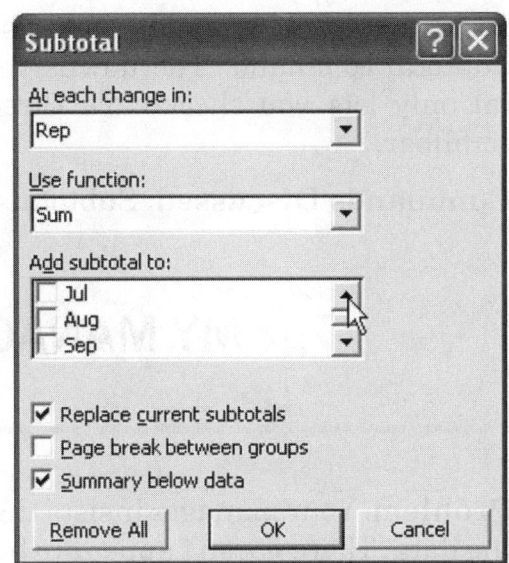

Fig. 690

Result: Subtotals are added to all of the columns at once, as shown in Fig. 691.

1 2 3		A	B	C	D	E	F
	1	**Rep**	**Customer**	**Jan**	**Feb**	**Mar**	**Apr**
	2	Bob	Bell Canada	20,992	9,970	57,797	49,839
	3	Bob	Compton Petroleum	72,030	27,714	22,737	48,059
	4	Bob	Exxon	13,438	65,812	10,137	52,216
	5	Bob	Sears	58,901	15,112	12,576	2,960
	6	Bob	Texaco	4,937	56,399	42,673	8,706
	7	Bob	Verizon	74,173	69,724	26,459	2,303
	8	**Bob Total**		244,471	244,731	172,379	164,083
	9	Joe	Air Canada	43,097	53,369	58,981	52,386
	10	Joe	Compaq	25,991	56,623	65,028	32,723
	11	Joe	Ford	47,662	30,635	58,536	29,054
	12	Joe	Sun Life Financial	42,172	43,469	30,493	17,100
	13	**Joe Total**		158,922	184,096	213,038	131,263
	14	Mary	Ainsworth	6,475	15,567	56,722	59,764
	15	Mary	Chevron	72,587	23,640	65,507	15,028
	16	Mary	Sears Canada	69,013	24,207	5,525	61,329
	17	Mary	SBC Communications	18,244	22,914	57,609	1,887
	18	Mary	Shell Canada	46,756	60,476	32,342	21,848
	19	**Mary Total**		213,075	146,804	217,705	159,856
	20	**Grand Total**		616,468	575,631	603,122	455,202

Fig. 691

Summary: You can add subtotals to many columns in one pass of the Subtotal command. The downside is that the Excel dialog for Subtotal only lets you checkmark three fields before you have to use the scrollbar.

Commands Discussed: Subtotals

MY MANAGER WANTS SUBTOTALS
ABOVE THE DATA

Problem: Your manager insists that subtotals for each rep appear above the data. There doesn't appear to be any hope of the manager being reassigned to Minsk soon.

Strategy: Luckily, someone on the Excel team at Microsoft must have worked for your manager once. There is a setting on the Subtotals dialog to move the totals to the top of the section being subtotaled.

As shown in Fig. 692, in the Subtotal dialog, uncheck the box for Summary Below Data.

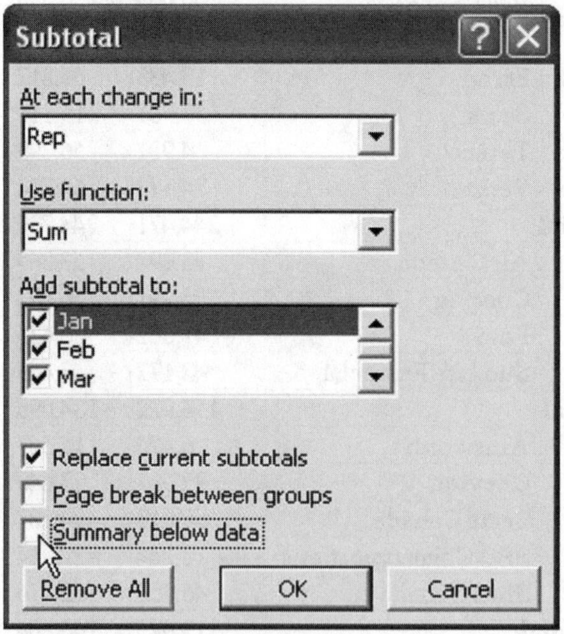

Fig. 692

Result: As shown in Fig. 693, the Grand Total appears at the top of the dataset and the subtotal for each manager appears before records for that manager.

1 2 3		A	B	C	D	E
	1	**Rep**	**Customer**	**Jan**	**Feb**	**Mar**
−	2	**Grand Total**		616,468	575,631	603,122
	3	**Bob Total**		244,471	244,731	172,379
	4	Bob	Bell Canada	20,992	9,970	57,797
	5	Bob	Compton Petroleum	72,030	27,714	22,737
	6	Bob	Exxon	13,438	65,812	10,137
	7	Bob	Sears	58,901	15,112	12,576
	8	Bob	Texaco	4,937	56,399	42,673
	9	Bob	Verizon	74,173	69,724	26,459
	10	**Joe Total**		158,922	184,096	213,038
	11	Joe	Air Canada	43,097	53,369	58,981
	12	Joe	Compaq	25,991	56,623	65,028
	13	Joe	Ford	47,662	30,635	58,536
	14	Joe	Sun Life Financial	42,172	43,469	30,493
	15	**Mary Total**		213,075	146,804	217,705
	16	Mary	Ainsworth	6,475	15,567	56,722
	17	Mary	Chevron	72,587	23,640	65,507
	18	Mary	Sears Canada	69,013	24,207	5,525
	19	Mary	SBC Communications	18,244	22,914	57,609
	20	Mary	Shell Canada	46,756	60,476	32,342

Fig. 693

Summary: You can easily add subtotals above each section being subtotaled.

Commands Discussed: Subtotals

ADD OTHER TEXT DATA TO THE AUTOMATIC SUBTOTAL LINES

Problem: Your dataset has Account number in column A and Customer name in column B. When you subtotal by Account and collapse using #2 Group & Outline button, you only see the Account numbers, as shown in Fig. 694. While you personally have memorized that B4504 is Bell Canada, your manager cannot seem to remember this. You need to add the customer name to the subtotal lines.

1 2 3		A	B	C	D
	1	Acct	Customer	Invoice	Revenue
+	6	A3108 Total			31,021
+	12	A4368 Total			60,461
+	17	B4504 Total			51,240
+	22	C4904 Total			39,250

Fig. 694

Strategy: This may seem convoluted, but it works. Follow these steps.

1) Collapse the report to summary view two by choosing the small #2 button above and to the left of cell A1.

2) You want to select all of the blank cells in column B. Using the mouse, drag from B6 down to the cell above the Grand Total row, as shown in Fig. 695.

3) This selects all of the cells from B6: B136. You actually need to select just the blanks. You can do this by using the Go To Special dialog. From the menu, select Edit – Go To. In the lower left corner of the Go To dialog, choose the Special

1 2 3		A	B	C
	1	Acct	Customer	Invoice
+	6	A3108 Total		
+	12	A4368 Total		
+	17	B4504 Total		
+	22	C4904 Total		
+	27	C8082 Total		
+	32	C9651 Total		
+	38	E9872 Total		
+	44	F7747 Total		
+	49	G1365 Total		
+	55	G9151 Total		
+	60	H0559 Total		
+	66	I7424 Total		
+	71	K3177 Total		
+	76	L8482 Total		
+	82	M3105 Total		
+	87	N7835 Total		
+	92	P2623 Total		
+	97	P5225 Total		
+	101	S1939 Total		
+	106	S2463 Total		
+	111	S2811 Total		
+	116	S4455 Total		
+	120	S6473 Total		
+	124	S9766 Total		
+	128	T3756 Total		
+	132	V6841 Total		
+	136	W1645 Total		
−	137	Grand Total		

Fig. 695

button. In the Go To Special dialog, select Blanks, as shown in Fig. 696.

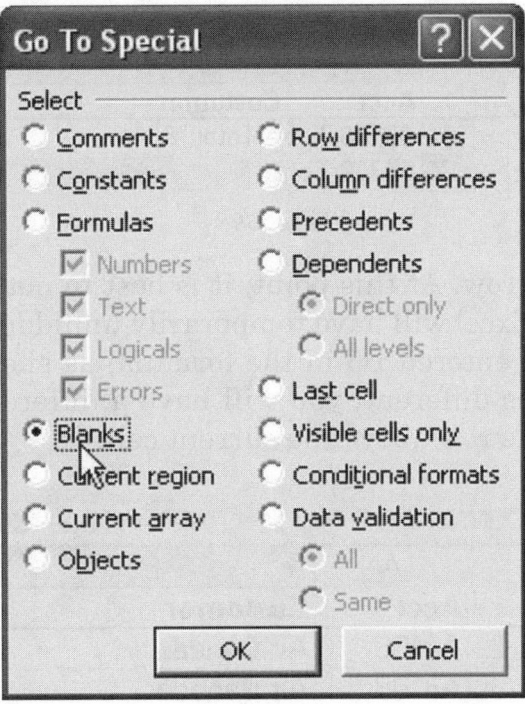

Fig. 696

4)   You have now selected just the blank column B cells in the subtotal rows, as shown in Fig. 697. Your goal now is to enter a formula in the blank cells that will copy the customer name in the hidden detail row above, down to the current cell.

	A	B	C	D
1	Acct	Customer	Invoice	Revenue
6	A3108 Total			31,021
12	A4368 Total			60,461
17	B4504 Total			51,240
22	C4904 Total			39,250
27	C8082 Total			31,369
32	C9651 Total			54,048

Fig. 697

Part
III

5)   Without changing the selection, start typing this formula as shown in Fig. 698: ="Total "&

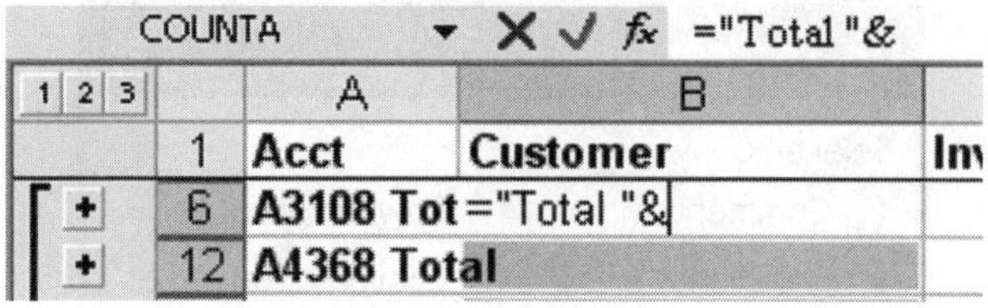

Fig. 698

6)   Hit the Up Arrow. At this point, it is best to not even look at your formula bar! Excel will have temporarily unhidden the hidden rows and will have entered B5 in the formula, as shown in Fig. 699. If your dataset is different, you will have a different formula, but it will still be one row above the current cell.

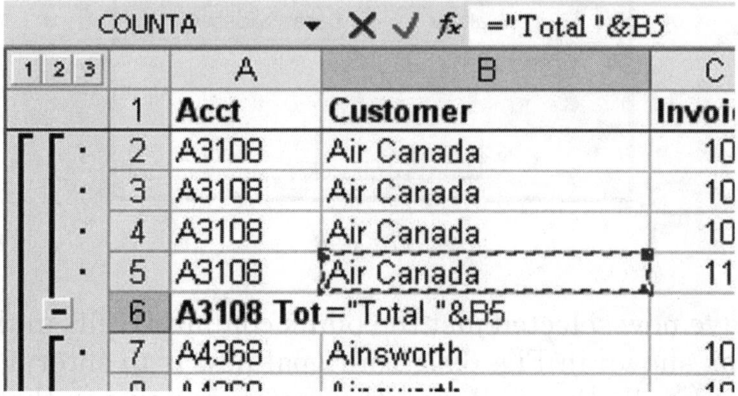

Fig. 699

7)   Your formula is done, but you do not want to hit Enter yet! First, you want to enter this relative formula in all of the selected blank cells.

Hit Ctrl+Enter. The formula will be entered in all subtotal rows, as shown in Fig. 700.

1 2 3		A	B	C	D
	1	Acct	Customer	Invoice	Revenue
+	6	A3108 Tot	Total Air Canada		31,021
+	12	A4368 Tot	Total Ainsworth		60,461
+	17	B4504 Tot	Total Bell Canada		51,240
+	22	C4904 Tot	Total Compaq		39,250
+	27	C8082 Tot	Total Compton Petroleum		31,369
+	32	C9651 Tot	Total Chevron		54,048
+	38	E9872 Tot	Total Exxon		68,200

Fig. 700

Gotcha: The Go To Special – Blanks step is radically important. If you fail to do this step, you will get a result such as the one shown in Fig. 701.

B	C	D
Customer	Invoice	Revenue
Total Air Canada		31,021
Total Total Total Total Total Total		60,461
Total Total Total Total Total Total		51,240
Total Total Total Total Total Total		39,250
Total Total Total Total Total Total		31,369
Total Total Total Total Total Total		54,048

Fig. 701

If you see this, you need to immediately do an Edit – Undo.

By not selecting just the blank cells, you effectively overwrote the hidden rows with your Ctrl+Enter.

As shown in Fig. 702, if you unhide the detail rows, you will see that you accidentally entered the formula in all of the detail rows and overwrote the customer names.

	A	B	C
1	Acct	Customer	Invoice
2	A3108	Air Canada	1057
3	A3108	Air Canada	1061
4	A3108	Air Canada	1090
5	A3108	Air Canada	1108
6	A3108 Tot	Total Air Canada	
7	A4368	Total Total Air Canada	1014
8	A4368	Total Total Total Air Ca	1015
9	A4368	Total Total Total Total A	1030
10	A4368	Total Total Total Total T	1054
11	A4368	Total Total Total Total T	1091
12	A4368 Tot	Total Total Total Total Total Total	

Fig. 702

Part III

Summary: Using Go To Special Blanks is an effective method for adding data to the subtotal rows. It would be a lot better if Excel allowed you to write an SQL-like query, such as Select First(Customer), but for now, the Blanks option will have to do the trick.

Commands Discussed: Go To Special – Blanks; Subtotals

BE WARY

Problem: By using the tips in this book, you will find yourself processing data faster than ever before. However, this might also make you mess up data faster than ever before.

Strategy: Save and Save often. Do a reasonableness test on your data often. If you work for a company with $100 Million in annual sales, a quarterly sales report should not show $200 Billion in sales.

Try to figure out problems as soon as they happen. Excel is an incredibly logical program. Everything happens for a reason. If you can figure out the reason, you will master it in no time. Every "Gotcha" in this book is here because I have been stung by this problem in the past.

In twenty years of spreadsheet work, there have only been a few times when I could not find a logical explanation for something. If you are truly stumped, describe the situation on a message board such as the one at MrExcel.com. The odds are that someone else has seen the same problem and has figured it out.

Summary: Be wary of your data processing steps and occasionally do a reasonableness test to make sure that your data still looks right. Save frequently with different file names if you are doing something new that you are unsure of. This way, you can go back to the "IncomeBeforeSub-totals.xls" if you think that you have done something wrong.

GENERAL PROTECTION FAULTS

Problem: You keep getting a GPF on a particular workbook.

Strategy: GPFs are the exceptions to the rule. I can rarely figure out what is causing a GPF. In version 2002, Excel became much better at being able to recover from GPFs.

As shown in Fig. 703, if Excel crashes and offers you the chance to report the problem, please do so. With millions of people using Excel, if everyone reports their errors, Microsoft will get a good statistical picture of the errors.

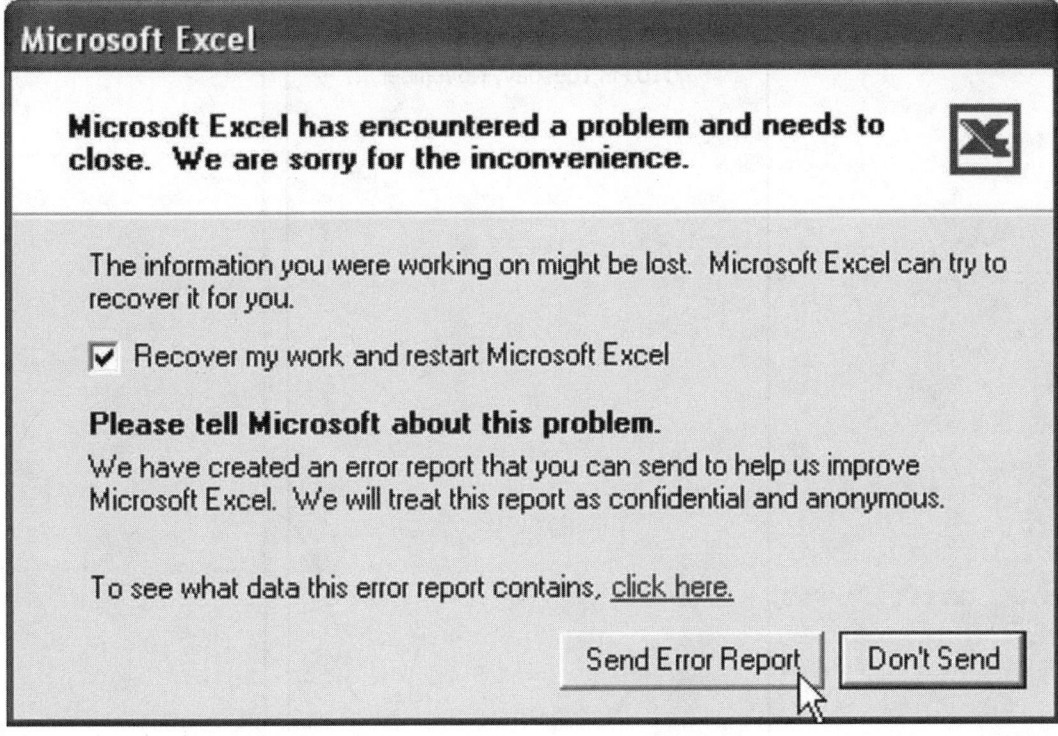

Fig. 703

This is particularly important if you are using a new version of the program or have recently installed a service pack.

If you keep getting one particular crash, check the Microsoft Knowledge Base. I remember one version of Excel that would crash about three steps after you had used the Edit – Find command in Excel. By the time that I realized the trend, Microsoft had acknowledged the problem and offered a HotFix, which was downloadable from the Knowledge Base.

After sending an error report, Excel 2002 or later will re-open and offer to load up the last version of your workbook, as shown in Fig. 704. You might also have the choice to open previously saved versions of the workbook.

Document Recovery

Excel has recovered the following files. Save the ones you wish to keep.

Available Files

GPF.xls [Original]
Last saved by user
7:10 PM Tuesday, November ...

[?] Which file do I want to save?

Close

Fig. 704

There are certain things that I know will cause Excel to crash. For instance, I added a cell comment in the GPF.xls workbook and then ran a simple Excel macro to delete all of the shapes on the worksheet. When I got the mouse pointer near the red triangle in the commented cell, Excel tried to display the comment shape. Since the macro had already deleted the shape, Excel crashed with a GPF.

Sometimes, particularly in Excel 2000 and earlier versions, I would encounter a spreadsheet which had simply become corrupt. It was able to open the worksheet, but if I tried to use File – Close or File – Save, Excel would crash. I learned that this sequence would save the data:

1)   Open the corrupt workbook.

2)   Create a new blank workbook.

3)   Copy data from the bad workbook to the new workbook.

4)   Use File – Save As to save the new workbook.

5)   Close the new workbook.

6)   Close the corrupt workbook, knowing it will crash. You can then use the saved version of the new workbook without having it crash.

Summary: Always report your crashes to Microsoft. If you keep getting a particular crash, check the Excel Knowledge Base to see if a HotFix is available.

CREATE SUBTOTALS BY PRODUCT
WITHIN REGION

Problem: In the dataset shown in Fig. 705, you want to add subtotals by two fields, such as Product and Region.

	A	B	C	D
1	Region	Product	Invoice	Revenue
2	West	DEF	1051	11982
3	Central	XYZ	1052	48370
4	East	ABC	1053	65770
5	East	XYZ	1054	69552
6	East	XYZ	1055	4358
7	East	ABC	1056	33875
8	East	DEF	1057	20200
9	West	ABC	1058	64782

Fig. 705

Strategy: This seems easy, but there is a trick to it. You want to add subtotals to the less detailed field first.

1)   Sort by product within region, as shown in Fig. 706.

	A	B	C	D
1	Region	Product	Invoice	Revenue
2	Central	ABC	1064	67357
3	Central	ABC	1075	60248
4	Central	DEF	1067	6497
5	Central	XYZ	1052	48370
6	Central	XYZ	1070	55612
7	East	ABC	1053	65770
8	East	ABC	1056	33875
9	East	ABC	1068	21977
10	East	DEF	1057	20200

Fig. 706

2)   Add a subtotal by Region, as shown in Fig. 707.

	A	B	C	D
1	Region	Product	Invoice	Revenue
2	Central	ABC	1064	67357
3	Central	ABC	1075	60248
4	Central	DEF	1067	6497
5	Central	XYZ	1052	48370
6	Central	XYZ	1070	55612
7	**Central Total**			238084
8	East	ABC	1053	65770
9	East	ABC	1056	33875
10	East	ABC	1068	21977
11	East	DEF	1057	20200

Fig. 707

3)   Select Data – Subtotals again. Change Region to Product. Be sure to uncheck the box for Replace Current Subtotals, as shown in Fig. 708.

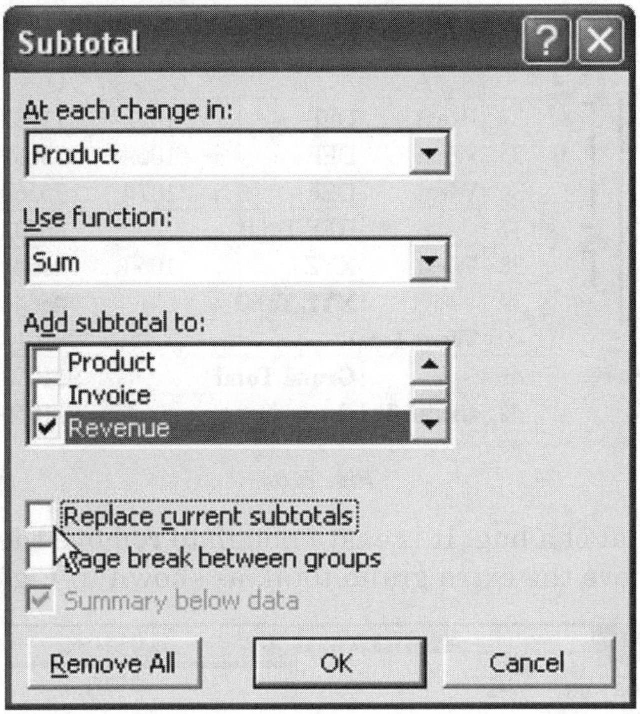

Fig. 708

Result: You now have two sets of subtotals. As shown in Fig. 709, there are now four Group & Outline buttons to the left of cell A1.

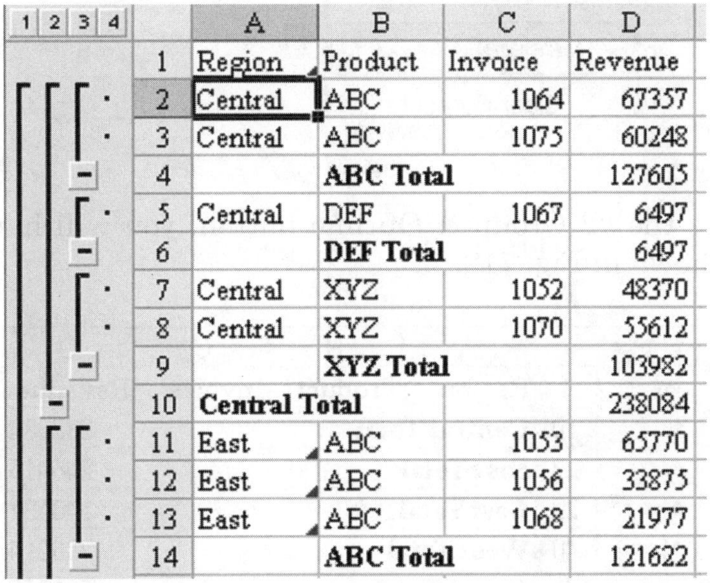

Fig. 709

There are also two grand total lines, as shown in Fig. 710.

1 2 3 4		A	B	C	D
·	34	West	DEF	1051	11982
·	35	West	DEF	1069	38161
·	36	West	DEF	1074	36560
−	37		**DEF Total**		86703
·	38	West	XYZ	1060	46644
−	39		**XYZ Total**		46644
−	40	**West Total**			286014
−	41		**Grand Total**		911050
	42	**Grand Total**			911050

Fig. 710

This is somewhat of a bug. It is easy enough to remove the second to the last line to remove the extra grand total, as shown in Fig. 711.

41			**Grand Total**		911050
42	✂	Cut			911050
43	▤	Copy			
44					
45	▣	Paste			
46		Paste Special…			
47					
48		Insert			
49		Delete			
50		Clear Contents			

Fig. 711

If you choose the #2 Group & Outline button, you will have totals by Region, as shown in Fig. 712.

1 2 3 4		A	B	C	D
	1	Region	Product	Invoice	Revenue
+	10	**Central Total**			238084
+	23	**East Total**			246415
+	29	**Govt Total**			140537
+	40	**West Total**			286014
−	41	**Grand Total**			911050

Fig. 712

If you choose the #3 Group & Outline button, you will have totals by
Region and Product, as shown in Fig. 713.

1 2 3 4		A	B	C	D
	1	Region	Product	Invoice	Revenue
+	4		ABC Total		127605
+	6		DEF Total		6497
+	9		XYZ Total		103982
−	10	Central Total			238084
+	14		ABC Total		121622
+	18		DEF Total		32013
+	22		XYZ Total		92780
−	23	East Total			246415
+	28		XYZ Total		140537
−	29	Govt Total			140537
+	33		ABC Total		152667
+	37		DEF Total		86703
+	39		XYZ Total		46644
−	40	West Total			286014
−	41	Grand Total			911050

Fig. 713

Additional Details:
Here is why it is impor-
tant to do the subtotals
in the right order. Say
that your company sells
three products. The Gov-
ernment region only buys
product XYZ. You might
have data that looks like
the data in Fig. 714. Note
that row 15 contains an
XYZ record for the East
and row 16 contains an
XYZ record for the Gov-
ernment region.

	A	B	C	D
1	Region	Product	Invoice	Revenue
9	East	ABC	1068	21977
10	East	DEF	1057	20200
11	East	DEF	1059	9566
12	East	DEF	1066	2247
13	East	XYZ	1054	69552
14	East	XYZ	1055	4358
15	East	XYZ	1072	18870
16	Govt	XYZ	1063	33118
17	Govt	XYZ	1065	35401
18	Govt	XYZ	1071	17927
19	Govt	XYZ	1073	54091
20	West	ABC	1058	64782

Fig. 714

If you subtotal by product first, the XYZ products from the East and the Government will be trapped in one subtotal in row 25, as shown in Fig. 715. This is an absolute mess.

1 2 3			A	B	C	D
		1	Region	Product	Invoice	Revenue
	•	15	East	DEF	1059	9566
	•	16	East	DEF	1066	2247
–		17		**DEF Total**		32013
	•	18	East	XYZ	1054	69552
	•	19	East	XYZ	1055	4358
	•	20	East	XYZ	1072	18870
	•	21	Govt	XYZ	1063	33118
	•	22	Govt	XYZ	1065	35401
	•	23	Govt	XYZ	1071	17927
	•	24	Govt	XYZ	1073	54091
–		25		**XYZ Total**		233317
	•	26	West	ABC	1058	64782
	•	27	West	ABC	1061	18361
	•	28	West	ABC	1062	69524
–		29		**ABC Total**		152667

Fig. 715

If you then total by Region, you will have set up Groups that make no sense. Note that the XYZ total in D32 is greater than the Government Region total in D31, as shown in Fig. 716.

1 2 3 4			A	B	C	D
		1	Region	Product	Invoice	Revenue
	+	16	**East Total**			121622
–		17		**ABC Total**		121622
	+	21	**East Total**			32013
–		22		**DEF Total**		32013
	+	26	**East Total**			92780
	+	31	**Govt Total**			140537
–		32		**XYZ Total**		233317
	+	36	**West Total**			152667
–		37		**ABC Total**		152667

Fig. 716

In Excel 95, there was no workaround for this problem. In Excel 97, they added the rule that XYZ rows separated by a blank row would be handled OK. Thus, you need to add subtotals by Region first.

Summary: You can create very powerful summary reports using two sets of subtotals. Remember to subtotal the outer grouping first and then the inner subtotals. On the second and subsequent calls to the Subtotal command, remember to uncheck the Replace Current Subtotals option.

MY MANAGER WANTS THE SUBTOTAL LINES IN BOLD PINK TAHOMA FONT

Problem: Your manager loves your reports with automatic subtotals. He wants the subtotal lines formatted in bold pink Tahoma 15 point font. Again, there is no hope for the manager to be transferred soon.

Part III

Strategy: Anonymously send your manager copies of job postings for other departments. In the meantime, follow these steps.

1) Add subtotals to the dataset.

2) Choose the #2 Group and Outline button to display only the subtotals, as shown in Fig. 717.

	A	B	C	D	E
1	Rep	Customer	Jan	Feb	Mar
8	Bob Total		244,471	244,731	172,379
13	Joe Total		158,922	184,096	213,038
19	Mary Total		213,075	146,804	217,705
20	Grand Total		616,468	575,631	603,122

Fig. 717

3) Select all data except the headings. In Fig. 717, this would mean dragging the mouse from A8 to N20. From the menu, select Edit–Go To. In the Go To dialog, choose Special. In the Go To Special dialog, choose Visible Cells Only, as shown in Fig. 718.

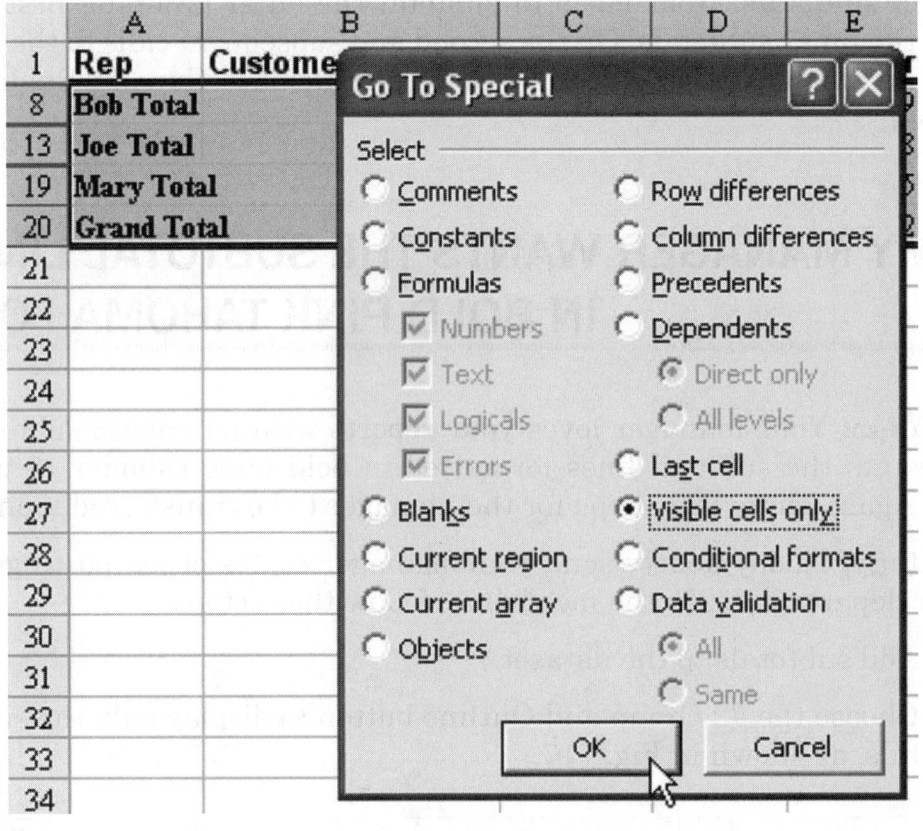

Fig. 718

Result: You will have selected only the total rows. You can now do any formatting changes necessary, as shown in Fig. 719.

		A	B	C	D
	1	Rep	Customer	Jan	Feb
+	8	Bob Total		244,471	244,731
+	13	Joe Total		158,922	184,096
+	19	Mary Total		213,075	146,804
−	20	Grand Total		616,468	575,631

Fig. 719

When you display the #3 Group & Outline button, only the subtotal rows will have the desired formatting, as shown in Fig. 720.

1 2 3		A	B	C
	1	Rep	Customer	Jan
	2	Bob	Bell Canada	20,992
	3	Bob	Compton Petroleum	72,030
	4	Bob	Exxon	13,438
	5	Bob	Sears	58,901
	6	Bob	Texaco	4,937
	7	Bob	Verizon	74,173
	8	**Bob Total**		**244,471**
	9	Joe	Air Canada	43,097
	10	Joe	Compaq	25,991
	11	Joe	Ford	47,662
	12	Joe	Sun Life Financial	42,172
	13	**Joe Total**		**158,922**

Fig. 720

Summary: Using the Visible Cells Only option of the Go To Special dialog, you can apply any particular formatting to just the subtotal rows.

MY MANAGER WANTS A BLANK LINE AFTER EVERY SUBTOTAL

Problem: Your manager wants you to add a blank line between sections of the subtotal report. This is a fairly standard request. Quite simply, data looks better when it is formatted this way.

Strategy: This is really hard. There is no built-in way to do this. I've tried many methods. I picked the three best methods to explain here.

Method 1: The first method is to try to fool the manager by making the total rows be double-height, with the totals vertically aligned to the top. This method may work if you are printing the report to give to the manager. It will give the appearance that a blank row has been inserted.

Part
III

1)   To do this easily, follow the steps in the preceding "bold pink Tahoma font" chapter. Add subtotals, collapse to level 2, select column A between the headings and grand total, Edit – Go To – Special– Visible Cells Only. You will then have selected just the subtotal rows, as shown in Fig. 721.

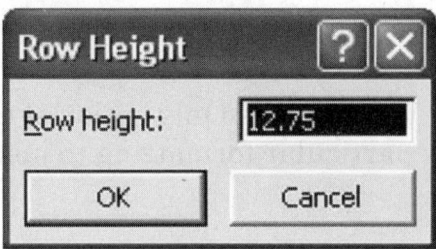

Fig. 721

2)   From the menu, select Format – Row – Height. Depending on your font, the row height will probably be between 12 and 14. The height shown here in Fig. 722 is 12.75.

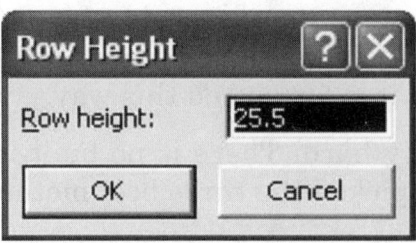

Fig. 722

3)   Mentally multiply by 2 and type 25.5 as the new height, as shown in Fig. 723.

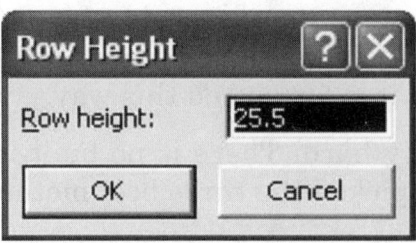

Fig. 723

This creates a fairly ugly intermediate result, as shown in Fig. 724.

	A	
1	Rep	Cust
8	Bob Total	
13	Joe Total	
19	Mary Total	
20	Grand Total	

Fig. 724

4) Select everything from the first subtotal to the last subtotal again, this time selecting all of the columns in the dataset. As shown in Fig. 725, use Edit – Go To – Special – Visible Cells Only.

Part III

	A	B	C	D	E
1	Rep	Customer	Jan	Feb	M
8	Bob Total		244,471	244,731	172,3
13	Joe Total		158,922	184,096	213,0
19	Mary Total		213,075	146,804	217,7
20	Grand Total		616,468	575,631	603,1

Fig. 725

5) Press Ctrl+1 on the keyboard to display the Format Cells dialog. Select the Alignment tab. By default, you will see that the Text Alignment – Vertical is set to Bottom, as shown in Fig. 726.

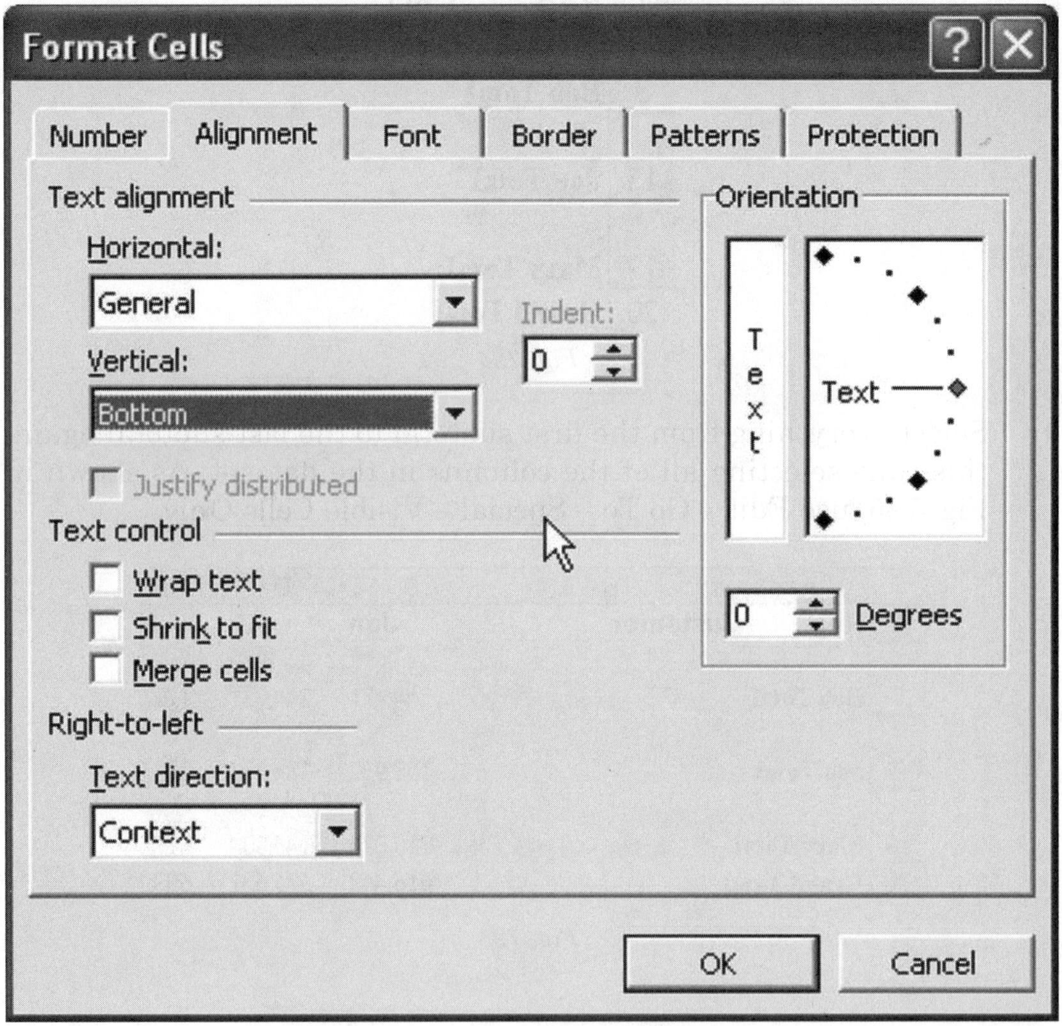

Format Cells
Number
Alignment
Font
Border
Patterns
Protection
Text alignment
Horizontal:
General
Indent:
0
Vertical:
Bottom
Justify distributed
Text control
Wrap text
Shrink to fit
Merge cells
Right-to-left
Text direction:
Context
Orientation
Text
Text
0
Degrees
OK
Cancel

Fig. 726

6) Choose the Vertical dropdown arrow. As shown in Fig. 727, you will appear to have choices for Center, Bottom, Justify, or Distributed.

Vertical:
Bottom
Center
Bottom
Justify
Distributed

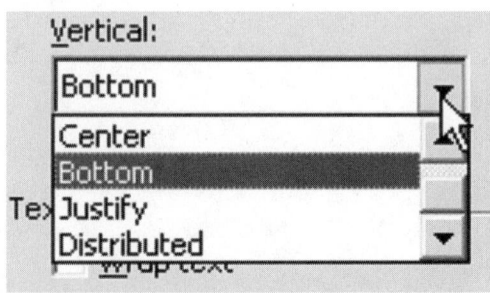

Fig. 727

7) Use the up scrollbar to display the other choice: Top, as shown in Fig. 728.

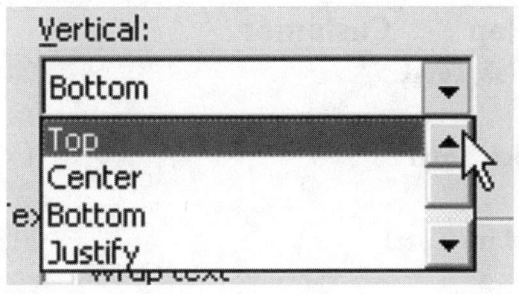

Fig. 728

8) Select Top and choose OK, as shown in Fig. 729.

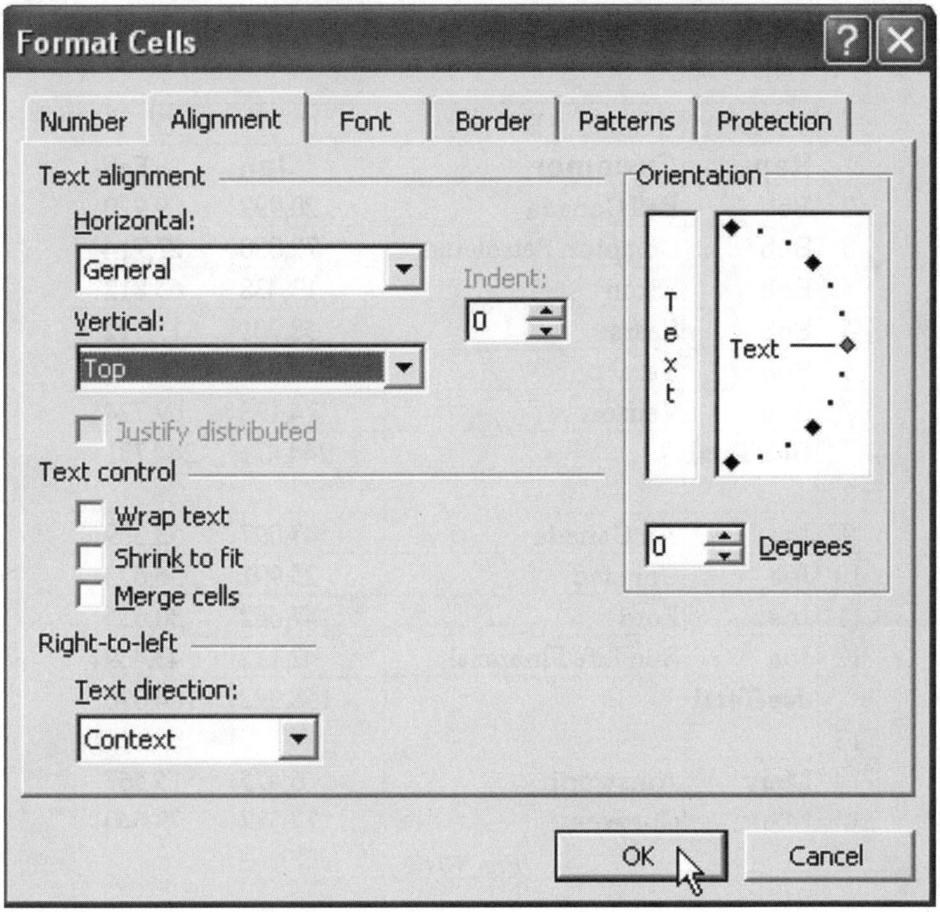

Fig. 729

As shown in Fig. 730, the intermediate result looks only slightly better.

	A	B	C
1	**Rep**	**Customer**	**Jan**
8	**Bob Total**		244,471
13	**Joe Total**		158,922
19	**Mary Total**		213,075
20	**Grand Total**		616,468

Fig. 730

9)   Choose the Group & Outline button #3 to display the detail rows again, as shown in Fig. 731.

	A	B	C	D
1	**Rep**	**Customer**	**Jan**	**Feb**
2	Bob	Bell Canada	20,992	9,970
3	Bob	Compton Petroleum	72,030	27,714
4	Bob	Exxon	13,438	65,812
5	Bob	Sears	58,901	15,112
6	Bob	Texaco	4,937	56,399
7	Bob	Verizon	74,173	69,724
8	**Bob Total**		244,471	244,731
9	Joe	Air Canada	43,097	53,369
10	Joe	Compaq	25,991	56,623
11	Joe	Ford	47,662	30,635
12	Joe	Sun Life Financial	42,172	43,469
13	**Joe Total**		158,922	184,096
14	Mary	Ainsworth	6,475	15,567
15	Mary	Chevron	72,587	23,640

Fig. 731

Although you can see that there is no blank row after the subtotals in rows 8 and 13, when you print the report for your manager, it will appear to have a blank row, as shown in Fig. 732.

Rep	Customer	Jan	Feb
Bob	Bell Canada	20,992	9,970
Bob	Compton Petroleum	72,030	27,714
Bob	Exxon	13,438	65,812
Bob	Sears	58,901	15,112
Bob	Texaco	4,937	56,399
Bob	Verizon	74,173	69,724
Bob Total		244,471	244,731
Joe	Air Canada	43,097	53,369
Joe	Compaq	25,991	56,623
Joe	Ford	47,662	30,635
Joe	Sun Life Financial	42,172	43,469
Joe Total		158,922	184,096
Mary	Ainsworth	6,475	15,567
Mary	Chevron	72,597	23,640

Fig. 732

Part III

Method 1 will not work if you have to send the dataset to the manager via e-mail. The manager may be smart enough to want to stop at each subtotal using the End key, and this will not work with the double-height rows.

Method 2: The second method is to use old-fashioned, brute force. Insert a blank row between each group method.

1) As shown in Fig. 733, go to cell A9.

	A	B
1	**Rep**	**Customer**
2	Bob	Bell Canada
3	Bob	Compton Petroleum
4	Bob	Exxon
5	Bob	Sears
6	Bob	Texaco
7	Bob	Verizon
8	**Bob Total**	
9	Joe	Air Canada
10	Joe	Compaq

Fig. 733

2)   Hold down Alt while you press I and then R. As shown in Fig. 734, this will insert a row above the current cell, using the Insert – Row command.

	A	B
1	**Rep**	**Customer**
2	Bob	Bell Canada
3	Bob	Compton Petroleum
4	Bob	Exxon
5	Bob	Sears
6	Bob	Texaco
7	Bob	Verizon
8	**Bob Total**	
9		
10	Joe	Canada
11	Joe	Compaq
12	Joe	Ford
13	Joe	Sun Life Financial
14	**Joe Total**	
15	Mary	Ainsworth

Fig. 734

3)   Go to cell A15 and insert another row. This method is easy when you have three sales reps as shown here in Fig. 735, but very tedious when you have 50 sales reps.

	A	B	C	D
1	**Rep**	**Customer**	**Jan**	
2	Bob	Bell Canada	20,992	9,
3	Bob	Compton Petroleum	72,030	27,
4	Bob	Exxon	13,438	65,
5	Bob	Sears	58,901	15,
6	Bob	Texaco	4,937	56,
7	Bob	Verizon	74,173	69,
8	**Bob Total**		244,471	244
9				
10	Joe	Air Canada	43,097	53,
11	Joe	Compaq	25,991	56,
12	Joe	Ford	47,662	30,
13	Joe	Sun Life Financial	42,172	43,
14	**Joe Total**		158,922	184
15				
16	Mary	Ainsworth	6,475	15,

Fig. 735

Method 3: The third method is to attempt to make method 2 faster. This is particularly important if you have 50 reps. Follow these steps.

1) Add subtotals. Collapse to Group & Outline level 2, as shown in Fig. 736.

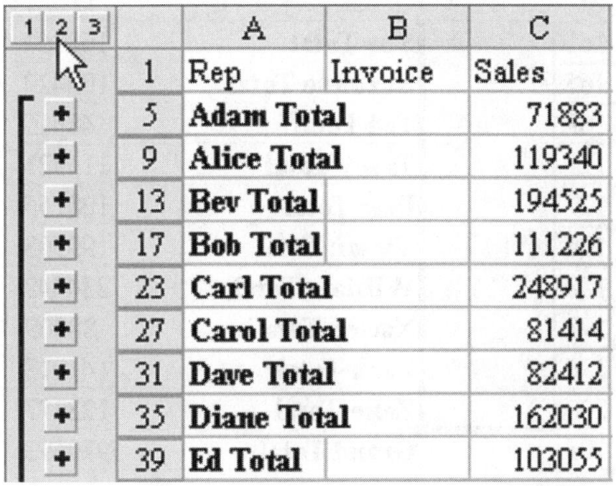

		A	B	C
	1	Rep	Invoice	Sales
+	5	**Adam Total**		71883
+	9	**Alice Total**		119340
+	13	**Bev Total**		194525
+	17	**Bob Total**		111226
+	23	**Carl Total**		248917
+	27	**Carol Total**		81414
+	31	**Dave Total**		82412
+	35	**Diane Total**		162030
+	39	**Ed Total**		103055

Fig. 736

Part III

2) Insert a new temporary blank column A to the left of the current column A, as shown in Fig. 737. To do this, select any cell in column A and choose Insert – Column.

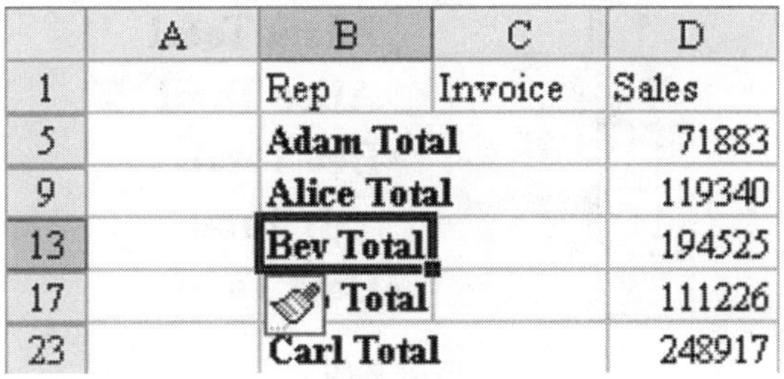

	A	B	C	D
1		Rep	Invoice	Sales
5		**Adam Total**		71883
9		**Alice Total**		119340
13		**Bev Total**		194525
17		**Total**		111226
23		**Carl Total**		248917

Fig. 737

3)   The goal is to enter an x next to each subtotal in column A. With the mouse, drag from A5 down to the last row with a subtotal in A, as shown in Fig. 738.

A5	▼	fx	
	A	B	C	D
161		Sue Total		168764
165		Suzanne Total		109429
169		Ted Total		48415
173		Tracy Total		115521
177		Uma Total		108155
182		Victor Total		199503
188		William Total		234448
192		Xavier Total		88909
196		Zach Total		141013
200		Zeke Total		123777
201		Grand Total		5979593

Fig. 738

4)   Select Edit – Go To – Special – Visible Cells Only, as shown in Fig. 739.

	A	B	
1		Rep	Inv
5		Adam Total	
9		Alice Total	
13		Bev Total	
17		Total	
23		Carl Total	

Fig. 739

5)   Type an x and hit Ctrl+Enter to place the x in all selected cells, as shown in Fig. 740.

	A	B	C
1		Rep	Invoic
5	x	Adam Total	
9	x	Alice Total	
13	x	Bev Total	

Fig. 740

6)   As shown in Fig. 741, choose the #3 Group & Outline button to un-
      hide the detail rows.

1 2 3		A	B	C	D
1			Rep	Invoice	Sales
2			Adam	1096	14511
3			Adam	1114	33873
4			Adam	1140	23499
5	x		**Adam Total**		71883
6			Alice	1142	19390
7			Alice	1193	53766
8			Alice	1215	46184
9	x		**Alice Total**		119340
10			Bev	1180	69506
11			Bev	1197	71264
12			Bev	1226	53755
13	x		**Bev Total**		194525

Fig. 741

7)   The next step is to move all of the "x" values down one cell. It is
      tempting to hit Ctrl+X to perform a Cut, but this will not work on
      non-adjacent cells, as shown in Fig. 742.

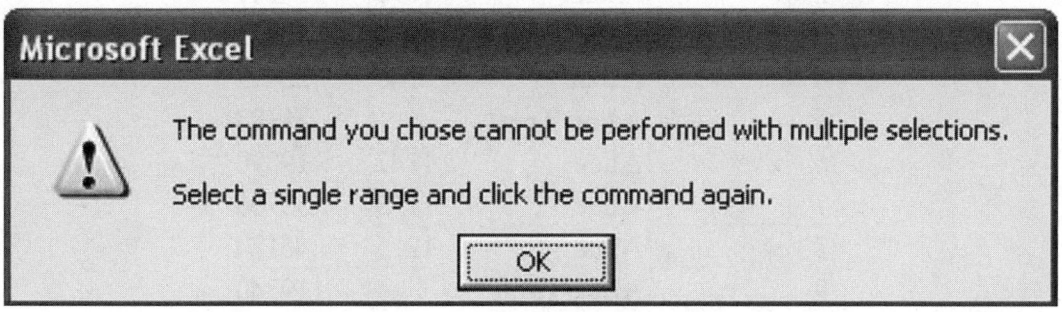

Fig. 742

Part III

8) Select from A5 through the last x in column A, as shown in Fig. 743.

	A	B
191		Xavier
192	x	**Xavier Total**
193		Zach
194		Zach
195		Zach
196	x	**Zach Total**
197		Zeke
198		Zeke
199		Zeke
200	x	**Zeke Total**
201		**Grand Total**

Fig. 743

9) Use Edit – Cut or Ctrl+X to cut the cells. Move down one cell to A6. Hit Ctrl+V or Edit – Paste to place the "x" cells on the first row of each subtotal group, as shown in Fig. 744.

	A	B	C	D
1		Rep	Invoice	Sales
2		Adam	1096	14511
3		Adam	1114	33873
4		Adam	1140	23499
5		**Adam Total**		71883
6	x	Alice	1142	19390
7		Alice	1193	53766
8		Alice	1215	46184
9		**Alice Total**		119340
10	x	Bev	1180	69506
11		Bev	1197	71264
12		Bev	1226	53755
13		**Bev Total**		194525
14	x	Bob	1113	11930

Fig. 744

10) You want to select all of the rows with an x in column A. Select the entire column by using the mouse on the gray "A" at the top of the column. Choose Edit – Go To – Special – Constants, as shown in Fig. 745.

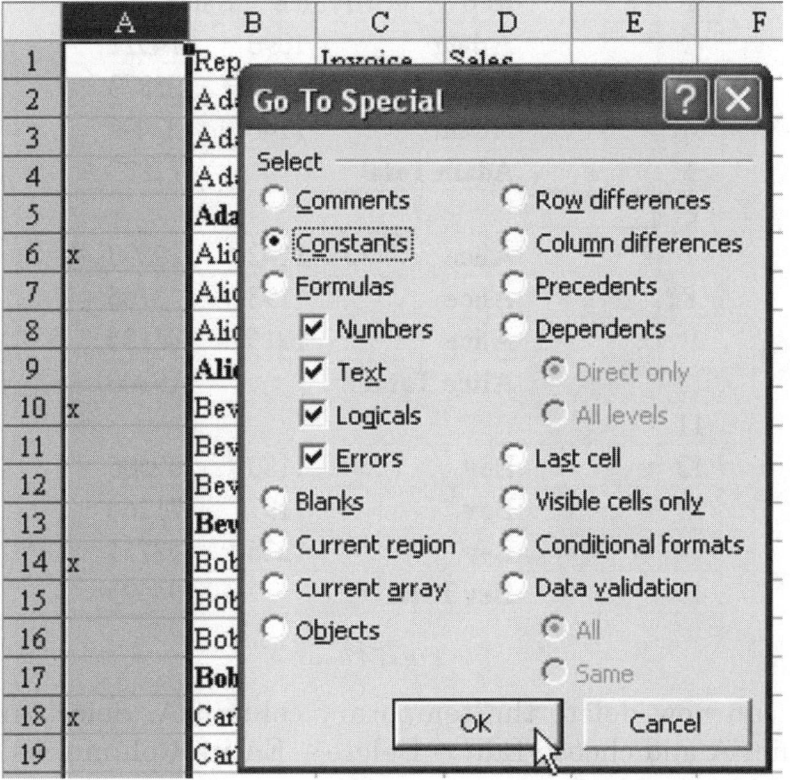

Fig. 745

You will have now selected just the first cell of each group, as shown in Fig. 746.

	A	B
1		Rep
2		Adam
3		Adam
4		Adam
5		**Adam** ˉ
6	x	Alice
7		Alice
8		Alice
9		**Alice** ˉ
10	x	Bev
11		Bev
12		Bev

Fig. 746

11) From the menu, select Insert – Row. You will have inserted 50 rows at the appropriate spots, as shown in Fig. 747.

	A	B	C	D
1		Rep	Invoice	Sales
2		Adam	1096	14511
3		Adam	1114	33873
4		Adam	1140	23499
5		**Adam Total**		71883
6				
7	x	Alice	1142	19390
8		Alice	1193	53766
9		Alice	1215	46184
10		**Alice Total**		119340
11				
12	x	Bev	1180	69506
13		Bev	1197	71264
14		Bev	1226	53755
15		**Bev Total**		194525

Fig. 747

12) You can now delete the temporary column A. Select any cell in column A and choose Edit – Delete – Entire Column, as shown in Fig. 748.

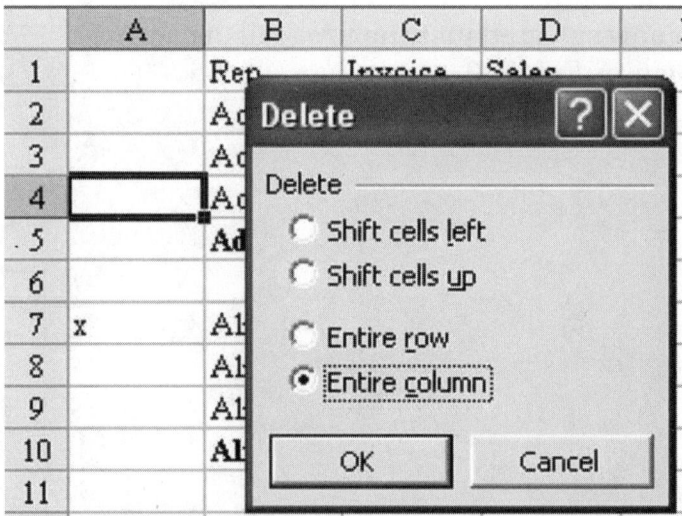

Fig. 748

Result: As shown in Fig. 749, you will have quickly added the blank rows requested by the manager.

	A	B	C
1	Rep	Invoice	Sales
2	Adam	1096	14511
3	Adam	1114	33873
4	Adam	1140	23499
5	**Adam Total**		71883
6			
7	Alice	1142	19390
8	Alice	1193	53766
9	Alice	1215	46184
10	**Alice Total**		119340
11			
12	Bev	1180	69506
13	Bev	1197	71264
14	Bev	1226	53755
15	**Bev Total**		194525
16			
17	Bob	1113	11930

Fig. 749

Gotcha: Once the blank rows are in, you may have a difficult time getting rid of the subtotals. As shown in Fig. 750, if you select cell A2 and choose Data – Subtotals – Remove All, Excel will only delete the first subtotal.

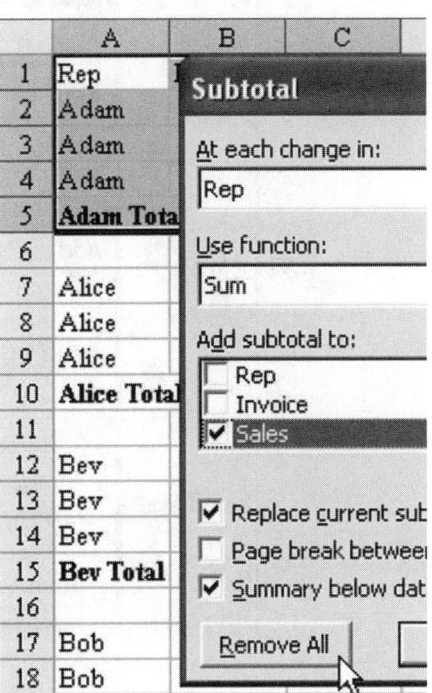

Fig. 750

In order to delete all of the subtotals, you will have to select the entire range before calling the Data Subtotals command. One fast way to do this is to click on the blank gray box above and to the left of cell A1. This box will select all cells in the worksheet, as shown in Fig. 751.

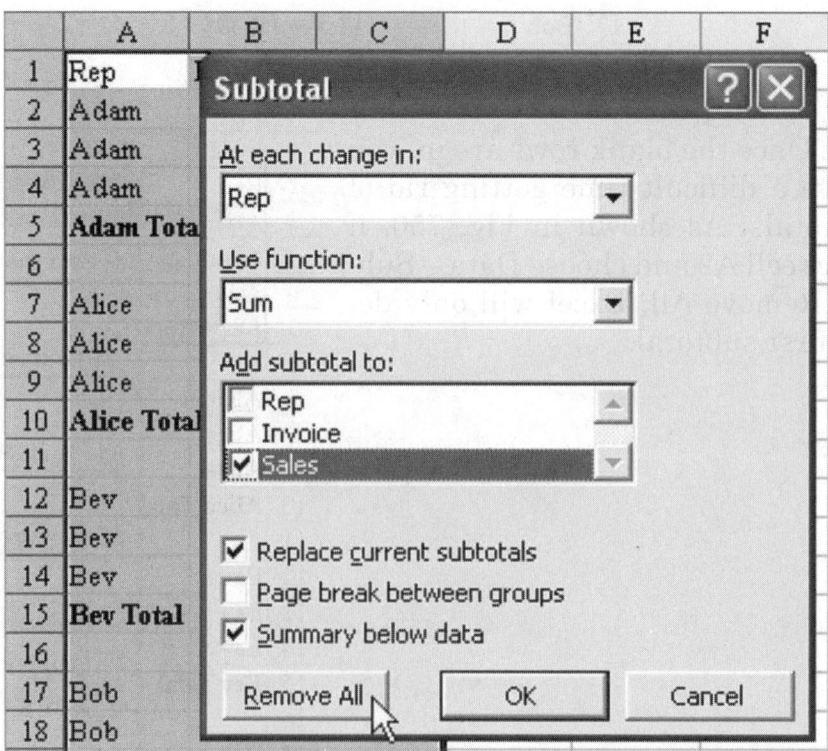

	A	B	C
1	Rep	Invoice	Sales
2	Adam	1096	14511
3	Adam	1114	33873
4	Adam	1140	23499
5	Adam Total		71883
6			
7	Alice	1142	19390

Fig. 751

Now when you choose Data – Subtotals, you will find that Excel has selected all of the subtotals. Click Remove All to remove the subtotals, as shown in Fig. 752.

Fig. 752

Summary: There are three methods for inserting a blank row between each group of subtotals. You can see that none of the three methods seem very appealing, which means that this fairly common request is fairly hard to do. However, with practice, you will find that the third method can be accomplished quickly.

Commands Discussed: Edit – Go To – Special – Visible Cells Only; Edit – Go To – Special – Constants; Edit – Cut; Edit – Paste; Insert – Row; Insert – Column

SUBTOTAL ONE COLUMN AND SUBAVERAGE ANOTHER COLUMN

Problem: In the dataset in Fig. 753, you want to create a subtotal of revenue. It does not make sense to subtotal the unit prices in column C. It might make sense to create an average price for each rep.

Part III

	A	B	C	D
1	Rep	Invoice	Price	Revenue
2	Adam	1096	4.17	14,511
3	Adam	1114	4.56	33,873
4	Adam	1140	4.83	23,499
5	Alice	1142	4.98	19,390
6	Alice	1193	4.31	53,766
7	Alice	1215	4.36	46,184
8	Bev	1180	4.56	69,506
9	Bev	1197	4.86	71,264
10	Bev	1226	4.81	53,755
11	Bob	1113	4.71	11,930

Fig. 753

Strategy: When you add subtotals to a dataset, the function used is the SUBTOTAL function. As shown in Fig. 754, the formula automatically added to cell D5 is =SUBTOTAL(9,D2:D4).

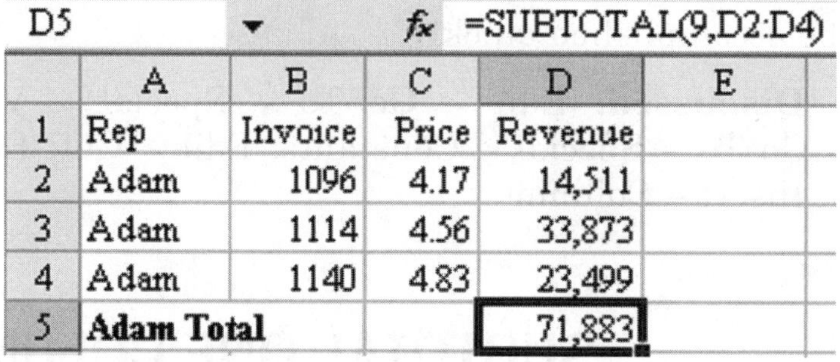

D5				f_x =SUBTOTAL(9,D2:D4)	
	A	B	C	D	E
1	Rep	Invoice	Price	Revenue	
2	Adam	1096	4.17	14,511	
3	Adam	1114	4.56	33,873	
4	Adam	1140	4.83	23,499	
5	**Adam Total**			71,883	

Fig. 754

Remove that subtotal and add a subtotal that averages the Price column. You can do this by changing the Use Function: dropdown from Sum to Average in the Subtotal dialog, as shown in Fig. 755.

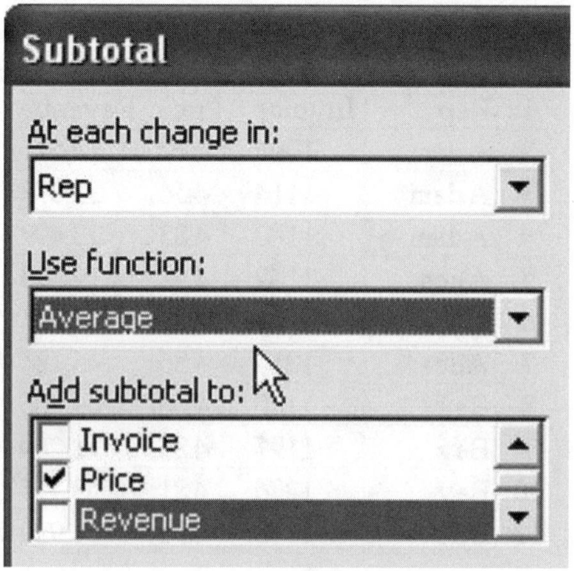

Fig. 755

Examine the formula entered in C5. Excel still uses the =SUBTOTAL() function, but the first parameter changes from a 9 to a 1, as shown in Fig. 756.

Fig. 756

You can imagine that after creating the SUBTOTAL function, the team at Microsoft realized that they also needed SUBAVERAGE, SUBMIN, SUBMAX, and SUBCOUNT. Rather than create nine different functions, they created one function. The first parameter indicates whether Excel should average, sum, count, min, or max, etc. Fig. 757 shows the complete table of values.

Function_Num	Function
1	AVERAGE
2	COUNT
3	COUNTA
4	MAX
5	MIN
6	PRODUCT
7	STDEV
8	STDEVP
9	SUM
10	VAR
11	VARP

Fig. 757

Note: *In Excel 2003, Microsoft added the 11 new function numbers. From 101 to 111, they do the same functions as 1 through 11, but ignore hidden rows.*

If you attempt to add a Sum subtotal to revenue and then add an Average subtotal to Price, the subtotals appear on two lines, as shown in Fig. 758. This may not be what you want.

1 2 3 4		A	B	C	D
	1	Rep	Invoice	Price	Revenue
	2	Adam	1096	4.17	14,511
	3	Adam	1114	4.56	33,873
	4	Adam	1140	4.83	23,499
	5	**Adam Average**		4.52	
	6	**Adam Total**			71,883
	7	Alice	1142	4.98	19,390
	8	Alice	1193	4.31	53,766
	9	Alice	1215	4.36	46,184
	10	**Alice Average**		4.55	
	11	**Alice Total**			119,340
	12	Bev	1180	4.56	69,506

Fig. 758

An alternate method is to add Sum subtotals to both columns. The intermediate result will not make sense for the Price column. Select column C and from the menu choose Edit – Replace.

As shown in Fig. 759, in the Find and Replace dialog, specify that you want to change every occurrence of =SUBTOTAL(9, to =SUBTOTAL(1,.

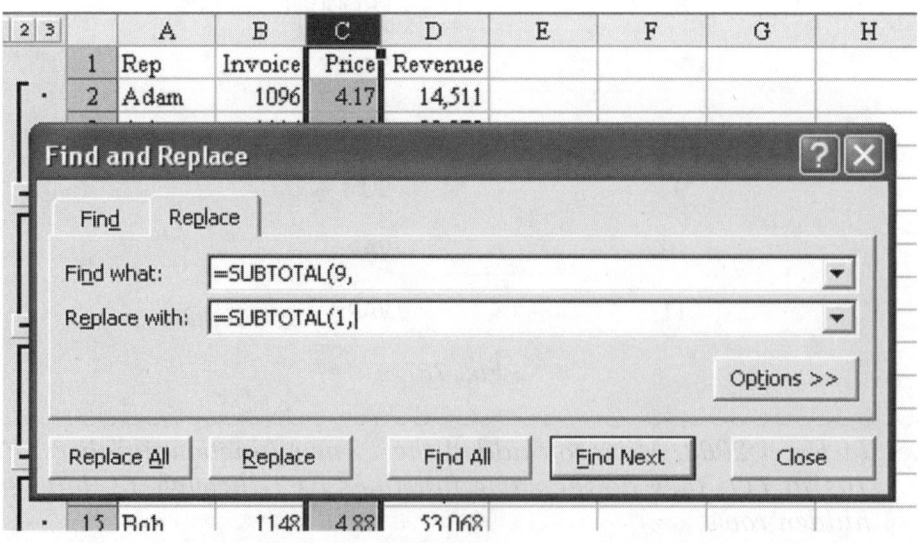

Fig. 759

It is important that you only select column C before you replace, other-wise you will replace the formulas in the Revenue column as well.

It is worth noting that the Find and Replace dialog remembers settings from the last time it was used in the current Excel session. There are settings in the Options>> button that are right by default, but might have been changed if you did a Replace or a Find since you launched Excel. Choose the Options>> button. Make sure that the Look In dropdown is set to Formulas. As shown in Fig. 760, make sure that the Match Entire Cell Contents checkbox is unchecked.

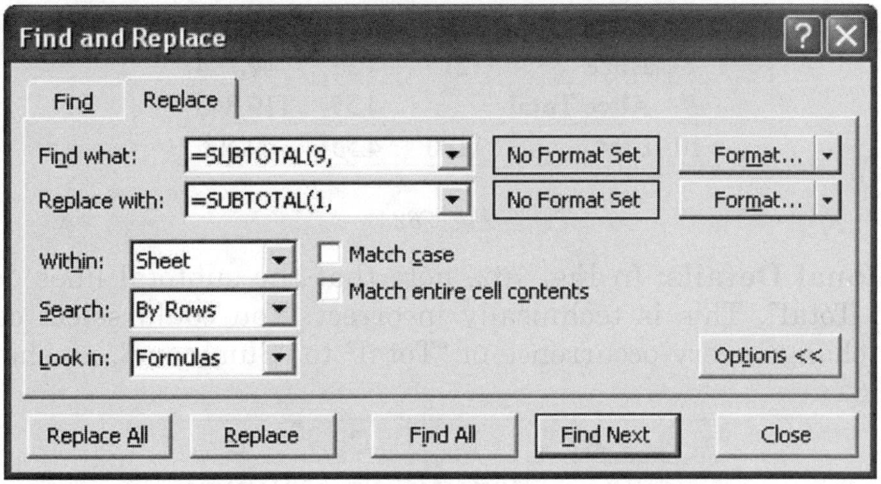

Fig. 760

Choose the Replace All button. Excel will confirm how many cells have been changed. As shown in Fig. 761, a good reasonableness test is to check whether your company has 47 sales reps.

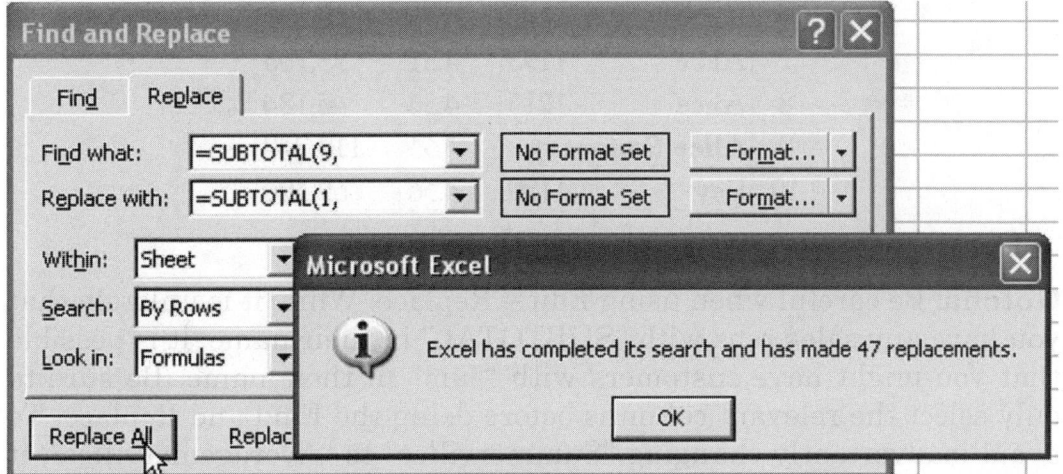

Fig. 761

Result: As shown in Fig. 762, the revenue is totaled and the prices are averaged on the subtotal lines.

	A	B	C	D
1	Rep	Invoice	Price	Revenue
2	Adam	1096	4.17	14,511
3	Adam	1114	4.56	33,873
4	Adam	1140	4.83	23,499
5	**Adam Total**		4.52	71,883
6	Alice	1142	4.98	19,390
7	Alice	1193	4.31	53,766
8	Alice	1215	4.36	46,184
9	**Alice Total**		4.55	119,340
10	Bev	1180	4.56	69,506

Fig. 762

Additional Details: In Fig. 762, note that the subtotal lines declare "Adam Total". This is technically incorrect. You could select column A and change every occurrence of "Total" to "Summary", as shown in Fig. 763.

	A	B	C	D
1	Rep	Invoice	Price	Revenue
2	Adam	1096	4.17	14,511
3	Adam	1114	4.56	33,873
4	Adam	1140	4.83	23,499
5	**Adam Summary**		4.52	71,883
6	Alice	1142	4.98	19,390
7	Alice	1193	4.31	53,766
8	Alice	1215	4.36	46,184
9	**Alice Summary**		4.55	119,340
10	Bev	1180	4.56	69,506

Fig. 763

Gotcha: Be careful when using Edit – Replace. While it is unlikely that you have any sales reps with "SUBTOTAL" in their name, it is possible that you might have customers with "sum" in their name. Be sure to only select the relevant columns before doing the Find and Replace. To avoid inadvertently changing "Summervilles" to "Averagemervilles", it helps to make sure that the text being changed is unique. You can usually do this by including the opening parenthesis in the original and changed text. Making sure to change "SUM(" to "AVERAGE(" is a simple but important step to prevent accidentally changing "summary" to "averagemary".

Summary: Use Edit – Replace to change the SUBTOTAL function from a sum to an average. This allows you to have one summary line per rep, with different types of subtotals.

Commands Discussed: Edit – Replace; Data – Subtotals

Functions Discussed: =SUBTOTAL()

HOW TO DO 40 DIFFERENT
WHAT-IF ANALYSES QUICKLY

Part
III

Problem: You want to buy a car. You want to compare eight price points and four loan terms to calculate the monthly payment amount.

Strategy: There are two methods. The cool method is to use a data table. As shown in Fig. 764, set up the worksheet as follows:

1) Enter one price in cell B2.

2) Enter one term in cell B3.

3) Enter the current annual interest rate in B4.

4) In cell B5, enter a formula to calculate a monthly payment:

=–PMT(B4/12,B3,B2)

Cell B5 is going to be the magic corner cell of your data table.

	B5	▼	f_x =-PMT(B4/12,B3,B2)	
	A	B	C	D	E
1					
2	Price	29995			
3	Term	48			
4	Interest	5.40%			
5	Payment	$696.21			

Fig. 764

5)   In cells B6:B9, enter the four possible terms that you would like to compare. In cells C5:L5, enter the possible prices that you hope to negotiate to, as shown in Fig. 765.

6)   Select the rectangular range of B5:L9. As shown in Fig. 765, the upper left corner of this range contains the formula to calculate your monthly payment.

	B5	▾			*fx* =-PMT(B4/12,B3,B2)								
	A	B	C	D	E	F	G	H	I	J	K	L
1												
2	Price	29995										
3	Term	48										
4	Interest	5.40%										
5	Payment	$696.21	29995	28995	28495	27995	27495	26995	26495	25995	25495	24995
6		36										
7		48										
8		60										
9		72										
10												

Fig. 765

7)   From the menu, select Data – Table. Excel will ask you to specify a row input cell. In other words, Excel will take each cell in the top row of the table and substitute it for this cell. Because these cells contain prices, choose cell B2 as the row input cell, as shown in Fig. 766.

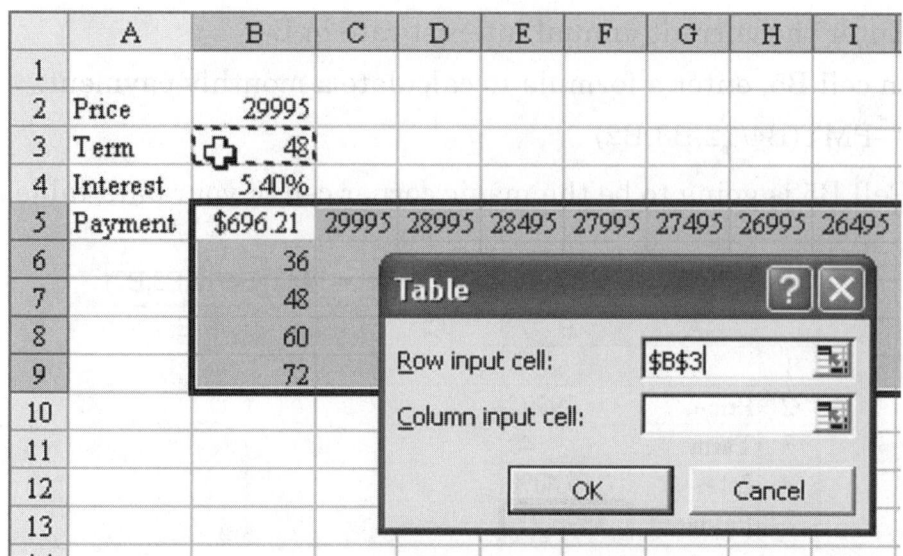

Fig. 766

8) Next, Excel wants to know where the cells in the first column should be used. Because B6:B9 contains terms, specify cell B3, as shown in Fig. 767. Choose OK.

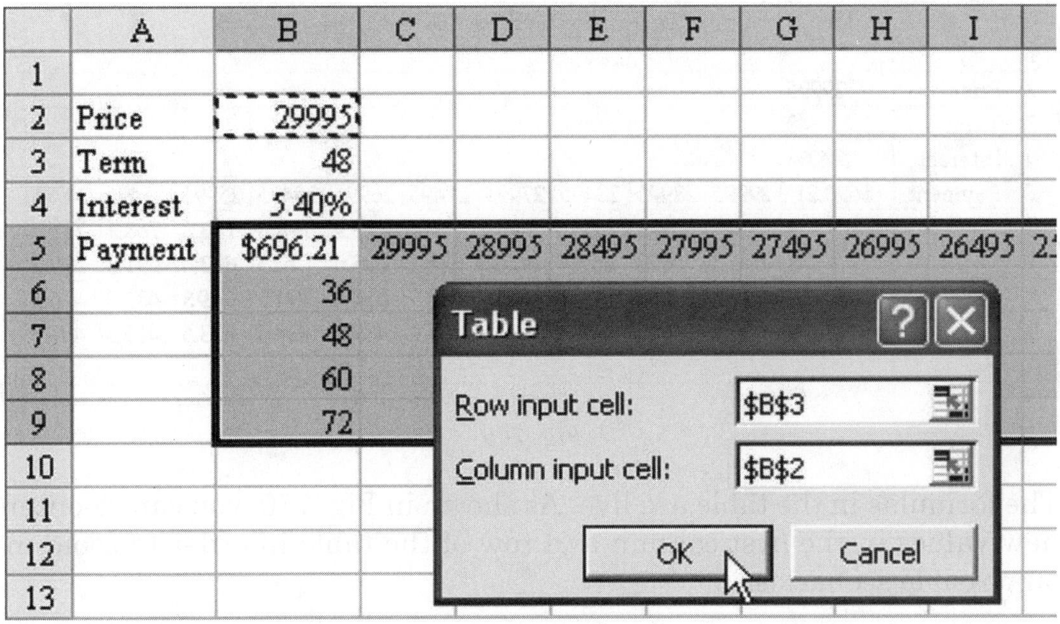

	A	B	C	D	E	F	G	H	I	
1										
2	Price	29995								
3	Term	48								
4	Interest	5.40%								
5	Payment	$696.21	29995	28995	28495	27995	27495	26995	26495	2!
6		36								
7		48								
8		60								
9		72								
10										
11										
12										
13										

Table

Row input cell: $B$3

Column input cell: $B$2

OK   Cancel

Fig. 767

Excel enters an array formula for you. You can see the monthly prices for many combinations of terms and price points, as shown in Fig. 768.

	A	B	C	D	E	F	G	H	I	J	K	L	
1													
2	Price	29995											
3	Term	48											
4	Interest	5.40%											
5	Payment	$696.21	29995	28995	28495	27995	27495	26995	26495	25995	25495	24995	
6			36	904.4	874.2	859.1	844.1	829	813.9	798.8	783.8	768.7	753.6
7			48	696.2	673	661.4	649.8	638.2	626.6	615	603.4	591.8	580.2
8			60	571.6	552.5	543	533.4	523.9	514.4	504.9	495.3	485.8	476.3
9			72	488.7	472.4	464.2	456.1	447.9	439.8	431.6	423.5	415.3	407.2
10													

Fig. 768

Part
III

If you are looking for a monthly payment of $495, you will have to either negotiate down to a price of $25,995 with a 60-month loan, or choose a 72-month loan, as shown in Fig. 769.

	A	B	C	D	E	F	G	H	I	J	K	L
1												
2	Price	29995										
3	Term	48										
4	Interest	5.40%										
5	Payment	$696.21	29995	28995	28495	27995	27495	26995	26495	25995	25495	24995
6		36	904.4	874.2	859.1	844.1	829	813.9	798.8	783.8	768.7	753.6
7		48	696.2	673	661.4	649.8	638.2	626.6	615	603.4	591.8	580.2
8		60	571.6	552.5	543	533.4	523.9	514.4	504.9	**495**	485.8	476.3
9		72	**489**	472.4	464.2	456.1	447.9	439.8	431.6	423.5	415.3	407.2
10												
11												

Fig. 769

The formulas in the table are live. As shown in Fig. 770, you can re-enter new values in the first column and row of the table in order to zoom in on possible scenarios.

$696.21	29995	29295	28795	28195	27695	27095	26595	25995	25495	24995
60	571.6	558.2	548.7	537.3	527.7	516.3	506.8	**495**	485.8	476.3
63	547.8	535.1	525.9	515	505.8	**495**	485.7	474.8	465.7	456.5
66	526.3	514	505.3	**495**	486	475.4	466.7	456.1	447.3	438.6
69	506.7	**495**	486.4	476.3	467.8	457.7	449.2	439.1	430.6	422.2

Fig. 770

Additional information: You can also change the formula in B5 and the table will update.

Summary: The Data Table command is a powerful command for comparing several what-if scenarios.

Commands Discussed: Data – Table

REMOVE BLANKS FR...

Problem: Someone has given you data pasted from Word. As shown in Fig. 771, there are a number of blank cells in the list. You want to eliminate the blank rows.

Strategy: If the sequence is not important, sort the entire data range. Excel will move all blank cells to the bottom of the sort range.

1) Move the cell pointer to A1. While holding down the Shift key, hit the End key and then the Home key. This should select the entire range of data in the spreadsheet.

2) From the menu, select Data – Sort. As shown in Fig. 772, indicate that your data does not have a header row in the Sort dialog box. Choose OK.

1	H
2	He
3	
4	Li
5	Be
6	B
7	C
8	N
9	O
10	F
11	Ne
12	
13	Na
14	Mg

Fig. 771

Part III

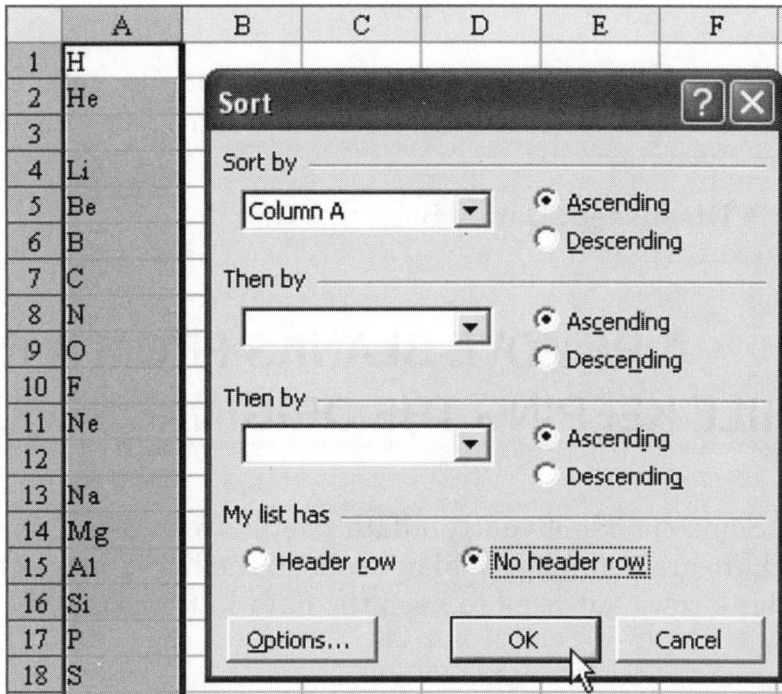

Fig. 772

...ved from the list, as shown in Fig. 773.

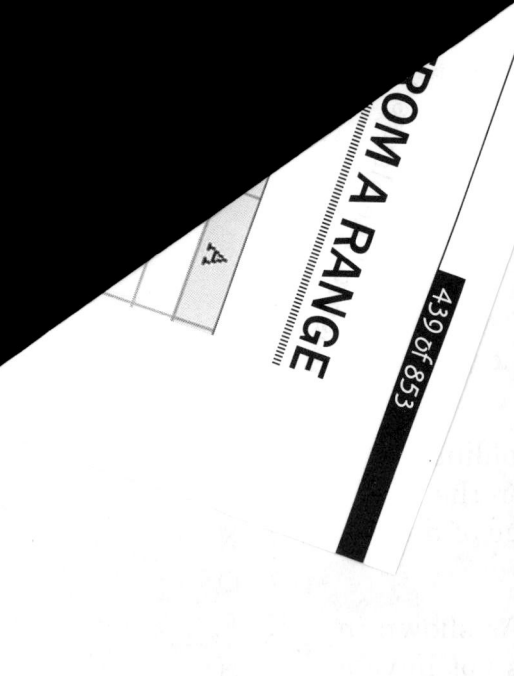

	A
1	Ac
2	Ag
3	Al
4	Am
5	Ar
6	As
7	At
8	Au
9	B
10	Ba
11	Be
12	Bh
13	Bi
14	Bk
15	Br
16	C
17	Ca

Fig. 773

Summary: Excel's Sort feature always moves blanks cells to the end of the sort. Sorting a column with blanks is a quick way to remove the blanks from the data.

Commands Discussed: Data – Sort

REMOVE BLANKS FROM A RANGE WHILE KEEPING THE ORIGINAL SEQUENCE

Problem: Someone has given you data pasted from Word, as shown in Fig. 774. There are a number of blank cells in the list. You want to eliminate the blank rows but need to keep the data in the original sequence.

	A
1	H
2	He
3	
4	Li
5	Be
6	B
7	C
8	N
9	O
10	F
11	Ne
12	
13	Na
14	Mg

Fig. 774

Part III

Strategy: The previous trick of sorting data to move the blanks to the end is effective, but it destroys the original sequence of the range. Before sorting, add a temporary column with the original sequence numbers so that the data can be sorted back. Follow these steps.

1) Insert a new row 1. Place the cell pointer in cell A1 and from the menu, select Insert – Rows. Since you have only one cell selected, only one row will be inserted.

2) In A1, enter a heading such as Symbol. In cell B1, enter a heading such as Sequence. Make both headings bold with Ctrl+B.

3) In cell B2, enter the number 1. In cell B3, enter the number 2. Select cells B2:B3, as shown in Fig. 775.

	A	B
1	**Symbol**	**Sequence**
2	H	1
3	He	2
4		

Fig. 775

...g down to the last row with data. The
...down to 129 in row 130, as shown in

...uq		125
Uup		126
Uuh		127
Uus		128
Uuo		129

Fig. 776

5) Nex... ...ta by column A. Select a single cell in column A
    and hit the ...utton in the Standard toolbar.

6) Hit the End key and then the Down Arrow key to ride the range
    down to the last cell in A with data. You will want to delete the
    rows below this last cell. These are the blank cells. It is important
    to delete the sequence numbers from B for the blank cells so that
    they do not sort back into the data in the next step. One way to
    delete these rows is to highlight the row numbers, right-click, and
    choose Delete, as shown in Fig. 777.

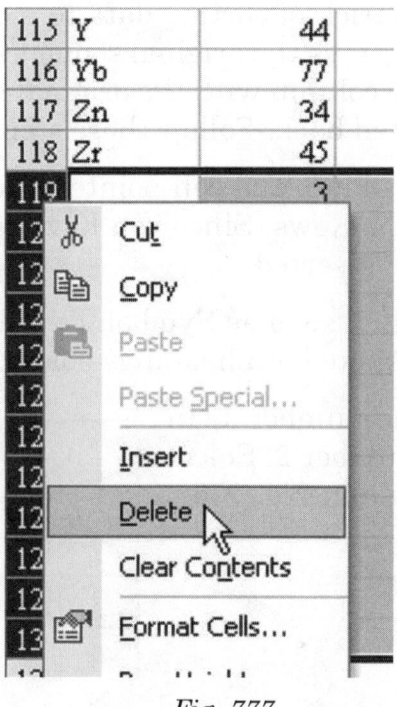

Fig. 777

7) Move the cell pointer to B2. Choose the AZ button in the Standard toolbar to sort the data into the original sequence without the blanks, as shown in Fig. 778.

	A	B
1	Symbol	Sequence
2	H	1
3	He	2
4	Li	4
5	Be	5
6	B	6

Fig. 778

8) You can now delete the temporary column B. From the menu, select Edit – Delete – Entire Column.

9) You can also delete the temporary row 1. Move to A1. From the menu, select Edit – Delete – Entire Row.

Result: The blanks will be removed from the list and the list will retain the original sequence.

Summary: To remove blanks while keeping the original sequence, add a temporary column with sequence numbers to allow the list to return to the original sequence.

Commands Discussed: Data – Sort

Part
III

INCREASE A RANGE BY TWO PERCENT

Problem: You run the repair department for a company. As shown in Fig. 779, you have a spreadsheet of prices. Your manager tells you to increase the price on all service contracts by two percent.

	A	B
1	Contract	Rate
2	K3504	7.23
3	K3350	10.38
4	K10761	7.48
5	K7205	5.48
6	K8213	7.9
7	K2561	7.53
8	K9684	9.03
9	K4979	10.13
10	K2966	5.22

Fig. 779

Strategy: In a blank cell, enter 102%, as shown in Fig. 780. Copy that cell and then use Paste Special Multiply to multiply all of the contract prices by this cell.

1) Find a blank cell, such as D1. Enter 102% in that cell.

2) Select D2 and choose Edit – Copy from the menu.

3) Select all of the rates in column B.

	A	B	C	D
1	Contract	Rate		102%
2	K3504	7.23		
3	K3350	10.38		
4	K10761	7.48		

Fig. 780

4) From the menu, select Edit – Paste Special. In the Paste Special dialog, choose Values and Multiply, as shown in Fig. 781.

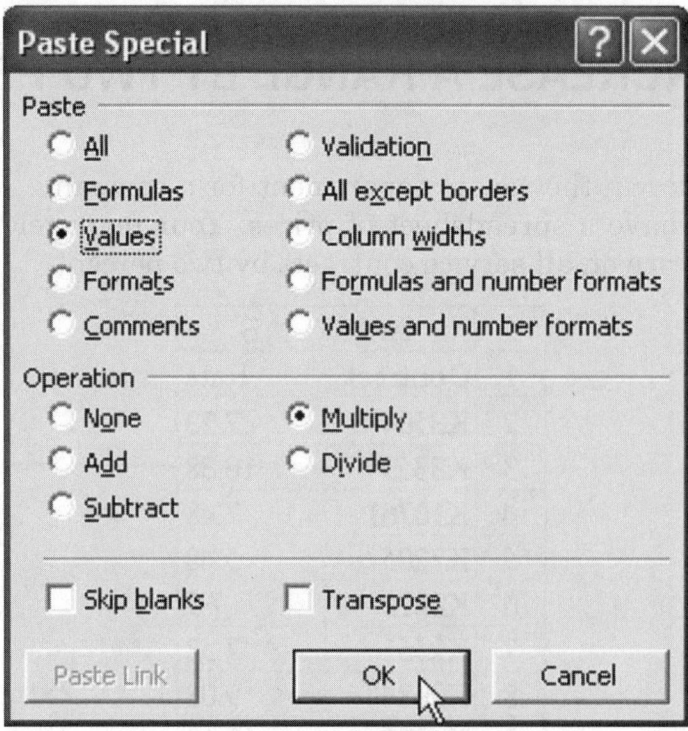

Fig. 781

Result: All of the values in column B are increased by 2 percent, as shown in Fig. 782.

Summary: Multiply an entire range by a single cell, using Paste Special – Multiply.

Commands Discussed: Edit – Paste Special – Multiply

	A	B
1	Contract	Rate
2	K3504	7.3746
3	K3350	10.5876
4	K10761	7.6296
5	K7205	5.5896
6	K8213	8.058
7	K2561	7.6806

Fig. 782

USE FIND AND REPLACE
TO FIND AN ASTERISK

Problem: Your largest customer is Wal*Mart. When you use Find or Find and Replace to search for Wal*Mart, Excel also finds Wallingsmart, as shown in Fig. 783.

Part III

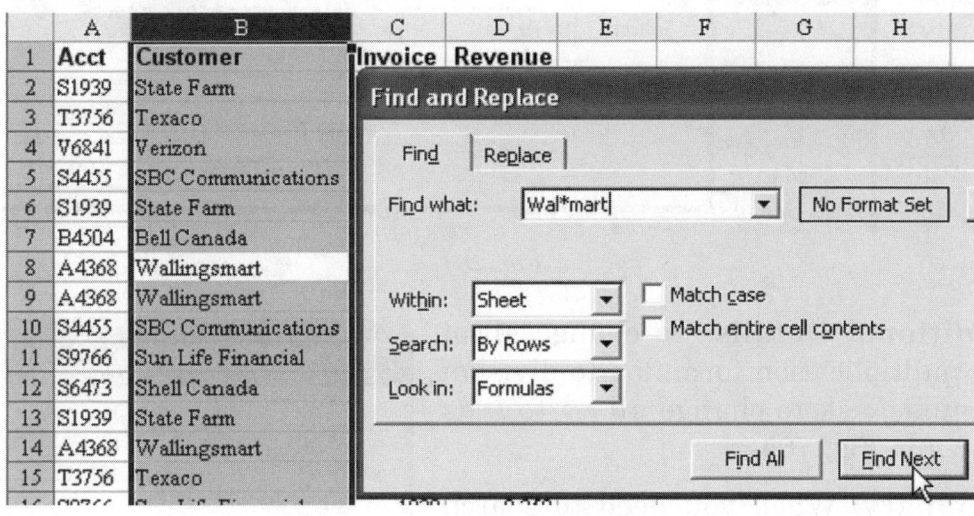

Fig. 783

This is because the * is seen as a wildcard character. What if you really want to search for an asterisk?

Strategy: There are three wildcard characters that can be used in the Find and Replace dialog.

If you include an asterisk, Excel will search for any number of characters where the asterisk is located. "Wal*mart" will find "Wal*mart" but also "Walton Williams is smart".

If you include a question mark, Excel will search for any one character. Searching for "?arl" will find both "Carl" and "Karl".

To really force Excel to search for an asterisk or a question mark, precede the asterisk by a tilde (~). When you search for "Wal~*mart", Excel will only find "Wal*mart", as shown in Fig. 784. If you search for "Who~?", Excel will only find "Who?" and not "whom".

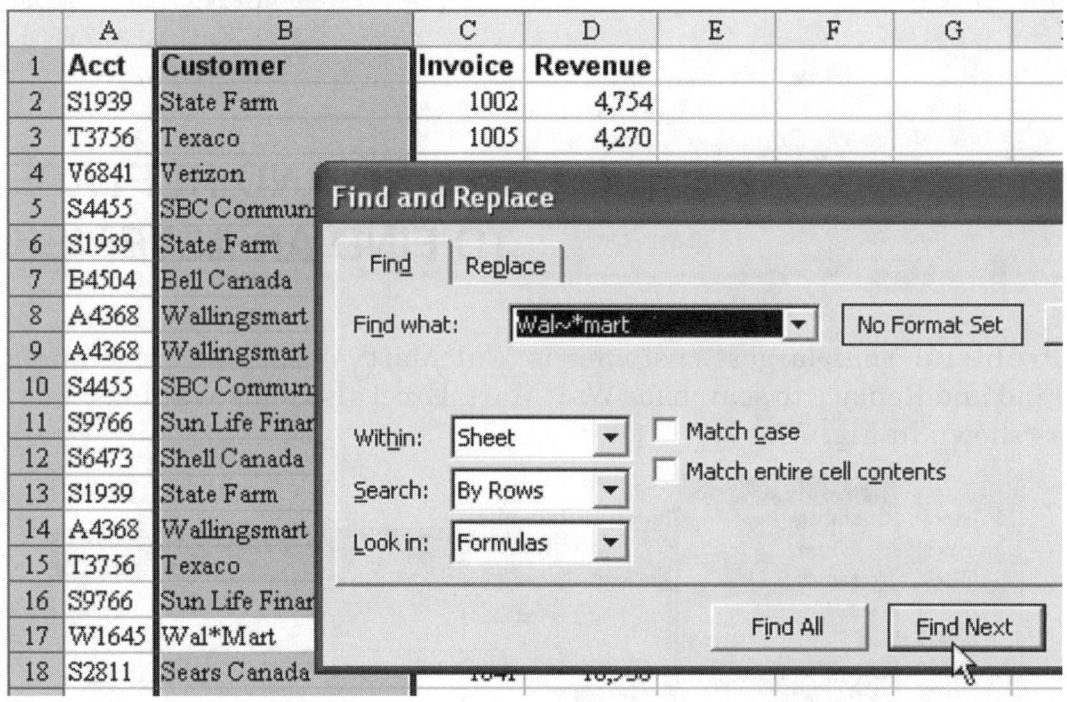

Fig. 784

Additional Details: To change all of the multiplication formulas to division formulas, ask to change all ~* to /, as shown in Fig. 785.

Summary: When you need to search for an actual question mark or an asterisk, precede the wildcard character with a tilde.

Commands Discussed: Edit – Replace; Edit – Find

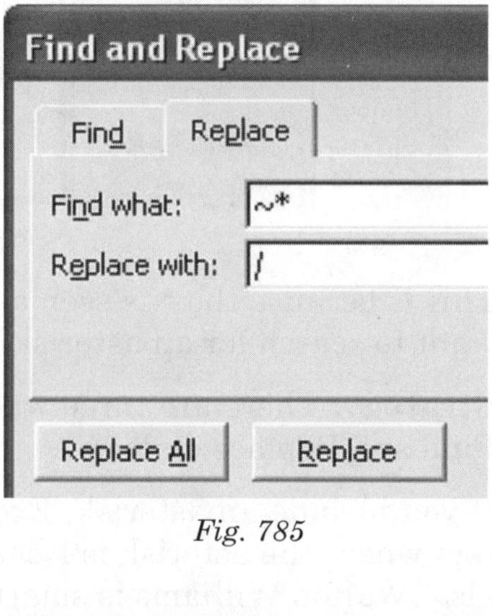

Fig. 785

USE A CUSTOM HEADER OF "PROFIT & LOSS"

Problem: As shown in Fig. 786, you add a custom header to your report of "Profit & Loss Report".

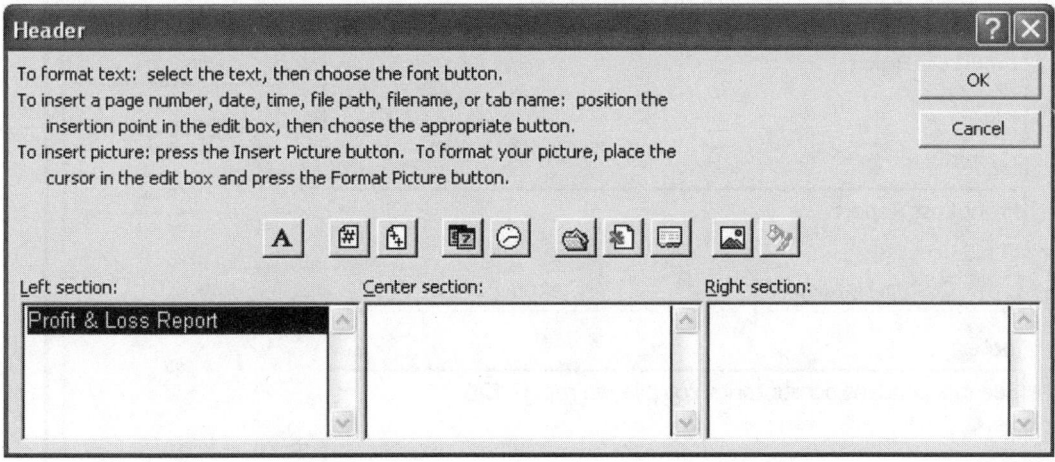

Fig. 786

When you print preview the document, the header says "Profit Loss Report", as shown in Fig. 787. The ampersand is missing.

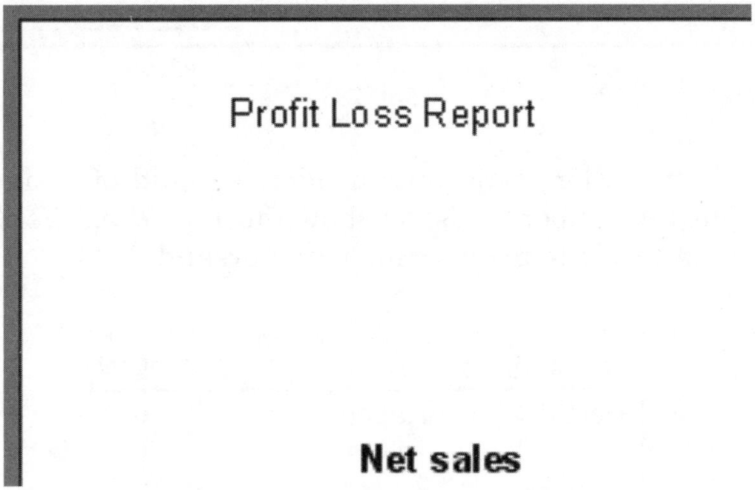

Profit Loss Report

Net sales

Fig. 787

Strategy: The ampersand is a special character in the custom header and footer field. Follow these steps.

1)   From the menu, select File – Page Setup. On the Header/Footer
     tab, select the Custom Header… button, as shown in Fig. 788.

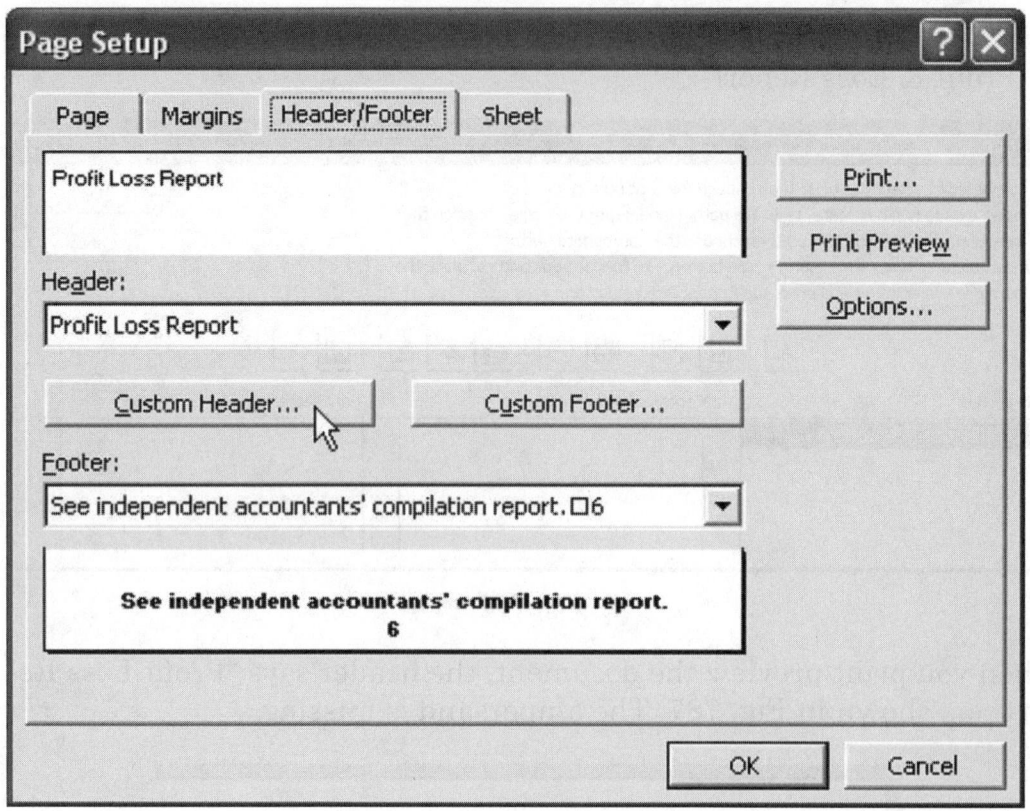

Fig. 788

2)   In the Left section, type your header. Instead of a single amper-
     sand, put two ampersands, as shown in Fig. 789. The && is actu-
     ally a secret code to print a single ampersand.

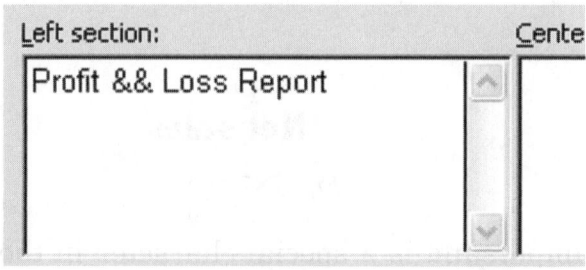

Fig. 789

Having two ampersands will give you the desired heading of "Profit &
Loss", as shown in Fig. 790.

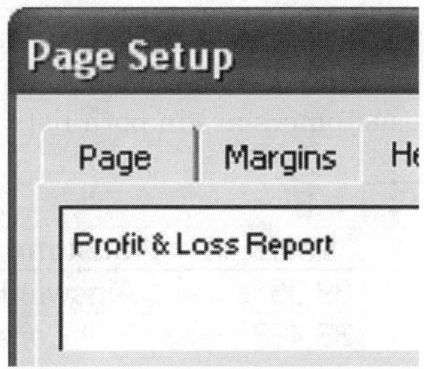

Fig. 790

Additional Details: The ampersand doesn't print because it is used
for all sorts of custom text fields in either the header or the footer. You
can build your own custom footers by using the icons or simply typing
&[Page] or &[Pages].

Summary: When you want to print an ampersand in a page header or
footer, use two ampersands.

Commands Discussed: File – Page Setup – Header/Footer

Part
III

USE CONSOLIDATION TO COMBINE TWO LISTS

Problem: Jerry and Tina each compiled sales figures from paper invoices, as shown in Fig. 791. You need to combine Jerry and Tina's list into a single list. Some customers are in both lists.

	A	B	C	D	E	
1	**Customer**	**Sales**		**Customer**	**Sales**	
2	Ainsworth	89,357		Ainsworth	74,514	
3	Air Canada	38,468		Bell Canada	63,539	
4	Bell Canada	94,742		Chevron	54,857	
5	Chevron	57,560		Compaq	82,488	
6	Compaq	58,467		General Motors	57,840	
7	Compton Petroleum	51,435		Kroger	40,896	
8	Exxon Mobil	52,974		Sun Life Financial	68,674	
9	Ford	75,517		Sun Life Financial	73,118	
10	General Motors	36,200		Verizon	57,888	
11	Gildan Activewear	88,577		Wal-Mart	69,170	
12	HP	61,304		Accelent Systems	84,420	
13	IBM	37,713		DigiKnow	50,924	
14	Kroger	69,883		Sequoia Financial	87,895	
15	Lucent	35,515		Shearer's Foods	44,510	
16	Molson, Inc	53,705		Zebra Skimmers	70,996	
17	Nortel Networks	49,669		3M	70,900	
18	P&G	68,858		Alcoa	50,709	
19	Shell Canada	83,174		Boeing	81,865	
20	Sun Life Financial	86,780		Citigroup	88,839	
21	Verizon	37,795		Exxon Mobil	41,736	
22	Wal-Mart	35,157		Intel	88,163	
23	Pfizer	39,880		Home Depot	63,528	
24						

Fig. 791

Strategy: Excel offers a great tool for consolidating data.

1) To use the tool, move the cell pointer to a blank area of the work-sheet. You will need a blank area with several rows and a few columns. In Fig. 792, G1 would be appropriate. Select cell G1. From the menu, select Data – Consolidate.

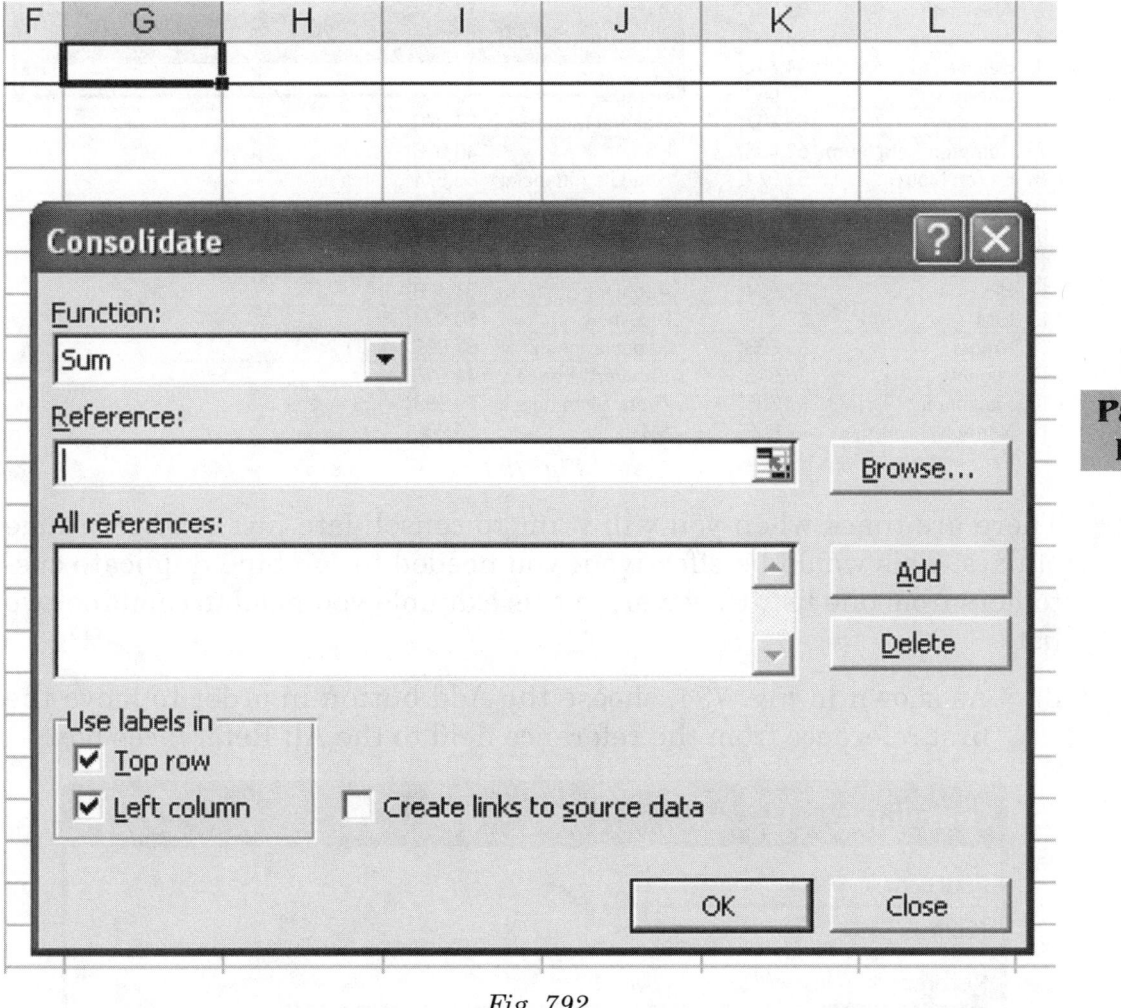

Fig. 792

Notice that both boxes for Use labels in are checked. This means that Excel relies on the headings to be the same and that the customer field is in the left column of each range.

Part
III

2)   Put the cursor in the Reference field. Click the Collapse button at the right end of the Reference field. With the mouse, select the first range: A1:B23. Choose the Collapse button again to return to the Consolidate Dialog. See Fig. 793.

	A	B	C	D	E	F	G	H	I
1	Customer	Sales		Customer	Sales				
2	Ainsworth	89,357		Ainsworth	74,514				
3	Air Canada	38,468							
4	Bell Canada	94,742							
5	Chevron	57,560							
6	Compaq	58,467		General Motors	57,840				
7	Compton Petroleum	51,435		Kroger	40,896				
8	Exxon Mobil	52,974		Sun Life Financial	68,674				
9	Ford	75,517		Sun Life Financial	73,118				
10	General Motors	36,200		Verizon	57,888				
11	Gildan Activewear	88,577		Wal-Mart	69,170				
12	HP	61,304		Accelent Systems	84,420				
13	IBM	37,713		DigiKnow	50,924				
14	Kroger	69,883		Sequoia Financial	87,895				
15	Lucent	35,515		Shearer's Foods	44,510				
16	Molson, Inc	53,705		Zebra Skimmers	70,996				
17	Nortel Networks	49,669		3M	70,900				

Consolidate - Reference: $A$1:$B$23

Fig. 793

There are times when you will want to consolidate just a single range of data. This would be effective if you needed to combine duplicate customers from one list. However, in this example you need to combine two lists.

3)   As shown in Fig. 794, choose the Add button in order to move the first reference from the reference field to the All References box.

Consolidate

Function:
Sum

Reference:
$A$1:$B$23

All references:

Browse...
Add
Delete

Fig. 794

4)   Once the first reference has been added to the All References box, choose the Collapse button again to specify the second reference, as shown in Fig. 795.

Fig. 795

5)   Use the mouse to select D1:E23. Choose the Collapse button to return to the Consolidate dialog. As shown in Fig. 796, choose the Add button to add the reference to the All References list.

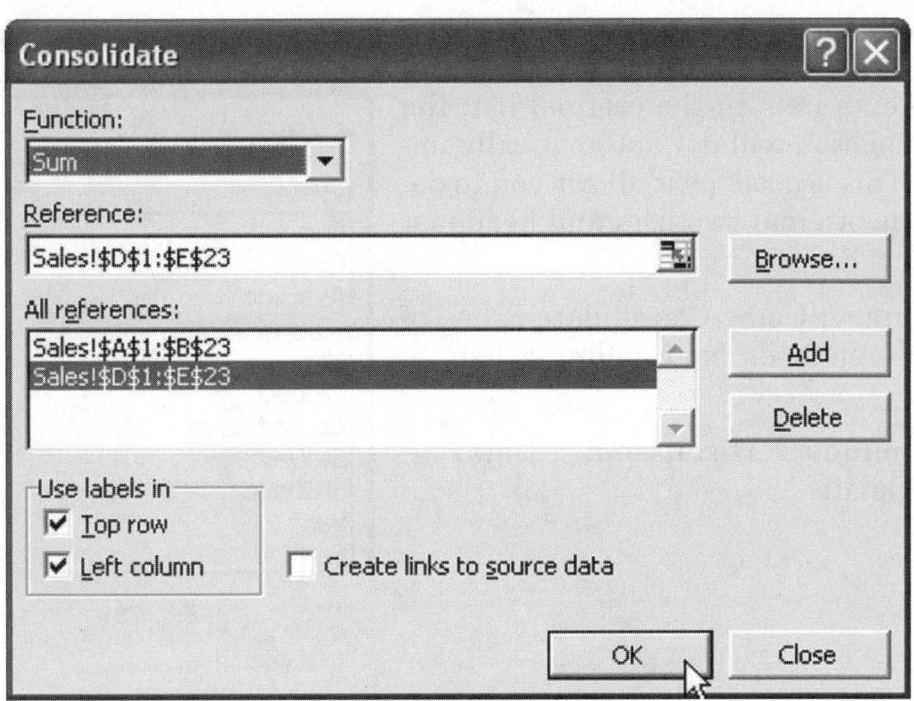

Fig. 796

6)　Choose OK. In a few seconds, Excel will return a brand new list that extends down and to the right from cell G1, as shown in Fig. 797. The list will contain one instance of each customer along with the total revenue from the customer.

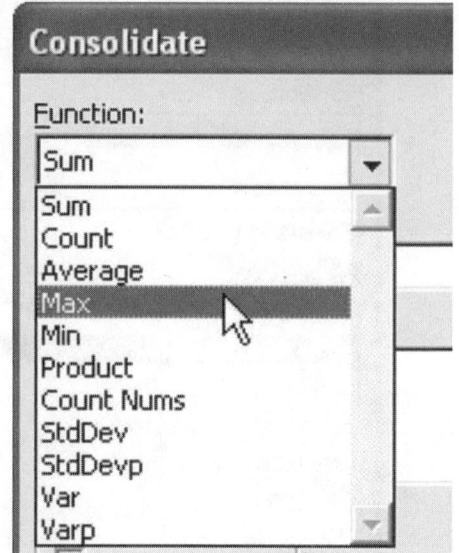

G	H
	Sales
Ainsworth	163,871
Air Canada	38,468
Bell Canac	158,281
Chevron	112,417
Compaq	140,955
Compton F	51,435
Accelent S	84,420
DigiKnow	50,924
Sequoia Fi	87,895
Shearer's F	44,510
Zebra Skin	70,996
3M	70,900
Alcoa	50,709
Boeing	81,865

Gotcha: The new list is not in any sequence. You can see it sort of starts out in the sequence of the first list, but then randomly inserts customers from the second list. You will probably want to sort the list alphabetically or by revenue. However, Excel always fails to fill in the label in the upper left corner of the consolidation. If you want to sort the result, you need to type the word Customer in cell G1.

Fig. 797

Additional Details: The function box in the Data Consolidation dialog offers many functions other than SUM, as shown in Fig. 798. For instance, if you wanted to find the largest purchase by each customer, you could use the MAX function.

The results of the consolidation shown in Fig. 797 are all static values. If you change an item in the original list, the consolidation will not automatically update. This is good, as it allows you to delete the original two lists and keep just the new list.

Summary: Using Consolidate is one of several methods for combining lists of data.

Commands Discussed: Data – Consolidate

Fig. 798

FIND TOTAL SALES BY CUSTOMER BY COMBINING DUPLICATES

Problem: You have an invoice register for the month. The report shows Account, Customer, Invoice, Sales, Cost, and Profit for each invoice, as shown in Fig. 799. You want to combine customers in order to produce a report of sales by customer.

	A	B	C	D	E	F
1	Acct	Customer	Invoice	Sales	COGS	Profit
2	H1247	Home Depot	1201	63,528	36,656	26,872
3	B5618	Boeing	1202	81,865	45,834	36,031
4	C2299	Compaq	1203	85,096	49,117	35,979
5	H1247	Home Depot	1204	72,410	42,238	30,172
6	Z1752	Zebra Skimmers	1205	70,996	39,783	31,213
7	D1891	DigiKnow	1206	58,784	33,747	25,037
8	K7539	Kroger	1207	40,896	22,563	18,333
9	K7539	Kroger	1208	49,463	28,283	21,180
10	A4509	Alcoa	1209	47,045	26,235	20,810
11	G5111	General Motors	1210	57,840	33,508	24,332
12	A5911	Accelent Systems	1211	84,420	50,120	34,300

Fig. 799

Part
III

Strategy: You can use Data Consolidation to solve this task. It is possible to consolidate a single list by using the labels in the left column. This will produce a report with one line per customer and totals of each numeric field.

1) Select a blank section of the worksheet. From the menu, select Data– Consolidate. In the reference field, select the complete range of your data, including the headings. Be sure that the Left Column option is checked, as shown in Fig. 800. Choose OK.

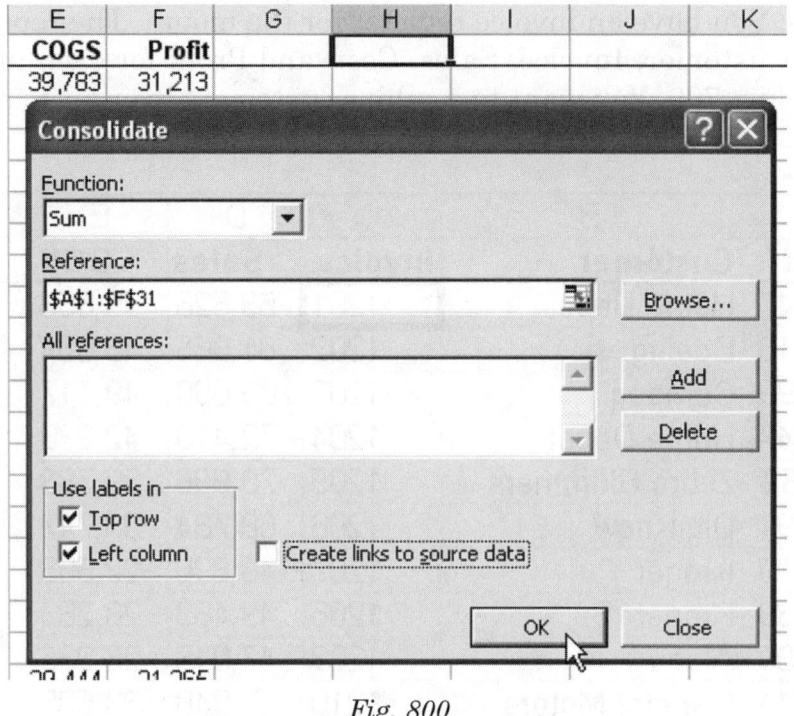

Fig. 800

2) As shown in Fig. 801, Excel will combine all identical account numbers together. The original data did not have to be sorted by account number.

H	I	J	K	L	M
	Customer	Invoice	Sales	COGS	Profit
D1891		2428	109,708	62,093	47,615
K7539		2415	90,359	50,846	39,513
A4509		2433	97,754	55,679	42,075
G5111		2433	115,816	67,055	48,761
A5911		2441	125,222	73,839	51,383
S3647		2441	127,899	71,138	56,761
E2257		2430	91,175	52,765	38,410
S4871		2441	132,452	76,017	56,435
C5484		2438	178,422	101,788	76,634
V7797		2444	116,418	68,740	47,678
I1622		2449	128,755	75,631	53,124

Fig. 801

Gotcha: Note that Excel did add up the invoice numbers in column J. This makes no sense.

3) Delete column J.

4) Excel did not fill in the label in the upper left corner of the table. Enter Acct in H1.

5) The Consolidate command is not smart enough to take the first or last instance of text fields. You will have to fill in the customer name, using a VLOOKUP function, as shown in Fig. 802. (For more information on VLOOKUP, see "Sorting with a Formula" on page 167.)

H	I	J	K	L
Acct	Customer	Sales	COGS	Profit
H1247	=vlookup(H2,$A$2:$B$31,2,false)			
B5618		141,633	79,910	61,
C2299		167,584	95,433	72,
717٢٦		1 44 ٦٦7	٥1 ٦٥٥	٢٥ (

Fig. 802

6) Copy the VLOOKUP function down by double-clicking the Fill handle. Change the VLOOKUP formula to values by copying I2:I16 and then using Edit – Paste Special Values.

7) The resulting dataset is in the same sequence as the customers in the original list. Choose a single cell in column I and click the AZ sort button to produce an alphabetical list by customer.

8)   Finally, the column widths are not automatically adjusted as the result of a consolidation. As shown in Fig. 803, you might want to double-click the right side of the I column heading in order to autofit the Customer column. Double-click when the mouse pointer looks like the dual-headed arrowed I-beam.

H	I	J	K	L
Acct	Customer	Sales	COGS	Profit
A5911	Accelent 9	125,222	73,839	51,383
A4509	Alcoa	97,754	55,679	42,075
B5618	Boeing	141,633	79,910	61,723
C5484	Citigroup	178,422	101,788	76,634
C2299	Compaq	167,584	95,433	72,151
D1891	DigiKnow	109,708	62,093	47,615
E2257	Exxon Mol	91,175	52,765	38,410
G5111	General M	115,816	67,055	48,761
H1247	Home Dep	135,938	78,894	57,044
I1622	Intel	128,755	75,631	53,124
K7539	Kroger	90,359	50,846	39,513
S3647	Sequoia Fi	127,899	71,138	56,761
S4871	Shearer's F	132,452	76,017	56,435
V7797	Verizon	116,418	68,740	47,678
Z1752	Zebra Skin	141,227	81,309	59,918

Fig. 803

Summary: Using Consolidate is a good method for combining duplicate customers while totaling many columns of numeric data.

Commands Discussed: Data – Consolidate

Functions Discussed: VLOOKUP

CREATE A SUMMARY OF FOUR LISTS

Problem: You have a list of Webelos scouts. As shown in Fig. 804, the list shows who attended various sessions at camp. You need to produce a master list of who attended which session.

	A	B	C	D	E	F	G
1				**Aquanaut**	**Artist**	**Citizen**	**Engineer**
2				Joey	Rowen	Nick	Matt
3				Zeke	Josh	Josh	Robby
4				Josh	Jake	Jake	Tim
5				Kyle	Jordan	Kyle	Josh
6				Dan	Zeke	Rowen	Zeke
7							

Fig. 804

Strategy: You can use Data Consolidation to solve this task.

1) Find a blank section of the worksheet. Enter headings for Name and Class. Copy all of the Aquanaut scouts to the list and assign a value of 1 in the Class column, as shown in Fig. 805.

	A	B	C	D	E
1	Name	Class		**Aquanaut**	**Artist**
2	Joey		1	Joey	Rowen
3	Zeke		1	Zeke	Josh
4	Josh		1	Josh	Jake
5	Kyle		1	Kyle	Jordan
6	Dan		1	Dan	Zeke
7					
8					

Fig. 805

Part III

2) Copy the Artist scouts below this list and assign a value of 10 in the class column. Copy the Citizen scouts below those with a value of 100. Copy the Engineer scouts below those with a value of 1000. Your list should look like Fig. 806.

	A	B
1	Name	Class
2	Joey	1
3	Zeke	1
4	Josh	1
5	Kyle	1
6	Dan	1
7	Rowen	10
8	Josh	10
9	Jake	10
10	Jordan	10
11	Zeke	10
12	Nick	100
13	Josh	100
14	Jake	100
15	Kyle	100
16	Rowen	100
17	Matt	1000
18	Robby	1000
19	Tim	1000
20	Josh	1000
21	Zeke	1000

Fig. 806

3)   Go to a blank section of the worksheet. From the menu, select
Data – Consolidate. Choose A1:B21 as the reference. Choose Top
Row and Left Column, as shown in Fig. 807. Choose OK.

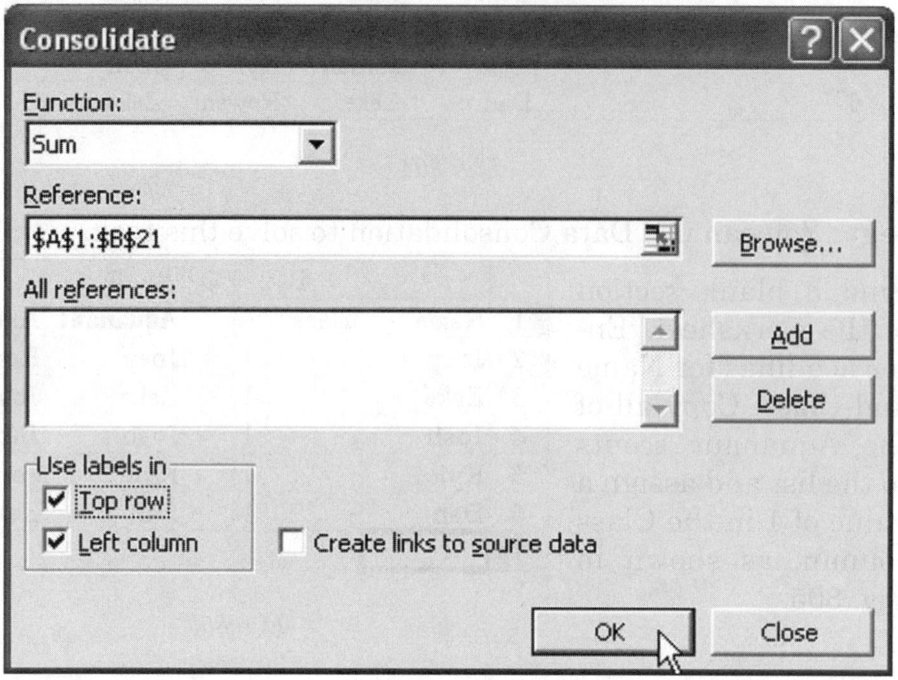

Fig. 807

Result: As shown in Fig. 808, any scouts with
1111 as the class attended all four sessions.
Scouts with 1000 attended only the Engineer session. Scouts with 1 attended only the Aquanaut
session.

	Class
Joey	1
Zeke	1011
Josh	1111
Kyle	101
Dan	1
Rowen	110
Jake	110
Jordan	10
Nick	100
Matt	1000
Robby	1000
Tim	1000

Fig. 808

Additional Details: You might want to assign a numeric format of "0000" to the result, as shown in Fig. 809.

Summary: Consolidation is one method for identifying who is in which list when you have many lists of data.

Cross Reference: Pivot tables also do a great job at this task.

Commands Discussed: Data – Consolidate

I	J
	Class
Joey	0001
Zeke	1011
Josh	1111
Kyle	0101
Dan	0001

Fig. 809

NUMBER EACH RECORD FOR A CUSTOMER, STARTING AT ONE FOR A NEW CUSTOMER

Part III

Problem: You have a list of invoice data, as shown in Fig. 810. You wish to number the records in such a way that the first invoice number for Ford is one. The next Ford invoice is two, and so on. When you get to a new customer, you want to start over at one.

	A	B	C	D	E	F	G	H	I
1	Invoice	Customer	Date	Region	Product	Quantity	Revenue	COGS	Profit
2	1010	Ford	1/1/04	East	XYZ	1000	22810.00	10220	12590
3	1011	Verizon	1/2/04	Central	DEF	100	2257.00	984	1273
4	1012	Verizon	1/2/04	East	ABC	500	10245.00	4235	6010
5	1013	Ainsworth	1/3/04	Central	XYZ	500	11240.00	5110	6130
6	1014	Ainsworth	1/4/04	Central	XYZ	400	9204.00	4088	5116
7	1015	Gildan Activew	1/4/04	East	DEF	800	18552.00	7872	10680
8	1016	Texaco	1/4/04	East	XYZ	400	9152.00	4088	5064
9	1017	IBM	1/5/04	Central	ABC	400	6860.00	3388	3472
10	1018	General Motors	1/7/04	East	ABC	400	8456.00	3388	5068
11	1019	State Farm	1/7/04	East	DEF	1000	21730.00	9840	11890
12	1020	Texaco	1/7/04	West	XYZ	600	13806.00	6132	7674
13	1021	General Motors	1/9/04	Central	ABC	800	16416.00	6776	9640
14	1022	HP	1/9/04	East	XYZ	900	21015.00	9198	11817
15	1023	Ainsworth	1/10/04	East	XYZ	900	21465.00	9198	12267

Fig. 810

Strategy: Sort the data by Customer. Insert a new temporary column A and add a heading called "Rec #", as shown in Fig. 811.

	A	B	C	D	E
1	Rec #	Invoice	Customer	Date	Region
2		1013	Ainsworth	1/3/04	Central
3		1014	Ainsworth	1/4/04	Central
4		1023	Ainsworth	1/10/04	East
5		1025	Ainsworth	1/12/04	West

Fig. 811

The formula in A2 is =IF(C2=C1,1+A1,1). In plain language, this formula says, "If the customer in C is equal to the customer above me, then add 1 to the cell above me. Otherwise, start at 1."

Result: Each group of customer invoices is numbered from 1 to N, as shown in Fig. 812.

A54   ▼   *fx* =IF(C54=C53,1+A53,1)

	A	B	C	D	E
1	Rec #	Invoice	Customer	Date	Regio
52	51	1562	Ainsworth	12/24/04	West
53	52	1566	Ainsworth	12/26/04	Centra
54	1	1143	Air Canada	3/31/04	West
55	2	1169	Air Canada	4/19/04	Centra
56	3	1368	Air Canada	8/24/04	West
57	4	1438	Air Canada	10/7/04	East
58	1	1165	Bell Canada	4/13/04	East
59	2	1271	Bell Canada	6/24/04	Centra
60	3	1382	Bell Canada	8/31/04	West
61	4	1479	Bell Canada	11/4/04	West
62	1	1086	Chevron	2/26/04	Centra

Fig. 812

As shown in Fig. 813, copy the formulas in column A and Paste Special – Values to change to numbers so that you can re-sort the data by Invoice Number.

	A	B	C	D
1	Rec #	Invoice	Customer	Date
2	1	1010	Ford	1/1/0⌐
3	1	1011	Verizon	1/2/0⌐
4	2	1012	Verizon	1/2/0⌐
5	1	1013	Ainsworth	1/3/0⌐
6	2	1014	Ainsworth	1/4/0⌐
7	1	1015	Gildan Activew⌐	1/4/0⌐
8	1	1016	Texaco	1/4/0⌐
9	1	1017	IBM	1/5/0⌐

Fig. 813

Alternate Strategy: A formula of =COUNTIF($C$2:C2,C2) will work without sorting.

Summary: The IF function is perfect for this task of comparing the current record to the record above.

Functions Discussed: =IF()

ADD A GROUP NUMBER
TO EACH SET OF RECORDS
WITH A UNIQUE CUSTOMER NUMBER

Problem: You have a list of invoice data. You wish to number the records in such a way that the invoices for the first customer all have a group number of 1. The invoices for the next customer all will have a group number of 2.

Strategy: Sort the data by customer. Add a new column A, with the heading of Group. In cell A2, enter the number 1 for Group #1. In cell A3, enter the formula that will be used for the rest of the records:

=IF(C3=C2,A2,1+A2)

In plain language, this formula says, "If the customer on this row equals the row above, then use the group number on the row above. Otherwise, add one to the group number above." Copy this formula down to all the other rows, as shown in Fig. 814.

	A	B	C	D	E	P
	A54	▼	fx	=IF(C54=C53,A53,1+A53)		
1	Group	Invoice	Customer	Date	Region	P
50	1	1538	Ainsworth	12/9/04	Central	D
51	1	1541	Ainsworth	12/10/04	East	D
52	1	1562	Ainsworth	12/24/04	West	D
53	1	1566	Ainsworth	12/26/04	Central	A
54	2	1143	Air Canada	3/31/04	West	A
55	2	1169	Air Canada	4/19/04	Central	X
56	2	1368	Air Canada	8/24/04	West	X
57	2	1438	Air Canada	10/7/04	East	D
58	3	1165	Bell Canada	4/13/04	East	D
59	3	1271	Bell Canada	6/24/04	Central	D
60	3	1382	Bell Canada	8/31/04	West	X
61	3	1479	Bell Canada	11/4/04	West	A
62	4	1086	Chevron	2/26/04	Central	D
63	4	1116	Chevron	3/15/04	East	A
64	4	1325	Chevron	7/29/04	West	A
65	4	1444	Chevron	10/12/04	West	X
66	5	1251	Compaq	6/6/04	Central	X

Fig. 814

Result: The records are all assigned a group number. Each customer has a unique group number.

In order to allow future sorting, copy the formulas in column A and use Paste Special – Values to convert the formulas to numbers.

Summary: Use the IF function to add a group number to each group of records.

Functions Discussed: =IF()

DEAL WITH DATA WHERE EACH RECORD TAKES FIVE PHYSICAL ROWS

Problem: Sometime back, in the days of COBOL, a programmer was dealing with the constraints of the physical width of a page. The programmer built a report where each record actually took up five lines of the report, as shown in Fig. 815. You now want to analyze this data in Excel.

	A	B	C	D	E	F	G
1	ACCT: 12345		INVOICE: 1010		DATE: 10/21/2005		
2	INVOICE TOTAL:		$125.00				
3	ABC CO						
4	123 S. MAIN STREET						
5	SALEM OH 44460						
6	---						
7	ACCT: 23456		INVOICE: 1011		DATE: 10/21/2005		
8	INVOICE TOTAL:		$175.00				
9	XYZ INC.						
10	456 N. BROADWAY						
11	SALEM OR 98754						
12	---						
13	ACCT: 34567		INVOICE: 1012		DATE: 10/23/2005		
14	INVOICE TOTAL:		$225.00				
15	HANEY & ASSOCIATES						
16	789 LUNDY LANE						
17	SALEM MA 12345						
18	---						

Fig. 815

Strategy: Your goal is to get the data back into one row per record. This process is possible. The process involves adding two new columns, one called Group number and one called Sequence.

Part
III

1) First, add a new Row 1. Insert two new columns A and B. Add headings as shown in Fig. 816 in A1:C1. The headings should be Group, Sequence, and Text.

	A	B	C
1	Group	Seq	Text
2			ACCT: 1:
3			INVOICE
4			ABC CO

Fig. 816

2) In column A, assign a Group number to each logical record.

One way to do this is to check to see if the first four characters of column C are "ACCT". If this is true, add one to the group number. In A2, enter the number 1. In A3, enter the formula =IF(LEFT(C3,4)="ACCT",1+A2,A2). Copy it down to all of the rows. This will neatly assign each logical group of records a group number, as shown in Fig. 817.

	A3		▼	*fx* =IF(LEFT(C3,4)="ACCT",1+A2,A2)		
	A	B	C	D	E	F	G
1	Group	Seq	Text				
2	1		ACCT: 12345		INVOICE: 1010		
3	1		INVOICE TOTAL:	$125.00			
4	1		ABC CO				
5	1		123 S. MAIN STREET				
6	1		SALEM OH 44460				
7	1		------------------------------------				
8	2		ACCT: 23456		INVOICE: 1011		
9	2		INVOICE TOTAL:	$175.00			
10	2		XYZ INC.				
11	2		456 N. BROADWAY				
12	2		SALEM OR 98754				
13	2		------------------------------------				
14	3		ACCT: 34567		INVOICE: 1012		
15	3		INVOICE TOTAL:	$225.00			
16	3		HANEY & ASSOCIATES				
17	3		789 LUNDY LANE				
18	3		SALEM MA 12345				

Fig. 817

3)   Next, design a formula for a sequence number.

In cell B2, enter the formula =IF(A2=A1,B1+1,1). Copy this down. This formula will number each record in the group, as shown in Fig. 818. It should ensure that all of the Account numbers are on a

B2			▼	f_x =IF(A2=A1,B1+1,1)	
	A	B	C	D	E
1	Group	Seq	Text		
2	1	1	ACCT: 12345		INVOIC
3	1	2	INVOICE TOTAL:	$125.0	
4	1	3	ABC CO		
5	1	4	123 S. MAIN STREET		
6	1	5	SALEM OH 44460		
7	1	6	------------------------		
8	2	1	ACCT: 23456		INVOIC
9	2	2	INVOICE TOTAL:	$175.0	
10	2	3	XYZ INC.		
11	2	4	456 N. BROADWAY		
12	2	5	SALEM OR 98754		
13	2	6	------------------------		
14	3	1	ACCT: 34567		INVOIC

Fig. 818

Sequence 1 record.

4)   This step is critical. Copy the formulas in columns A and B and paste them back, using Paste Special Values. This will ensure that you can safely sort the data.

5) Sort the data by the Sequence number in column B. Your data will look like Fig. 819.

	A	B	C	D	E	F	G	H	I
1	Group	Seq	Text						
2	1	1	ACCT: 12345		INVOICE: 1010		DATE:	10/21/2005	
3	2	1	ACCT: 23456		INVOICE: 1011		DATE:	10/21/2005	
4	3	1	ACCT: 34567		INVOICE: 1012		DATE:	10/23/2005	
5	4	1	ACCT: 45678		INVOICE: 1013		DATE:	10/24/2005	
6	5	1	ACCT: 56789		INVOICE: 1014		DATE:	10/24/2005	
7	6	1	ACCT: 67890		INVOICE: 1015		DATE:	10/26/2005	
8	1	2	INVOICE TOTAL:	$125.00					
9	2	2	INVOICE TOTAL:	$175.00					
10	3	2	INVOICE TOTAL:	$225.00					
11	4	2	INVOICE TOTAL:	$425.00					
12	5	2	INVOICE TOTAL:	$25.00					
13	6	2	INVOICE TOTAL:	$185.00					
14	1	3	ABC CO						
15	2	3	XYZ INC.						
16	3	3	HANEY & ASSOCIATES						
17	4	3	FRIEDLINE FRYERS						
18	5	3	EASTERN POOLS						
19	6	3	BONNIE DOON						
20	1	4	123 S. MAIN STREET						
21	2	4	456 N. BROADWAY						

Fig. 819

You have now managed to intelligently segregate the data so that all similar records are together. A contiguous range of C2:C7 contains all of the first rows from each record. All of the line 1 records have three fields that really should be parsed into three separate columns. You can easily do this with the Text to Columns Wizard.

6) Select cells C2:C7. From the menu, select Data – Text to Columns. Select Fixed Width and Next, as shown in Fig. 820.

Fig. 820

7) Excel should properly guess where your columns are, as shown in
    Fig. 821. Click Next.

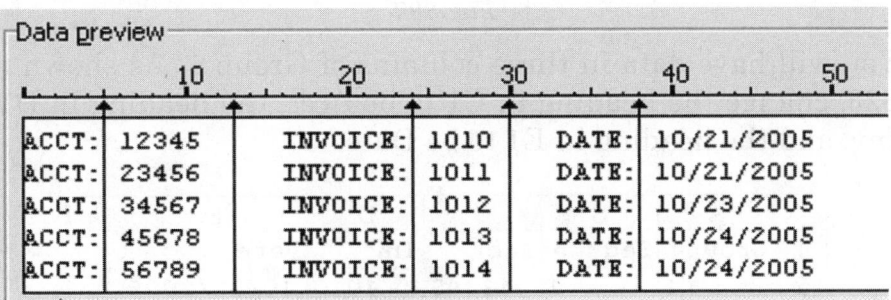

Fig. 821

Part
III

8) Choose the heading for each column and define a data format. You don't really need the word ACCT each time, so choose to Skip the first, third, and fifth fields. Make the sixth field a date. When your information looks like Fig. 822, choose Finish.

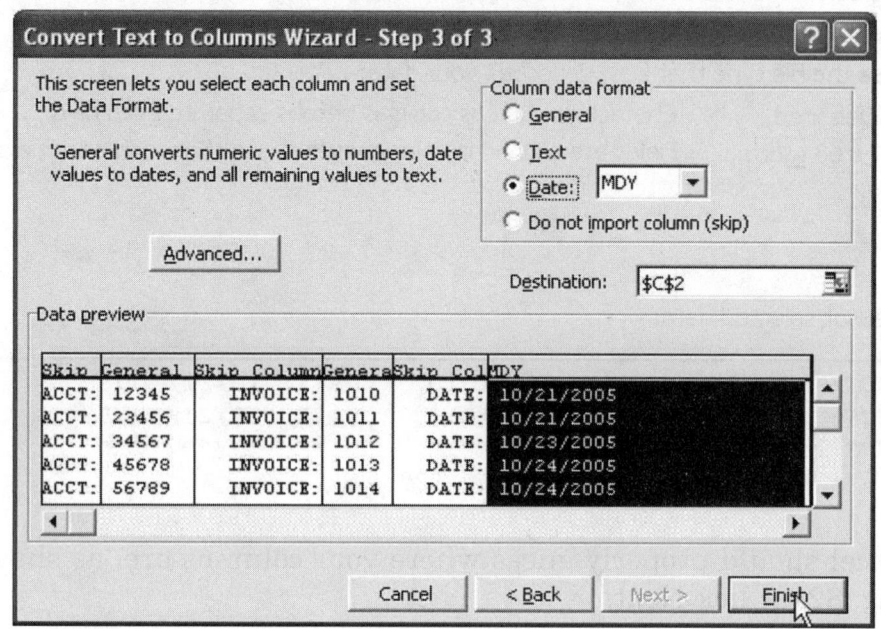

Fig. 822

9) You will have data in three columns of Group 1. As shown in Fig. 823, change the heading in C1 to be Acct, the heading in D1 to be Inv, and the heading in E1 to be Date.

	A	B	C	D	E	
1	Group	Seq	Acct	Inv	Date	
2	1	1	12345	1010	10/21/2005	
3	2	1	23456	1011	10/21/2005	
4	3	1	34567	1012	10/23/2005	
5	4	1	45678	1013	10/24/2005	
6	5	1	56789	1014	10/24/2005	
7	6	1	67890	1015	10/26/2005	
8	1	2	INVOICE	TOTAL:	$125.00	
9	2	2	INVOICE	TOTAL:	$175.00	
10	3	2	INVOICE	TOTAL:	$225.00	
11	4	2	INVOICE	TOTAL:	$425.00	
12	5	2	INVOICE	TOTAL:	$25.00	
13	6	2	INVOICE	TOTAL:	$185.00	

Fig. 823

10) Next, select A8:C13. Cut and paste in F2. Add headings in F1:H1 of Group, Seq, and Total, as shown in Fig. 824.

E	F	G	H	I	J	K
Date	Group	Seq	Total			
10/21/2005	1	2	INVOICE	TOTAL:	$125.00	
10/21/2005	2	2	INVOICE	TOTAL:	$175.00	
10/23/2005	3	2	INVOICE	TOTAL:	$225.00	
10/24/2005	4	2	INVOICE	TOTAL:	$425.00	
10/24/2005	5	2	INVOICE	TOTAL:	$25.00	
10/26/2005	6	2	INVOICE	TOTAL:	$185.00	

Fig. 824

11) Select H2:H6 and choose Data – Text to Columns. In Step 1, select Fixed Width and choose Next. In Step 2, Excel offers to split your data into three fields. There is no need to have one column for the word Invoice and another column for the word Total. As shown in Fig. 825, double-click the line between Invoice and Total to delete the line.

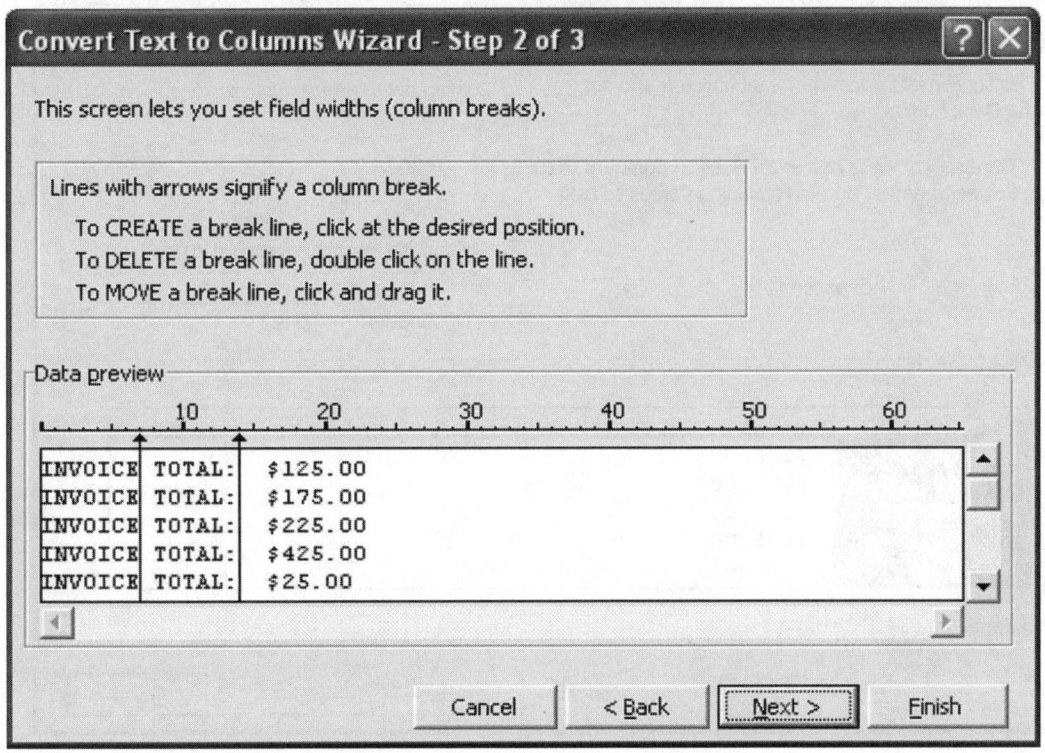

Fig. 825

12) After double-clicking the first line, it is deleted. Choose Next, as shown in Fig. 826.

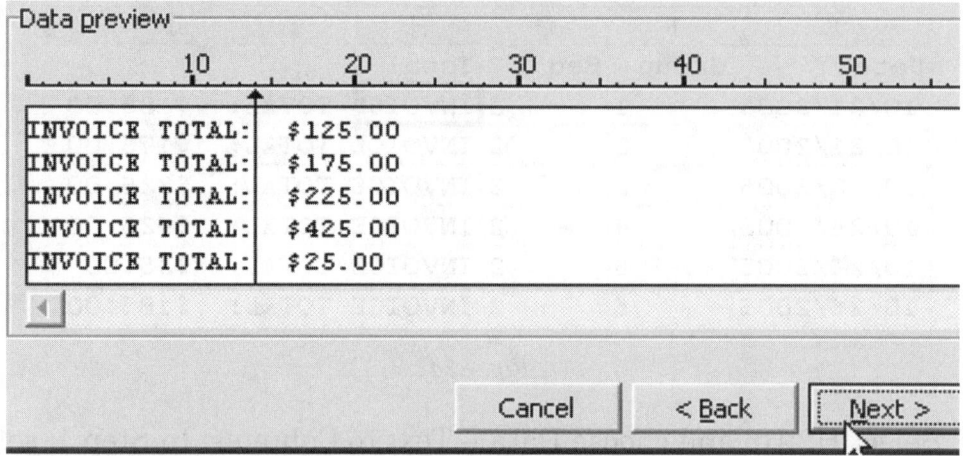

Fig. 826

13) In Step 3, choose to skip the field with "Invoice Total" and choose Finish, as shown in Fig. 827.

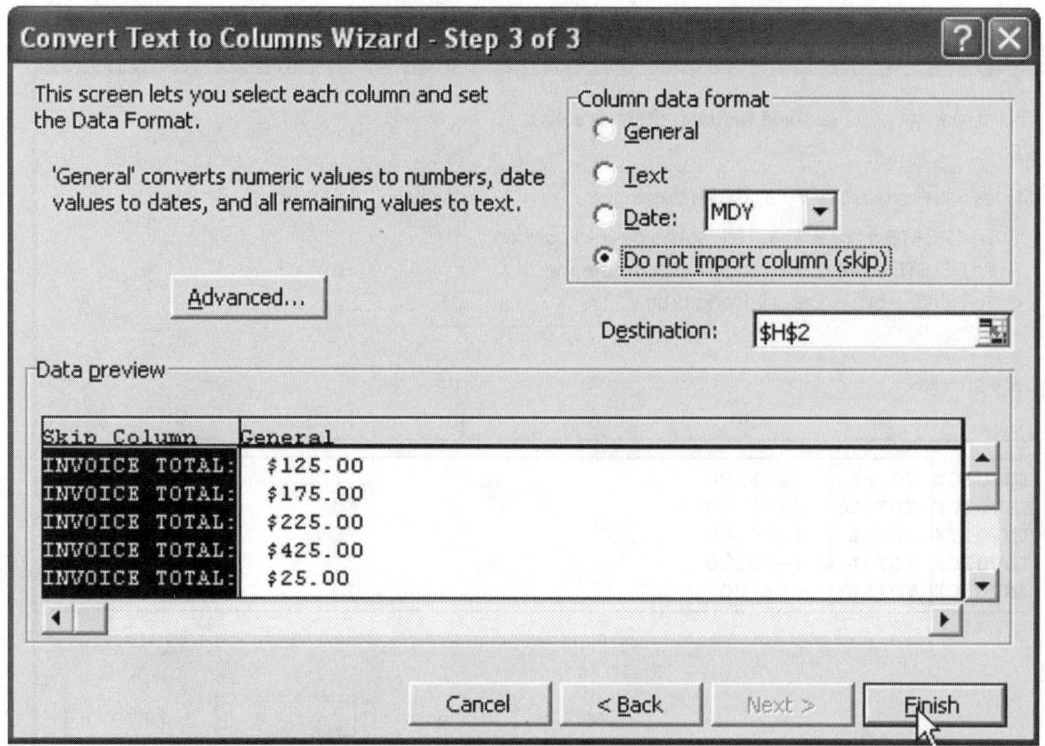

Fig. 827

14) Select the Group 3 records, as shown in Fig. 828.

13			
14	1	3	ABC CO
15	2	3	XYZ INC.
16	3	3	HANEY & ASSOCIATES
17	4	3	FRIEDLINE FRYERS
18	5	3	EASTERN POOLS
19	6	3	BONNIE DOON

Fig. 828

15) Copy them to I2. The headings in I1:K1 are Group, Seq, and Name, as shown in Fig. 829.

	A	B	C	D	E	F	G	H	I	J	K	L	M
1	Group	Seq	Acct	Inv	Date	Group	Seq	Total	Group	Seq	Name		
2	1	1	12345	1010	10/21/2005	1	2	$125.00	1	3	ABC CO		
3	2	1	23456	1011	10/21/2005	2	2	$175.00	2	3	XYZ INC.		
4	3	1	34567	1012	10/23/2005	3	2	$225.00	3	3	HANEY & ASSOCIATES		
5	4	1	45678	1013	10/24/2005	4	2	$425.00	4	3	FRIEDLINE FRYERS		
6	5	1	56789	1014	10/24/2005	5	2	$25.00	5	3	EASTERN POOLS		
7	6	1	67890	1015	10/26/2005	6	2	$185.00	6	3	BONNIE DOON		
8													

Fig. 829

16) Select the Group 4 records. Cut and paste in L2.

17) Select the Group 5 records. Cut and paste in O2.

18) As shown in Fig. 830, the Group 6 records have no data – they are just dashed lines. You can delete these rows.

32	1	6	----------
33	2	6	----------
34	3	6	----------
35	4	6	----------
36	5	6	----------
37	6	6	----------
38			

Fig. 830

Part
III

You now have all the fields, one line per record. You also have the words Group and Sequence taking up about five columns each. Before you delete the Group and Sequence columns, let's make sure that everything worked correctly. The Group numbers in columns A, F, I, L, and O should all match.

19) As shown in Fig. 831, in a blank column at the end, enter a large AND function as shown below. Copy this formula down to all rows:

=AND(A2=F2,F2=I2,I2=L2,L2=O2)

=AND(A2=F2,F2=I2,I2=L2,L2=O2)

O	P	Q	R
Group	Seq	City ST ZIP	
1	5	SALEM OH 44460	TRUE
2	5	SALEM OR 98754	TRUE
3	5	SALEM MA 12345	TRUE
4	5	SALEM WV 32145	TRUE

Fig. 831

20) A value of True means that you have successfully put all of the Group 1 records back together. To test if all of the rows have True, enter the formula =AND(R2:R99) in cell R1. As shown in Fig. 832, if this formula is True, then you've crosschecked that all of the rows match up.

fx =AND(R2:R7)

Q	R
ST ZIP	TRUE
OH 44460	TRUE
OR 98754	TRUE
MA 12345	TRUE
WV 32145	TRUE

Fig. 832

21) At this point, you can delete the columns that you don't need. As shown in Fig. 833, delete columns R, P, O, M, L, J, I, G, F, B, and A.

	A	B	C	D	E	F	G	H	I	J	K	L	M	N	O	P	Q	R
1	Group	Seq	Acct	Inv	Date	Group	Seq	Total	Group	Seq	Name	Group	Seq	Address	Group	Seq	City ST ZIP	TRUE
2	1	1	12345	1010	10/21/2005	1	2	$125.00	1	3	ABC CO	1	4	123 S. MAIN STREET	1	5	SALEM OH 44460	TRUE
3	2	1	23456	1011	10/21/2005	2	2	$175.00	2	3	XYZ INC.	2	4	456 N. BROADWAY	2	5	SALEM OR 98754	TRUE
4	3	1	34567	1012	10/23/2005	3	2	$225.00	3	3	HANEY & ASSOCIATES	3	4	789 LUNDY LANE	3	5	SALEM MA 12345	TRUE
5	4	1	45678	1013	10/24/2005	4	2	$425.00	4	3	FRIEDLINE FRYERS	4	4	987 KING CHURCH	4	5	SALEM WV 32145	TRUE

Fig. 833

Result: You now have a sortable, filterable, and reportable version of the original dataset. Each record consists of one row in Excel, as shown in Fig. 834.

	A	B	C	D	E	F	G
1	Acct	Inv	Date	Total	Name	Address	City ST ZIP
2	12345	1010	10/21/2005	$125.00	ABC CO	123 S. MAIN STREET	SALEM OH 44460
3	23456	1011	10/21/2005	$175.00	XYZ INC.	456 N. BROADWAY	SALEM OR 98754
4	34567	1012	10/23/2005	$225.00	HANEY & ASSOCIATES	789 LUNDY LANE	SALEM MA 12345
5	45678	1013	10/24/2005	$425.00	FRIEDLINE FRYERS	987 KING CHURCH	SALEM WV 32145
6	56789	1014	10/24/2005	$25.00	EASTERN POOLS	654 FAIR AVE	SALEM IL 60187
7	67890	1015	10/26/2005	$185.00	BONNIE DOON	321 PERSHING	SALEM IN 46875

Fig. 834

Part III

Summary: This process is convoluted. However, if you are presented with data as shown in the original example, the only way to quickly add up figures or to produce a report is to follow steps similar to the ones shown in this topic.

Commands Discussed: Data – Text to Columns

Functions Discussed: =IF(); =AND(); =LEFT()

ADD A CUSTOMER NUMBER
TO EACH DETAIL RECORD

Problem: You've imported a dataset where they list the customer number once in column A and then have any number of invoice detail records. At the end of the first customer, they put the next customer number in column A and then have the detail records for that customer, as shown in Fig. 835. This is a common data format, but it is horrible in Excel. You cannot sort this dataset. You need to add the customer information to each record.

	A	B	C	D	E	F	G
1	Invoice	Date	Quantity	Product	Revenue	COGS	Profit
2	Acct A4651 Air Canada						
3	1533	31-Mar-04	300	ABC	5859.00	2541	3318
4	1559	19-Apr-04	200	XYZ	4948.00	2044	2904
5	1756	24-Aug-04	800	XYZ	17856.00	8176	9680
6	1828	7-Oct-04	100	DEF	2358.00	984	1374
7	Acct A8736 Ainsworth						
8	1404	3-Jan-04	500	XYZ	11240.00	5110	6130
9	1405	4-Jan-04	400	XYZ	9204.00	4088	5116
10	1414	10-Jan-04	900	XYZ	21465.00	9198	12267
11	1416	12-Jan-04	400	XYZ	9144.00	4088	5056

Fig. 835

Strategy:

1) Insert new columns A and B. Add headings of Acct and Customer, as shown in Fig. 836.

	A	B	C	D	E
1	Acct	Customer	Invoice	Date	Quantity
2			Acct A4651 Air Canada		
3			1533	31-Mar-04	300
4			1559	19-Apr-04	200
5			1756	24-Aug-04	800
6			1828	7-Oct-04	100
7			Acct A8736 Ainsworth		
8			1404	3-Jan-04	500

Fig. 836

Here is the basic logic of what Excel want to do in plain language: Look at the first four characters of column C. If they are equal to "Acct", then this row has customer information. Take data from that cell and move it to column A. Otherwise, if the first four characters are anything other than "Acct", use the same account information from the previous row's column A.

The formula to do this for cell A2 is as follows:

=IF(LEFT(C2,4)="Acct",MID(C2,6,5),A1)

2)   Enter this formula into cell A2 and copy it down through column A.

As shown in Fig. 837, as you copy this formula down, it does the job. In cell A2, the IF condition is true and data is extracted from C2. In cell A3, the condition is not true, so the value from A2 is used. Down in cell A7, a new customer number is found so the data from C7 is used in A7. Cells A8 through A59 get the customer number from A7.

Part III

A2			*fx* =IF(LEFT(C2,4)="Acct",MID(C2,6,5),A1)			
	A	B	C	D	E	F	R
1	Acct	Customer	Invoice	Date	Quantity	Product	R
2	A4651		Acct A4651 Air Canada				
3	A4651		1533	31-Mar-04	300	ABC	!
4	A4651		1559	19-Apr-04	200	XYZ	!
5	A4651		1756	24-Aug-04	800	XYZ	1i
6	A4651		1828	7-Oct-04	100	DEF	:
7	A8736		Acct A8736 Ainsworth				
8	A8736		1404	3-Jan-04	500	XYZ	1·
9	A8736		1405	4-Jan-04	400	XYZ	!
10	A8736		1414	10-Jan-04	900	XYZ	2·

Fig. 837

Similar logic is needed in column B. In this case, though, you need to grab the customer name. You know that the word "Acct" and the space that follows it take up five characters. You know that your account number is another five characters and then there is a space before the customer name. Thus, you want to ignore the first 11 characters of cell C2.

You can use a formula of =MID(C2,12,50) to skip the first 11 characters and return the next 50 characters of the customer name. However, this formula will add spaces to the end of the customer name to ensure that you have 50 characters in the result. You really don't want all of those trailing spaces. The =TRIM() function will remove leading and trailing spaces from text.

Use =TRIM(MID(C2,12,50)) as the formula to extract a customer name. Use this formula as the True portion of the IF function. As shown in Fig. 838, the formula in B2, copied down through column B, is as follows:

=IF(LEFT(C2,4)="Acct",TRIM(MID(C2,12,50)),B1)

3) Enter this formula into cell B2 and copy it down through column B.

	B65	▼	fx	=IF(LEFT(C65,4)="Acct",TRIM(MID(C65,12,50)),B64)			
	A	B	C	D	E	F	
1	**Acct**	**Customer**	**Invoice**	**Date**	**Quantity**	**Product**	**Rev**
62	B3529	Bell Canada	1662	24-Jun-04	200	DEF	40
63	B3529	Bell Canada	1773	31-Aug-04	800	XYZ	180
64	B3529	Bell Canada	1871	4-Nov-04	800	ABC	151
65	C434	Compton Petroleum	**Acct C4341 Compton Petroleum**				
66	C4341	Compton Petroleum	1696	17-Jul-04	200	ABC	41
67	C4341	Compton Petroleum	1724	3-Aug-04	600	XYZ	139
68	C4341	Compton Petroleum	1782	8-Sep-04	100	DEF	20
69	C4341	Compton Petroleum	1851	21-Oct-04	500	DEF	112
70	C7849	Compaq	**Acct C7849 Compaq**				
71	C7849	Compaq	1642	6-Jun-04	400	XYZ	90
72	C7849	Compaq	1733	6-Aug-04	200	DEF	43
73	C7849	Compaq	1885	15-Nov-04	1000	ABC	172
74	C7849	Compaq	1900	24-Nov-04	400	XYZ	85
75	C8297	Chevron	**Acct C8297 Chevron**				
76	C8297	Chevron	1477	26-Feb-04	900	DEF	206
77	C8297	Chevron	1506	15-Mar-04	400	ABC	81
78	C8297	Chevron	1717	29-Jul-04	1000	ABC	182
79	C8297	Chevron	1835	12-Oct-04	300	XYZ	70
80	E3310	Exxon	**Acct E3310 Exxon**				
81	E3310	Exxon	1424	17-Jan-04	300	DEF	59

Fig. 838

You have now successfully filled in account and customer. You need to change these formulas to values.

4) Highlight columns A and B. Hit Ctrl+C to copy. Choose Edit – Paste Special – Values to convert the formulas to values.

The last task is to remove all of the customer heading rows. As you look for a method to isolate the heading rows, you will notice that heading rows are the only rows with blank cells in column D. You can move the blanks to the end of a dataset by sorting the data by column D.

5) Select the heading in D1. Hit the AZ sort button to sort ascending by Date. Any rows without a value in column D will automatically sort to the bottom of the dataset, as shown in Fig. 839.

6) From D1, press the End key and then the Down Arrow key twice. The cell pointer will be located on the first customer heading. Delete all of the rows below row 564.

Part III

1	Acct	Customer	Invoice	Date	Quantity	Proc
556	W7256	Wal-Mart	1955	24-Dec-04	200	XYZ
557	A8736	Ainsworth	1956	26-Dec-04	100	ABC
558	E3310	Exxon	1957	26-Dec-04	600	XYZ
559	S2571	SBC Communication	1958	26-Dec-04	500	XYZ
560	W7256	Wal-Mart	1959	26-Dec-04	700	DEF
561	S2328	Sun Life Financial	1960	27-Dec-04	500	ABC
562	G1394	General Motors	1961	28-Dec-04	600	ABC
563	G1394	General Motors	1962	28-Dec-04	600	ABC
564	G1394	General Motors	1963	28-Dec-04	900	ABC
565	A4651	Air Canada	Acct A4651 Air Canada			
566	A8736	Ainsworth	Acct A8736 Ainsworth			
567	B3529	Bell Canada	Acct B3529 Bell Canada			
568	C4341	Compton Petroleum	Acct C4341 Compton Petroleum			
569	C7849	Compaq	Acct C7849 Compaq			
570	C8297	Chevron	Acct C8297 Chevron			
571	E3310	Exxon	Acct E3310 Exxon			
572	F8417	Ford	Acct F8417 Ford			
573	G1394	General Motors	Acct G1394 General Motors			
574	G7759	Gildan Activewear	Acct G7759 Gildan Activewear			
575	H2221	HP	Acct H2221 HP			

Fig. 839

Result: You have a clean dataset with customer information on every row, as shown in Fig. 840. You can sort this data and otherwise use it for data analysis.

	A	B	C	D	E	F	G	H	I
1	Acct	Customer	Invoice	Date	Quantity	Product	Revenue	COGS	Profit
2	F8417	Ford	1401	1-Jan-04	1000	XYZ	22810.00	10220	12590
3	V8627	Verizon	1402	2-Jan-04	100	DEF	2257.00	984	1273
4	V8627	Verizon	1403	2-Jan-04	500	ABC	10245.00	4235	6010
5	A8736	Ainsworth	1404	3-Jan-04	500	XYZ	11240.00	5110	6130
6	A8736	Ainsworth	1405	4-Jan-04	400	XYZ	9204.00	4088	5116
7	G7759	Gildan Activewear	1406	4-Jan-04	800	DEF	18552.00	7872	10680
8	T5952	Texaco	1407	4-Jan-04	400	XYZ	9152.00	4088	5064

Fig. 840

Summary: A couple of formulas with IF functions help to snap this data into shape.

Commands Discussed: =IF(); =LEFT(); =MID()

USE A PIVOT TABLE
TO SUMMARIZE DETAILED DATA

Problem: You have 50,000 rows of sales data, as shown in Fig. 841. You want to produce a summary report showing sales by region and product.

	A	B	C	D	E	F	G	H
1	Region	Product	Date	Customer	Quantity	Revenue	COGS	Profit
2	East	XYZ	1-Jan-04	Ford	1000	22810	10220	12590
3	Central	DEF	2-Jan-04	Verizon	100	2257	984	1273
4	East	ABC	2-Jan-04	Verizon	500	10245	4235	6010
5	Central	XYZ	3-Jan-04	Ainsworth	500	11240	5110	6130
6	Central	XYZ	4-Jan-04	Ainsworth	400	9204	4088	5116
7	East	DEF	4-Jan-04	Gildan Activewear	800	18552	7872	10680
8	East	XYZ	4-Jan-04	Texaco	400	9152	4088	5064

Fig. 841

Strategy: Use a pivot table. As Excel's most powerful feature, pivot tables are well suited to this type of analysis. Follow these steps.

1) Ensure that your data is in list format. It is important that every heading be unique.

2) Select a single cell in the database. From the Data menu, select Pivot Table and Pivot Chart Report....

3) Choose Next in Wizard Step 1 to confirm that your data is in Excel, as shown in Fig. 842.

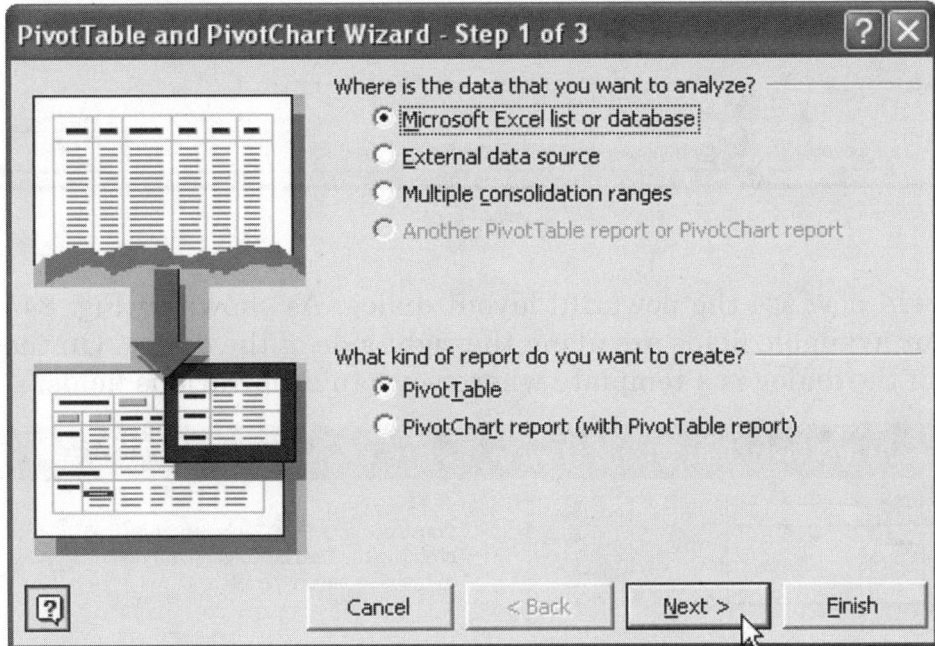

Fig. 842

4) In Step 2, Excel's intellisense will guess the range of your data. It is usually correct. Choose Next, as shown in Fig. 843.

Fig. 843

5)   In Wizard Step 3, choose the Layout button in the lower left corner, as shown in Fig. 844.

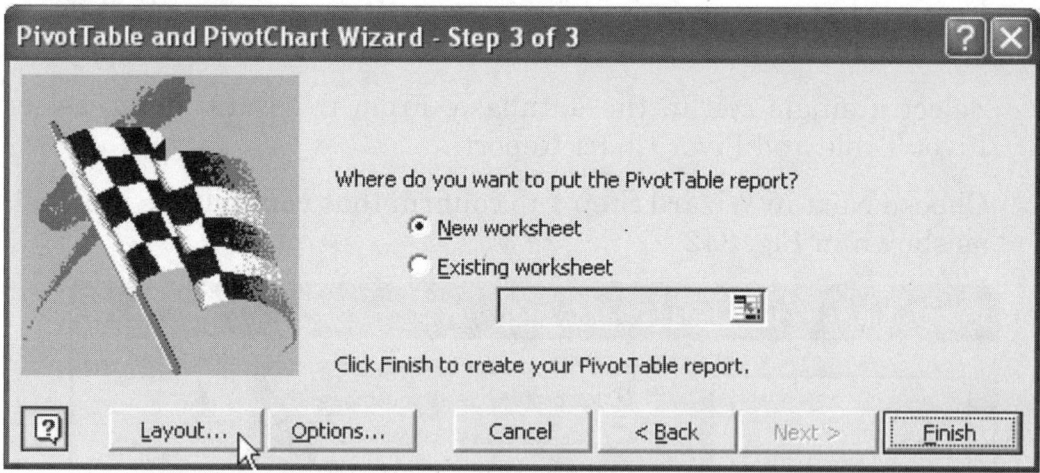

Fig. 844

You will now see the powerful layout dialog. As shown in Fig. 845, all of your available fields are along the right side of the dialog. On the left side of the dialog is a template where you can drop various fields.

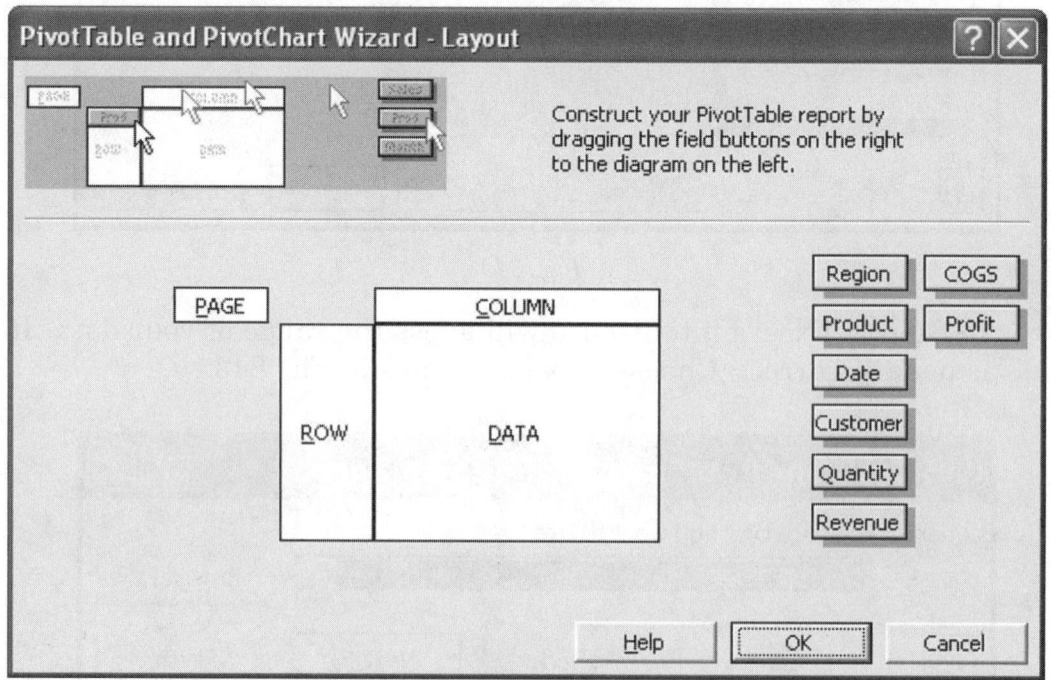

Fig. 845

To build your pivot table, you will drag a field to the proper location. In this case you will want to have products going down the side of the report and regions going across the top.

6) Drag the Product field from the Field list and drop it in the Row area of the layout, as shown in Fig. 846.

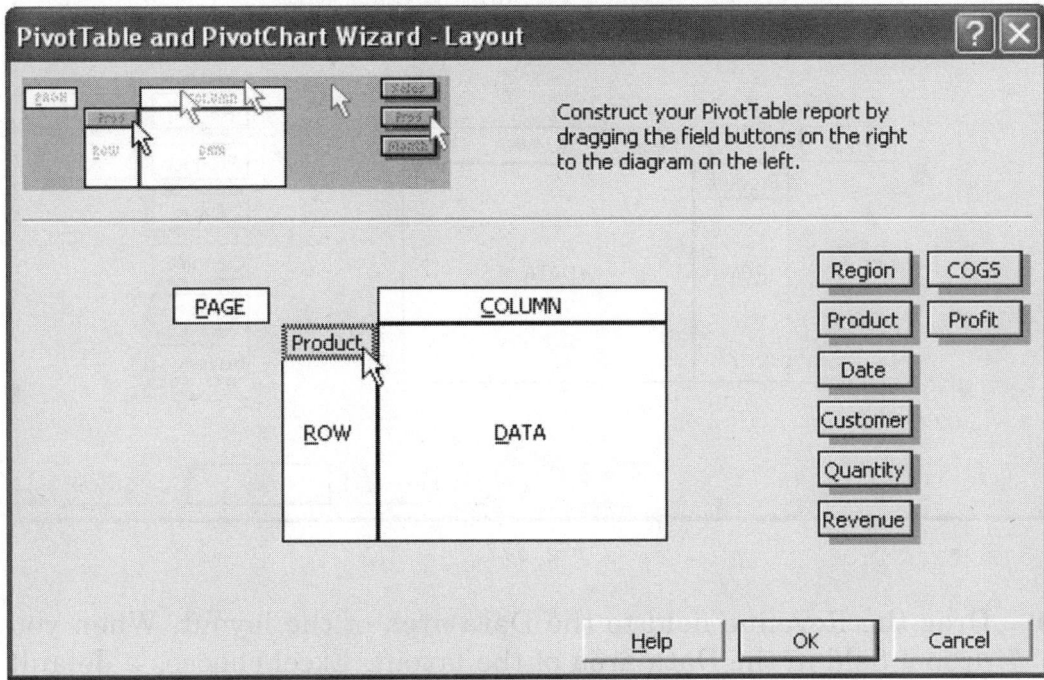

Fig. 846

Part III

7)   Drag the Region field from the Field list and drop it in the Column area of the layout, as shown in Fig. 847.

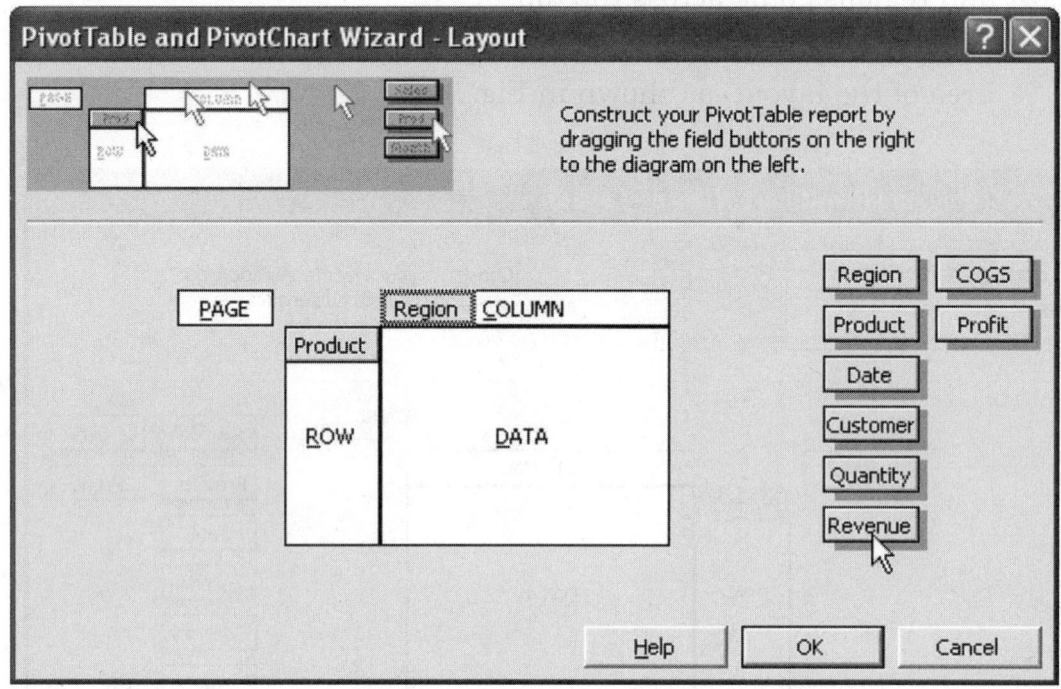

Fig. 847

8)   Drag the Revenue field to the Data area of the layout. When you drop a field in the Data area of the layout, Excel chooses a default operation. In this case, Excel correctly chose Sum of Revenue, as shown in Fig. 848. However, if Excel encounters any cells with text or blanks, it will instead choose to use Count of Revenue.

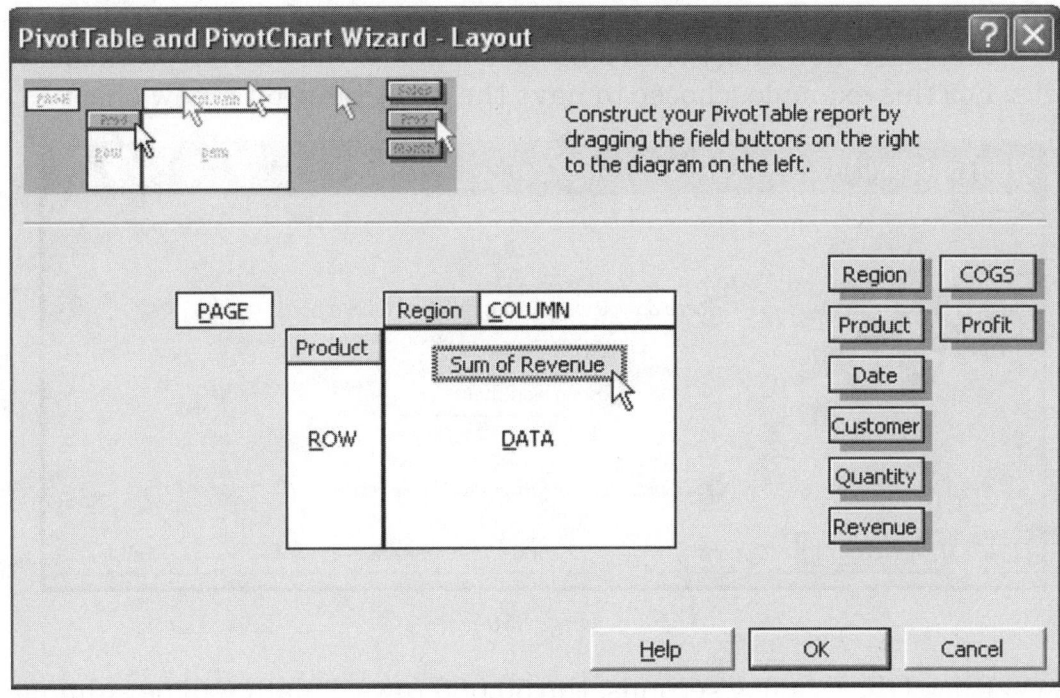

Fig. 848

9)   If Excel's guess for the function in the Data area is incorrect, dou-
      ble click the field to display the PivotTable Field dialog, as shown
      in Fig. 849. Select the correct function for summarization. Choose
      OK to close the Layout dialog. You will be back in Step 3 of the
      Wizard.

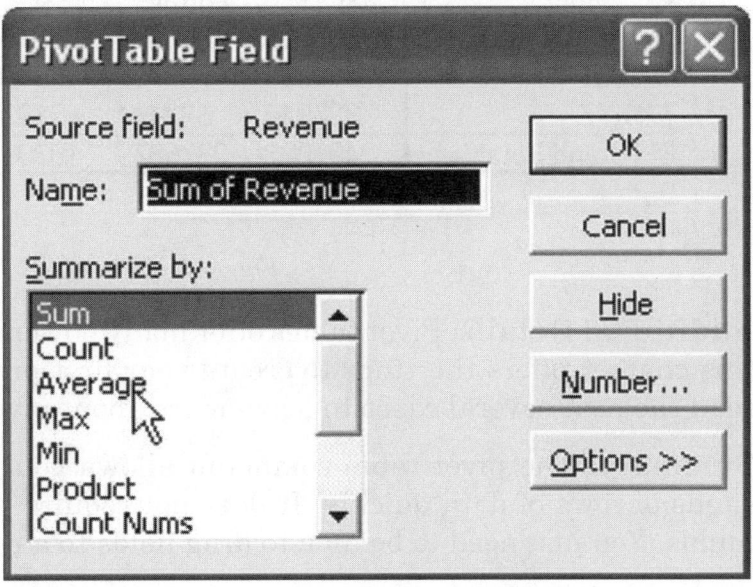

Fig. 849

10) As shown in Fig. 850, you are given a choice of creating the pivot table on a new sheet or in a blank section of the current worksheet. For this example, choose to have the pivot table on a new sheet.

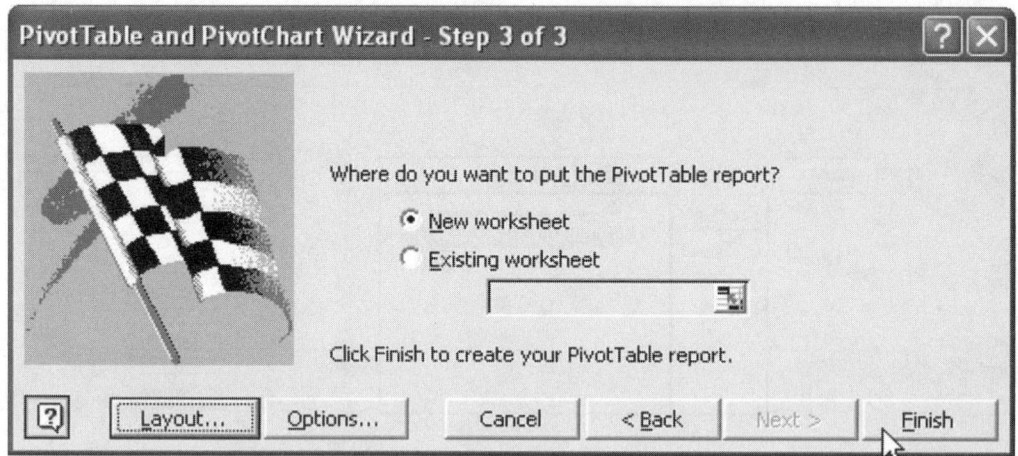

Fig. 850

11) Click OK. In a few seconds, the 50,000 rows of data will be summarized and presented on a new worksheet, as shown in Fig. 851.

	A	B	C	D	E
1		Drop Page Fields Here			
2					
3	Sum of Revenue	Region ▼			
4	Product ▼	East	Central	West	Grand Total
5	ABC	703255	766469	631646	2101370
6	DEF	891799	776996	494919	2163714
7	XYZ	897949	832414	712365	2442728
8	Grand Total	2493003	2375879	1838930	6707812
9					
10					

Fig. 851

Additional Details: Pivot tables offer many powerful options. Although this chapter offers the steps to create your first pivot table, you should read the next several cases to learn more about pivot tables.

Summary: The pivot table command allows you to summarize thousands of rows of data quickly. It does not require you to know any formulas. You just need to be able to drag fields to a report.

Commands Discussed: Data – Pivot Table

YOUR MANAGER WANTS
YOUR REPORT CHANGED

Problem: You present your first pivot table report, as shown in Fig. 852, to your manager. He says, "This is almost perfect, but could you have the products going across the top and the regions going down the side?"

	A	B	C	D	E
1					
2					
3	Sum of Revenue	Region ▼			
4	Product ▼	East	Central	West	Grand Total
5	ABC	703255	766469	631646	2101370
6	DEF	891799	776996	494919	2163714
7	XYZ	897949	832414	712365	2442728
8	Grand Total	2493003	2375879	1838930	6707812
9					

Fig. 852

Strategy: Pivot tables make this easy.

1) On the worksheet, click on the gray Product field, then drag and drop it next to Region, as shown in Fig. 853.

	A	B	C	D	E
1					
2					
3	Sum of Revenue	Region ▼			
4	Product ▼	East	Central	West	Grand Total
5	ABC	703255	766469	631646	2101370
6	DEF	891799	776996	494919	2163714
7	XYZ	897949	832414	712365	2442728
8	Grand Total	2493003	2375879	1838930	6707812
9					

Fig. 853

Part
III

2) When you release the mouse button, the pivot table will instantly redraw, as shown in Fig. 854.

	A	B	C	D	E	F
1						Drop Page F
2						
3	Sum of Revenue	Product ▼	Region ▼			
4		ABC			ABC Total	DEF
5		East	Central	West		East Ce
6	Total	703255	766469	631646	2101370	891799	77

Fig. 854

3) Using the mouse, grab the gray Region field, then drag and drop it to the left of cell A4, as shown in Fig. 855.

	A	B	C	D
1				
2				
3	Sum of Revenue	Product ▼	Region ▼	①
4		ABC		
5		East	Central	West
6	Total	703255	766469	631646
7				

Fig. 855

4) When you release the mouse button, the pivot table will redraw, as shown in Fig. 856.

	A	B	C	D	E
1					
2					
3	Sum of Revenue	Product ▼			
4	Region ▼	ABC	DEF	XYZ	Grand Total
5	East	703255	891799	897949	2493003
6	Central	766469	776996	832414	2375879
7	West	631646	494919	712365	1838930
8	Grand Total	2101370	2163714	2442728	6707812

Fig. 856

Result: With two movements of the mouse, you have created a new report for the manager.

Additional Details: Watch the mouse pointer as you drag fields around a pivot table. There are five possible cursors. As shown in Fig. 857, the blue portion of the cursor shows where the field will be dropped when you release the mouse button. In the following image, the first cursor shows a field about to be dropped in the Row area. The second cursor shows a field about to be dropped in the Column area. The third cursor shows a field about to be dropped in the Data area. The fourth cursor shows a field about to be dropped in the Page area (discussed later). The fifth cursor shows a field about to be removed from the pivot table – this happens if you drag the field too far outside of the boundary of the pivot table.

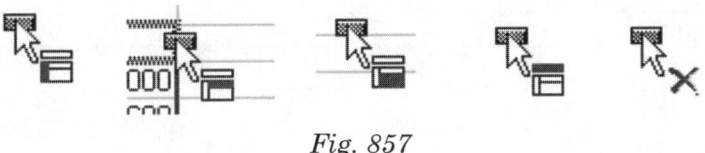

Fig. 857

Summary: The first amazing feature of pivot tables is that they can summarize massive amounts of data very quickly. This topic shows the second amazing feature – pivot tables can be quickly changed to show another view of the data.

Commands Discussed: Data – Pivot Table

MOVE OR CHANGE PART OF A PIVOT TABLE

Problem: If you try to insert a row in a pivot table, you are greeted with a message saying that you cannot change, move, or insert cells in a pivot table, as shown in Fig. 858.

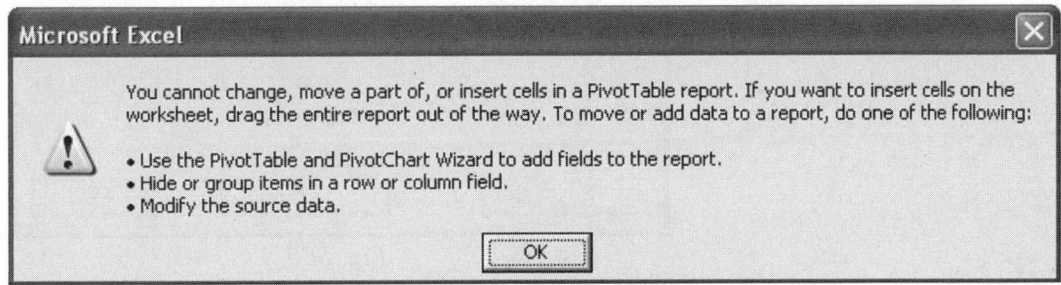

Fig. 858

Strategy: This is correct; you cannot do a lot of things to a finished pivot table. While the flexibility of pivot tables is awesome, sometimes you just want to take the results of the pivot table and turn off the pivot features. If you want to take the data and re-use it somewhere else, you can convert the pivot table to regular data using Paste Special Values. Follow these steps.

1) Select the entire pivot table, as shown in Fig. 859. Be sure to include the two blank rows at the top of the table (known as the Page area).

	A	B	C	D	E
1	Drop Page Fields Here				
2					
3	Sum of Revenue	Product ▼			
4	Region ▼	ABC	DEF	XYZ	Grand Total
5	East	703255	891799	897949	2493003
6	Central	766469	776996	832414	2375879
7	West	631646	494919	712365	1838930
8	Grand Total	2101370	2163714	2442728	6707812
9					

Fig. 859

2) Hit Ctrl+C to copy.

3) From the menu, select Edit – Paste Special – Values – OK, as shown in Fig. 860.

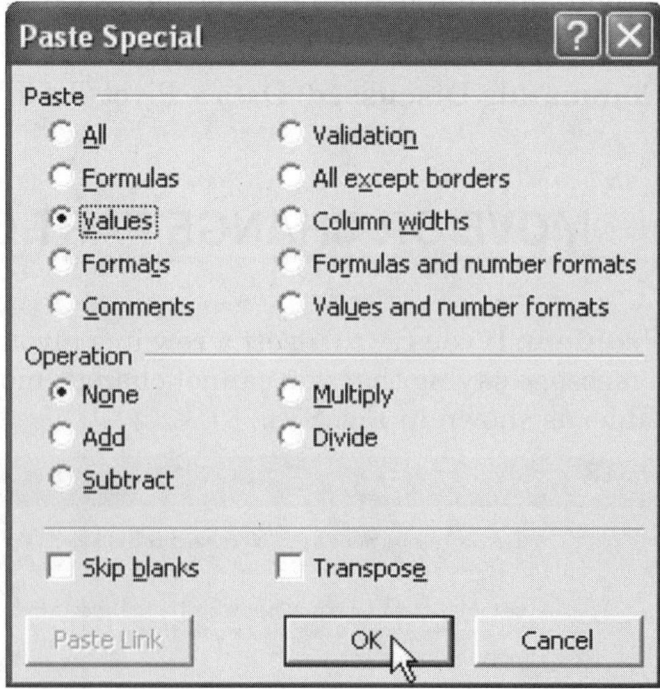

Fig. 860

This action will change the pivot table from a live pivot table to just values in cells. You can now insert rows and columns to your heart's content, as shown in Fig. 861.

	A	B	C	D	E	F
1						
2						
3	Sum of Revenue	Product				
4	Region	ABC	DEF	XYZ		Grand Total
5	East	703255	891799	897949		2493003
6	Central	766469	776996	832414		2375879
7	West	631646	494919	712365		1838930
8						
9	**Grand Total**	**2101370**	**2163714**	**2442728**		**6707812**
10						

Fig. 861

Summary: When doing data analysis, it is common to use a pivot table to get the result, but then to convert the pivot table from a live table to static values using Paste Special Values.

Part III

Commands Discussed: Data – Pivot Table; Edit – Paste Special

SEE DETAIL BEHIND ONE NUMBER IN A PIVOT TABLE

Problem: One number in the Pivot Table seems to be wrong. For example, maybe the Government region does not typically buy a certain product line from you, yet they are shown with that product in the report, as shown in Fig. 862.

	A	B	C	D	E	F
1						
2						
3	Sum of Revenue	Region ▼				
4	Product ▼	East	Central	West	Government	Grand Total
5	ABC	703255	766469	631646	10290	2111660
6	DEF	891799	776996	494919		2163714
7	XYZ	897949	832414	712365	24685	2467413
8	Grand Total	2493003	2375879	1838930	34975	6742787

Fig. 862

Strategy: You can see the detail behind any number in a pivot table by double-clicking on the number. If the $10,290 in sales of product ABC to the government seems unusual, double-click cell E5. As shown in Fig. 863, a new worksheet is inserted with all of the records that make up the $10,290. In this case, it is just one record, which seems to have been coded to the wrong region.

	A	B	C	D	E	F	G	H
1	Region	Product	Date	Customer	Quantity	Revenue	COGS	Profit
2	Government	ABC	12/28/2004	General Motors	600	10290	5082	5208
3								

Fig. 863

Additional Information: If you double-click on a number in the total row or total column, you will see all of the records that make up that number. Drilling down on E8 in the original pivot table will show the records that make up the $34,975, as shown in Fig. 864.

	A	B	C	D	E	F	G	H
1	Region	Product	Date	Customer	Quantity	Revenue	COGS	Profit
2	Government	ABC	12/28/2004	General Motors	600	10290	5082	5208
3	Government	XYZ	12/27/2004	IBIS	700	15225	7154	8071
4	Government	XYZ	12/27/2004	IBIS	500	9460	4235	5225
5								

Fig. 864

Gotcha: Each drill down creates a new worksheet. The new worksheet is just a snapshot in time of what made up the original number. If you detect a wrong number in the drill down report, you need to go back to the original data to make the correction.

Summary: Given the power to summarize data in a pivot table, you are likely to spot information that might point to a problem in the underlying data. With 50,000 rows of data, it is likely that someone miscoded the region on a few of the records. Until you look at a pivot table with a quick summary, it is hard to spot obvious problems like the one shown here. When you see a number that seems suspicious in a pivot table, double-click the number to drill down and see the records behind the data.

Commands Discussed: Data – Pivot Table

UPDATE DATA BEHIND A PIVOT TABLE

Problem: You discovered that some of the underlying data in the pivot table is wrong. After correcting the number, the pivot table does not appear to include the change, as shown in Fig. 865.

	A	B	C	D	E	F
1		Drop Page Fields Here				
2						
3	Sum of Revenue	Region ▼				
4	Product ▼	East	Central	West	Government	Grand Total
5	ABC	703255	766469	631646	10290	2111660
6	DEF	891799	776996	494919		2163714
7	XYZ	897949	832414	712365	24685	2467413
8	Grand Total	2493003	2375879	1838930	34975	6742787
9						
10						
11	PivotTable ▼ ×					
12	PivotTable ▼					
13						

Fig. 865

Strategy: This is one of the important things to understand about pivot tables. When you create the pivot table, all of the data is loaded into memory to allow it to calculate quickly. When you change the data on the original worksheet, it does not automatically update the pivot table.

Select a cell in the pivot table. The PivotTable toolbar will appear. As shown in Fig. 866, choose the Red exclamation point on the toolbar to recalculate the pivot table from the worksheet data.

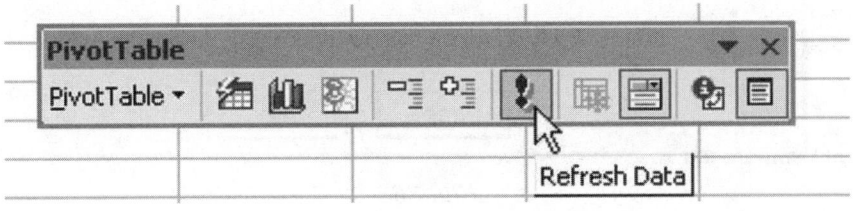

Fig. 866

Part
III

Result: The pivot table is updated, as shown in Fig. 867.

	A	B	C	D	E	F
1	Drop Page Fields Here					
2						
3	Sum of Revenue	Region ▼				
4	Product ▼	East	Central	West	Government	Grand Total
5	ABC	703255	776759	631646		2111660
6	DEF	891799	776996	494919		2163714
7	XYZ	897949	832414	712365	24685	2467413
8	Grand Total	2493003	2386169	1838930	24685	6742787
9						

Fig. 867

Additional Details: If you make changes to the underlying data, it could cause the table to grow. For example, if you re-classify some records from the East region to the Southeast region, be aware that choosing the Refresh button will cause the table to grow by one column. If there happens to be other data in that column, Excel will warn you and ask if it is OK to overwrite those cells, as shown in Fig. 868.

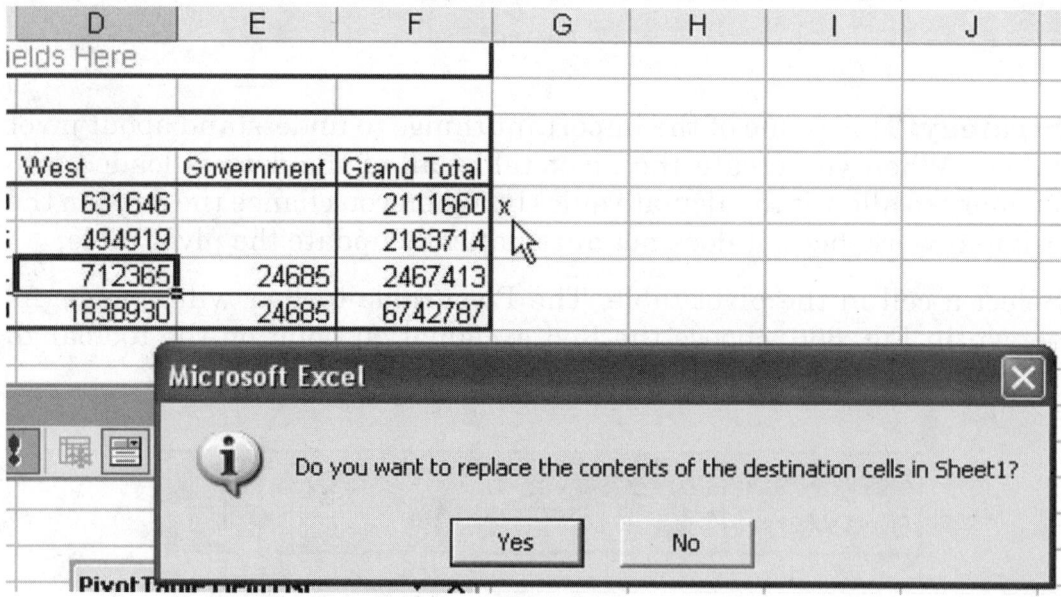

Fig. 868

Summary: Changes to the underlying data do not automatically get calculated in the pivot table. You must choose the red exclamation icon in the toolbar to have Excel re-read the original data.

Commands Discussed: Data – Pivot Table

REPLACE BLANKS
IN A PIVOT TABLE WITH ZEROES

Problem: Since you had no sales of a particular product in a particular region, Excel leaves those cells in the pivot table blank, as shown in Fig. 869. This seems like a really bad idea. You've learned in this book that if your data has blanks instead of zeroes, Excel will assume that a column is a text column. It is really ironic that Microsoft would dare to use a blank cell in the middle of numeric results.

	A	B	C	D	E
1					
2					
3	Sum of Revenue	Product ▼			
4	Region ▼	ABC	DEF	XYZ	Grand Total
5	East	703255	891799	882724	2477778
6	Central	776759	776996	832414	2386169
7	West	631646	494919	712365	1838930
8	Government			24685	24685
9	Southeast	15225			15225
10	Grand Total	2126885	2163714	2452188	6742787
11					

Fig. 869

Part
III

Strategy: When pivot tables first came out, there was no way to correct this. After much outcry from accountants everywhere, Microsoft gave us two ways to solve the problem.

Method 1: If you discover the problem after the fact in a completed pivot table, follow these steps.

1)   Select one cell in the pivot table in order to display the PivotTable toolbar. From the toolbar, use the PivotTable dropdown and select the Table Options menu item, as shown in Fig. 870.

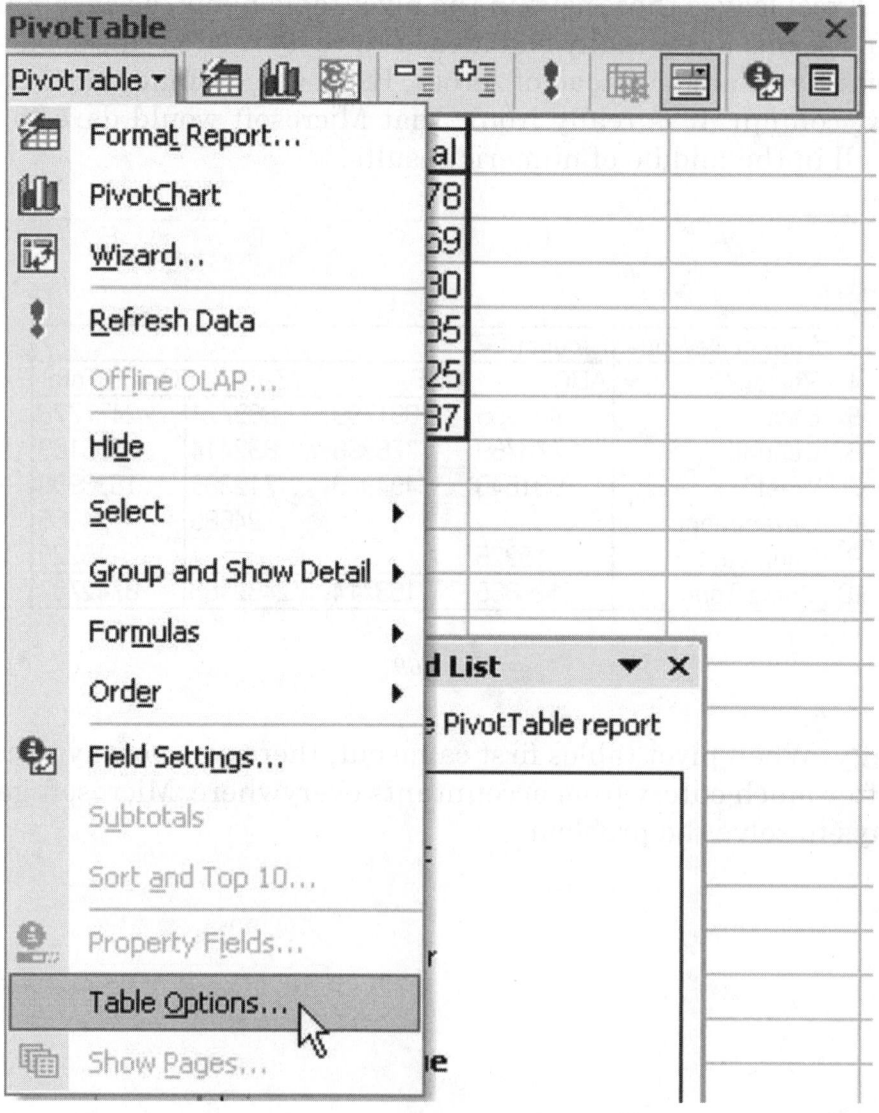

Fig. 870

2)   In the Table Options dialog, on the right side, locate the field called For Empty Cells, Show:, as shown in Fig. 871.

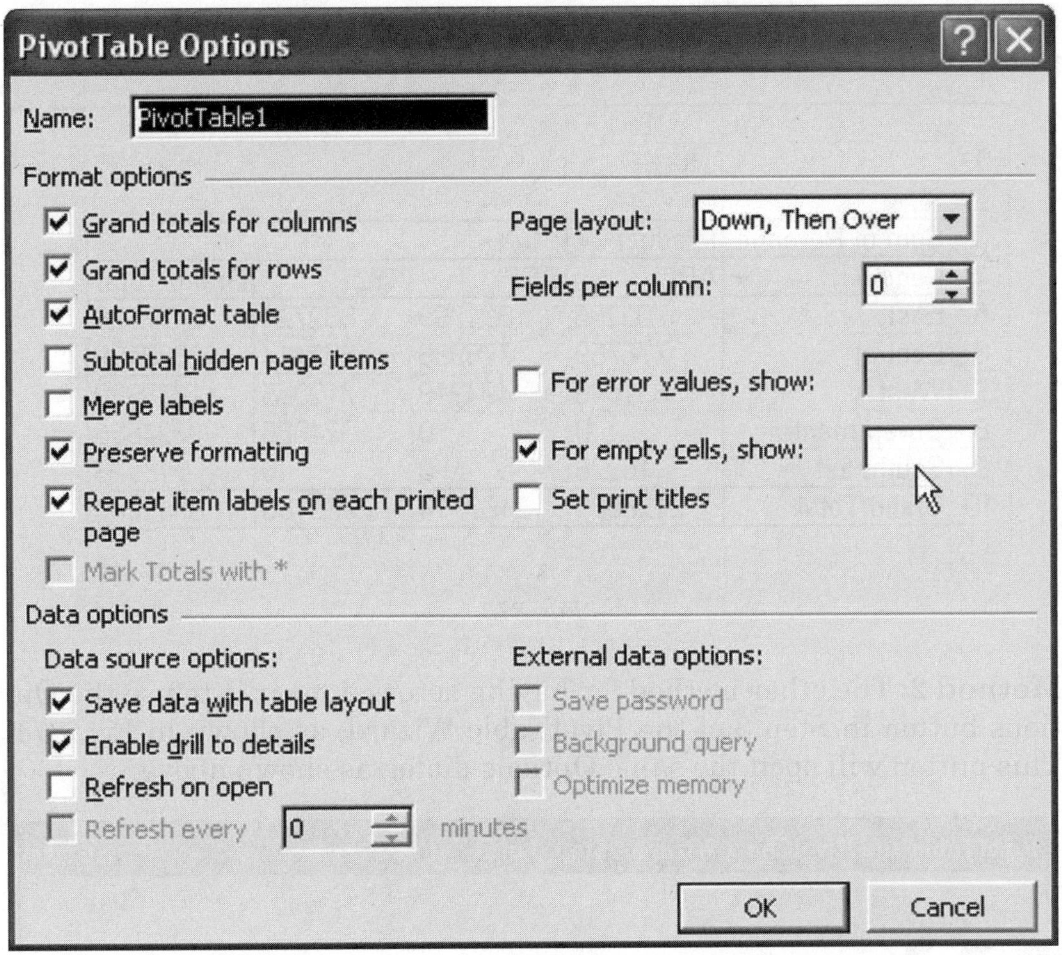

PivotTable Options   [?] [X]

Name: PivotTable1

Format options

☑ Grand totals for columns   Page layout: Down, Then Over ▼

☑ Grand totals for rows   Fields per column: 0 ▲▼
☑ AutoFormat table
☐ Subtotal hidden page items
                                    ☐ For error values, show: [   ]
☐ Merge labels

☑ Preserve formatting   ☑ For empty cells, show: [   ]

☑ Repeat item labels on each printed   ☐ Set print titles
   page

☐ Mark Totals with *

Data options

Data source options: External data options: **Part**
                                                                              III
☑ Save data with table layout   ☐ Save password

☑ Enable drill to details   ☐ Background query

☐ Refresh on open   ☐ Optimize memory

☐ Refresh every   0   ▲▼ minutes

                                          [OK   ]   [Cancel]

Fig. 871

3) By default, this setting is
   blank. Type a zero in the
   textbox and choose OK, as
   shown in Fig. 872.

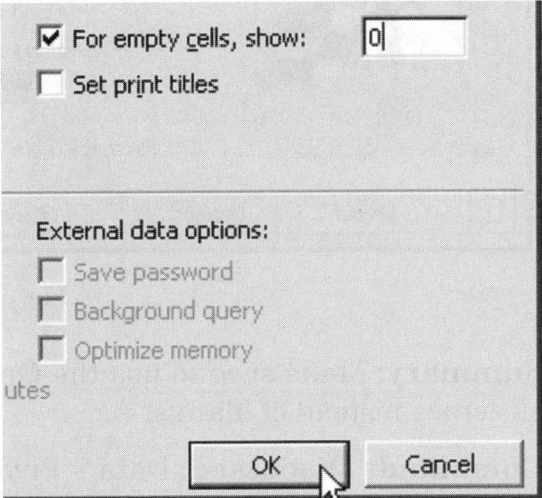

Fig. 872

Result: As you see in Fig. 873, blanks in the data section of the pivot table are shown as zeroes.

	A	B	C	D	E
1					
2					
3	Sum of Revenue	Product ▼			
4	Region ▼	ABC	DEF	XYZ	Grand Total
5	East	703255	891799	882724	2477778
6	Central	776759	776996	832414	2386169
7	West	631646	494919	712365	1838930
8	Government	0	0	24685	24685
9	Southeast	15225	0	0	15225
10	Grand Total	2126885	2163714	2452188	6742787
11					

Fig. 873

Method 2: The other method for having zeroes appear is to use the Options button in Step 3 of the PivotTable Wizard, as shown in Fig. 874. This button will open the same Options dialog as shown above.

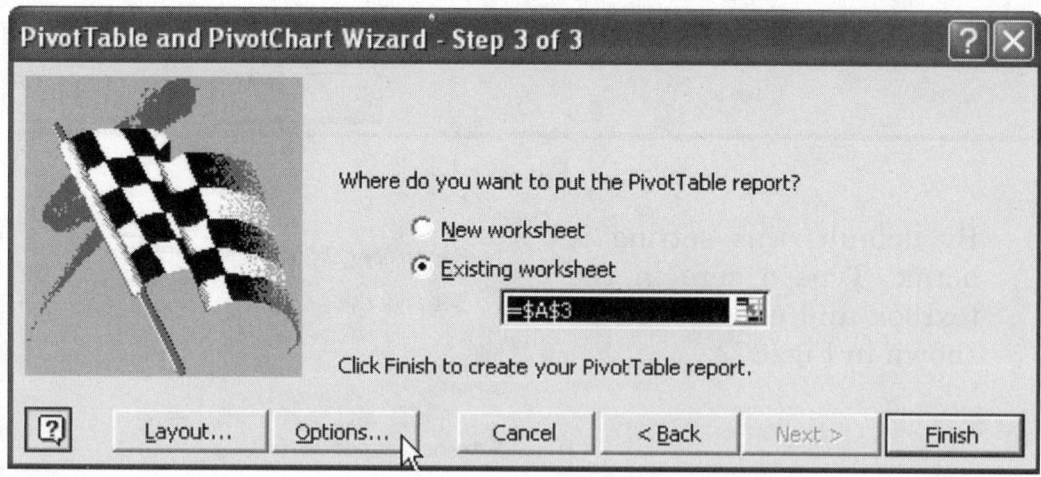

Fig. 874

Summary: Make sure to use the Options dialog to display empty cells as zeroes instead of blanks.

Commands Discussed: Data – Pivot Table

ADD OR REMOVE FIELDS
FROM AN EXISTING PIVOT TABLE

Problem: You've seen how easy it is to rearrange an existing pivot table, swapping Region and Product fields, as shown in Fig. 875. Now, what if you want to replace the Region field with the Customer field?

	A	B	C	D	E
1	Drop Page Fields Here				
2					
3	Sum of Revenue	Product ▼			
4	Region ▼	ABC	DEF	XYZ	Grand Total
5	East	703255	891799	882724	2477778
6	Central	776759	776996	832414	2386169
7	West	631646	494919	712365	1838930
8	Government	0	0	24685	24685
9	Southeast	15225	0	0	15225
10	Grand Total	2126885	2163714	2452188	6742787
11					

Fig. 875

Strategy: In order to remove the Region field from the pivot table, click on the gray Region button and drag it off the pivot table, as shown in Fig. 876. The mouse pointer will eventually change to include a red X, which is synonymous with Delete.

2		
3	Sum of Revenue	Product ▼
4	Region ▼	ⓘ C
5	East	70325!
6	Central	77675!
7	West	63164!
8	Government	!
9	Southeast	1522!
10	Grand Total	2126688!
11		
12		
13		
14		

Fig. 876

Part
III

This will remove the Region field from the pivot table, as shown in Fig. 877.

	A	B	C	D	E
1	Drop Page Fields Here				
2					
3	Sum of Revenue	Product ▼			
4		ABC	DEF	XYZ	Grand Total
5	Total	2126885	2163714	2452188	6742787
6					

Fig. 877

Select any cell in the pivot table and the PivotTable Field List will appear. This list is one of the things that look different in various versions of Excel. In Excel 2002 and 2003, the list is a floating box, as shown in Fig. 878, that appears when you select a cell in the pivot table.

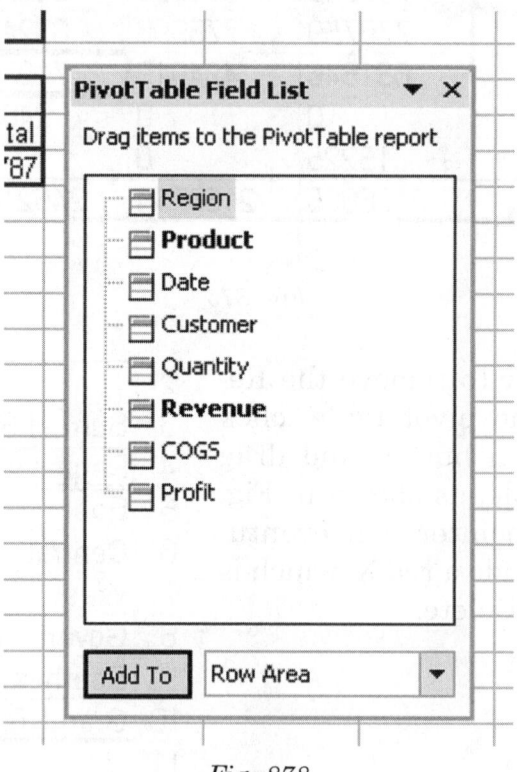

Fig. 878

In Excel 2000 and earlier versions, the Field List appears as a part of the PivotTable toolbar, as shown in Fig. 879. The toolbar expands whenever you select a cell in the pivot table.

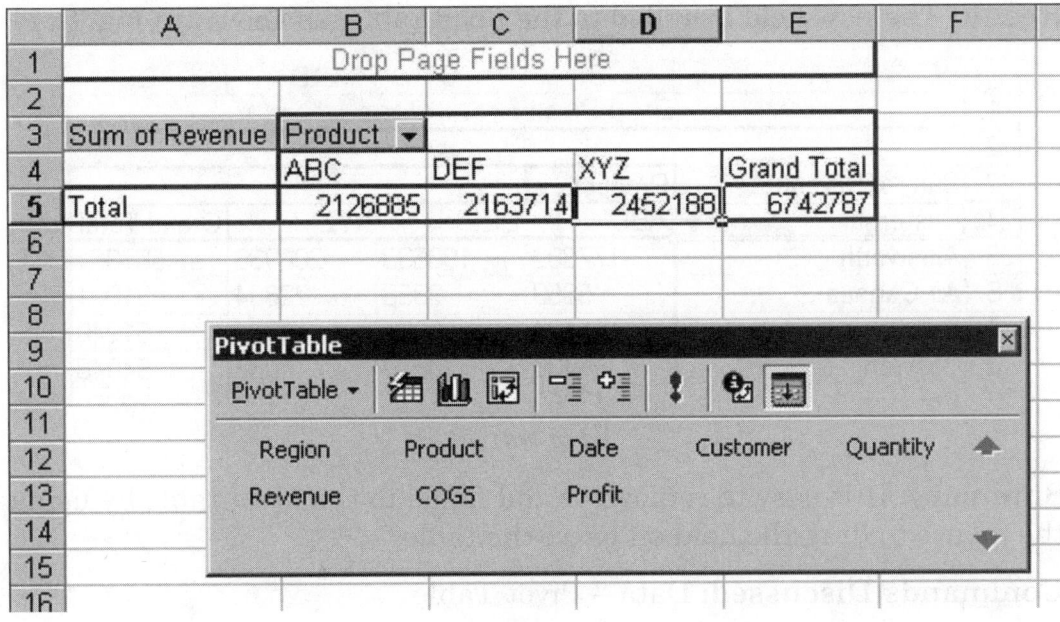

Fig. 879

To add the customer field, drag the field from the Field List and drop it in the correct area on the pivot table, as shown in Fig. 880.

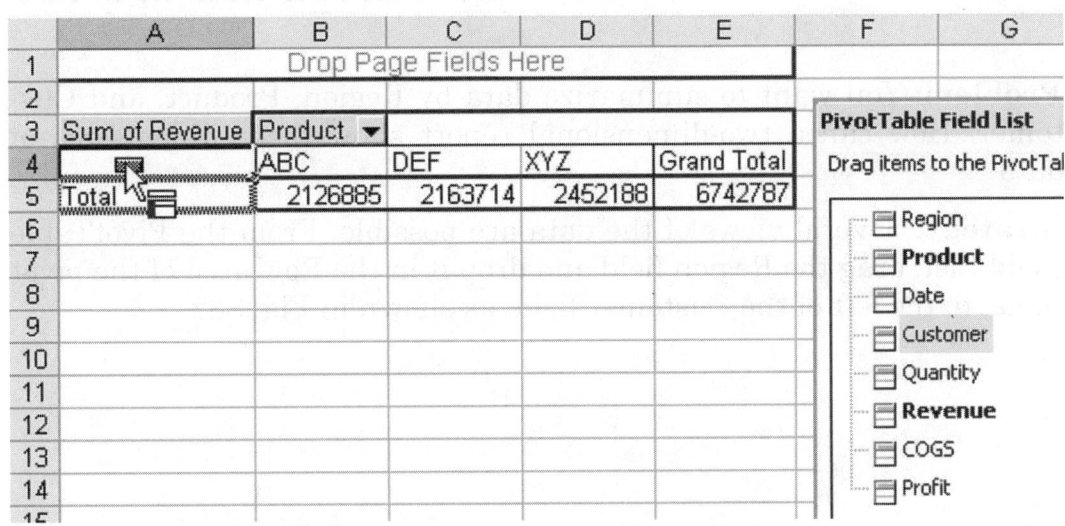

Fig. 880

Result: The new field is added to the pivot table, as shown in Fig. 881.

	A	B	C	D	E
1		Drop Page Fields Here			
2					
3	Sum of Revenue	Product ▼			
4	Customer ▼	ABC	DEF	XYZ	Grand Total
5	Ainsworth	177382	190533	200936	568851
6	Air Canada	5859	2358	22804	31021
7	Bell Canada	15104	18064	18072	51240
8	Chevron	26406	20610	7032	54048
9	Camnaa	17250	4380	17620	39250

Fig. 881

Summary: It is easy to remove or add fields to the pivot table by using the mouse to drag the field off or on the table.

Commands Discussed: Data – Pivot Table

SUMMARIZE PIVOT TABLE DATA BY THREE MEASURES

Problem: You want to summarize data by Region, Product, and Customer. How can a two-dimensional report show three dimensions of data?

Strategy: Several views of the data are possible. From the PivotTable Field List, drag the Region field and drop it in the Row area of the pivot table, to the left of the Customer field, as shown in Fig. 882.

	A	B	C	D	E	F
1			Drop Page Fields Here			
2						
3	Sum of Revenue		Product ▼			
4	Region ▼	Customer ▼	ABC	DEF	XYZ	Grand Total
5	East	Ainsworth	61660	90978	79438	232076
6		Air Canada	0	2358	0	2358
7		Bell Canada	0	14004	0	14004
8		Chevron	8116	0	0	8116
9		Compaq	0	4380	0	4380
10		Compton Petroleum	0	2029	0	2029
11		Exxon	60556	98295	70789	229640
12		Ford	27550	75977	72440	175967
13		General Motors	69040	132844	58279	260163
14		Gildan Activewear	0	18552	0	18552
15		HP	17840	0	21015	38855
16		IBM	39273	60637	65860	165770
17		Kroger	1819	0	2538	4357
18		Lucent	0	14497	0	14497
19		Molson, Inc	69991	82029	93061	245081
20		Nortel Networks	89960	14580	99350	203890
21		P&G	0	17757	0	17757
22		Phillip Morris	0	10760	0	10760
23		SBC Communications	14440	0	24420	38860
24		Sears	0	4282	0	4282
25		Sears Canada	5532	0	18264	23796
26		Shell Canada	9635	0	16936	26571
27		State Farm	0	21730	0	21730
28		Sun Life Financial	75912	51445	72625	199982
29		Texaco	7136	0	9152	16288
30		Verizon	64527	18577	101459	184563
31		Wal-Mart	80268	156088	77098	313454
32	East Total		703255	891799	882724	2477778

Fig. 882

Part
III

Another option is to drag the third measure to the Column area of the pivot table, as shown in Fig. 883.

	A	B	C	D	E	F	G
1							
2							
3	Sum of Revenue	Region ▼	Product ▼				
4		East				East Total	Central
5	Customer ▼	ABC	DEF	XYZ			ABC	DEF
6	Ainsworth	61660	90978	79438	232076	77683	49816
7	Air Canada	0	2358	0	2358	0	0
8	Bell Canada	0	14004	0	14004	0	4060
9	Chevron	8116	0	0	8116	0	20610
10	Compaq	0	4380	0	4380	0	0
11	Compton Petroleum	0	2029	0	2029	0	11220
12	Exxon	60556	98295	70789	229640	136774	57857
13	Ford	27550	75977	72440	175967	90995	67173
14	General Motors	69040	132844	58279	260163	135028	47373

Fig. 883

Even with this view, the report looks different if you move the Region field and drop it to the right of the Product field, as shown in Fig. 884.

	A	B	C	D	E	F	G
1							Drop
2							
3	Sum of Revenue	Product ▼	Region ▼ ①				
4		ABC				ABC Total	DEF
5	Customer ▼	East	Central	West	Southeast		East
6	Ainsworth	61660	77683	38039	0	177382	90978
7	Air Canada	0	0	5859	0	5859	2358
8	Bell Canada	0	0	15104	0	15104	14004
9	Chevron	8116	0	18290	0	26406	0
10	Compaq	0	0	17250	0	17250	4380
11	Compton Petroleum	0	0	4158	0	4158	2029
12	Exxon	60556	136774	96808	0	294138	98295
13	Ford	27550	90995	72440	0	191630	75977

Fig. 884

Summary: You can use more than one field along either the row or column axis of the pivot table to produce more complex summaries.

Commands Discussed: Data – Pivot Table

MAKE PIVOT TABLES BE TALLER THAN WIDE

Problem: An Excel worksheet has 256 columns and 65,536 rows. As you start adding fields to a pivot table, it is possible to quickly run out of columns, as shown in Fig. 885. If you want a report with products, customers and regions, it can quickly get large. Three Regions x 10 Products x 300 customers would require 900 columns.

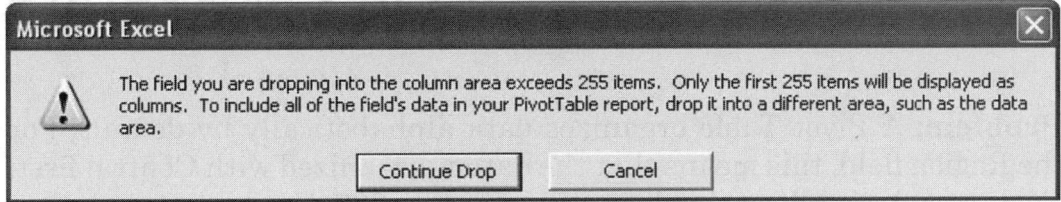

Fig. 885

Strategy: Make your pivot tables tall instead of wide. If you have most of the measures in the Row area of the pivot table, it is far less likely that you will run out of room for the table.

Part III

As shown in Fig. 886, this 668-row table fits fine going down the rows, but would fail if we tried to have it going across the columns.

	A	B	C	D
657			30-May-04	19152
658			5-Jun-04	4264
659			2-Jul-04	22716
660			6-Jul-04	8580
661			2-Oct-04	12760
662			4-Oct-04	24070
663			6-Oct-04	15715
664			19-Dec-04	18560
665			24-Dec-04	4690
666		XYZ Total		288409
667	Wal-Mart Total			869454
668	Grand Total			6742787

Fig. 886

Summary: If you are going to have a combination of fields that will be larger than 255 columns, build the table to have these fields going down the rows.

Commands Discussed: Data – Pivot Table

MANUALLY RESEQUENCE THE ORDER OF DATA IN A PIVOT TABLE

Problem: A Pivot Table organizes data alphabetically by default. For the Region field, this means that the data is organized with Central first, East second, and West third, as shown in Fig. 887. Your manager wants the regions to appear in the order of "East, Central, West". Unless you can convince the company to change the name of the Central region to the Middle region, the regions will not appear in the proper order. After unsuccessfully lobbying to have the Central region renamed to Middle, you need to find a way to have the following table sequenced with the East region first.

	A	B	C	D	E
1					
2					
3	Sum of Revenue	Region ▼			
4	Product ▼	Central	East	West	Grand Total
5	ABC	776759	703255	631646	2111660
6	DEF	776996	891799	494919	2163714
7	XYZ	832414	882724	712365	2427503
8	Grand Total	2386169	2477778	1838930	6702877

Fig. 887

Strategy: It is amazing that this trick works.

1)   Select cell B4 in the pivot table, as shown in Fig. 888.

	A	B	C
1		Drop Page Field	
2			
3	Sum of Revenue	Region ▼	
4	Product ▼	Central	East
5	ABC	776759	703:
6	DEF	776996	891:

Fig. 888

2) Right in cell B4, start typing the word "East", as shown in Fig. 889.

	A	B	C
1		Drop Page Fields H	
2			
3	Sum of Revenue	Region ▼	
4	Product ▼	East|	East
5	ABC	776759	703255
6	DEF	776996	891799

Fig. 889

3) When you hit Enter, Excel senses what you are trying to do. All of the data from the East region moves to Column B. Excel automatically moves the Central region heading and data to column C, as shown in Fig. 890.

	A	B	C	D	E
1					
2					
3	Sum of Revenue	Region ▼			
4	Product ▼	East	Central	West	Grand Total
5	ABC	703255	776759	631646	2111660
6	DEF	891799	776996	494919	2163714
7	XYZ	882724	832414	712365	2427503
8	Grand Total	2477778	2386169	1838930	6702877

Fig. 890

You can easily use this trick to resequence the fields into whatever order is necessary.

Additional Details: The technique shown above will only change the Region sequence in a single pivot table. If you would like to change the sequence in all future pivot tables, create a custom list.

1) In a blank area of the worksheet, type your regions in the desired order in a column. Enter East in one cell, Central in the next cell, and West in the next cell. Select these three cells.

2) From the menu, select Tools – Options. Go to the Custom Lists tab. At the bottom of the Custom Lists tab, there is a section called Import List from Cells. Your selected range will be in this field. As shown in Fig. 891, choose the Import button to add a custom list of East, Central, West.

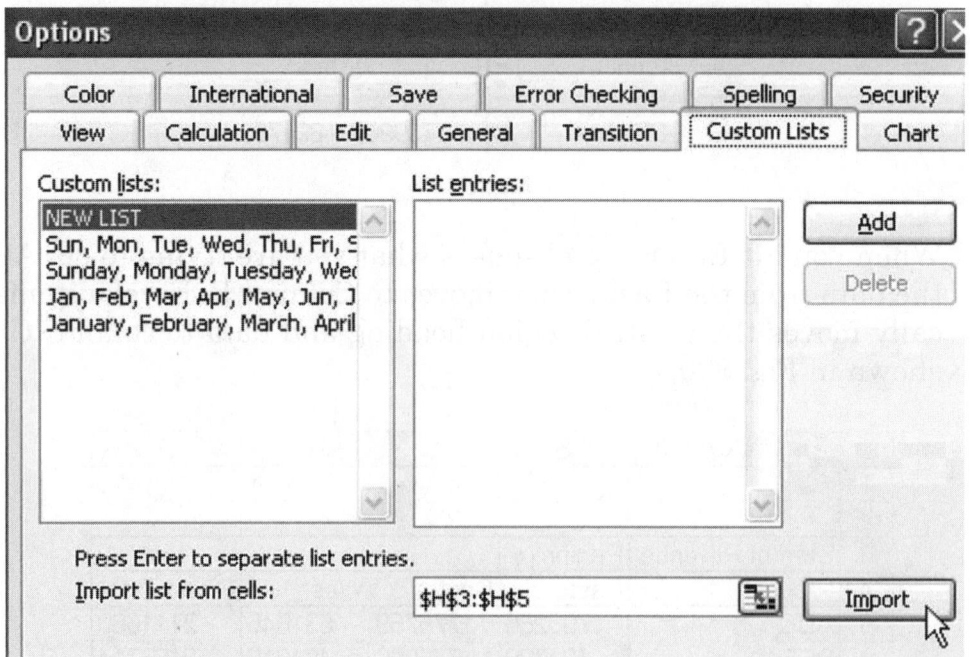

Fig. 891

All future pivot tables will automatically sort into East, Central, West sequence.

Summary: The manual sort feature of a pivot table is astounding. Simply type a heading in a new place to have Excel turn on manual sequencing of the data.

Commands Discussed: Data – Pivot Table

PRESENT A PIVOT TABLE
IN HIGH-TO-LOW ORDER BY REVENUE

Problem: A Pivot Table organizes data alphabetically by default, as shown in Fig. 892. You want to produce a report sorted high-to-low by Revenue.

	A	B	C	D	E
1	Drop Page Fields Here				
2					
3	Sum of Revenue	Region ▼			
4	Customer ▼	Central	East	West	Grand Total
5	Ainsworth	223540	232076	113235	568851
6	Air Canada	4948	2358	23715	31021
7	Bell Canada	4060	14004	33176	51240
8	Chevron	20610	8116	25322	54048
9	Compaq	9064	4380	25806	39250
10	Compton Petroleum	11220	2029	18120	31369

Fig. 892

Strategy: Each pivot field offers a sort option. To access the Sort options for the pivot field, follow these steps.

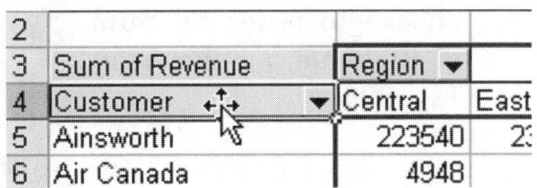

2			
3	Sum of Revenue	Region ▼	
4	Customer ⤢ ▼	Central	East
5	Ainsworth	223540	2:
6	Air Canada	4948	

Fig. 893

1) As shown in Fig. 893, double-click the Customer field in the pivot table.

2) This brings up the PivotTable Field dialog. Choose the Advanced button on the right side, as shown in Fig. 894.

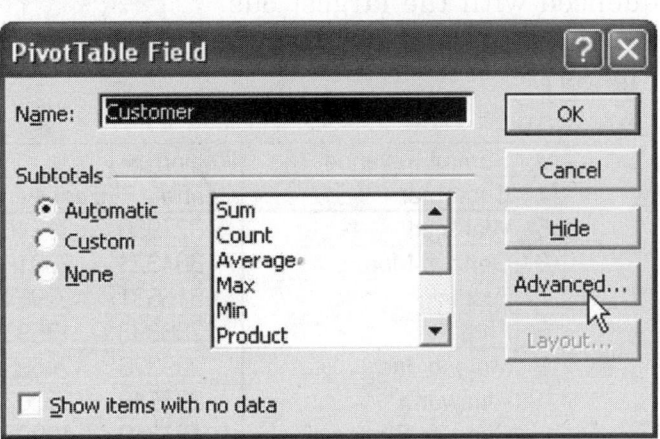

Fig. 894

Part III

3)   As shown the PivotTable Field Advanced Options dialog in Fig. 895, you can see that the default sort is Manual. This option lets you resequence items by dragging or retyping. In the current example, you want to choose Descending.

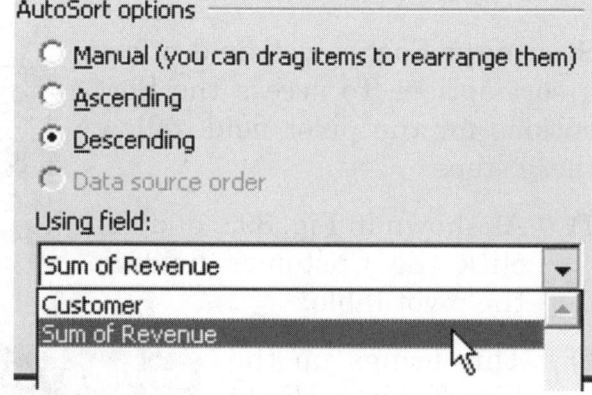

Fig. 895

4)   Use the dropdown in the Using Field: area to choose to order by Sum of Revenue, as shown in Fig. 896.

Result: The report is sequenced with the largest customers at the top, as shown in Fig. 897.

Fig. 896

3	Sum of Revenue	Region ▼			
4	Customer ▼	Central	East	West	Grand Total
5	Wal-Mart	327958	313454	228042	869454
6	General Motors	304323	260163	195967	760453
7	Exxon	315631	229640	159088	704359
8	Ford	288393	175967	158434	622794
9	Molson, Inc	209326	245081	159107	613514
10	Ainsworth	223540	232076	113235	568851
11	Sun Life Financial	151310	199982	147645	498937
12	IBM				

Fig. 897

Summary: The AutoSort options are fairly well hidden, but offer a variety of sorting options for each field in a pivot table.

Commands Discussed: Data – PivotTable – AutoSort

LIMIT A PIVOT REPORT
TO SHOW JUST THE TOP 12 CUSTOMERS

Problem: Many times, a customer report will have hundreds of customers. If you are preparing a report for the senior vice president of sales, he may not care about the 400 customers who bought spare batteries this month. For most of the senior vice presidents of sales that I know, they like to see only the top 10 or 20 customers each month.

Strategy: There is a Top 10 AutoShow feature available in pivot tables. Follow these steps.

Part
III

1) Double-click the Customer field in the pivot table. This brings up the PivotTable Field dialog. Choose the Advanced button, as shown in Fig. 898.

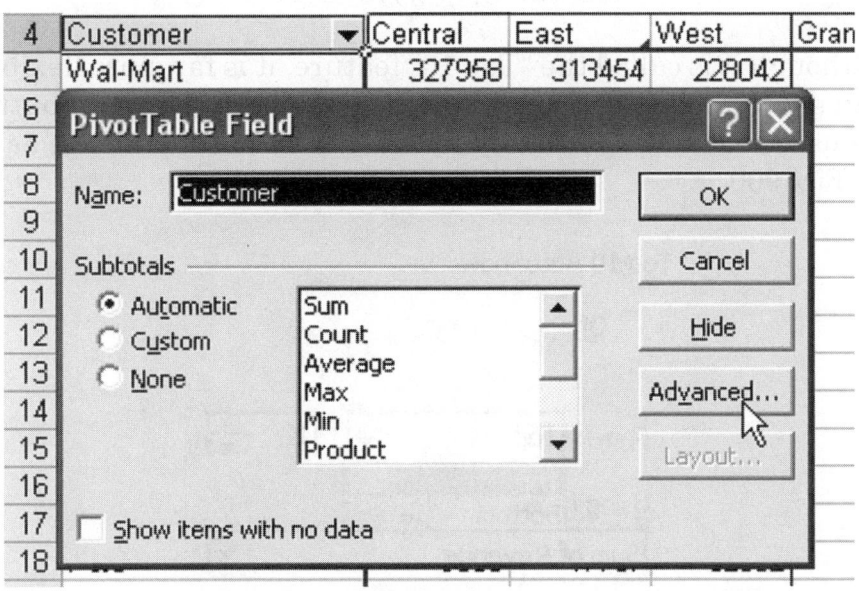

Fig. 898

2) This brings up the PivotTable Field Advanced Options. On the right side of this dialog is the Top 10 AutoShow, as shown in Fig. 899. By default, this feature is turned off for each field. Click to turn this option on.

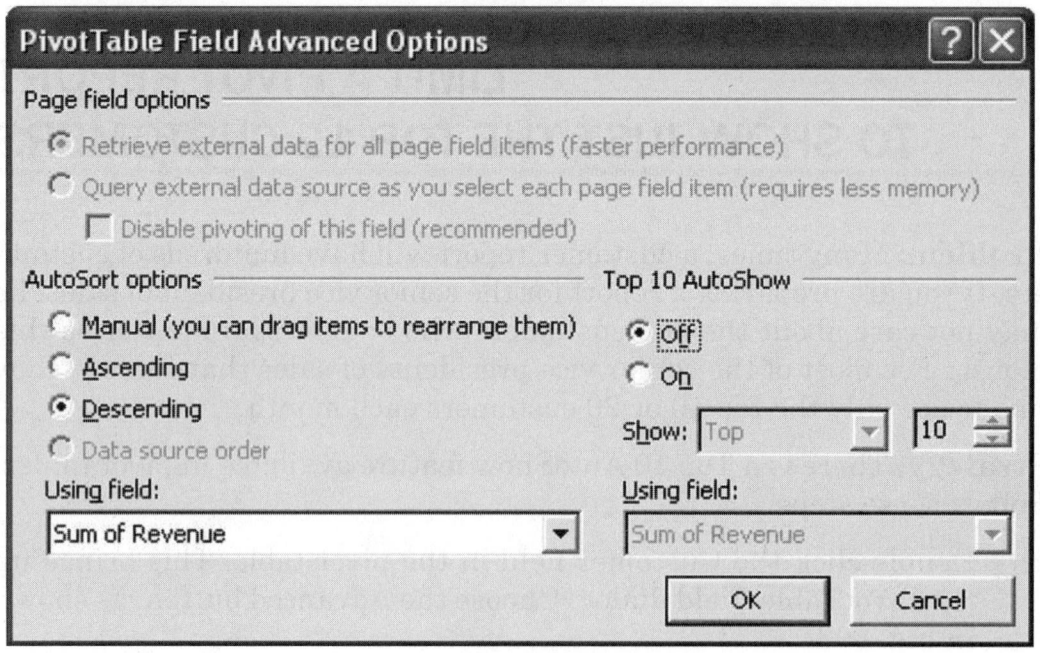

Fig. 899

3) Although it is called the "Top 10" feature, it is far more flexible. You can show either the Top or Bottom customers. The spin button can be used to change 10 to any number. Select Top and 12, as shown in Fig. 900.

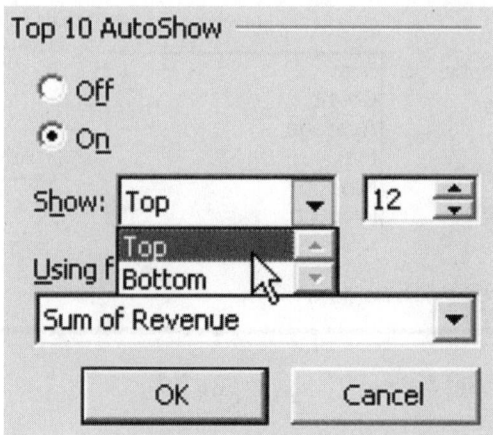

Fig. 900

4)   Choose OK to close the Advance dialog. Choose OK to close the
      Field dialog.

Result: The report will be filtered to show just the top 12 customers, as
shown in Fig. 901.

3	Sum of Revenue	Region ▾			
4	**Customer** ▾	Central	East	West	Grand Total
5	Wal-Mart	327958	313454	228042	869454
6	General Motors	304323	260163	195967	760453
7	Exxon	315631	229640	159088	704359
8	Ford	288393	175967	158434	622794
9	Molson, Inc	209326	245081	159107	613514
10	Ainsworth	223540	232076	113235	568851
11	Sun Life Financial	151310	199982	147645	498937
12	IBM	157637	165770	103942	427349
13	Nortel Networks	109320	203890	77891	391101
14	Verizon	100748	184563	105667	390978
15	SBC Communications	22140	38860	11680	72680
16	Shell Canada	20950	26571	24130	71651
17	Grand Total	2231276	2276017	1484828	5992121

Fig. 901

Additional Information: It is not obvious from this book, but the customer heading is in a blue font to indicate that the customer list has
been filtered.

Gotcha: If there is a tie for twelfth place, the list may contain 13 customers. I have seen situations where the pivot table is limited to one
obscure product that was only purchased by a few customers. This can
create a huge multi-way tie at $0 for twelfth place, resulting in hun-
dreds of customers in the report.

Summary: The AutoShow option allows you to dynamically limit a report to the top five or bottom 12 items in a report.

Commands Discussed: Data – PivotTable – AutoShow

Part
III

QUICKLY PRODUCE REPORTS
FOR EACH REGION

Problem: You need to send a customer report to each regional manager in your company, as shown in Fig. 902. You want each manager to see sales only in his region.

	A	B	C	D	E
1		Drop Page Fields Here			
2					
3	Sum of Revenue	Product ▼			
4	Customer ▼	ABC	DEF	XYZ	Grand Total
5	Air Canada	5859	2358	22804	31021
6	Compton Petroleum	4158	13249	13962	31369
7	Texaco	7136	4270	22958	34364
8	Sears	8940	4282	21488	34710

Fig. 902

Strategy: The Page Field area of the pivot table can enable such a report. Drag the Region field from the PivotTable Field List and drop it above the pivot table, in the area called Drop Page Fields Here, as shown in Fig. 903.

	A	B	C	D	E
1		Drop Page Fields Here			
2					
3	Sum of Revenue	Product ▼			
4	Customer ▼	ABC	DEF	XYZ	Grand

Fig. 903

At first glance, nothing has really changed. All of the numbers in the pivot table are the same, as shown in Fig. 904.

	A	B	C	D	E
1	Region	(All) ▼			
2					
3	Sum of Revenue	Product ▼			
4	Customer ▼	ABC	DEF	XYZ	Grand Total
5	Air Canada	5859	2358	22804	31021
6	Compton Petroleum	4158	13249	13962	31369
7	Texaco	7136	4270	22958	34364
8	Sears	8940	4282	21488	34710
9	Compaq	17250	4380	17620	39250

Fig. 904

However, if you use the dropdown next to Region to select the East region, the report will update to show just the customers from the East region, as shown in Fig. 905. Print this report and send it to the East regional manager.

Part III

	A	B	C	D	E
1	Region	East ▼			
2					
3	Sum of Revenue	Product ▼			
4	Customer ▼	ABC	DEF	XYZ	Grand Total
5	Ainsworth	61660	90978	79438	232076
6	Air Canada	0	2358	0	2358
7	Bell Canada	0	14004	0	14004
8	Chevron	8116	0	0	8116
9	Compaq	0	4380	0	4380

Fig. 905

To produce the report for Central, simply change the Region dropdown from East to Central. Repeat for each region.

Summary: Using Page Fields allows you to quickly filter a report to one choice from a given field.

Commands Discussed: Pivot Table – Page Fields

CREATE AN AD-HOC REPORTING TOOL

Problem: You have an operations manager who is famous for asking many ad-hoc questions. One day, he will want to know who bought XYZ product. The next day, he will want to know all sales to Air Canada.

Strategy: Build a pivot table report with many fields in the Page Field area, as shown in Fig. 906. The manager can use this to answer just about any ad-hoc query that he can dream up.

	A	B
1	Region	(All) ▼
2	Product	(All) ▼
3	Customer	(All) ▼
4	Date	(All) ▼
5		
6	Data ▼	Total
7	Sum of Revenue	6702877
8	Sum of Quantity	313800
9	Sum of COGS	2976322
10	Sum of Profit	3726555
11		

Fig. 906

The operations manager can easily figure out how many ABC products were shipped to the East Region on a given date, as shown in Fig. 907.

Summary: Using many Page Fields allows you to quickly filter a report to answer ad-hoc queries.

Commands Discussed: Pivot Table – Page Fields

	A	B
1	Region	East ▼
2	Product	ABC ▼
3	Customer	(All) ▼
4	Date	2-Jan-04 ▼
5		
6	Data ▼	Total
7	Sum of Revenue	10245
8	Sum of Quantity	500
9	Sum of COGS	4235
10	Sum of Profit	6010
11		

Fig. 907

CREATE A UNIQUE LIST OF CUSTOMERS WITH A PIVOT TABLE

Problem: You need to create a unique list of customers from a large list.

Strategy: Build a Pivot Table report with Customer in the Row area of the layout. Because the Pivot Table creates a summary report, the first column of the table will include the unique list of customers.

From the Data menu, select Pivot Table and Pivot Chart report. Choose Next in Step 1 and Step 2. In Step 3, choose Layout and drag the customer field to the Row area, as shown in Fig. 908.

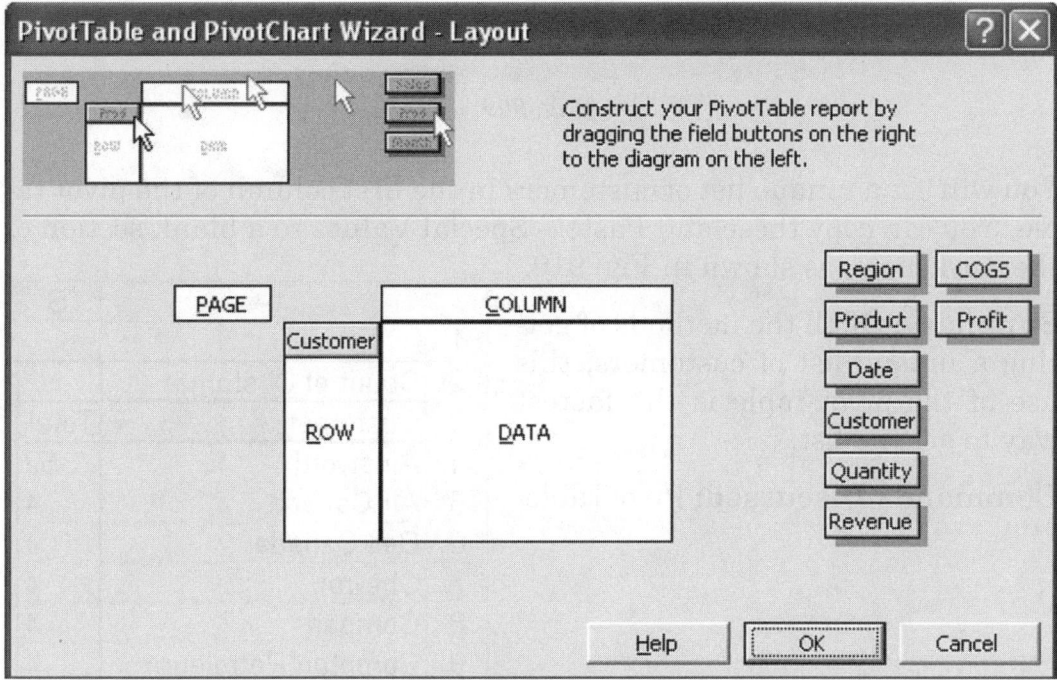

Fig. 908

You don't want a field in the Data area, but Excel will not let you out of the wizard without selecting something for the Data field. From the field list on the right, drag a second copy of the Customer field to the Data area, as shown in Fig. 909. This will give you a count of how many times each customer appears. While you don't need a count, remember you are just making Excel happy so it will give you the list of customers.

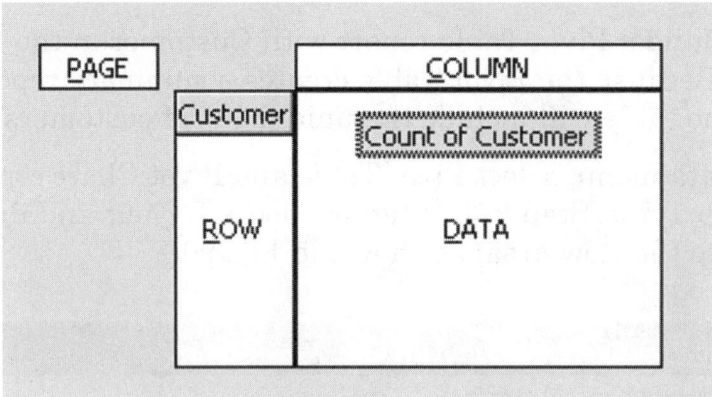

Fig. 909

You will get a unique list of customers in the first column of the pivot table. You can copy these and Paste – Special Values to a blank section of the worksheet, as shown in Fig. 910.

Summary: Of all the methods of getting a unique list of customers, this use of the pivot table is the fastest way to get the list.

Commands Discussed: PivotTable

	A	B
1		
2	Count of Customer	
3	Customer ▼	Total
4	Ainsworth	52
5	Air Canada	4
6	Bell Canada	4
7	Chevron	4
8	Compaq	4
9	Compton Petroleum	4
10	Exxon	66
11	Ford	56
12	General Motors	61
13	Gildan Activewear	4
14	HP	4
15	IBM	44

Fig. 910

CREATE A PIVOT TABLE WITH FEWER CLICKS

Problem: Even though pivot tables are the fastest way to summarize data, you are looking for an even faster way to create pivot tables.

Strategy: This method is only available in Excel 2000 and newer versions. Follow these steps.

1)   Select a single cell in the original data, as shown in Fig. 911.

	A	B	C	D
1	**Region**	**Product**	**Date**	**Customer**
2	East	XYZ	1-Jan-04	Ford
3	Central	DEF	2-Jan-04	Verizon
4	East	ABC	2-Jan-04	Verizon

Fig. 911

Part III

2)   From the menu, select Data – PivotTable. Click Finish, as shown in Fig. 912.

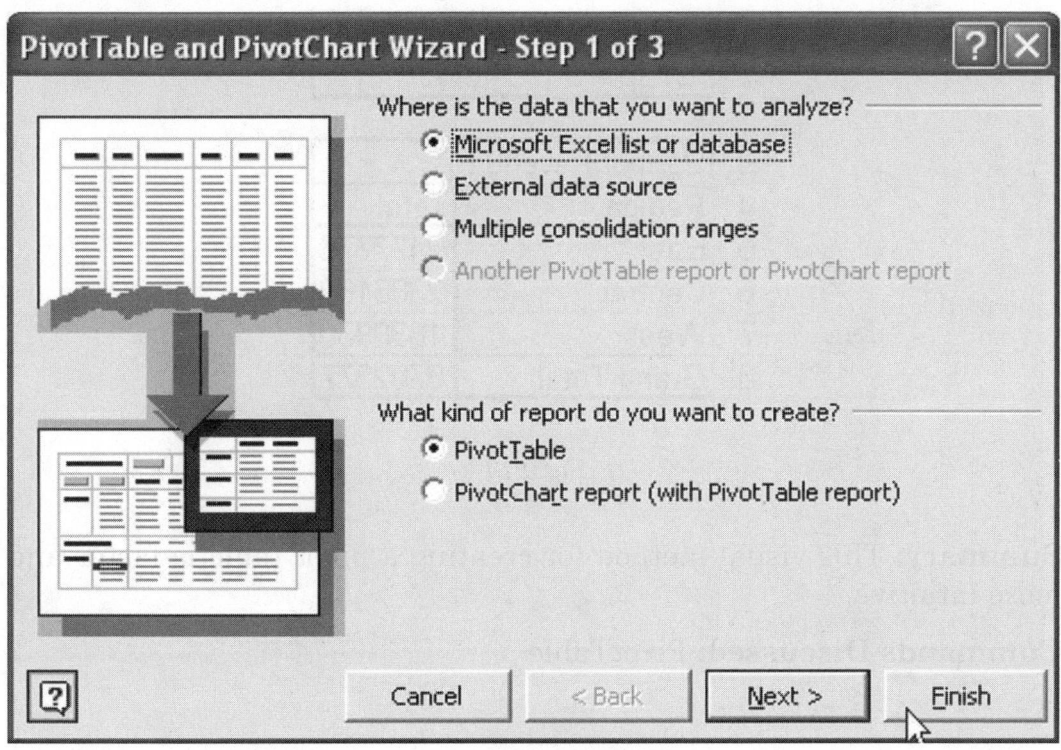

Fig. 912

You are given a blank pivot table on a new sheet, as shown in Fig. 913.

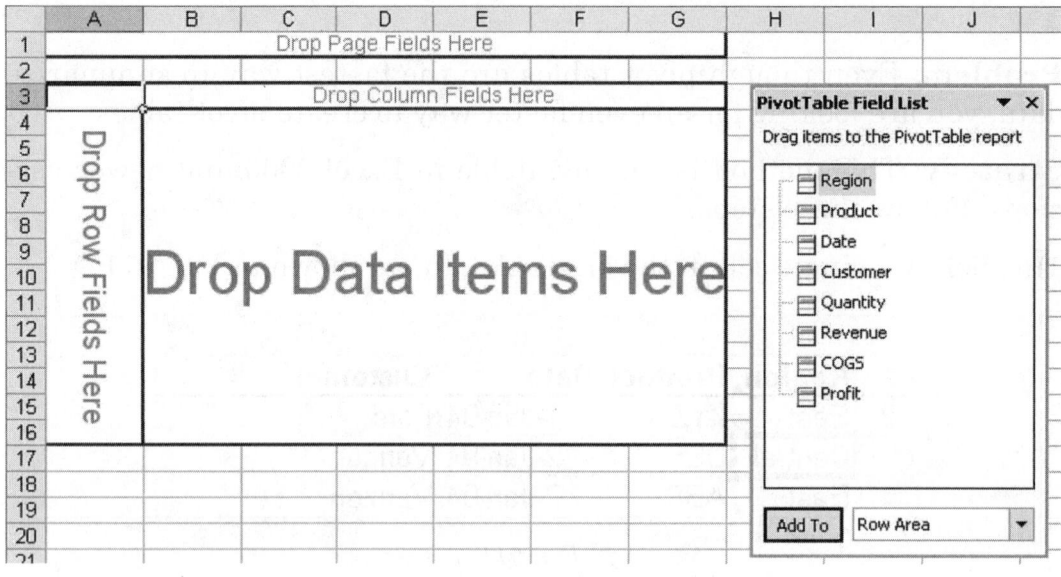

Fig. 913

3)   Drag fields from the field list to the table, as shown in Fig. 914.

	A	B
1	Drop Page Fields Here	
2		
3	Sum of Revenue	
4	Region ▼	Total
5	East	2477778
6	Central	2386169
7	West	1838930
8	Grand Total	6702877
9		

Fig. 914

Summary: This visual method for creating a pivot table is faster and more intuitive.

Commands Discussed: PivotTable

CREATE A REPORT SHOWING COUNT, MIN, MAX, AVERAGE, ETC.

Problem: All of the Pivot Table examples shown thus far are for summing revenue. What if you need to find out the average sale by customer or the smallest sale?

Strategy: Pivot tables offer a variety of calculation options. Double-click the Sum of Revenue button to change the calculation from Sum to any other calculation, as shown in Fig. 915.

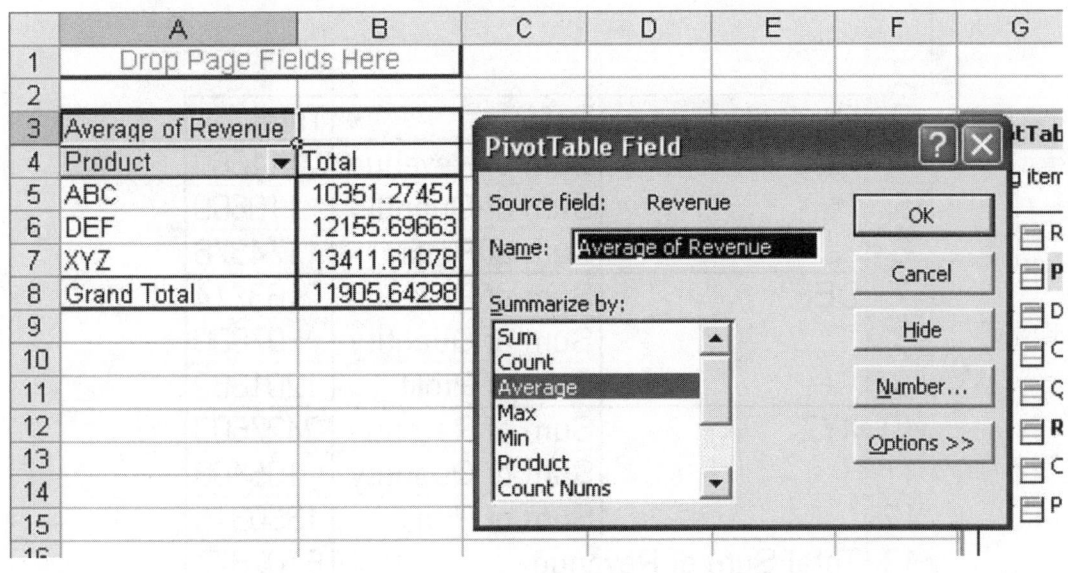

Fig. 915

Additional Information: There is no built-in way to create a median for a pivot table. I've heard this question a few times. If you absolutely need to create a median in a pivot table, contact MrExcel Consulting – we've custom written pivot-table-like reports that do medians.

Summary: Pivot tables can create averages; find the smallest sale, largest sale, and the number of sales. Use the Summarize By field in the PivotTable Field dialog.

Commands Discussed: PivotTable

USE MULTIPLE DATA FIELDS
AS A COLUMN FIELD

Problem: When you create a table with two or more Data fields, Excel will default to having the various Data fields be like the innermost Row field, as shown in Fig. 916. This is not the most useful view of the data. It would be preferable to have the three data columns going across the columns for each product.

	A	B	C
1			
2			
3	Product ▼	Data ▼	Total
4	ABC	Sum of Revenue	2111660
5		Sum of Quantity	110600
6		Sum of Profit	1174878
7	DEF	Sum of Revenue	2163714
8		Sum of Quantity	97800
9		Sum of Profit	1201362
10	XYZ	Sum of Revenue	2427503
11		Sum of Quantity	105400
12		Sum of Profit	1350315
13	Total Sum of Revenue		6702877
14	Total Sum of Quantity		313800
15	Total Sum of Profit		3726555
16			

Fig. 916

Strategy: When you have more than one field in the Data area, you will find that a new button appears on the pivot table that is called Data, as shown in Fig. 917. You can drag the Data button from the Row field to the Column field.

	A	B	C	D
1				
2				
3		Data ▼		
4	Product ▼	Sum of Revenue	Sum of Quantity	Sum of Profit
5	ABC	2111660	110600	1174878
6	DEF	2163714	97800	1201362
7	XYZ	2427503	105400	1350315
8	Grand Total	6702877	313800	3726555
9				

Fig. 917

Summary: Although the default view of the pivot report for multiple Data fields is unusual, you can easily correct it by moving the Data field to the Column area.

Commands Discussed: Data – PivotTable

Part III

COMPARE FOUR WAYS TO SHOW TWO DATA FIELDS IN A PIVOT TABLE

Problem: When you create a pivot table with two fields and two Data fields, Excel uses this very ugly default view of the data, as shown in Fig. 918.

	A	B	C	D	E	F
1			Drop Page Fields Here			
2						
3			Region ▼	①		
4	Product ▼	Data ▼	East	Central	West	Grand Total
5	ABC	Sum of Revenue	703255	776759	631646	2111660
6		Sum of Quantity	36500	40800	33300	110600
7		Sum of Profit	394100	431183	349595	1174878
8	DEF	Sum of Revenue	891799	776996	494919	2163714
9		Sum of Quantity	40300	34900	22600	97800
10		Sum of Profit	495247	433580	272535	1201362
11	XYZ	Sum of Revenue	882724	832414	712365	2427503
12		Sum of Quantity	38900	36200	30300	105400
13		Sum of Profit	485166	462450	402699	1350315
14	Total Sum of Revenue		2477778	2386169	1838930	6702877
15	Total Sum of Quantity		115700	111900	86200	313800
16	Total Sum of Profit		1374513	1327213	1024829	3726555
17						

Fig. 918

Strategy: There is really no good strategy to deal with this problem. Excel offers four ways to view this report and none of them is entirely acceptable.

As shown in Fig. 919, in the second view, the Data field is dragged to be the first Column field. I don't like the fact that they show revenue in columns B through D, but then you have to scroll all the way over to column K for the total revenue.

> **Note:** *The numbers below are reformatted to make the columns narrower so the entire report can fit in this page.*

	A	B	C	D	E	F	G	H	I	J	K	L	M
1													
2													
3		Data ▾	Regi ▾										
4		Sum of Revenue			Sum of Quantity			Sum of Profit			Total Sum of Revenue	Total S	Total Sur
5	Product ▾	East	Central	West	East	Central	West	East	Central	West			
6	ABC	703K	777K	632K	37K	41K	33K	394K	431K	350K	2,112K	111K	1,175K
7	DEF	892K	777K	495K	40K	35K	23K	495K	434K	273K	2,164K	98K	1,201K
8	XYZ	883K	832K	712K	39K	36K	30K	485K	462K	403K	2,428K	105K	1,350K
9	Grand Total	2,478K	2,386K	1,839K	116K	112K	86K	1,375K	1,327K	1,025K	6,703K	314K	3,727K

Fig. 919

In the third view, the Data field is dragged to be the second Column field, as shown in Fig. 920. This view keeps all of East together, then all of Central, then all of West.

	A	B	C	D	E	F	G	H	I	J	K	L	M
1													
2													
3		Region ▾	Data ▾										
4		East			Central			West			Total Sum of Revenue	Sum of Quantity	Sum of Profit
5	Product ▾	Sum of Revenue	Sum of Quantity	Sum of Profit	of Revenue	n of Quantity	m of Profit	of Revenue	m of Quantity	n of Profit			
6	ABC	703K	37K	394K	777K	41K	431K	632K	33K	350K	2,112K	111K	1,175K
7	DEF	892K	40K	495K	777K	35K	434K	495K	23K	273K	2,164K	98K	1,201K
8	XYZ	883K	39K	485K	832K	36K	462K	712K	30K	403K	2,428K	105K	1,350K
9	Grand Total	2,478K	116K	1,375K	2,386K	112K	1,327K	1,839K	86K	1,025K	6,703K	314K	3,727K

Fig. 920

For the final view, drag the Data field to be the outermost Row field, as shown in Fig. 921. This view is pretty good, although it would be preferable to have the total Sum of Revenue appear after row 7 instead of all the way at the end.

	A	B	C	D	E	F
1						
2						
3			Region ▼			
4	Data ▼	Product ▼	East	Central	West	Grand Total
5	Sum of Reve	ABC	703K	777K	632K	2,112K
6		DEF	892K	777K	495K	2,164K
7		XYZ	883K	832K	712K	2,428K
8	Sum of Quar	ABC	37K	41K	33K	111K
9		DEF	40K	35K	23K	98K
10		XYZ	39K	36K	30K	105K
11	Sum of Profi	ABC	394K	431K	350K	1,175K
12		DEF	495K	434K	273K	1,201K
13		XYZ	485K	462K	403K	1,350K
14	Total Sum of Revenue		2,478K	2,386K	1,839K	6,703K
15	Total Sum of Quantity		116K	112K	86K	314K
16	Total Sum of Profit		1,375K	1,327K	1,025K	3,727K

Fig. 921

Part
III

Summary: When you have two fields and two data types in a pivot table, there are four possible options for displaying the data. None of the options is perfect. It might be easier to create the report without totals and add them yourself after changing to values.

Commands Discussed: Data – PivotTable

GROUP DAILY DATES UP BY MONTH IN A PIVOT TABLE

Problem: Your dataset has a date on which each item was shipped. When you produce a pivot table with that field, it provides sales by day, as shown in Fig. 922. The plant manager loves sales by day, but everyone else in the company would rather see sales by month.

	A	B	C	D	E
1	Drop Page Fields Here				
2					
3	Sum of Revenue	Product ▼			
4	Date ▼	ABC	DEF	XYZ	Grand Total
5	1-Jan-04	0	0	22,810	22,810
6	2-Jan-04	10,245	2,257	0	12,502
7	3-Jan-04	0	0	11,240	11,240
8	4-Jan-04	0	18,552	18,356	36,908
9	5-Jan-04	6,860	0	0	6,860
10	7-Jan-04	8,456	21,730	13,806	43,992
11	9-Jan-04	16,416	0	21,015	37,431
12	10-Jan-04	0	0	42,903	42,903
13	12-Jan-04	6,267	0	9,144	15,411

Fig. 922

Strategy: You can group daily dates to show year, quarter, and month. Build a pivot table with dates in the Row area of the pivot table.

1) Right-click the Date heading. From the popup menu, choose Group and Show Detail and then Group, as shown in Fig. 923.

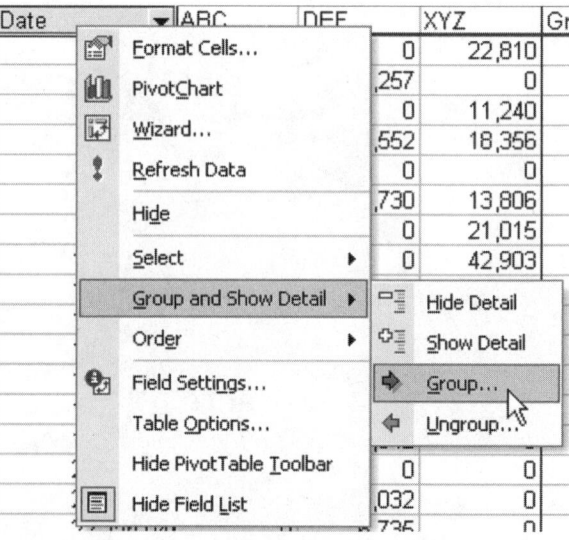

Fig. 923

2)   The Grouping dialog defaults to select Months. If your data spans more than one year, it is crucial that you also select years. For this example, select Months, Quarters, and Years, as shown in Fig. 924.

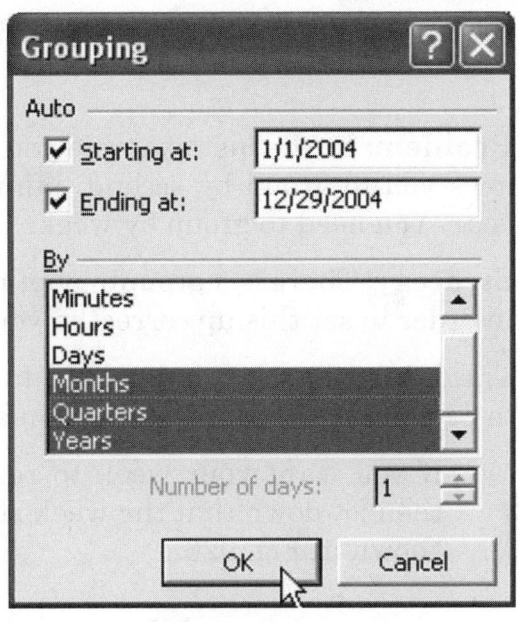

Result: The Date field is now replaced with Months. There are two new fields in the PivotTable Field List – one for Quarters and one for Years, as shown in Fig. 925.

Fig. 924

	A	B	C	D	E	F	G	H	I	J
1				Drop Page Fields Here						
2										
3	Sum of Revenue			Product ▼						
4	Years ▼	Quarters ▼	Date ▼	ABC	DEF	XYZ	Grand Total			
5	2004	Qtr1	Jan	262,726	94,413	173,607	530,746			
6			Feb	171,194	174,365	220,483	566,042			
7			Mar	119,131	185,336	181,890	486,357			
8		Qtr2	Apr	182,134	157,101	229,408	568,643			
9			May	194,643	212,803	212,073	619,519			
10			Jun	145,088	143,024	119,340	407,452			
11		Qtr3	Jul	154,812	264,976	261,830	681,618			
12			Aug	184,452	136,723	277,461	598,636			
13			Sep	189,193	207,730	76,593	473,516			
14		Qtr4	Oct	196,345	173,816	243,071	613,232			
15			Nov	106,523	259,841	167,388	533,752			
16			Dec	205,419	153,586	264,359	623,364			
17	Grand Total			2,111,660	2,163,714	2,427,503	6,702,877			
18										
19										
20										

PivotTable Field List ▼ ×

Drag items to the PivotTable report

- Region
- **Product**
- **Date**
- Customer
- Quantity
- **Revenue**
- COGS
- Profit
- **Quarters**
- **Years**

Add To   Row Area ▼

Fig. 925

Gotcha: If you fail to include Years in the grouping, data from both Jan 2004 and Jan 2005 will be reported as "Jan". Unless you are doing a seasonality analysis, this is rarely what you need.

Summary: The Group feature is excellent for turning a daily report into a monthly or quarterly report.

Commands Discussed: PivotTable – Group and Show Detail – Group

GROUP BY WEEK IN A PIVOT TABLE

Problem: In the last example you noticed that the Grouping dialog allows you to group by second, minute, hour, day, month, quarter, and year. You need to group by week.

Strategy: There is a grouping option that will group by week. However, in order to set this up correctly, you will have to grab a calendar.

The dataset has data going back to January 1, 2004. Look on a calendar to determine that this date fell on a Thursday.

1)   If you want your week to report from Monday through Sunday, then jot down that the week should start on December 29, 2003, as shown in Fig. 926.

Fig. 926

2)   Create a pivot table with dates in the Row area. Right-click the date, choose Group and Show Detail and then Group.

3)   In the Grouping dialog, Excel defaults to showing the entire range of dates of the dataset. If you left the Starting at: field unchanged, as shown in Fig. 927, your weeks would all start on Thursday. As shown in Fig. 928, change the 1/1/2004 date to 12/29/2003 to have your weeks start on Monday.

Fig. 927

4)   Unselect the Months selection by choosing it with the mouse. Select
      the Days choice. This will ungray the Number of Days: field at the
      bottom of the dialog. Use the spin button to move up to 7 days. See
      Fig. 928.

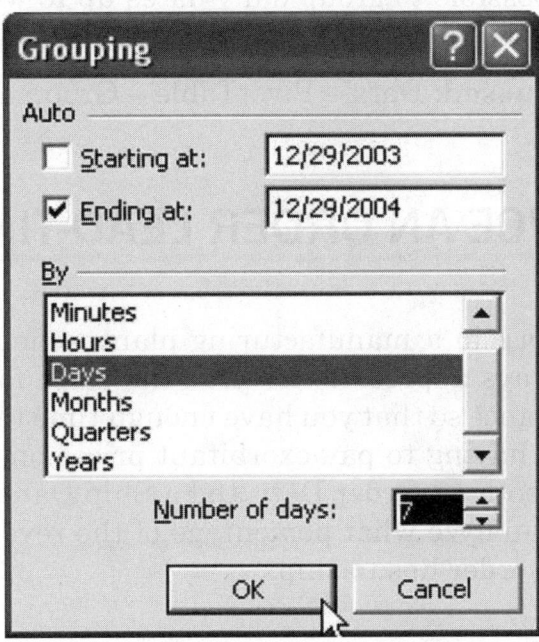

Fig. 928

**Part
III**

Result: The report is redrawn as a weekly report, as shown in Fig. 929.

	A	B	C	D	E
1	Drop Page Fields Here				
2					
3	Sum of Revenue	Region ▼			
4	Date ▼	East	Central	West	Grand Total
5	12/29/2003 - 1/4/2004	60,759	22,701	0	83,460
6	1/5/2004 - 1/11/2004	72,666	44,714	13,806	131,186
7	1/12/2004 - 1/18/2004	29,335	29,895	28,254	87,484
8	1/19/2004 - 1/25/2004	41,450	38,275	40,160	119,885
9	1/26/2004 - 2/1/2004	86,404	20,489	24,782	131,675
10	2/2/2004 - 2/8/2004	27,753	19,411	37,050	84,214

Fig. 929

Additional Details: Excel does not add a "Week" field to the PivotTable Field List. Instead, the field formerly containing dates now contains weeks, but is still called Date.

Gotcha: Once you group by weeks, you can no longer group by month, quarter, year, or any other selection.

Summary: It is possible to group daily dates up to weeks by using the Number of Days field in the Grouping dialog.

Commands Discussed: Data – PivotTable – Group and Show Detail

PRODUCE AN ORDER LEAD-TIME REPORT

Problem: You work in a manufacturing plant, scheduling orders and material. You always appreciate it when the sales force gets orders a few months in advance so that you have enough time to get material into the plant without having to pay exorbitant prices on the gray market. Your dataset has both an Order Date and a Ship Date, as shown in Fig. 930. You want to analyze what percentage of the revenue comes in two months before the order has to ship.

	A	B	C	D	E
1	**Region**	**Product**	**OrdDate**	**ShipDate**	**Customer**
2	East	XYZ	12-Nov-03	1-Jan-04	Ford
3	Central	DEF	6-Nov-03	2-Jan-04	Verizon
4	East	ABC	27-Oct-03	2-Jan-04	Verizon
5	Central	XYZ	2-Nov-03	3-Jan-04	Ainsworth
6	Central	XYZ	30-Sep-03	4-Jan-04	Ainsworth
7	East	DEF	20-Oct-03	4-Jan-04	Gildan Activewear

Fig. 930

Strategy: You would like to build a pivot table report with OrdDate in the Column area, ShipDate in the Row area, and Revenue in the Data area. However, both of the date fields have more than 255 points, so you cannot initially produce a report with dates going across the columns.

1) Initially, drag the OrdDate field to the Row area, as shown in Fig. 931.

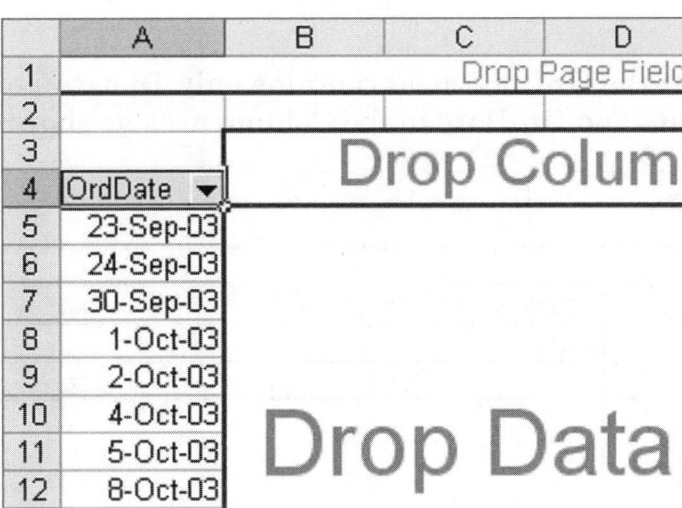

Fig. 931

2) Right-click OrdDate. Choose Group and Show Detail – Group. Choose to Group by Months and Years, as shown in Fig. 932.

Fig. 932

3) Now that the OrdDate field contains only 16 data points, you can drag Years and OrdDate to the Column area as shown in Fig. 933.

	A	B	C	D	E	F
1						
2						
3		Years ▼	OrdDate ▼			
4		2003				2004
5		Sep	Oct	Nov	Dec	Jan
6						
7						
8						
9						
10						

Fig. 933

4) Next, drag the ShipDate field to the Row area, as shown in Fig. 934.

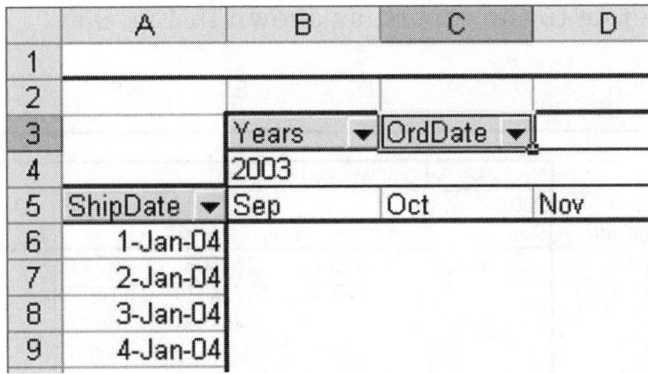

Fig. 934

5)   Right-click ShipDate. Choose Group and Show Detail and then Group. Group by Months and Years, as shown in Fig. 935.

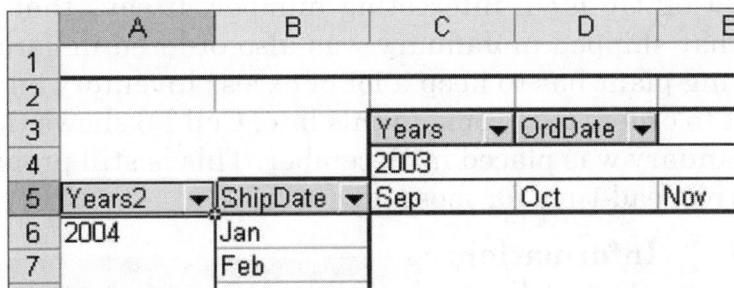

Fig. 935

It is interesting that the OrdDate fields get a name of "Years". When you group the Ship-Date field, the second field is called "Years2", as shown in Fig. 936. There is really nothing in the PivotTable Field List to help you remember which Year goes with which date.

It might help to write a note in the worksheet to help you remember that you grouped ShipDate second and that the Years2 field is associated with ShipDate instead of Ord-Date.

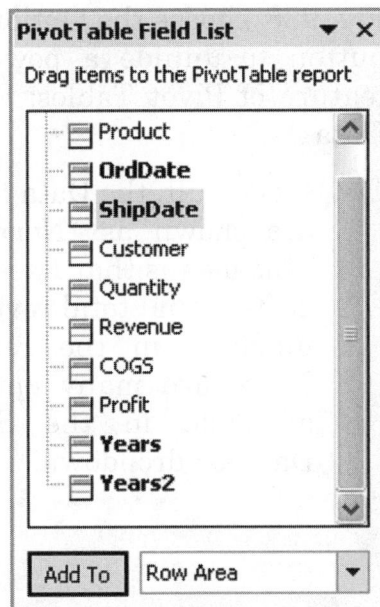

Fig. 936

6)   Drag Revenue to the report, as shown in Fig. 937.

	A	B	C	D	E	F	G	H
1								
2								
3	Sum of Reve		Years ▼	OrdDate ▼				
4			2003				2004	
5	Years2 ▼	ShipDate ▼	Sep	Oct	Nov	Dec	Jan	Feb
6	2004	Jan	32832	191608	153506	92432	60368	
7		Feb		19964	175461	114523	186286	69808
8		Mar			45143	88699	139027	94511
9		Apr				48770	128287	154154
10		May					86405	142692
11		Jun						30467

Fig. 937

In Fig. 937, Cell G6 is an interesting number. It says that $60,368 of the orders that shipped in January was also ordered in January. Your manufacturing plant has to keep a lot of excess inventory on hand to be able to react to orders that come in this late. Cell F6 shows that $92K of orders for January was placed in December. This is still probably inside the cumulative lead-time for most products.

Additional Information: Double-click the Sum of Revenue button to display the Pivot-Table Field dialog. As shown in Fig. 938, choose the Options>> button to unhide a powerful feature of Pivot Tables: Show Data As.

1)   By default, the Data fields are shown as "Normal". This means that Excel reports actual total revenue numbers in the report. There are many options available in the Show Data as: dropdown.

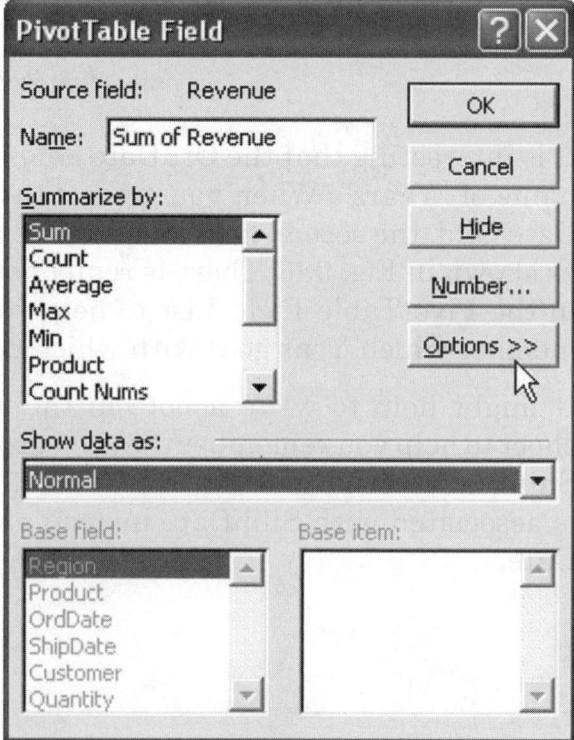

Fig. 938

2)   In this case, choose Percentage (%) of Row, as shown in Fig. 939.

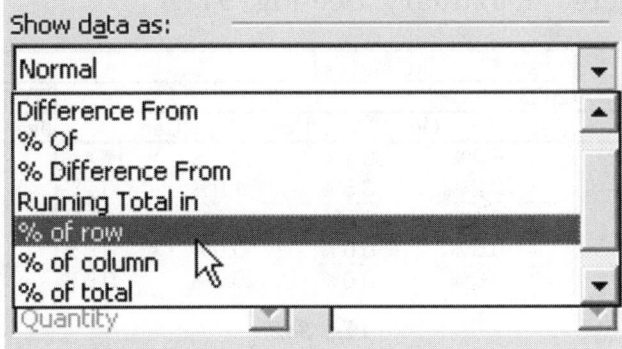

Fig. 939

3)   Before closing the PivotTable Field dialog, choose the button for Number..., as shown in Fig. 940.

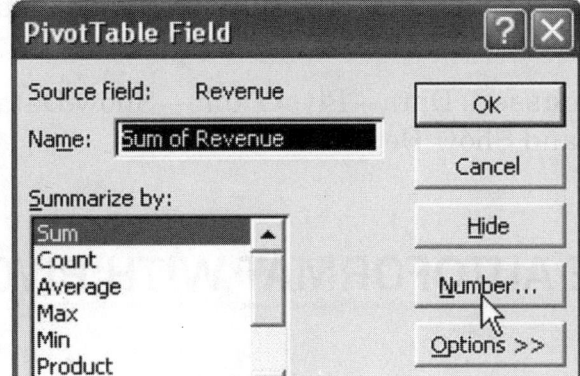

Fig. 940

4)   Choose Percentage with one decimal place, as shown in Fig. 941. Choose OK to close the Format Cells dialog, then OK to close the PivotTable Field dialog.

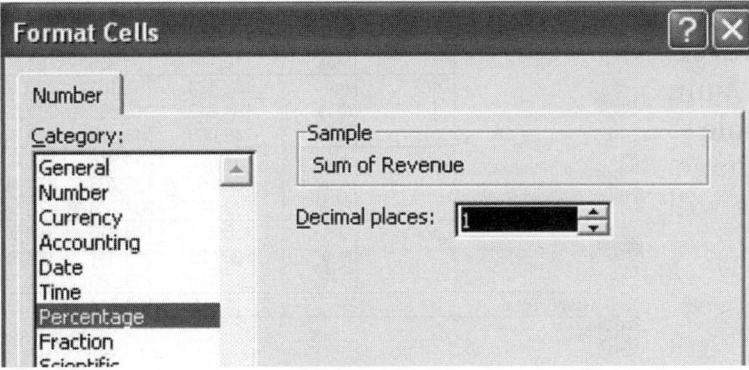

Fig. 941

Result: The pivot table shows that 11.4 percent of January 2004 shipments were ordered in January. See Fig. 942.

Sum of Reve		Years ▼	OrdDate ▼					
		2003					2004	
Years2 ▼	ShipDate ▼	Sep	Oct	Nov	Dec		Jan	Feb
2004	Jan	6.2%	36.1%	28.9%	17.4%		11.4%	0.0%
	Feb	0.0%	3.5%	31.0%	20.2%		32.9%	12.3%
	Mar	0.0%	0.0%	9.3%	18.2%		28.6%	19.4%
	Apr	0.0%	0.0%	0.0%	8.6%		22.6%	27.1%
	May	0.0%	0.0%	0.0%	0.0%		13.9%	23.0%

Fig. 942

Summary: This report required several techniques. Two different Date fields were grouped by month and year. You also had to double-click the Sum of Revenue field to set the number format and to change the reporting from Normal to Percentage of Row. This type of report will be very useful to all schedulers in manufacturing plants.

Commands Discussed: Data – PivotTable – Show Data As; Data – PivotTable – Group and Show Detail

USE AUTOFORMAT WITH PIVOT TABLES

Problem: Due to the dynamic nature of pivot tables, it is fairly hard to format them. As shown in Fig. 943, you might want to format the headings in D4:F4 with a particular format because they are column headings. However, when you spin the pivot table to another shape, the formats will be lost.

	A	B	C	D	E	F	G
1							
2							
3	Sum of Revenue			Product ▼			
4	Years ▼	Quarters ▼	Date ▼	**ABC**	**DEF**	**XYZ**	Grand Total
5	2004	Qtr1	Jan	262,726	94,413	173,607	530,746
6			Feb	171,194	174,365	220,483	566,042
7			Mar	119,131	185,336	181,890	486,357
8		Qtr2	Apr	182,134	157,101	229,408	568,643
9			May	194,643	212,803	212,073	619,519
10			Jun	145,088	143,024	119,340	407,452
11		Qtr3	Jul	154,812	264,976	261,830	681,618
12			Aug	184,452	136,723	277,461	598,636
13			Sep	189,193	207,730	76,593	473,516
14		Qtr4	Oct	196,345	173,816	243,071	613,232
15			Nov	106,523	259,841	167,388	533,752
16			Dec	205,419	153,586	264,359	623,364
17	Grand Total			2,111,660	2,163,714	2,427,503	6,702,877
18							
19							

Fig. 943

Strategy: Use one of the 22 built-in AutoFormats for pivot tables. Even if you don't normally use AutoFormat in regular Excel, you should consider it in pivot tables.

1)   Use the Format Report button on the PivotTable toolbar, as shown in Fig. 944.

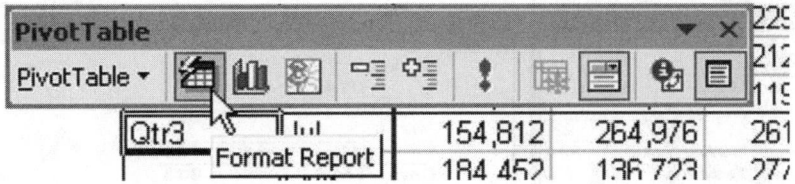

Fig. 944

The AutoFormat dialog box initially shows six different report layouts. The examples show the formatting on a report with four fields in the Column area. As shown in Fig. 945, in Report 1, they are showing you that the innermost level (Zone) would have a normal black font on white. The next level (Area) would have a black font on a gray background. The outermost level (Qtr) would have a bold font.

Part III

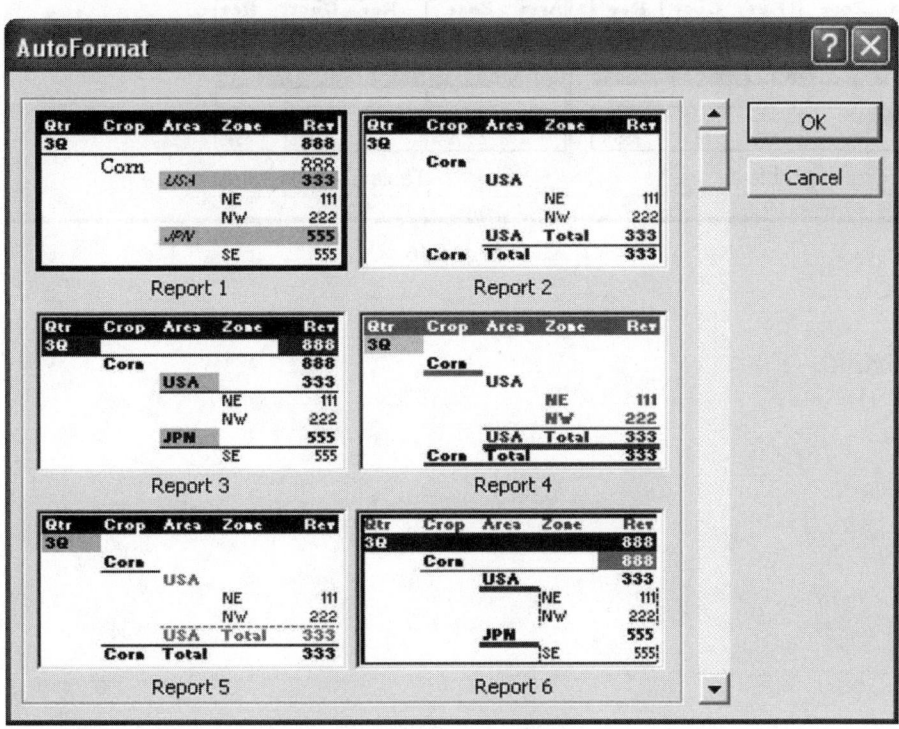

Fig. 945

2)   As shown in Fig. 946, use the scroll bar to see the formats for Report 7 through Report 10 and Tables 1 through Table 2.

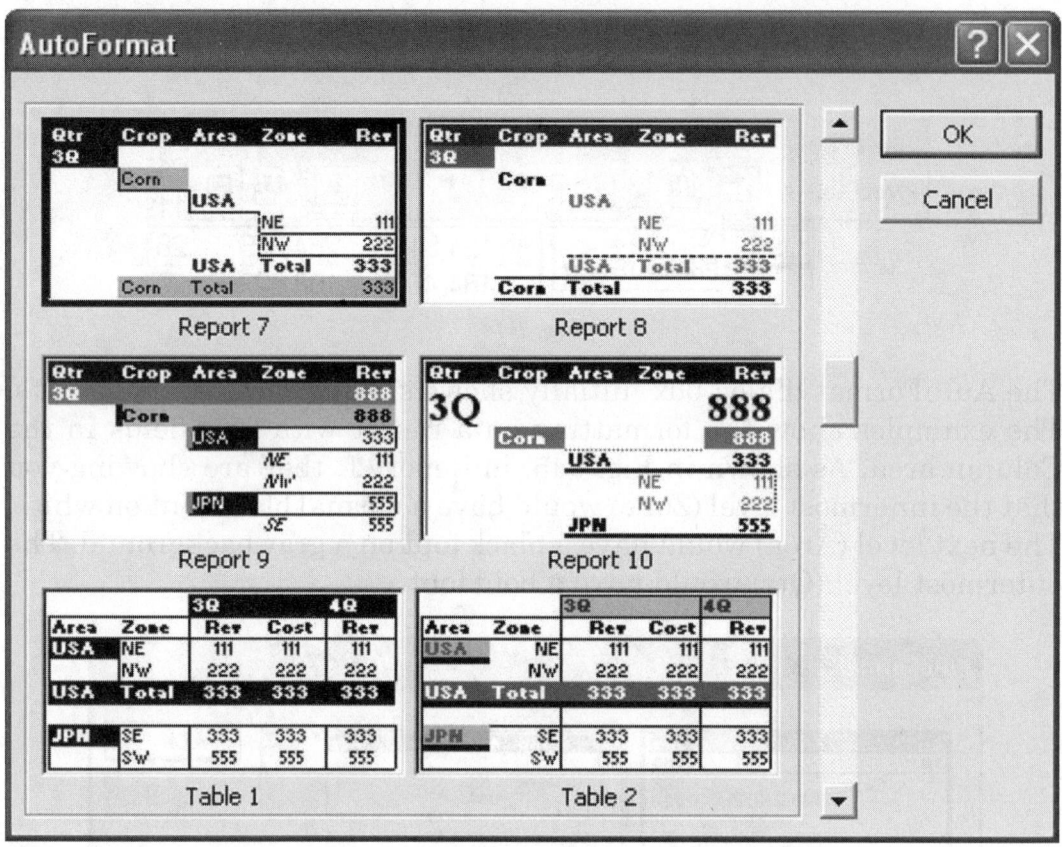

Fig. 946

Fig. 947 shows Table 3 through Table 8.

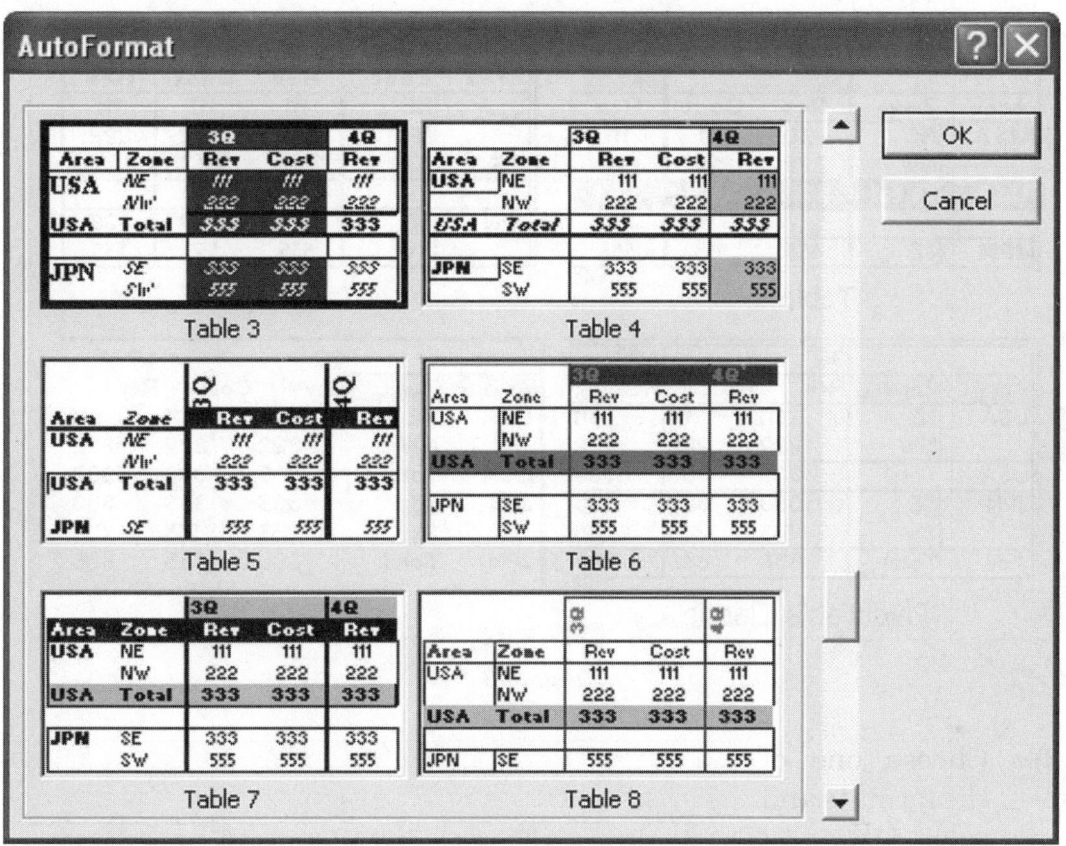

Fig. 947

The last few options are Table 9, Table 10, PivotTable Classic, and None, as shown in Fig. 948.

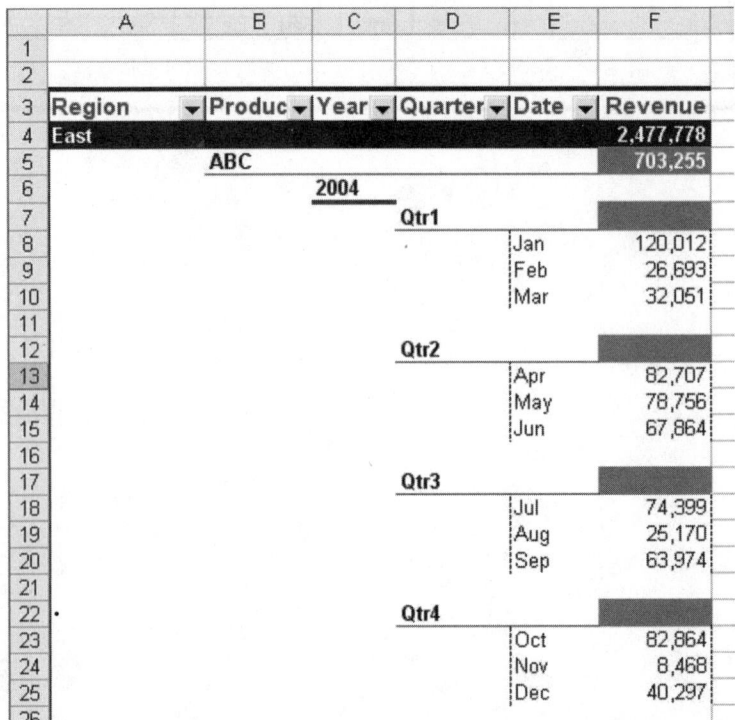

Table 9

Area	Zone	3Q Rev	Cost	4Q Rev
USA	NE	111	111	111
	NW	222	222	222
USA	Total	333	333	333
JPN	SE	555	555	555

Table 10

Area	Zone	3Q Rev	Cost	4Q Rev
USA	NE	111	111	111
	NW	222	222	222
USA	Total	333	333	333
JPN	SE	333	333	333
	SW	555	555	555

PivotTable Classic

Area	Zone	3Q Rev	Cost	4Q Rev
USA	NE	111	111	111
	NW	222	222	222
USA	Total	333	333	333
JPN	SE	333	333	333
	SW	555	555	555
JPN	Total	888	888	888

None

Area	Zone	3Q Rev	Cost	4Q Rev
USA	NE	111	111	111
	NW	222	222	222
USA	Total	333	333	333
JPN	SE	333	333	333
	SW	555	555	555
JPN	Total	888	888	888

Fig. 948

3) Choose one of the formats and select OK.

Result: You can quickly apply a new look to the data. Fig. 949 shows Report 6.

	A	B	C	D	E	F
3	Region	Produc	Year	Quarter	Date	Revenue
4	East					2,477,778
5		ABC				703,255
6			2004			
7				Qtr1		
8					Jan	120,012
9					Feb	26,693
10					Mar	32,051
12				Qtr2		
13					Apr	82,707
14					May	78,756
15					Jun	67,864
17				Qtr3		
18					Jul	74,399
19					Aug	25,170
20					Sep	63,974
22				Qtr4		
23					Oct	82,864
24					Nov	8,468
25					Dec	40,297

Fig. 949

If you don't like one look, choose the Format Report icon again and select a different look. Fig. 950 shows Table 7.

	Revenue				Region ▼			
	Product ▼	Years ▼	Quar ▼	Date ▼	East	Central	West	Grand Total
5	ABC	2004	Qtr1	Jan	120,012	80,003	62,711	262,726
6				Feb	26,693	77,108	67,393	171,194
7				Mar	32,051	47,033	40,047	119,131
8			Qtr2	Apr	82,707	48,376	51,051	182,134
9				May	78,756	52,761	63,126	194,643
10				Jun	67,864	36,902	40,322	145,088
11			Qtr3	Jul	74,399	23,391	57,022	154,812
12				Aug	25,170	79,862	79,420	184,452
13				Sep	63,974	79,144	46,075	189,193
14			Qtr4	Oct	82,864	87,351	26,130	196,345
15				Nov	8,468	46,953	51,102	106,523
16				Dec	40,297	117,875	47,247	205,419
17	ABC Total				703,255	776,759	631,646	2,111,660

Fig. 950

Even with these formats, you can still pivot the report as usual. Here, as shown in Fig. 951, the Product field moves up to the Column area, Region is removed, and Customer is added to the Row area.

	A	B	C	D	E	F	G	H
1				Drop Page Fields Here				
2								
3	Revenue				Product ▼			
4	Customer ▼	Years ▼	Quar ▼	Date ▼	ABC	DEF	XYZ	Grand Total
5	Ainsworth	2004	Qtr1	Jan	10,445	0	51,053	61,498
6				Feb	0	44,492	20,940	65,432
7				Mar	7,132	34,960	13,404	55,496
8			Qtr2	Apr	29,616	8,776	0	38,392
9				May	25,682	0	29,303	54,985
10				Jun	42,112	0	0	42,112
11			Qtr3	Jul	0	21,555	34,944	56,499
12				Aug	15,544	0	11,064	26,608
13				Sep	19,453	9,672	22,014	51,139
14			Qtr4	Oct	13,397	18,663	0	32,060
15				Nov	12,140	24,356	18,214	54,710
16				Dec	1,861	28,059	0	29,920
17	Ainsworth Total				177,382	190,533	200,936	568,851
18								
19	Air Canada	2004	Qtr1	Mar	5,859	0	0	5,859
20			Qtr2	Apr	0	0	4,948	4,948
21			Qtr3	Aug	0	0	17,856	17,856
22			Qtr4	Oct	0	2,358	0	2,358
23	Air Canada Total				5,859	2,358	22,804	31,021

Fig. 951

Summary: For years, I used pivot tables because of their ability to quickly produce summary reports. In recent versions of Excel, Microsoft has improved the pivot table by offering great looking ways to format the summary reports.

Commands Discussed: PivotTable – Format Report

SPECIFY A NUMBER FORMAT FOR A PIVOTTABLE FIELD

Problem: In a pivot table, a Data field will tend to inherit the numeric formatting assigned to the data in the original dataset. This may not always be correct. At a detail level, it might be appropriate to see invoice amounts in dollars and cents, as shown in Fig. 952. However, at a summary level, you might prefer to show numbers in thousands.

	A	B
1		
2		
3	Sum of Revenue	
4	Product ▼	Total
5	ABC	2111660.00
6	DEF	2163714.00
7	XYZ	2427503.00
8	Grand Total	6702877.00

Fig. 952

Strategy:

1) Assign a numeric format to the pivot field. Double-click the Sum of Revenue button to display the PivotTable Field dialog.

2) Choose the Number... button, as shown in Fig. 953. Choosing the Number... button will bring up an abbreviated version of the Format Cells dialog with only the Number tab.

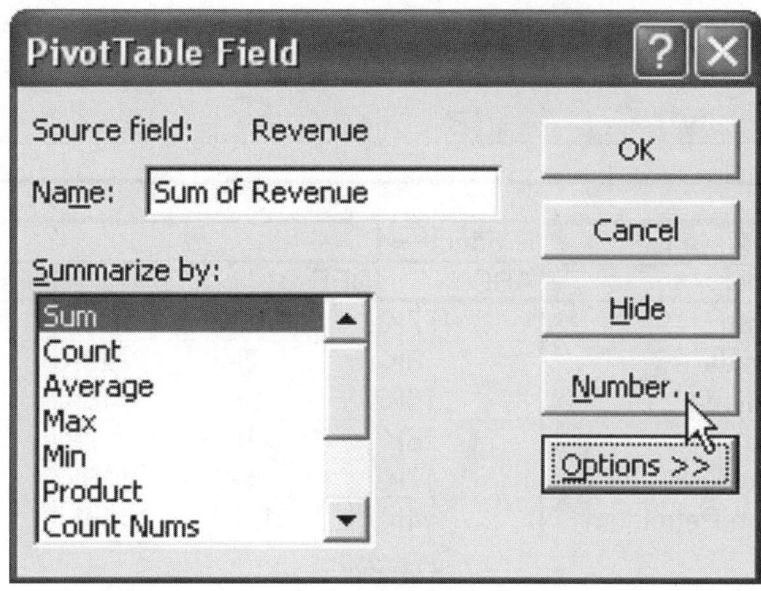

Fig. 953

3)   Choose an appropriate numeric format and select OK, as shown in
Fig. 954.

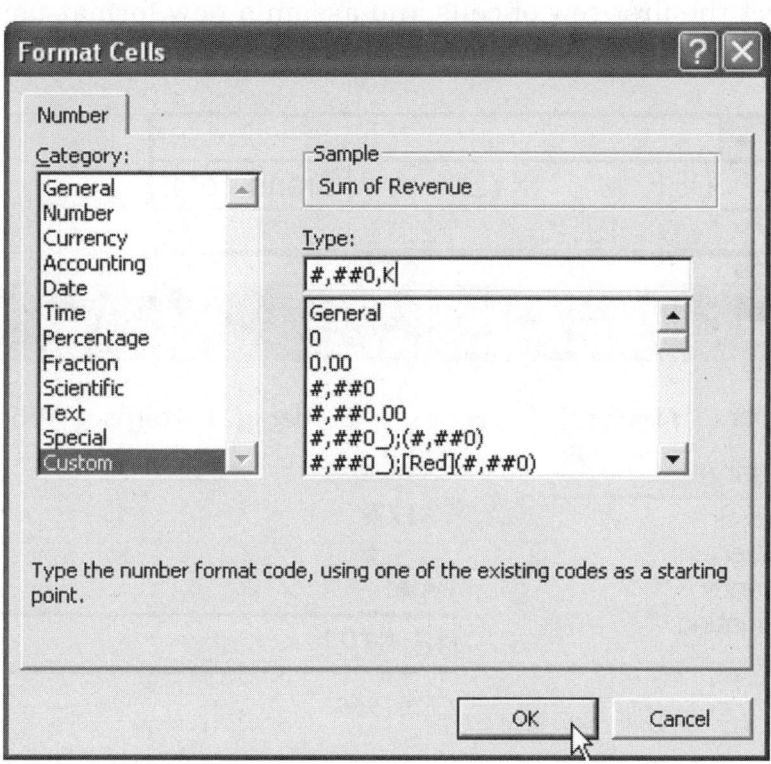

Fig. 954

Result: As shown in Fig. 955, the Revenue field will now always show the selected format, no matter how the pivot table is changed.

	A	B	C	D	E
1	Drop Page Fields Here				
2					
3	Sum of Revenue	Product ▼			
4	Customer ▼	ABC	DEF	XYZ	Grand Total
5	Ainsworth	177K	191K	201K	569K
6	Air Canada	6K	2K	23K	31K
7	Bell Canada	15K	18K	18K	51K
8	Chevron	26K	21K	7K	54K
9	Compaq	17K	4K	18K	39K
10	Compton Petroleum	4K	13K	14K	31K

Fig. 955

Gotcha: One of the conventions in formatting says that you should include a currency symbol on only the first and total rows of a dataset. There is not a good way to do this with a pivot table. Use the numeric formatting attached to the Product button to assign a currency format. Then, select the first row of cells and assign a new format using Ctrl+1 to display the Format Cells dialog, as shown in Fig. 956.

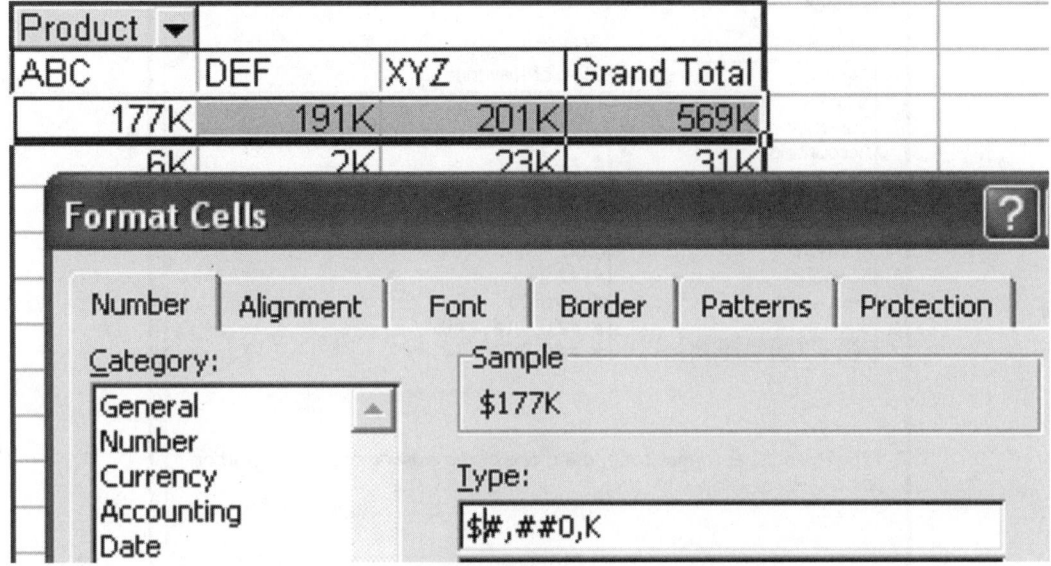

Fig. 956

This will work initially, as shown in Fig. 957.

	A	B	C	D	E
1					
2					
3	Sum of Revenue	Product ▼			
4	Customer ▼	ABC	DEF	XYZ	Grand Total
5	Ainsworth	$177K	$191K	$201K	$569K
6	Air Canada	6K	2K	23K	31K
7	Bell Canada	15K	18K	18K	51K
8	Chevron	26K	21K	7K	54K

Fig. 957

If you later resequence the pivot table, such as sorting by revenue, the special formatting will move into the pivot table instead of staying with the first row, as shown in Fig. 958.

3	Sum of Revenue	Product ▼			
4	Customer ▼	ABC	DEF	XYZ	Grand Total
5	Wal-Mart	277K	304K	288K	869K
6	General Motors	291K	233K	236K	760K
7	Exxon	294K	185K	225K	704K
8	Ford	192K	186K	245K	623K
9	Molson, Inc	204K	204K	206K	614K
10	Ainsworth	$177K	$191K	$201K	$569K
11	Sun Life Financial	142K	183K	174K	499K
12	IBM	100K	178K	150K	427K
13	Nortel Networks	114K	133K	144K	391K

Fig. 958

Summary: You can control numeric formatting in a pivot table by using the PivotTable Field dialog.

Commands Discussed: PivotTable – Pivot Field – Number

SUPPRESS TOTALS IN A PIVOT TABLE

Problem: Pivot tables are sometimes used just as an intermediate step in order to reach another result. If you are going to be copying the data to a new workbook that will be used as a new dataset, then all of the totals by month, region, and year will tend to get in the way, as shown in Fig. 959.

	A	B	C	D
1	Drop Page Fields Here			
2				
3	Sum of Revenue			
4	Date ▼	Region ▼	Product ▼	Total
5	Jan	East	ABC	120K
6			DEF	76K
7			XYZ	77K
8		East Total		273K
9		Central	ABC	80K
10			DEF	2K
11			XYZ	74K
12		Central Total		156K
13		West	ABC	63K
14			DEF	16K
15			XYZ	23K
16		West Total		101K
17	Jan Total			531K
18	Feb	East	ABC	27K
19			DEF	92K
20			XYZ	80K

Fig. 959

Strategy: You can turn off subtotals for any field.

1) Double-click the Date field. Change the Subtotals setting from Automatic to None, as shown in Fig. 960.

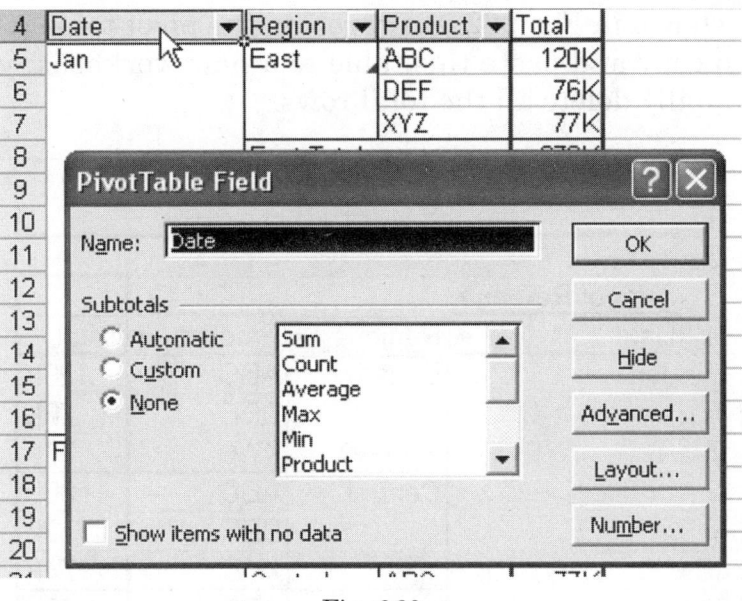

Fig. 960

2) Double-click the Region field. Change the Subtotals from Automatic to None, as shown in Fig. 961.

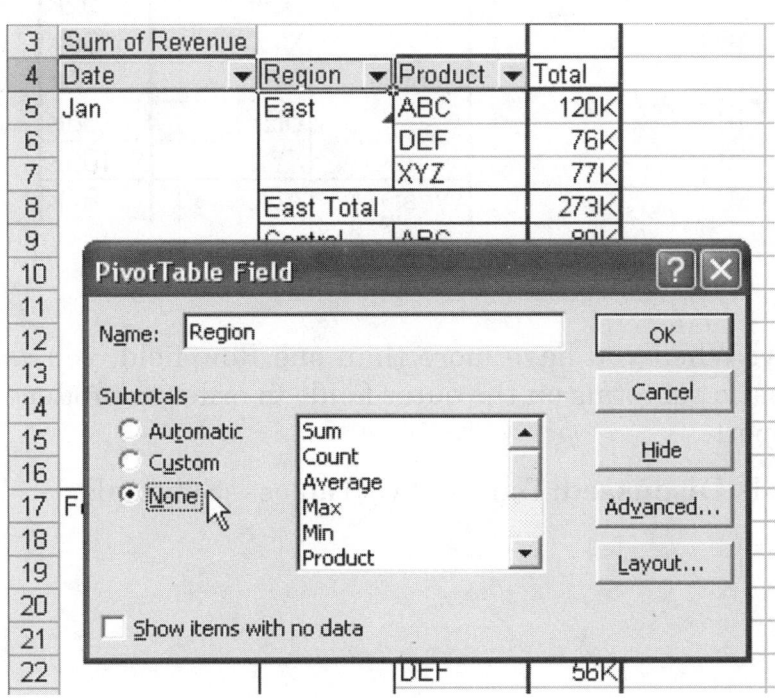

Fig. 961

Result: As shown in Fig. 962, every row in the pivot table is now a data point. If you copy and paste this table to a new workbook, you will not have to manually delete all the total rows.

	A	B	C	D
1	Drop Page Fields Here			
2				
3	Sum of Revenue			
4	Date ▼	Region ▼	Product ▼	Total
5	Jan	East	ABC	120K
6			DEF	76K
7			XYZ	77K
8		Central	ABC	80K
9			DEF	2K
10			XYZ	74K
11		West	ABC	63K
12			DEF	16K
13			XYZ	23K
14	Feb	East	ABC	27K
15			DEF	92K
16			XYZ	80K
17		Central	ABC	77K
18			DEF	56K
19			XYZ	105K
20		West	ABC	67K

Fig. 962

Summary: When you have more than one Row field, you can remove the automatic subtotals on the outer fields in order to produce a cleaner looking report.

Commands Discussed: Data – PivotTables – Subtotals

ELIMINATE BLANKS IN THE OUTLINE FORMAT OF A PIVOT TABLE

Problem: You have created a pivot table report and want to use this data as a database in another workbook. The pivot table report always uses this outline format. It may look great, but it is not conducive to data analysis. As shown in Fig. 963, you really need the Jan heading to be copied to A6:A13, and the East label to be in B6 and B7.

	A	B	C	D
1	Drop Page Fields Here			
2				
3	Sum of Revenue			
4	Date ▼	Region ▼	Product ▼	Total
5	Jan	East	ABC	120K
6			DEF	76K
7			XYZ	77K
8		Central	ABC	80K
9			DEF	2K
10			XYZ	74K
11		West	ABC	63K
12			DEF	16K
13			XYZ	23K
14	Feb	East	ABC	27K
15			DEF	92K
16			XYZ	80K
17		Central	ABC	77K
18			DEF	56K
19			XYZ	105K
20		West	ABC	67K
21			DEF	26K
22			XYZ	36K

Fig. 963

Part III

Strategy: To fill in the blank cells in the outline of the pivot table, you must make a values-only copy of the pivot table. Insert a new worksheet. Copy A4: D111 from the pivot table. On the new sheet, use Edit – Paste Special – Values in order to convert the pivot table to static values, as shown in Fig. 964.

	A	B	C	D
1	Date	Region	Product	Total
2	Jan	East	ABC	120012
3			DEF	76347
4			XYZ	76843
5		Central	ABC	80003
6			DEF	2257
7			XYZ	73814
8		West	ABC	62711
9			DEF	15809
10			XYZ	22950
11	Feb	East	ABC	26693
12			DEF	92441
13			XYZ	79822

Fig. 964

In this case, you need to fill in the blank cells in columns A and B with the value from the cell above. Follow these steps.

1)   Select cells A3:B108, as shown in Fig. 965.

	A	B	C
1	Date	Region	Produc
2	Jan	East	ABC
3			DEF
4			XYZ
5		Central	ABC
6			DEF
7			XYZ
8		West	ABC
9			DEF

Fig. 965

2)   Press the F5 key to display the Go To dialog. In the lower left corner, choose the Special... button, as shown in Fig. 966.

Fig. 966

3)   On the Go To Special dialog, choose Blanks from the first column
     and then choose OK, as shown in Fig. 967.

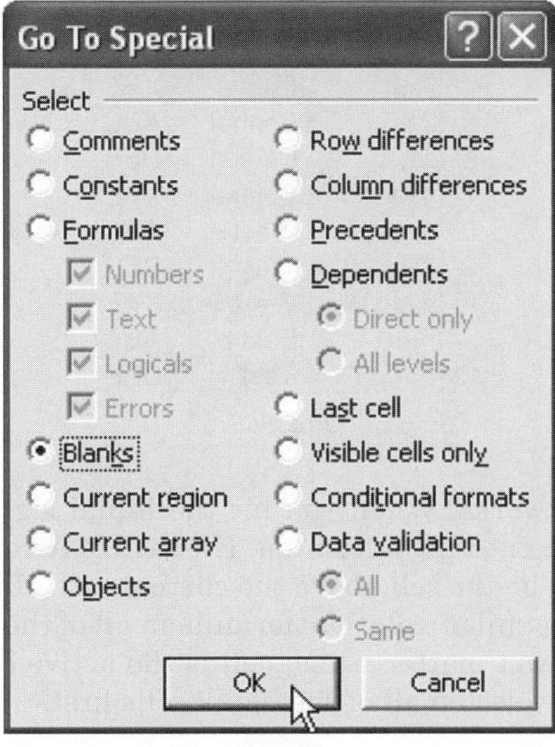

Fig. 967

4)   This next part is confusing, but it works. Type an Equal sign. Hit
     the Up Arrow, as shown in Fig. 968.

	A	B	C	D
2	Jan	East	ABC	120012
3		=B2	DEF	76347
4			XYZ	76843
5		Central	ABC	80003
6			DEF	2257
7			XYZ	73814
8		West	ABC	62711
9			DEF	15809
10			XYZ	22950

Fig. 968

5)   Press Ctrl+Enter, and you get the result shown in Fig. 969.

	A	B	C
2	Jan	East	ABC
3	Jan	East	DEF
4	Jan	East	XYZ
5	Jan	Central	ABC
6	Jan	Central	DEF
7	Jan	Central	XYZ
8	Jan	West	ABC
9	Jan	West	DEF
10	Jan	West	XYZ
11	Feb	East	ABC
12	Feb	East	DEF

Fig. 969

Here is why this works. When you hit the Equal sign, you are telling Excel that you are entering a formula. Hit the Up Arrow, and Excel will make the formula be the cell above the current cell. Hit Ctrl+Enter and Excel will enter a similar (relative) formula in all of the cells of the selection. It really doesn't matter which cell is the active cell, provided you have successfully selected all of the blank cells first.

6)   The next step is to convert all of those new formulas to values. You are tempted to use Ctrl+C and Edit – Paste Special – Values right now, but the Copy command cannot be used on multiple selections, as shown in Fig. 970.

Fig. 970

7)   Reselect A3:B108. Ctrl+C to copy. Edit – Paste Special Values to convert the formulas to values.

Result: You have a nice solid block of data with value in all of the rows for Region and Date, as shown in Fig. 971. This data is now suitable for sorting and filtering.

	A	B	C	D
1	Date	Region	Product	Total
2	Jan	East	ABC	120012
3	Jan	East	DEF	76347
4	Jan	East	XYZ	76843
5	Jan	Central	ABC	80003
6	Jan	Central	DEF	2257
7	Jan	Central	XYZ	73814
8	Jan	West	ABC	62711
9	Jan	West	DEF	15809
10	Jan	West	XYZ	22950
11	Feb	East	ABC	26693
12	Feb	East	DEF	92441
13	Feb	East	XYZ	79822

Fig. 971

Part III

Summary: The steps above seem very convoluted. However, they can easily be mastered and carried out in less than a minute. They are the key to taking the results of a pivot table and creating a useful block of data for further analysis.

Commands Discussed: Edit – Copy; Go To Special – Blanks; Ctrl+Enter

USE A PIVOT TABLE TO COMPARE TWO LISTS

Problem: You have last week's report of forecasted orders. You receive a new forecast report. As shown in Fig. 972, you need to determine which forecasts are new, which forecasts were changed, and which forecasts were deleted.

	A	B	C	D	E	F
1	Forecast Last Week				Forecast This Week	
2						
3	**Customer**	**Forecast**			**Customer**	**Forecast**
4	Compton Petroleum	32,937			Ainsworth	25,450
5	Exxon	68,200			Bell Canada	32,565
6	Ford	2,629			Chevron	45,240
7	General Motors	54,569			Compaq	45,215
8	Gildan Activewear	44,432			Compton Petrole	32,937
9	HP	55,251			Exxon	68,200
10	IBM	28,910			Ford	2,629
11	Kroger	46,717			General Motors	54,569
12	Lucent	65,881			Gildan Activewea	44,432
13	Molson, Inc	47,733			HP	55,251
14	Nortel Networks	49,459			Kroger	46,717
15	P&G	60,299			Lucent	65,881
16	Shell Canada	47,521			Molson, Inc	47,733
17	Sun Life Financial	21,578			P&G	50,000
18	Verizon	35,367			Shell Canada	60,000
19	Wal-Mart	27,862			Sun Life Financi:	21,578
20					Verizon	35,367
21					Wal-Mart	27,862

Fig. 972

Strategy: Copy the two lists into a single list, with a third column to indicate whether the forecast is from this week or last week. Create a pivot table and the new/deleted/changed forecasts will be readily apparent. Follow these steps.

1)   Add a heading in C3 called Source. Assign the value of "Last Week" in C4:C19, as shown in Fig. 973.

	A	B	C
1	Forecast Last Week		
2			
3	**Customer**	**Forecast**	**Source**
4	Compton Petroleum	32,937	Last Week
5	Exxon	68,200	Last Week
6	Ford	2,629	Last Week
7	General Motors	54,569	Last Week
8	Gildan Activewear	44,432	Last Week
9	HP	55,251	Last Week
10	IBM	28,910	Last Week
11	Kroger	46,717	Last Week
12	Lucent	65,881	Last Week
13	Molson, Inc	47,733	Last Week
14	Nortel Networks	49,459	Last Week
15	P&G	60,299	Last Week
16	Shell Canada	47,521	Last Week
17	Sun Life Financial	21,578	Last Week
18	Verizon	35,367	Last Week
19	Wal-Mart	27,862	Last Week
20			

Fig. 973

Part III

2) Copy the data from columns E and F to A20. In C20:C37, enter the value of This Week, as shown in Fig. 974.

	A	B	C
1	Forecast Last Week		
2			
3	**Customer**	**Forecast**	**Source**
9	HP	55,251	Last Week
10	IBM	28,910	Last Week
11	Kroger	46,717	Last Week
12	Lucent	65,881	Last Week
13	Molson, Inc	47,733	Last Week
14	Nortel Networks	49,459	Last Week
15	P&G	60,299	Last Week
16	Shell Canada	47,521	Last Week
17	Sun Life Financial	21,578	Last Week
18	Verizon	35,367	Last Week
19	Wal-Mart	27,862	Last Week
20	Ainsworth	25,450	This Week
21	Bell Canada	32,565	This Week
22	Chevron	45,240	This Week
23	Compaq	45,215	This Week
24	Compton Petroleum	32,937	This Week
25	Exxon	68,200	This Week

Fig. 974

3) Create a Pivot Table. Put Customer in the Row area, Source in the Column area, and Forecast in the Data area.

4) In the PivotTable Options, turn off Grand Total for Rows. As shown in Fig. 975, you will have a comparison of the two lists.

	A	B	C
1	Drop Page Fields Here		
2			
3	Sum of Forecast	Source ▼	
4	Customer ▼	Last Week	This Week
5	Ainsworth		25450
6	Bell Canada		32565
7	Chevron		45240
8	Compaq		45215
9	Compton Petroleum	32937	32937
10	Exxon	68200	68200
11	Ford	2629	2629
12	General Motors	54569	54569
13	Gildan Activewear	44432	44432
14	HP	55251	55251
15	IBM	28910	
16	Kroger	46717	46717
17	Lucent	65881	65881
18	Molson, Inc	47733	47733
19	Nortel Networks	49459	
20	P&G	60299	50000
21	Shell Canada	47521	60000
22	Sun Life Financial	21578	21578
23	Verizon	35367	35367
24	Wal-Mart	27862	27862
25	Grand Total	689345	761626
26			

Fig. 975

Results: For any cells without an entry in Last Week, the forecast is new. For any forecast without an entry in column C, the forecast was deleted. For any forecast where columns B and C do not match, the forecast was changed.

Gotcha: It would be nice to add a formula in column D that shows the difference between Last Week and This Week. However, if you use the method of highlighting a cell in the pivot table with the mouse or arrow keys while you enter the formula, Excel automatically changes the B5 reference to a GetPivotData function. Instead of getting a simple formula like =C5–B5, you get a complicated formula with GetPivotData formulas, as shown in Fig. 976.

D5	▼	*fx* =GETPIVOTDATA("Forecast",$A$3,"Customer","Ainsworth",

	A	B	"Source","This Week")-GETPIVOTDATA("Forecast",$A$3,		
1			"Customer","Ainsworth","Source","Last Week")		
2					
3	Sum of Forecast	Source ▼			
4	Customer ▼	Last Week	This Week		
5	Ainsworth		25450	25450	
6	Bell Canada		32565		
7	Chevron		45240		
8	Compaq		45215		
9	Compton Petroleum	32937	32937		

Fig. 976

Part III

As you copy this formula from D5 to D6, it does not have a relative reference. As shown in Fig. 977, the results will be wrong in the rest of the rows.

D6	▼	*fx* =GETPIVOTDATA("Forecast",$A$3,"Customer","Ainsworth",

	A	B	"Source","This Week")-GETPIVOTDATA("Forecast",$A$3,		
1			"Customer","Ainsworth","Source","Last Week")		
2					
3	Sum of Forecast	Source ▼			
4	Customer ▼	Last Week	This Week		
5	Ainsworth		25450	25450	
6	Bell Canada		32565	25450	
7	Chevron		45240	25450	
8	Compaq		45215	25450	
9	Compton Petroleum	32937	32937	25450	
10	Exxon	68200	68200	25450	
11	Ford	2629	2629	25450	
12	General Motors	54569	54569	25450	
13	Gildan Activewear	44432	44432	25450	

Fig. 977

You have two options in order to enter a regular formula outside of the pivot table.

First option: You can actually type =D5–C5 as the formula.

Second option: Alternatively, you can add a button to a toolbar to permanently turn off the automatic creation of GetPivotData functions. From the menu, select Tools – Customize. Choose the Commands tab. In the Category dropdown, choose Data. Scroll all the way to the bottom of the Commands list. There is an icon for Generate GetPivotData. Drag this icon from the Customize dialog and drop it on one of the toolbars, as shown in Fig. 978.

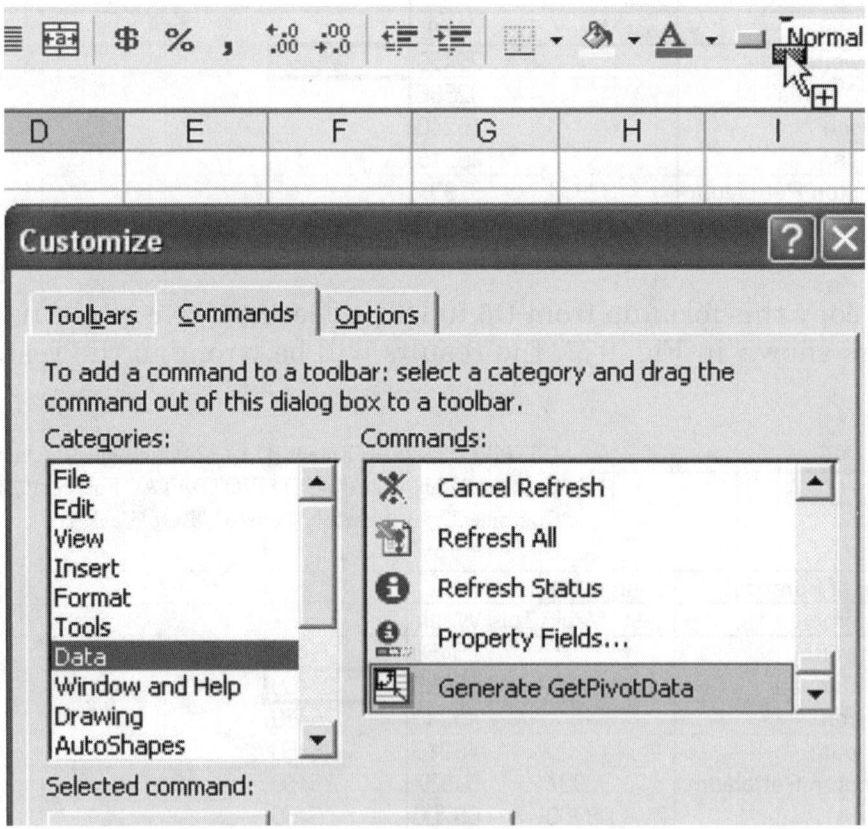

Fig. 978

You can now turn off the creation of GetPivotData functions automatically by selecting the item in the toolbar, as shown in Fig. 979.

Fig. 979

Summary: In addition to using VLOOKUP or Data Consolidation, you can use pivot tables as a quick way of comparing two or more lists. The trick is to add a new temporary column identifying the source of each record and then to use the Source column as a Column field.

Commands Discussed: Data – PivotTable; Generate GetPivotData

CALCULATED FIELDS IN A PIVOT TABLE

Problem: You need to include a calculation in the pivot table that is not in your underlying data. Your data includes Quantity Sold, Revenue, and Cost, as shown in Fig. 980. You would like to report Gross Profit and Average Price.

Part III

	A	B	C	D	E	F
1	**Region**	**Product**	**Customer**	**Quantity**	**Revenue**	**COGS**
539	East	XYZ	Ford	500	10380.00	5110
540	East	XYZ	IBM	300	6732.00	3066
541	East	XYZ	IBM	300	6744.00	3066
542	Central	ABC	Exxon	900	15651.00	7623
543	Central	ABC	Ford	700	13552.00	5929
544	East	ABC	Nortel Networks	600	11274.00	5082
545	West	ABC	Ford	800	14408.00	6776
546	West	XYZ	Wal-Mart	800	18560.00	8176
547	Central	ABC	Exxon	300	5847.00	2541

Fig. 980

Strategy: You can add a calculated field to a pivot table. Follow these steps.

1) Build a pivot table.

2) From the PivotTable toolbar, select PivotTable – Formula – Calculated Field, as shown in Fig. 981.

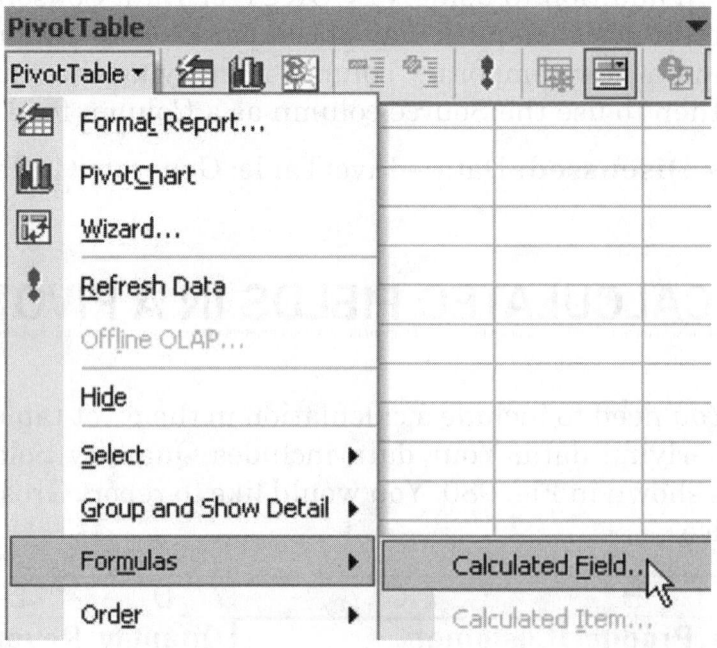

Fig. 981

3) Type a name for the field, in this case, Profit. Enter the calculation =Revenue–COGS. Choose the Add button, as shown in Fig. 982.

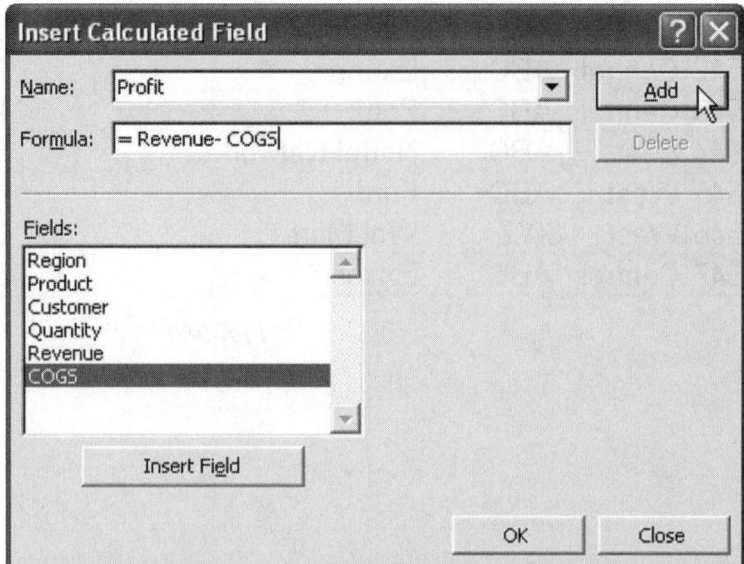

Fig. 982

4)   Here is the formula for Gross Profit Percent. See Fig. 983.

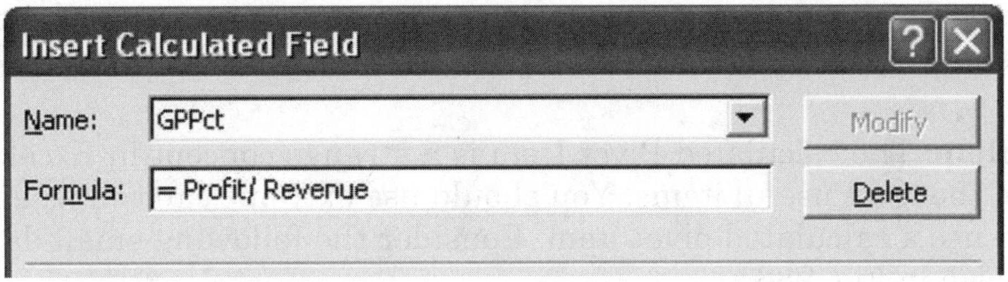

Insert Calculated Field   ? ✕

Name: GPPct   ▼   Modify

Formula: = Profit/ Revenue   Delete

Fig. 983

5)   The formula for Average Price is shown in Fig. 984.

Insert Calculated Field   ? ✕

Name: AveragePrice   ▼   Add

Formula: = Revenue/ Quantity   Delete

Fig. 984

The resulting pivot table includes all of the fields, as shown in Fig. 985.

3		Data ▼					
4	Product ▼	Sum of Revenue	Sum of COGS	Sum of Profit	Sum of GPPct	Sum of Quantity	Sum of AveragePrice
5	ABC	2111660	936782	1174878	55.6%	110600	19.09276673
6	DEF	2163714	962352	1201362	55.5%	97800	22.12386503
7	XYZ	2427503	1077188	1350315	55.6%	105400	23.03133776
8	Grand Total	6702877	2976322	3726555	55.6%	313800	21.36034736
9							

Fig. 985

Gotcha: The label Sum of GPPct is somewhat misleading, as is Sum of Average Price. In reality, Excel finds the sum of Revenue, finds the sum of Quantity, and then divides the values on the total line in order to get the average price. This makes calculated fields fine for any calculations that follow the Associative law of mathematics. If you actually wanted to have Excel do all of the individual average prices and then sum them up, it would be impossible in a pivot table.

Summary: Calculated Fields add a new measure that can be reported in the Data area of a PivotTable for all Measures.

Commands Discussed: PivotTable – Formula – Calculated Field

ADD A CALCULATED ITEM
TO GROUP ITEMS IN A PIVOT TABLE

Problem: The calculated Pivot Item is a strange concept in Excel. It is one of the least useful items. You should use extreme caution when trying to use a calculated pivot item. Consider the following small dataset as shown in Fig. 986.

	A	B
1	**Product**	**Quantity**
2	ABC	1
3	ABC	2
4	DEF	4
5	DEF	8
6	DEF	16
7	XYZ	32
8	XYZ	64
9		

Fig. 986

Your company has three product lines. The Hartville division manufactures ABC and DEF. The Norwalk division manufactures XYZ. As shown in Fig. 987, you have a pivot table showing sales by product. Remember that the total of items sold is 127.

	A	B	C
1	Drop Page Fields Here		
2			
3	Sum of Quantity		
4	Product ▼	Total	
5	ABC	3	
6	DEF	28	
7	XYZ	96	
8	Grand Total	127	

Fig. 987

Strategy: You've read that you can add a calculated item along the Product division to total ABC and DEF in order to get a total for the Hartville plant.

From the PivotTable toolbar, you select PivotTable – Formula – Calculated Item, as shown in Fig. 988.

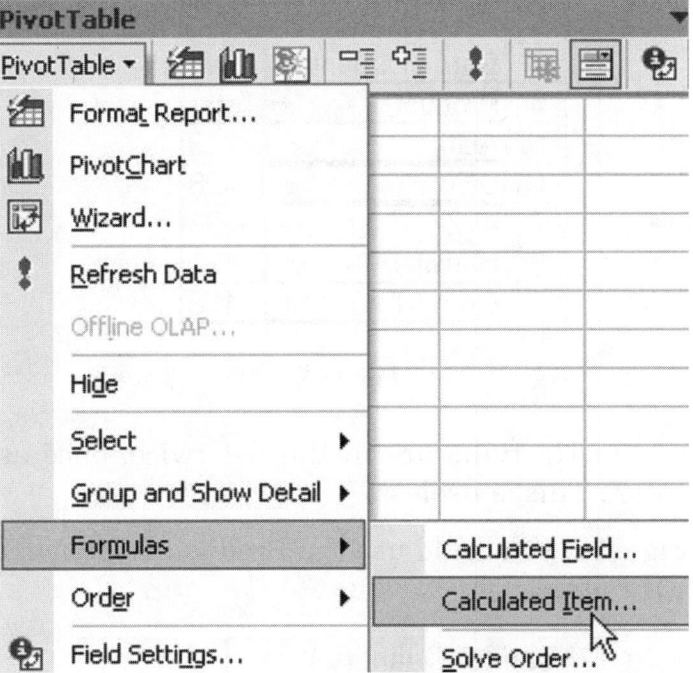

Fig. 988

In the Insert Calculated Item dialog, you define an item called Hartville, which is the total of ABC + DEF, as shown in Fig. 989.

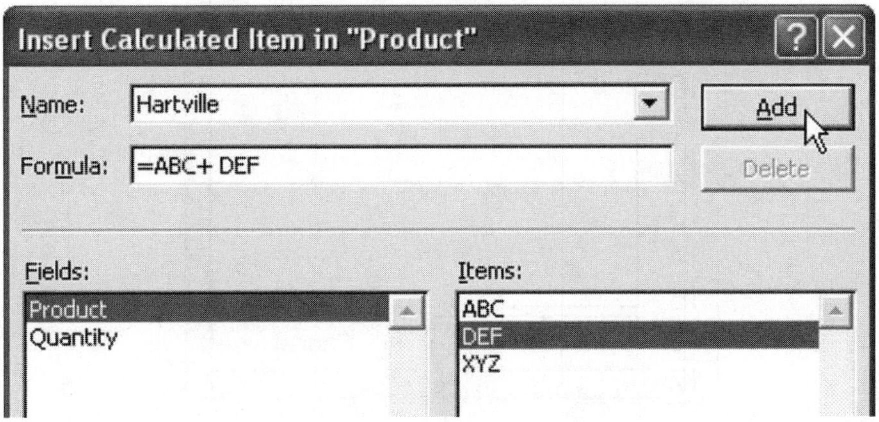

Fig. 989

However, when you view the resulting pivot table, the total is now wrong. Instead of having 127 items sold, the pivot table reports that the total is 158, as shown in Fig. 990.

	A	B
1	Drop Page Fields Here	
2		
3	Sum of Quantity	
4	Product ▼	Total
5	ABC	3
6	DEF	28
7	XYZ	96
8	Hartville	31
9	Grand Total	158
10		

Fig. 990

The items made in Hartville are in the list twice, once as "ABC" and once in "Hartville". This is useless.

As shown in Fig. 991, you could use the Product dropdown and uncheck the ABC and DEF items.

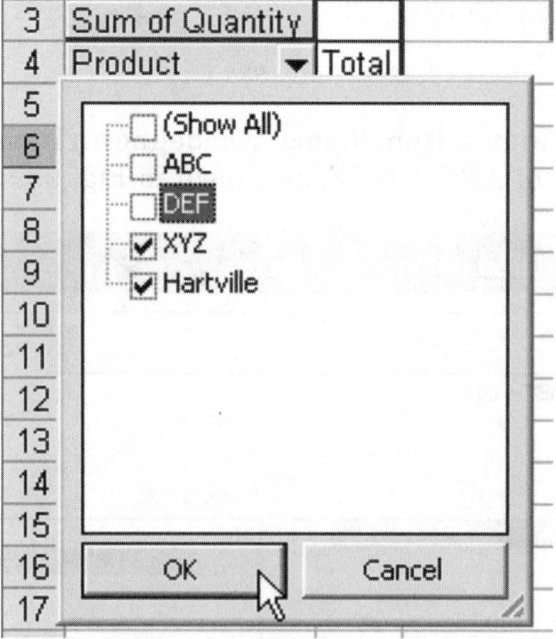

Fig. 991

The resulting pivot table shows the correct total of 127, as shown in Fig. 992.

	A	B	
1	Drop Page Fields Here		
2			
3	Sum of Quantity		
4	Product ▼	Total	
5	XYZ	96	
6	Hartville	31	
7	Grand Total	127	
8			

Fig. 992

Additional Details: I cannot think of a single example where a Calculated Item would actually be useful.

Instead of trying to use a Calculated Item, add a Plant column to the original data. You can now produce a report that shows both the plant location and the products made at the plant and the total of 127 will be correct, as shown in Fig. 993.

	A	B	C
1	Drop Page Fields Here		
2			
3	Sum of Qua		
4	Plant ▼	Product ▼	Total
5	Hartville	ABC	3
6		DEF	28
7	Hartville Total		31
8	Norwalk	XYZ	96
9	Norwalk Total		96
10	Grand Total		127
11			

Fig. 993

Summary: Calculated Pivot Items sound like they should be useful, but they are not.

Commands Discussed: Pivot Table – Formulas – Calculated Item

QUICKLY CREATE CHARTS FOR ANY REGION

Problem: You need to create similar charts for each sales region from the transactional data shown in Fig. 994.

	A	B	C	D	E	F
1	Region	Product	Date	Customer	Quantity	Revenue
2	East	XYZ	Jul-04	Nortel Networks	1000	25350
3	West	XYZ	May-04	Sun Life Financial	1000	25310
4	Central	XYZ	Feb-04	Wal-Mart	1000	25140
5	West	XYZ	Feb-04	General Motors	1000	25080

Fig. 994

Strategy: There have been many pivot table examples in the book. It is also possible to make a chart that relies on a pivot table.

1)   Select a single cell in your data and choose Data – PivotTable and PivotChart. In Step 1 of the Wizard, change the last option button to create a pivot chart, as shown in Fig. 995. Hit Next.

Fig. 995

2)   Confirm the data range in Step 2. Choose Next, as shown in
     Fig. 996.

Fig. 996

3)   In Step 3, choose Finish, as shown in Fig. 997.

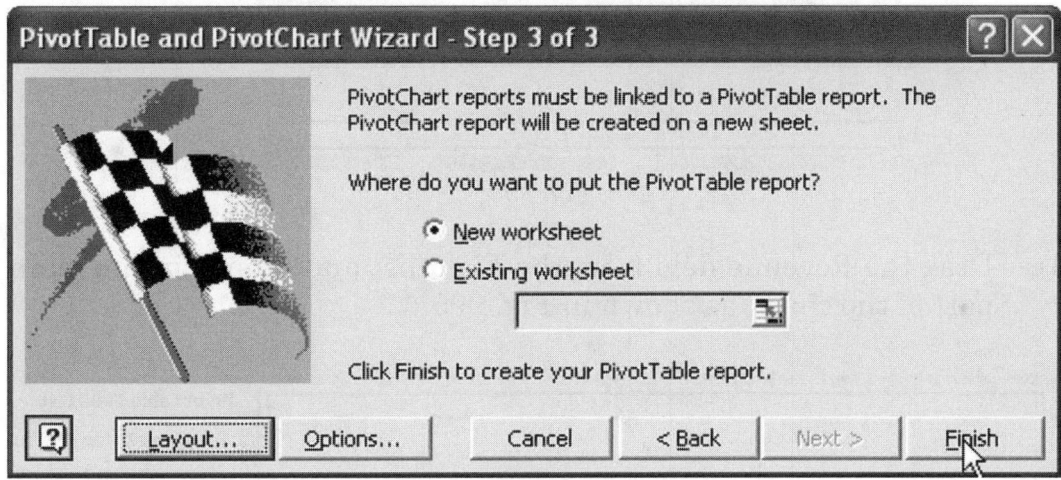

Fig. 997

You will be presented with a blank pivot chart, as shown in Fig. 998.

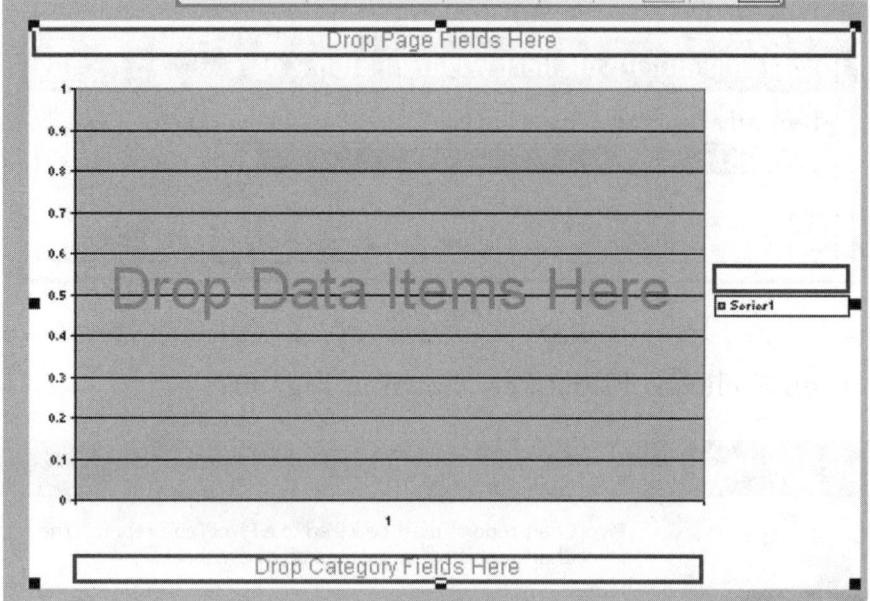

Fig. 998

4)   Drag the Revenue field from the Field list and drop it in the main part of the chart, as shown in Fig. 999.

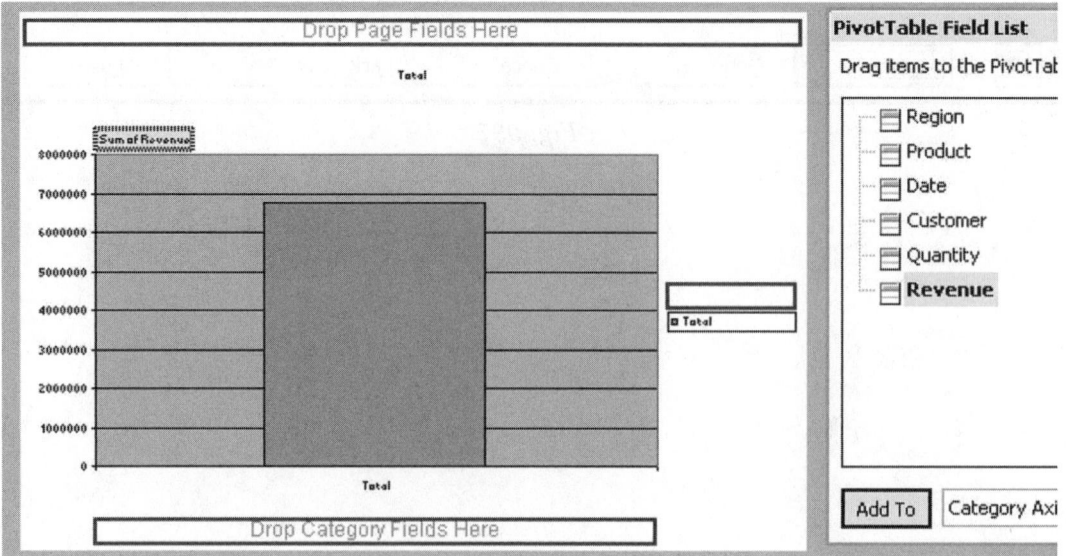

Fig. 999

5) Drag the Date field and drop it in the Category Fields area, as shown in Fig. 1000.

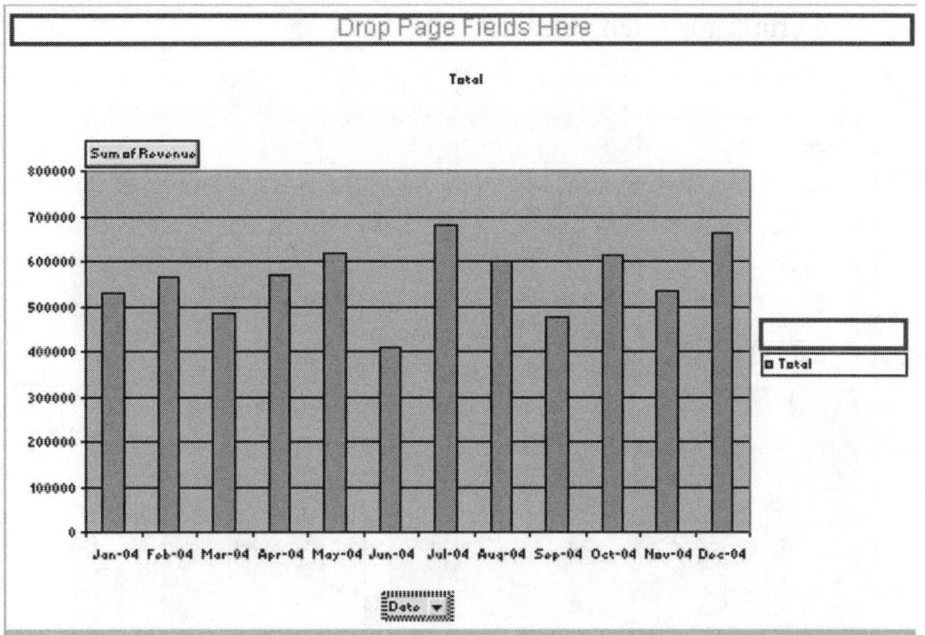

Fig. 1000

6) Drag the Product field and drop it in the blue box near the legend on the right side of the chart, as shown in Fig. 1001.

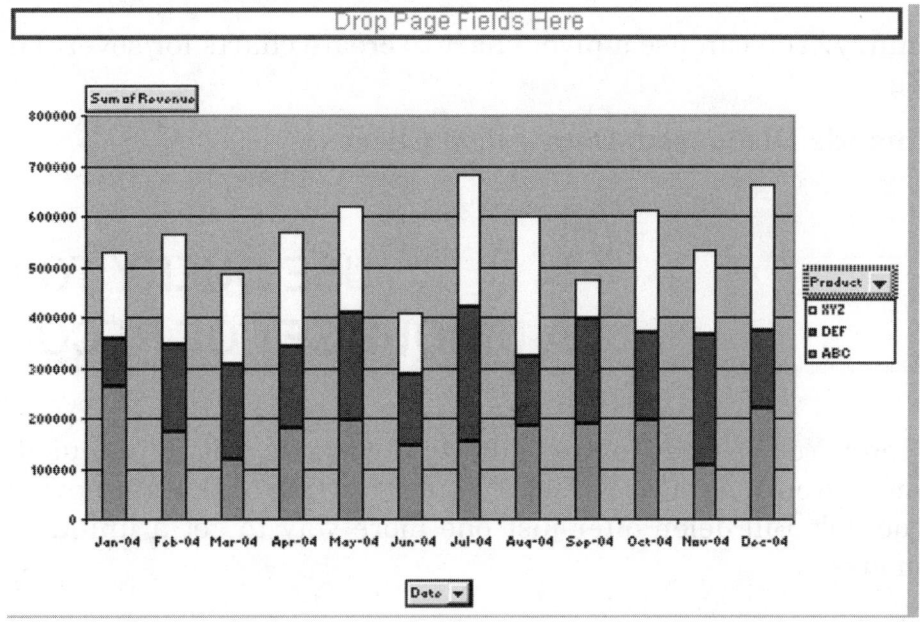

Fig. 1001

7)   Drag the Region field and drop it in the Page Fields area.

Result: As shown in Fig. 1002, you can change the Region field to quickly produce a chart for each region.

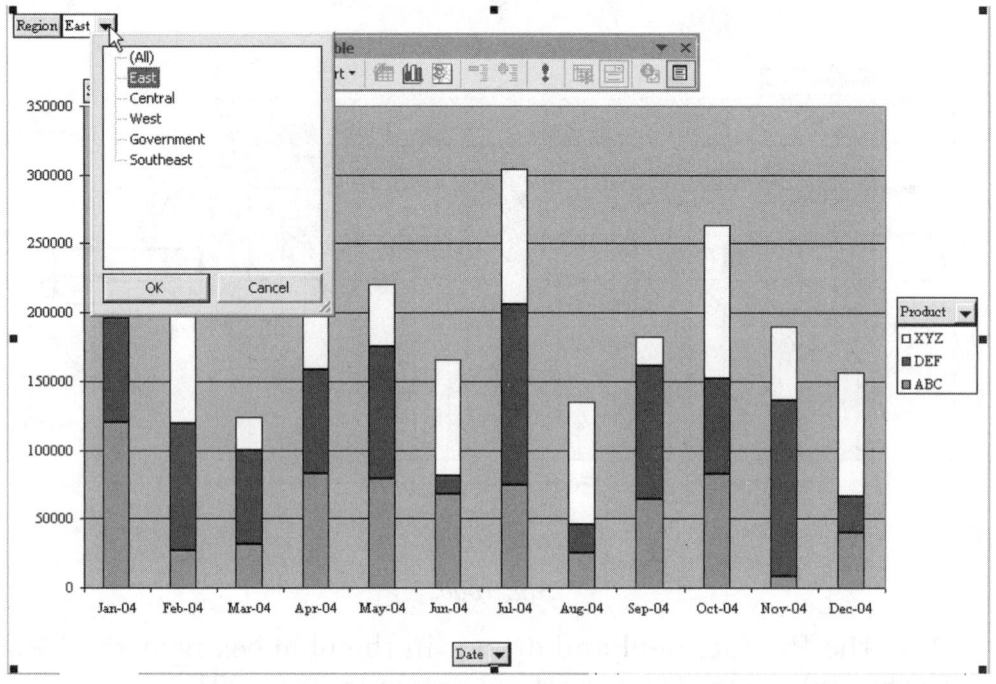

Fig. 1002

Summary: You can use a pivot chart to create charts for several different regions.

Commands Discussed: Data – PivotChart

USE QUERY TO GET
A UNIQUE SET OF RECORDS

Problem: You've seen many different ways to get a unique list of customers from a dataset in Excel. You are sitting back right now, thinking, couldn't Bill Jelen offer just one more way to get a unique list of customers?

Strategy: I have to bring this up, because it is fast and fairly cool. It is also a way to get a list of customers from a closed file. The trick is to use Microsoft Query. Now, Microsoft Query is not in the default install of Excel. So, if you didn't do a complete install, you are going to have to find the installation CDs to add Microsoft Query to your installation of Excel.

Basically, Microsoft Query is a way to run some SQL against an external file. I am sure that Microsoft envisioned this would be an Access table or an ODBC datasource, but, of course, someone figured out that the external file could be another Excel workbook. Here is how you would set this up.

1) Let's say you have a workbook called SalesData.xls. It has one worksheet called Data. The worksheet contains a bunch of records in columns A through H, as shown in Fig. 1003. Select the data in A:H. Give the table a range name of MyData.

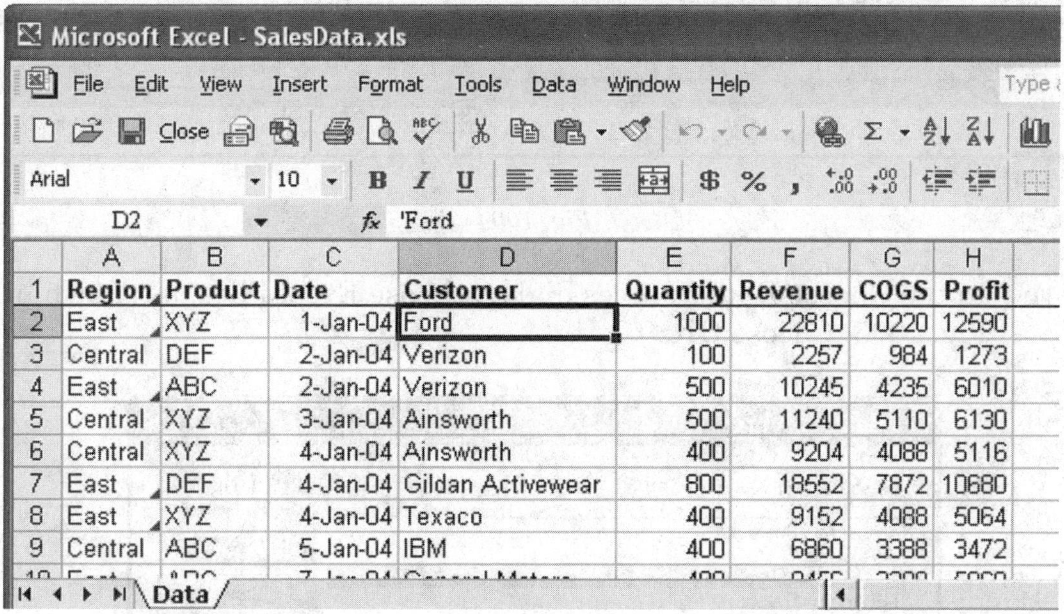

Fig. 1003

2) Save and Close SalesData.xls.

3)   In a new workbook, select Data – Get External Data – New Database Query, as shown in Fig. 1004.

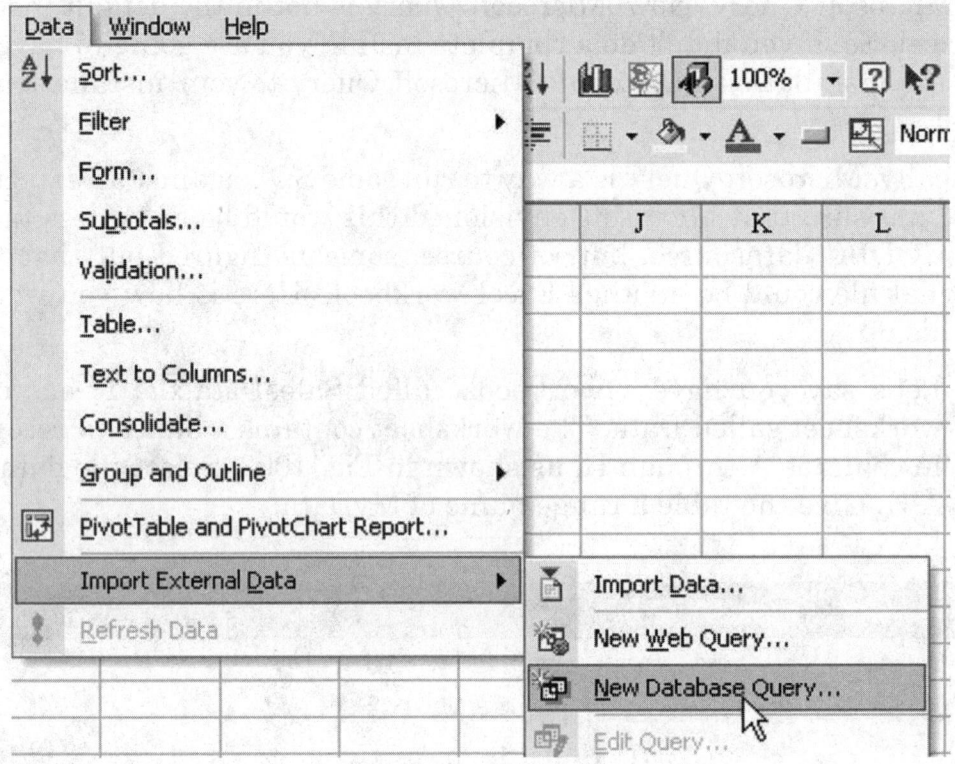

Fig. 1004

4)   In the Choose Data Sources dialog, choose Excel Files, as shown in Fig. 1005. Choose OK.

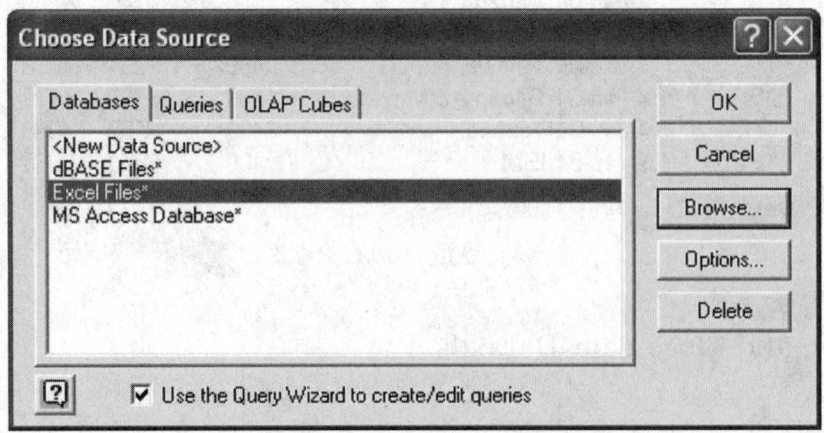

Fig. 1005

5) Laugh at the retro Select Workbook dialog. Then, browse to find SalesData.xls, as shown in Fig. 1006. Choose OK.

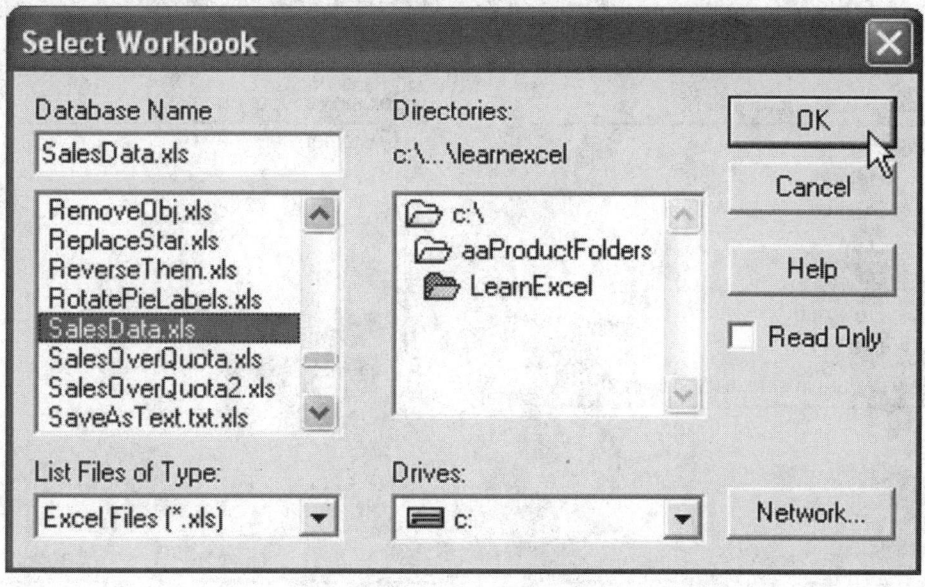

Fig. 1006

6) As shown in Fig. 1007, select the Customer field in the left list and hit the Right Arrow button to move Customer over to the Query.

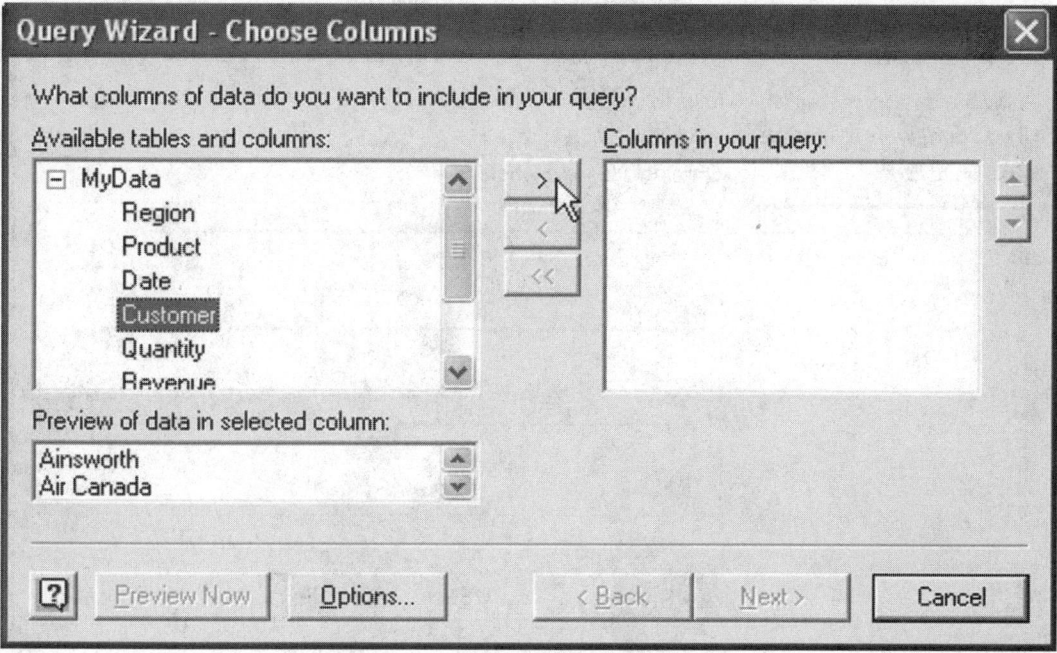

Fig. 1007

7)　　Choose the Next button, as shown in Fig. 1008.

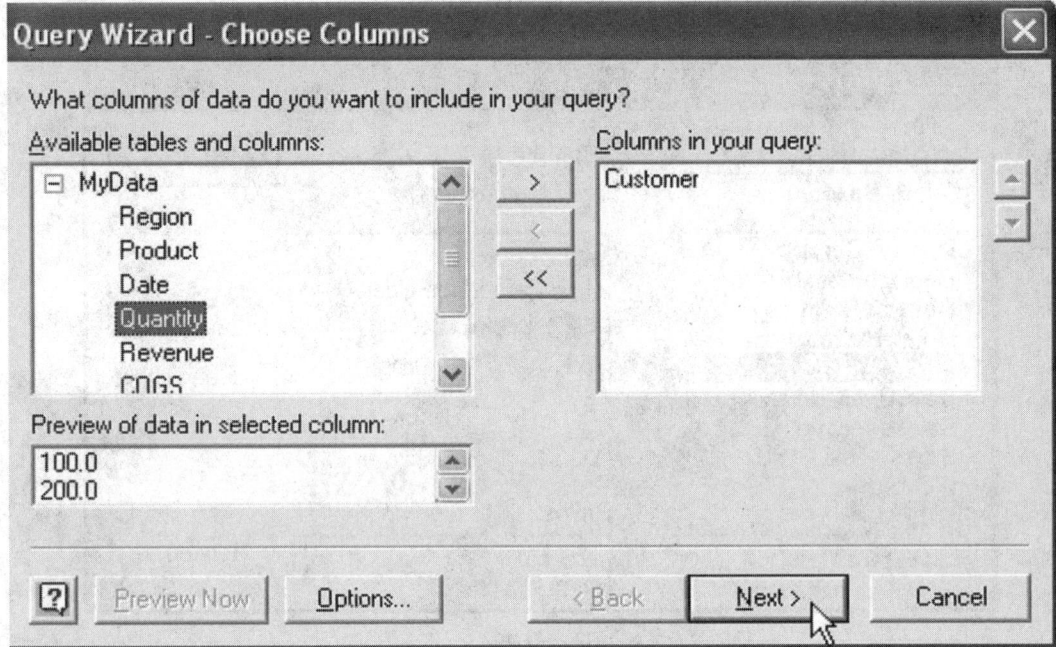

Fig. 1008

8)　　Choose Next to skip the Filter section. See Fig. 1009.

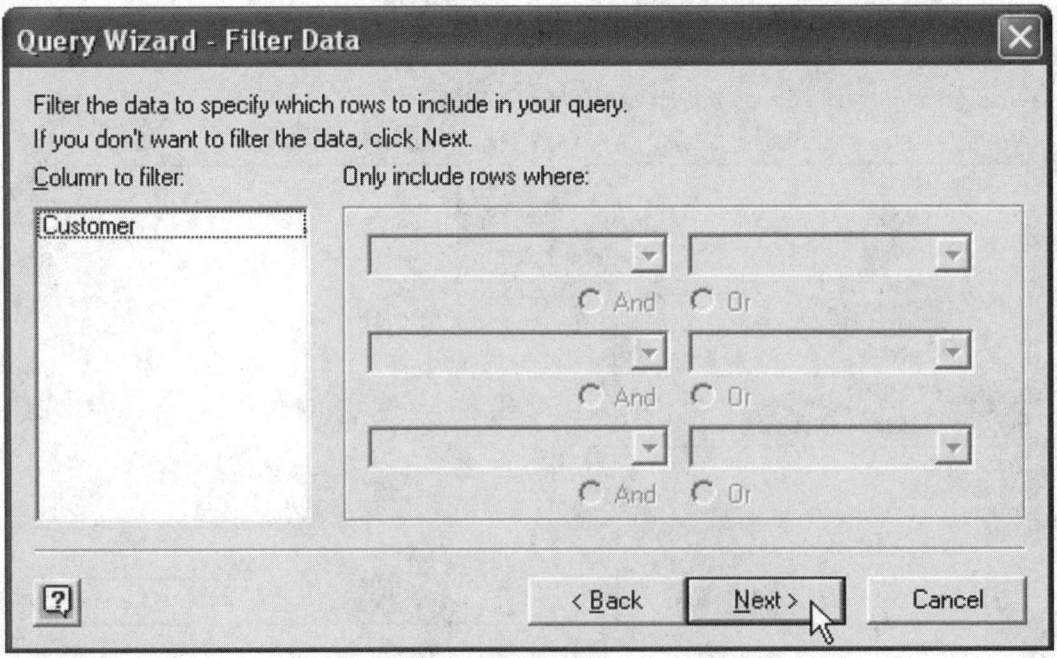

Fig. 1009

9)   Choose to Sort Ascending by Customer, as shown in Fig. 1010. Click Next.

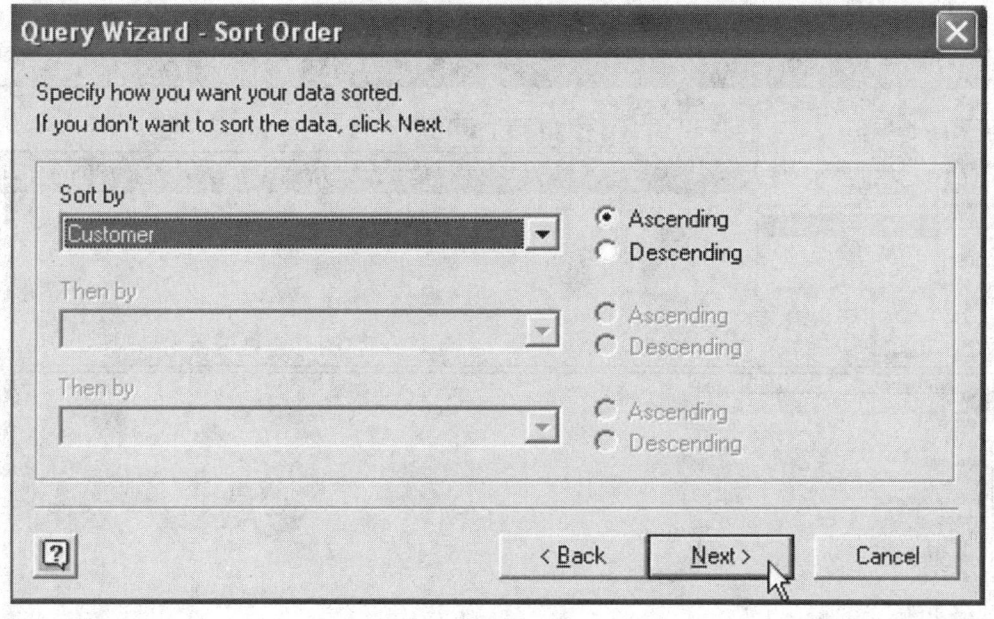

Fig. 1010

10)   Since you want unique records only, you need to edit the query in Microsoft Query. As shown in Fig. 1011, choose this option and then choose Finish.

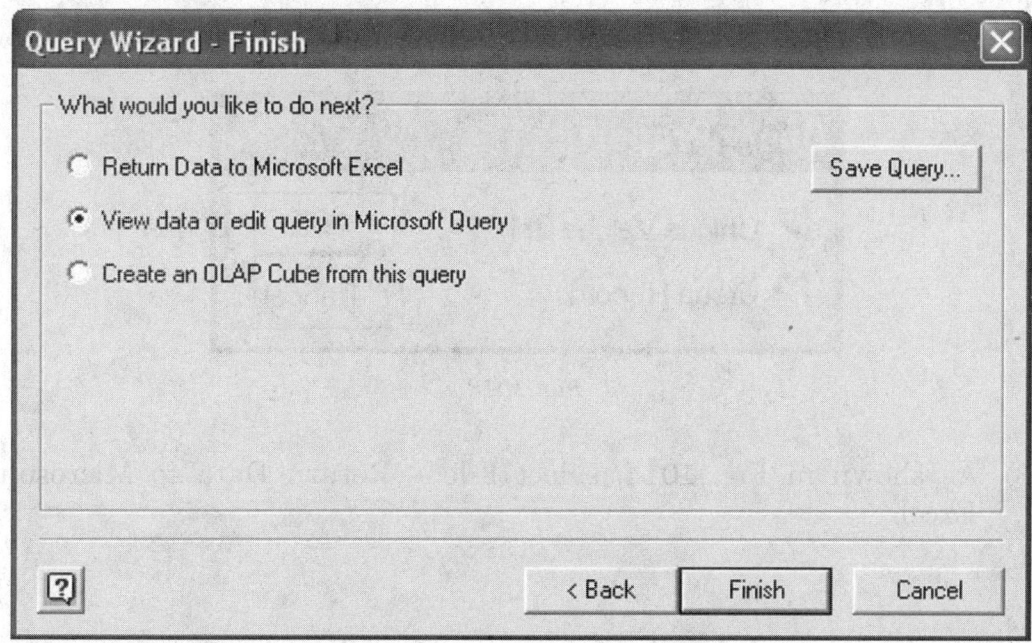

Fig. 1011

11) The Microsoft Query window opens. From the Microsoft Query menu, select View – Query Properties, as shown in Fig. 1012.

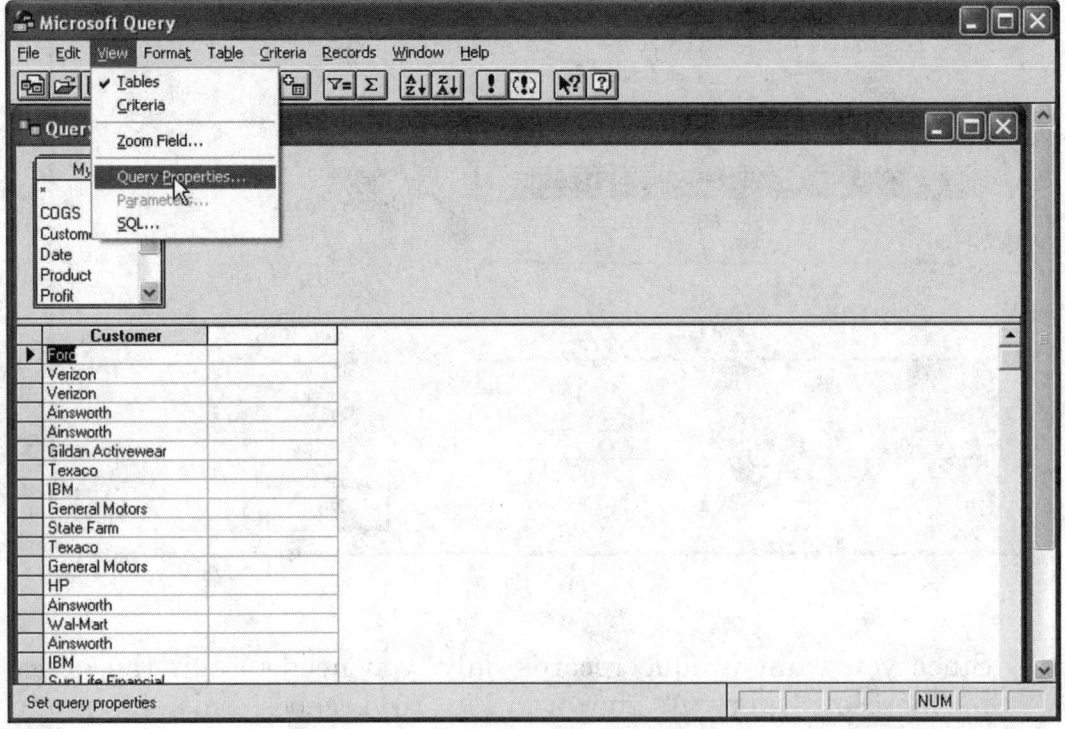

Fig. 1012

12) As shown in Fig. 1013, choose Unique Values Only and then OK.

Fig. 1013

13) As shown in Fig. 1014, select File – Return Data to Microsoft Excel.

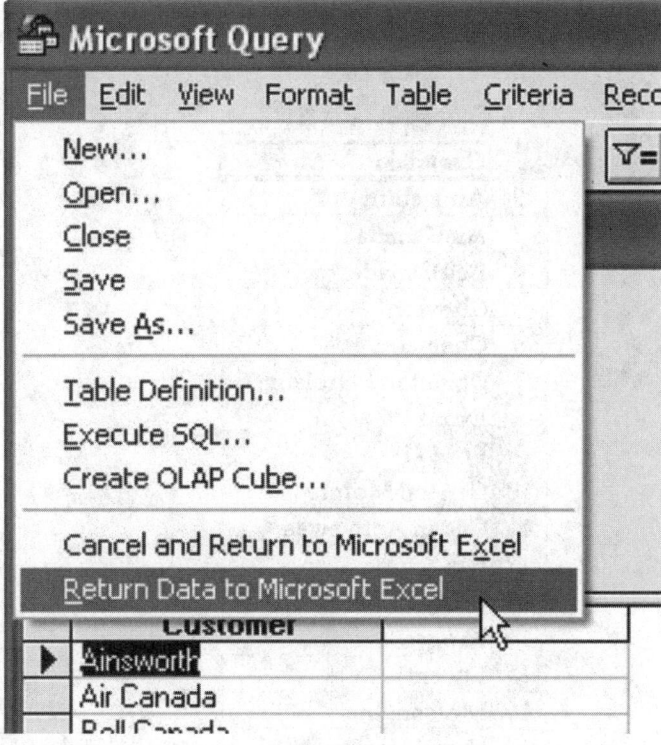

Fig. 1014

14) Choose where you would like to place the imported data, as shown in Fig. 1015. Choose OK.

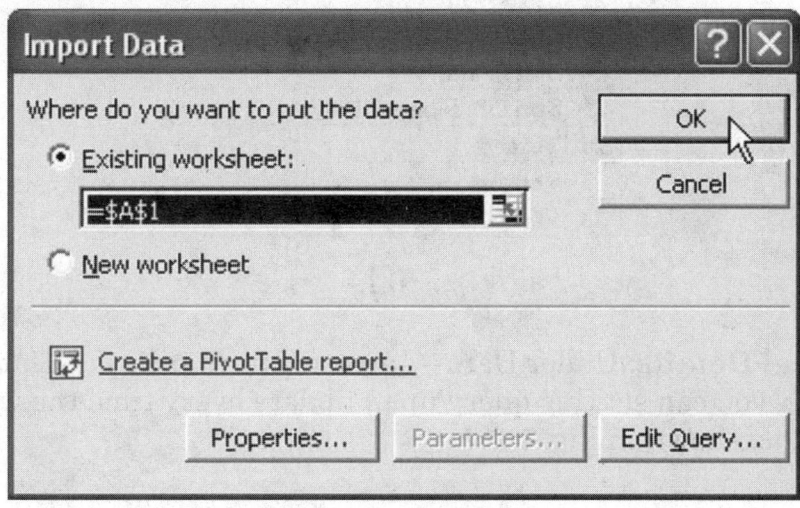

Fig. 1015

Result: You have a unique list of customers from the closed Excel file.
See Fig. 1016.

	A	B
1	**Customer**	
2	Ainsworth	
3	Air Canada	
4	Bell Canada	
5	Chevron	
6	Compaq	
7	Compton Petroleum	
8	Exxon	
9	Ford	
10	General Motors	
11	Gildan Activewear	
12	HP	
13	IBM	
14	Kroger	
15	Lucent	
16	Molson, Inc	
17	Nortel Networks	
18	P&G	
19	Phillip Morris	
20	SBC Communications	
21	Sears	
22	Sears Canada	
23	Shell Canada	
24	State Farm	
25	Sun Life Financial	
26	Texaco	
27	Verizon	
28	Wal-Mart	
29		

Fig. 1016

Additional Details: Under Data – Import External Data – Data Range
Properties, you can set this query up to update every time the workbook
is opened, as shown in Fig. 1017.

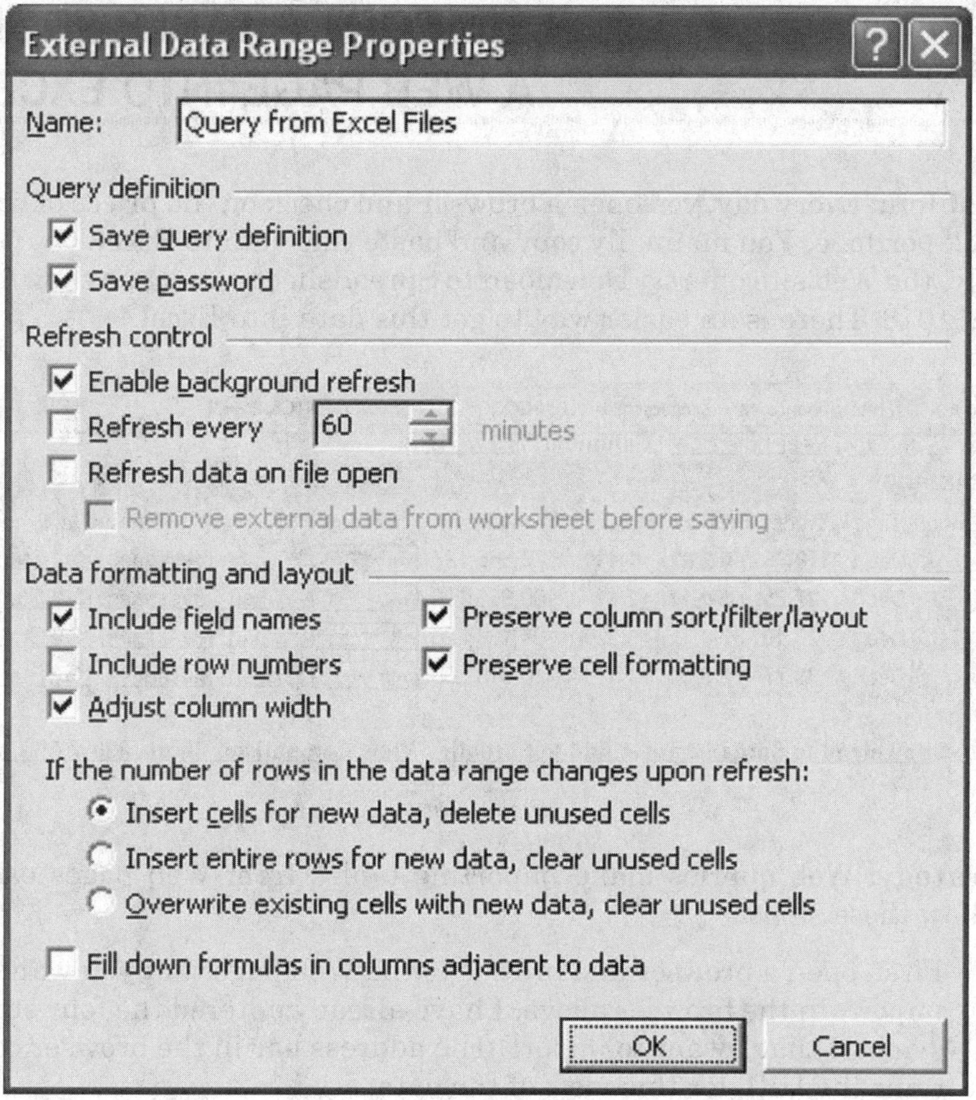

External Data Range Properties   ? X

Name: Query from Excel Files

Query definition
☑ Save query definition
☑ Save password

Refresh control
☑ Enable background refresh
☐ Refresh every   60 ⏫⏬ minutes
☐ Refresh data on file open
☐ Remove external data from worksheet before saving

Data formatting and layout
☑ Include field names   ☑ Preserve column sort/filter/layout
☐ Include row numbers   ☑ Preserve cell formatting
☑ Adjust column width

If the number of rows in the data range changes upon refresh:
◉ Insert cells for new data, delete unused cells
○ Insert entire rows for new data, clear unused cells
○ Overwrite existing cells with new data, clear unused cells

☐ Fill down formulas in columns adjacent to data

[OK]   [Cancel]

Fig. 1017

Part
III

Summary: The Data Query tool provides a way to import data from Access, Excel, or ODBC data sources.

Commands Discussed: Data – Import External Data – New Database Query

IMPORT A TABLE FROM A WEB PAGE INTO EXCEL

Problem: Every day, you open a browser and check on the prices of your stock portfolio. You manually copy and paste this data to Excel. Or, possibly, the Web site offers a Download to Spreadsheet option, as shown in Fig. 1018. There is an easier way to get this data into Excel.

Address	http://finance.yahoo.com/q/cq?d=v1&s=GOOG%2c+MSFT%2c+INTC%2c+KO	Go

View: <u>Summary</u> | <u>Real-Time ECN</u> | **Columnar** [<u>New View</u>]

Columnar

Symbol	Time	Trade	Change	% Chg	Volume	Intraday	Related Info
<u>GOOG</u>	Dec 1	**179.96**	↓2.02	-1.11%	7,868,147		<u>Chart</u>, <u>Messages</u>, <u>Key Stats</u>
<u>MSFT</u>	Dec 1	**27.25**	↑0.44	+1.64%	100,955,120		<u>Chart</u>, <u>Messages</u>, <u>Key Stats</u>
<u>INTC</u>	Dec 1	**23.10**	↑0.72	+3.22%	84,187,728		<u>Chart</u>, <u>Messages</u>, <u>Key Stats</u>
<u>KO</u>	Dec 1	**39.77**	↑0.46	+1.17%	10,010,500		<u>Chart</u>, <u>Messages</u>, <u>Key Stats</u>

⬆ **<u>Download to Spreadsheet</u>** ✉ **<u>Add to Portfolio</u>** - **<u>View Comparison Chart</u>** - **<u>View All Cha</u>**

Fig. 1018

Strategy: Web queries make importing tables from Web pages easy. Follow these steps:

1) First, open a browser and browse to the Web page that you want to import. In the browser above, I have already entered the four stock symbols that I want to import. The address bar in the browser contains the URL for this view of the data.

2) Start with a new Workbook. From the menu, select Data – Import External Data – New Web Query, as shown in Fig. 1019.

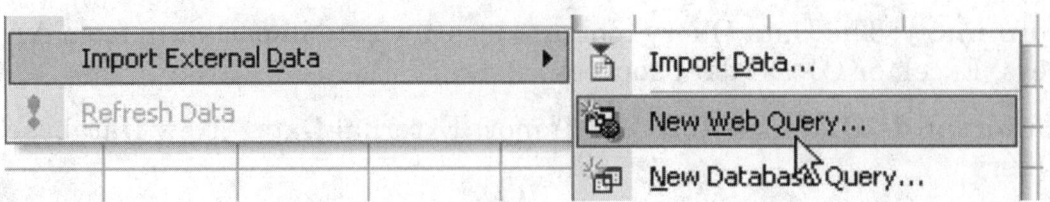

Fig. 1019

The New Web Query dialog box will appear with your usual home page in the browser. See Fig. 1020.

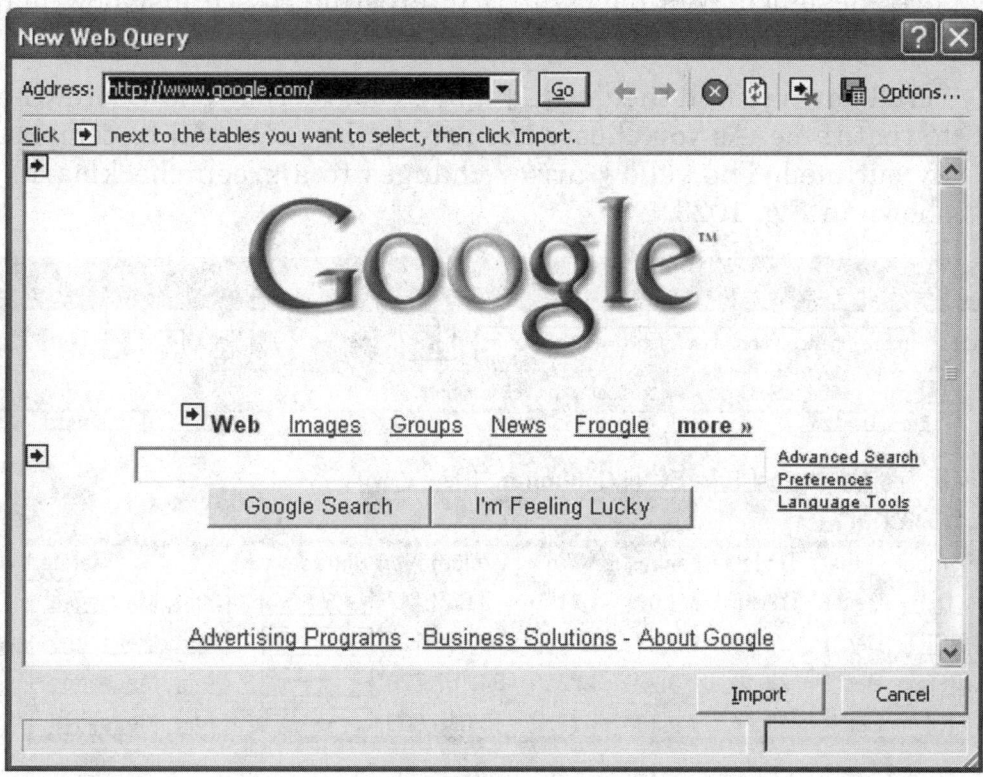

Fig. 1020

3)   Switch to your regular browser with Alt+Tab. Highlight the correct address in the address bar and hit Ctrl+C to copy this address to the clipboard, as shown in Fig. 1021.

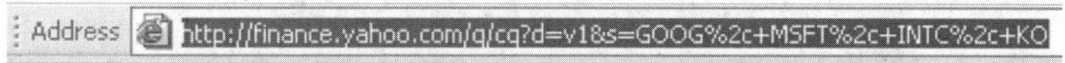

Fig. 1021

4)   Switch back to Excel with Alt+Tab. Hit Ctrl+V to paste the address into the formula bar, as shown in Fig. 1022. Choose the Go button.

Fig. 1022

The desired Web page will appear in the dialog box. There will be a yellow box with a black arrow next to each table on the Web page. If you have ever designed Web pages, it is interesting to see just how many tables the designer used to create the page.

5)   Scroll down to find the desired table. Choose the yellow arrow next to that table. As you choose the arrow, the table will be temporarily outlined. The yellow arrow changes to a green checkmark, as shown in Fig. 1023.

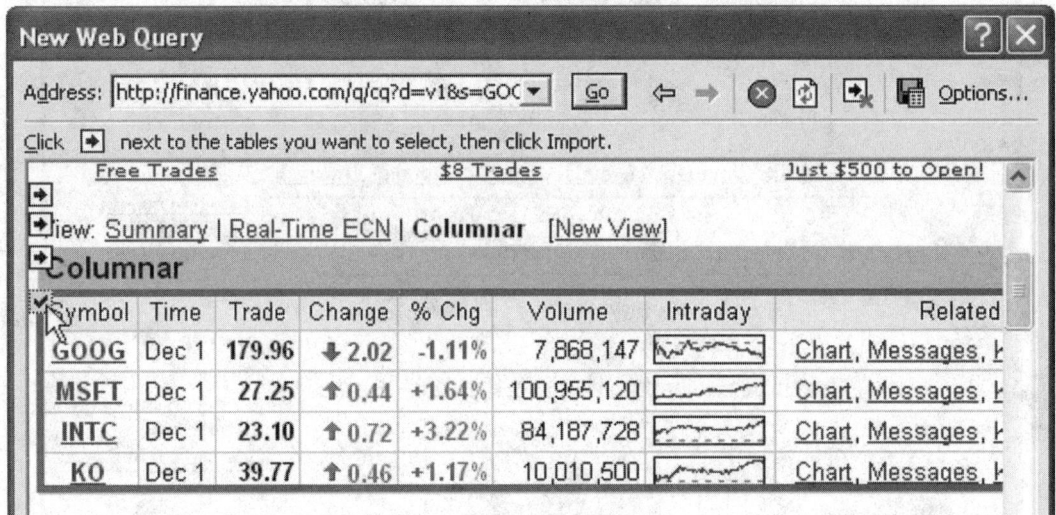

Fig. 1023

6)   Choose the Import button. Excel will ask where you want the data imported, as shown in Fig. 1024.

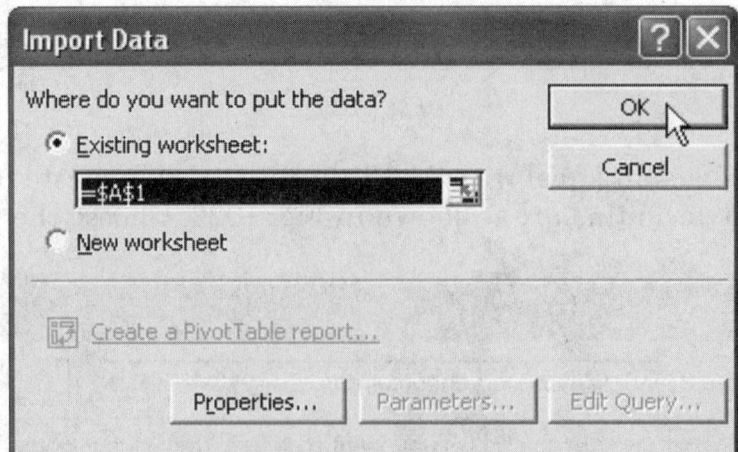

Fig. 1024

The dialog box disappears. For a few seconds, you see a strange value in cell A1, followed by "Getting Data…". In 1-10 seconds, the spreadsheet will redraw with a current version of the data from the Web page, as shown in Fig. 1025.

	A	B	C	D	E	F	G	H
1	Symbol	Time	Trade	Change	% Chg	Volume	Intraday	Related Info
2	GOOG	1-Dec	179.96	Down 2.02	-1.11%	7,868,147		Chart, Messages, Key Stats, More
3	MSFT	1-Dec	27.25	Up 0.44	1.64%	100,955,120		Chart, Messages, Key Stats, More
4	INTC	1-Dec	23.1	Up 0.72	3.22%	84,187,728		Chart, Messages, Key Stats, More
5	KO	1-Dec	39.77	Up 0.46	1.17%	10,010,500		Chart, Messages, Key Stats, More

Fig. 1025

7) To refresh the data at any time, return to this worksheet. Use Data – Refresh Data, as shown in Fig. 1026.

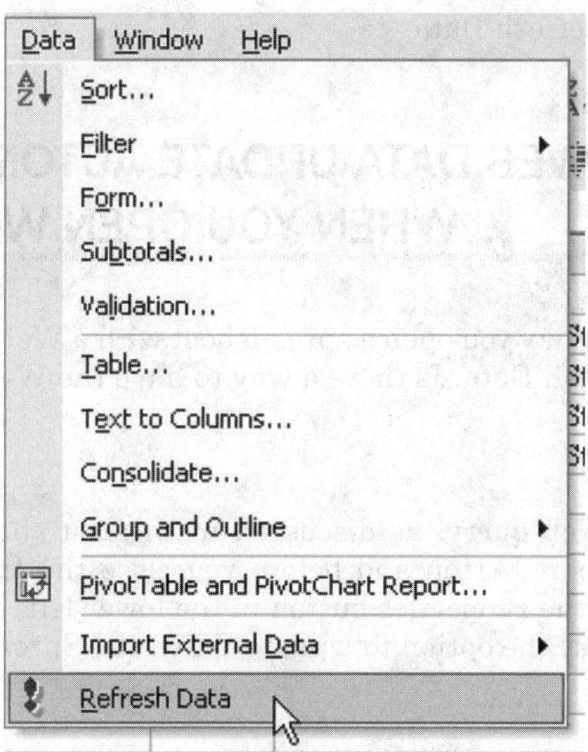

Fig. 1026

LEARN EXCEL FROM MR EXCEL

Additional Information: You can add numbers and formulas adjacent to the Web query. For example, you might add a column for the number of shares you hold and then calculate a value, as shown in Fig. 1027.

	J2	▼		fx	=I2*C2				
	C	D	E	F	G	H	I	J
1	Trade	Change	% Chg	Volume	Intraday	Related Info	My Share	Value
2	179.96	Down 2.02	-1.11%	7,868,147		Chart, Messages, Key Stats, More	10	1799.6
3	27.25	Up 0.44	1.64%	100,955,120		Chart, Messages, Key Stats, More	100	2725
4	23.1	Up 0.72	3.22%	84,187,728		Chart, Messages, Key Stats, More	100	2310
5	39.77	Up 0.46	1.17%	10,010,500		Chart, Messages, Key Stats, More	100	3977
6							Total:	10811.6

Fig. 1027

Summary: Web queries offer an easy way to regularly import data from a Web page into Excel.

Commands Discussed: Data – Import External Data – New Web Query; Data – Refresh Data

HAVE WEB DATA UPDATE AUTOMATICALLY WHEN YOU OPEN WORKBOOK

Problem: Every day you open a spreadsheet with a Web page query and use Data – Refresh Data. Is there a way to have the Web Query refresh automatically?

Strategy:

1) Set up a Web query, as discussed in the last chapter. After you hit the Import button and before you close the Import Data dialog, choose the Properties button in the lower left, as shown in Fig. 1028. Choose the option to Update When the Spreadsheet Opens.

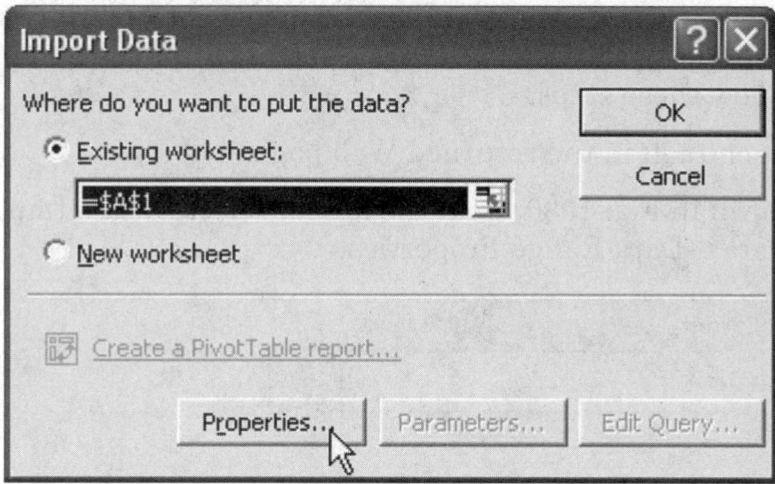

Fig. 1028

2)   The External Data Range Properties dialog will display. In the Refresh Control section, choose the option to Refresh Data on File Open, as shown in Fig. 1029.

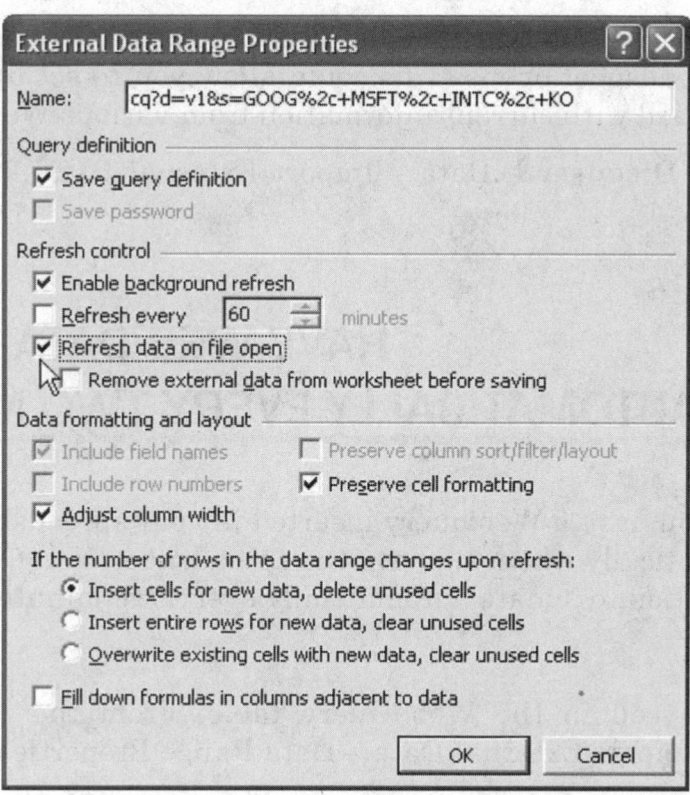

Fig. 1029

Additional Details: If you have a Web query set up and you need to access the Properties dialog to change a setting after the query has been defined, follow these steps.

1)   Select one cell in the returned Web page.

2)   As shown in Fig. 1030, from the menu, select Data – Import External Data – Data Range Properties.

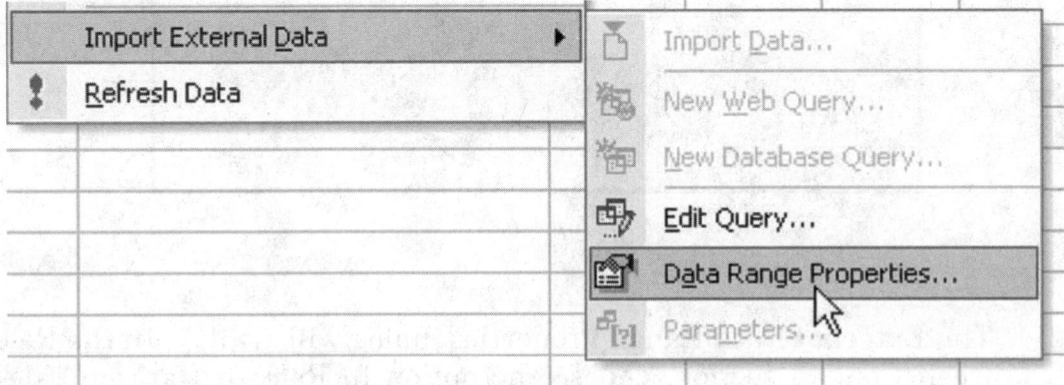

Fig. 1030

Summary: A Web query can be defined to update automatically every time the spreadsheet opens. This could allow you to set up a management dashboard with current information from various Web pages.

Commands Discussed: Data – Import External Data – Data Range Properties

HAVE WEB DATA UPDATE
AUTOMATICALLY EVERY TWO MINUTES

Problem: You have a Web query inserted in your spreadsheet that updates automatically when you open the spreadsheet. You would like the Web information to update automatically every two minutes.

Strategy:

1)   Select a cell in the Web Query table. From the menu, select Data – Import External Data – Data Range Properties.

2) From the External Range Properties dialog box, in the Refresh Contol section, select the Refresh Every option. Change the spin button to 2 minutes, as shown in Fig. 1031.

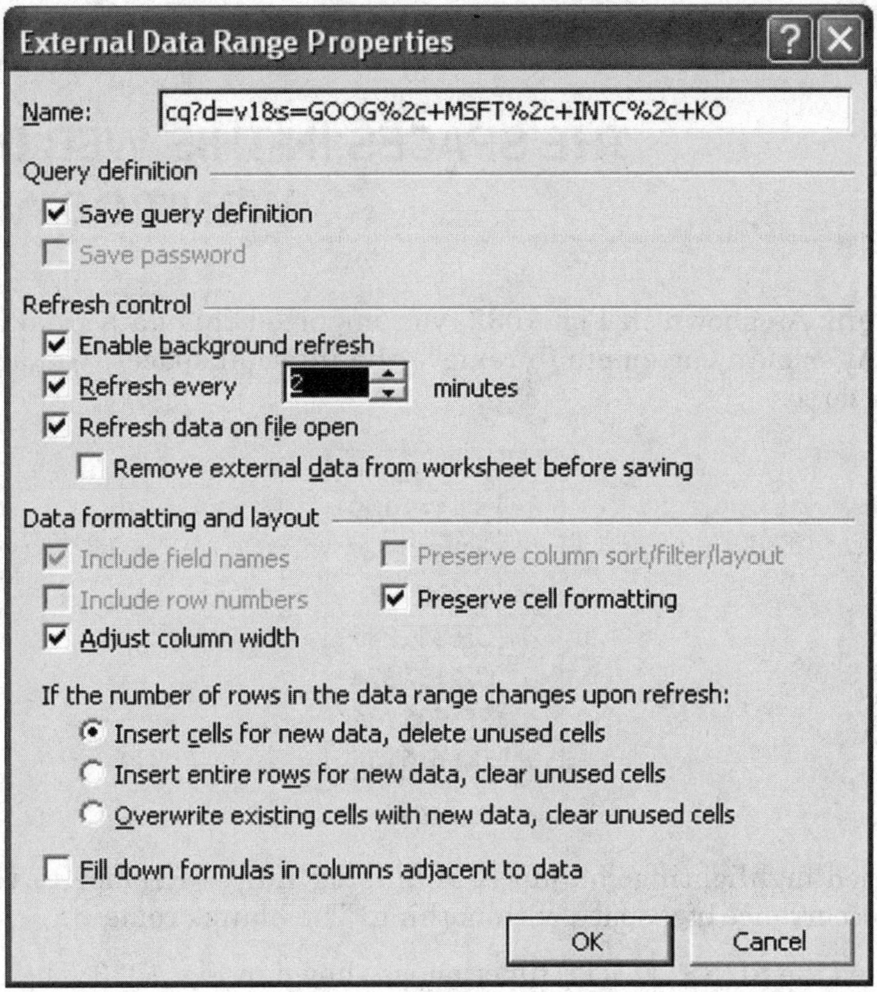

Fig. 1031

Gotcha: A refresh cannot happen if you are in Edit mode. If you start to enter a cell in the worksheet, get a telephone call, and head off to a meeting without completing the cell, Excel cannot update the query.

Gotcha: You may want to open a second instance of Excel and have the AutoRefresh query retrieved above in its own window. If you are trying to work in the same instance of Excel, the pause that occurs every two minutes while Excel refreshes is maddening.

Summary: To have a web query automatically update periodically, use the properties box and select the AutoRefresh button.

Commands Discussed: Date – Get External Data – Data Range Properties

THE SPACES IN THIS WEB DATA WON'T GO AWAY

Problem: As shown in Fig. 1032, you imported this data from a Web page. After many attempts to remove the internal spaces, you are still unable do so.

	A
1	AJ 335 986
2	AV 797 147
3	CJ 541 149
4	CR 846 746
5	CZ 137 324
6	FD 605 706
7	JM 615 876

Fig. 1032

You tried highlighting column A and using Edit – Replace to replace every occurrence of a space with nothing. The blanks remain.

You tried the SUBSTITUTE function, as shown in Fig. 1033. The blanks remain.

B1   fx =SUBSTITUTE(A1," ","")

	A	B	C	D	E
1	AJ 335 986	AJ 335 986			
2	AV 797 147	AV 797 147			
3	CJ 541 149	CJ 541 149			
4	CR 846 746	CR 846 746			
5	CZ 137 324	CZ 137 324			

Fig. 1033

If you go to cell A1 and type AJ Space 335 Space 986, the formula in column B will work, as shown in Fig. 1034.

B1		▼		f_x =SUBSTITUTE(A1," ","")	
	A	B	C	D	E
1	AJ 335 986	AJ335986			
2	AV 797 147	AV 797 147			

Fig. 1034

What is going on? Why won't the formula work on numbers pasted from the Web page?

Strategy: You can do some investigative work. Every character in the alphabet is assigned a number. A capital letter "A" is really character code 65. Normally, a space is character code 32.

In order to find the character code for a character, you can use the CODE function. To isolate the third character in cell A1, you would use =MID(A2,3,1). To find the character code for that value, you would use =CODE(MID(A2,3,1)).

As shown in Fig. 1035, this formula confirms that the value typed into cell A1 contains a space (character code 32) in the third position.

C1		▼		f_x =CODE(MID(A1,3,1))	
	A	B	C	D	E
1	AJ 335 986	AJ335986	32		
2	AV 797 147	AV 797 147			
3	CJ 541 149	CJ 541 149			
4	CR 846 746	CR 846 746			

Fig. 1035

Now, copy that formula down to the other cells. As shown in Fig. 1036, all of the other cells have a character code 160 in the third position!

C2		▼		f_x =CODE(MID(A2,3,1))	
	A	B	C	D	E
1	AJ 335 986	AJ335986	32		
2	AV 797 147	AV 797 147	160		
3	CJ 541 149	CJ 541 149	160		
4	CR 846 746	CR 846 746	160		
5	CZ 137 324	CZ 137 324	160		
6	FD 605 706	FD 605 706	160		

Fig. 1036

Part
III

This explains why your attempts to change a space to nothing wouldn't work. The cells in A don't contain spaces.

A little research shows that character 160 is a non-breaking space. This is a space where you do not want the browser to start a new line between those words. The Nbsp character is very common on Web pages.

So, how can you use Character 160 in Edit – Replace? Here is one method.

Method 1:

1) Go to a blank cell in the worksheet and use the =CHAR(160) formula, as shown in Fig. 1037. You won't see anything in the cell, but the formula bar will show that you have a formula hidden there.

	=CHAR(160)	
C	D	E
32		
160		
160		

Fig. 1037

2) Copy this cell.

3) Select your range of Web data. From the menu, choose Edit – Replace, as shown in Fig. 1038.

	A	B	C
1	AJ 335 986	AJ335986	32
2	AV 797 147	AV 797 147	160
3	CJ 541 149	CJ 541 149	160
4	CR 846 746	CR 846 746	16
5	CZ 137 324	CZ 137 324	16
6	FD 605 706	FD 605 706	16
7	JM 615 876	JM 615 876	16
8	JS 729 656	JS 729 656	16
9	JW 575 238	JW 575 238	16
10	KF 574 928	KF 574 928	16
11	LG 831 760	LG 831 760	16
12	LZ 928 105	LZ 928 105	16
13	MC 429 519	MC 429 519	16
14	MD 152 951	MD 152 951	16
15	NJ 838 134	NJ 838 134	16
16	OP 817 204	OP 817 204	16
17	PD 105 934	PD 105 934	16
18	SH 514 666	SH 514 666	166

Find and Replace — Find / Replace — Find what: — Replace with: — Within: Sheet — Search: By Rows — Look in: Formulas — Replace All — Replace

Fig. 1038

4) In the Find what box, hit Ctrl+V to paste the non-breaking space. Again, you won't see anything that is there. Leave the Replace with box blank. Choose Replace All.

Result: As shown in Fig. 1039, the unwanted spaces are removed.

2	AV797147
3	CJ541149
4	CR846746
5	CZ137324
6	FD605706
7	JM615876
8	JS729656
9	JW575238
10	KF574928
11	LG831760
12	LZ928105
13	MC429519

Fig. 1039

Method 2: The other solution is to use the SUBSTITUTE function, as shown in Fig. 1040.

B2		▼	*fx* =SUBSTITUTE(A2,CHAR(160),"")		
	A	B	C	D	E	F
1	AJ 335 986	AJ335986	32			
2	AV 797 147	AV797147	160			
3	CJ 541 149	CJ541149	160			
4	CR 846 746	CR846746	160			
5	CZ 137 324	CZ137324	160			
6	FD 605 706	FD605706	160			

Fig. 1040

Summary: Although character 160 is the usual culprit for this problem, using the CODE function will allow you to find the character code for any such offending character.

Functions Discussed: =CODE(); =CHAR(); =SUBSTITUTE()

Part
III

USE A BUILT-IN DATA ENTRY FORM

Problem: You need to do data entry in Excel. You have a lot of records to key or to edit, as shown in Fig. 1041. Can you easily create a dialog to help with this?

	A	B	C	D	E	F	G	H
1	Invoice	Customer	Region	Rep	Merchandise	Tax	Freight	Total
2	1201	RST Pty Ltd.	Southern	Mary	280	39.2	14.95	334.15
3	1202	NOP Pty Ltd.	Northern Territory	Terry	237	33.18	14.95	285.13
4	1203	EFG Pty Ltd.	NSW	Joe	257	35.98	14.95	307.93
5	1204	EFG Pty Ltd.	NSW	Joe	523	73.22	29.95	626.17
6	1205	STU Pty Ltd.	Southern	Mary	266	37.24	14.95	318.19
7	1206	OPQ Pty Ltd.	OZ	Mary	577	80.78	29.95	687.73
8	1207	GHI Pty Ltd.	Western	Terry	895	125.3	29.95	1050.25
9	1208	HIJ Pty Ltd.	Northern Territory	Terry	328	45.92	14.95	388.87
10	1209	STU Pty Ltd.	Southern	Mary	220	30.8	14.95	265.75
11	1210	NOP Pty Ltd.	Northern Territory	Terry	1006	140.84	34.95	1181.79
12	1211	GHI Pty Ltd.	Western	Terry	630	88.2	29.95	748.15
13	1212	MNO Pty Ltd.	Northern Territory	Terry	963	134.82	29.95	1127.77
14	1213	NOP Pty Ltd.	Northern Territory	Terry	703	98.42	29.95	831.37
15	1214	FGH Pty Ltd.	Queensland	Joe	113	15.82	14.95	143.77

Fig. 1041

Strategy: Using Excel VBA, you can build very complex dialog boxes for data entry. However, even without knowing VBA, you can use a simple built-in dialog for entering data.

1) Select a cell in your data. Choose Data – Form. As shown in Fig. 1042, Excel will display a dialog box with your fields. Use the Next and Previous buttons to move through the dataset.

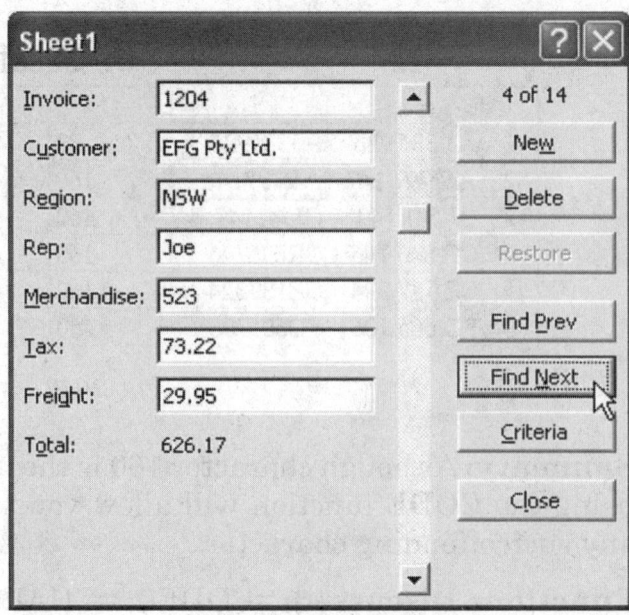

Fig. 1042

2)   To add a record, choose the New button. The Total field does not fill in until you choose Previous or Next to enter this record. When you come back to the record, the total will be filled in, as shown in Fig. 1043.

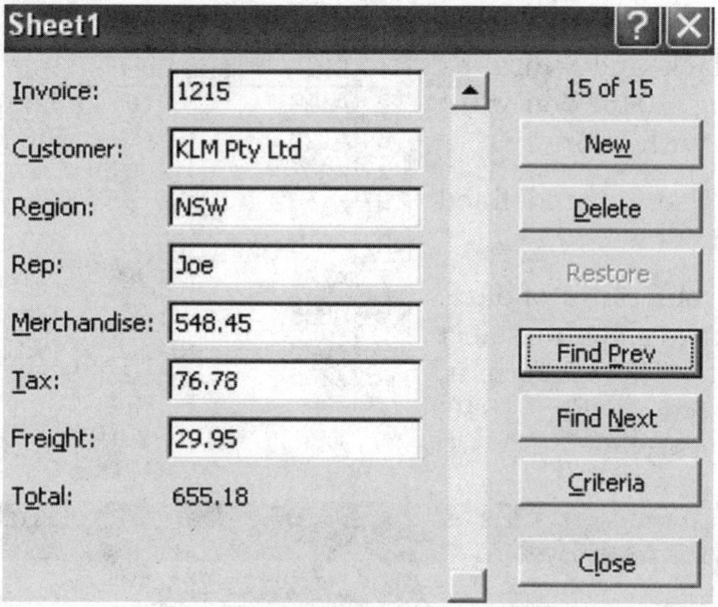

Fig. 1043

Additional information: The Criteria button will allow you to limit the Next and Previous buttons to only contain records. For instance, to show just those records where the sales rep is Joe.

Enter the criteria of Joe and choose the Form button to be able to scroll through just the Joe records, as shown in Fig. 1044.

Summary: To use a dialog box to help key records, select a cell in your data, choose Data – Form.

Commands Discussed: Data – Form

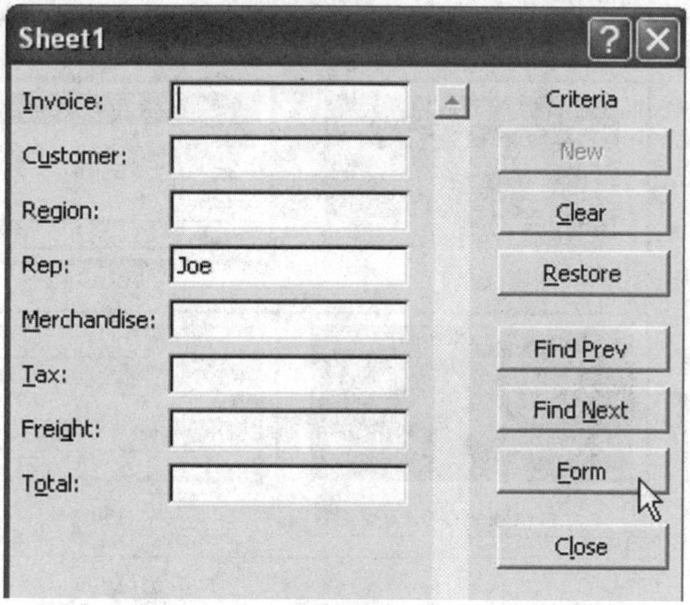

Fig. 1044

Part III

TRANSFORM BLACK AND WHITE
SPREADSHEETS INTO COLOR

Problem: Your worksheet is boring black and white, as shown in Fig. 1045. You want to jazz it up with color.

Strategy: Use a predefined AutoFormat.

1) Select your range of data. From the menu, select Format – AutoFormat. As shown in Fig. 1046, choose a style.

	A	B	C	D
1	**SKU**	**Mfg Cost**	**Part 1**	**List Price**
2	A409	209.03	421.06	425
3	A322	157.98	318.96	320
4	A356	18.97	40.94	45
5	A460	88.38	179.76	180
6	A976	165.08	333.16	335
7	A764	134.16	271.32	275
8	A865	71.02	145.04	150
9	A628	94.52	192.04	195
10	A196	190.05	383.1	385

Fig. 1045

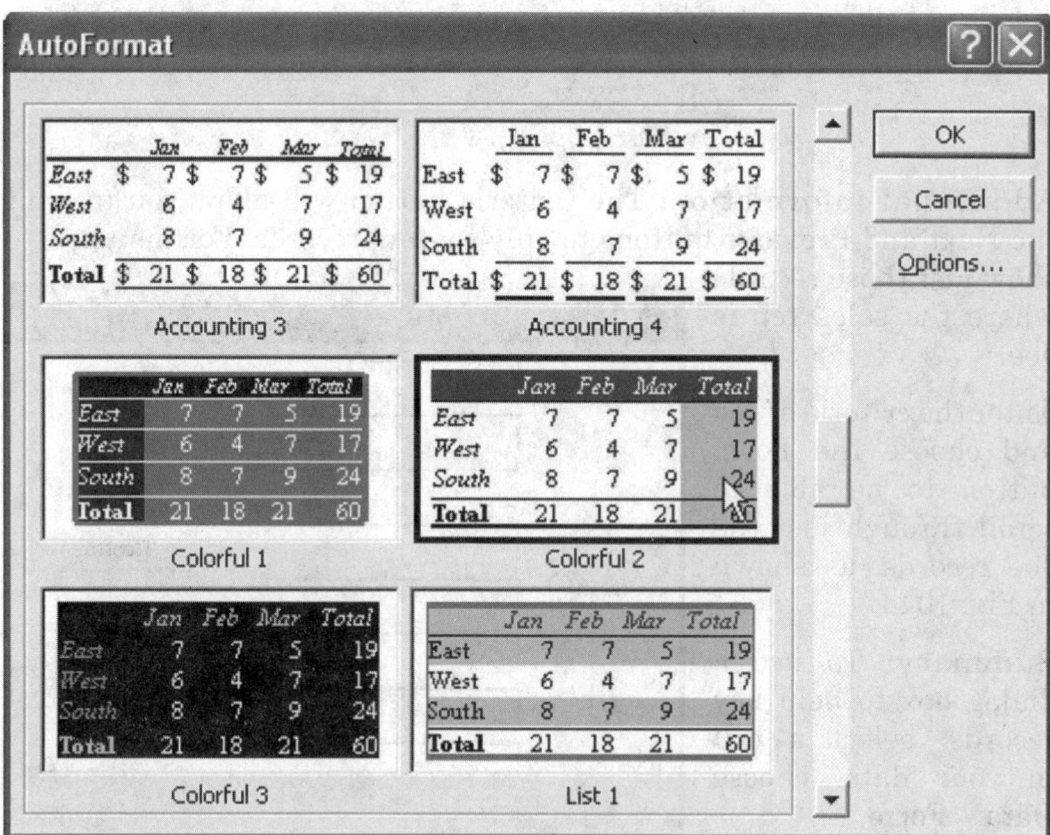

Fig. 1046

2) Choose the Options button. As shown in Fig. 1047, in the options section of the dialog, you can choose whether the format should apply to everything or, perhaps, everything except borders.

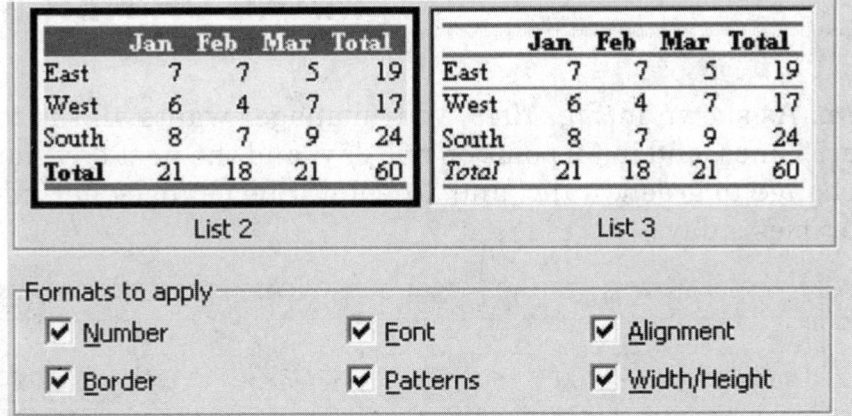

Fig. 1047

Result: Your worksheet is formatted in just a few clicks, as shown in Fig. 1048.

	A	B	C	D
1	SKU	Mfg Cost	Part 1	List Price
2	A409	209.03	421.06	425
3	A322	157.98	318.96	320
4	A356	18.97	40.94	45
5	A460	88.38	179.76	180
6	A976	165.08	333.16	335
7	A764	134.16	271.32	275
8	A865	71.02	145.04	150
9	A628	94.52	192.04	195
10	A196	190.05	383.1	385

Fig. 1048

Summary: The AutoFormat dialog offers many built-in formats to quickly transform a black and white spreadsheet to something neatly formatted.

Commands Discussed: Format – AutoFormat

YOUR MANAGER IS OBSESSED WITH FORMATTING AND CANNOT MAKE UP HER MIND

Problem: As shown in Fig. 1049, your manager wants all the totals in bold blue, Times, and in 12 point on one day, and the next day she wants you to change to green, italic, and 10 point. She changes her mind two to three times a day.

	A	B	C	D	E	F
1						
2	Product A	Q1	Q2	Q3	Q4	Total
3	England	1507	1677	1902	2155	7241
4	N. Ireland	358	409	458	510	1735
5	Scotland	423	482	534	598	2037
6	Wales	447	507	557	629	2140
7	Total A	2735	3075	3451	3892	13153
8						
9	Product B	Q1	Q2	Q3	Q4	Total
10	England	1733	1954	2184	2430	8301
11	N. Ireland	495	564	623	687	2369
12	Scotland	500	559	631	721	2411
13	Wales	506	580	653	734	2473
14	Total B	3234	3657	4091	4572	15554
15						

Fig. 1049

Strategy: Calm down and put the resume away; you can tame this problem in two ways.

Method 1: The first method, for Excel 2002 and later versions, is to use Find and Replace for Formats.

1)   From the menu, select Edit – Replace. In the Find and Replace dialog, choose the Options>> button, as shown in Fig. 1050.

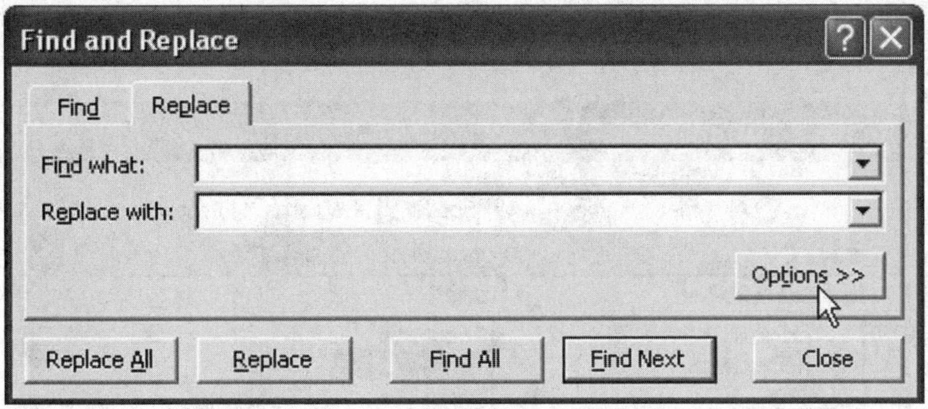

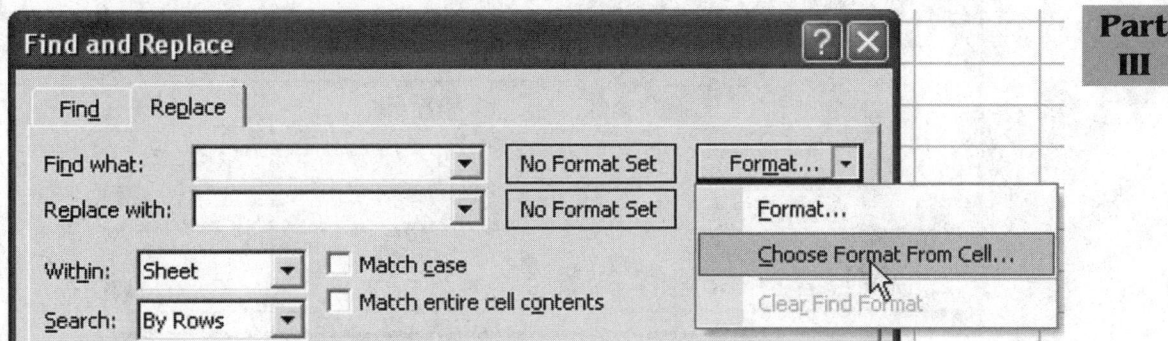

Fig. 1050

2)   Leave the Find What and Replace With boxes blank. On the right side, choose the dropdown next to the top Format... button. Select Choose Format From Cell, as shown in Fig. 1051.

Fig. 1051

3)   Using the eyedropper, select the cell with the current totals format. See Fig. 1052.

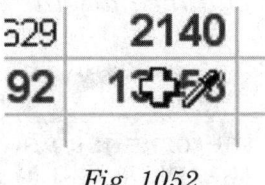

Fig. 1052

4)   Choose the second Format... button. Specify the new format to be used for the replacement, as shown in Fig. 1053.

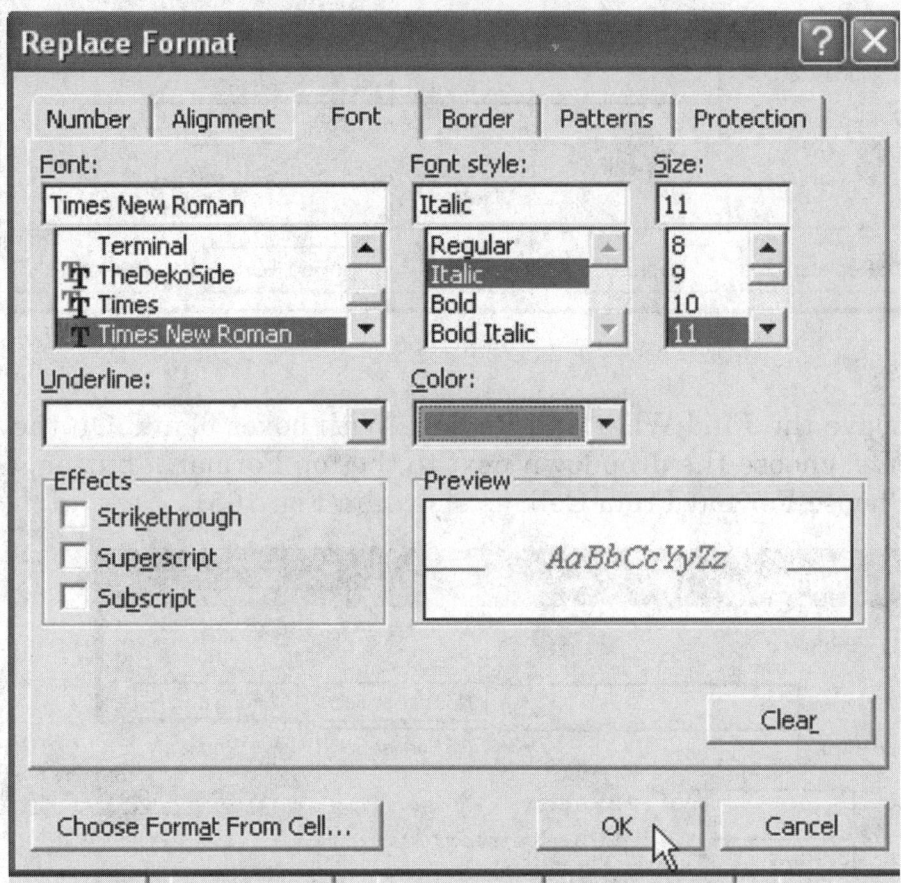

Fig. 1053

Tip   *To make a format similar to the original, select Choose Format From Cell and then change only the elements that you want to be different.*

5)   After specifying both the original and new formats, choose the Replace All button in the Find and Replace dialog, as shown in Fig. 1054.

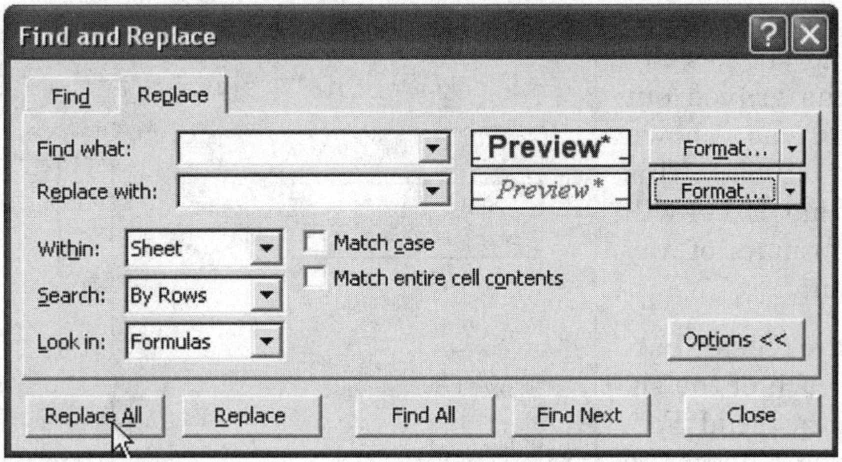

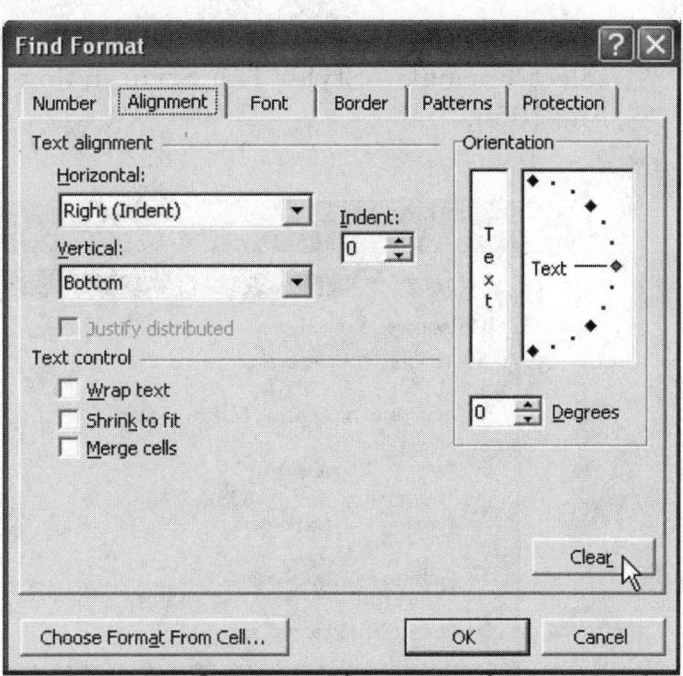

Fig. 1054

Gotcha: When you choose the format from an existing cell, Excel picks up all of the formats. When you perform the Replace, if a format does not match exactly, the cell is not replaced. For example, in Fig. 1055, the cells in column A were left-justified instead of right-justified. They were not replaced.

N. Ireland	495	564
Scotland	500	559
Wales	506	580
Total B	*3234*	*3657*

Fig. 1055

Part III

The workaround: To tell Excel that you want to change all of the blue, 12 point cells, irrespective of the alignment, you can Select Format from Cell, but then use the Clear button on the Alignment tab to clear all of the Alignment choices, as shown in Fig. 1056.

Fig. 1056

After choosing Clear, all of the choices are set to the grayed out checkbox, as shown in Fig. 1057. This means that Excel will choose formats of any alignment.

There are Clear buttons on each of the six tabs of the Find Format dialog. Choose the Clear button for any attributes that you do not need to replace.

Method 2: Use styles. Styles are popular in Word. Since Microsoft leaves the Style dropdown off the Formatting toolbar, many do not realize that you can use styles in Excel.

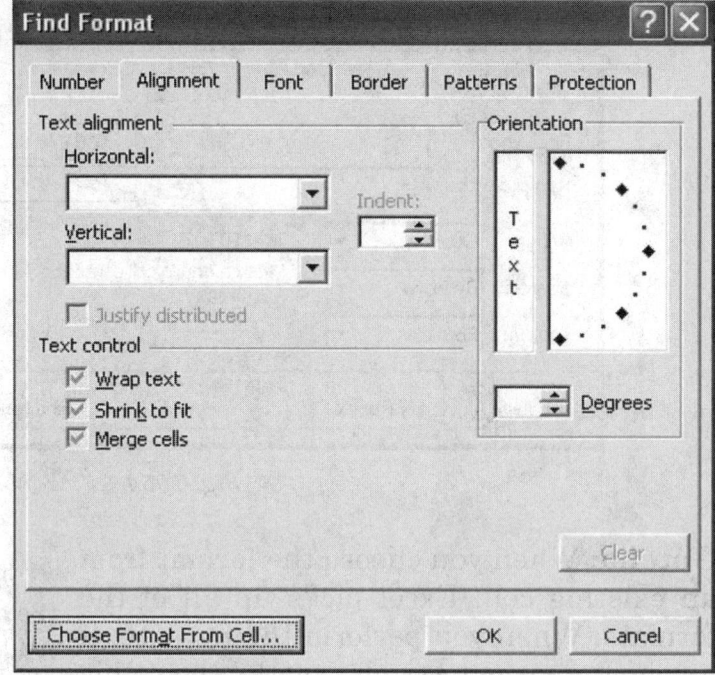

Fig. 1057

1)   First, you need to set up a style for your totals. From the menu, select Format – Style. The Style dialog is displayed, as shown in Fig. 1058.

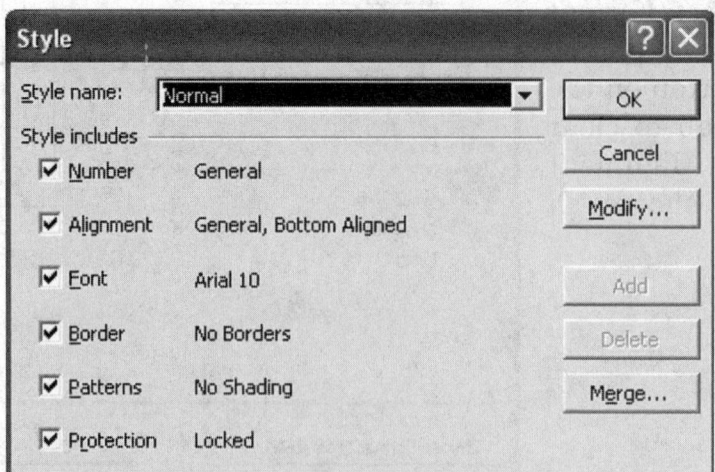

Fig. 1058

2) Type a new style name such as MyTotalStyle in the Style drop-down. Choose the Modify button. Use the Format button to set up the format *du jour*; Red, Times Italic, 11 point. See Fig. 1059.

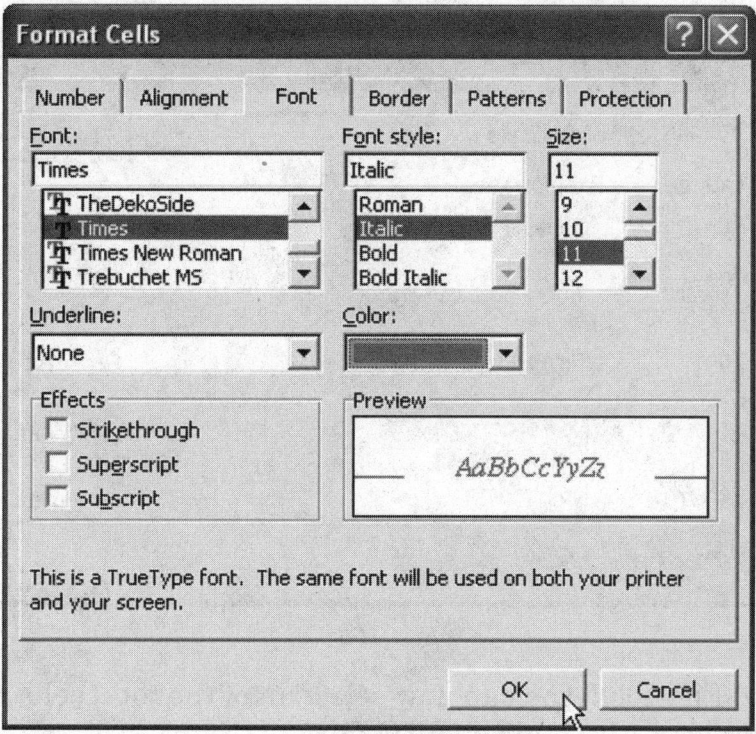

Fig. 1059

Caution: *Since a format applies to a single cell, you cannot select Inside borders on the Border tab.*

3) Choose OK to close the Format Cells dialog.

Examine the choices in the Style box. You want your style to be Red, Italic, and 11 point, but you do not want the style to include right alignment, as shown in Fig. 1060.

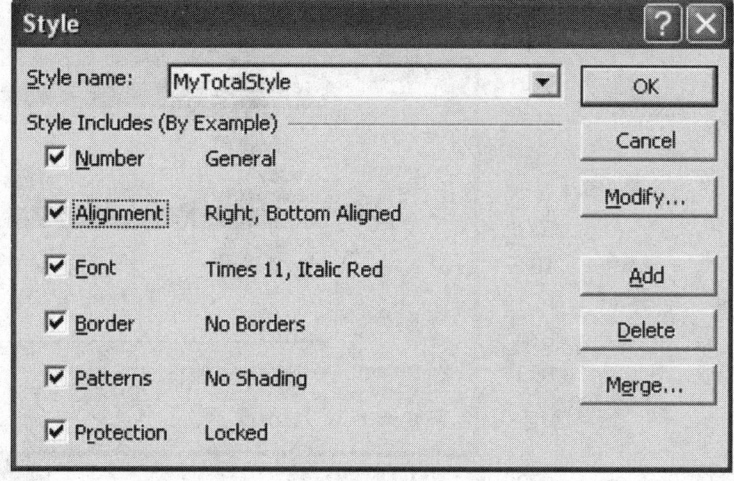

Fig. 1060

4) Uncheck the Alignment tab.

5) **Important:** To finish adding the style, choose the Add button, as shown in Fig. 1061.

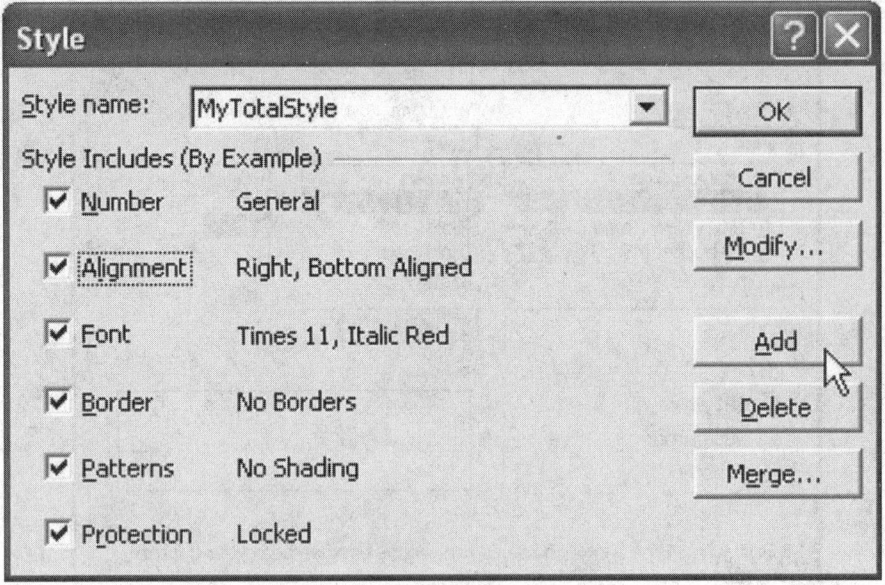

Fig. 1061

As shown in Fig. 1062, you can now select all of the total cells and choose Format – Styles – MyTotalStyle – OK.

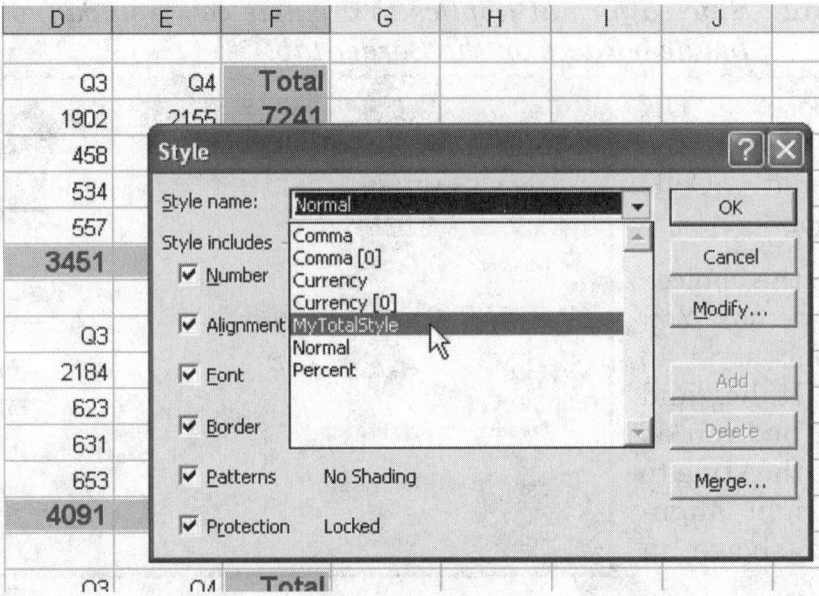

Fig. 1062

The next day, when your manager wants the total cells to be green, 14 point Tahoma, with double accounting underlines, the process is simple. First, select one of the Total cells. From the menu select Format – Styles – MyTotalStyle – Modify. Change the format and choose OK. All cells formatted with the MyTotalStyle format will change to the new format, as shown in Fig. 1063.

	A	B	C	D	E	F
1						
2	Product A	Q1	Q2	Q3	Q4	Total
3	England	1507	1677	1902	2155	7241
4	N. Ireland	358	409	458	510	1735
5	Scotland	423	482	534	598	2037
6	Wales	447	507	557	629	2140
7	Total A	2735	3075	3451	3892	13153

Fig. 1063

Summary: You can use Styles to manage constantly changing formats, or use the Edit – Replace – Formats option in Excel 2002 and later versions to change formats.

Commands Discussed: Edit – Replace – Format; Format – Styles – Add; Format – Styles – Modify

Part
III

PART 4

MAKING THINGS
LOOK GOOD

CREATE A CHART WITH ONE CLICK

Problem: You have to create a bunch of charts. You usually select all of the defaults in the Chart Wizard. Can you speed up the process?

Strategy: You can create a chart with one keystroke! Select the data, including the headings and row labels, as shown in Fig. 1064.

	A	B	C	D	E	F
1						
2		Jan-06	Feb-06	Mar-06	Apr-06	May-06
3	East	12,000	13,200	14,520	15,972	17,569
4	Central	17,000	19,550	22,483	25,855	29,733
5	West	8,000	8,400	8,820	9,261	9,724

Fig. 1064

Press the F11 key. The data is charted on a new chart sheet, as shown in Fig. 1065.

Part
IV

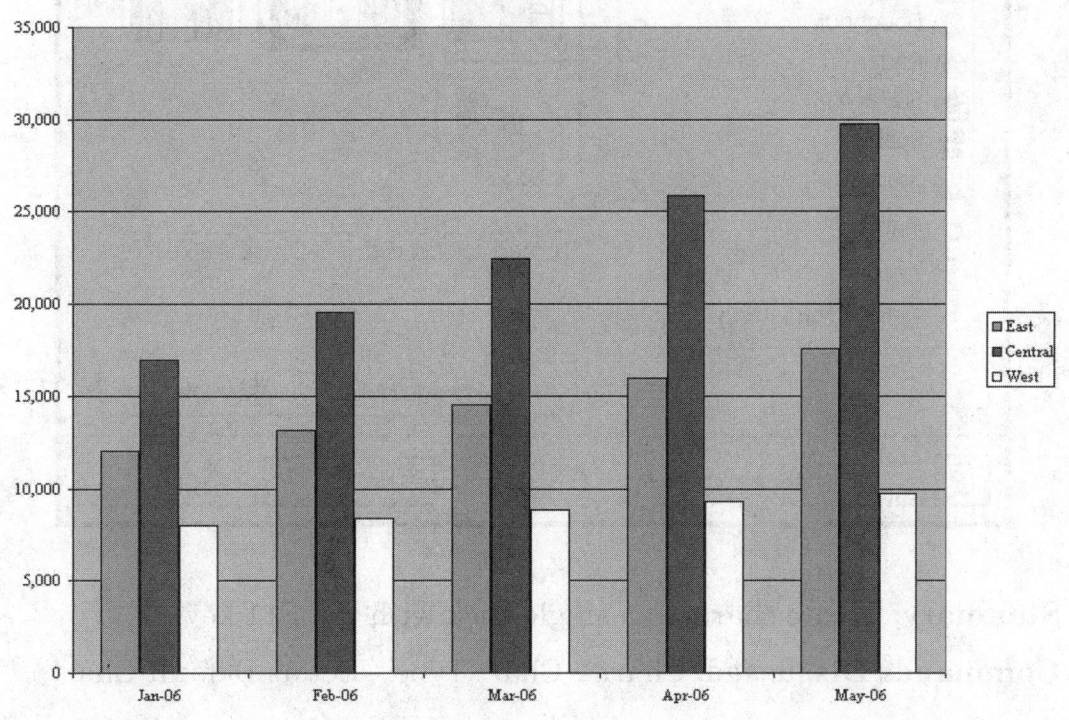

Fig. 1065

Caution: *If your data includes dates as labels, the upper left corner cell of the data range should be blank. Do not include a heading such as "Date" there.*

Additional Details: You can change the type of chart created with the single keystroke. While a chart is active, choose Chart – Chart Type. Select a Chart type and choose the button for Set as Default Chart, as shown in Fig. 1066. All future one-click charts will be created as this type.

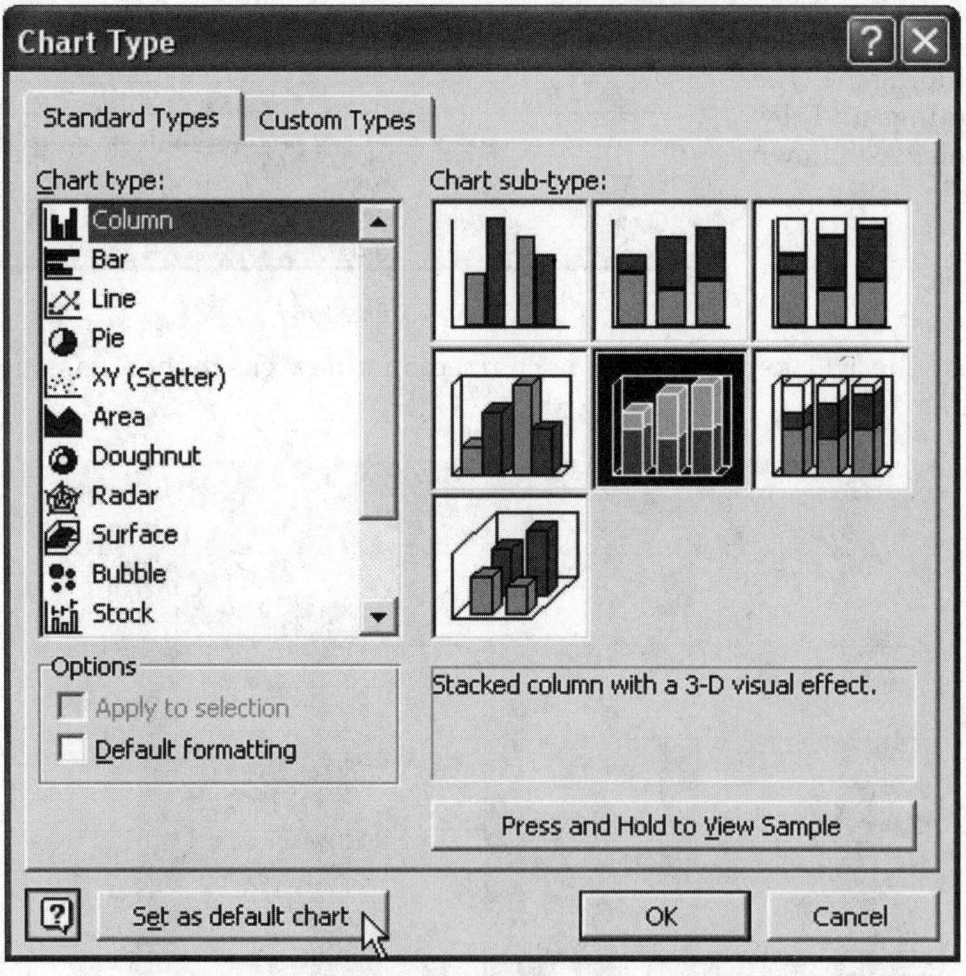

Fig. 1066

Summary: Create charts in a single click with the F11 key.

Commands Discussed: Chart – Chart Type – Set as Default Chart

CHANGE A CHART FROM
A CHART SHEET TO AN EMBEDDED CHART

Problem: You created a chart with the F11 key. You need this chart to be an embedded chart. How can you change the location of the chart?

Strategy:

1) Right-click the chart. Choose Location, as shown in Fig. 1067.

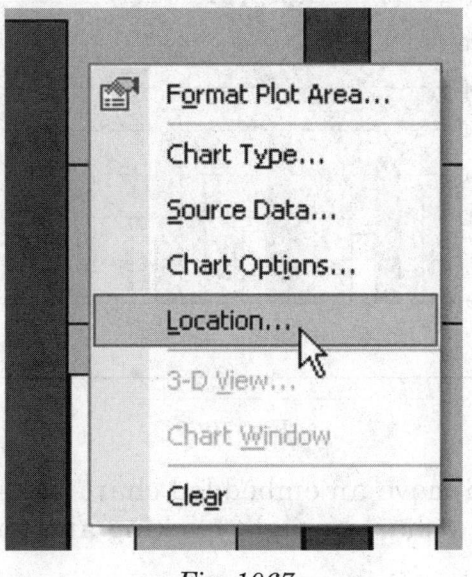

Fig. 1067

Part IV

2) As shown in Fig. 1068, in the Chart Location dialog, choose a new location.

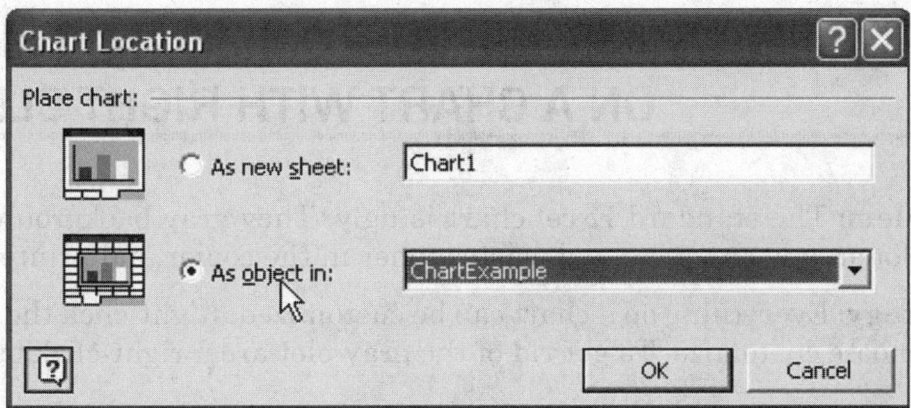

Fig. 1068

Gotcha: When you move a chart from a chart sheet to an embedded object, the size and scale of the chart changes, as shown in Fig. 1069. It is best to move the chart to its final location before customizing it.

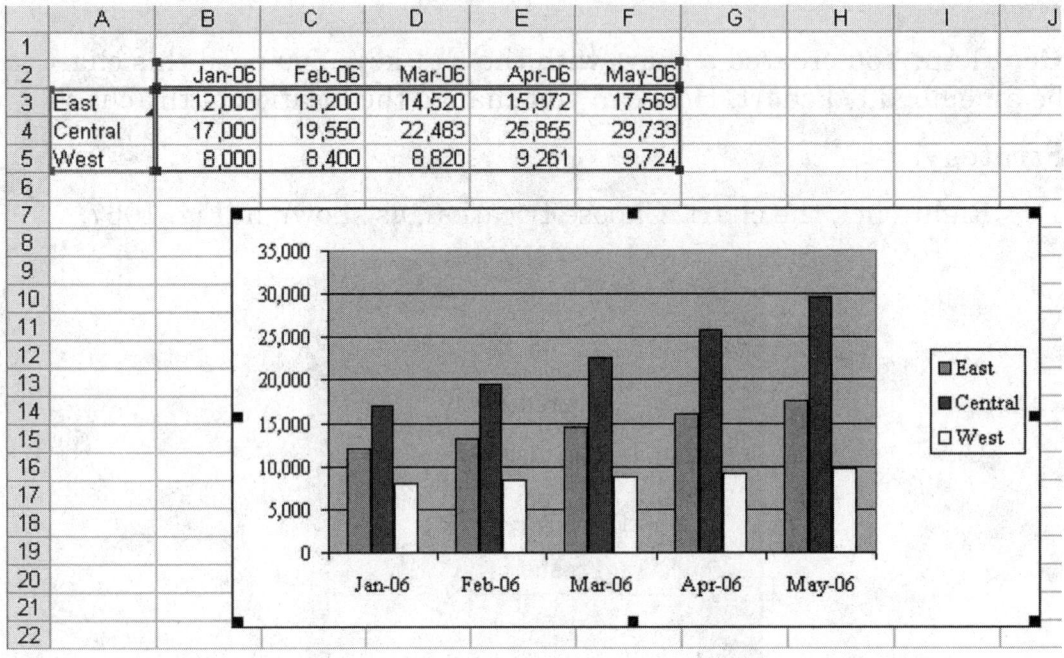

Fig. 1069

Summary: You can move an embedded chart to its own chart sheet or back to an embedded chart by right-clicking and choosing the Location option.

Commands Discussed: Chart – Chart Location

CUSTOMIZE ANYTHING
ON A CHART WITH RIGHT-CLICK

Problem: The standard Excel chart is ugly. They gray background on the plot area is annoying and wastes toner in the copier and printer.

Strategy: Everything on a chart can be customized. Right-click the item and choose customize. To get rid of the gray plot area, right-click on the middle of nothing in the chart and choose Format Plot Area, as shown in Fig. 1070.

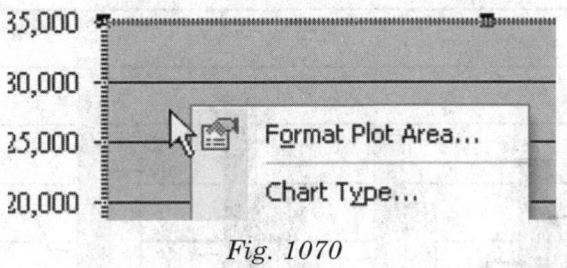

Fig. 1070

In the Format dialog, choose the white color to eliminate the gray background, as shown in Fig. 1071.

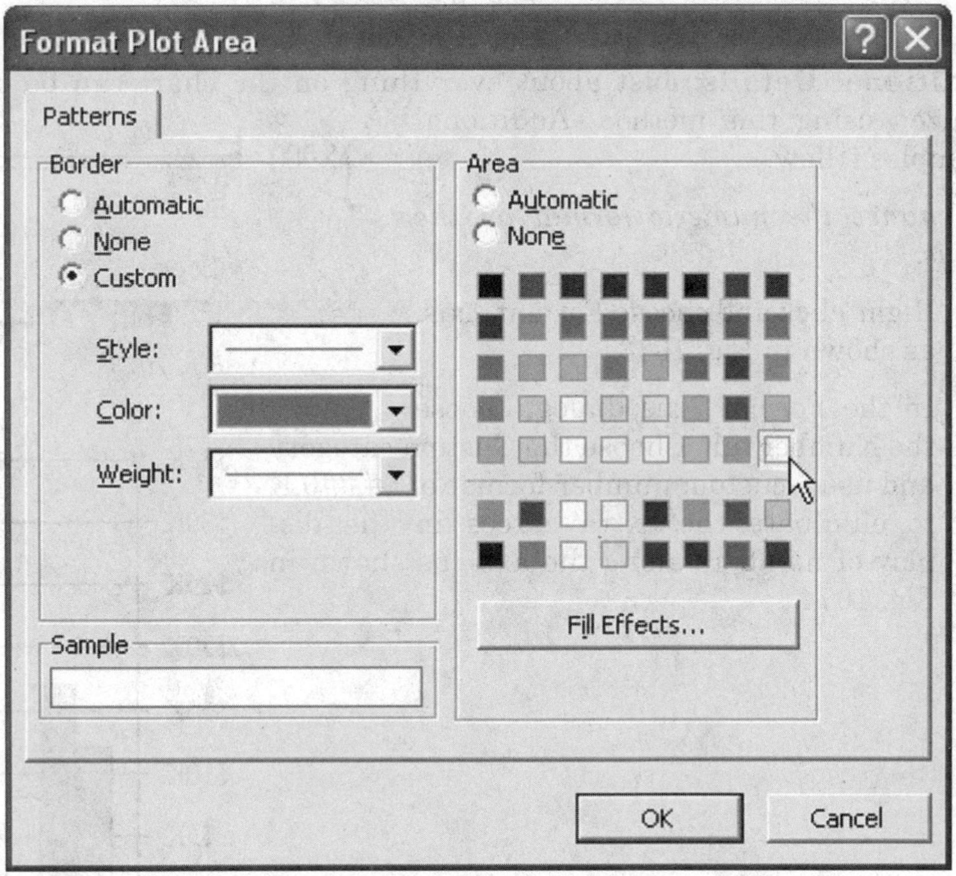

Fig. 1071

Result: As shown in Fig. 1072, the gray background is gone.

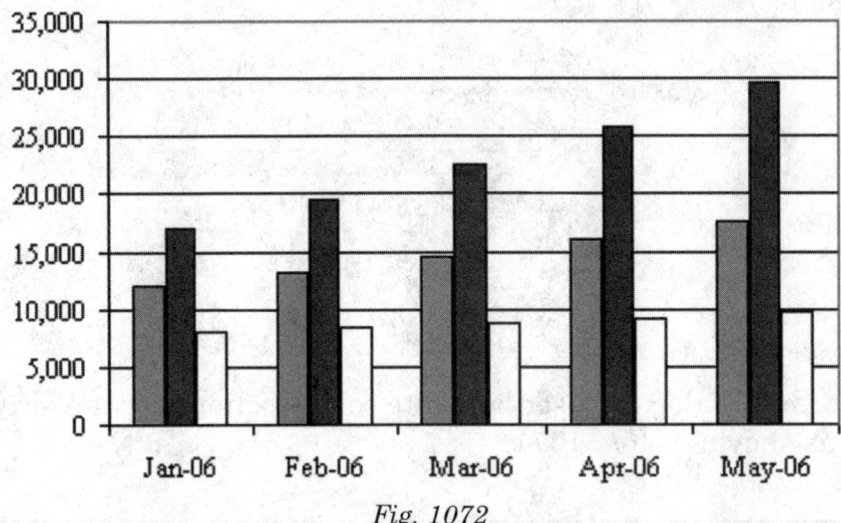

Fig. 1072

Additional Details: Just about everything on the chart can be customized using this method. Additional examples follow.

To change the numeric format on the y-axis:

Fig. 1073

1)   Right-click and choose Format Axis, as shown in Fig. 1073.

2)   In the Format Axis dialog, choose the Number tab. Choose the Custom category and use a custom number format of $#,##0,K to eliminate the extra zeroes in the display of numbers along the axis, as shown in Fig. 1074.

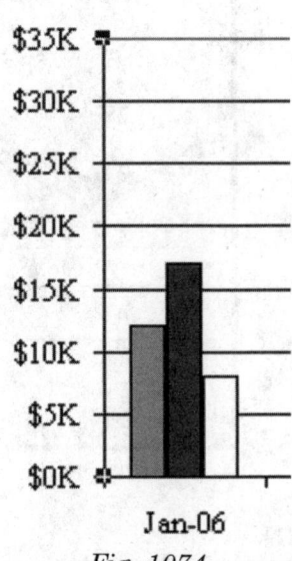

Fig. 1074

3)   You can drag the legend from its location along the side and drop it in a blank area of the chart, as shown in Fig. 1075.

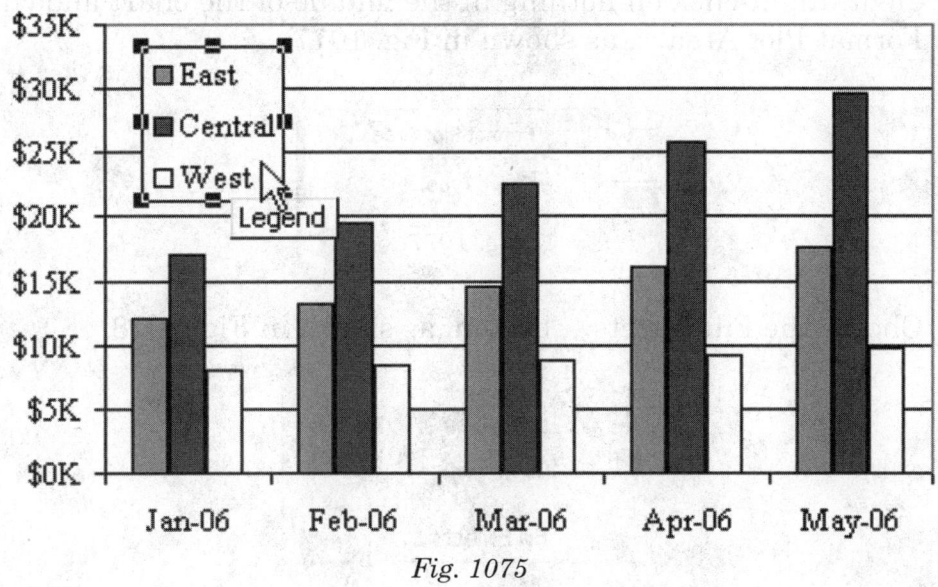

Fig. 1075

4)   You can then drag the right edge of the chart to the right, to fill the area that used to be taken up by the legend, as shown in Fig. 1076.

Part IV

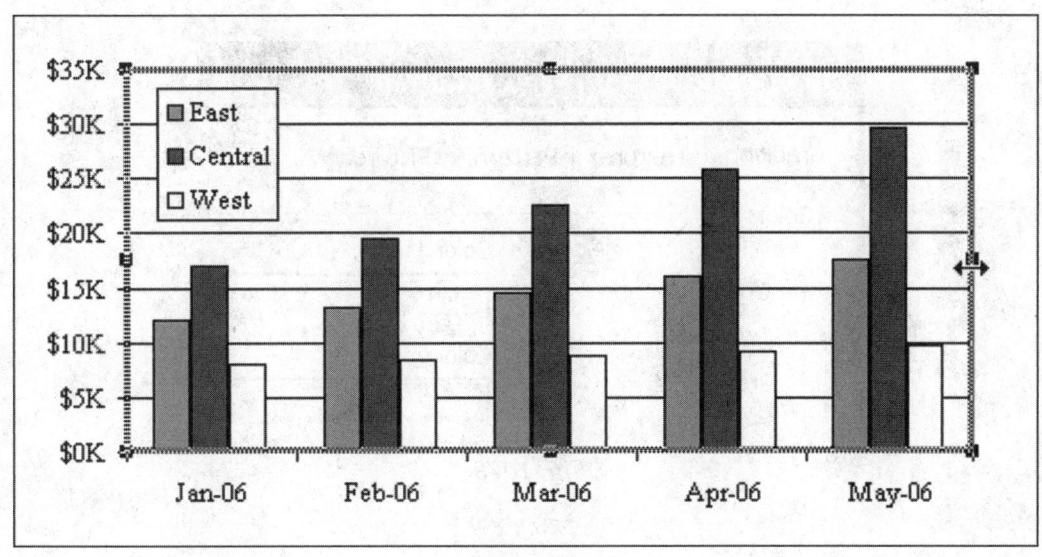

Fig. 1076

To change the background on the plot area:

1) Instead of a boring white plot area, you can use an interesting gradient. Right-click on nothing in the middle of the chart and choose Format Plot Area..., as shown in Fig. 1077.

Fig. 1077

2) Choose the Fill Effects... button, as shown in Fig. 1078.

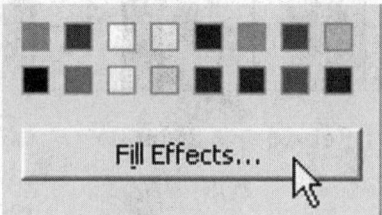

Fig. 1078

3) In the Fill Effects dialog, choose the Gradient tab. Choose Two Colors. I like a gradient from green to white for revenue charts, as shown in Fig. 1079.

Fill Effects

| Gradient | Texture | Pattern | Picture |

Colors

○ One color
● Two colors
○ Preset

Color 1:
Color 2:

Fig. 1079

To change the look of the data series:

1)   Single-click any bar to select the entire data series. Right-click and choose Format Data Series, as shown in Fig. 1080.

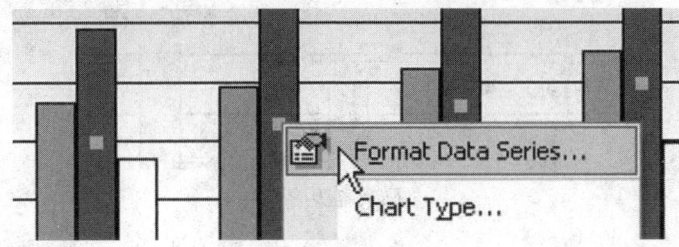

Fig. 1080

2)   You can now change the color for that series of bars. Or, you can add a data label to the bar, as shown in Fig. 1081.

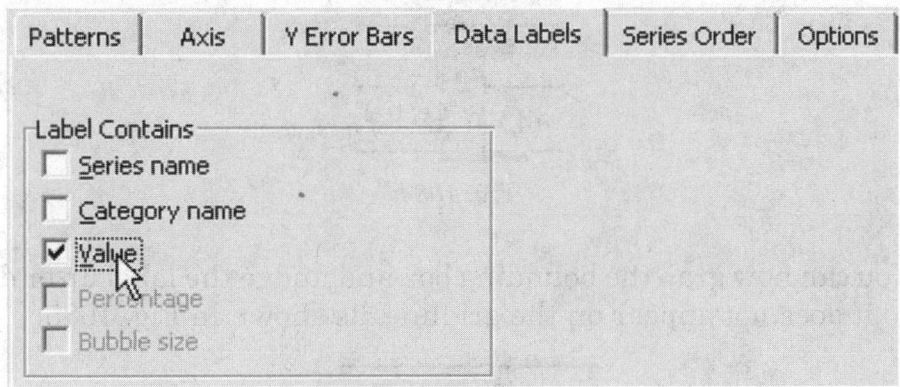

Fig. 1081

To change the look of a data point and its label:

1)   What if there is one single bar that needs explaining? Single-click the bar to select the whole series. Then, do a second single-click to select just the data point. You can right-click and select Format Data Point..., as shown in Fig. 1082.

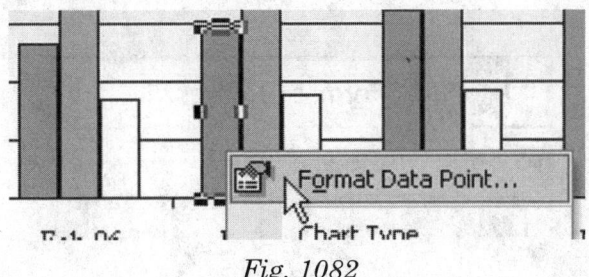

Fig. 1082

2)   If the data labels run into the axis, you can easily move them. The first click on a data label will select all of the data labels for that series, as shown in Fig. 1083.

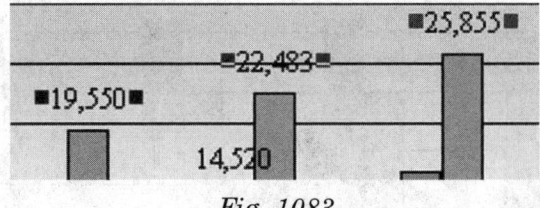

Fig. 1083

3)   A second single-click on the one data label will select just that label, as shown in Fig. 1084.

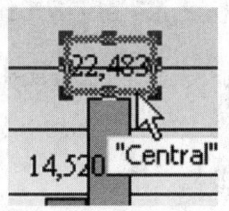

Fig. 1084

4)   You can now grab the bounding box and nudge the label up or down, so it does not appear on the gridline, as shown in Fig. 1085.

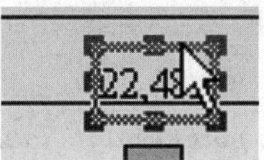

Fig. 1085

To control gridline formatting:

1)   As you might expect, you can change the gridlines by right-clicking on a gridline and choosing format gridlines, as shown in Fig. 1086.

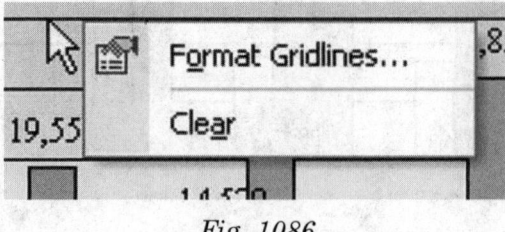

Fig. 1086

2)   Change the gridlines to be dotted lines instead of solid, as shown in
     Fig. 1087.

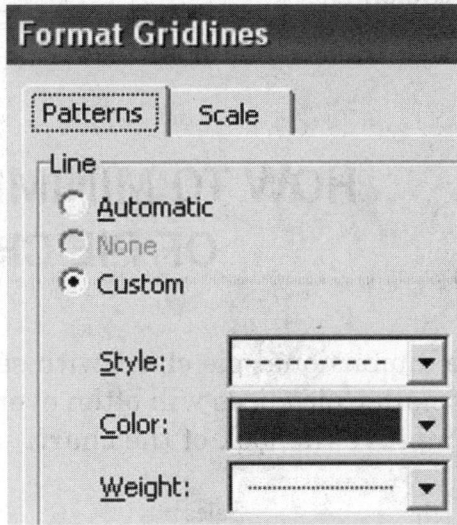

Fig. 1087

As shown in Fig. 1088, the resulting chart may be even more hideous
than the default Excel chart, but at least you can take pride that it is
hideousness that you created, instead of being forced to accept the Excel
default.

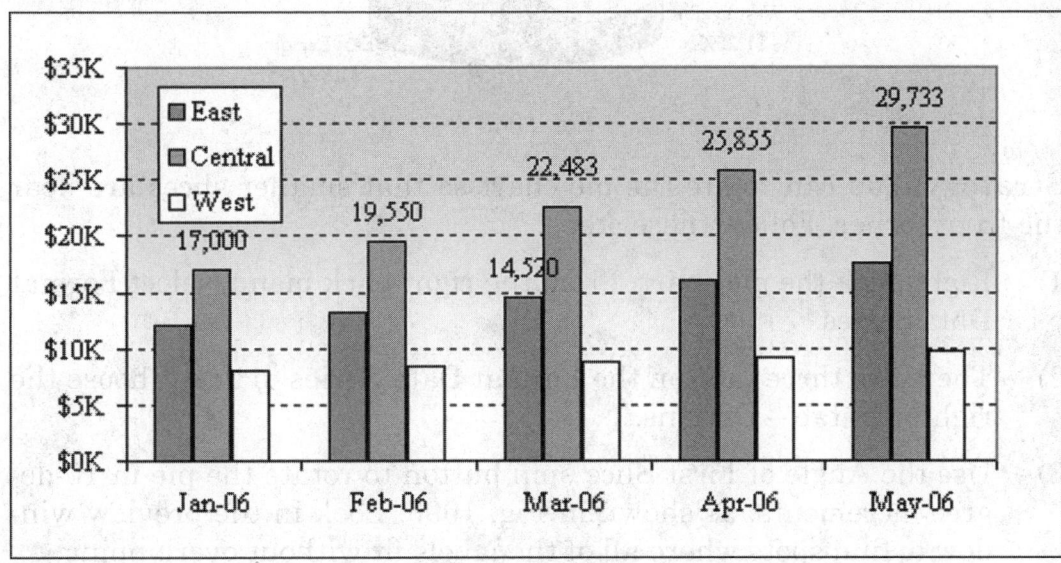

Fig. 1088

Summary: You have ultimate control of nearly everything on a chart. Few of these choices can be changed through the Chart menu. You have to right-click around the chart.

Commands Discussed: Chart – Customize

HOW TO MINIMIZE OVERLAP OF PIE CHART LABELS

Problem: On a three-dimensional pie chart with several small pie slices, the labels for the smaller pie slices will often overwrite each other, as shown in Fig. 1089. Improve the look of the chart.

Sales

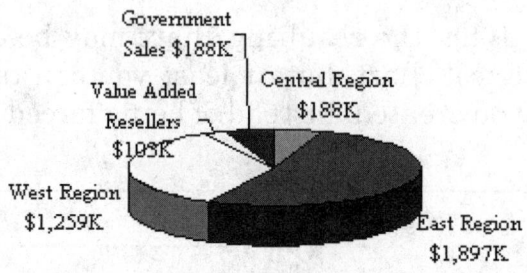

Fig. 1089

Strategy: You can rotate the pie chart so that smaller slices are near the front corner. Follow these steps.

1) Right-click the pie chart. From the right-click menu, select Format Data Series.

2) There are three tabs on the Format Data Series dialog. Choose the rightmost tab – Options.

3) Use the Angle of First Slice spin button to rotate the pie in 10-degree increments, as shown in Fig. 1090. Look in the preview window to find spots where all of the labels fit without overlapping.

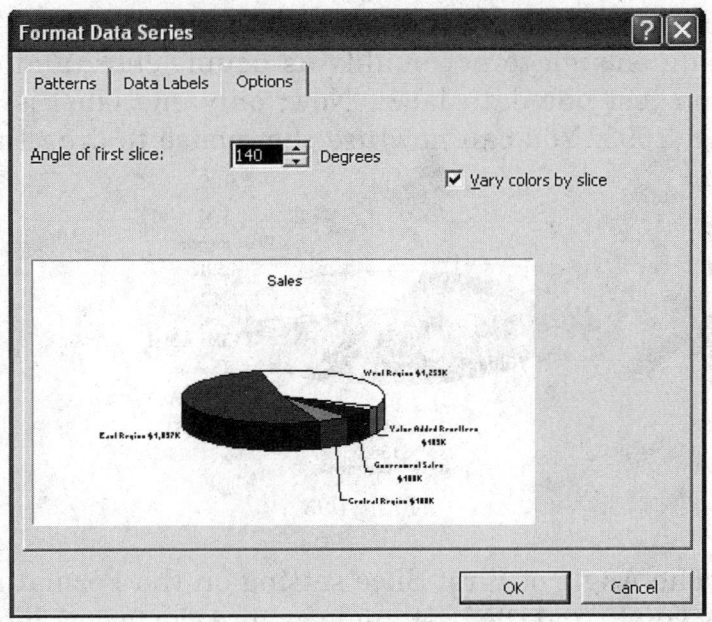

Fig. 1090

4)   Choose OK to close the Format Data Series dialog.

Result: All of the data labels are visible, as shown in Fig. 1091.

Alternate Strategy: Using the mouse, click on one of the data labels. Black Fill handles will surround all of the labels. Right-click any label and choose Format Data Labels, as shown in Fig. 1092. You can now change the font of all labels.

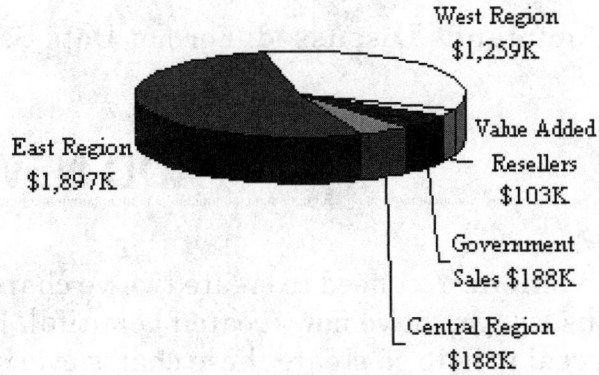

Fig. 1091

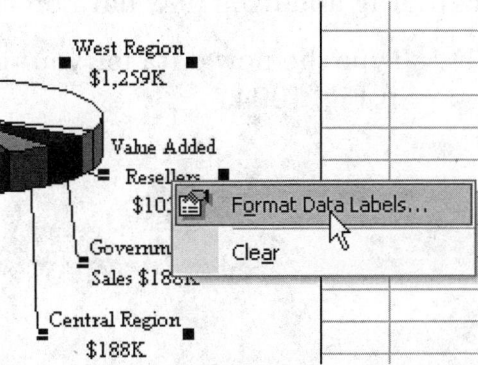

Fig. 1092

Alternate Strategy: Single-click on a data label to select all data labels. Wait long enough to not qualify as double-click, and do a second single-click on just one data label. Now, only one label is selected, as shown in Fig. 1093. You can now use the mouse to drag the label to a new position.

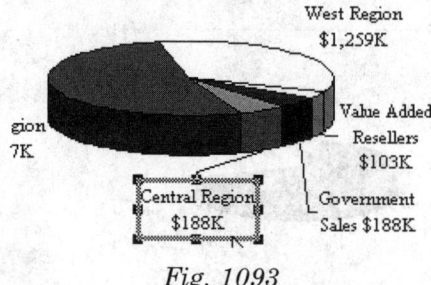

Fig. 1093

Summary: The Angle of First Slice setting on the Format Data Series dialog allows you to find the best angle, where the fewest labels overlap. You can then use the Format Data Labels to change the font or simply move one data label out of the way.

Commands Discussed: Format Data Series; Format Data Labels

ADD NEW DATA TO A CHART

Problem: You need to create twelve charts every month. Using a previous tip, you have now created beautiful, highly customized charts. It is a real pain to re-create these charts every month.

Strategy: If your chart is located as an embedded object on a sheet, you can drag and drop new data on the chart.

1) Type the new data for your chart adjacent to the old data, as shown in Fig. 1094.

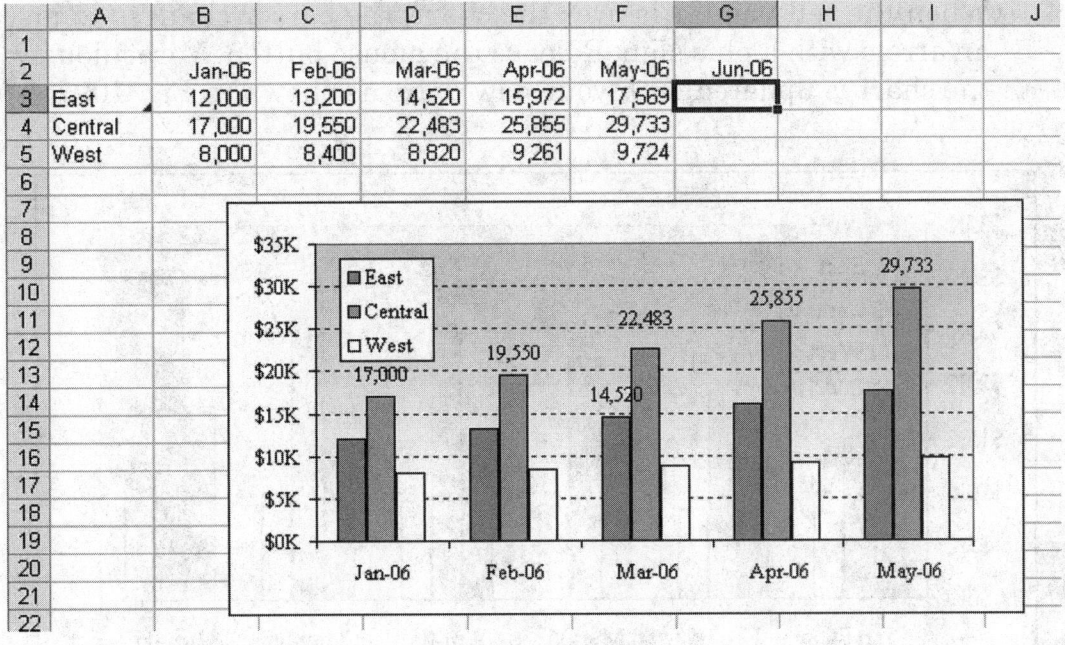

Fig. 1094

2) Select the entire range, including the new heading for the new month, as shown in Fig. 1095.

3) Using the mouse, grab anywhere on the thick black border (but do not grab the square Fill handle in the lower right). Start to drag the border down towards the chart, as shown in Fig. 1096.

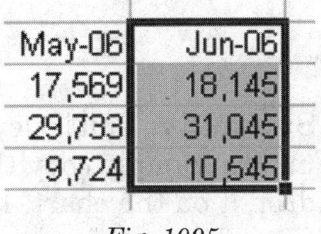

Fig. 1095

Part IV

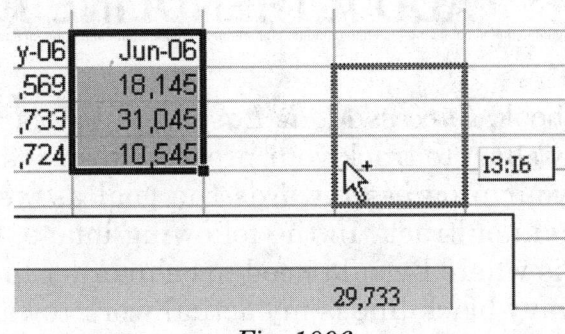

Fig. 1096

4) When the cell pointer is over the chart, the cursor changes to just an arrow with a plus sign. Release the mouse button. Miraculously, the chart is updated with your new data, as shown in Fig. 1097.

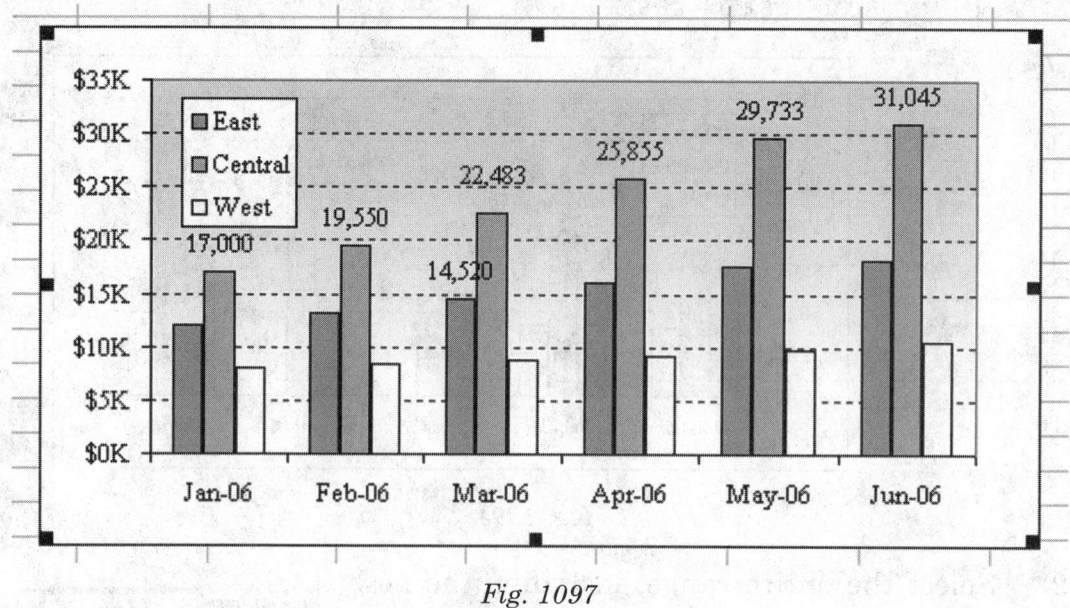

Fig. 1097

Summary: You'll never have to waste hours creating new charts each month. Simply copy the new data adjacent to the old data and drag and drop it on the chart. I first saw this trick in a demo at a Microsoft seminar. The "wow" factor was amazing.

ADD A TRENDLINE TO A CHART

Problem: In his book, *Success Made Easy*, retail guru Ron Martin suggests using a daily chart to track your progress towards a goal. His typical chart shows your progress towards the goal as well as where you need to be to remain on track. In the following image, the straight line is the track. This is where I would need to be in order to finish by the set goal. The thick, wavy black line is my actual work towards the goal.

As shown in Fig. 1098, I can see from the chart that I am not working on track to meet the goal. However, my question is: What would happen if I continued to work at my current pace? By how much would I miss the goal on 1 December?

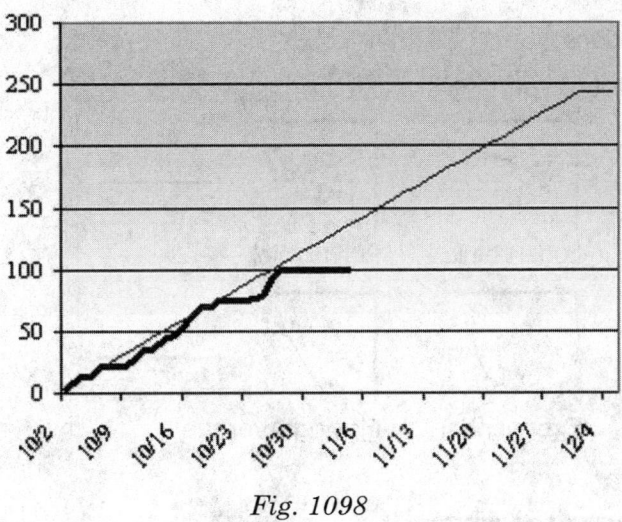

Fig. 1098

Strategy: Excel makes it easy to add a trendline to charted data.

1)   Right-click the graphed line for actual results. From the menu that appears, choose Add Trendline..., as shown in Fig. 1099.

**Part
IV**

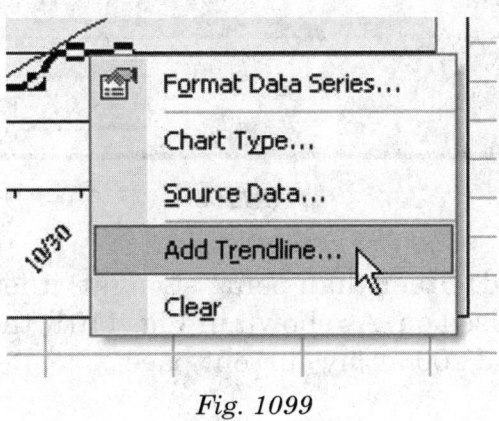

Fig. 1099

2)   In the Add Trendline dialog, you can accept the defaults, as shown
      in Fig. 1100. Click OK.

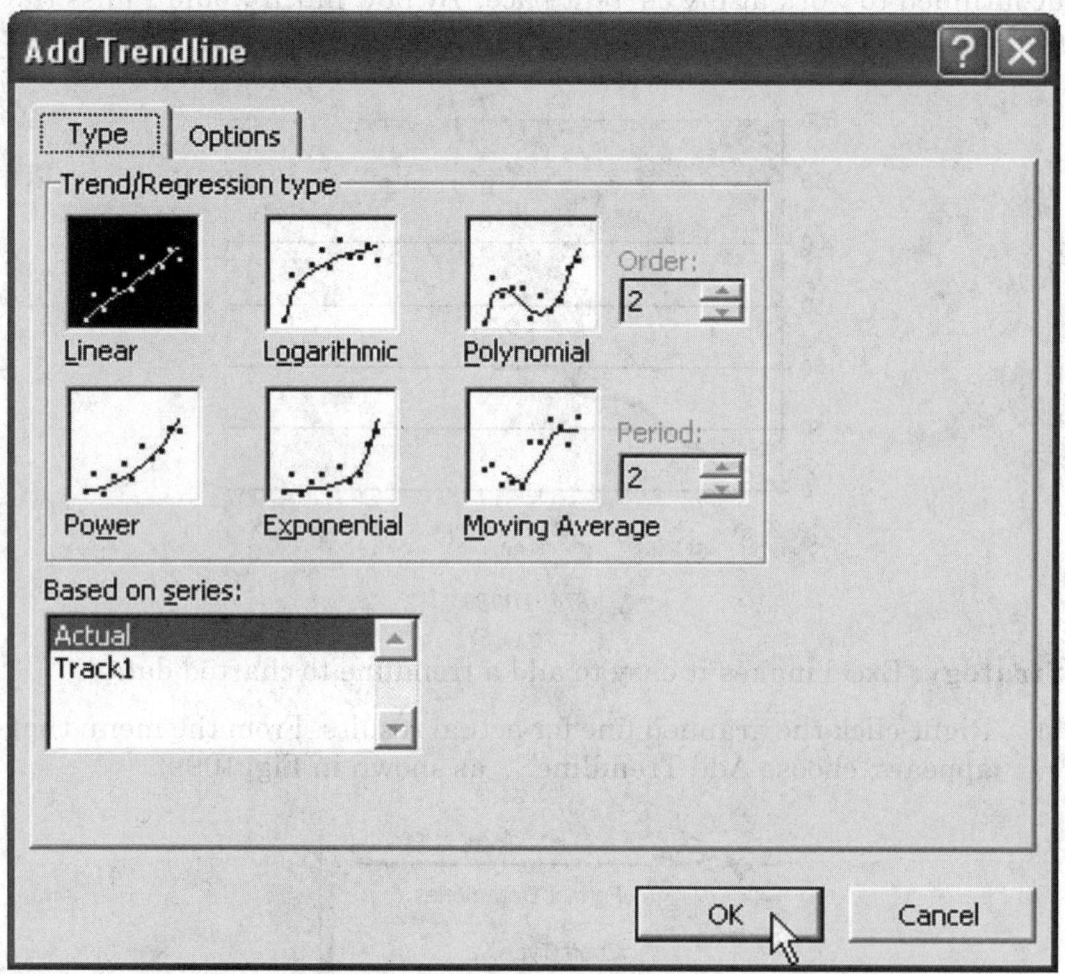

Fig. 1100

A trendline is added. Other than being straight, it looks very much like
the line that it is based on. As shown in Fig. 1101, the line tells me that
I will only be around 200 at my current pace.

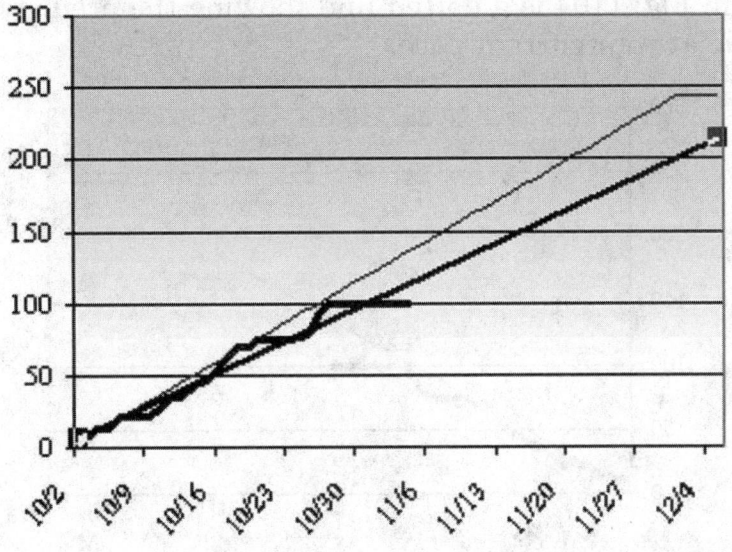

Fig. 1101

3) Since the trendline is only a forecast, I like to format it with a dotted style so that I know it is just a prediction. Right-click the trendline and choose Format Trendline..., as shown in Fig. 1102.

Fig. 1102

Part IV

4) Choose a thin weight in red and a dotted style, as shown in Fig. 1103.

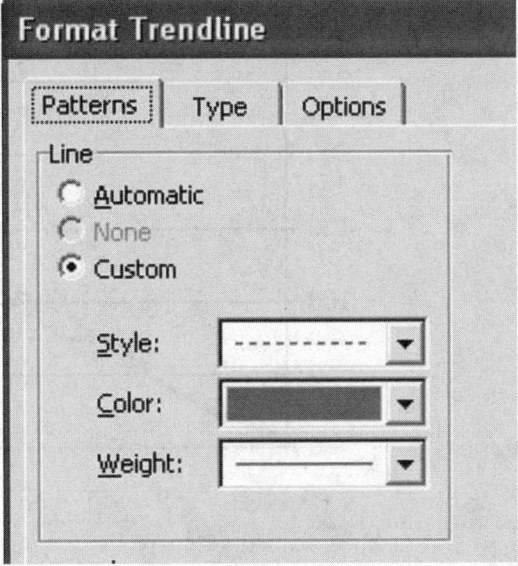

Fig. 1103

The result in Fig. 1104 is a dotted line showing the predicted results if you continue at your current pace.

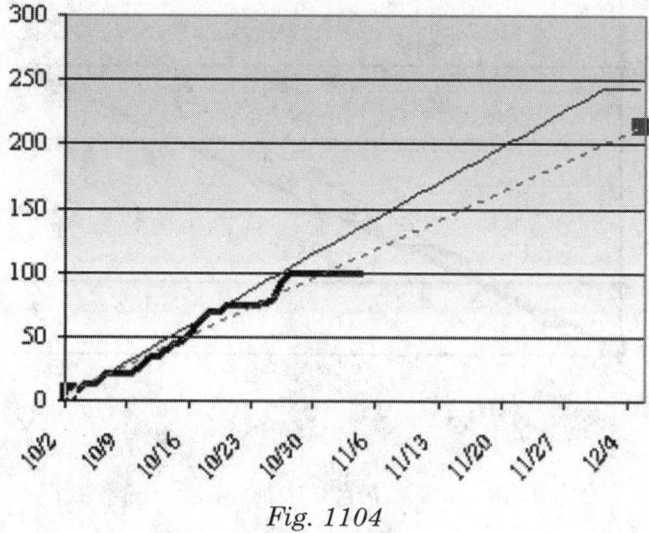

Fig. 1104

As you continue to plug in actual data, the trendline will redraw. After seeing the above chart, I was nervous about missing my goal and really put it into hyperdrive for the next few days. Even though the Actual line is above the Track line, the dotted trendline is still predicting I will miss the goal. That is because the trendline sees all of those days between 10/30 and 11/5 where I did nothing, as shown in Fig. 1105. It can predict that those days might happen again.

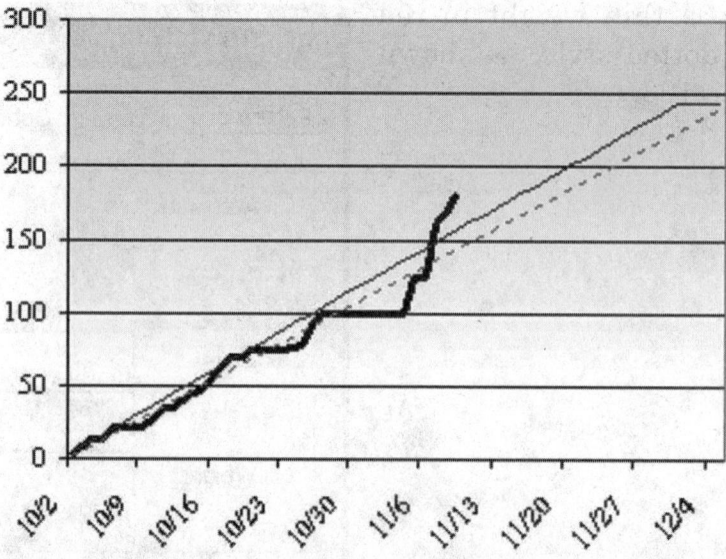

Fig. 1105

My reaction was to continue working at a pace to finish the project ahead of schedule. Finally, the red trendline acknowledged that I might beat the schedule, as shown in Fig. 1106.

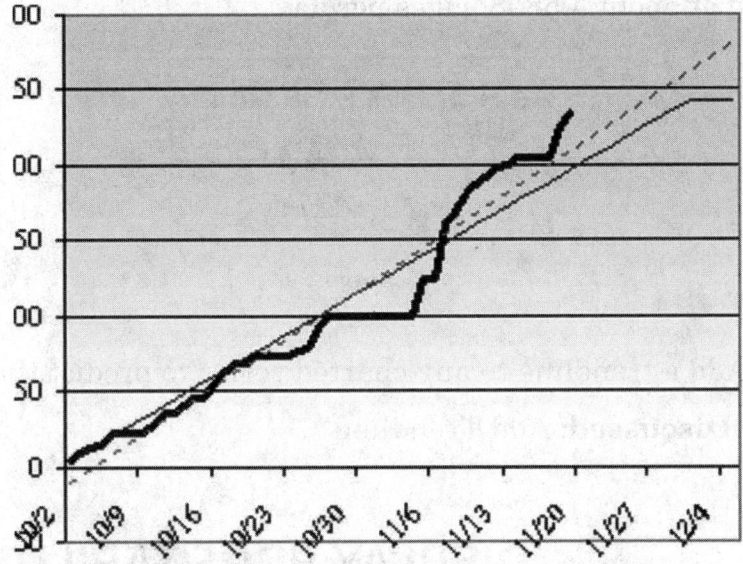

Fig. 1106

Additional Details: Right-click the trendline and choose Format Trendline. On the Options tab, you can choose to display the equation on the chart, as shown in Fig. 1107.

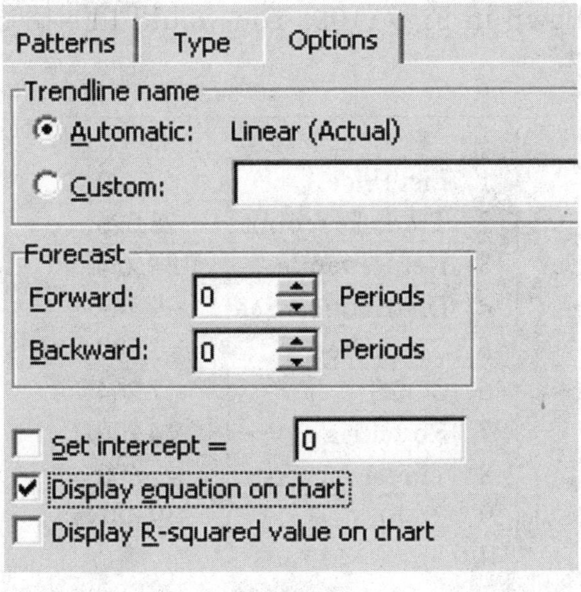

Part IV

Fig. 1107

Result: As shown in Fig. 1108, the chart will include an equation in the y=Mx+b format. The y-intercept in the equation is fairly crazy because the x-axis is a date field. However, the slope of the line shows that I have been working at about 4.5808 pages per day.

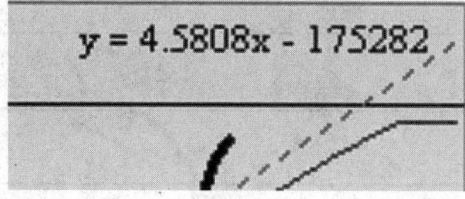

$$y = 4.5808x - 175282$$

Fig. 1108

Summary: Add a trendline to any charted series to predict the future.

Commands Discussed: Add Trendline

DISPLAY PROFITABILITY IN A PROFIT WATERFALL CHART

Problem: Your sales team is ready to make a large sale. You have done an analysis of the list price, discount, revenue, and all the internal costs of the sale, as shown in Fig. 1109. You would like to present this in a meaningful chart.

	A	B
1	List Price	62,280
2	Trade Discount	28,026
3	Net Revenue	34,254
4	Distribution Fee	9,249
5	Co-op Fee	3,000
6	COGS	7,264
7	Royalties	4,700
8	Travel	600
9	Profit	9,441
10		

Fig. 1109

Strategy: Use a Profit Waterfall Chart. This chart has three solid bars, representing List Price, Net Revenue, and Profit. Between those bars are floating bars that show how each individual expense item eats away the profit of the deal, as shown in Fig. 1110.

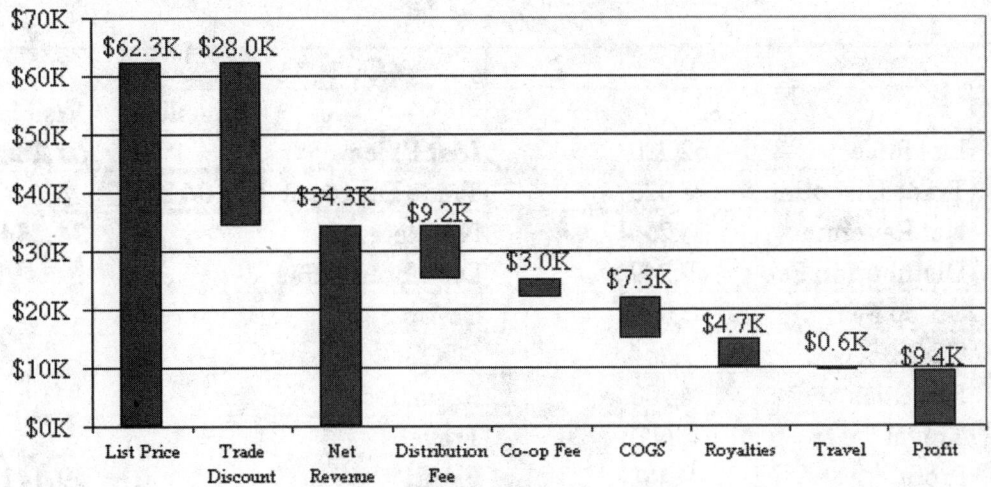

Fig. 1110

The trick to make the middle bars float is to use a stacked bar chart. The first series of bars will be changed into an invisible color without any lines in order to make the bars in the second series appear to float. The second series is that of the actual bars that will appear on the chart.

1) Set up a new range that will be used to create the chart. Copy the labels from column A to this range.

2) There are three bars that will need to touch the x-axis. For these three bars, the invisible series needs to be zero. The height of the bar is the same as the value in column B, as shown in Fig. 1111.

	A	B	C	D	E	F
1					Invisible	Visible
2	List Price	62,280		**List Price**	0	62,280
3	Trade Discount	28,026		Trade Discount		
4	Net Revenue	34,254		**Net Revenue**	0	34,254
5	Distribution Fee	9,249		Distribution Fee		
6	Co-op Fee	3,000		Co-op Fee		
7	COGS	7,264		COGS		
8	Royalties	4,700		Royalties		
9	Travel	600		Travel		
10	Profit	9,441		**Profit**	0	9,441
11						

Fig. 1111

3)   The goal for Trade Discount is to have a floating bar that extends from 62,280 down to 34,254. In order to have the bar float at this level, you will need an invisible bar that is 34,254 tall. In cell E3, enter the formula of =F4, as shown in Fig. 1112.

	E3	▼		f_x =+F4		
	A	B	C	D	E	F
1					Invisible	Visible
2	List Price	62,280		**List Price**	0	**62,280**
3	Trade Discount	28,026		Trade Discount	34,254	
4	Net Revenue	34,254		**Net Revenue**	0	**34,254**
5	Distribution Fee	9,249		Distribution Fee		
6	Co-op Fee	3,000		Co-op Fee		
7	COGS	7,264		COGS		
8	Royalties	4,700		Royalties		
9	Travel	600		Travel		
10	Profit	9,441		**Profit**	0	**9,441**
11						

Fig. 1112

4)   The height of the floating bar needs to extend from 34,254 to 62,280. Set the formula in F3 to =F2–E3, as shown in Fig. 1113.

	F3	▼		f_x =+F2-E3		
	A	B	C	D	E	F
1					Invisible	Visible
2	List Price	62,280		**List Price**	0	**62,280**
3	Trade Discount	28,026		Trade Discount	34,254	28,026
4	Net Revenue	34,254		**Net Revenue**	0	**34,254**
5	Distribution Fee	9,249		Distribution Fee		
6	Co-op Fee	3,000		Co-op Fee		

Fig. 1113

5)   After the Net Revenue bar come all the SG&A expenses. The height of each floating bar will be the amount of the expense. In F5 enter a formula of =B5. Copy this down to cells F6:F9, as shown in Fig. 1114.

F5   ▼   *fx* =B5

	A	B	C	D	E	F
1					Invisible	Visible
2	List Price	62,280		**List Price**	0	**62,280**
3	Trade Discount	28,026		Trade Discount	34,254	28,026
4	Net Revenue	34,254		**Net Revenue**	0	**34,254**
5	Distribution Fee	9,249		Distribution Fee		9,249
6	Co-op Fee	3,000		Co-op Fee		3,000
7	COGS	7,264		COGS		7,264
8	Royalties	4,700		Royalties		4,700
9	Travel	600		Travel		600
10	Profit	9,441		**Profit**	0	**9,441**

Fig. 1114

6)   The formula for the invisible portion of the bars always seems hard to figure out. In this case, if you start at the final bar, it might be easier. The Travel expense bar, representing $600, needs to float just above the profit level of 9441. Thus, the formula in E9 will be =F10, as shown in Fig. 1115.

Part IV

E9   ▼   *fx* =F10

	A	B	C	D	E	F
1					Invisible	Visible
2	List Price	62,280		**List Price**	0	**62,280**
3	Trade Discount	28,026		Trade Discount	34,254	28,026
4	Net Revenue	34,254		**Net Revenue**	0	**34,254**
5	Distribution Fee	9,249		Distribution Fee		9,249
6	Co-op Fee	3,000		Co-op Fee		3,000
7	COGS	7,264		COGS		7,264
8	Royalties	4,700		Royalties		4,700
9	Travel	600		Travel	9,441	600
10	Profit	9,441		**Profit**	0	**9,441**
11						

Fig. 1115

7) The Royalties bar of $4700 needs to float just above the level of the Travel bar. The height of the Travel bar is the height of the invisible bar (9441 in E9) and the height of the visible bar (500 in F9). The formula for E8 is =E9+F9, as shown in Fig. 1116.

E8	▼	fx	=E9+F9		
	A	B	C	D	E	F
1					Invisible	Visible
2	List Price	62,280		List Price	0	62,280
3	Trade Discount	28,026		Trade Discount	34,254	28,026
4	Net Revenue	34,254		Net Revenue	0	34,254
5	Distribution Fee	9,249		Distribution Fee		9,249
6	Co-op Fee	3,000		Co-op Fee		3,000
7	COGS	7,264		COGS		7,264
8	Royalties	4,700		Royalties	10,041	4,700
9	Travel	600		Travel	9,441	600
10	Profit	9,441		Profit	0	9,441

Fig. 1116

8) You now have a formula that can be copied. Copy E8 to the blank cells in E7:E5.

9) Select the range of data from D1 to F10, as shown in Fig. 1117.

D	E	F
	Invisible	Visible
List Price	0	62,280
Trade Discount	34,254	28,026
Net Revenue	0	34,254
Distribution Fee	25,005	9,249
Co-op Fee	22,005	3,000
COGS	14,741	7,264
Royalties	10,041	4,700
Travel	9,441	600
Profit	0	9,441

Fig. 1117

10) From the menu, select Insert – Chart. Choose a Column chart and then in the Chart Sub-type box choose a Stacked chart, as shown in Fig. 1118.

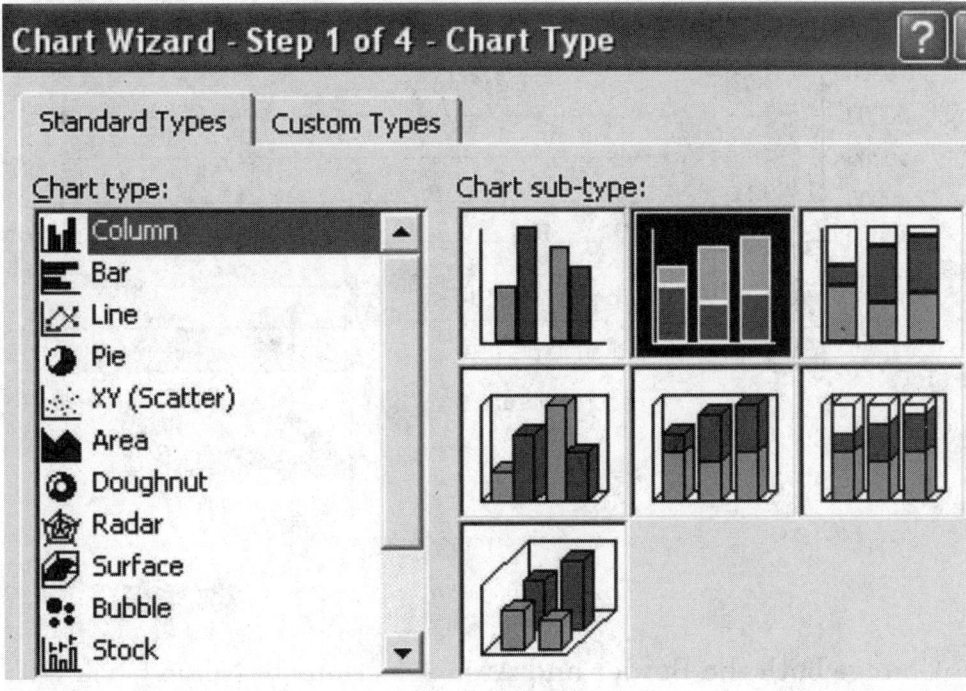

Fig. 1118

11) Choose Finish to accept the remaining default settings. The following chart, as shown in Fig. 1119, will appear.

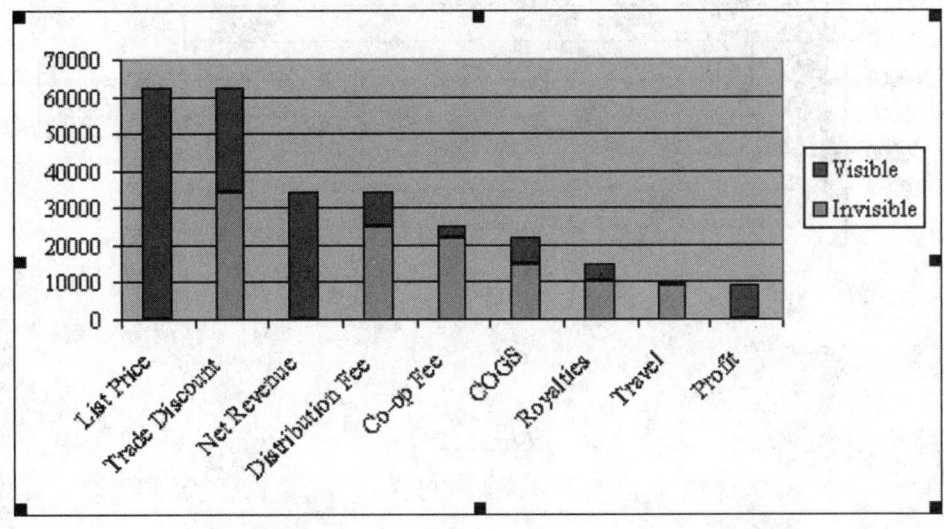

Fig. 1119

12) In the second bar, use the mouse to click on the lower portion of the bar. This is the section that should be invisible. All of the blue bars will be selected. Right-click and choose Format Data Series..., as shown in Fig. 1120.

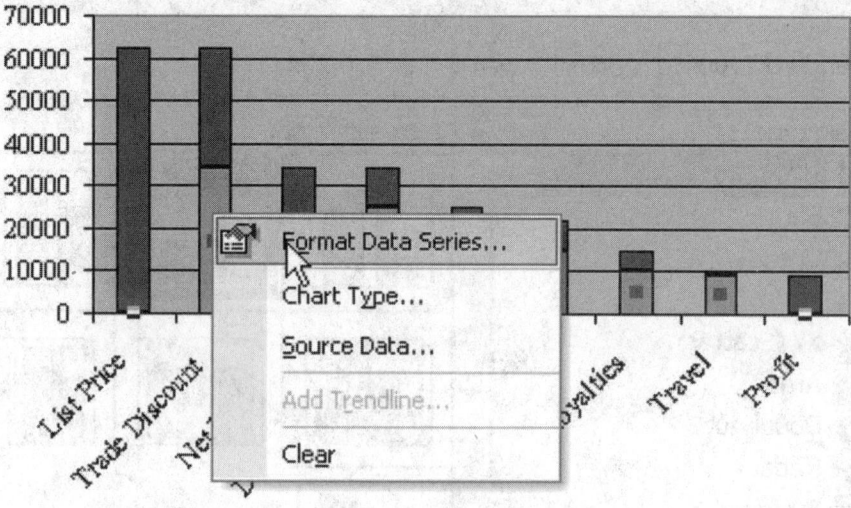

Fig. 1120

13) Change both the Border and Area selections to None. Click OK. As shown in Fig. 1121, the bars in the invisible series will now truly be invisible.

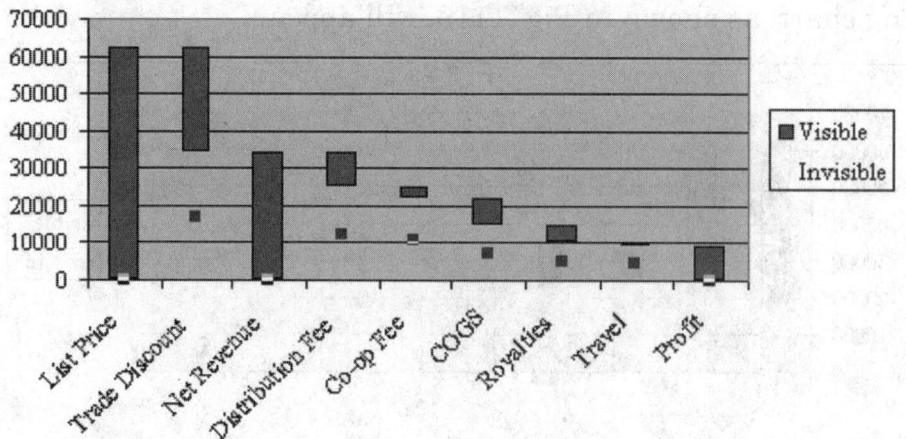

Fig. 1121

The point of the Profit Waterfall Chart is to illustrate to your VP of sales that, although this is a $60K deal, the net profit is less than $10K.

Additional Details: There are a number of steps to make the chart look more presentable.

1) Remove the legend.

   Click in the legend and hit the Delete key on the keyboard.

2) Format the y-axis in thousands.

   Right-click the numbers along the side of the chart. Choose Format Axis. In the Number tab, change to a custom format of $#,##0,K, as shown in Fig. 1122.

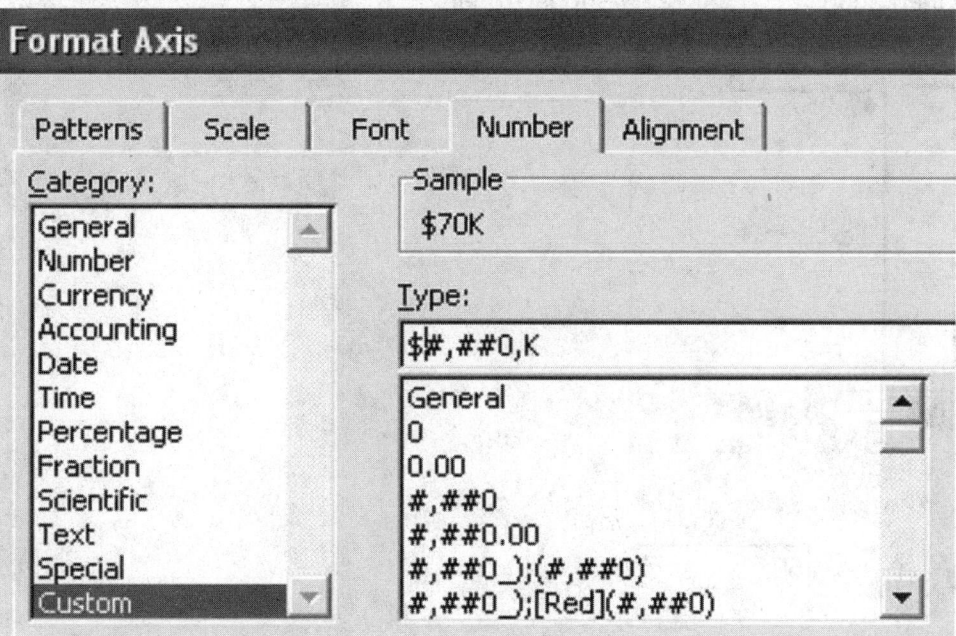

Fig. 1122

3) Get rid of the gray background.

   Right-click on the chart but in a blank area. Do not click on a grid-line, a line, or a bar. Choose Format Plot Area. Change the Area to None.

4) Make the chart larger.

   Click just inside the chart border. Grab a Fill handle and make the chart wider.

Part IV

5) Fix the labels along the bottom of the chart.

    Right-click the labels along the x-axis and choose Format Axis.

6) On the Font tab, change the font to 8 points. On the Alignment tab, you want to turn off the Automatic rotation. The only way to do this is to use the spin button to move the rotation percentage up to 1 degree and then back down to 0 degrees, as shown in Fig. 1123.

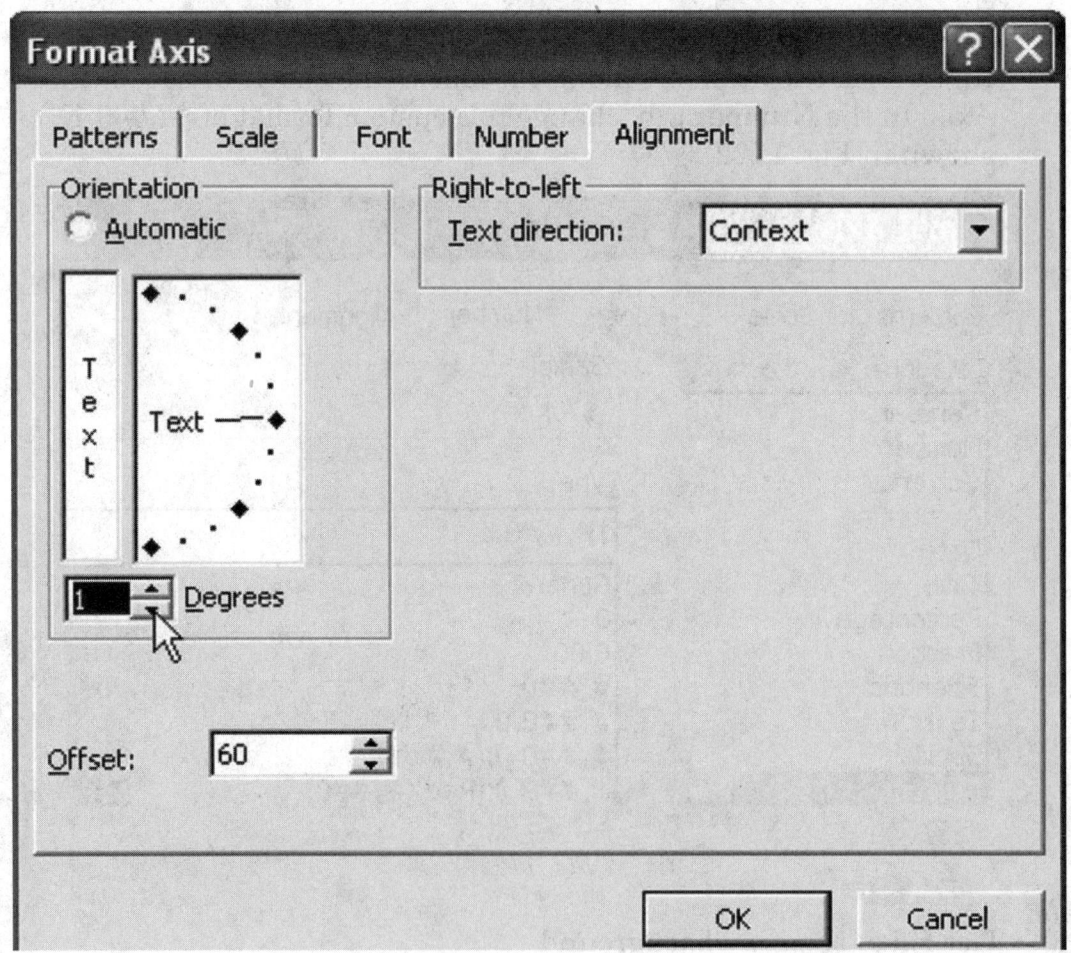

Fig. 1123

This will force the labels to appear horizontal instead of at an angle.

Gotcha: Excel might decide to display only every other label along the x-axis. Keep making the chart larger horizontally until you can see all of the labels.

Result: As shown in Fig. 1124, you get a Profit Waterfall Chart that demonstrates the true profit on the deal.

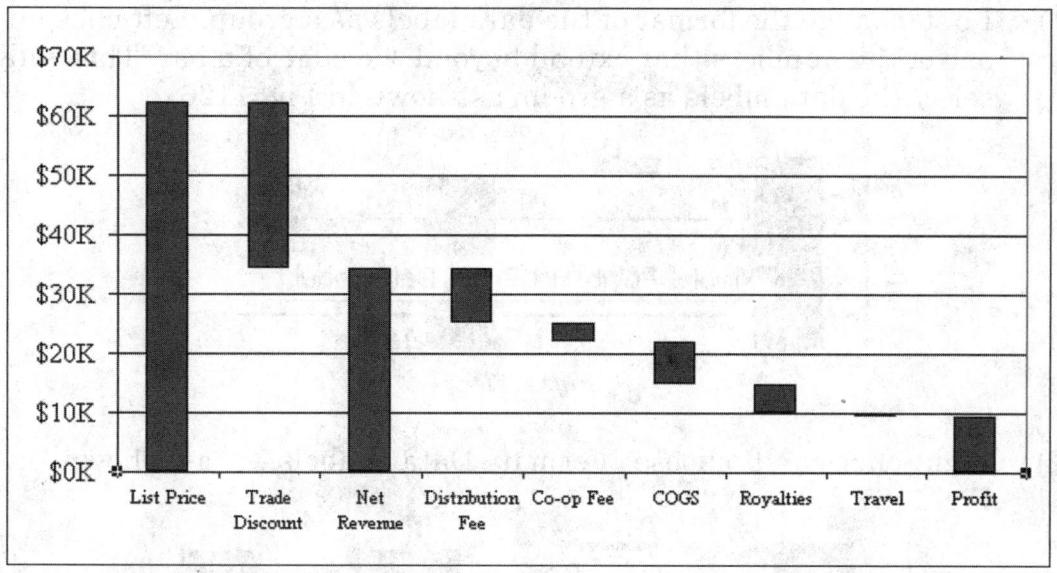

Fig. 1124

Additional Details: Normally, you would want to display values on top of each bar. In a regular bar chart, you would select the visible series and then right-click to choose Format Series. On the Data Labels tab, choose the Value setting, as shown in Fig. 1125.

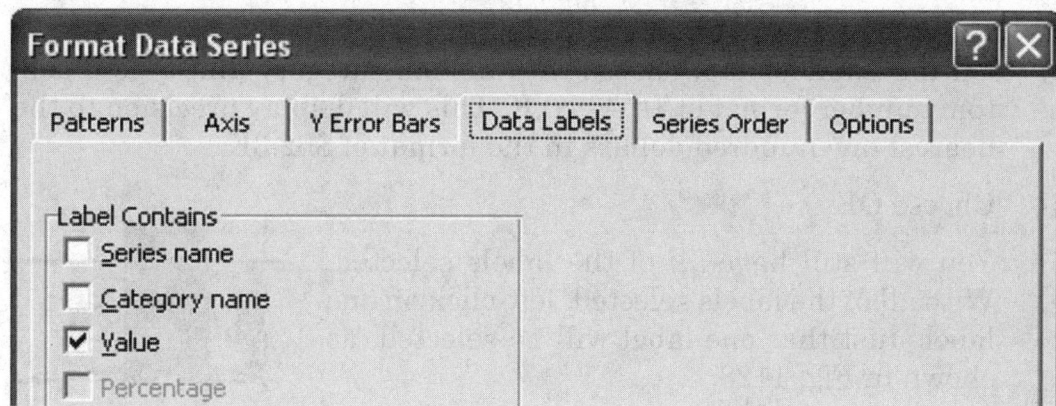

Fig. 1125

However, because this chart is actually a stacked column chart, Excel does not display the values on top of each bar. Instead, it displays the values in the middle of each bar. This is frustrating. It can be fixed, although it is a bit tedious. Follow these steps.

1)   First, change the format of the data labels as a group. Left-click on one of the numbers that extend beyond the edge of a bar. This will select the data labels as a group, as shown in Fig. 1126.

Fig. 1126

2)   Right-click and choose Format Data Labels..., as shown in Fig. 1127.

Fig. 1127

3)   On the Number tab, choose the Custom category and type a custom number format of $#,##0.0,K. This will display precision to the nearest one hundred dollars in the format of $62.3K.

4)   Choose OK.

5)   You will still have all of the labels selected. With all of the labels selected, left-click on one label. Just that one label will be selected, as shown in Fig. 1128.

List Price

Fig. 1128

6)   You can now grab the border of the label and drag it to the proper location above the bar, as shown in Fig. 1129.

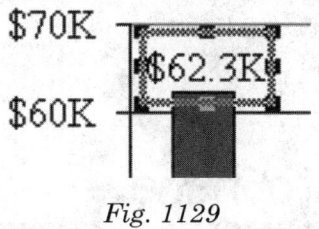

Fig. 1129

7)   Click the next label. Drag it to the proper location. Repeat for each data label. You will eventually have this chart, as shown in Fig. 1130.

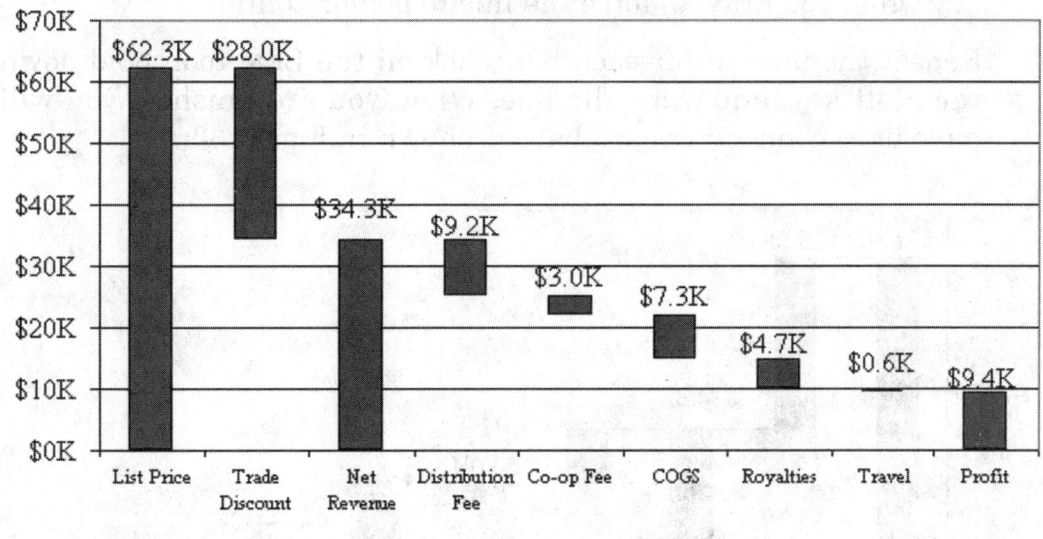

Fig. 1130

Part IV

Optional: Some people prefer the Waterfall chart without gridlines and with lines from one bar to the next.

1)   To remove gridlines, right-click on a gridline and choose Clear, as shown in Fig. 1131.

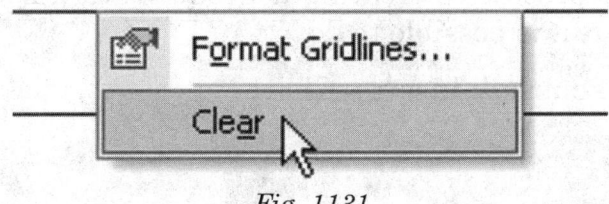

Fig. 1131

2)   Display the Drawing toolbar with View – Toolbars – Drawing. From the Drawing toolbar, click on the Line tool, as shown in Fig. 1132.

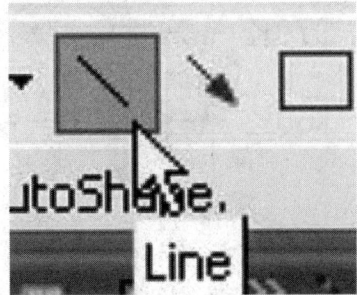

Fig. 1132

3)   Carefully draw a line from one bar to the next. Hold down the Shift key while you draw to force the line to be horizontal.

4)   Repeat the process for each bar: click on the Line tool, hold down the Shift key, and draw the line. When you are finished, you will have lines connecting each bar, as shown in Fig. 1133.

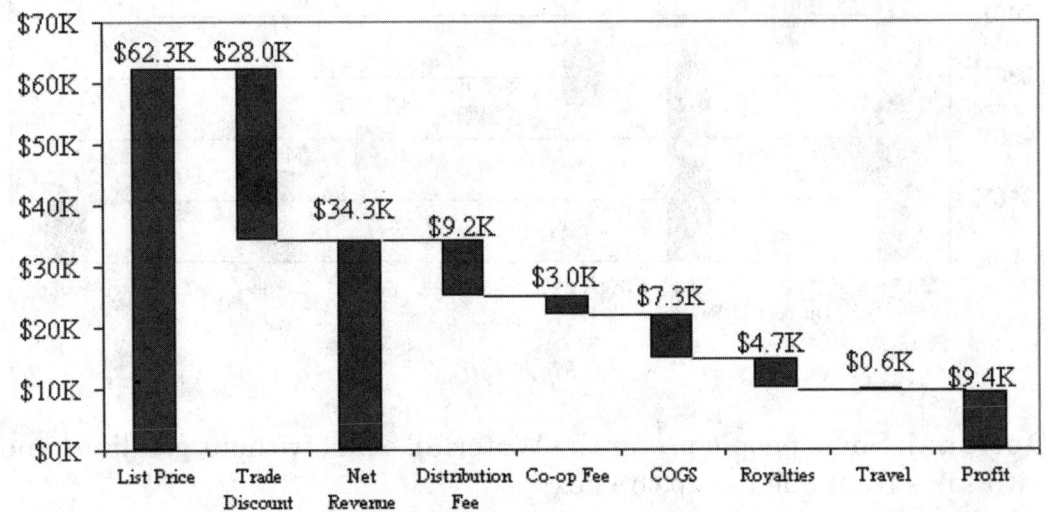

Fig. 1133

Summary: The process of creating a Profit Waterfall Chart is somewhat tedious, but it is possible to do.

Commands Discussed: Insert – Chart

FOR EACH CELL IN COLUMN A, HAVE THREE ROWS IN COLUMN B

Problem: For each cell in column A, you want three rows in columns B and C, as shown in Fig. 1134. You also want to be able to perform calculations with the values in column C.

	A	B	C
	Andy	Quota	1000
		Actual	1200
1		Variance	200
	Ben	Quota	900
		Actual	500
2		Variance	-400

Fig. 1134

Strategy: One common attempt is to use the Alt+Enter trick to enter three lines of data in column B. However, this will not work well in column C. Although the numbers are displayed fine, there is no way to have the numbers in C calculate automatically.

A better option is to merge cells A1:A3 into a single cell. You can then let the data in B fill B1:B3.

1) Select cells A1:A3. Choose Ctrl+1 to display Format Cells. On the Alignment tab, select Merge Cells, as shown in Fig. 1135.

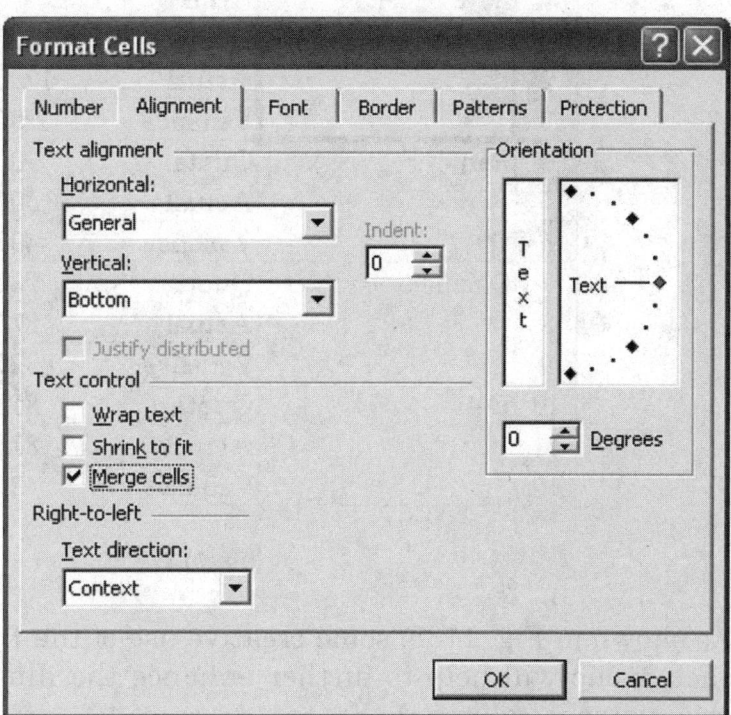

Fig. 1135

Gotcha: Notice that the vertical alignment defaults to the bottom. This looks OK in a normal-height cell, but not so good in a triple-height cell.

2)   Change the vertical alignment to top or center, as shown in Fig. 1136.

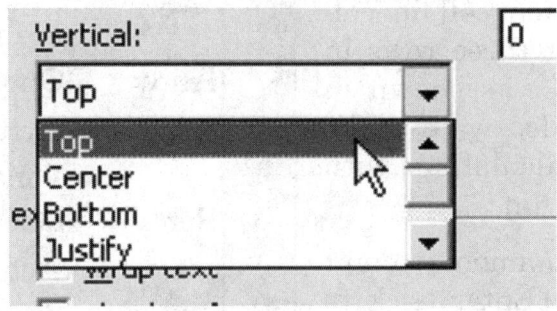

Fig. 1136

3)   If you have several rows that need this formatting, copy the merged A1:A3 cell. Highlight A3:A6 and use Edit – Paste Special – Formats. Repeat for each section that needs a similar format. You will soon have a worksheet that appears to have three rows in column B for every entry in column A, as shown in Fig. 1137.

	A	B	C	D
1	Andy	Quota	1000	
2		Actual	1200	
3		Variance	200	
4	Ben	Quota	900	
5		Actual	500	
6		Variance	-400	
7	Charlie	Quota	900	
8		Actual	875	
9		Variance	-25	
10	Del	Quota	850	
11		Actual	875	
12		Variance	25	

Fig. 1137

As shown in Fig. 1138, some creative use of the Borders setting around each group will help to further enhance the illusion of three rows for each value in column A.

Summary: To have three cells in column B, next to one cell in column A, use the Merge command on cells A1:A3.

Commands Discussed: Merge Cells

	A	B	C
1	Andy	Quota	1000
2		Actual	1200
3		Variance	200
4	Ben	Quota	900
5		Actual	500
6		Variance	-400
7	Charlie	Quota	900
8		Actual	875
9		Variance	-25
10	Del	Quota	850
11		Actual	875
12		Variance	25

Fig. 1138

COPY FORMATTING TO A NEW RANGE

Problem: You have several similar report sections on a spreadsheet. Once you get the first report nicely formatted, you would like to copy the format to the other reports. See Fig. 1139.

	A	B	C	D	E
1	UNIT SALES				
2		East	Central	West	Total
3	Widgets	44	11	83	138
4	Sprockets	71	59	52	182
5	Wheels	16	99	57	172
6	Total	131	169	192	492
7					
8	DOLLAR SALES				
9		East	Central	West	Total
10	Widgets	62.48	15.62	117.86	195.96
11	Sprockets	180.34	149.86	132.08	462.28
12	Wheels	256	1584	912	2752
13	Total	498.82	1749.48	1161.94	3410.24
14					
15	TOTAL COST				
16		East	Central	West	Total
17	Widgets	29.99	7.5	56.57	94.06
18	Sprockets	86.56	71.93	63.4	221.89
19	Wheels	122.88	760.32	437.76	1320.96
20	Total	239.43	839.75	557.73	1636.91

Part IV

Fig. 1139

Strategy: Use Paste Special Formats to copy just the formats from one range to another.

1)   Select cells A1:E6. From the menu, select Edit – Copy.

2)   Select the upper left corner of the next section. With the cell pointer in A8, select Edit – Paste Special – Formats, as shown in Fig. 1140.

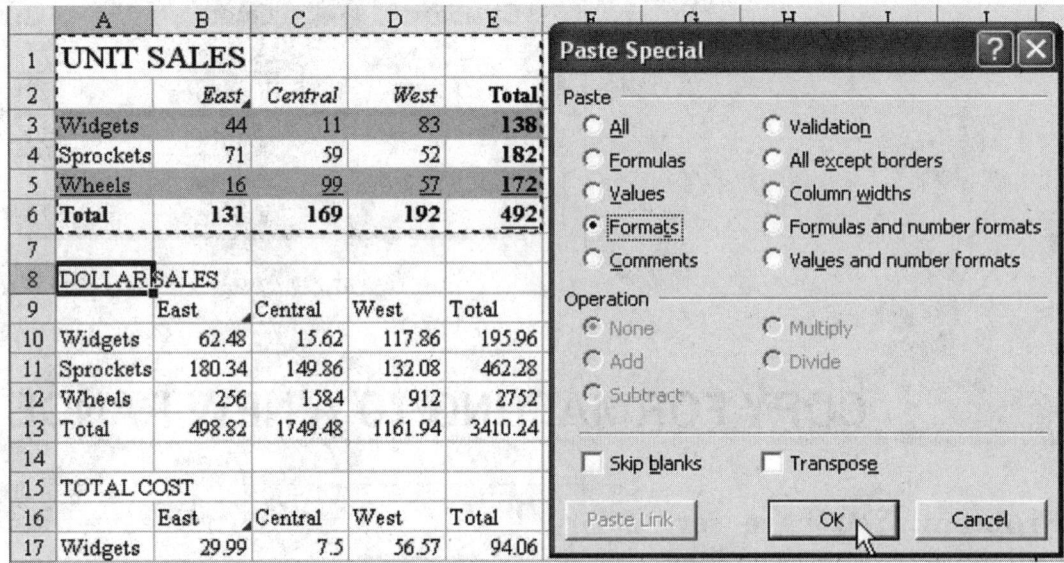

Fig. 1140

3)   Move the cell pointer to A15. Repeat the Edit – Paste Special – Formats command to format the Cost section of the report. Repeat for any additional sections.

Result: As shown in Fig. 1141, the cell formats will be copied, but not their values or formulas.

	A	B	C	D	E
1	UNIT SALES				
2		East	Central	West	Total
3	Widgets	44	11	83	138
4	Sprockets	71	59	52	182
5	Wheels	16	99	57	172
6	Total	131	169	192	492
7					
8	DOLLAR SALES				
9		East	Central	West	Total
10	Widgets	62.48	15.62	117.86	195.96
11	Sprockets	180.34	149.86	132.08	462.28
12	Wheels	256	1584	912	2752
13	Total	498.82	1749.48	1161.94	3410.24
14					
15	TOTAL COST				
16		East	Central	West	Total
17	Widgets	29.99	7.5	56.57	94.06
18	Sprockets	86.56	71.93	63.4	221.89
19	Wheels	122.88	760.32	437.76	1320.96
20	Total	239.43	839.75	557.73	1636.91
21					
22	GROSS PROFIT				
23		East	Central	West	Total
24	Widgets	32.49	8.12	61.29	101.9
25	Sprockets	93.78	77.93	68.68	240.39
26	Wheels	133.12	823.68	474.24	1431.04
27	Total	259.39	909.73	604.21	1773.33

Fig. 1141

Part
IV

Summary: After you've taken the time to nicely format one range, you can copy the formatting to other ranges by using the Paste Special Formats command.

Commands Discussed: Edit – Paste Special Formats

COPY WITHOUT CHANGING BORDERS

Problem: You have built a report in Excel and used numerous borders to outline the data, as shown in Fig. 1142. After entering a formula to calculate profit in E3, you want to copy the formula down to E4 through E7.

	A	B	C	D	E
1					
2		Week	Sales	COGS	Profit
3		1	$18,972	$8,537	$10,435
4		2	17,074	8,195	
5		3	15,366	7,375	
6		4	13,829	6,637	
7		5	12,446	5,974	
8		Total	$77,687	$36,718	$10,435
9					

Fig. 1142

However, because cell E3 has a top border, copying the formula causes all of the cells in E4 through E7 to also have a top border, ruining the effect of your borders, as shown in Fig. 1143.

Week		Sales	COGS	Profit
	1	$18,972	$8,537	$10,435
	2	17,074	8,195	$8,879
	3	15,366	7,375	$7,991
	4	13,829	6,637	$7,192
	5	12,446	5,974	$6,472
Total		$77,687	$36,718	$40,969

Fig. 1143

Strategy: Use Edit – Paste Special – All except borders to copy the formula and the numeric formatting, but to not disturb the borders. See Fig. 1144.

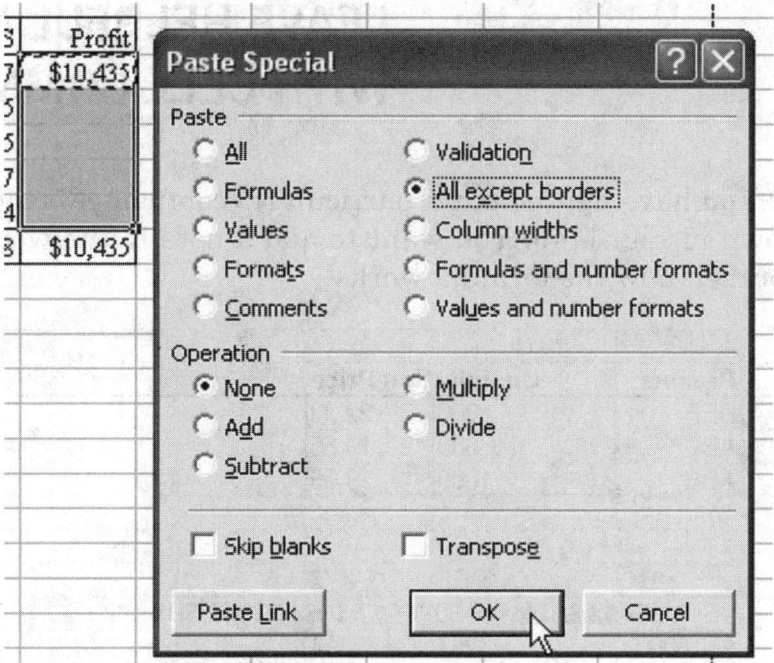

Fig. 1144

Result: As shown in Fig. 1145, the formula is successfully copied, but the borders remain as they were.

Week	Sales	COGS	Profit
1	$18,972	$8,537	$10,435
2	17,074	8,195	$8,879
3	15,366	7,375	$7,991
4	13,829	6,637	$7,192
5	12,446	5,974	$6,472
Total	$77,687	$36,718	$40,969

Fig. 1145

Alternate Strategy: In the above dataset, it appears that you had decided to show the currency symbol on only the first row and the total row. In this case, it might have been more appropriate to use Paste Special – Formulas to just copy the formula.

Summary: To copy without disrupting borders, use the Paste Special – All Except Borders option.

Commands Discussed: Edit – Paste Special – All Except Borders; Edit – Paste Special – Formulas

LEAVE HELPFUL NOTES
WITH CELL COMMENTS

Problem: You have figured out a particularly confusing formula in Excel, as shown in Fig. 1146. You want to add a note to the worksheet to remind yourself how the formula works.

	A	B	C	D	E	F	G	H
1	**Region**	**Product**	**Quantity**	**Unit Price**				
44	East	DEF	300	22.38				
45	East	ABC	800	19.55				
46	West	ABC	1000	19.25				
47								
48	Revenue							
49		ABC	DEF	XYZ				
50	East	=SUM(($A$2:$A$46=$A50)*$C$2:$C$46*$D$2:$D$46*($B$2:$B$46=B$49))						
51	Central	80003	2257	73814				
52	West	62711	15809	22950				
53								

Fig. 1146

Strategy: Use a cell comment. In addition to 16.7 million cells on a worksheet, you can also store a comment for every cell. Typically, cell comments show up as a red triangle in the corner of the cell. Hover the mouse over the cell and the comment will appear.

1) Select the cell where you want to add the comment. From the menu, select Insert – Comment. A comment box appears with your name in bold on line 1, as shown in Fig. 1147.

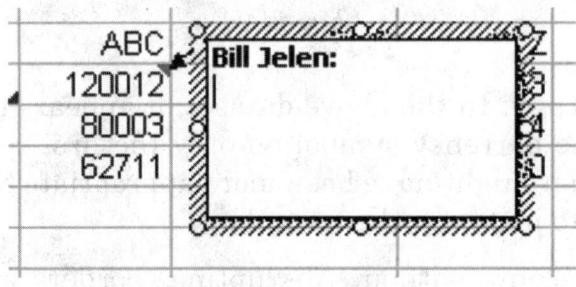

Fig. 1147

2)   Type a comment, as shown in Fig. 1148.

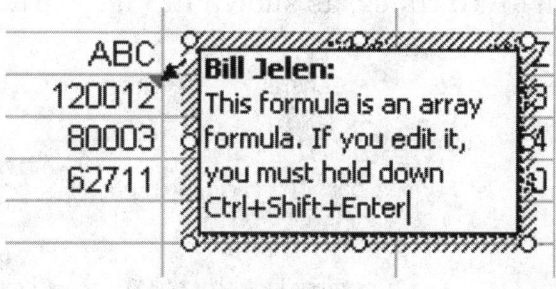

Fig. 1148

3)   Click the mouse outside the comment box to complete the entry of the comment. Only a red triangle remains in the cell to indicate the presence of a comment there, as shown in Fig. 1149.

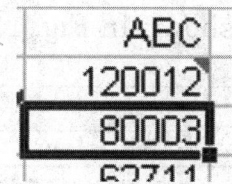

Fig. 1149

Part IV

When you hover your mousepointer over the cell with the red triangle, your comment box will pop up like a tooltip, as shown in Fig. 1150.

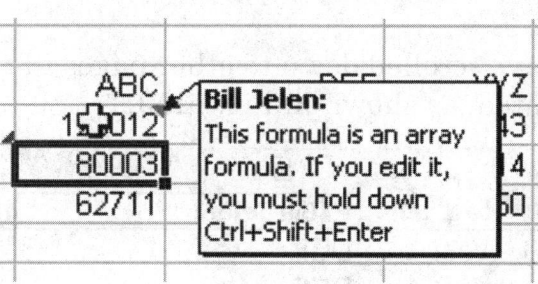

Fig. 1150

Additional Details: To delete a comment, right-click the cell and choose Delete Comment. To edit a comment, right-click the cell and choose Edit Comment.

The above information is based on the assumption that you are using the default settings for comments. There are additional settings available on the View tab of the Tools – Options dialog. On this tab, you can suppress the appearance of the red comment indicator or force all comments to be shown at all times, as shown in Fig. 1151.

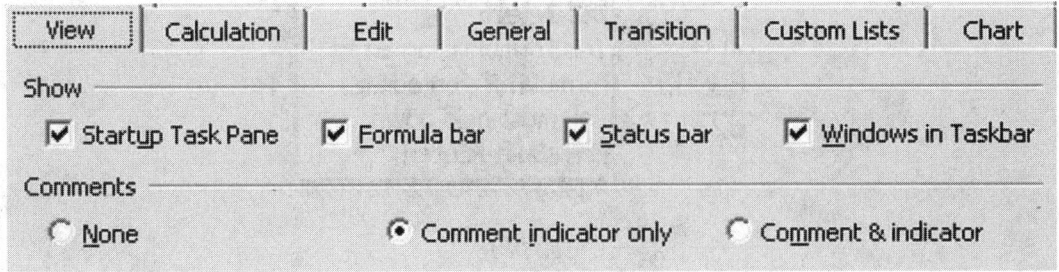

Fig. 1151

Gotcha: If you have a comment in a row above the freeze panes line, you will notice a bug. The comment will appear normally if you have scrolled the worksheet to the top, as shown in Fig. 1152.

	A	B	C
1	Region	P	**Bill Jelen:**
2	East	XY	Valid values are East,
3	Central	DI	Central, or West
4	East	AI	
5	Central	XY	

Fig. 1152

However, if you have scrolled down to other pages in the worksheet, the comment is truncated, as shown in Fig. 1153.

	A	B	C
1	Region	P	**Bill Jelen:**	ty
30	West	DEF	300
31	West	DEF	300

Fig. 1153

Summary: Adding comments to a cell is a great way to leave notes for yourself to help you remember something about a formula later.

Commands Discussed: Insert – Comment

CHANGE APPEARANCE OF CELL COMMENTS

Problem: You type a very long comment into a cell. The comment is longer than the comment box will display, as shown in Fig. 1154.

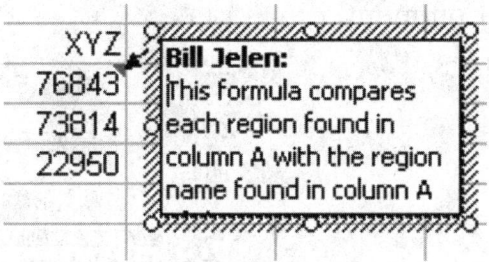

Fig. 1154

Strategy: You actually have complete control over the size and appearance of the comment box. Right-click the border of the comment and choose Format Comment.

Caution: *Watch for a strange behavior when formatting comments. If you notice the image in Fig. 1154, the border around the comment is comprised of diagonal lines. If you right-click and choose Format Comment when the diagonal lines appear, you will get this truncated version of the Format Comment dialog, as shown in Fig. 1155. The only options available are on the Font tab.*

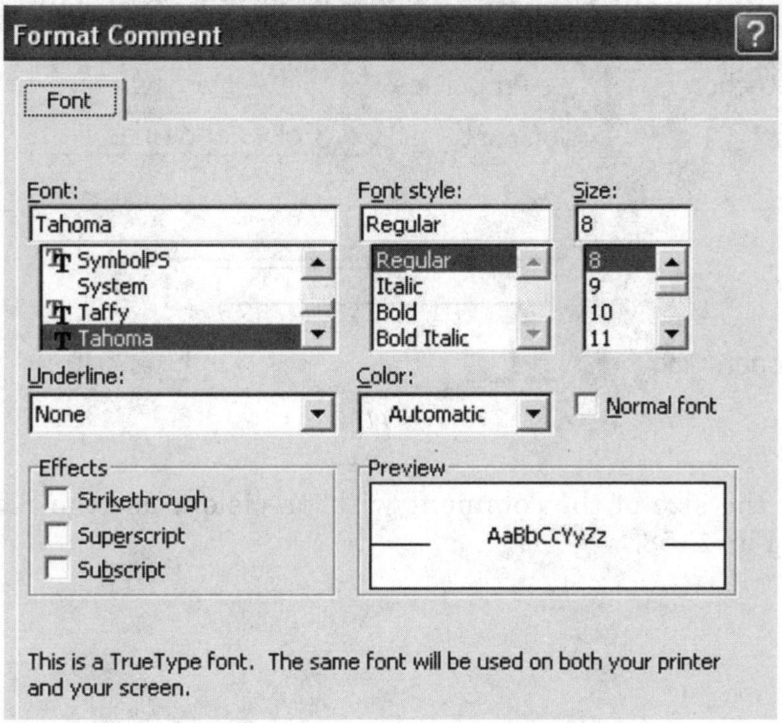

Part
IV

Fig. 1155

To get the complete set of formatting options, you must first left-click on the diagonal lines border. This will change the diagonal lines to dots as shown in Fig. 1156. You can now right-click the dots and choose Format Comment.

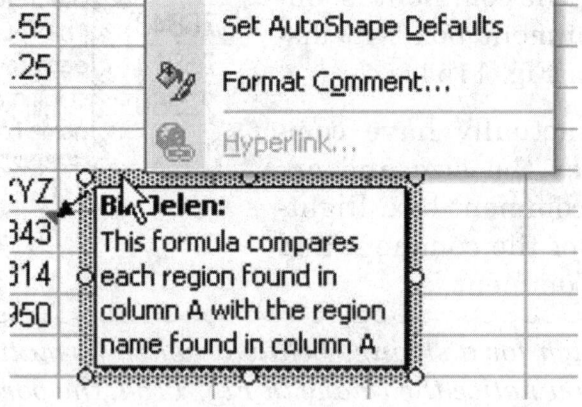

Fig. 1156

This will display the complete Format Comment dialog, as shown in Fig. 1157.

Format Comment			?
Protection	Properties	Margins	Web
Font	Alignment	Colors and Lines	Size

Fill

Color: [   ] ▼

Transparency: ◄ [   ]   ► [0 %] ▲▼

Fig. 1157

To adjust the size of the comment with precision, use the Size tab, as shown in Fig. 1158.

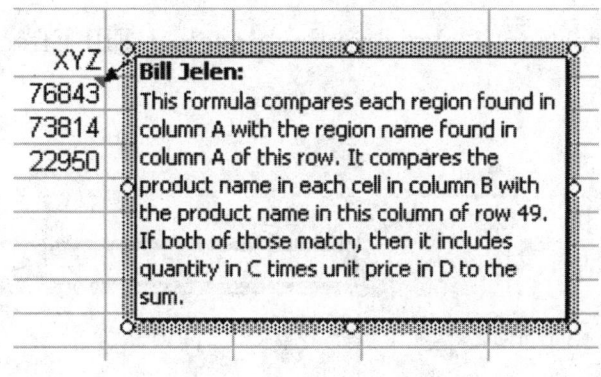

Fig. 1158

Enter a new size so that the entire comment will appear, as shown in Fig. 1159.

Bill Jelen:
This formula compares each region found in column A with the region name found in column A of this row. It compares the product name in each cell in column B with the product name in this column of row 49. If both of those match, then it includes quantity in C times unit price in D to the sum.

Fig. 1159

Additional Details: It is also possible to change the boring yellow comment as shown above to a nicely formatted comment. The following comment has a green-to-white gradient and is semi-transparent so that you can see the underlying cells below the comment, as shown in Fig. 1160.

$\{=SUM((\$A\$2:\$A\$46=\$A50)*\$C\$2:\$C\$46*\$D\$2:\$D\$46*(\$B\$2:\$B\$46=D\$49))\}$

C	D	E	F	G	H	I
Quantity	Unit Price					
DEF	XYZ					
76347	76843					
2257	73814					
15809	22950					

Bill Jelen:
This formula compares each region found in column A with the region name found in column A of this row. It compares the product name in each cell in column B with the product name in this column of row 49. If both of those match, then it includes quantity in C times unit price in D to the sum.

Fig. 1160

Part IV

1)   On the Format Comment dialog, go to the Colors and Lines tab, as
     shown in Fig. 1161.

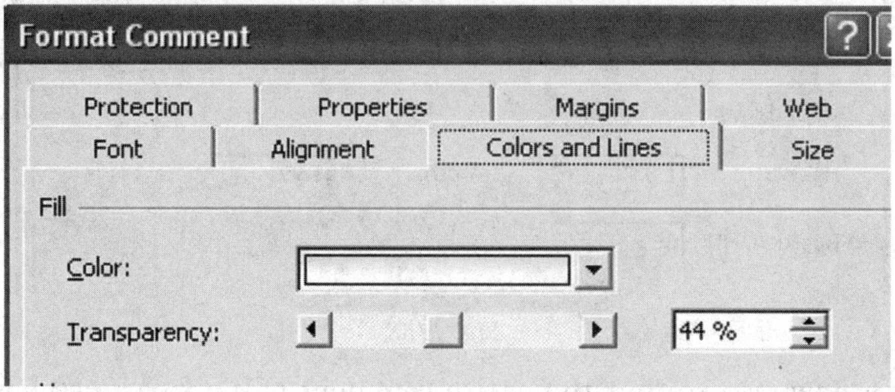

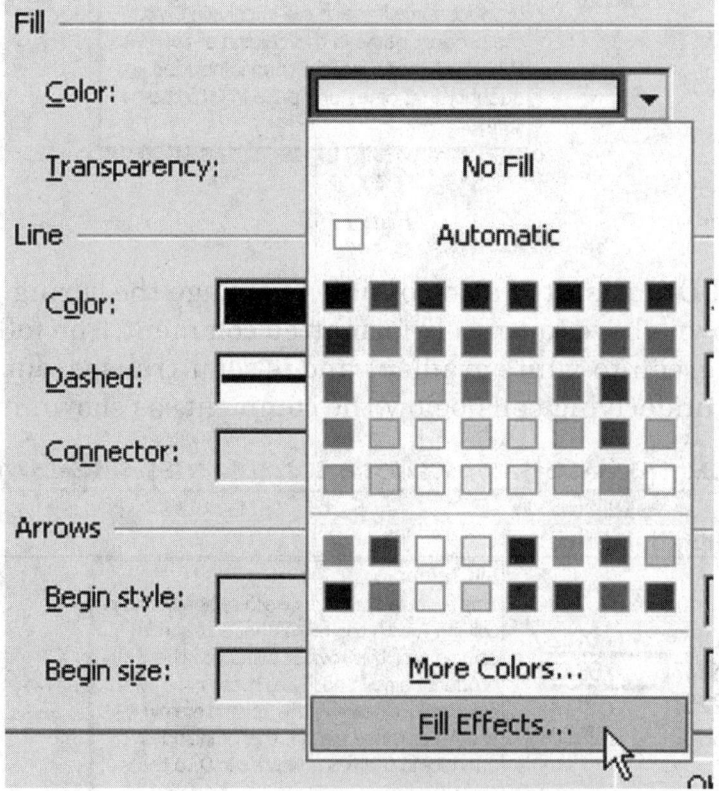

Fig. 1161

2)   In the Fill section, Color dropdown, select Fill Effects, as shown in
     Fig. 1162.

Fig. 1162

3) On the Fill Effects dialog, choose the Gradient tab. Choose Two Colors, green for Color 1 and white for Color 2. You can adjust the transparency for each color independently, as shown in Fig. 1163.

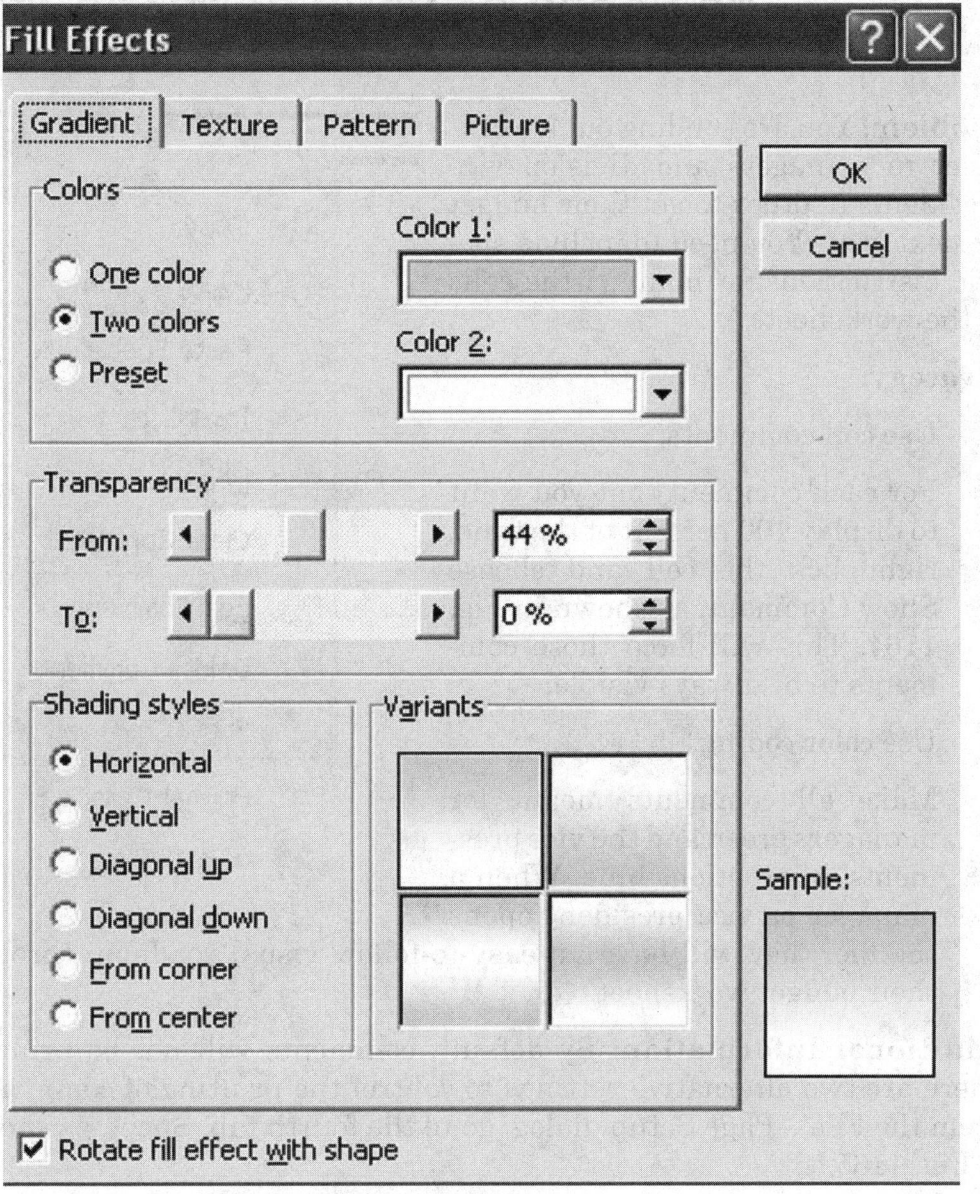

Fig. 1163

Summary: You can replace the default yellow comments with a variety of sizes and formats to increase interest in the workbook.

Commands Discussed: Format Comments

FORCE CERTAIN COMMENTS TO BE ALWAYS VISIBLE TO PROVIDE A HELP SYSTEM TO USERS OF YOUR SPREADSHEET

Problem: You are sending out a worksheet to managers and division vice presidents in order to get their budget for next year. You need to include specific instructions for many of the cells in the worksheet.

Strategy:

1) Use cell comments.

    For each comment that you want to display 100 percent of the time, right-click the cell and choose Show Comment, as shown in Fig. 1164. This will force those comments to be always visible.

2) Use color coding.

    Make all comments meant for managers green and the vice presidents' instructions blue. When a manager or vice president opens the file, they will have an easy-to-follow visual roadmap through their budget worksheet.

Fig. 1164

Additional Information: By default, comments will not be printed. There are two alternative settings to control the printing of comments. From the File – Page Setup dialog, go to the fourth tab, Sheet, as shown in Fig. 1165.

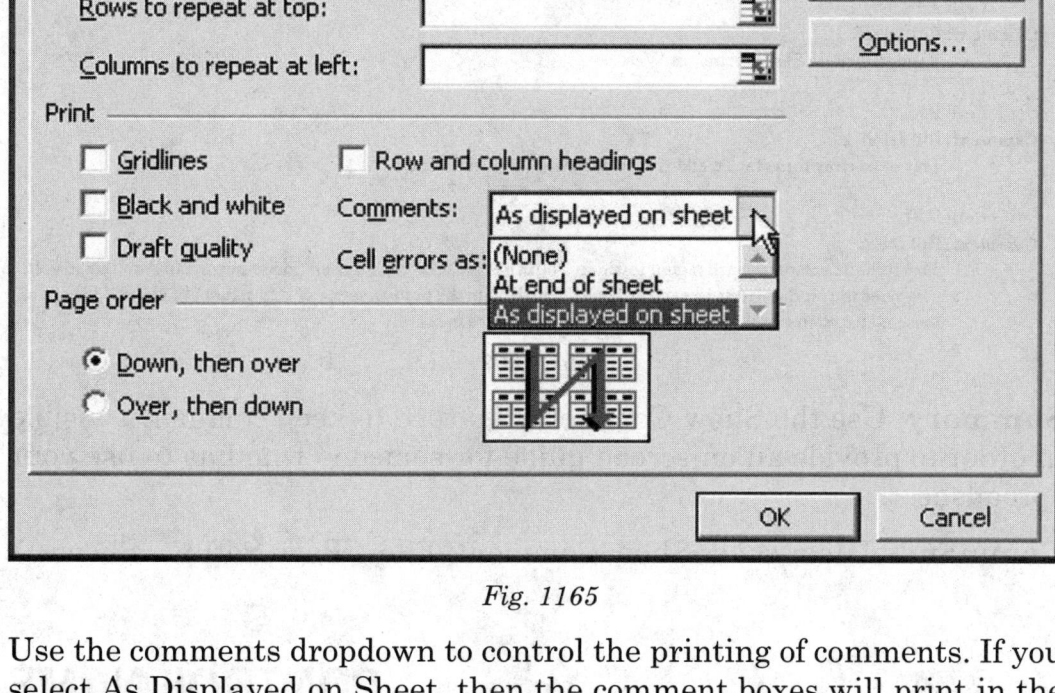

Fig. 1165

Use the comments dropdown to control the printing of comments. If you select As Displayed on Sheet, then the comment boxes will print in the size and format that you have set up for all of the displayed comments, as shown in Fig. 1166. This setting will not print comments that are hidden with only the red triangle visible.

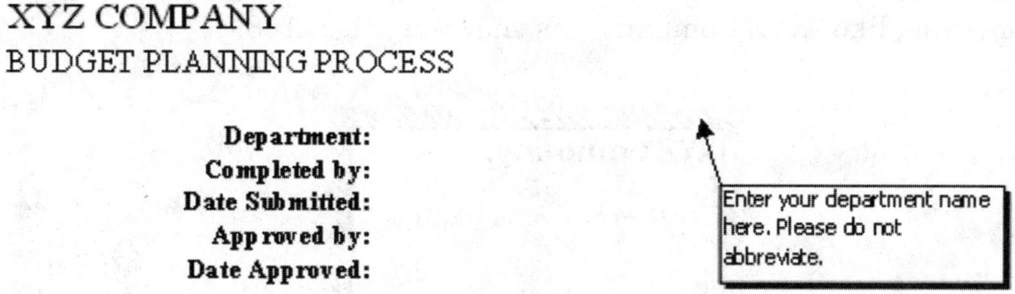

XYZ COMPANY
BUDGET PLANNING PROCESS

Department:
Completed by:
Date Submitted:
Approved by:
Date Approved:

Enter your department name here. Please do not abbreviate.

Fig. 1166

If you select At End of Sheet, the comments will print in a separate section at the end of the printout, as shown in Fig. 1167. The only drawback with this method is that the comment printout indicates that a certain comment is attached to cell A50. Unless you print row and column headings, there is no way for the reader of the printed document to know which value on the sheet is located in cell A50.

Cell: A1
Comment: Bill Jelen:
        Valid values are East, Central, or West

Cell: B50
Comment: Bill Jelen:
        This is an array formula. To edit it, you must use Ctrl+Shift+Enter

Cell: D50
Comment: Bill Jelen:
        This formula compares each region found in Column A with the region name found in column A of this row. It compares the product name in each cell in column B with the product name of this column of row 49. If both of those match, then it includes quantity in C times the price in D.

Fig. 1167

Summary: Use the Show Comments feature to keep comments visible in order to provide an on-screen guide for someone who has to use your spreadsheet.

Commands Discussed: Show Comment; File – Page Setup – Sheet

CONTROL NAME THAT APPEARS IN COMMENTS

Problem: When you insert a comment, the name displayed in bold is something like "XYZ Company", as shown in Fig. 1168.

Fig. 1168

Strategy: You can change the name that is displayed in the comment.

From the menu, go to Tools – Options – General. At the bottom of the General tab is a field called User Name, as shown in Fig. 1169. Change this field to the name you would like displayed in the comment.

At startup, open all files in:

User name: XYZ Company

Fig. 1169

Additional Information: It is impossible to suppress the name appearing in the comment. Even if you change the above field to a blank, Excel will pick up the computer user name.

If you want to have a comment without the name, select the name and press Delete or simply backspace through the name. Typically, the name will appear in bold and the comment that you type will appear in normal font, as shown in Fig. 1170.

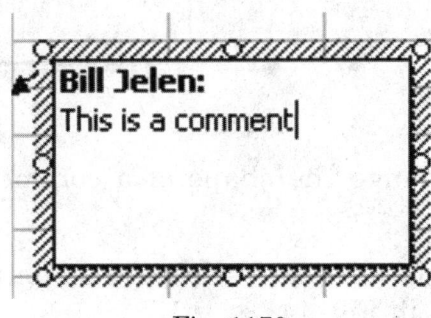

Bill Jelen:
This is a comment

Fig. 1170

When you backspace through the name and then begin to type, Excel will be in bold mode and any comment that you type will appear in bold, as shown in Fig. 1171.

This is a comment

Fig. 1171

To turn off the bold mode, hit Ctrl+B before you begin to type the comment.

Summary: You can change the name that appears in the comment by using the General tab of the options dialog.

Commands Discussed: Tools – Options – General

CHANGE SHAPE OF COMMENT TO A STAR

Problem: As shown in Fig. 1172, you have a comment in a cell. Jazz up your spreadsheet by changing the shape of the comment into a starburst or any other AutoShape.

2003	2004	Growth	
1897091	2108490	11.⬚%	Congratulations on 11.1% Growth!

Fig. 1172

Strategy: You can change the shape of a comment. Follow these instructions.

1)   From the cell, right-click and select Edit Comment. Diagonal lines appear, as shown in Fig. 1173.

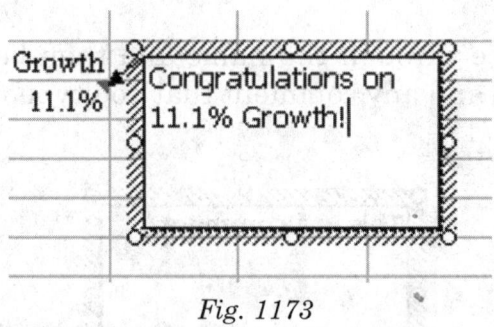

Growth	
11.1%	Congratulations on 11.1% Growth!

Fig. 1173

2)   Click on the diagonal lines to change the comment from edit text mode to edit mode, as shown in Fig. 1174.

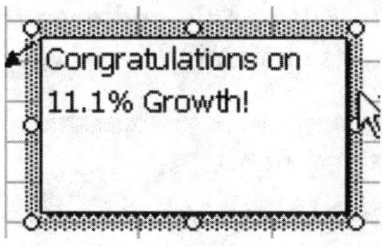

Fig. 1174

3)   If you do not have the Drawing toolbar displayed, choose View –
     Toolbars – Drawing from the menu.

4)   On the left side of the Drawing toolbar is a dropdown called Draw.
     Choose this dropdown. From the menu, select Change AutoShape.

5)   From the flyout menu, choose Stars and Banners. From the next
     flyout choose Explosion 2, as shown in Fig. 1175.

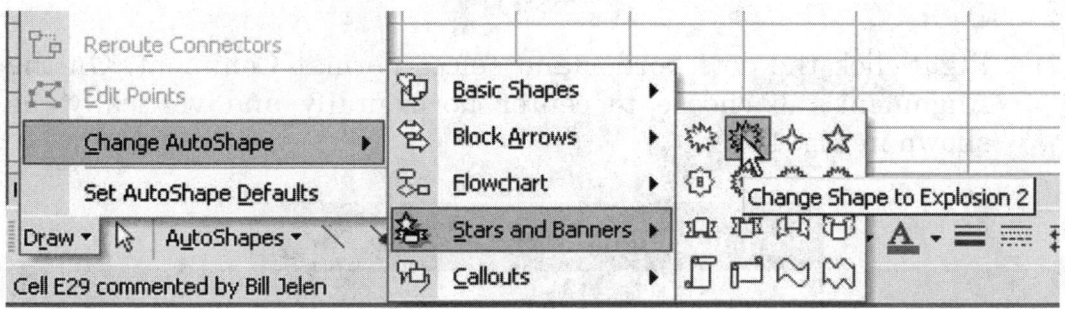

Fig. 1175

The comment will change from a rectangle to a starburst, as shown in
Fig. 1176.

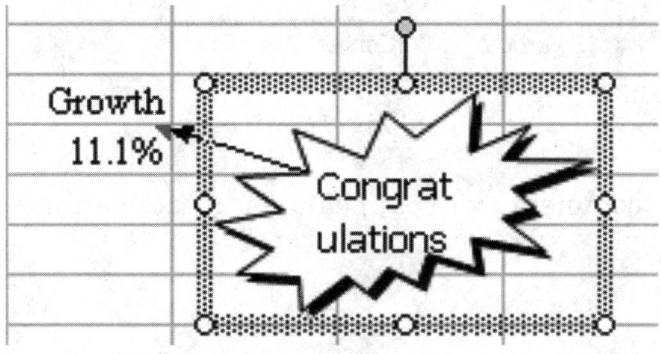

Fig. 1176

6)   Grab a corner white Fill handle and drag to make the shape large enough for the text, as shown in Fig. 1177.

Fig. 1177

7)   Right-click the dots border and select Format Comment. On the Alignment tab choose to center horizontally and vertically, as shown in Fig. 1178.

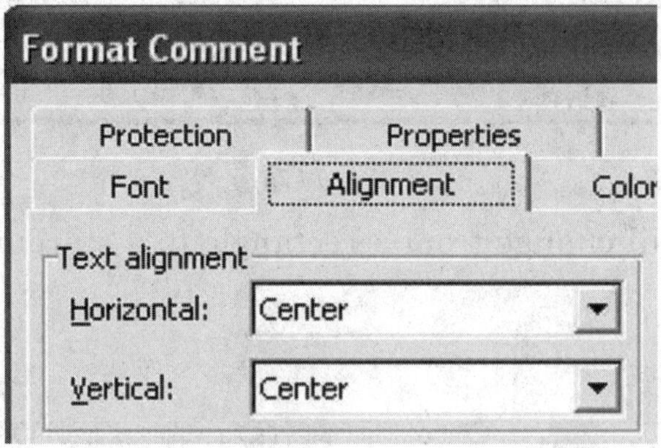

Fig. 1178

Result: The comment will appear as a starburst, as shown in Fig. 1179.

Fig. 1179

Additional Information: Grab the green rotate handle and rotate until you have the shape that best fits the text, as shown in Fig. 1180.

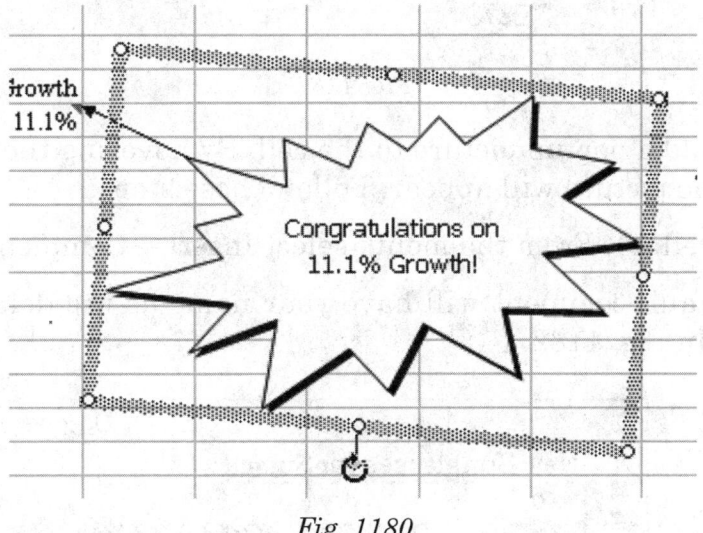

Fig. 1180

Part
IV

Summary: Using the Draw button on the Drawing toolbar, you can control the shape of a comment.

Commands Discussed: View – Toolbars; Draw – Change AutoShape

ADD A POP-UP PICTURE
OF AN ITEM IN A CELL

Problem: As shown in Fig. 1181, you have a product catalog in Excel. Your sales reps will show the list of items to the buyer in a retail store. It is a pain to go back and forth between Excel and the product catalog. Can you have pictures appear on demand in Excel?

	A	B	C
1	New Sunglasses for Summer		
2			
3	Item #	Order	
4	SG073		
5	SG197		
6	SG207		
7	SG878		

Fig. 1181

Strategy: Add a pop-up picture to the cell. By hovering the mouse over an item #, the picture will appear. Follow these steps.

1)   Select cell A4. From the menu, select Insert – Comment.

The default comment will have your name as the default text, as shown in Fig. 1182.

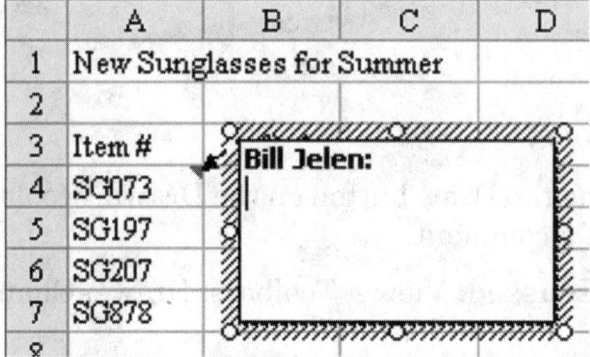

Fig. 1182

2) Backspace to clear out the text in the comment.

3) Using the mouse, click on the diagonal-lines border in order to change the border to a series of dots, as shown in Fig. 1183.

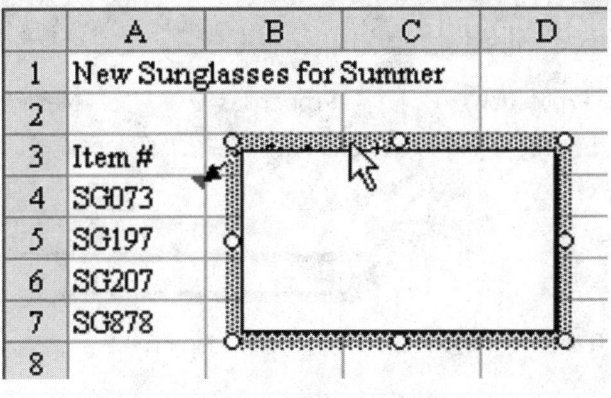

Fig. 1183

4) Right-click the dotted border and select Format Comment, as shown in Fig. 1184.

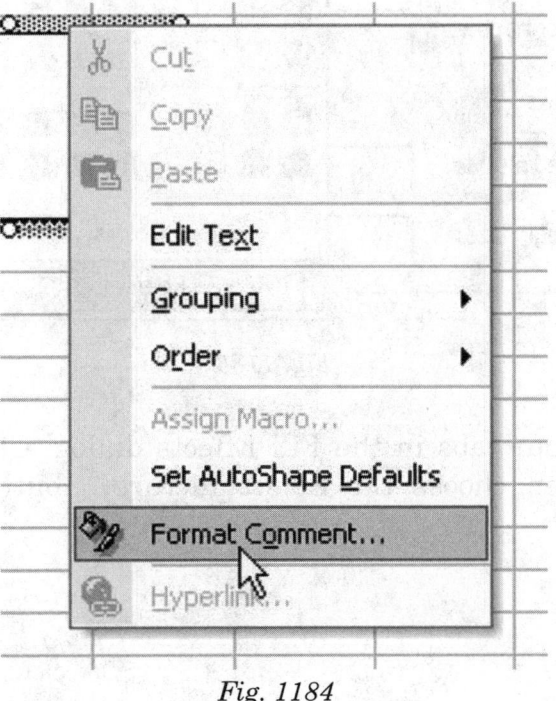

Fig. 1184

5) There are eight tabs in the Format Comment dialog. Go to the Colors and Lines tab. In the Fill Color dropdown, choose Fill Effects..., as shown in Fig. 1185.

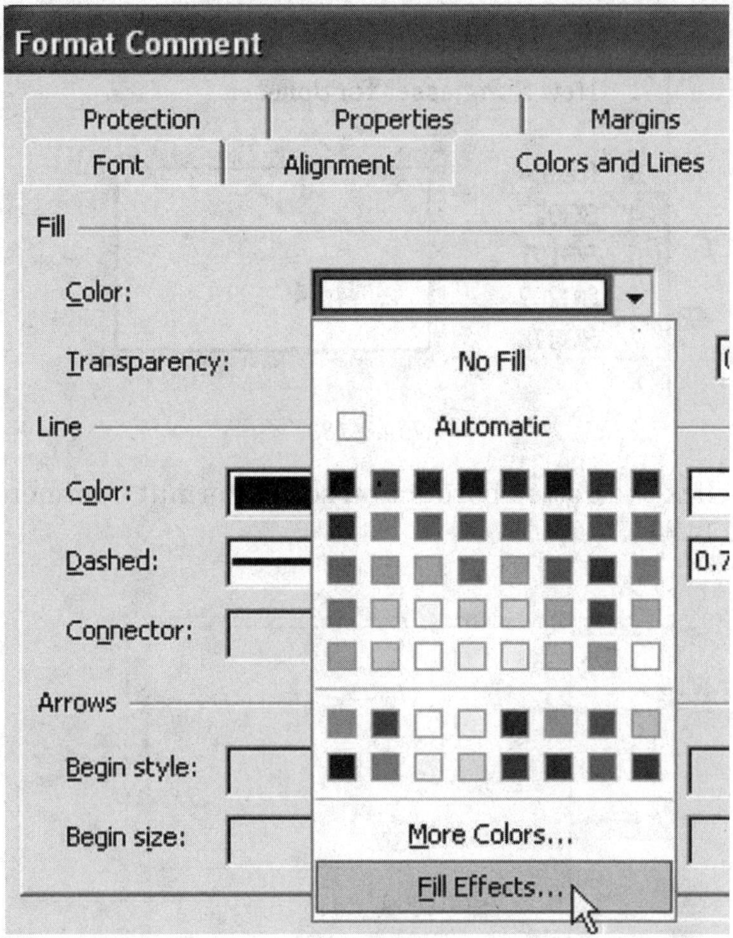

Fig. 1185

6) There are four tabs in the Fill Effects dialog. Choose the Picture tab and then choose the Select Picture... button, as shown in Fig. 1186.

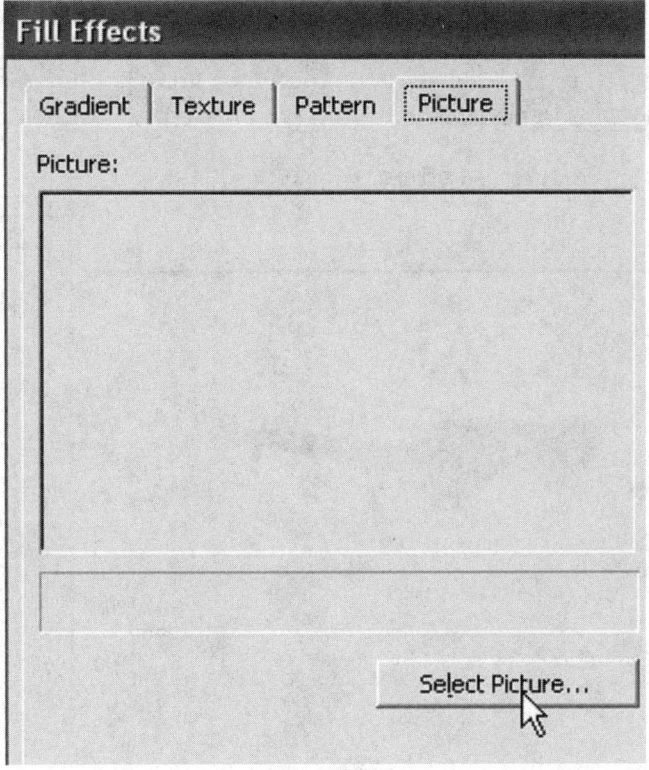

Fig. 1186

Part IV

7) Browse to the location where you have product pictures stored. Select a digital image of the item. Choose Insert, as shown in Fig. 1187.

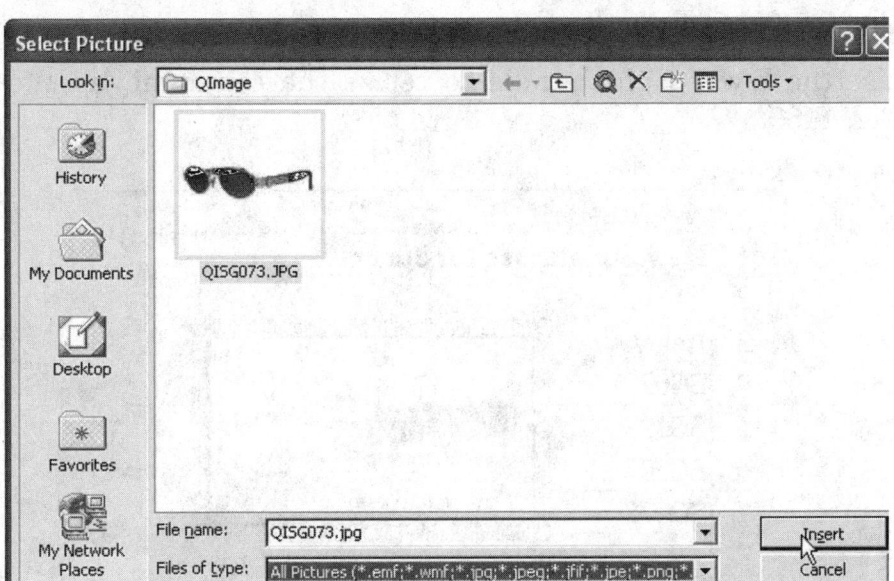

Fig. 1187

8)   On the Fill Effects tab, select OK, as shown in Fig. 1188.

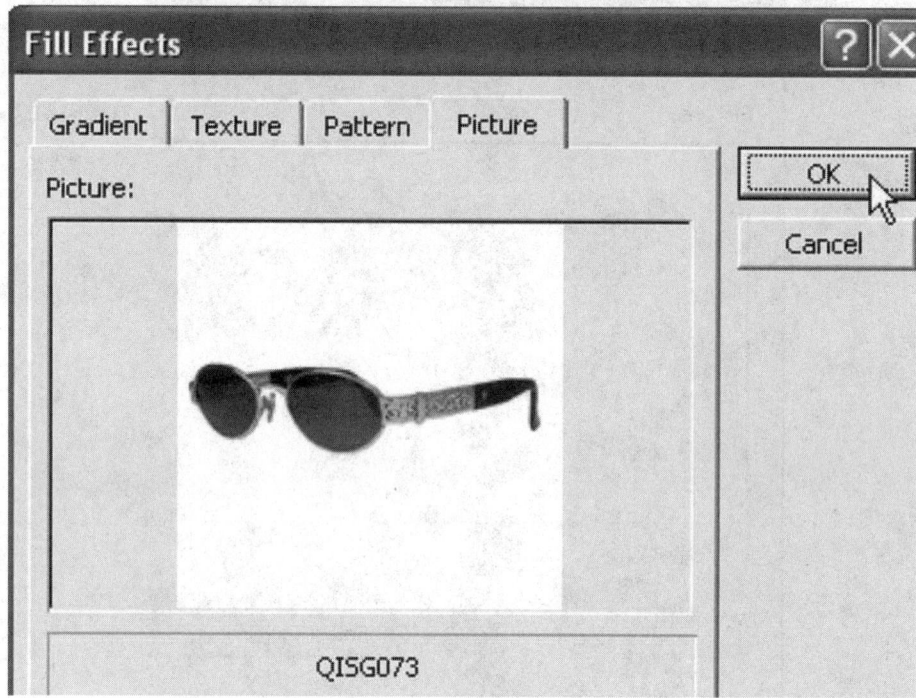

Fig. 1188

As you return to the Format Comment dialog, a squished version of the image will appear in the Color dropdown. Don't worry – the actual comment will look better.

9)   Choose OK to close the Format Comment tab.

10) Use the lower right handle to resize the comment, as shown in Fig. 1189.

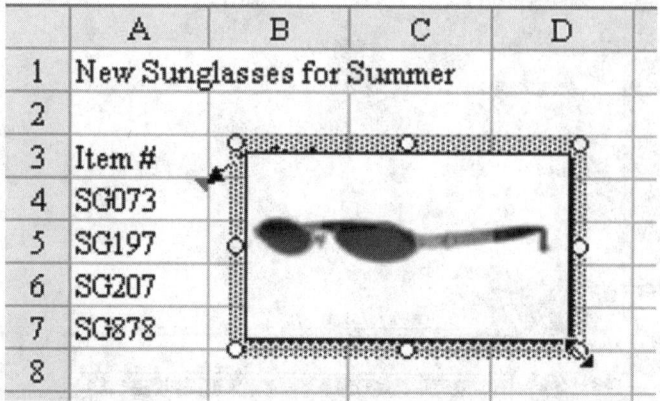

Fig. 1189

A red triangle appears in cell A4, as shown in Fig. 1190.

	A	B	C
1	New Sunglasses for Summer		
2			
3	Item #	Order	
4	SG073		
5	SG197		
6	SG207		
7	SG878		
8			

Fig. 1190

As promised, a picture of the product appears when you hover the mouse icon over the cell, as shown in Fig. 1191.

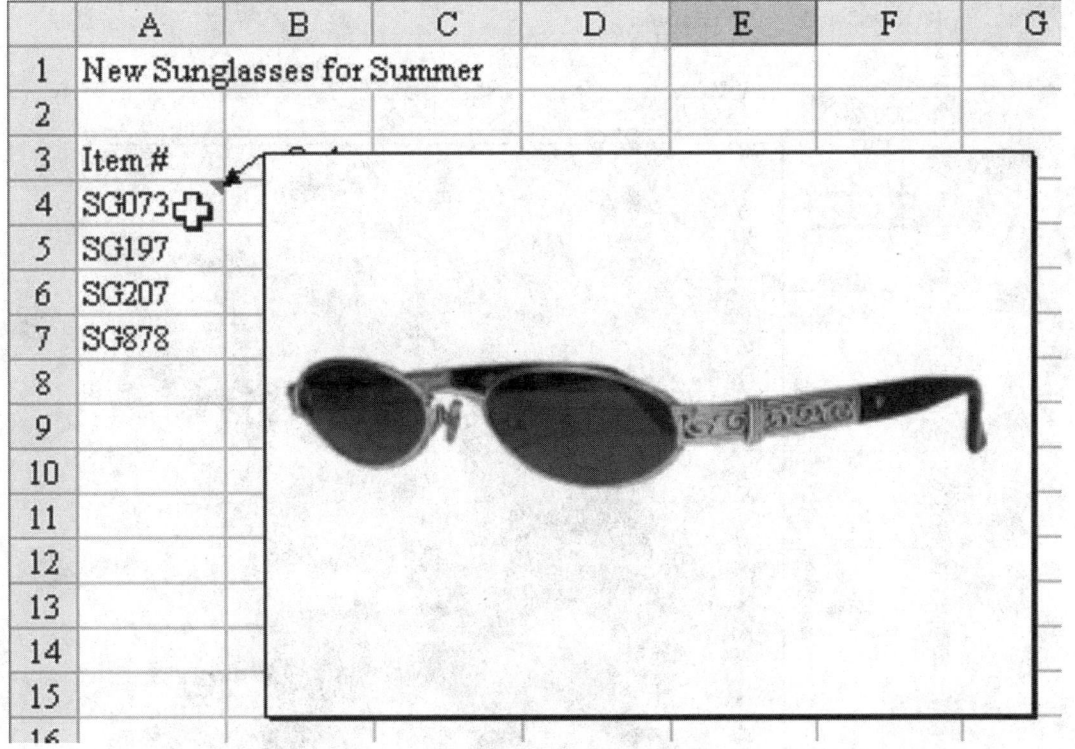

Fig. 1191

Part
IV

11) Repeat these steps for each item in the catalog.

Summary: Everyone thinks of Excel as being strictly for numbers. Adding pop-up pictures is a great trick to make your spreadsheets more of a sales tool.

Commands Discussed: Insert Comment; Format Comment

ADD A POP-UP PICTURE TO MULTIPLE CELLS

Problem: You gave this book to your manager for Boss' Day. He saw the previous trick, about adding a pop-up picture to a cell, and wants you to add pictures to dozens of cells, as shown in Fig. 1192. Adding pictures is one of the most tedious tasks in Excel.

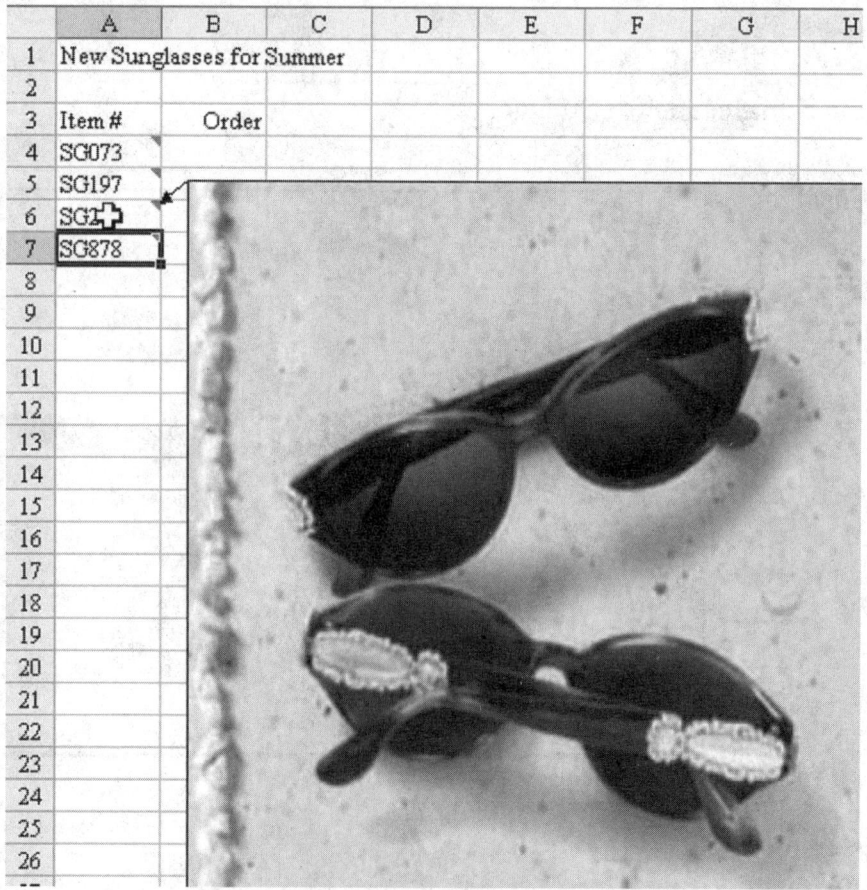

Fig. 1192

Strategy: A VBA macro can be used to speed up a lot of jobs. I would never attempt this particular task without it, especially because the macro is so simple.

Enter these few lines of code in the VBA Editor. Select the dozens of cells. Run the macro. Pictures are added to every cell in the selection.

```
Sub AddABunch()

For Each cell In Selection

    MyPic = "C:\Qimage\QI" & cell.Value & ".jpg"

    With cell.AddComment

        .Shape.Fill.UserPicture MyPic

        .Shape.Height = 300

        .Shape.Width = 300

    End With

Next cell

End Sub
```

Additional Details: For the complete guide to learning VBA, check out *VBA & Macros for Microsoft Excel* from QUE.

The above macro works because all of our company pictures are in the same folder with a common naming scheme.

Summary: A few lines of VBA code can turn a horribly monotonous job into a few seconds of work.

Commands Discussed: VBA

Part
IV

CHANGE THE BACKGROUND
OF THE WORKSHEET

Problem: Excel looks boring. You generally have black text on white background, with gray lines. If you have an opening menu worksheet in your workbook, you can change the background to any picture.

Strategy: From the menu, select Format – Sheet – Background. Choose any image from your computer. The image will be tiled to form the background, as shown in Fig. 1193.

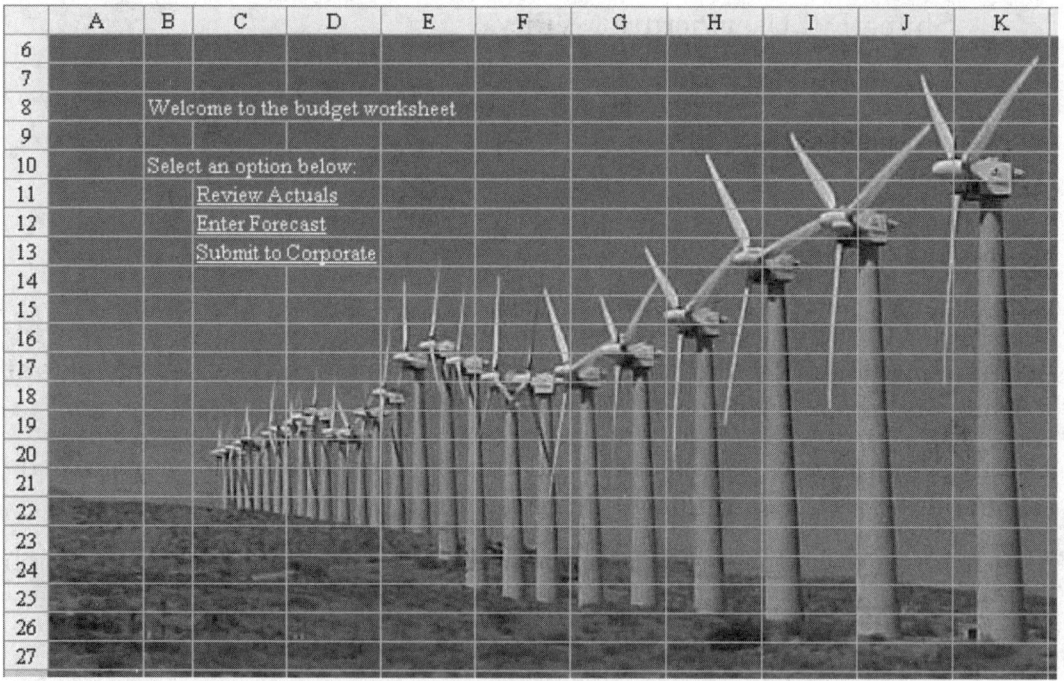

Fig. 1193

You might wish to turn off the gridline display on this menu. Go to Tools – Options – View. In the lower left corner, turn off the Gridlines display, as shown in Fig. 1194.

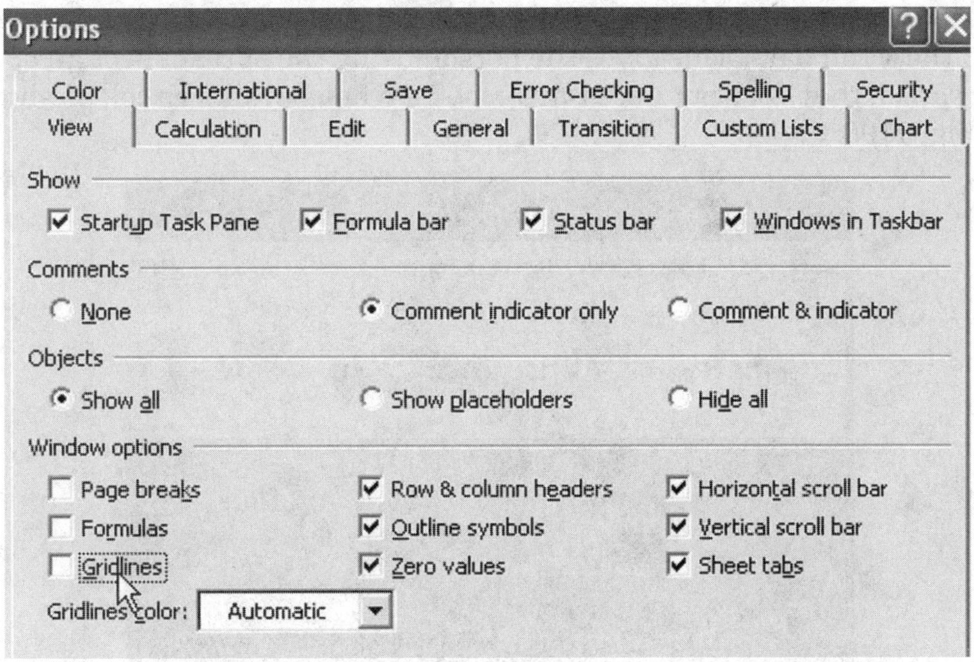

Fig. 1194

This will present a cleaner view of the worksheet, as shown in Fig. 1195.

Part IV

Fig. 1195

Optionally, you might turn off the sheet tabs, row and column headers, and the scroll bars. This gives the person using the spreadsheet an opening screen that does not necessarily look a whole lot like Excel, as shown in Fig. 1196.

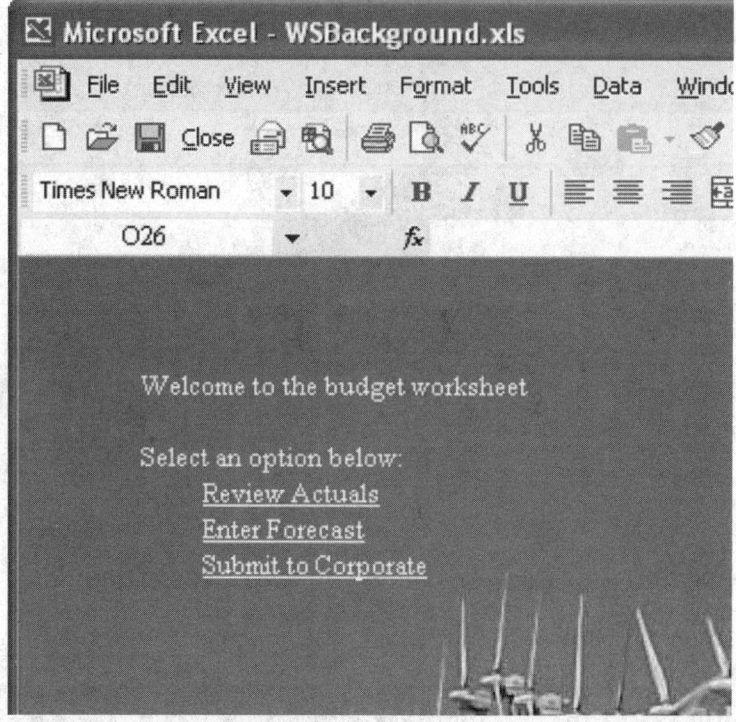

Fig. 1196

Some people also like to uncheck the Formula Bar and Status Bar from the View menu, as shown in Fig. 1197. Personally, I think this is going too far. After all, someone has to use the Forecast sheet that is also in this book. If you turn off all of the scroll bars, formula bar, status bar, and index tabs, it will be pretty hard to actually use Excel. The Row & Column Headers is independent of the worksheet, but all of the other settings apply to the whole workbook.

You do not want an Excel rookie to be forced to use Excel without a formula bar or status bar. This is the second worksheet in the workbook. Even though you made most of the changes to the Menu worksheet, they apply to the entire workbook.

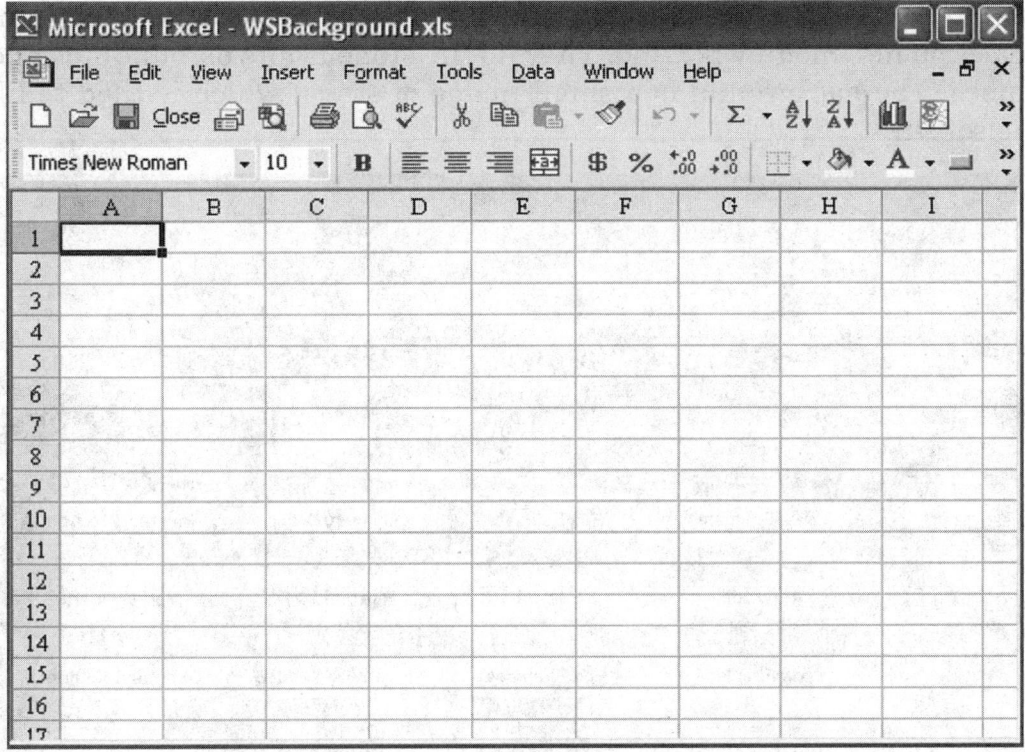

Fig. 1197

Gotcha: The background will never print. The following chapter, Add a Printable Background to Your Spreadsheet, explains how to create a background that will print.

Additional Information: In order to change the background image on the worksheet, you must remove the first image. From the menu, select Format – Sheet – Delete Background, as shown in Fig. 1198.

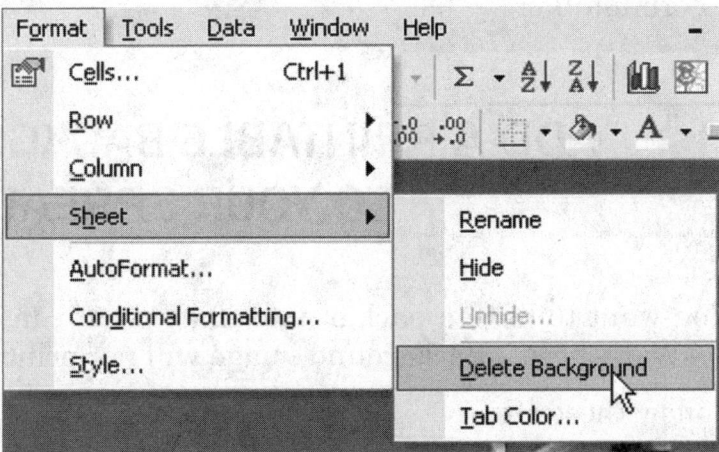

Fig. 1198

As shown in Fig. 1199, here is a menu that was built for Bedrock Construction in Uniontown, Ohio. They do the stone fronts on buildings and homes. The background is a small image of stone, which is tiled to fill the screen.

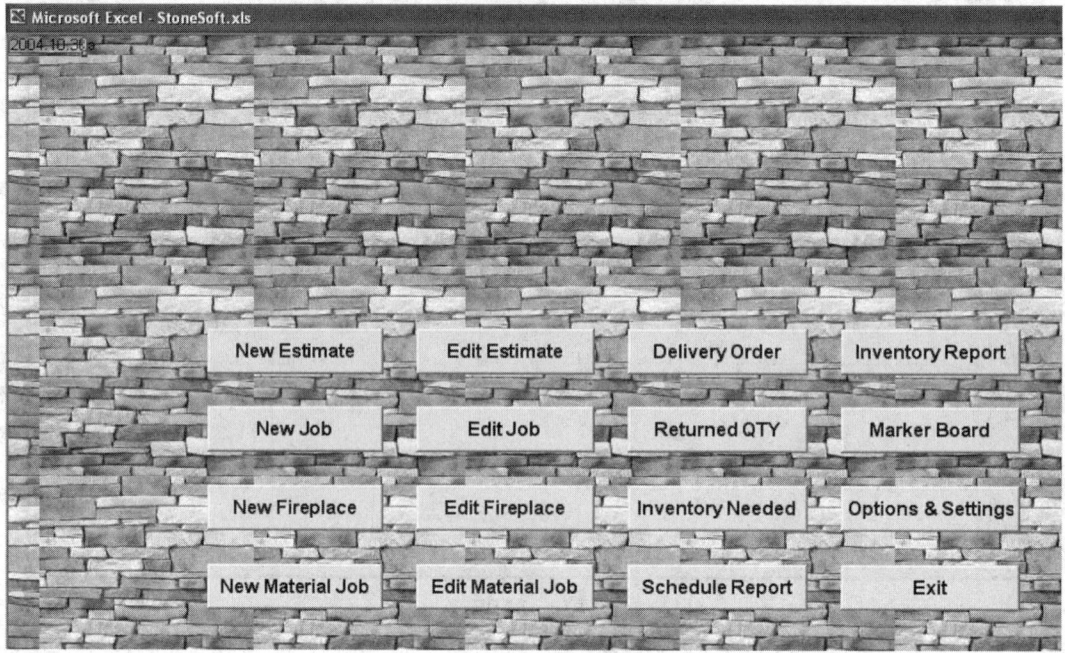

Fig. 1199

Summary: Make Excel look less sterile by adding a background image to the worksheet.

Commands Discussed: Format – Sheet – Background; Format – Sheet – Remove – Background; Tools – Options – View; View – Status Bar; View – Formula Bar

ADD A PRINTABLE BACKGROUND TO YOUR SPREADSHEET

Problem: You want to have a background image that can be printed. The Format – Worksheet – Background image will not print.

Strategy: Follow these steps:

1) Display the Drawing toolbar.

2) Click on the Rectangle tool. Draw a white rectangle to cover your print area, as shown in Fig. 1200.

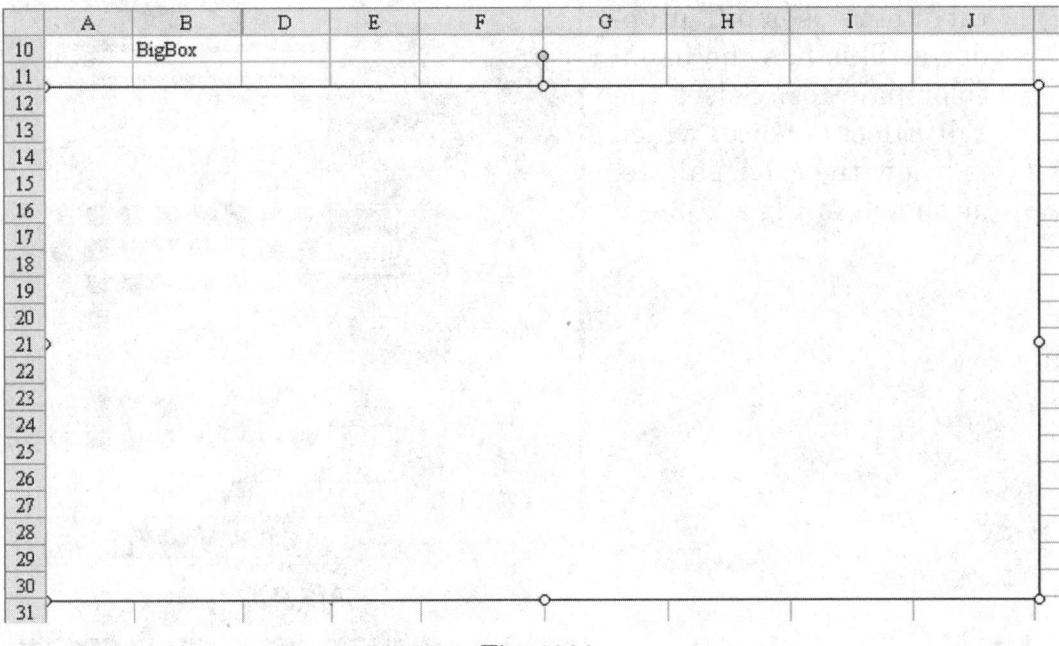

Fig. 1200

3) Select the Line Color icon and choose No Line, as shown in Fig. 1201.

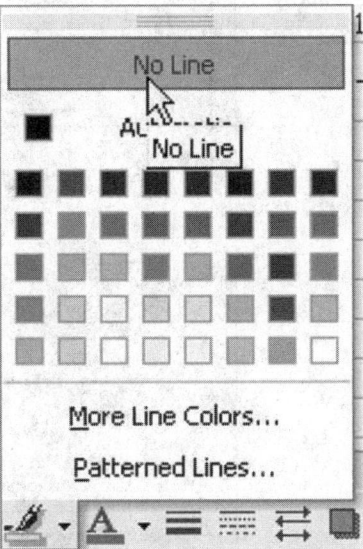

Fig. 1201

4) Right-click the rectangle and choose Format AutoShape.

5) On the Colors and Lines tab, there is a fill drop-down. This has the usual color palettes. Select the Fill Effects choice, which is below the color palette, as shown in Fig. 1202.

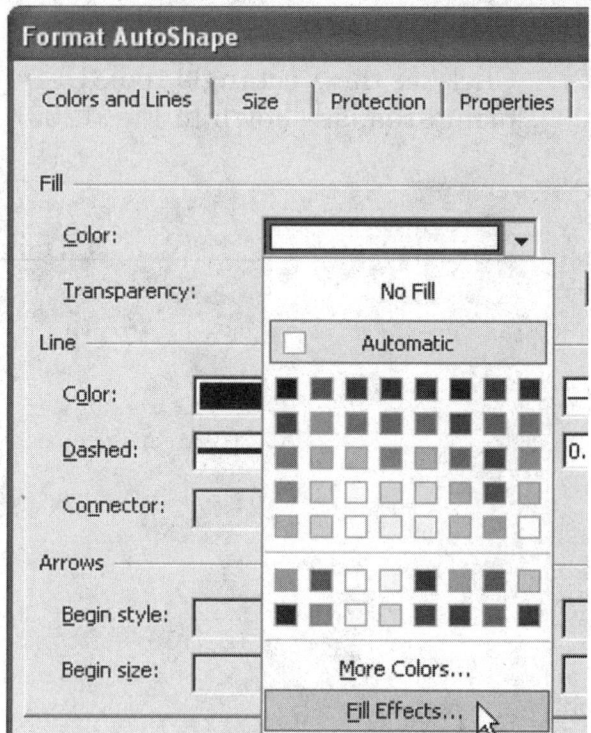

Fig. 1202

6) There are four tabs in Fill Effects. Choose Picture, the rightmost tab. Choose the Select Picture button. Select your picture, as shown in Fig. 1203.

7) In the lower left corner, select Lock Picture Aspect Ratio. Choose OK to close fill effects.

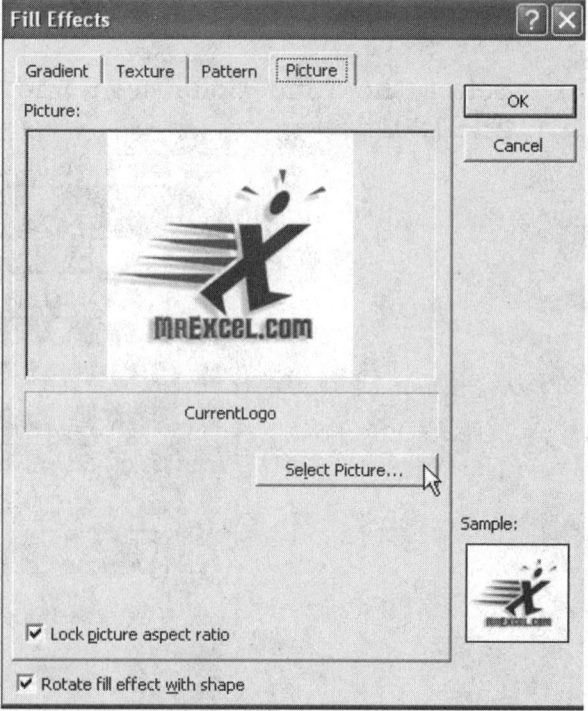

Fig. 1203

8) Back on the Format AutoShape dialog, move the transparency slider from 0 to 80, as shown in Fig. 1204.

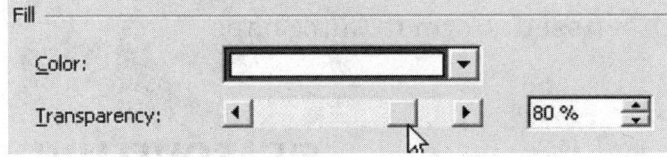

Fig. 1204

9) On the Properties tab of the Dialog, check to make sure the item will print, as shown in Fig. 1205.

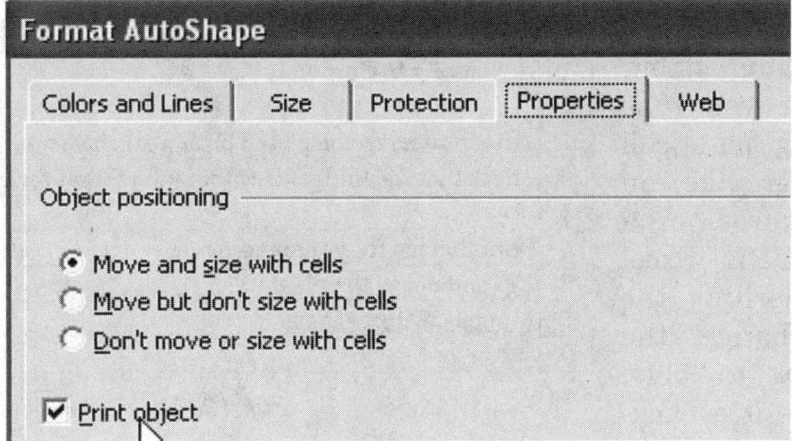

Fig. 1205

10) Choose OK to Close the Format AutoShape tab.

Result: As shown in Fig. 1206, you've added a background that can be printed.

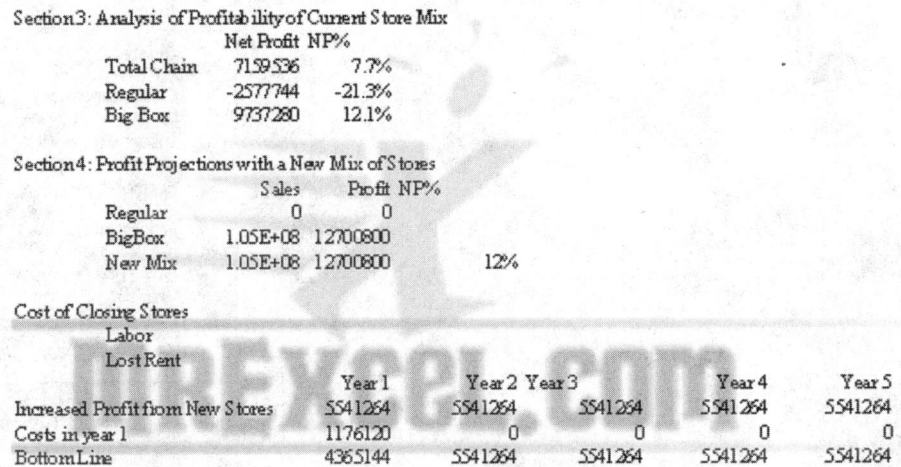

Fig. 1206

Summary: With this technique, you can add a semi-transparent background that will print behind your spreadsheet.

Commands Discussed: Format AutoShape

REMOVE HYPERLINKS
AUTOMATICALLY INSERTED BY EXCEL

Problem: Excel has an annoying habit. Whenever you type something in a cell that looks like an e-mail address or a website URL, Excel will underline the value, change the font color to blue, and make it a clickable hyperlink, as shown in Fig. 1207.

	A	B	C	D	E	F
1	Submitting to Corporate					
2						
3	After you have completed both worksheets, be sure to					
4	check that the budget is within your target for the year.					
5						
6	Print this file for your records.					
7	Zip and e-mail the file to:					
8	budget@MrExcel.com					
9						

Fig. 1207

Strategy: As shown in Fig. 1208, to remove the hyperlink, right-click the cell and choose Remove Hyperlink.

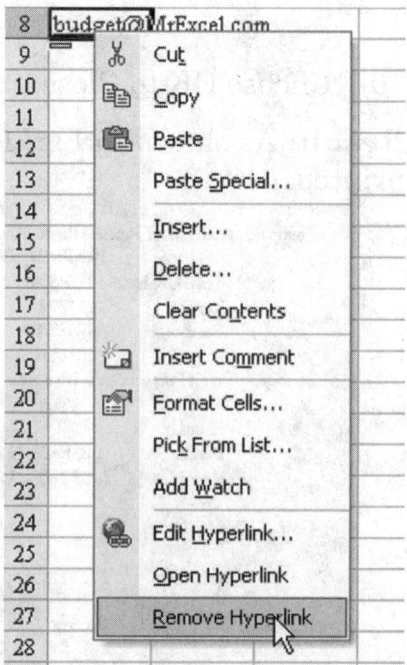

Fig. 1208

To prevent Excel from adding hyperlinks in the first place, go to Tools – AutoCorrect Options. On the tab for Autoformat as you Type, uncheck the Internet and Network Paths with Hyperlinks, as shown in Fig. 1209.

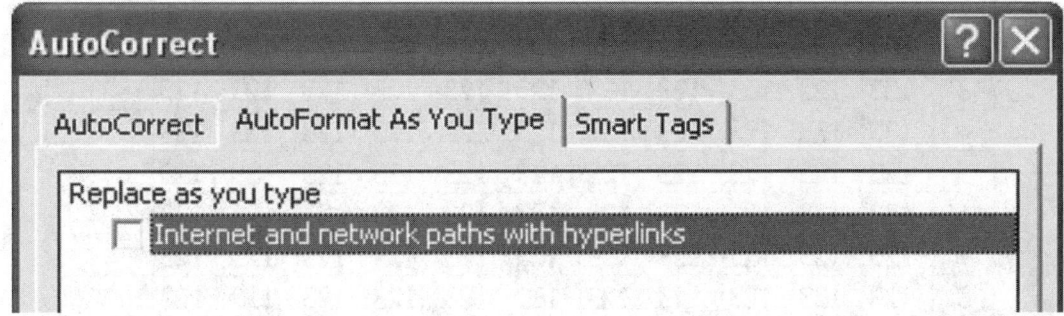

Fig. 1209

Summary: There is an easy way to prevent Excel from automatically inserting hyperlinks.

Commands Discussed: Tools – AutoCorrect Options

CHANGE WIDTH OF ALL COLUMNS IN ONE COMMAND

Part
IV

Problem: You have a large model set up in Excel. Some of the columns are hidden. You want to globally change the width of all unhidden columns to a width of 4. As shown in Fig. 1210, if you choose all columns in the worksheet and use Format – Column Width, the hidden columns will unhide.

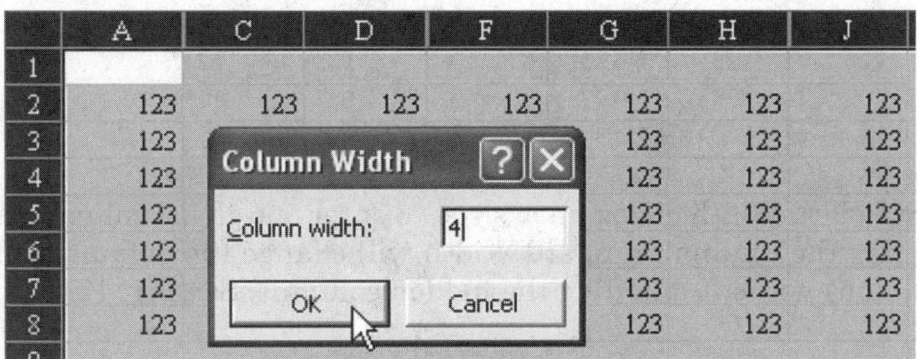

Fig. 1210

When you change the column width globally, using Format – Column Width, the hidden columns will unhide, as shown in Fig. 1211.

	A	B	C	D	E	F	G	H	I	J	K	L
1												
2	123	123	123	123	123	123	123	123	123	123	123	
3	123	123	123	123	123	123	123	123	123	123	123	
4	123	123	123	123	123	123	123	123	123	123	123	
5	123	123	123	123	123	123	123	123	123	123	123	
6	123	123	123	123	123	123	123	123	123	123	123	
7	123	123	123	123	123	123	123	123	123	123	123	
8	123	123	123	123	123	123	123	123	123	123	123	
9												
10												

Fig. 1211

Strategy: Use Format – Column – Standard Width, as shown in Fig. 1212.

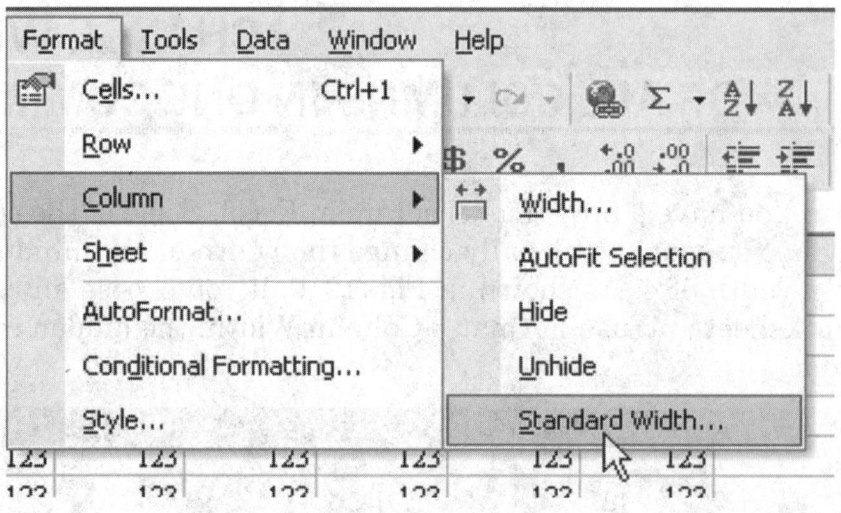

Fig. 1212

The Standard Width dialog allows you to enter one global column width. Changing the column Standard Width will change the default width of all columns without unhiding the hidden columns. See Fig. 1213.

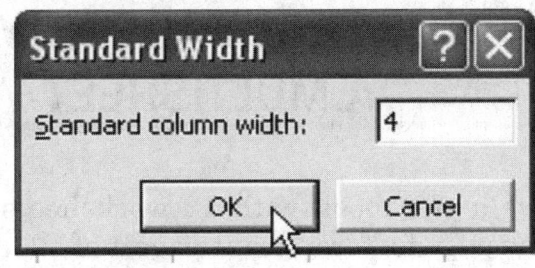

Fig. 1213

Result: All of the columns will have a width of 4, as shown in Fig. 1214.

	A	C	D	F	G	H	J
1	123	123	123	123	123	123	123
2	123	123	123	123	123	123	123
3	123	123	123	123	123	123	123

Fig. 1214

Additional Information: Changing the standard width will change the width of hidden columns. When they are later unhidden, they will have the correct width, as shown in Fig. 1215.

D	E	F
123	123	123
123	123	123

Fig. 1215

Part IV

Gotcha: The Standard Width does not change the widths of columns that have previously been changed. For example, open a new workbook. Manually change column C to be 20 wide. Use Format Column Standard Width to be 1 wide. All of the columns except C will be changed, as shown in Fig. 1216.

	A	B	C	D	E	F	G	H	I	J	K	L	M	N
1														
2														
3														
4														

Fig. 1216

Summary: Use Standard Width to globally adjust the width of all columns without unhiding hidden columns.

Commands Discussed: Format – Column – Standard Width

CONTROL PAGE NUMBERING IN A MULTISHEET WORKBOOK

Problem: You have a workbook with 12 worksheets, one per month. Although you set the page footer to print page 1 of 12, every sheet prints with page 1 of 1, as shown in Fig. 1217.

Page 1 of 1

December

	Dec-05	Prior Year	Delta
Net sales	0	0	0

Fig. 1217

Strategy: The key to making this work is to print the entire workbook at once. Organize the Worksheets so that they are in the proper order for printing, with the worksheet for the first page on the left. Instead of using the Print icon, select File – Print. You will then have an option to print the entire workbook, as shown in Fig. 1218.

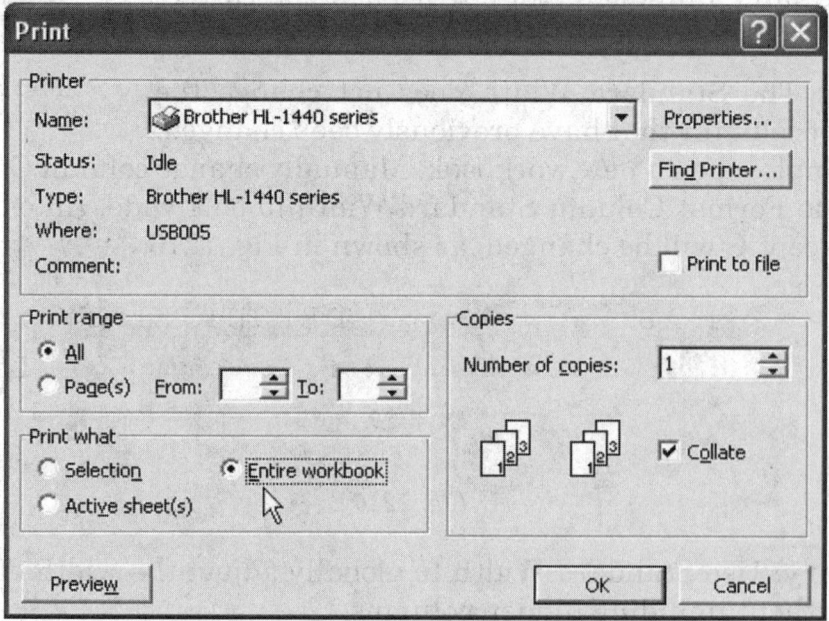

Fig. 1218

Result: As shown in Fig. 1219, the page numbers will reflect 1 of 12, 2 of 12, etc.

December

	Dec-05	Prior Year	Delta
Net sales	0	0	0

Fig. 1219

Alternate Strategy: If you only need to print a few sheets, select the first sheet. Hold down Ctrl while selecting other sheets. You can now use the File – Print and choose Active Sheets to print the selected sheets, as shown in Fig. 1220.

Fig. 1220

Summary: To ensure your worksheet pages print with the proper page numbers, use File – Print to select printing the entire worksheet.

Commands Discussed: File – Print

**Part
IV**

USE WHITE COLOR FOR FONTS TO HIDE DATA

Problem: As shown in Fig. 1221, your workbook needs extra columns in order to show a graph. You would prefer to hide this information from the user.

	I	J	K	L	M	N	O
	DATE	Weight	Food	ACTIVITY	To Chart	TrendLine	Actually At
	Wednesday 9/1/2004	226.00		BB 1 hour	226.00	226.00	226
	Thursday 9/2/2004	224.00		Walk 20 Min	224	225.31	224
	Friday 9/3/2004	226.00	Meatloaf, sandwich, pizza	Nothing	226	224.62	226
	Saturday 9/4/2004	229.00	Junk food at game; 3 chix legs	Walked at game	229	223.93	229
	Sunday 9/5/2004	224.00			224	223.24	224
	Monday 9/6/2004				#N/A	222.55	224
	Tuesday 9/7/2004				#N/A	221.86	224
	Wednesday 9/8/2004				#N/A	221.17	224

Fig. 1221

Strategy: Highlight the extra cells and choose white text color. Use the dropdown next to the Font Color icon, as shown in Fig. 1222.

Fig. 1222

When you choose the dropdown instead of the icon, you can choose a white color, as shown in Fig. 1223.

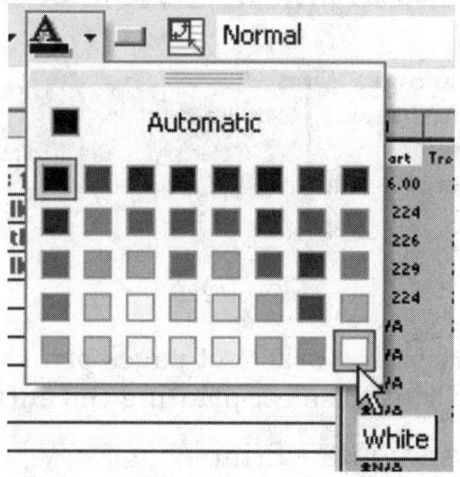

Fig. 1223

As shown in column M & N of Fig. 1224, this will prevent the cells from being seen or from printing (assuming the cell background color is also white).

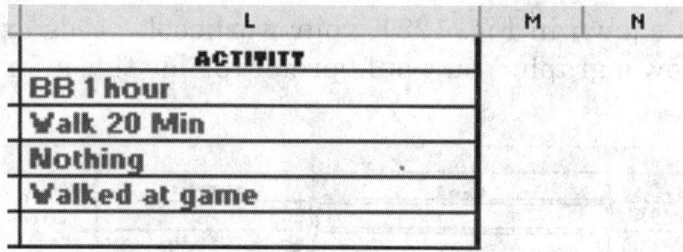

Fig. 1224

Additional information: If you need to troubleshoot these cells, reselect the columns. As shown in Fig. 1225, against the dark highlighting you can see the results in white.

Summary: Selecting an area and choosing white text will prevent the cells from printing and the user from seeing them.

Commands Discussed: Format – Cells – Color

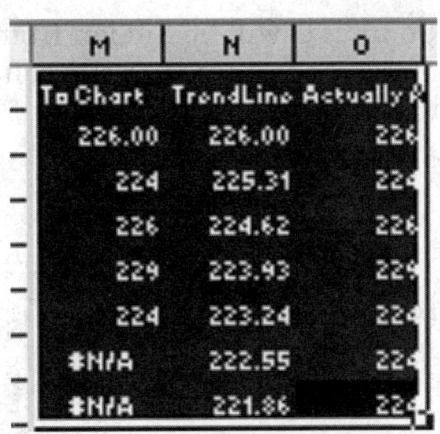

Fig. 1225

HIDE AND UNHIDE DATA

Problem: As shown in Fig. 1226, you need to hide data in a worksheet but you don't want to delete it.

	A	B	C	D
1	Section 1: Historical Trends (Per Month)			
2				
3		Store Type	Size	Rent
4		Regular	1200	2400
5		BigBox	2600	5200
6				

Fig. 1226

Part
IV

Strategy: Another method for hiding data to simplify a worksheet is to physically hide a row or column.

1) In the spreadsheet below, you might want to hide column C. To do this, select a cell in column C. From the menu, select Format – Column – Hide, as shown in Fig. 1227.

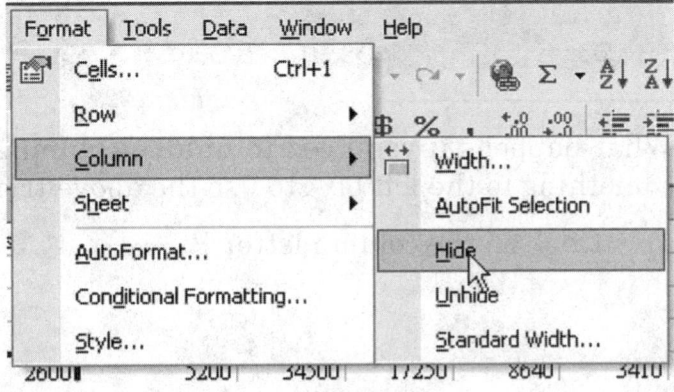

Fig. 1227

Column C will be hidden from the user. As shown in Fig. 1228, it is interesting to note that the cell pointer has disappeared. This is because the active cell is still in C5.

	C5		▼	*fx*	2600	
	A	B	D		E	
1	Section 1: Historical Trends (Per Month)					
2						
3		Store Type		Rent	S	
4		Regular		2400	1:	
5		BigBox		5200	3₄	

Fig. 1228

2)   Simply hit the Left or Right Arrow key to move to a visible column to get the cell pointer back.

3)   To unhide column C, click on the "B" heading and drag to the right to select the entire range of B:D. From the menu, select Format – Column – Unhide, as shown in Fig. 1229.

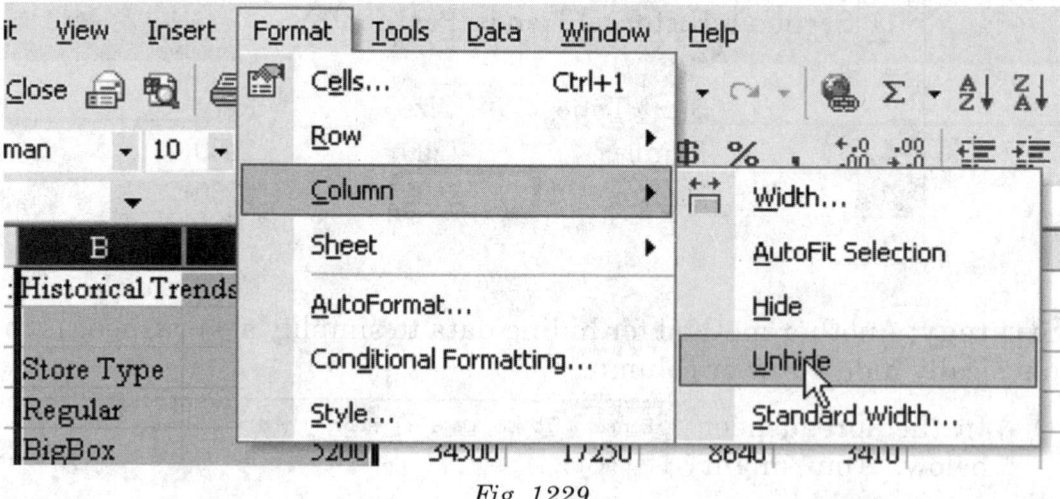

Fig. 1229

What happens if you need to unhide column A? You can't really select something to the left of A to use the above trick, so follow these steps:

1)   Click on the column letter B.

2)   As shown in Fig. 1230, drag up and to the left so that the mouse is above row 1. The difference is subtle but you have now selected columns B and A. Use Format – Column – Unhide.

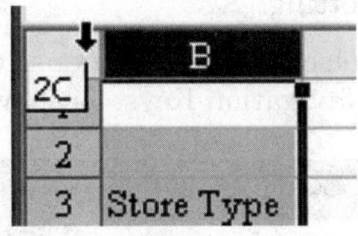

Fig. 1230

Summary: To hide data in a worksheet without deleting it, select the column to hide and use Format – Column – Hide. To unhide the column select and highlight the entire columns on either side of it and use Format – Column – Unhide.

Commands Discussed: Format – Column – Hide; Format – Column – Unhide

TEMPORARILY SEE
A HIDDEN COLUMN WITHOUT UNHIDING

Part
IV

Problem: You have data hidden in column E, as shown in Fig. 1231. You want to quickly view data in the hidden column without actually unhiding it.

	A	B	D	E
1	Section 1: Historical Trends (Per Month)			
2				
3		Store Type	Rent	Sales
4		Regular	2400	12456
5		BigBox	5200	34500
6				

Fig. 1231

Strategy: Use this trick to temporarily view a hidden column. Note that this trick only works if you use Transition Navigation Keys. If you regularly work with hidden data, this cool trick might be enough to tip you over to turning on this setting.

1) From the menu, select Tools – Options. On the Transition tab, choose Transition Navigation Keys, as shown in Fig. 1232.

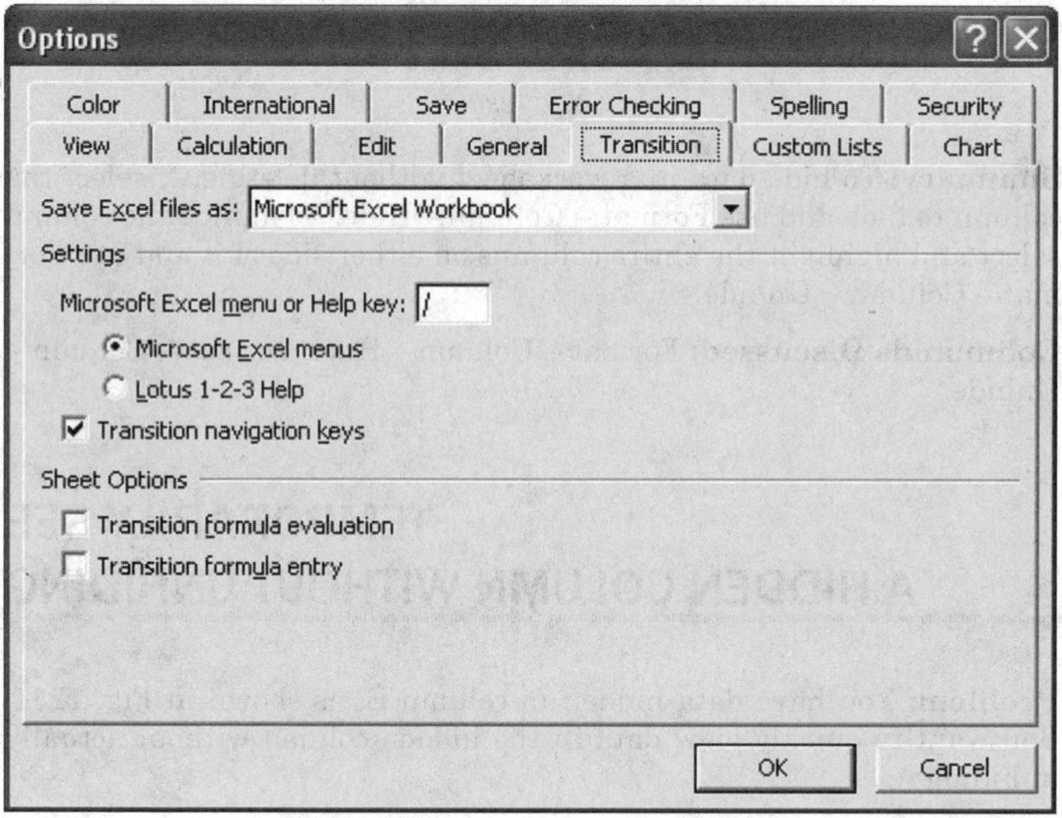

Fig. 1232

2) In the image, column C is hidden. Place the cell pointer in column D, in a blank cell. Type the Equal sign to start entering a formula.

3) Hit the Left Arrow key as if you were going to enter a formula using the arrow keys. Excel magically unhides the hidden columns, as shown in Fig. 1233. You can now arrow through the worksheet to look at hidden data.

4) When you are done, hit the Esc key to cancel entering the formula. The hidden ranges will be hidden again.

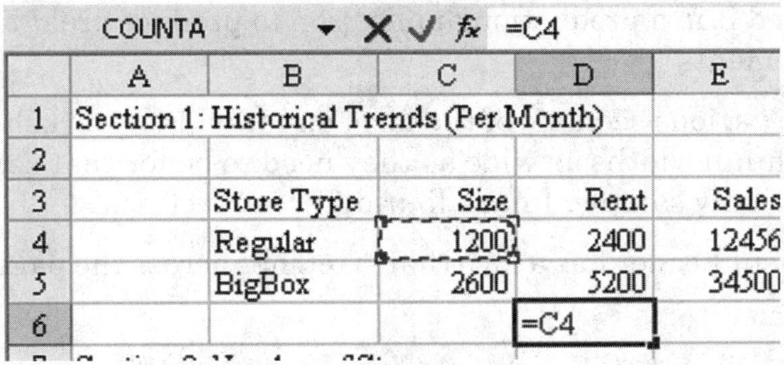

Fig. 1233

Gotcha: Beware, users could employ this method to see hidden data. To avoid this behavior, you need to protect the worksheet.

Gotcha: This behavior can be incredibly annoying. If you are in cell D3 and hope to enter a formula of =2*A3, you might think this is only five keystrokes:

=, 2, *, Left Arrow, Enter (a total of five strokes)

However, when you actually try to do this, after the fourth keystroke the hidden columns will open. You usually just catch this out of the corner of your eye, as you incorrectly enter =2*D3 in the formula.

Summary: To quickly view hidden data in a worksheet, select a cell in the column to the hidden data's immediate right, type an Equal sign, and then hit the Left Arrow key.

Commands Discussed: Tools – Options – Transition

BUILD COMPLEX REPORTS WHERE COLUMNS IN SECTION 1 DON'T LINE UP WITH SECTION 2

Problem: You need to duplicate a fairly complex form. The form has several sections. The column widths needed for the first section do not line up with the column widths needed for the other two sections.

Strategy: This is a wildly amazing and obscure solution. It has been floating around Excel Web sites for years as a novelty. However, we recently used it in a production application to produce great looking customer statements.

1)   Set up various sections of the form on individual worksheets. Make the column widths as wide as they need to be for that section of the form. In my sample, I have four different sections.

The statement header has a logo that stretches across the page, as shown in Fig. 1234.

Fig. 1234

The next section has five columns, as shown in Fig. 1235.

	A	B	C	D	E
1	Section 1: Orders Shipped this Period				
2					
3	Date	Invoice #	Your Reference #	Via	Total
4	11/2/2004	1021	PO AJHOIP	FedEx Ground	225
5	11/4/2004	1027	PO KJKJLK	FedEx Ground	499
6	11/8/2004	1030	PO YUOIU	FedEx Ground	510
7	11/9/2004	1031	PO KJL DADS	FedEx Ground	461
8	11/13/2004	1034	Verbal per Marc	FedEx Next Day	410
9	11/17/2004	1038	PO 9LKJD	FedEx Ground	546
10	Total Shipments				2651
11					

Fig. 1235

The next section has just three columns, as shown in Fig. 1236.

	A	B	C	D	E
1	Section 2: Payments Received This Period				
2					
3	Date	Ck#	Total		
4	11/2/2004	113783	272		
5	11/4/2004	113865	161		
6	11/8/2004	113919	600		
7	11/9/2004	113990	244		
8	11/13/2004	114070	114		
9	11/17/2004	114168	485		
10	Total Payments		1876		
11					

Fig. 1236

The final section has six columns, as shown in Fig. 1237.

	A	B	C	D	E	F
1	Section 3: Outstanding Invoices from Prior Periods					
2						
3	Date	Invoice #	Original Amount	Amt Paid	Amt Due	Your Reference #
4	1/10/2004	601	1029	929	100	PO AJHOIP
5	4/3/2004	685	393	0	393	PO YUOIU
6	4/20/2004	702	203	200	3	Verbal per Marc
7	5/18/2004	730	850	100	750	PO KJL DADS
8	9/6/2004	841	251	0	251	PO 9LKJD
9	10/10/2004	875	946	875	71	PO KJKJLK
10	Total Due from Prior Periods				1568	

Fig. 1237

You will build a printable statement on the worksheet that has the company header. On that page, you will paste three linked pictures that give a view of the back worksheets.

2) As shown in Fig. 1238, select the cells for Section 1. Use Ctrl+C to copy.

	A	B	C	D	E
1	Section 1: Orders Shipped this Period				
2					
3	Date	Invoice #	Your Reference #	Via	Total
4	11/2/2004	1021	PO AJHOIP	FedEx Ground	225
5	11/4/2004	1027	PO KJKJLK	FedEx Ground	499
6	11/8/2004	1030	PO YUOIU	FedEx Ground	510
7	11/9/2004	1031	PO KJL DADS	FedEx Ground	461
8	11/13/2004	1034	Verbal per Marc	FedEx Next Day	410
9	11/17/2004	1038	PO 9LKJD	FedEx Ground	546
10	Total Shipments				2651
11					

Fig. 1238

Part
IV

3)   Go to cell A7 on the main worksheet. Hold down the Shift key while
     you select the Edit menu. A secret option will appear in the menu
     for Paste Picture Link, as shown in Fig. 1239.

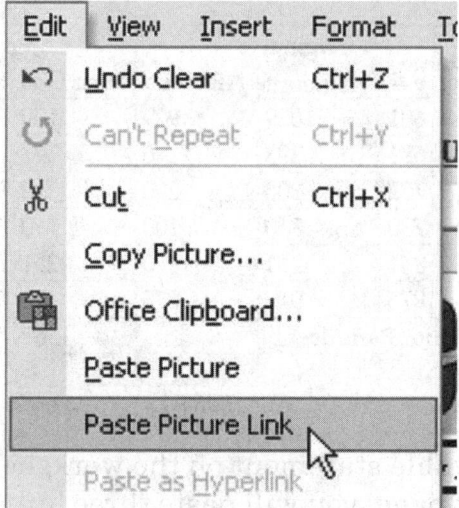

Fig. 1239

You will now have a live picture on Sheet1 of the cells on Sheet2, as
shown in Fig. 1240.

	A	B	C	D	E	F	G	H	I	J
1										
2					MREXCEL CONSULTING					
3										
4										
5				13386 Judy Ave NW, Uniontown OH 44685 , USA						
6										
7			Section 1: Orders Shipped this Period							
8										
9		Date		Invoice #	Your Reference #	Via		Total		
10		11/2/2004		1021	PO AJHOIP	FedEx Ground		225		
11		11/4/2004		1027	PO KJKJLK	FedEx Ground		499		
12		11/8/2004		1030	PO YUOIU	FedEx Ground		510		
13		11/9/2004		1031	PO KJL DADS	FedEx Ground		461		
14		11/13/2004		1034	Verbal per Marc	FedEx Next Day		410		
15		11/17/2004		1038	PO 9LKJD	FedEx Ground		546		
16		Total Shipments						2651		
17										
18										

Fig. 1240

4)   You can drag this picture so that it is centered on the page.

5)   Select A18:H18 and then select Format – Cells – Border. Choose
      a thick border and click the bottom Border section to draw a thick
      border along the bottom of row 18, as shown in Fig. 1241.

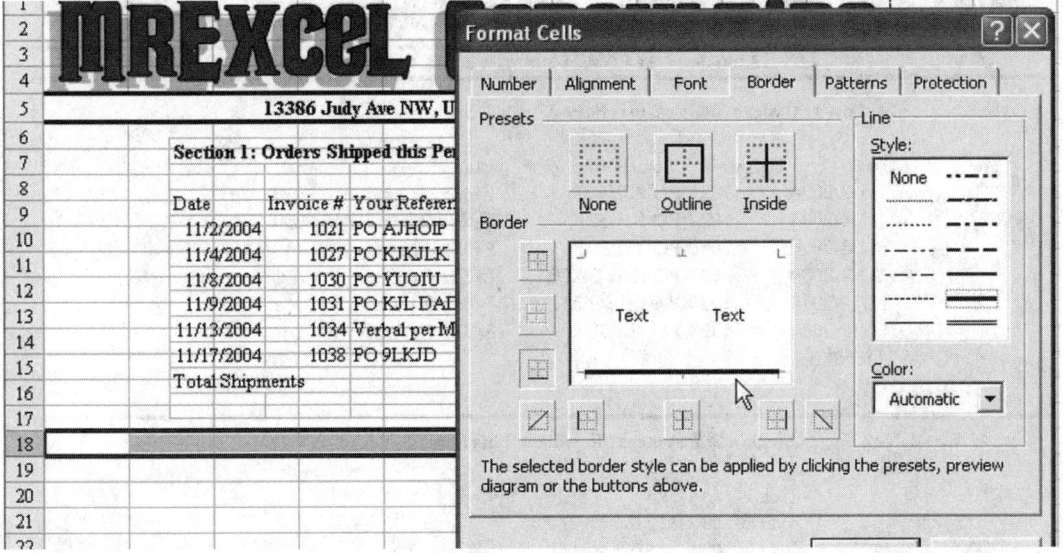

Fig. 1241

Part
IV

6)   Repeat for Section 2: Go to Sheet3. Select the Cells. Hit Ctrl+C to
      Copy. Return to Sheet1, cell A20. Hold down the Shift key while
      you do Edit – Paste Picture Link.

7)   Repeat for Section 3.

The pictures in the new sheet can be resized so that all have the same
width or you can simply center them on the page.

Result: You can print one unified form that does not look like it came from Excel. As shown in Fig. 1242, fields in section 2 are not necessarily lined up with fields in sheet 1.

MREXCEL CONSULTING

13386 Judy Ave NW, Uniontown OH 44685 , USA

Section 1: Orders Shipped this Period

Date	Invoice #	Your Reference #	Via	Total
11/2/2004	1021	PO AJHOIP	FedEx Ground	225
11/4/2004	1027	PO KJKJLK	FedEx Ground	324
11/8/2004	1030	PO YUOIU	FedEx Ground	113
11/9/2004	1031	PO KJL DADS	FedEx Ground	498
11/13/2004	1034	Verbal per Marc	FedEx Next Day	531
11/17/2004	1038	PO 9LKJD	FedEx Ground	869
Total Shipments				2560

Section 2: Payments Received This Period

Date	Ck#	Total
11/2/2004	113783	272
11/4/2004	113865	161
11/8/2004	113919	600
11/9/2004	113990	244
11/13/2004	114070	114
11/17/2004	114168	485
Total Payments		1876

Section 3: Outstanding Invoices from Prior Periods

Date	Invoice #	Original Amount	Amt Paid	Amt Due	Your Reference #
1/10/2004	601	1029	929	100	PO AJHOIP
4/3/2004	685	393	0	393	PO YUOIU
4/20/2004	702	203	200	3	Verbal per Marc
5/18/2004	730	850	100	750	PO KJL DADS

Fig. 1242

Additional Details: In our real statement application, the process of putting together the sections is handled by a VBA macro. This macro can paste a different number of rows each time.

Summary: Using the obscure Paste Picture Link command from the Shift+Edit menu allows you to paste a live picture of cells in a new section of the workbook. In this case, you can use this to avoid trying to align Section 1 column widths with Section 3 column widths.

Commands Discussed: Shift+Edit – Insert Picture Link; Format – Cells – Border

PASTE A LIVE PICTURE OF A CELL

Problem: You have a massively large spreadsheet. You are working on calculations in the top of the spreadsheet, but need to monitor a result in W842. It is a pain to travel back and forth to monitor that cell.

Strategy: Take a picture of the cell and paste it where you can keep and eye on it.

1)   As shown in Fig. 1243, select the cell W842. Hit Ctrl+C to copy.

	W841	▼	f_x
	V	W	
841		Final Result	
842	5,005,926.47	5,055,985.73	
843			

Fig. 1243

2)   Return to the top of the worksheet. Select an area with a few blank cells. Hold down the Shift key while you access the Edit menu. A Paste Picture Link choice is magically available, as shown in Fig. 1244.

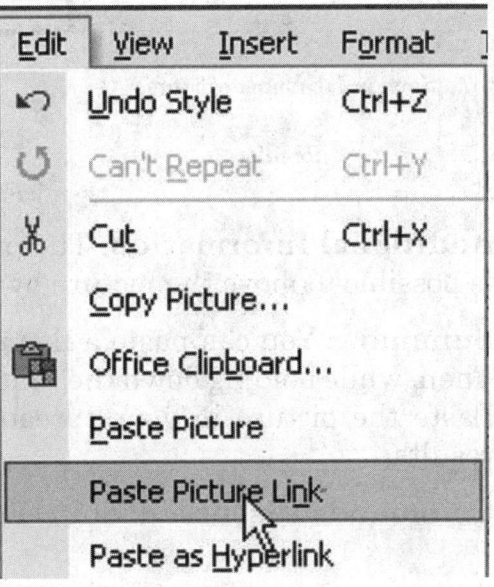

Fig. 1244

3) Choose Paste Picture Link. A live picture of the cell will be pasted, as shown in Fig. 1245.

	A	B	D	E	F	G	H
1	Section 1: Historical Trends (Per Month)						
2							
3		Store Type	Rent	Sales	Profit	Labor	Net
4		Regular	2400	12456	6228	6480	-2652
5		BigBox	5200	34500	17250	8640	3410
6							
7	Section 2: Number of Stores					Final Result	
8						5,055,985.73	
9		Regular					
10		BigBox					

Fig. 1245

As you make changes and the calculations cause the result to change, the picture will update, as shown in Fig. 1246.

	E5	▼		fx	36500		
	A	B	D	E	F	G	H
1	Section 1: Historical Trends (Per Month)						
2							
3		Store Type	Rent	Sales	Profit	Labor	Net
4		Regular	2400	12456	6228	6480	-2652
5		BigBox	5200	36500	18250	8640	4410
6							
7	Section 2: Number of Stores					Final Result	
8						5,975,966.76	
9		Regular					

Fig. 1246

Additional Information: The picture can be of multiple cells. Also, it is possible to move the picture by dragging it to a new location.

Summary: You can paste a live picture of distant cells. Copy the cells. Then, while holding down the Shift key, select Edit – Paste Picture Link. Paste the picture in your spreadsheet where you need to monitor its results.

Commands Discussed: Shift+Edit – Paste Picture Link

MONITOR FAR-OFF CELLS
IN EXCEL 2002 AND LATER VERSIONS

Problem: You have a massively large spreadsheet. You are working on calculations in the top of the spreadsheet, but need to monitor results in several other worksheets. It is a pain to travel back and forth to monitor those cells.

Strategy: Microsoft added the Watch Window in Excel 2002. This window is a favorite tool of VBA programmers and Microsoft added it to the regular Excel interface.

1) From the menu, select Tools – Formula Auditing – Show Watch Window, as shown in Fig. 1247.

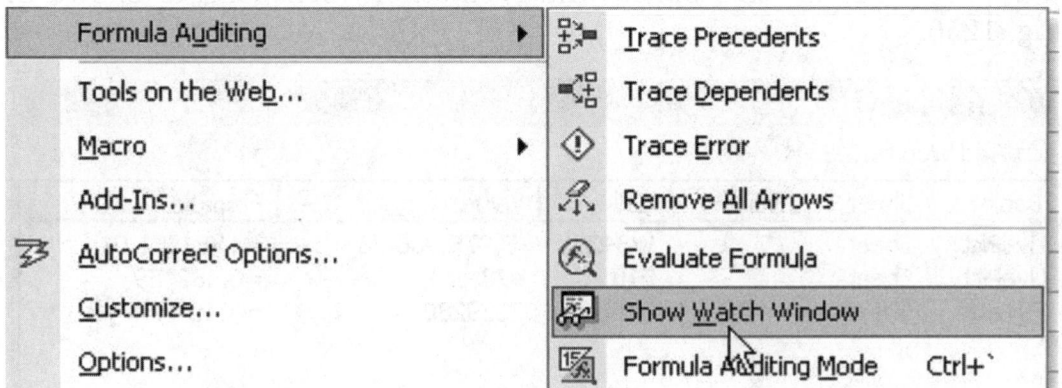

Fig. 1247

2) The Watch Window is a floating dialog box that you can move around your screen. Select Add Watch..., as shown in Fig. 1248.

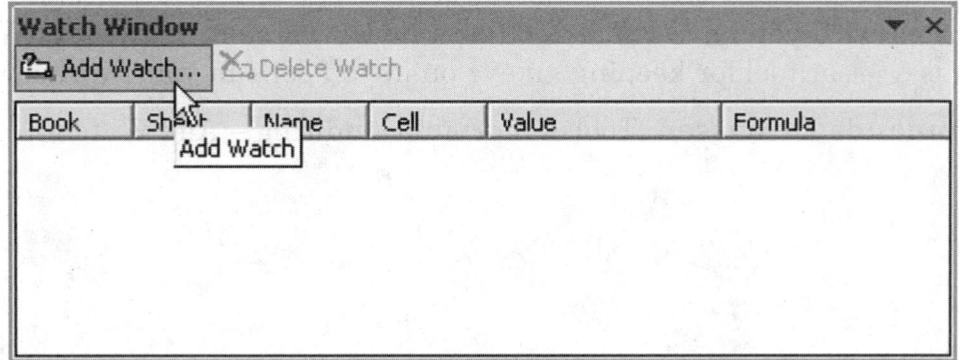

Fig. 1248

Part
IV

3) Using the Add Watch dialog, navigate to and touch the cell that you want to watch. Alternatively, you can first navigate to the cell, select Add Watch and choose Add, as shown in Fig. 1249

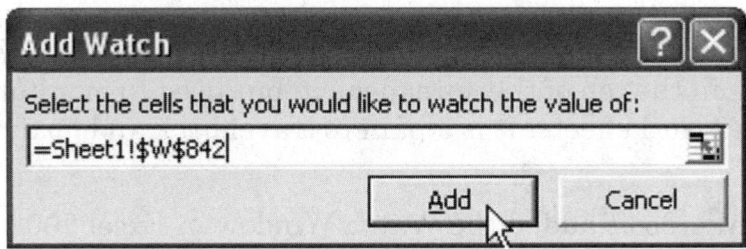

Fig. 1249

For each cell that you Add to the Add Watch dialog, you can always see the formula and the result of that formula in the Watch window. You can add cells from other sheets and even other workbooks, as shown in Fig. 1250.

Watch Window ▾ ✕

📋 Add Watch... ✂ Delete Watch

Book	Sheet	Name	Cell	Value	Formula
LivePict...	Sheet1		W842	5,975,966.76	=+V842*1.01
LivePict...	Sheet2		F10	473.324	=0.482*F9
F9Test...	Sheet1		D16	7529280	=(C10*H5)*12

Fig. 1250

Summary: If you have Excel 2002 or a newer version, the Watch Window is a great tool for keeping an eye on far-off cells in your worksheet.

Commands Discussed: Tools – Formula Auditing – Add Watch

ADD A PAGE BREAK
AT EACH CHANGE IN CUSTOMER

Problem: Your data is sorted by customer in column A, as shown in Fig. 1251. You want to put each customer on a different page.

	A	B	C	D	E	F
1	**Customer**	**Region**	**Date**	**Quantity**	**Product**	**Revenue**
2	Ainsworth	Central	3-Jan-04	500	XYZ	11240
3	Ainsworth	Central	4-Jan-04	400	XYZ	9204
4	Ainsworth	Central	6-Feb-04	200	DEF	4280
5	Ainsworth	East	6-Feb-04	900	DEF	21708
6	Ainsworth	Central	20-Feb-04	800	DEF	18504
7	Ainsworth	East	24-Feb-04	1000	XYZ	20940
8	Ainsworth	East	2-Mar-04	400	XYZ	8620
9	Air Canada	West	31-Mar-04	300	ABC	5859
10	Air Canada	Central	19-Apr-04	200	XYZ	4948
11	Air Canada	West	24-Aug-04	800	XYZ	17856
12	Air Canada	East	7-Oct-04	100	DEF	2358
13	Bell Canada	East	13-Apr-04	600	DEF	14004
14	Bell Canada	Central	24-Jun-04	200	DEF	4060
15	Bell Canada	West	31-Aug-04	800	XYZ	18072
16	Bell Canada	West	4-Nov-04	800	ABC	15104
17	Chevron	Central	26-Feb-04	900	DEF	20610

Fig. 1251

Strategy: The easiest way to do this is to add a subtotal by using the Data – Subtotals command. You can choose to have a page break between groups, as shown in Fig. 1252.

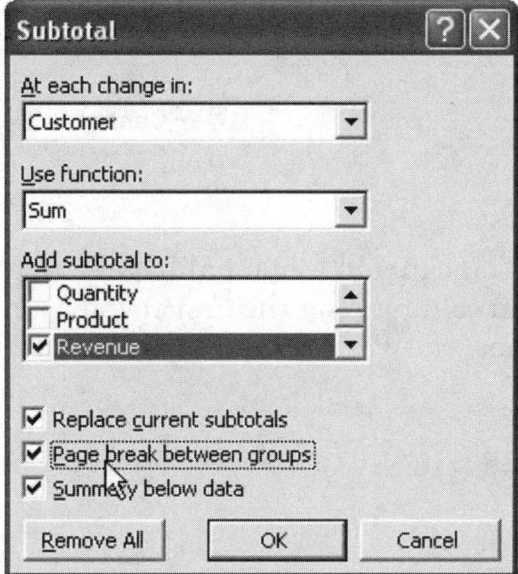

Fig. 1252

Part
IV

However, let's assume that you cannot use the automatic Subtotals feature for some reason. It helps to understand page breaks.

Excel page breaks can either be automatic or manual. If you use the Print Preview icon, as shown in Fig. 1253, and then close the Print Preview window, Excel will draw in the automatic page breaks. The Print Preview icon is in the Standard toolbar.

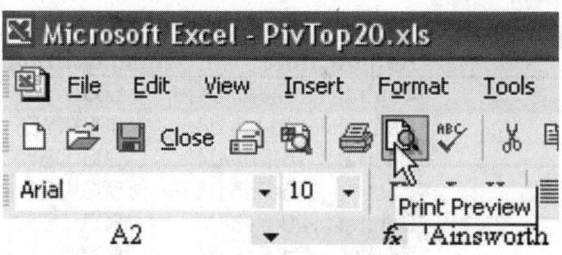

Fig. 1253

In this particular report, it turns out that with the margins and print size, Excel would normally offer an automatic page break after row 52. After you do a Print Preview, Excel draws in a dashed line after row 52 to indicate that this is an automatic page break, as shown in Fig. 1254.

	A	B	C	D	E	F	
1	Customer	Region	Date	Quantity	Product	Revenue	
50	Exxon	West	23-May-04	200	XYZ	4388	
51	Exxon	East	25-May-04	600	DEF	12048	
52	Exxon	West	28-May-04	900	ABC	17964	
53	Exxon	West	12-Jun-04	600	ABC	10404	
54	Exxon	West	23-Jun-04	100	ABC	1882	
55	Exxon	Central	25-Jun-04	700	ABC	13734	

Fig. 1254

You can add a manual page break to any row. Position the cell pointer in column A on the first row for a new customer. From the menu, select Insert – Page Break, as shown in Fig. 1255.

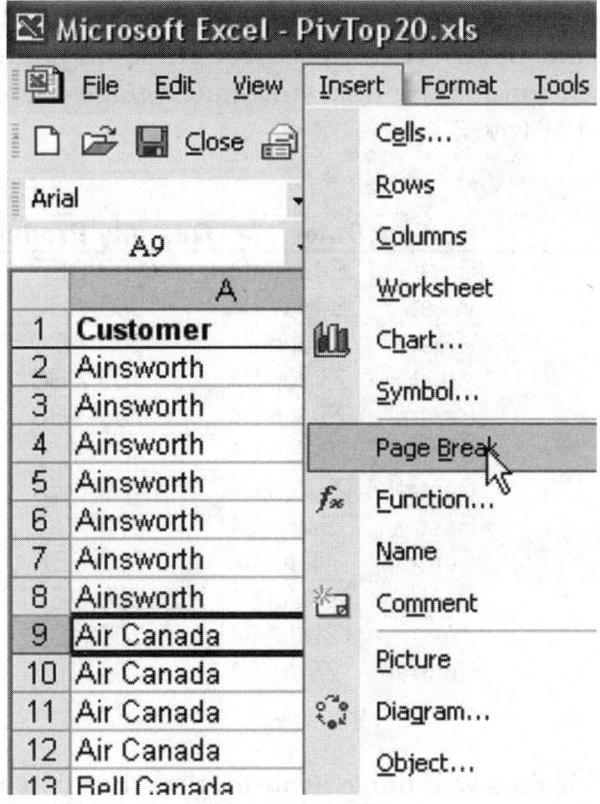

Fig. 1255

Excel draws in a dotted line above the cell pointer to indicate that there is a page break after row 8, as shown in Fig. 1256.

	A	B	C	D	E	F
1	Customer	Region	Date	Quantity	Product	Revenue
2	Ainsworth	Central	3-Jan-04	500	XYZ	11240
3	Ainsworth	Central	4-Jan-04	400	XYZ	9204
4	Ainsworth	Central	6-Feb-04	200	DEF	4280
5	Ainsworth	East	6-Feb-04	900	DEF	21708
6	Ainsworth	Central	20-Feb-04	800	DEF	18504
7	Ainsworth	East	24-Feb-04	1000	XYZ	20940
8	Ainsworth	East	2-Mar-04	400	XYZ	8620
9	Air Canada	West	31-Mar-04	300	ABC	5859
10	Air Canada	Central	19-Apr-04	200	XYZ	4948

Fig. 1256

Since you've added a manual page break after row 8, Excel automatically calculates that it can fit rows 9 through 60 on page 2. As shown in Fig. 1257, the location for the next automatic page break is now shown at row 60 instead of row 52.

	A	B	C	D	E	F
1	Customer	Region	Date	Quantity	Product	Revenue
51	Exxon	East	25-May-04	600	DEF	12048
52	Exxon	West	28-May-04	900	ABC	17964
53	Exxon	West	12-Jun-04	600	ABC	10404
54	Exxon	West	23-Jun-04	100	ABC	1882
55	Exxon	Central	25-Jun-04	700	ABC	13734
56	Exxon	Central	26-Jun-04	400	XYZ	8804
57	Exxon	Central	29-Jun-04	100	DEF	2231
58	Exxon	East	29-Jun-04	500	XYZ	12425
59	Exxon	Central	4-Jul-04	700	DEF	16303
60	Exxon	East	7-Jul-04	900	DEF	21168
61	Exxon	West	21-Jul-04	200	ABC	3390
62	Exxon	Central	27-Jul-04	200	XYZ	4722

Fig. 1257

Automatic Page Breaks will move around. Say that you change the margins for the page, using File – Page Setup – Margins – Bottom, as shown in Fig. 1258.

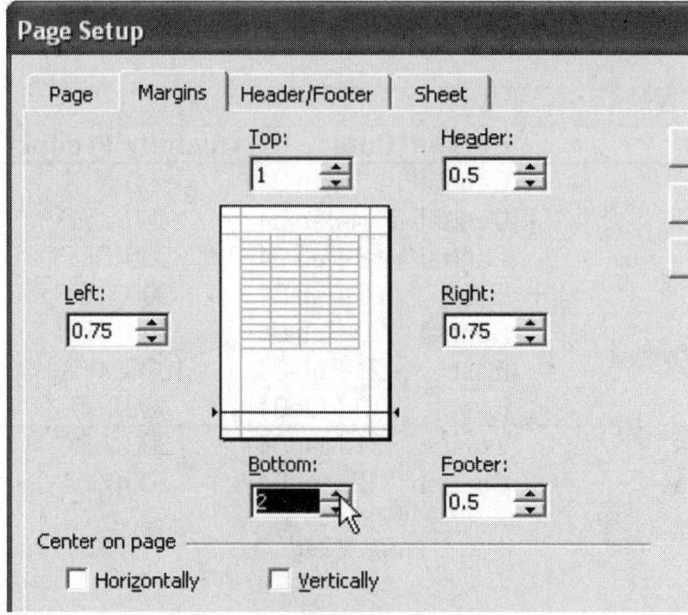

Fig. 1258

As shown in Fig. 1259, Excel will now calculate that the end of the second page is at row 54.

	A	B	C	D	E	F
1	**Customer**	**Region**	**Date**	**Quantity**	**Product**	**Revenue**
51	Exxon	East	25-May-04	600	DEF	12048
52	Exxon	West	28-May-04	900	ABC	17964
53	Exxon	West	12-Jun-04	600	ABC	10404
54	Exxon	West	23-Jun-04	100	ABC	1882
55	Exxon	Central	25-Jun-04	700	ABC	13734
56	Exxon	Central	26-Jun-04	400	XYZ	8804

Fig. 1259

Unlike Automatic Page Breaks, the Manual Page Break will never move.

To add the rest of the page breaks, move the cell pointer to the next cell in column A that has a new customer. From the menu, select Insert – Pagebreak. (Since you have 50 of these to insert, you might want to use the keyboard shortcut: Alt+IB.

Additional Details: Selecting each new customer is tedious. Microsoft has given you a shortcut for finding the next cell in the current column that is different from the active cell. However, it is difficult to use this shortcut. You will have to decide if it is worth the hassle.

Start with the cell pointer on Texaco. Hit Ctrl+Shift+Down Arrow to select all of the cells below the current cell. Type the F5 key. Press the Special button. Select Column Differences, as shown in Fig. 1260.

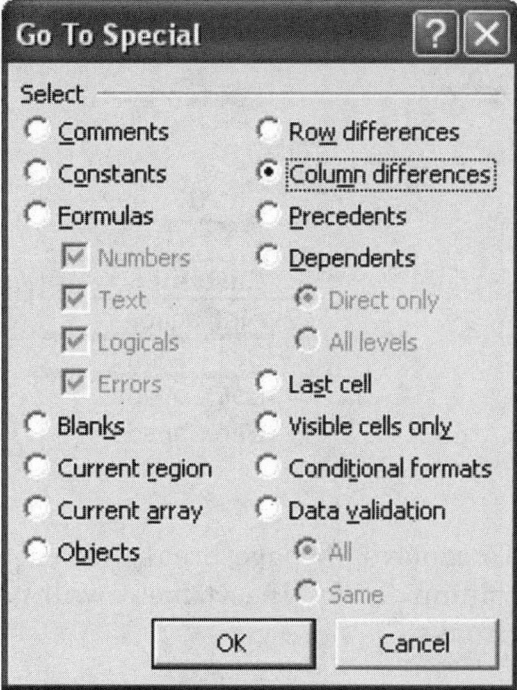

Fig. 1260

As shown in Fig. 1261, the cell pointer will move to the first row with Verizon.

	A	B
1	**Customer**	**Regio**
419	Verizon	Centra
420	Verizon	East
421	Verizon	East

Fig. 1261

You can use the Insert – PageBreak command. This whole series of events can be repeated by holding down the Alt key while you type EGSM. Release the Alt key to hit Enter. Hold down the Alt key while you type IB. If you have hundreds of page breaks to add, mastering this keystroke might be worth the time.

Additional Details: To remove a manual page break, you should put the cell pointer in the first cell under the manual page break. When the cell pointer is in this location, the Insert Menu offers a Remove Page Break option, as shown in Fig. 1262.

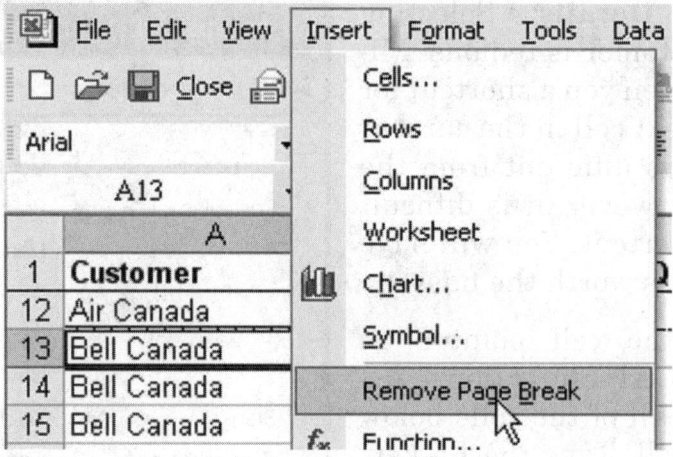

Fig. 1262

To remove all page breaks, select all cells using the box to the left of column A. The Insert menu will now offer an option to Reset All Page Breaks.

Gotcha: To insert a row page break, you must either select the entire row or have the cell pointer in column A. If you select Insert Page Break from cell C9, Excel will insert a horizontal page break above row 9 and also a vertical page break to the left of column C, as shown in Fig. 1263. This is rarely what you want.

	A	B	C	Q
1	**Customer**	**Region**	**Date**	**Q**
2	Ainsworth	Central	3-Jan-04	
3	Ainsworth	Central	4-Jan-04	
4	Ainsworth	Central	6-Feb-04	
5	Ainsworth	East	6-Feb-04	
6	Ainsworth	Central	20-Feb-04	
7	Ainsworth	East	24-Feb-04	
8	Ainsworth	East	2-Mar-04	
9	Air Canada	West	31-Mar-04	
10	Air Canada	Central	19-Apr-04	

Fig. 1263

Summary: Excel offers two kinds of page breaks. Automatic Page Breaks are calculated on the fly, based on row height and margins of the current page. Manual Page Breaks that you add are permanent and will not move.

Commands Discussed: Insert – Page Break; Edit – Go To – Special – Column Differences; Insert – Remove Page Break; Insert – Reset All Page Breaks; File – Page Setup – Margins

Part
IV

USE HORIZONTAL PAGE BREAKS EVEN WHEN YOU USE FIT TO N PAGES WIDE

Problem: In general, if you use the Fit to N pages option, your manual page breaks are ignored.

As shown in Fig. 1264, the File – Page Setup dialog offers a scaling choice, where you can fit the report to be 1 page wide.

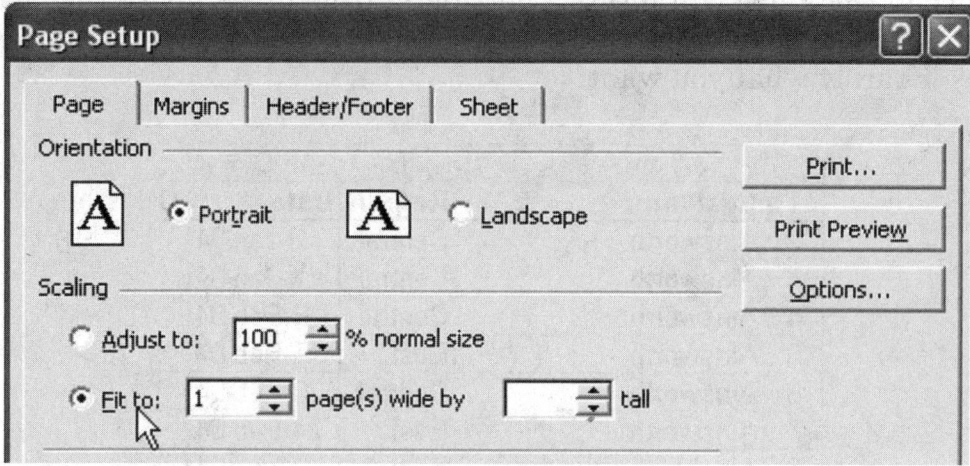

Fig. 1264

However, when you use this option, Excel 2000 and earlier versions will not display your manual page breaks!

Strategy: There is a workaround.

1)   Select the Fit to: scaling option.

2)   Do a Print Preview. Close the Print Preview.

3)   Go back to File – Page Setup. As shown in Fig. 1265, the Adjust to: option will be filled in with the proper adjustment to force the report to fit to one page wide.

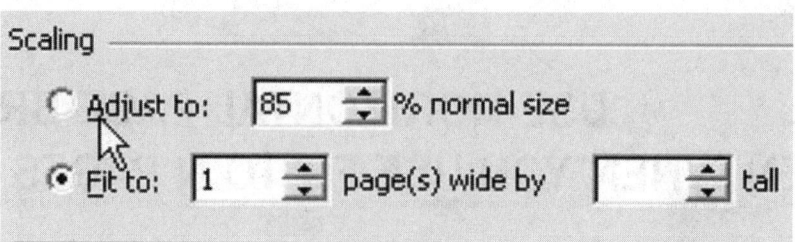

Fig. 1265

4)   Choose the Adjust to option. Your manual page breaks will display correctly.

Gotcha: If you adjust column widths, you will need to repeat these steps.

Summary: The missing manual page break appears to be a bug in Excel 2000 and earlier version. Using the techniques described here, you can overcome the problem.

Commands Discussed: File – Page Setup – Page

HIDE ERROR CELLS WHEN PRINTING

Problem: You have a formula that does division. Occasionally, the divisor cell is zero, so you have a couple of Div/0 value errors, as shown in Fig. 1266. You just need to print this without the errors to get the report to the staff meeting, without having to rewrite all the formulas to test if the divisor is zero. What can you do?

D2	▼	f_x =B2/C2		
	A	B	C	D
1	Region	Revenue	Units	Average
2	City of London	265.3	70	3.79
3	Barking and Dagenham	167.9	46	3.65
4	Barnet	179.01	51	3.51
5	Bexley	0	0	#DIV/0!
6	Brent	315.06	89	3.54
7	Bromley	318.75	85	3.75
8	Camden	248.88	68	3.66
9	Croydon	0	0	#DIV/0!

Fig. 1266

Part IV

Strategy: Go to File – Page Setup. Go to the Sheet tab. There is a dropdown for (Print) Cell Errors As:. Choose this dropdown and select <blank>, as shown in Fig. 1267.

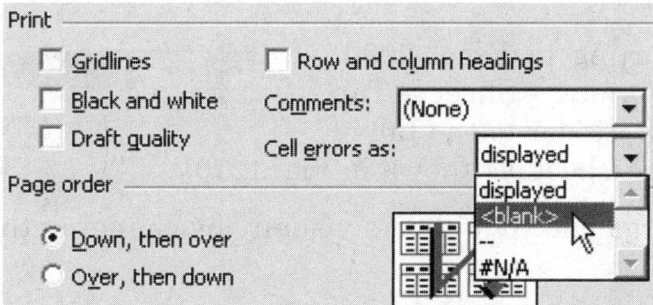

Fig. 1267

Result: Although the error will still appear in the worksheet, when you print, the error cells will print as blanks, as shown in Fig. 1268.

Region	Revenue	Units	Average
City of London	265.3	70	3.79
Barking and Dagenham	167.9	46	3.65
Barnet	179.01	51	3.51
Bexley	0	0	
Brent	315.06	89	3.54
Bromley	318.75	85	3.75
Camden	248.88	68	3.66
Croydon	0	0	
Ealing	260.13	69	3.77

Fig. 1268

Alternate Strategy: Perhaps the "right" way to solve this problem is to change the formula to test if the divisor is zero. In this case, a proper formula would be =IF(C2=0,"",B2/C2).

Summary: To print a worksheet without the error cells, change the setting on the Sheet tab of the Page Setup dialog.

Commands Discussed: File – Page Setup – Sheet

ORGANIZE YOUR
WORKSHEET TABS WITH COLOR

Problem: As shown in Fig. 1269, you have a lot of tabs in the workbook. Can you highlight the frequently used tabs in red?

\ Land / Capital / Sale / Rent / ChkList \ **ProjSumm** / ScenA / Storage /

Fig. 1269

Strategy: Starting in Excel 2000, you can use Format – Sheet – Tab Color to assign a color to the tab of the current worksheet, as shown in Fig. 1270.

/ ChkList / ProjSumm \ **ScenA** /

Fig. 1270

Summary: Organize your sheets visually by changing the color of the sheet tabs.

Commands Discussed: Format – Sheet – Tab Color

COPY CELL FORMATTING,
INCLUDING COLUMN WIDTHS

Problem: You have one section of a report set up, including custom column widths, as shown in Fig. 1271.

	A	B	C	D	E	F	G
1			Manufactured in Harrow				
2							
3					Model		
4			A		B		C
5	Display		12		42		42
6	Engine		0		0		112.5
7	PCB		18		22		41
8	RAM		8		56		56
9	Other Mat'l		11.17		18.15		21.45
10	Total Matl		49.17		138.15		272.95
11							
12	Labor		8.24		12.45		15.24
13							
14	Overhead		34.608		52.29		64.008
15							
16	Total MLO		92.018		202.89		352.198
17							
18	Target Price		368.07		811.56		1408.79

Fig. 1271

Part IV

As shown in Fig. 1272, when you copy and paste to a new section of the workbook, the column widths do not get pasted.

I	J	K	L	M	N	O
		Manufactured in Trent				
				Model		
		A		B		C
Display		12		42		42
Engine		0		0		112.5
PCB		18		22		41

Fig. 1272

Strategy: Use the Format Painter icon. This is a cool trick, but it is hard to use. Carefully follow these steps.

1) Select the columns with the original formatted data. Choose the Format Painter icon, which looks like a whiskbroom, as shown in Fig. 1273.

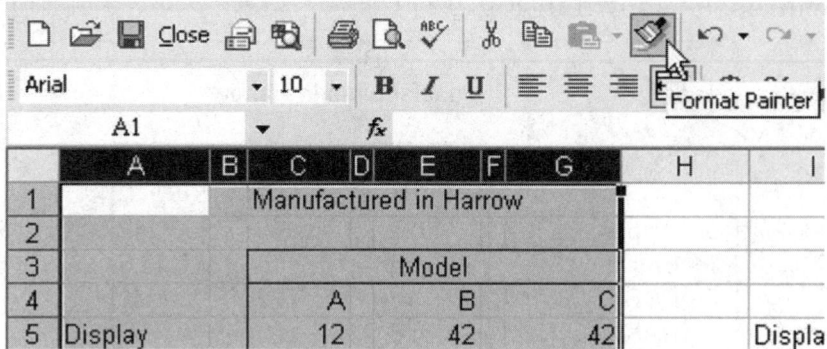

Fig. 1273

2) Use the scroll bars to move so that you can see all of the new range in the window. Even if it would be more convenient to navigate using the Arrow or Tab keys, you have to avoid selecting any cells or columns until the next step.

3) Click on the first new column and drag to select the same number of columns. As you are dragging, the mouse pointer changes to the whiskbroom icon, as shown in Fig. 1274.

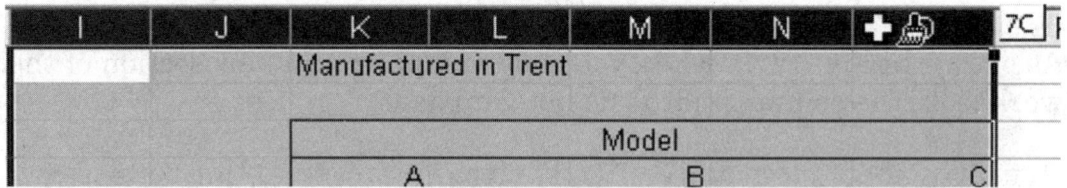

Fig. 1274

4) When you release the mouse button, the formats, including font, colors, borders, and cell height, and width, will be copied, as shown in Fig. 1275.

I	J	K	L	M	N	O
		Manufactured in Trent				
				Model		
		A		B		C
Display		12		42		42
Engine		0		0		112.5
PCB		18		22		41

Fig. 1275

Summary: Use the Format Painter tool to copy formats, including column widths.

Commands Discussed: Format Painter tool

WHY DOES EXCEL MARK ALL MY TRUE CELLS WITH AN INDICATOR?

Problem: In Excel 2002, you start noticing crazy cells being marked with a purple indicator. As shown in Fig. 1276, why is every TRUE value marked?

	A	B	C	D	E	F
1	Invoice	Product	Price	Qty	Total	Bonus
2	2010	Jacket	225	14	3150	TRUE
3	2011	Jacket	225	8	1800	TRUE
4	2012	Jacket	225	11	2475	TRUE
5	2013	Cap	25	6	150	FALSE
6	2014	Jacket	225	17	3825	TRUE
7	2015	Jacket	225	3	675	FALSE

Fig. 1276

Part IV

Strategy: We've become used to red indicators for cell comments and green indicators for Excel errors. Why is Excel marking all of these seemingly innocent values?

Well, those are smart tags. If you enter a stock market ticker symbol in a cell, Excel adds a smart tag indicator, as shown in Fig. 1277.

Fig. 1277

The smart tag lets you insert the stock price for the symbol, as shown in Fig. 1278.

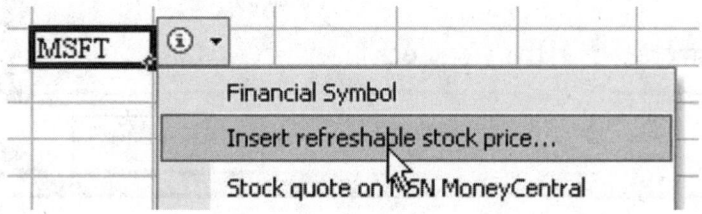

Fig. 1278

This is fine, but even cells that just look like ticker symbols are marked. The Truetime company went public in 1999 with the ticker symbol TRUE. Symmetricon bought them out in 2002. The TRUE ticker is no longer valid, yet everyone using Excel 2002 or 2003 has to put up with the annoying SmartTags on their logical formulas. No offense to the Truetime Company, but I really don't want to mark every TRUE cell with their stock price.

If you use many logical formulas, you will find that there are a lot of false positives in Smart Tags.

In Excel 2002, your only choice was to turn off the Financial Smart Tag. Use Tools – AutoCorrect Options – Smart Tags and uncheck the MSN MoneyCentral Financial Symbols, as shown in Fig. 1279.

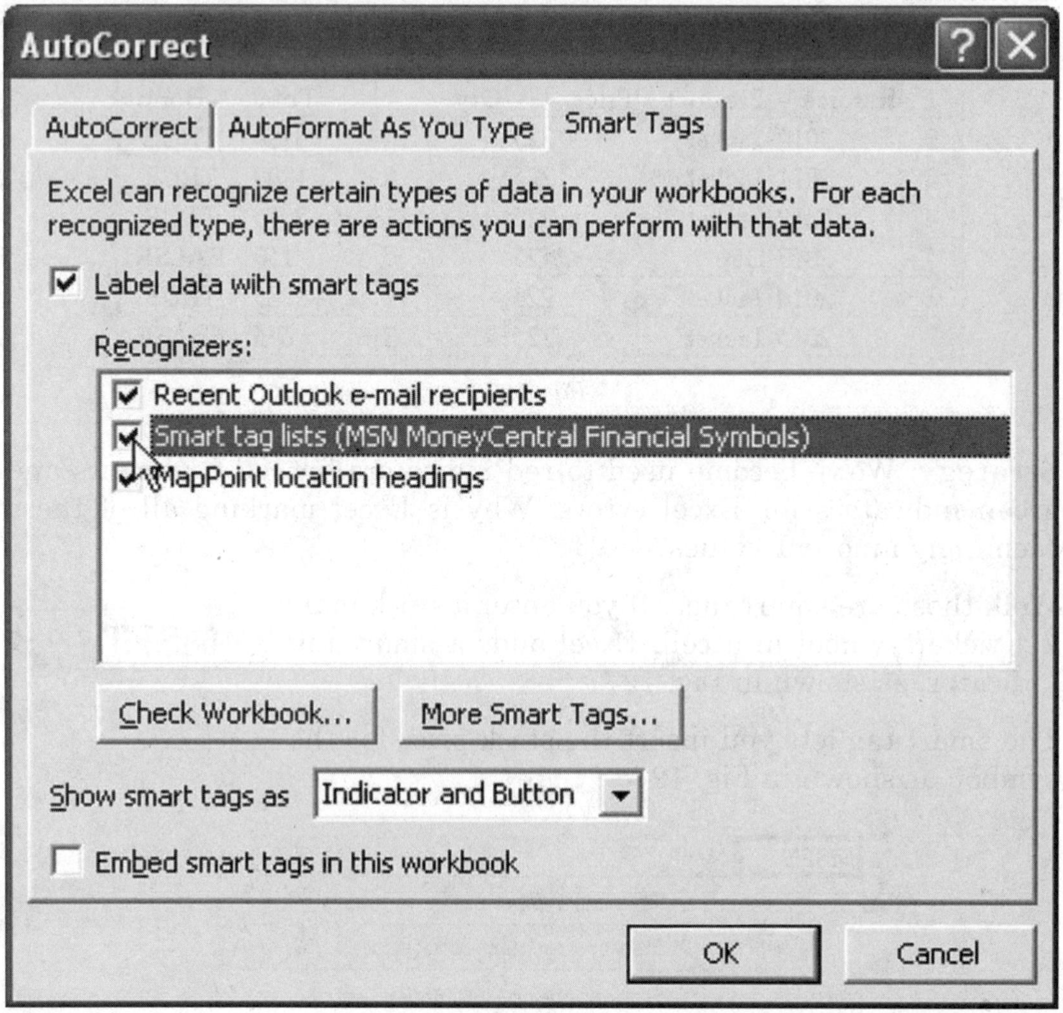

Fig. 1279

In Excel 2003, the smart tag itself now has an option to stop recognizing TRUE as a Smart Tag, as shown in Fig. 1280.

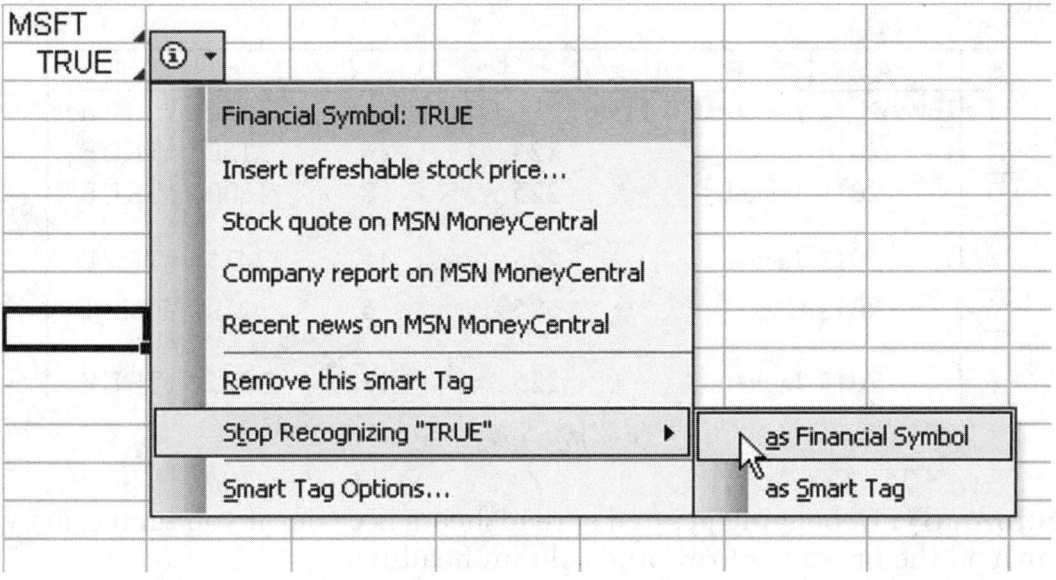

Fig. 1280

Summary: In Excel 2002, you can turn off the Financial Smart Tag. In Excel 2003 and later versions, you can turn off the Smart Tag for specific values.

Commands Discussed: Tools – Auto correct – Smart Tags

DEBUG FROM A PRINTED SPREADSHEET

Problem: You need to proofread cells in your spreadsheet. It would be easier to do this from a printed piece of paper but, at the same time, you need to see the row numbers and column letters in the printout.

Strategy: You can print row numbers and column letters. From the File menu, select File – Page Setup – Sheet – (Print) Row and Column Headings, as shown in Fig. 1281.

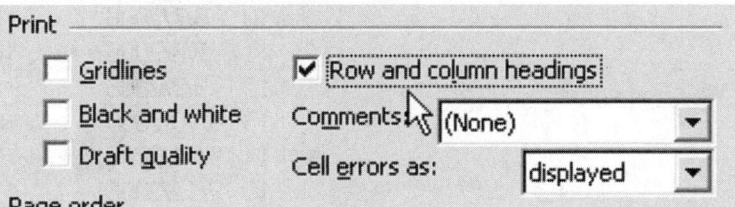

Fig. 1281

Part IV

Result: As shown in Fig. 1282, the printed copy of the spreadsheet will show letters A, B, C, and D across the top and row numbers down the side.

	A	B	C	D	E	F
1	Invoice	Product	Price	Qty	Total	Bonus
2	2010	Jacket	225	14	3150	TRUE
3	2011	Jacket	225	8	1800	TRUE
4	2012	Jacket	225	11	2475	TRUE
5	2013	Cap	25	6	150	FALSE
6	2014	Jacket	225	17	3825	TRUE

Fig. 1282

Summary: Debugging printed spreadsheets is easier if you temporarily turn on the printing of row and column headings.

Commands Discussed: File – Page Setup – Sheet – Row and Column Headings

COPIED FORMULA HAS STRANGE BORDERS

Problem: You copied a formula and the borders look out of place in the paste area. In the image below, you copied D4 and pasted to D5:D34. The top border from D4 was copied to every cell in the paste area, as shown in Fig. 1283.

	A	B	C	D
1				
2				
3	Date	Units	Dollars	Average
4	9/1/2006	84	312.48	3.72
5	9/2/2006	75	274.5	3.66
6	9/3/2006	0	0	0
7	9/4/2006	24	87.6	3.65
8	9/5/2006	63	236.25	3.75
9	9/6/2006	18	67.14	3.73
10	9/7/2006	18	65.52	3.64
11	9/8/2006	104	395.2	3.8
12	9/9/2006	49	175.42	3.58
13	9/10/2006	60	221.4	3.69
14	9/11/2006	92	348.68	3.79
15	9/12/2006	139	494.84	3.56

Fig. 1283

Strategy: After the fact, you need to clear the borders and start over again. Select the range with the unwanted formats. From the menu, select Edit – Clear – Formats, as shown in Fig. 1284.

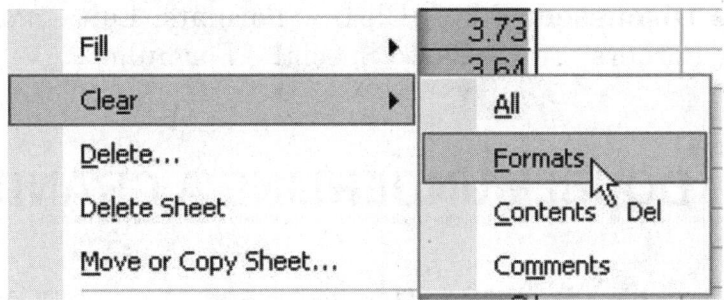

Fig. 1284

As shown in Fig. 1285, this will clear all of the borders, which is seldom what you want.

Additional Details: To prevent the problem in the first place, instead of pasting the cells, use either Edit – Paste Special – Formulas or Edit – Paste Special – All Except Borders to copy the formulas without the border or formatting, as shown in Fig. 1286.

C	D
Dollars	Average
312.48	3.72
274.5	3.66
0	0
87.6	3.65
236.25	3.75
67.14	3.73
65.52	3.64
395.2	3.8

Fig. 1285

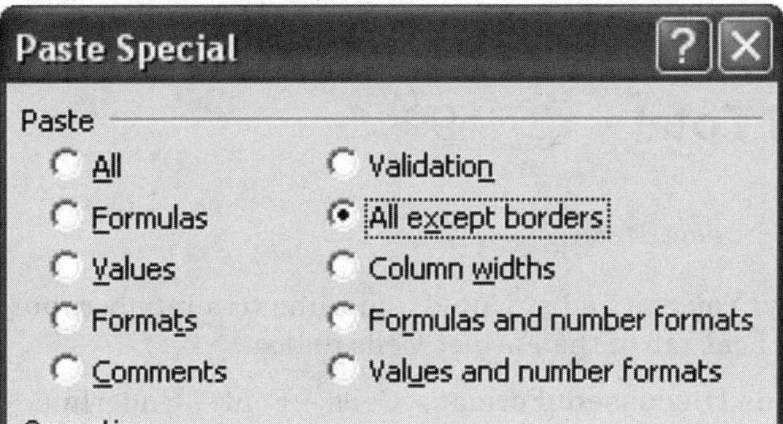

Fig. 1286

Summary: It is better to use Paste Special to prevent borders from getting copied into your data range. If you discover this too late, use Edit – Clear – Formats to get rid of unwanted borders.

Commands Discussed: Edit – Clear – Formats; Edit – Paste Special – All Except Borders; Edit – Paste Special – Formulas

DOUBLE UNDERLINE A GRAND TOTAL

Problem: Your boss is a CPA. He says you should double underline the grand total in a report. As the results show in Fig. 1287, you only have an underline icon on the Formatting toolbar.

8		
9	**Product B**	Total
10	England	8,301
11	N. Ireland	2,369
12	Scotland	2,411
13	Wales	2,473
14	Total B	15,554
15		
16	**Product C**	Total
17	England	5,031
18	N. Ireland	1,420
19	Scotland	1,413
20	Wales	1,028
21	Total C	8,892
22		
23	**Grand Total**	37,599

Fig. 1287

Strategy: Select the Grand Total cell. From the menu, select Format – Cells – Font. In the Underline dropdown, choose double or double accounting. The cell will have a double underline, as shown in Fig. 1288.

Grand Total	37,599

Fig. 1288

Summary: You can add a double underline to a number, but you have to use the Font tab of the Format Cells dialog.

Commands Discussed: Format – Cells – Font – Underline

USE THE BORDER TAB
IN THE FORMAT CELLS DIALOG

Problem: Borders drive you insane. How do you actually use the Border tab of the Format Cells toolbar, shown in Fig. 1289?

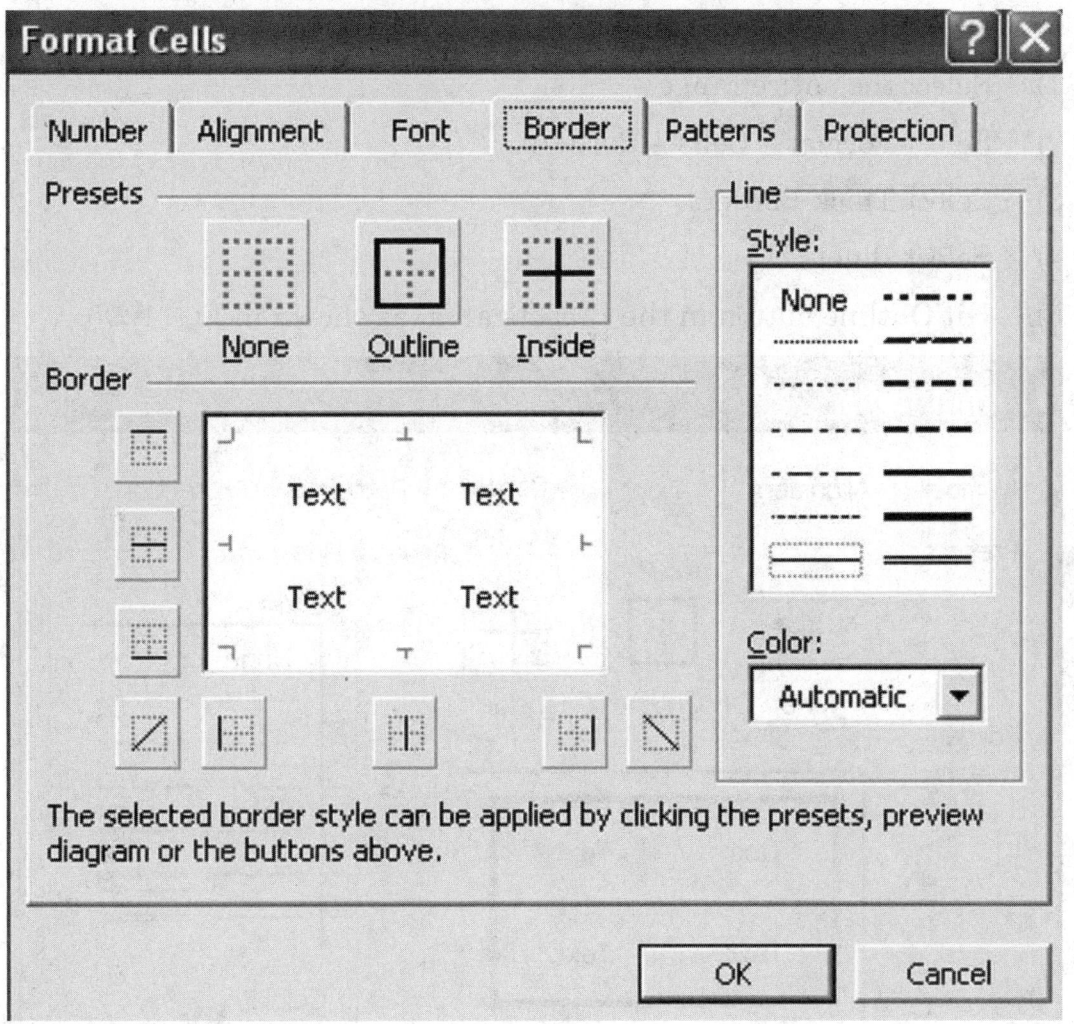

Fig. 1289

Strategy: The trick is to select the color and weight before you draw any borders. Once you've selected a color and the heavy line style, then you can begin drawing borders.

The large white area shows four sides plus a center horizontal and center vertical border. The center borders only make sense if you are formatting a range of cells. If you are formatting a single cell, choosing the center horizontal bar will not draw a border through the center of the cell.

Additional Details: Here is a typical example. Say that you want a thick blue border around a selection. You want a narrow green border around all cells inside the selection. Follow these steps:

1)   Select the entire range.

2)   Select Format – Cells – Borders.

3)   Select Thick Border.

4)   Select Blue.

5)   Hit Outline button in the Presets area, as shown in Fig. 1290.

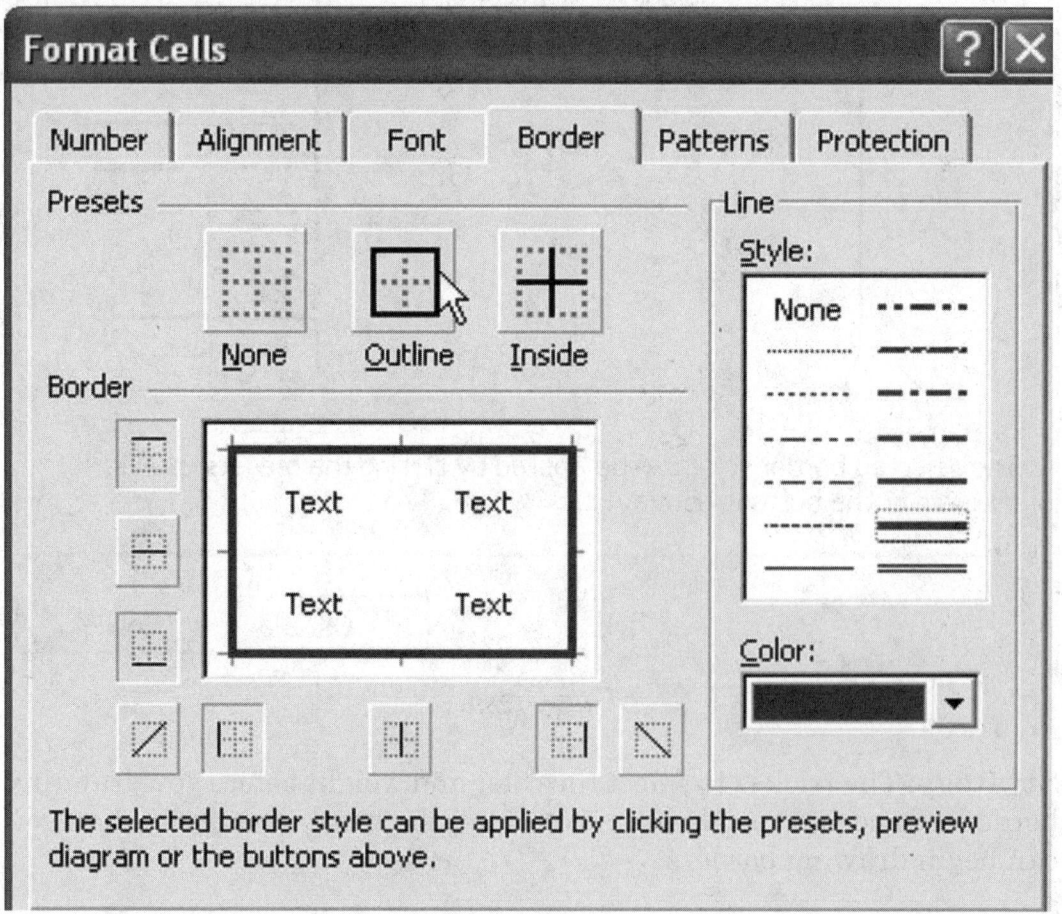

Fig. 1290

6) Select the thin border for the Style and select green for the color.

7) Choose Inside button in the Presets area, as shown in Fig. 1291.

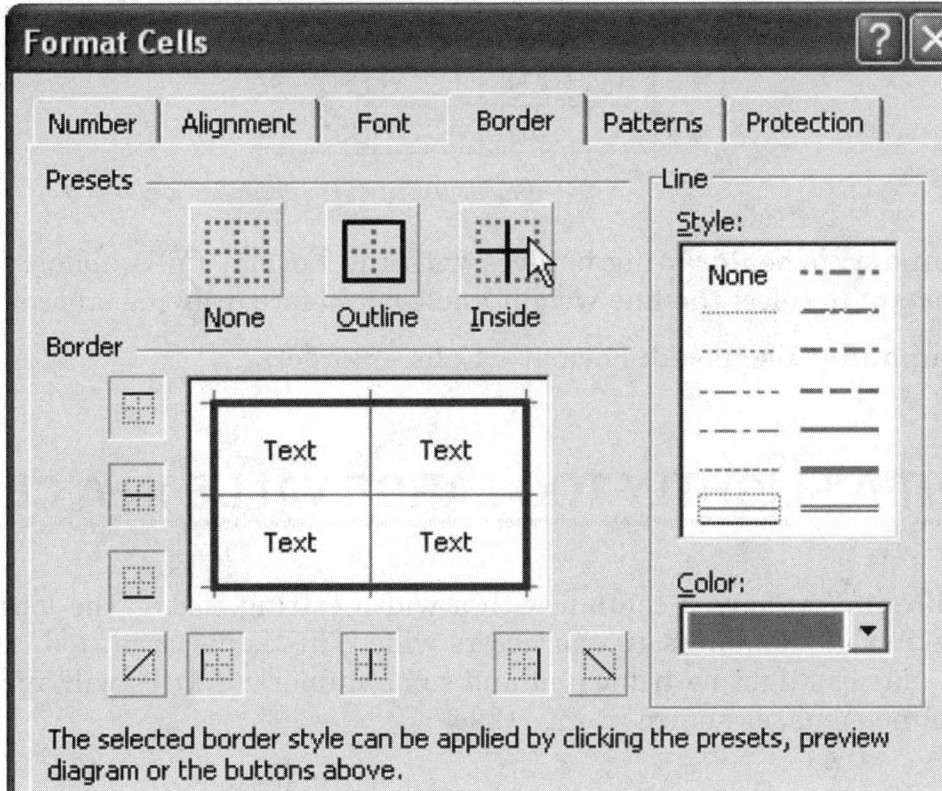

Fig. 1291

8) Choose OK to apply the format to the selected range, as shown in Fig. 1292.

	A	B	C	D	E
1					
2	Region	Books	DVD	VHS	Total
3	Western Australia	177	710	152	1,039
4	South Australia	794	289	69	1,152
5	Northern Territory	425	164	184	773
6	Queensland	919	588	896	2,403
7	New South Wales	425	978	713	2,116
8	Victoria	90	892	771	1,753
9	Tasmania	462	855	363	1,680
10	Total	3,292	4,476	3,148	10,916
11					

Fig. 1292

Part
IV

Additional Details: Choose the small buttons around the outside to select individual border formats. This group also includes diagonal cross through borders. The diagonal borders apply to individual cells only, as shown in Fig. 1293.

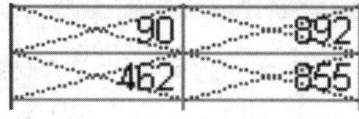

Fig. 1293

Summary: When drawing borders with the Format Cells dialog, it is important to select the line weight and color before drawing a border.

Commands Discussed: Format – Cells – Borders

FIT A SLIGHTLY TOO-LARGE VALUE IN A CELL

Problem: You have a column with a width setting of 8.5. The longest value in that column is 10 characters wide. This is just a bit too large. Text entries might be truncated and some numeric entries will appear as pound signs, as shown in Fig. 1294.

	C5	▼	*fx*	10205684.5
	A	B	C	D
1	Invoice	Customer	Sales	Date
2	1901	ABC, Inc.	4,974,374	9/12/2005
3	1902	TUVW, Ir	1,586,688	9/12/2005
4	1903	BCD, Inc.	2,140,258	9/12/2005
5	1904	JKLM, In	#######	9/13/2005
6	1905	FGH, Inc.	2,497,515	9/13/2005
7	1906	STUV, Inc	7,626,554	9/13/2005
8	1907	CDE, Inc.	9,908,921	9/14/2005

Fig. 1294

Strategy: Excel offers a Shrink to Fit option. Select the cells that are too large. From the menu, select Format – Cells. On the Alignment tab, choose Shrink to Fit from the Text Control section, as shown in Fig. 1295.

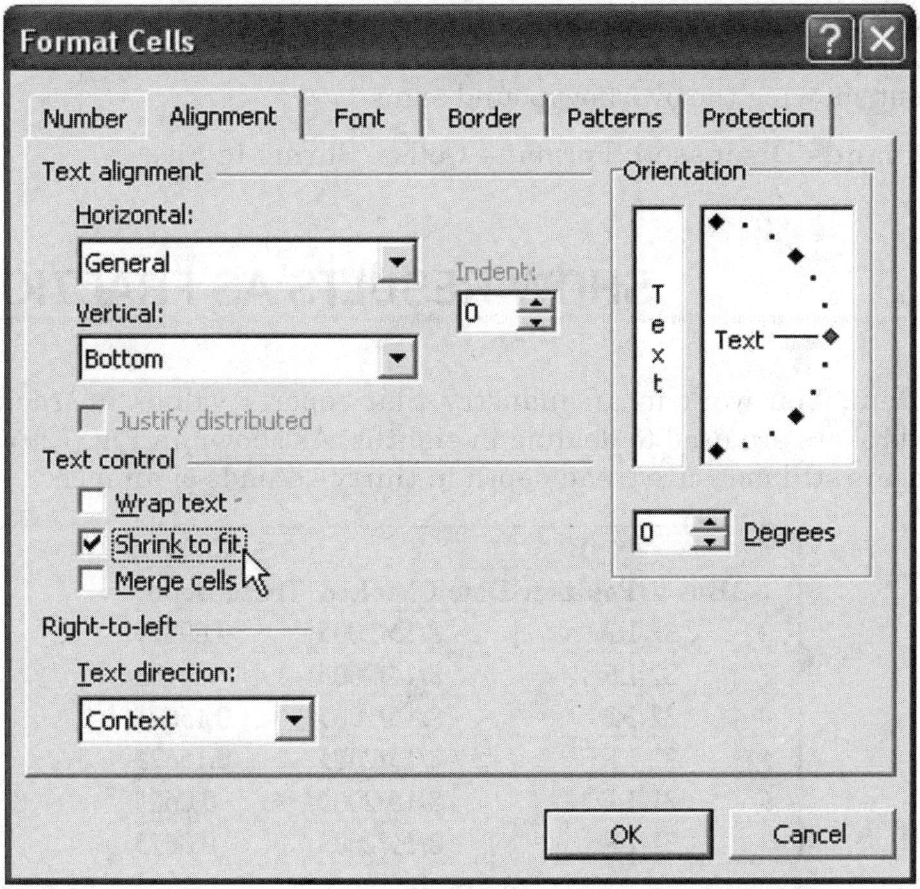

Fig. 1295

Result: The cells are displayed in a smaller font when they become too wide for the column, as shown in Fig. 1296. This is preferable to having the numbers displayed as ######.

	A	B	C	D
1	**Invoice**	**Customer**	**Sales**	**Date**
2	1901	ABC, Inc.	4,974,374	9/12/2
3	1902	TUVW, Ir	1,586,688	9/12/2
4	1903	BCD, Inc.	2,140,258	9/12/2
5	1904	JKLM, Inc.	10,205,685	9/13/2
6	1905	FGH, Inc.	2,497,515	9/13/2

Fig. 1296

Summary: When you have just a few cells that are too large for the column, use the Shrink to Fit option to allow the values to display properly without showing the overflow pound signs.

Commands Discussed: Format – Cells – Shrink to Fit

SHOW RESULTS AS FRACTIONS

Problem: You work in an industry that reports values in fractions. Stockbrokers are used to dealing in eighths. As shown in Fig. 1297, tire engineers still measure tread depth in thirty-seconds of an inch.

	A	B	C	D
1	Bus #	Position	Date Checked	Tread Depth
2	32	RF	8/15/2005	0.09375
3	32	LF	8/15/2005	0.125
4	32	RR	8/15/2005	0.15625
5	32	LR	8/15/2005	0.15625
6	31	RF	8/15/2005	0.0625
7	31	LF	8/15/2005	0.0625

Fig. 1297

Strategy: There are number formats for fractions. There are nine standard fractional formats available in the Format Cells dialog box, as shown in Fig. 1298.

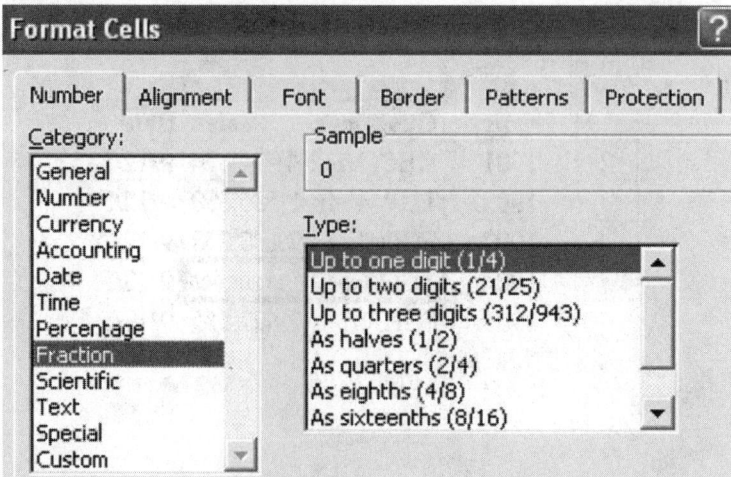

Fig. 1298

Beyond the seven shown in Fig. 1298, Excel offers standard formats for tenths and hundredths. Unfortunately, there is not a standard format for thirty-seconds.

There probably is a custom numeric format to handle thirty-seconds. Here is how to figure it out.

1)   Select the standard format for sixteenths, as shown in Fig. 1299.

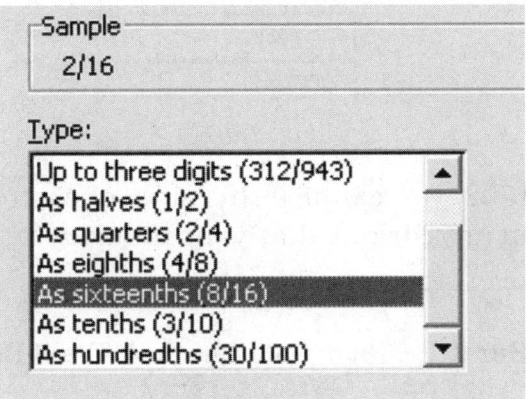

Fig. 1299

2)   Then, in the Category list, scroll down and select Custom. As shown in Fig. 1300, you will see that the custom number format code for sixteenths is # ??/16.

Part
IV

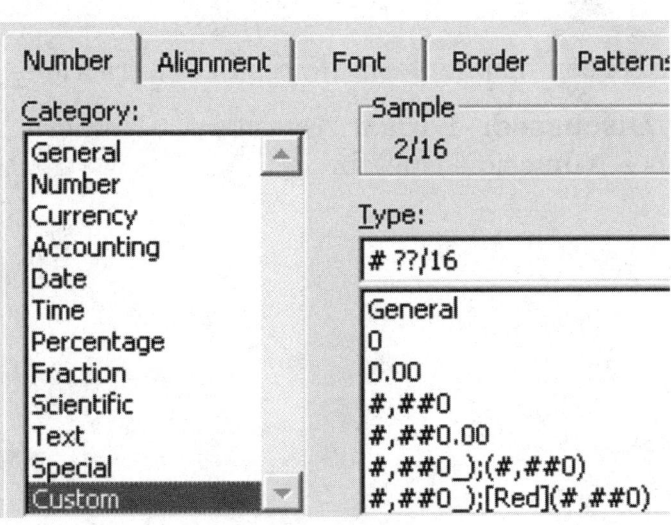

Fig. 1300

3)   From this, you can deduce that # ??/32 might be a valid number format. Click into the Type: box and change the 16 to 32. The Sample area will immediately confirm that you have hit upon the correct format for thirty-seconds, as shown in Fig. 1301.

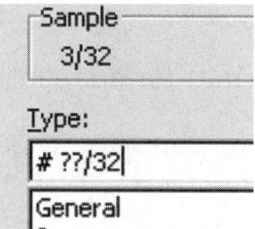

Fig. 1301

As shown in Fig. 1302, you can use this style of custom numeric format to build fractions in any format that your industry regularly uses.

	A	B	C	D
1	Bus #	Position	Date Checked	Tread Depth
2	32	RF	8/15/2005	3/32
3	32	LF	8/15/2005	4/32
4	32	RR	8/15/2005	5/32
5	32	LR	8/15/2005	5/32
6	31	RF	8/15/2005	2/32
7	31	LF	8/15/2005	2/32

Fig. 1302

Summary: Excel can display formula results as fractions.

Commands Discussed: Format – Cells – Numeric – Fractions; Format – Cells – Numeric – Custom

COLOR ALL SALES GREEN
FOR A DAY IF TOTAL SALES > $999

Problem: Your company offers a bonus pool on any day where the total sales exceed $1,000. You have invoice data by date, as shown in Fig. 1303. You would like to highlight all records for the days that meet $1,000 in sales.

Strategy: You can use conditional formatting to perform a complex task such as this. But first, before getting into conditional formatting, you should develop the formula that you will need.

1) The first task is to add a column that will total all sales for this day. As shown in Fig. 1304, the SUMIF function can do this. There are three arguments in the SUMIF function: =SUMIF($A$2:$A$30,A2,$C$2:$C$30).

	A	B	C
1	Date	Invoice	Sales $
2	12/1/2004	1506	82
3	12/1/2004	1507	172
4	12/1/2004	1508	202
5	12/1/2004	1509	155
6	12/2/2004	1510	107
7	12/2/2004	1511	249
8	12/2/2004	1512	156
9	12/2/2004	1513	450
10	12/2/2004	1514	227
11	12/3/2004	1515	125
12	12/3/2004	1516	239
13	12/3/2004	1517	115
14	12/3/2004	1518	82
15	12/3/2004	1519	236
16	12/4/2004	1520	218

Fig. 1303

Part IV

	A	B	C	D	E	F
1	Date	Invoice	Sales $	Total for Today		
2	12/1/2004	1506	82	=SUMIF($A$2:$A$30,A2,$C$2:$C$30)		
3	12/1/2004	1507	172			
4	12/1/2004	1508	202			

Fig. 1304

This function tells Excel to examine each cell in A2:A30. If the cell value is equal to cell A2, then it adds up the corresponding cell from C2:C30.

There are a lot of dollar signs in the formula. As you copy the formula down in your temporary column D, you want the ranges in the first and third parameter to be frozen. In our temporary formula in column D, there is no reason to freeze the A2 in the second parameter. However, in the conditional format dialog, this formula will be applied to cells in

A, B, and C, so it is important to freeze the second parameter to column A.

2)   In this case, you should edit the formula and add a $ before A2, as shown in Fig. 1305.

	A	B	C	D	E	F
1	Date	Invoice	Sales $	Total for Today		
2	12/1/2004	1506	82	=SUMIF($A$2:$A$30,$A2,$C$2:$C$30)		
3	12/1/2004	1507	172			

Fig. 1305

3)   Enter the formula in D2. Double-click the Fill handle to copy the formula down. In Fig. 1306, you can see that every row contains the total sales for that day.

	A	B	C	D
1	Date	Invoice	Sales $	Total for Today
2	12/1/2004	1506	82	611
3	12/1/2004	1507	172	611
4	12/1/2004	1508	202	611
5	12/1/2004	1509	155	611
6	12/2/2004	1510	107	1189
7	12/2/2004	1511	249	1189
8	12/2/2004	1512	156	1189
9	12/2/2004	1513	450	1189
10	12/2/2004	1514	227	1189
11	12/3/2004	1515	125	797
12	12/3/2004	1516	239	797
13	12/3/2004	1517	115	797
14	12/3/2004	1518	82	797
15	12/3/2004	1519	236	797
16	12/4/2004	1520	218	1017

Sheet1 \ Sheet2

Draw ▾   AutoShapes ▾

Ready   Sum=1189

Fig. 1306

4)   As a reasonableness test, highlight the sales for the December 2. The status bar at the bottom of the Excel window confirms that the total of these cells is $1,189.

5) The formula for conditional formats requires a formula that evaluates to either TRUE or FALSE. Add a new formula in column E. As shown in Fig. 1307, the formula in E2 is =D2>=1000.

E2				*fx* =D2>=1000	
	A	B	C	D	E
1	Date	Invoice	Sales $	Total for Today	Over $1000?
2	12/1/2004	1506	82	611	FALSE
3	12/1/2004	1507	172	611	FALSE

Fig. 1307

6) You can combine these two formulas into a single formula, as shown in Fig. 1308.

D2				*fx* =(SUMIF($A$2:$A$30,$A2,$C$2:$C$30))>=1000			
	A	B	C	D	E	F	G
1	Date	Invoice	Sales $	Over $1000?			
2	12/1/2004	1506	82	FALSE			
3	12/1/2004	1507	172	FALSE			
4	12/1/2004	1508	202	FALSE			
5	12/1/2004	1509	155	FALSE			
6	12/2/2004	1510	107	TRUE			

Fig. 1308

You now want to set up the conditional format. Follow these steps.

1) It is easiest if you copy the formula that is working. Go to cell D2. Hit the F2 key to put the formula in Edit mode. In the formula bar, drag to highlight the entire formula, as shown in Fig. 1309.

COUNTA			✕ ✓ *fx*	=(SUMIF($A$2:$A$30,$A2,$C$2:$C$30))>=1000			
	A	B	C	D	E	F	G
1	Date	Invoice	Sales $	Over $1000?			
2	12/1/2004	1506	82	=(SUMIF($A$2:$A$30,$A2,$C$2:$C$30))>=1000			
3	12/1/2004	1507	172	FALSE			

Fig. 1309

2) Hit Ctrl+C to copy the formula from the formula bar. Copying from the formula bar allows the text of the formula to stay on the clipboard after you hit the Esc key.

3) Hit the Esc key to exit Edit mode.

Part
IV

4) Select cells A2:C30. From the menu, select Format – Conditional Format.

The Conditional Format dialog initially displays a format suitable for specifying that a cell contains a value between two other values, as shown in Fig. 1310. This is the easier version of conditional formatting, but it is the less powerful.

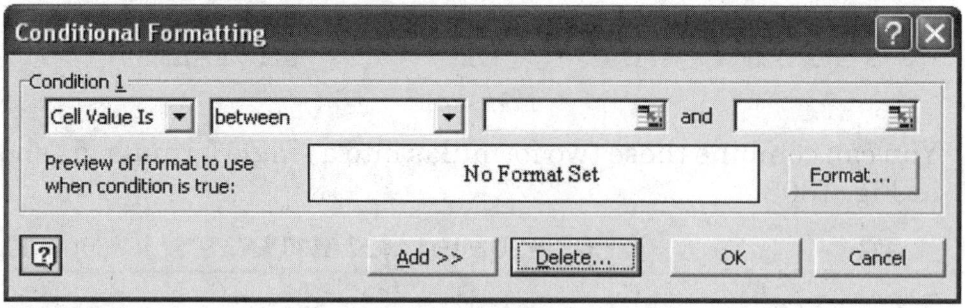

Fig. 1310

5) To access the more powerful version, use the dropdown to change "Cell Value Is" to "Formula Is", as shown in Fig. 1311.

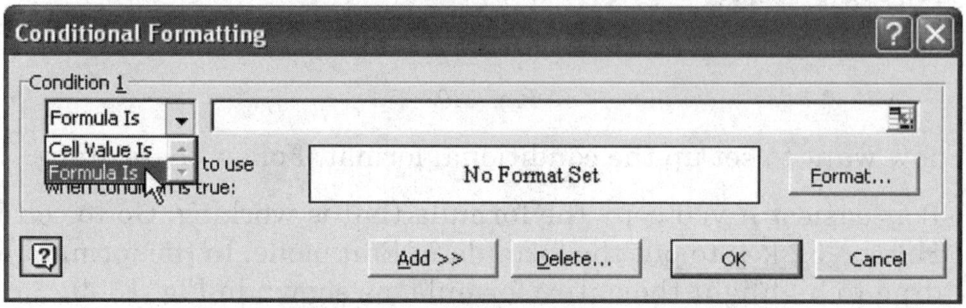

Fig. 1311

6) Click in the formula box, and hit Ctrl+V to paste the formula from the formula bar, as shown in Fig. 1312.

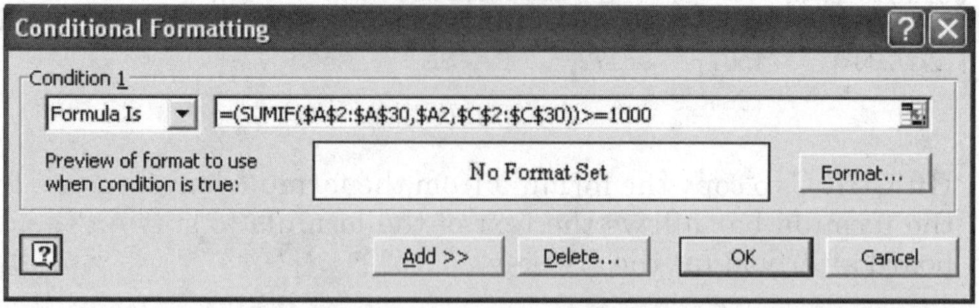

Fig. 1312

7) Next, you have to set up a unique format that should be used if the condition is True. Choose the Format... button. As shown in Fig. 1313, you will be given a dialog where you can customize the Font, Border, or Patterns.

8) Choose the Patterns tab. Select a green color and choose OK.

9) Choose OK to close the Conditional Format dialog.

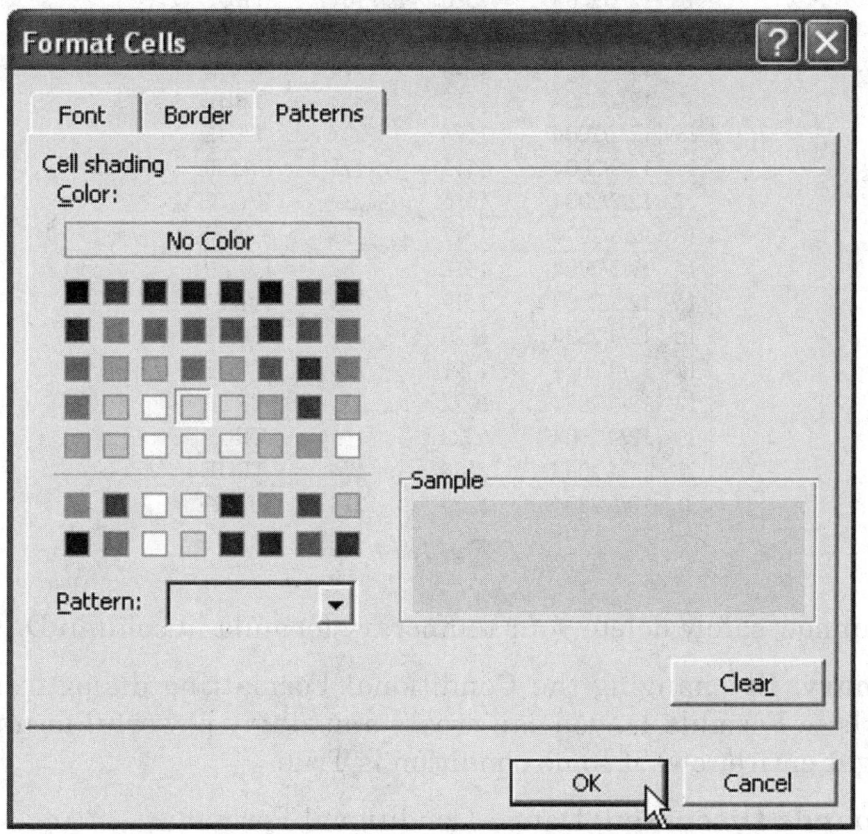

Fig. 1313

Part
IV

If everything worked OK, you will see that all of the rows for the second, fourth, and sixth are highlighted in green, as shown in Fig. 1314.

	A	B	C	D
2	12/1/2004	1506	82	FALSE
3	12/1/2004	1507	172	FALSE
4	12/1/2004	1508	202	FALSE
5	12/1/2004	1509	155	FALSE
6	12/2/2004	1510	107	TRUE
7	12/2/2004	1511	249	TRUE
8	12/2/2004	1512	156	TRUE
9	12/2/2004	1513	450	TRUE
10	12/2/2004	1514	227	TRUE
11	12/3/2004	1515	125	FALSE
12	12/3/2004	1516	239	FALSE
13	12/3/2004	1517	115	FALSE
14	12/3/2004	1518	82	FALSE
15	12/3/2004	1519	236	FALSE
16	12/4/2004	1520	218	TRUE
17	12/4/2004	1521	225	TRUE
18	12/4/2004	1522	235	TRUE
19	12/4/2004	1523	165	TRUE
20	12/4/2004	1524	174	TRUE
21	12/5/2004	1525	214	FALSE

Fig. 1314

You can now safely delete your temporary formula in column D.

Summary: By changing the Conditional Formatting dialog from Cell Value Is to Formula Is, you can create amazingly powerful formulas to highlight entire rows if some condition is True.

Commands Discussed: Data – Conditional Format

Functions Discussed: =SUMIF()

COLOR SALES
FOR A DAY THAT EXCEEDS $999

Problem: The owner of a retail store offers a five percent bonus when sales for a day exceed $1,000. In the dataset shown in Fig. 1315, you want to color all cells that are eligible for the bonus.

Strategy: In this case, you want to use SUMIF to keep a running total of all rows above the current row. If those rows are over $1,000, then the current row is eligible for the bonus.

1) It is easier to understand this formula if you enter it on the last row of the dataset, as shown in Fig. 1316.

This formula is similar to the formula in the last example, with one crucial difference. In the last example, the first and third ranges were examining all of the rows from A2 to A30 every time. This time, the top of the first range is locked at $A$2, but the bottom of

	A	B	C
1	Date	Invoice	Sales $
2	12/1/2004	1506	82
3	12/1/2004	1507	172
4	12/1/2004	1508	202
5	12/1/2004	1509	155
6	12/2/2004	1510	107
7	12/2/2004	1511	249
8	12/2/2004	1512	156
9	12/2/2004	1513	450
10	12/2/2004	1514	227
11	12/3/2004	1515	125
12	12/3/2004	1516	239
13	12/3/2004	1517	115
14	12/3/2004	1518	82
15	12/3/2004	1519	236
16	12/4/2004	1520	218

Fig. 1315

Part
IV

	A	B	C	D	E	F	G
1	Date	Invoice	Sales $	Over $1K			
20	12/4/2004	1524	174				
21	12/5/2004	1525	214				
22	12/5/2004	1526	21				
23	12/5/2004	1527	220				
24	12/6/2004	1528	240				
25	12/6/2004	1529	456				
26	12/6/2004	1530	219				
27	12/6/2004	1531	154				
28	12/6/2004	1532	37				
29	12/6/2004	1533	163				
30	12/6/2004	1533	163	=SUMIF($A$2:$A29,$A30,$C$2:$C29)			

Fig. 1316

the range is pointing to the row above the current row. The $A29 reference says that we are always looking at column A, but the reference will change to reflect the row above the current row.

2)   Copy D30 up to all of the other rows. This formula does not work in the first row of the dataset, so leave cell D2 blank, as shown in Fig. 1317.

	A	B	C	D
1	Date	Invoice	Sales $	Over $1K
2	12/1/2004	1506	82	
3	12/1/2004	1507	172	82
4	12/1/2004	1508	202	254
5	12/1/2004	1509	155	456
6	12/2/2004	1510	107	0
7	12/2/2004	1511	249	107
8	12/2/2004	1512	156	356
9	12/2/2004	1513	650	512
10	12/2/2004	1514	227	1162
11	12/3/2004	1515	125	0

Fig. 1317

The formula keeps a running total of all prior sales that day. In cell D5, the $456 means that the three prior sales of $82+172+202 totaled $456. In Fig. 1317, the bonus program would only kick in on the sale made in row 10.

3)   Edit the formula in D3 and add a test to see if this result is greater than or equal to 1000. You will have to add a leading parenthesis at the front and add)>=1000 at the end, as shown in Fig. 1318.

	A	B	C	D	E	F	G
1	Date	Invoice	Sales $	Over $1K			
2	12/1/2004	1506	82				
3	12/1/2004	1507	172	=(SUMIF($A$2:$A2,$A3,$C$2:$C2))>=1000			
4	12/1/2004	1508	202	FALSE			
5	12/1/2004	1509	155	FALSE			
6	12/2/2004	1510	107	FALSE			

Fig. 1318

4) Copy this formula down and you have a formula that evaluates to TRUE or FALSE. The True values are sales eligible for the bonus.

You now want to set up the conditional format. Follow these steps.

1) It is easiest if you copy the formula that is working. Go to cell D3. Hit the F2 key to put the formula in Edit mode. In the formula bar, drag to highlight the entire formula.

2) Hit Ctrl+C to copy the formula from the formula bar. Copying from the formula bar allows the text of the formula to stay on the clipboard after you hit the Esc key.

3) Hit the Esc key to exit Edit mode.

4) Select cells A3:C30.

5) From the menu, select Format – Conditional Format. Use the drop-down to change "Cell Value Is" to "Formula Is".

6) Click in the Formula box, and hit Ctrl+V to paste the formula from the formula bar, as shown in Fig. 1319.

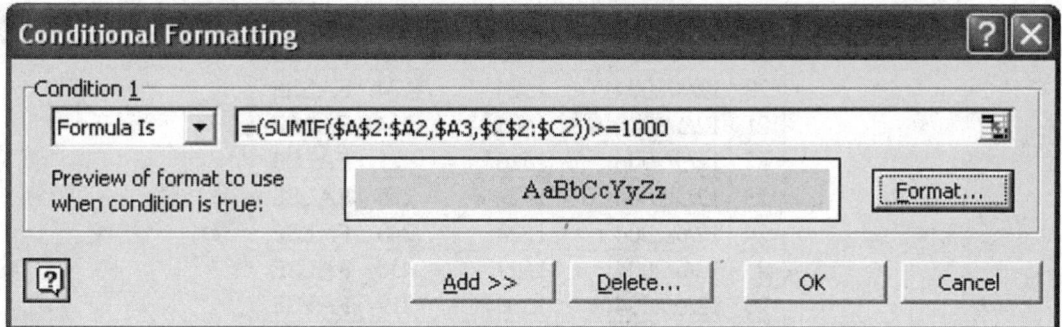

Fig. 1319

7) Choose the Format... button. Choose Green on the Patterns tab. Choose OK to close the Format Cells dialog. Choose OK to close the Conditional Format dialog.

Part IV

Result: Sales that occurred after $1000 in sales for a particular day are highlighted in green, as shown in Fig. 1320.

	A	B	C	D
1	Date	Invoice	Sales $	Over $1K
2	12/1/2004	1506	82	
3	12/1/2004	1507	172	FALSE
4	12/1/2004	1508	202	FALSE
5	12/1/2004	1509	155	FALSE
6	12/2/2004	1510	107	FALSE
7	12/2/2004	1511	249	FALSE
8	12/2/2004	1512	156	FALSE
9	12/2/2004	1513	650	FALSE
10	12/2/2004	1514	227	TRUE
11	12/3/2004	1515	125	FALSE
12	12/3/2004	1516	239	FALSE
13	12/3/2004	1517	115	FALSE
14	12/3/2004	1518	82	FALSE
15	12/3/2004	1519	236	FALSE
16	12/4/2004	1520	218	FALSE
17	12/4/2004	1521	225	FALSE
18	12/4/2004	1522	235	FALSE
19	12/4/2004	1523	165	FALSE
20	12/4/2004	1524	174	FALSE
21	12/5/2004	1525	214	FALSE
22	12/5/2004	1526	21	FALSE
23	12/5/2004	1527	220	FALSE
24	12/6/2004	1528	240	FALSE
25	12/6/2004	1529	456	FALSE
26	12/6/2004	1530	219	FALSE
27	12/6/2004	1531	154	FALSE
28	12/6/2004	1532	37	TRUE
29	12/6/2004	1533	163	TRUE

Fig. 1320

You can now safely delete your temporary formula in column D.

Summary: By changing the Conditional Formatting dialog from Cell Value Is to Formula Is, you can create amazingly powerful formulas to highlight entire rows if some condition is true.

Commands Discussed: Data – Conditional Format

Functions Discussed: =SUMIF()

TURN OFF WRAP TEXT IN PASTED DATA

Problem: If you regularly paste information from web pages, you might be frustrated at the way Excel wraps text in the cells. In Fig. 1321, column A is not wide enough for the date and column B is wrapped so that you can only see a few rows on the screen. Using AutoFit to make the columns wider will not work when the cells have their Wrap Text property turned on.

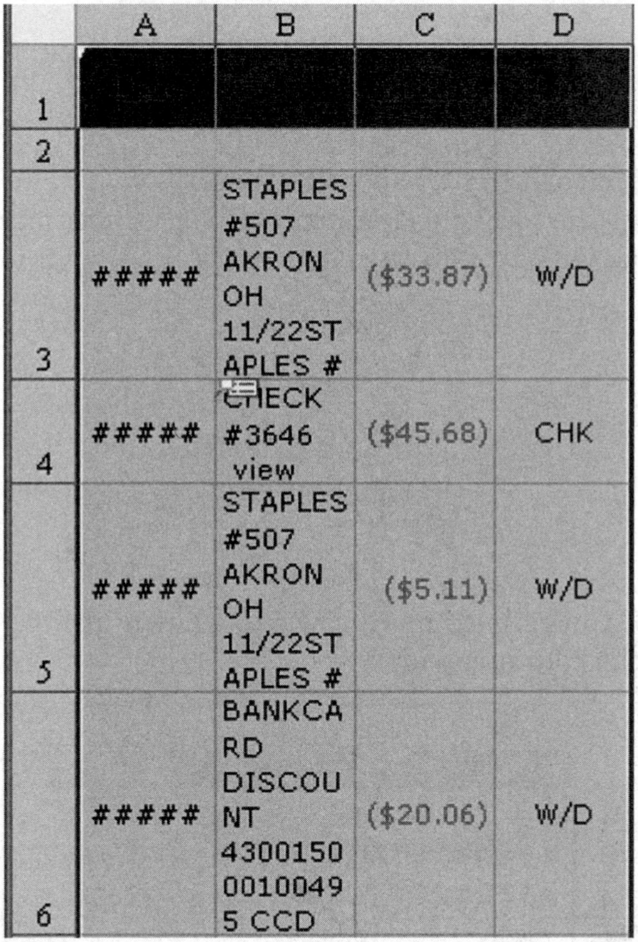

	A	B	C	D
1				
2				
3	#####	STAPLES #507 AKRON OH 11/22ST APLES #	($33.87)	W/D
4	#####	CHECK #3646 view	($45.68)	CHK
5	#####	STAPLES #507 AKRON OH 11/22ST APLES #	($5.11)	W/D
6	#####	BANKCA RD DISCOU NT 4300150 0010049 5 CCD	($20.06)	W/D

Fig. 1321

Part
IV

Strategy: Follow these steps to correct this.

1) First, hit Ctrl+1 to open the Format Cells dialog. On the Alignment tab, look in the Text Control section. The Wrap Text choice is probably a grey checkmark, as shown in Fig. 1322. This means that for some cells in the selection, the Wrap Text property is on, and for others it is off.

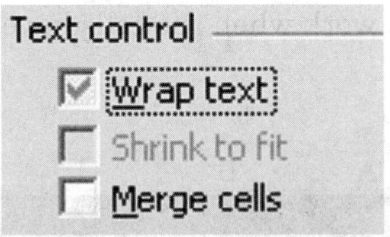

Fig. 1322

2) You want to turn the Wrap text property off. The first mouse click will change the grey checkmark to a black checkmark. The second mouse click will turn off the checkmark, as shown in Fig. 1323.

Fig. 1323

After this step, you can see more rows, as shown in Fig. 1324. You still need to make the columns wider.

	A	B	C	D
1				
2				
3	#####	STAPLES	($33.87)	W/D
4	#####	CHECK #	($45.68)	CHK
5	#####	STAPLES	($5.11)	W/D
6	#####	BANKCAF	($20.06)	W/D
7	#####	BANKCAF	$786.47	DEP

Fig. 1324

3) From the menu, select Format – Column – Autofit Selection. You can now see the bank statement, as shown in Fig. 1325.

	A	B	C	D
1	Date	Description	Amount	Type
2				
3	11/24/2004	STAPLES #507 AKRON OH 11/22STAPLES #	($33.87)	W/D
4	11/24/2004	CHECK #3646 view	($45.68)	CHK
5	11/24/2004	STAPLES #507 AKRON OH 11/22STAPLES #	($5.11)	W/D
6	11/24/2004	BANKCARD DISCOUNT 430015000100495 CCD	($20.06)	W/D

Fig. 1325

Summary: Data pasted from web pages will often have the Wrap Text property turned on. This prevents the AutoFit selection command from working.

Commands Discussed: Format – Cells – Alignment – Wrap Text; Format – Column – AutoFit

DELETE ALL PICTURES IN PASTED DATA

Problem: You copy data from your bank's Web page into Excel. On the Web page, the bank has little "check" icons that let you view a physical copy of the check, as shown in Fig. 1326.

Date ▼	Descrip
10/22/2004	TICKLING KEYS 1341
10/22/2004	CHECK #3622 📧 view
10/22/2004	BANKCARD DISC
10/22/2004	BANKCARD MTOT

Fig. 1326

Part
IV

As shown in Fig. 1327, this check icon shows up as an annoying image in your Excel workbook. How can you delete all of these images in one step?

Date	Payee
10/22/2004	TICKLING KEYS 1341
10/22/2004	CHECK #3622 view
10/22/2004	BANKCARD DISC
10/22/2004	BANKCARD MTOT

Fig. 1327

Strategy: There is a tool in the Drawing toolbar that allows you to select all images in a rectangular area.

1)   To display the Drawing toolbar, select View – Toolbars – Drawing. On the left side of the Drawing toolbar is a white arrow, as shown in Fig. 1328. This is called the Select Objects tool.

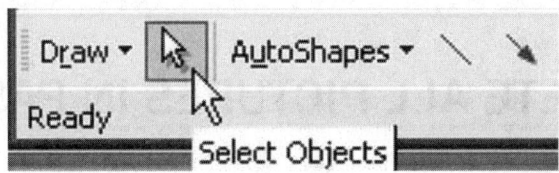

Fig. 1328

2)   Choose the Select Objects tool. When you are in Select Objects mode, the white arrow will have a blue square around it, as shown in Fig. 1328.

3)   Using the mouse, start highlighting above and to the left of the first cell with the check icon. Drag down and to the right to highlight all of the cells with the check icons. As shown in Fig. 1329, all of the drawing objects in the rectangle will be selected.

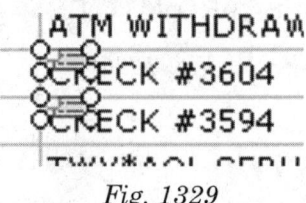

Fig. 1329

4)   Hit the Delete key on the keyboard to delete all of the selected objects at once.

Gotcha: You have to remember to turn off the Select Objects mode by choosing the white arrow in the Drawing toolbar again. It is very annoying to try to select cells and have the mouse not respond to clicking when you forget to turn the white arrow off.

Summary: Use the Drawing toolbar to select all images in a rectangular range.

Commands Discussed: View – Toolbars – Drawing

DRAW AN ARROW TO VISUALLY ILLUSTRATE THAT TWO CELLS ARE CONNECTED

Problem: You have a large spreadsheet with many calculations. Results from section 1 are carried forward to cells on section 2. It would help to graphically illustrate that one cell flows to the calculation of another.

Strategy: Use the Drawing toolbar, as shown in Fig. 1330. If this is not visible at the bottom of your worksheet, then use View – Toolbars – Drawing. The toolbar typically appears at the bottom of the screen. Use the Arrow tool shown here.

Fig. 1330

1) Click in the origin cell and drag to the final cell. When you release the mouse button, an arrow will appear, pointing from the first cell to the end cell, as shown in Fig. 1331.

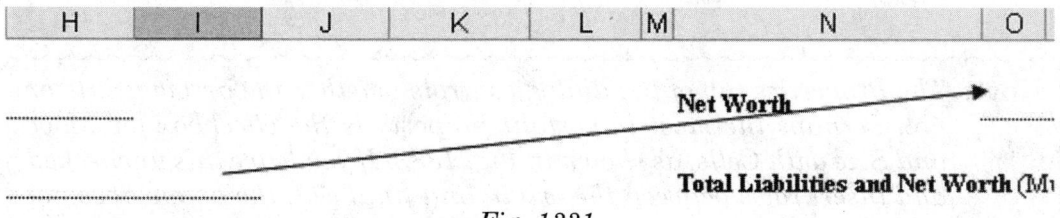

Fig. 1331

2) Use your mouse pointer to click on the line. Selection handles will appear. Right click and choose Format Drawing Object.

3) As shown in Fig. 1332, in the Format dialog you can customize line width, arrow style, color, etc.

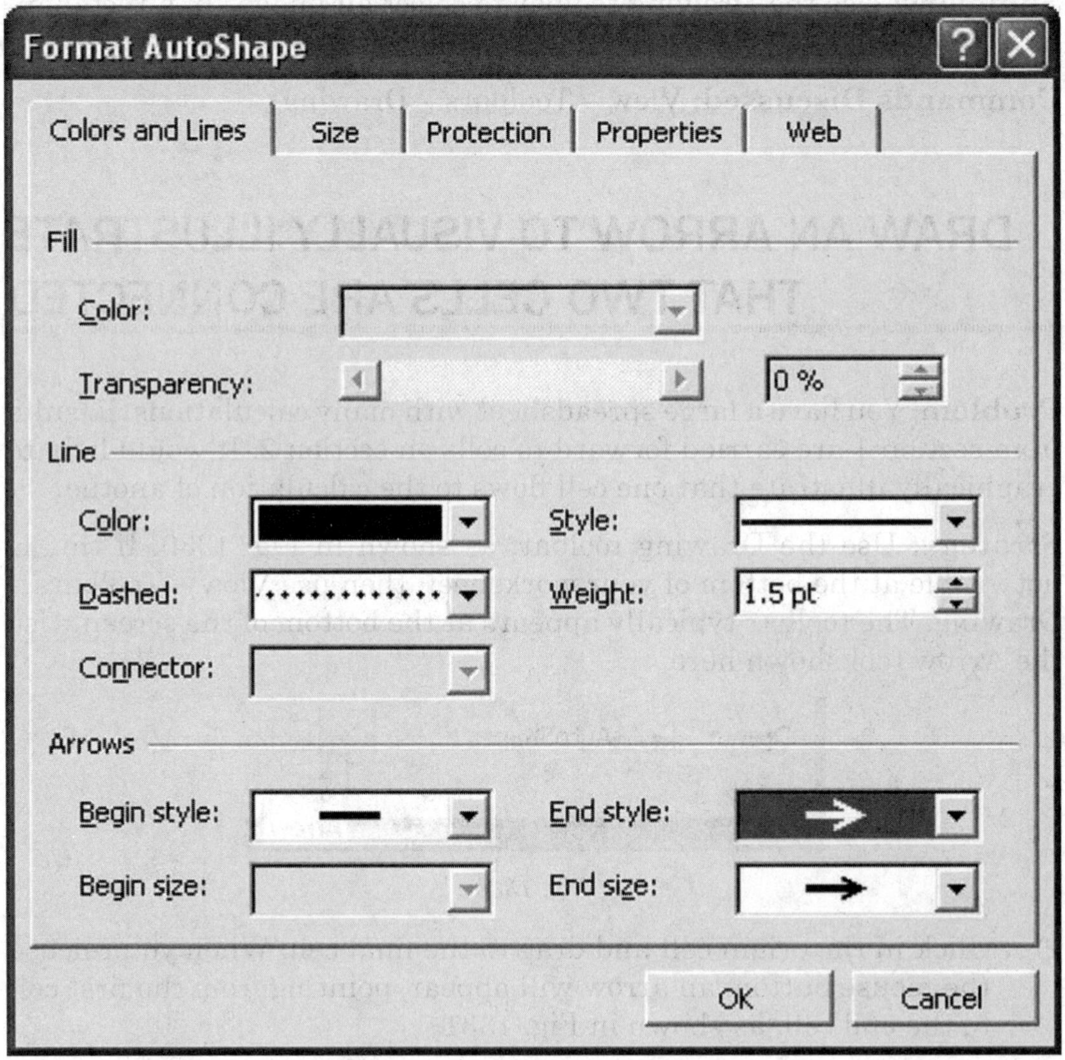

Fig. 1332

> **Note:** *The Properties tab of the dialog controls whether the arrow prints or not. Perhaps the most important property is the checkbox for Move and Size with Cells, as shown in Fig. 1333. If you leave this unchecked and insert rows between the origin and final cell, the arrow does not resize to keep pointing at the final cell.*

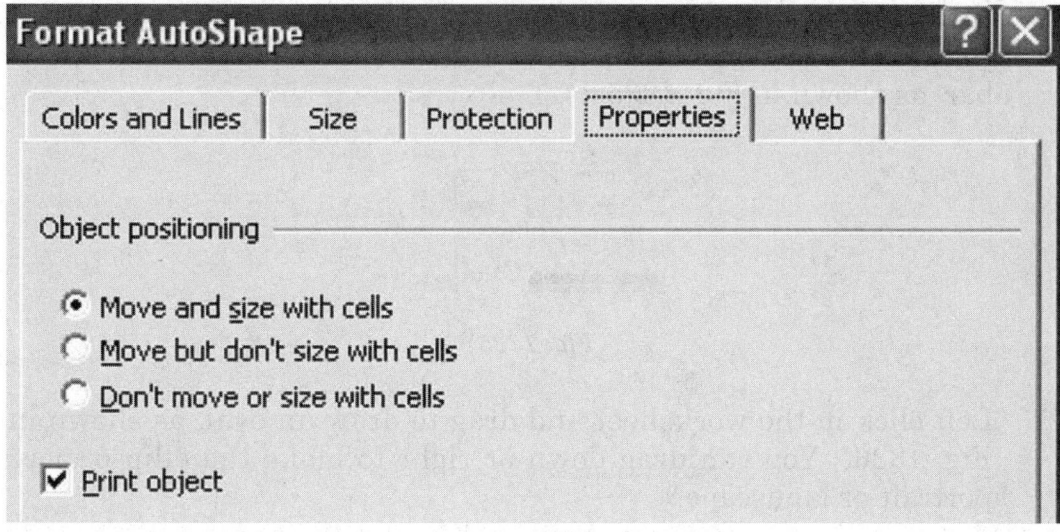

Fig. 1333

Summary: Create a variety of arrows to help graphically illustrate the flow of your spreadsheet.

Commands Discussed: View – Toolbars

ADD AN AUTOSHAPE TO YOUR WORKSHEET

Part
IV

Problem: Excel offers an excellent calculation tool. However, some people are more visually oriented, and their eyes glaze over when given a large white sheet with black numbers. You can use graphics to call attention to certain numbers.

Strategy: Use AutoShapes. If the Drawing toolbar is not displayed, use View – Toolbars – Drawing. The Drawing toolbar is typically docked to the bottom of the worksheet, as shown in Fig. 1334.

Fig. 1334

1)   The Drawing toolbar itself offers five standard shapes – Line, Arrow, Rectangle, Oval, and Textbox. Choose the Oval tool in the toolbar, as shown in Fig. 1335.

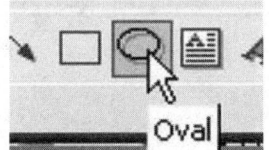

Fig. 1335

2)   Left-click in the worksheet and drag to draw an oval, as shown in Fig. 1336. You can drag down or right to make the ellipse more portrait or landscape.

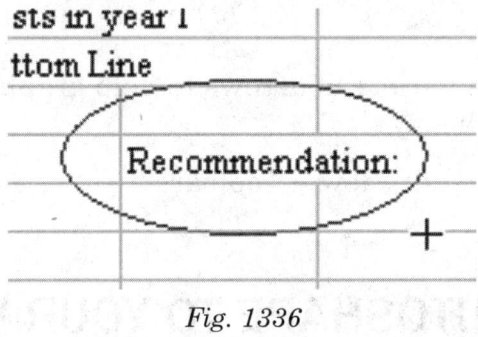

Fig. 1336

As shown in Fig. 1337, by default, the AutoShape is filled with white and covers up text.

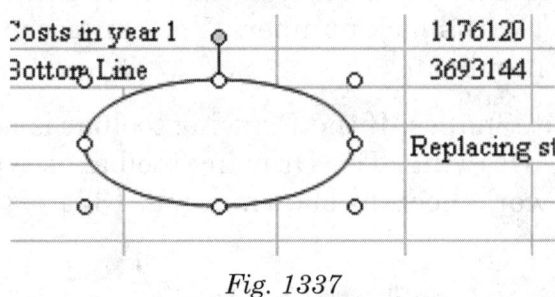

Fig. 1337

3)   Use the dropdown next to the paint bucket in the Drawing toolbar. Select No Fill from the list, as shown in Fig. 1338.

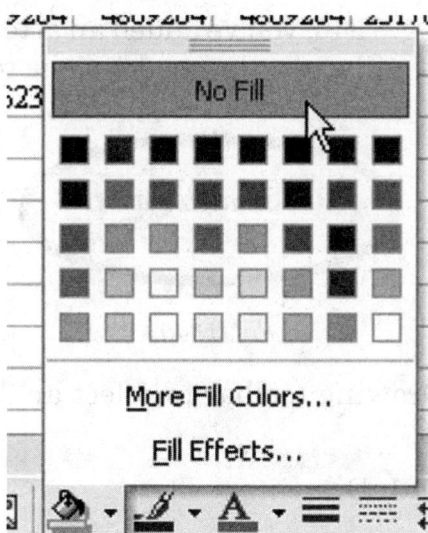

Fig. 1338

4)   Use the LineStyle icon and choose a thicker line, perhaps 3 point, as shown in Fig. 1339.

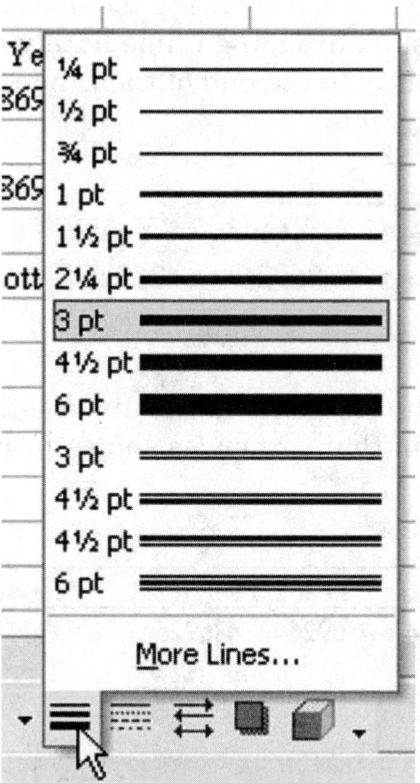

Fig. 1339

Result: As shown in Fig. 1340, you've added an attention-grabbing shape to the worksheet. This will draw the reader's eye to the conclusion.

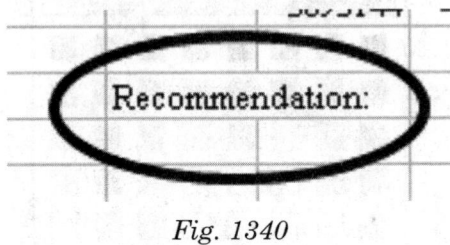

Fig. 1340

Summary: Use the Drawing toolbar to select an AutoShape and insert it into your worksheet.

Commands Discussed: Drawing toolbar

DRAW PERFECT CIRCLES

Problem: The oval tool in the Drawing toolbar is hard to use. With the rectangle tool, if you start dragging immediately above a cell, as shown in Fig. 1341, you can drag to the end of the range and effectively draw a perfect rectangle every time.

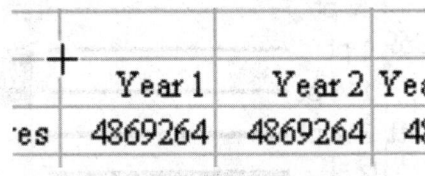

Fig. 1341

If you start drawing the rectangle in the upper left corner of the cell, the AutoShape will start in that corner, as shown in Fig. 1342.

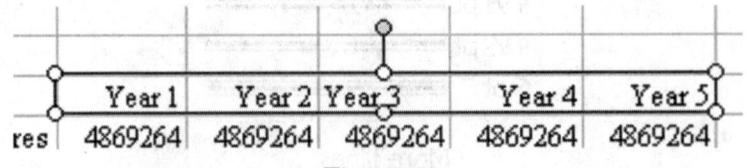

Fig. 1342

However, if you start drawing a circle in the same spot, the oval that you draw will not completely include the text in the cells, as shown in Fig. 1343.

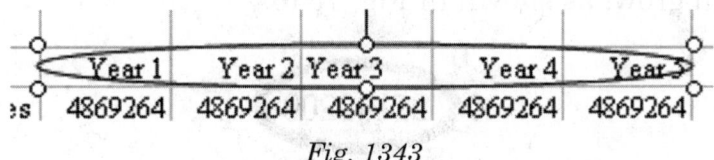

Fig. 1343

Strategy: There are a few special keys that work well when drawing ovals.

First, to force an oval to be a perfect circle, hold down the Shift key while you draw and release the mouse button, as shown in Fig. 1344.

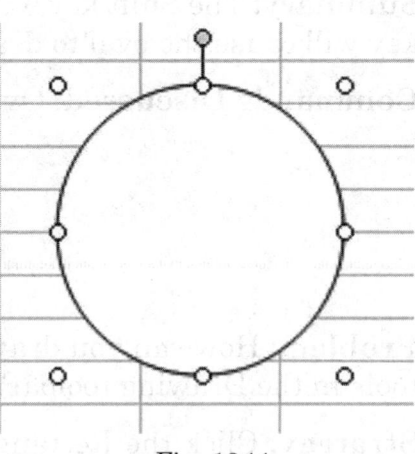

Second, a circle or oval is hard to draw. In order to draw the circle shown in Fig. 1345, you would have to start at the upper left corner of K15. This is non-intuitive, because all of the area in black is covered when you drag the circle tool to draw the circle. How can you know how far above your data to start in order to include all of the data?

Fig. 1344

Part
IV

	J	K	L	M
14				
15				
16				
17				
18				
19				
20				
21				
22				
23				
24				
25				

Fig. 1345

One solution is to hold down the Ctrl key when you draw the oval (or the Ctrl+Shift keys to draw a circle). Then, instead of starting in the left corner, start directly in the middle of the circle. As you drag outward, the circle will grow, as shown in Fig. 1346.

Fig. 1346

Summary: The Shift key will cause an oval to draw as a circle. The Ctrl key will cause the oval to draw outwards from the original point.

Commands Discussed: Oval Tool

DRAW PERFECT SQUARES

Problem: How can you draw a perfect square by using the AutoShape tools in the Drawing toolbar?

Strategy: Click the Rectangle tool in the Drawing toolbar. Before you left-click in the worksheet, hold down the Shift key. Keeping it held down, draw the rectangle. Release the mouse button, then release the Shift key.

Result: A perfect square will be drawn, as shown in Fig. 1347.

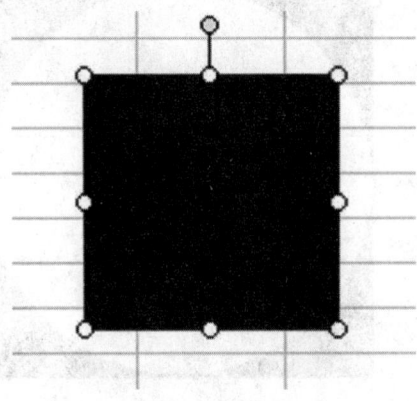

Fig. 1347

Additional Details: If you want to resize a square, hold down the Shift key while you drag a corner handle. This will force Excel to keep the shape a square.

Additional Details: If you need to produce many identically sized squares, follow these steps.

1) First, draw one square as shown in Fig. 1347. Next, hold down the Ctrl key. Click on the first square and drag to move a copy of the square to a new location. You will now have two identical squares.

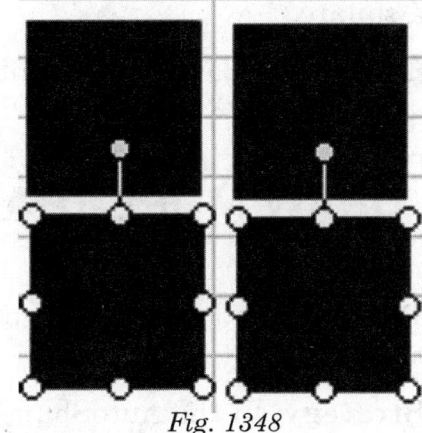

2) Hold down the Ctrl key and click on the new square. Both squares will be selected. Hold down the Ctrl key and drag the two squares to create a copy of both. You will now have four squares, as shown in Fig. 1348.

Fig. 1348

3) Hold down the Ctrl key and choose the original two squares to add them to the selection. You will now have all four squares selected. Hold down the Ctrl key, click and drag to make a copy of the four squares, as shown in Fig. 1349.

Part IV

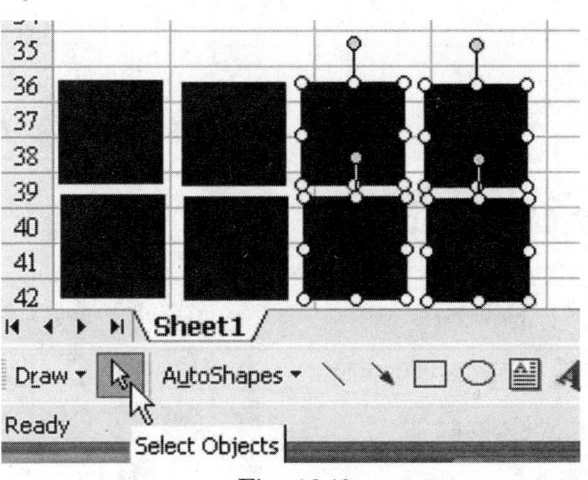

Fig. 1349

4) If you need to keep copying, you will want to select all eight squares. The fastest way to do this is to use the Select Objects arrow in the Drawing toolbar. Select this icon, then drag a box around all of the squares to select them all. Ctrl+Drag to copy the eight squares to be 16 squares.

5) When you are finally done, choose the white Select Object arrow again to exit the Select Objects mode.

Summary: Use the Shift key while drawing a rectangle to force it to be a square.

Commands Discussed: Shift; Ctrl; Ctrl+Drag

DRAW MORE THAN THE FOUR BASIC SHAPES

Problem: You need a shape other than the four basic AutoShapes in the Drawing toolbar.

Strategy: In the AutoShapes dropdown, there are seven flyout menus available. Of these, five menus offer additional shapes.

1) Select the AutoShape dropdown on the toolbar, as shown in Fig. 1350.

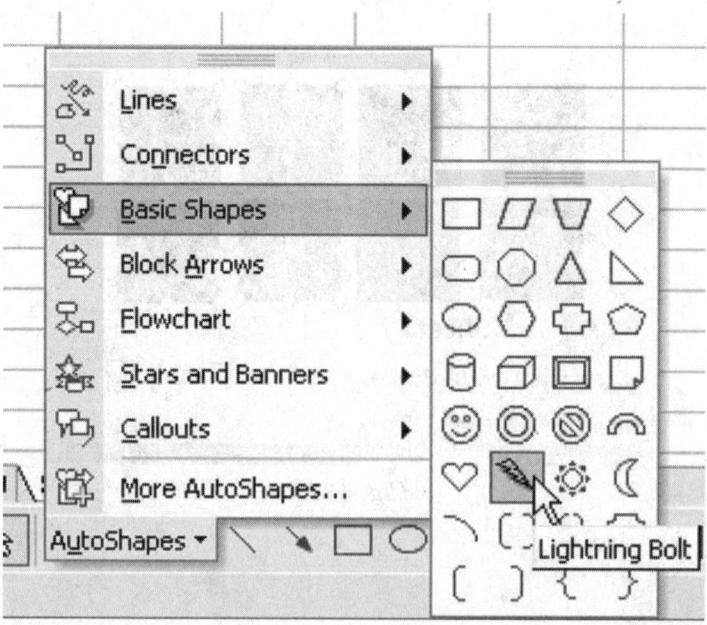

Fig. 1350

2) Choose the basic shapes choice. Choose the lightning bolt. As shown in Fig. 1351, left-click in your worksheet and drag to draw a lightning bolt.

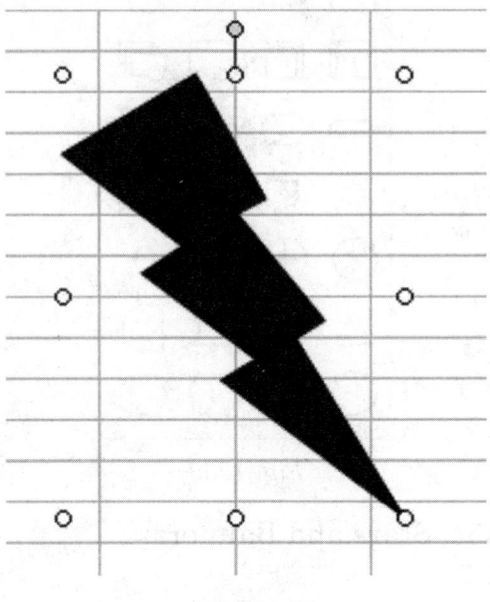

Fig. 1351

Additional Details: The other shapes available are shown below.

As shown in Fig. 1352, Block Arrows:

Fig. 1352

Part
IV

As shown in Fig. 1353, Flowchart symbols:

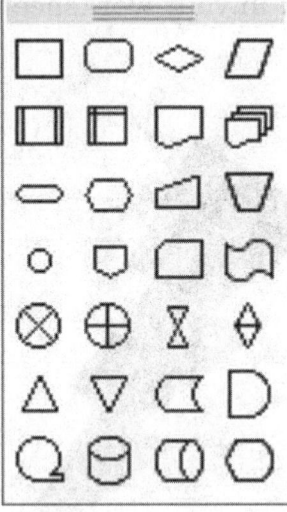

Fig. 1353

As shown in Fig. 1354, Stars and Banners:

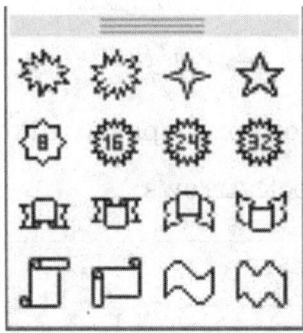

Fig. 1354

As shown in Fig. 1355, Callouts. These special shapes have an anchor point that is attached to one cell. As you move the shape, it continues to be anchored to the original cell.

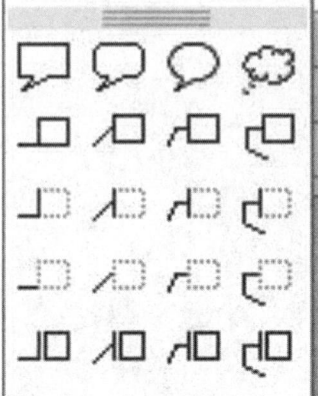

Fig. 1355

The More AutoShapes option opens the Insert Clipart task pane, with a number of vector-based line drawings available, as shown in Fig. 1356.

Fig. 1356

Summary: Use the AutoShape dropdown option to select from additional AutoShapes offered in Excel.

Commands Discussed: AutoShape dropdown

CHANGE AN EXISTING AUTOSHAPE

Problem: How can you change an existing AutoShape to a new shape?

Strategy: There is an extra step involved if your AutoShape can accept text.

Part
IV

1)   Using the mouse, click on the AutoShape. If you immediately get nine resize handles, as shown in Fig. 1357, then your AutoShape does not accept text. Skip the next step.

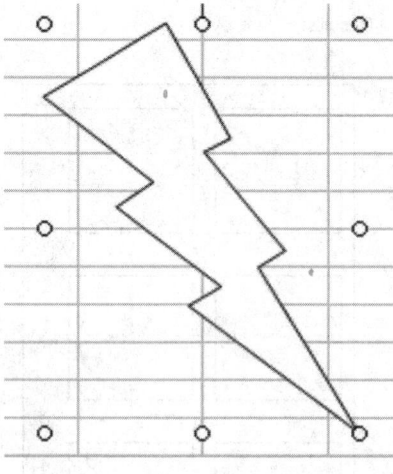

Fig. 1357

However, if you click on the AutoShape and the shape is surrounded by diagonal lines, then you have a text-enabled AutoShape, as shown in Fig. 1358.

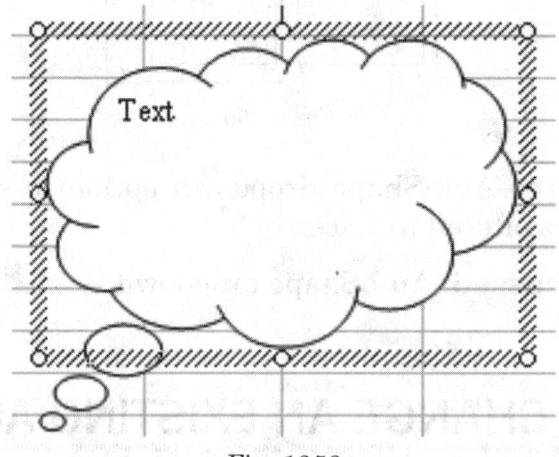

Fig. 1358

2)   In text-enabled AutoShapes, the first click will put the shape in text-edit mode. This is represented by the diagonal lines in the border. In order to select the shape, you need to click again on the diagonal lines. This will change the diagonal lines to dotted lines, as shown in Fig. 1359.

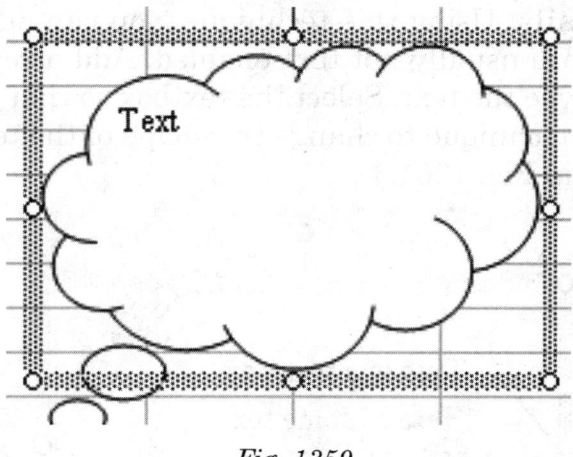

Fig. 1359

3)   After the shape is selected, select Draw – Change AutoShape from the Drawing toolbar and choose another AutoShape, as shown in Fig. 1360.

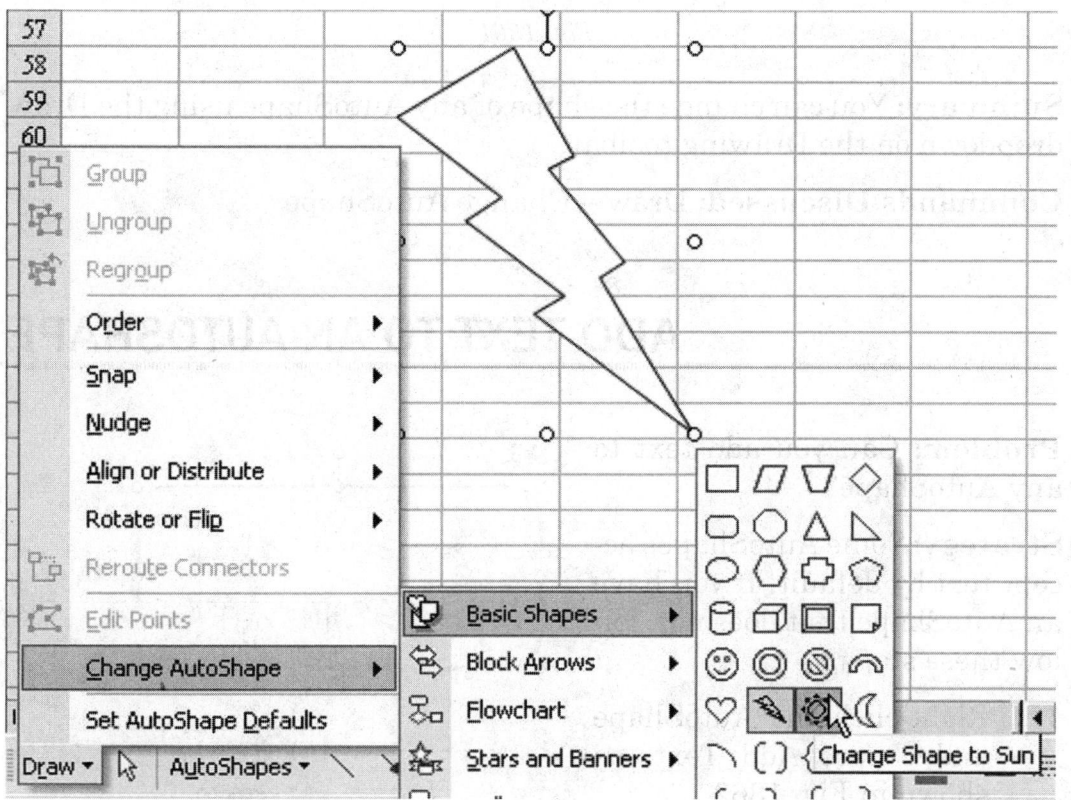

Fig. 1360

Additional Details: Using this technique, you can add text to any of the shapes that are usually not text-enabled. Add a regular textbox to the worksheet. Type the text. Select the textbox so that it is surrounded by dots. Use this technique to change the shape of the textbox to a basic shape, as shown in Fig. 1361.

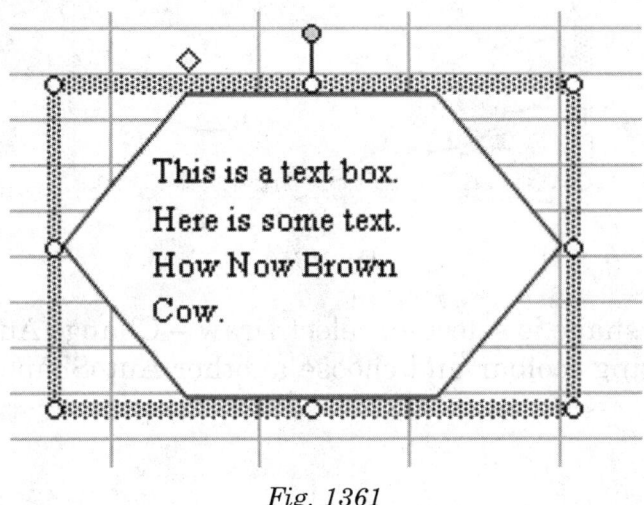

Fig. 1361

Summary: You can change the shape of any AutoShape using the Draw dropdown on the Drawing toolbar.

Commands Discussed: Draw – Change AutoShape

ADD TEXT TO AN AUTOSHAPE

Problem: Can you add text to any AutoShape?

Strategy: Some AutoShapes accept text by default. If you have an AutoShape that does not, follow these steps.

1) Right-click the AutoShape and choose Add Text, as shown in Fig. 1362.

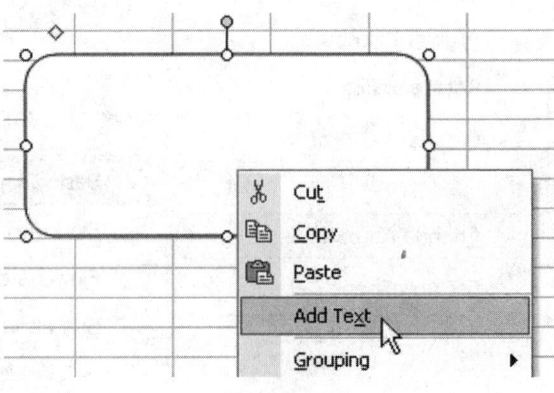

Fig. 1362

2) Click on the AutoShape. Type some text, as shown in Fig. 1363.

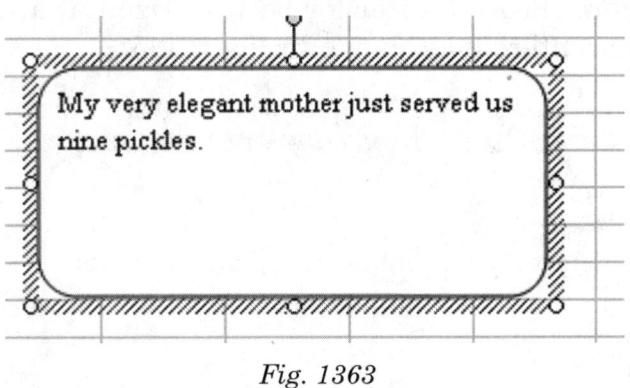

Fig. 1363

Additional Information: To center and then bold the text, follow these steps.

1) The text box is surrounded by diagonal lines. Click on the diagonal lines to change them to dots. Right-click on the dots and choose Format AutoShape, as shown in Fig. 1364.

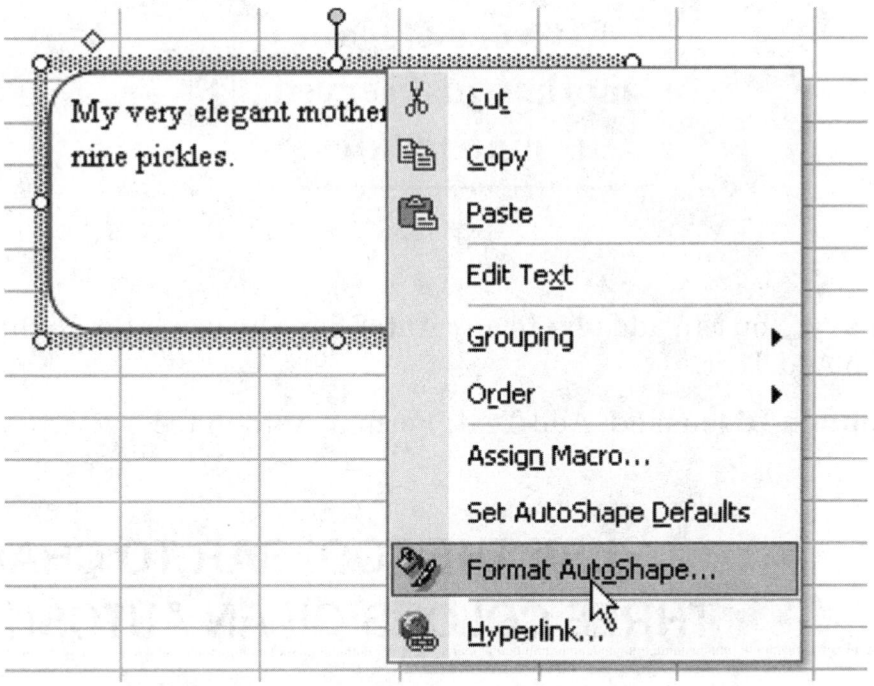

Fig. 1364

2)   In the Format dialog, go to the Alignment tab. In the Text Align-
     ment section, choose Center for both Horizontal and Vertical. The
     text will be centered, as shown in Fig. 1365.

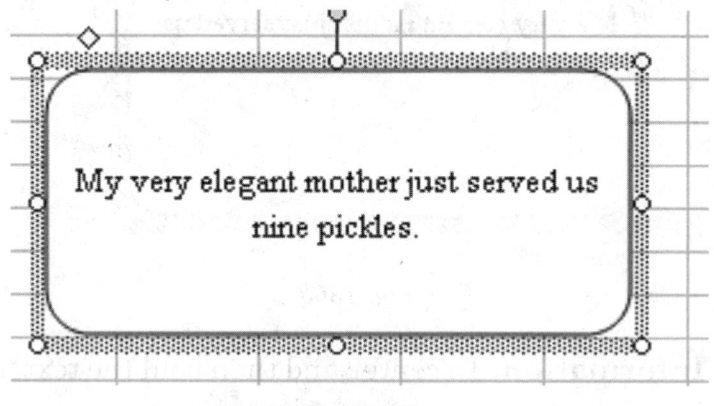

Fig. 1365

3)   To make a bolder text, go to font tab, choose a color, 18pt, font, and
     bold to create the result shown in Fig. 1366.

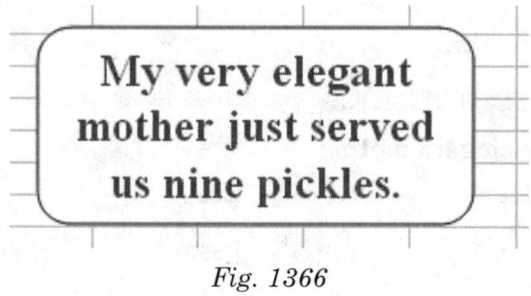

Fig. 1366

Summary: You can add text to any AutoShape by using the Right-Click
menu to Add Text.

Commands Discussed: Add Text; Format AutoShape

USE THE TOOLBAR TO CHANGE
THREE COLORS OF AN AUTOSHAPE

Problem: Is there a quick way to change the colors of an AutoShape, as
shown in Fig. 1367?

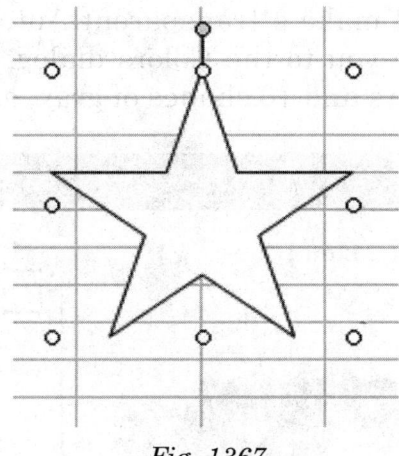

Fig. 1367

Strategy: Towards the right side of the Drawing toolbar there are three buttons to control the Fill Color, Line Color, and Text Color of the AutoShape.

The Fill Color icon is the paint bucket. Touch the paint bucket to use the most recently used color. Otherwise, use the dropdown to access 40 different colors, as shown in Fig. 1368.

Part
IV

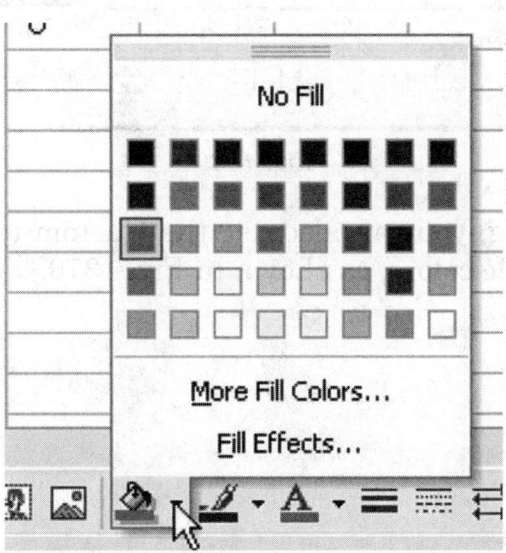

Fig. 1368

The No Fill option will make a transparent AutoShape. The More Fill Colors option will take you to the Colors dialog, where you can select from 127 standard colors and 16 shades of gray, as shown in Fig. 1369.

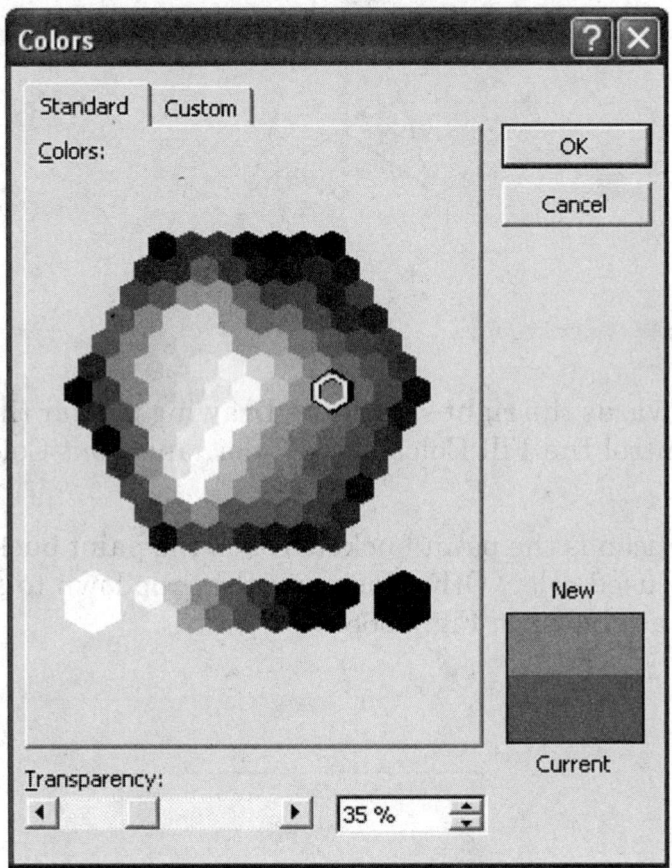

Fig. 1369

On the Color dialog, you can also use the Custom tab to create any of 16.5 million possible colors, as shown in Fig. 1370.

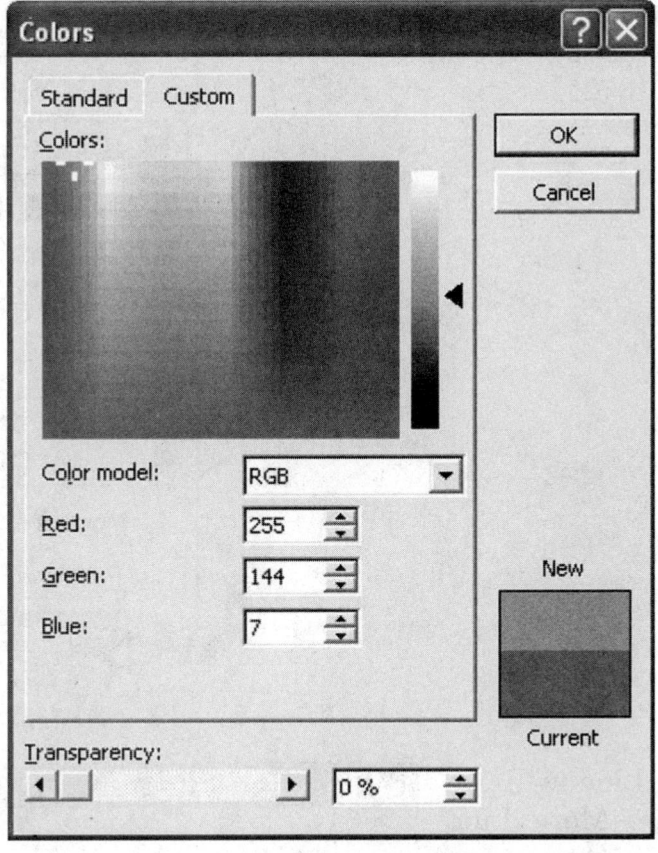

Fig. 1370

If you choose Fill Effects, you can choose any gradient, texture, pattern, or picture to fill the AutoShape, as shown in Fig. 1371.

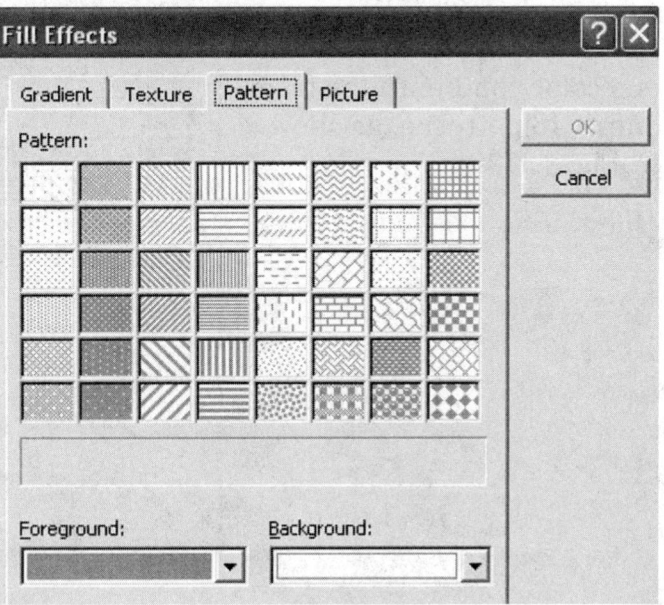

Fig. 1371

The Line Color icon in the Drawing toolbar is used to change the line color, as
shown in Fig. 1372.

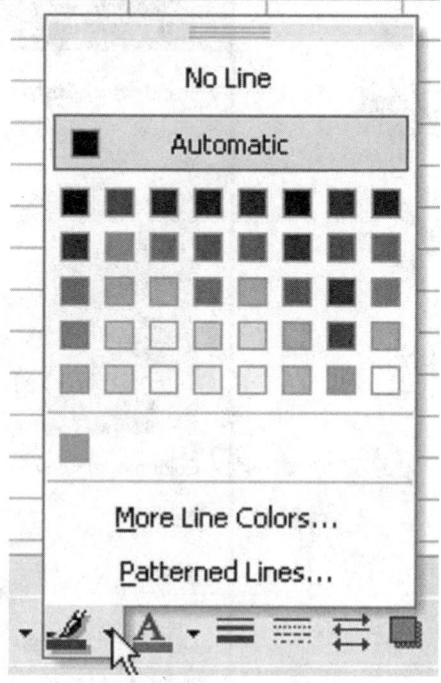

Fig. 1372

Choosing No Line will re-
move the line. More Line
Colors offers the same custom color choices as the Fill
Area dialog. The Patterned
Lines option allows for various color combinations from
one of 48 patterns, as shown
in Fig. 1373.

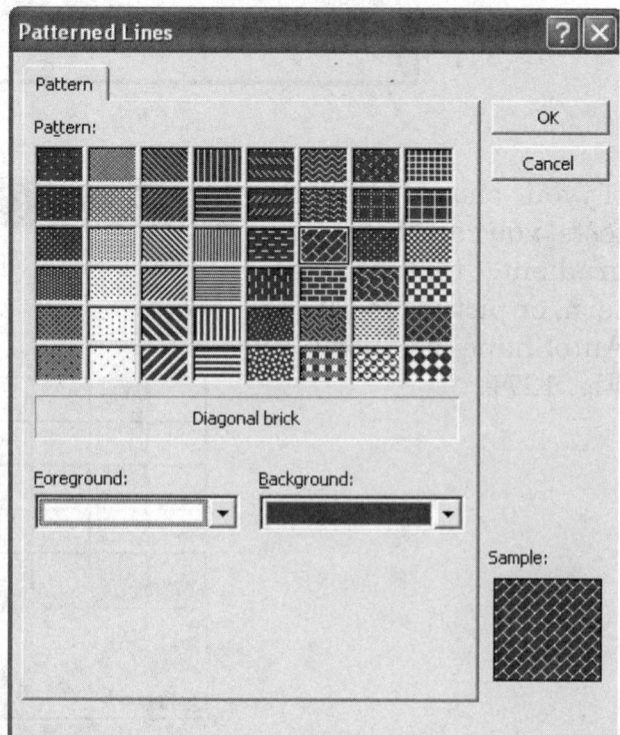

Fig. 1373

If you have an AutoShape with Text, you can adjust the text color by using the Font Color dropdown, as shown in Fig. 1374.

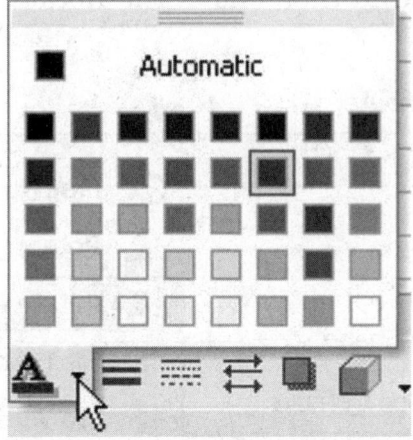

Fig. 1374

Summary: To change the color format of an AutoShape, use the three buttons on the right side of the toolbar.

Commands Discussed: Drawing – Fill Color

ROTATE AN AUTOSHAPE

Problem: How do I rotate an AutoShape?

Strategy: When you select an AutoShape, a green circle appears, as shown in Fig. 1375. Grab the green arrow, click, and rotate. This is a free rotation; you can rotate it in 360 degrees.

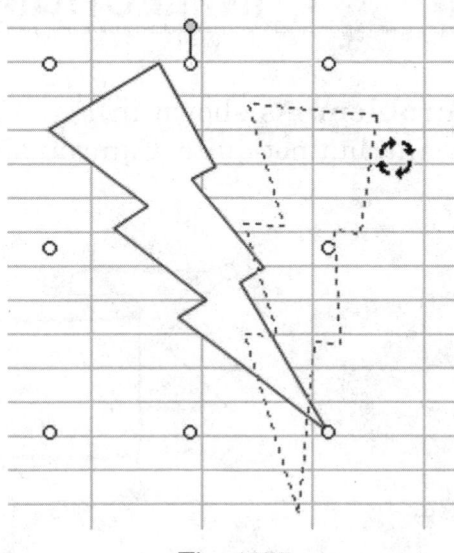

Fig. 1375

Additional Information: If you need to rotate exactly 90, 180, or 270 degrees, use the Draw dropdown on the left side of the Drawing toolbar. Choose Rotate or Flip and then one of the Rotate or Flip commands, as shown in Fig. 1376.

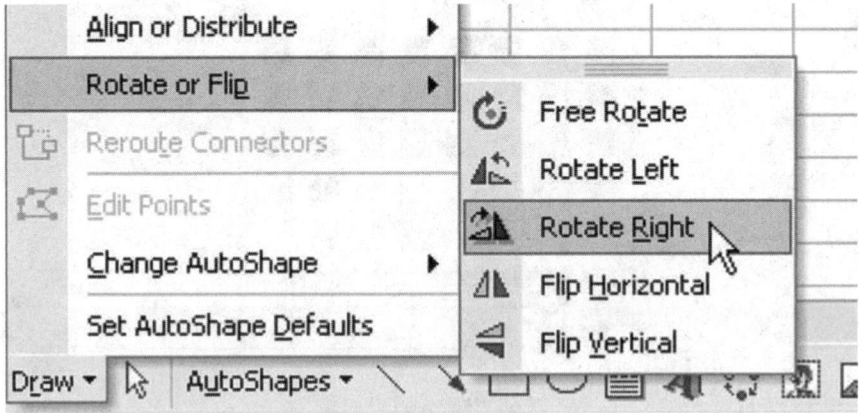

Fig. 1376

Summary: To rotate an AutoShape, select and use the green handle to rotate.

Commands Discussed: Draw – Rotate or Flip

ALTER THE KEY
INFLECTION POINT IN AN AUTOSHAPE

Problem: As shown in Fig. 1377, the AutoShape is almost what you want, but not quite. Can you adjust it to a narrower banner?

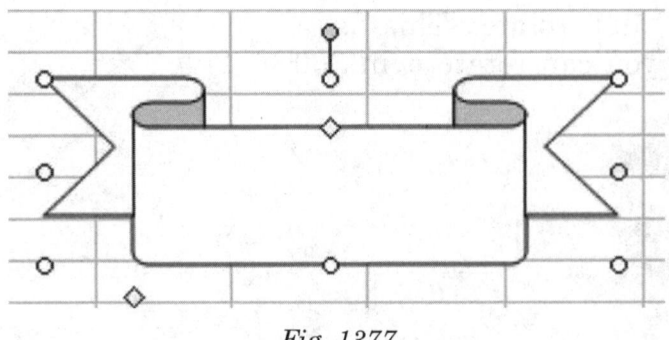

Fig. 1377

Strategy: For many AutoShapes, you can select the shape and it offers one or more yellow diamond-shaped handles. This yellow handle allows you to adjust the inflection point in shapes. In the image above, the lower left diamond handle will allow you to control how much overlap appears on the back ribbon.

As shown in Fig. 1378, you can make the front portion of the ribbon shorter,

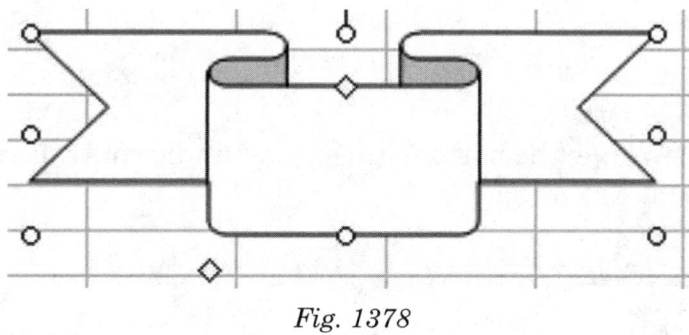

Fig. 1378

or longer, as shown in Fig. 1379.

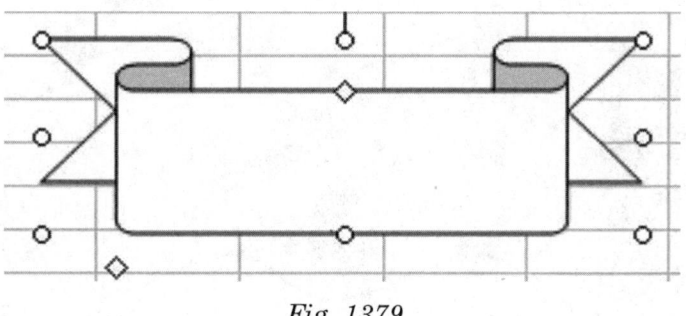

Fig. 1379

Part
IV

This shape offers a top inflection point. This can make the "fold" of the ribbon narrower, as shown in Fig. 1380

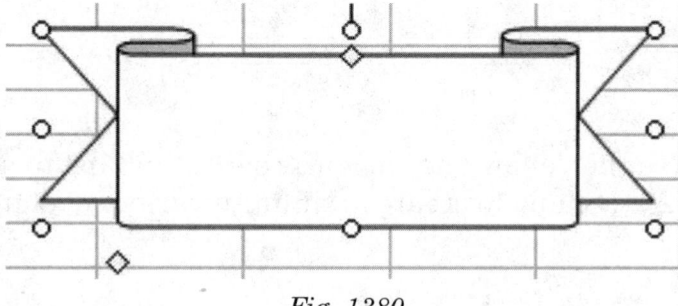

Fig. 1380

or thicker, as shown in Fig. 1381.

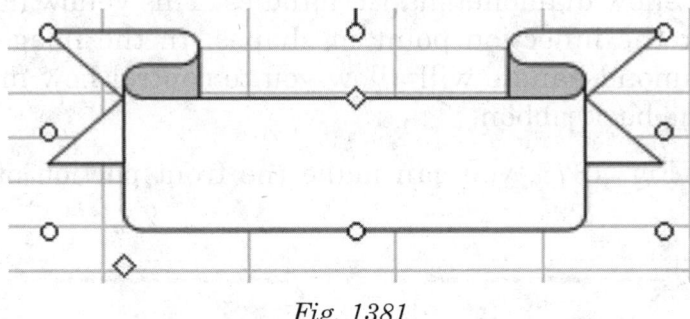

Fig. 1381

For the Double Wave, the bottom inflection handle controls tilt, as shown in Fig. 1382 and Fig. 1383.

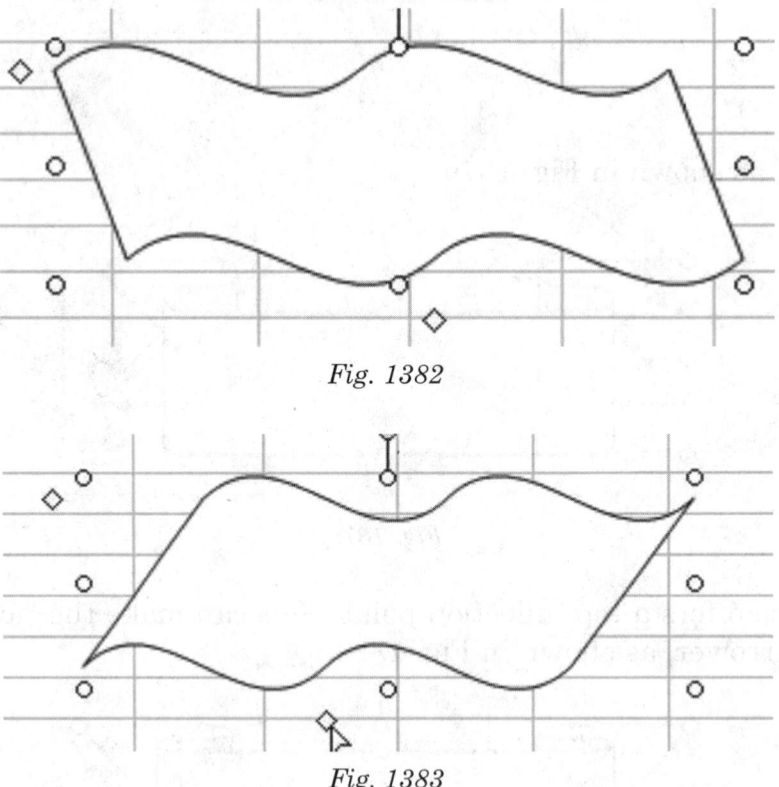

Fig. 1382

Fig. 1383

Summary: Use the yellow handle with the AutoShape to adjust the inflection of an AutoShape to create an infinite variety of shapes.

ADD A SHADOW TO AN AUTOSHAPE

Problem: How do you add a shadow to an AutoShape?

Strategy: Click the Shadow dropdown on the Drawing toolbar. A list of available shadow styles appears, as shown in Fig. 1384. Select one of the shadow styles to add a shadow.

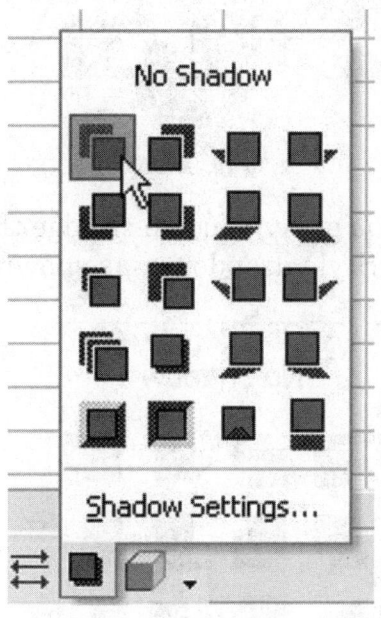

Fig. 1384

Part
IV

There are a variety of shadows available. Fig. 1385 shows the Shadow Style 1.

Fig. 1385

Fig. 1386 shows Shadow Style 3

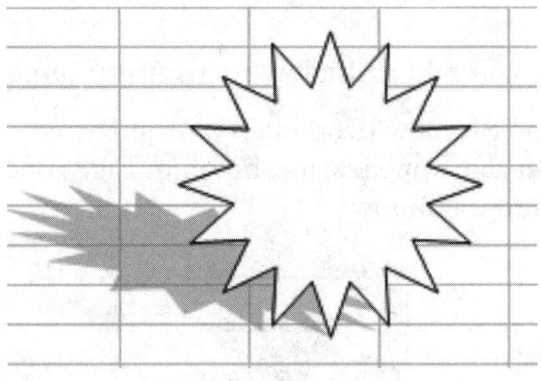

Fig. 1386

By default, the shadow is gray. You can change this. Select Shadow Settings from the Shadow Style dropdown, as shown in Fig. 1387.

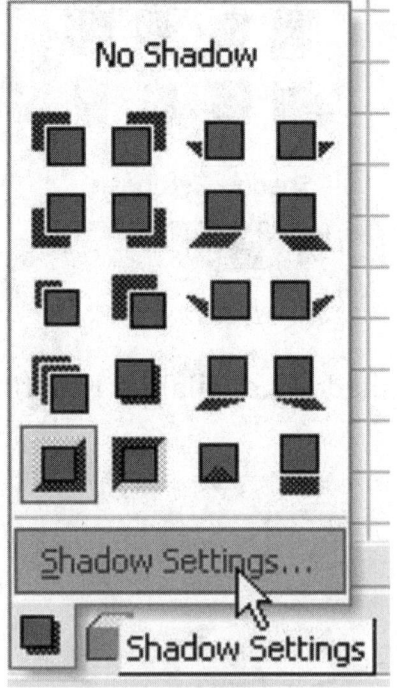

Fig. 1387

As shown in Fig. 1388, this will display the Shadow Settings toolbar.

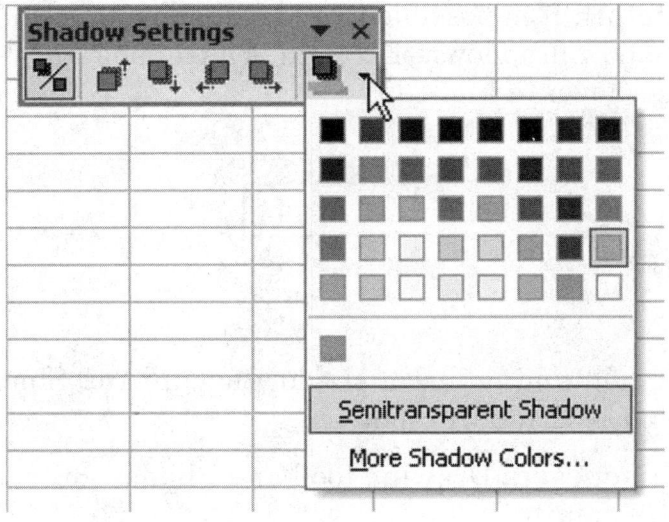

Fig. 1388

You can change the color of the shadow in this toolbar. In addition, there are four buttons that allow you to adjust the x and y offset of the shadow, as shown in Fig. 1389.

Fig. 1389

If you nudge the shadow further up and to the left, it gives the impression that the shape is floating above the page, as shown in Fig. 1390.

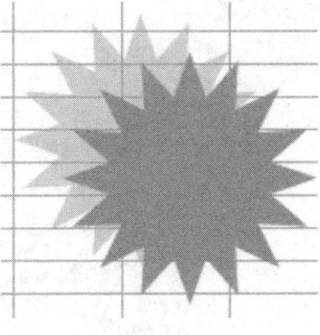

Fig. 1390

Additional Detail: It is possible to add a shadow to a cell. Select a cell and use the shadow dropdown. Excel adds a transparent rectangle with the shadow, as shown in Fig. 1391.

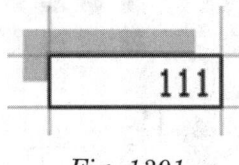

Fig. 1391

Summary: To add and adjust a shadow for an AutoShape, select the Drawing tool bar – Shadow dropdown.

Commands Discussed: Drawing toolbar – Shadow dropdown; Shadow AutoShape – Customize

ADD A 3-D EFFECT TO AN AUTOSHAPE

Problem: How do I add a 3-D effect to an AutoShape?

Strategy: From the Drawing toolbar, select the 3-D dropdown. As shown in Fig. 1392, there are a variety of 3-D effects available.

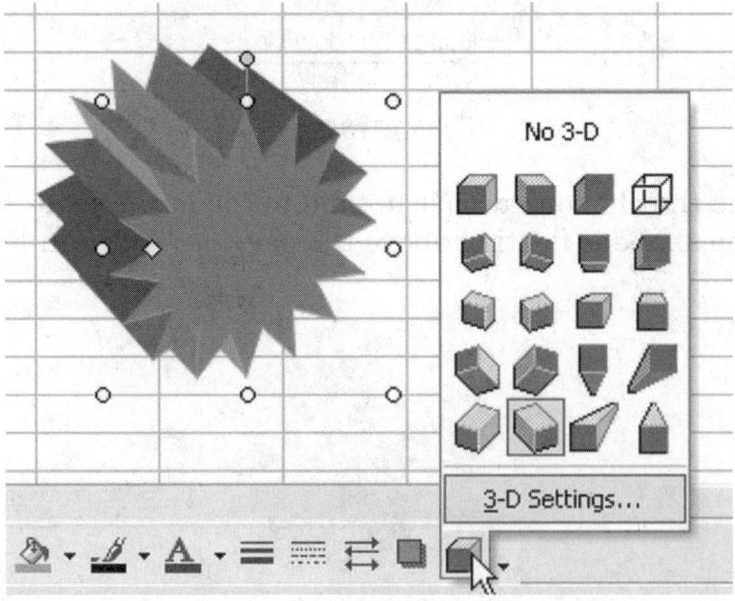

Fig. 1392

I realize this is Excel and not PhotoShop, but you still have a fair amount of control. Choose the 3-D settings button from the dropdown to display the 3-D Settings toolbar, as shown in Fig. 1393.

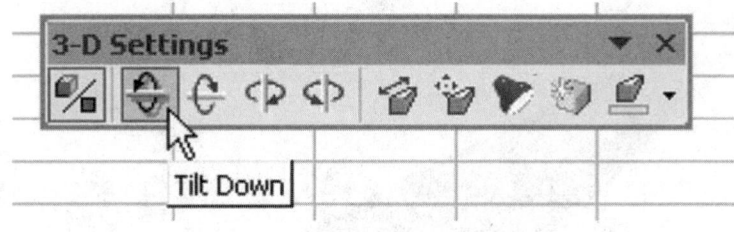

Fig. 1393

The first icon turns the 3-D effect on or off. The next four icons control the tilt and rotation of the effect. Each click on the Tilt or Rotate icons rotates the shape five degrees.

The depth icon controls the depth of the 3-D effect. You can choose from presets or enter a custom value from 9600 to –600, as shown in Fig. 1394.

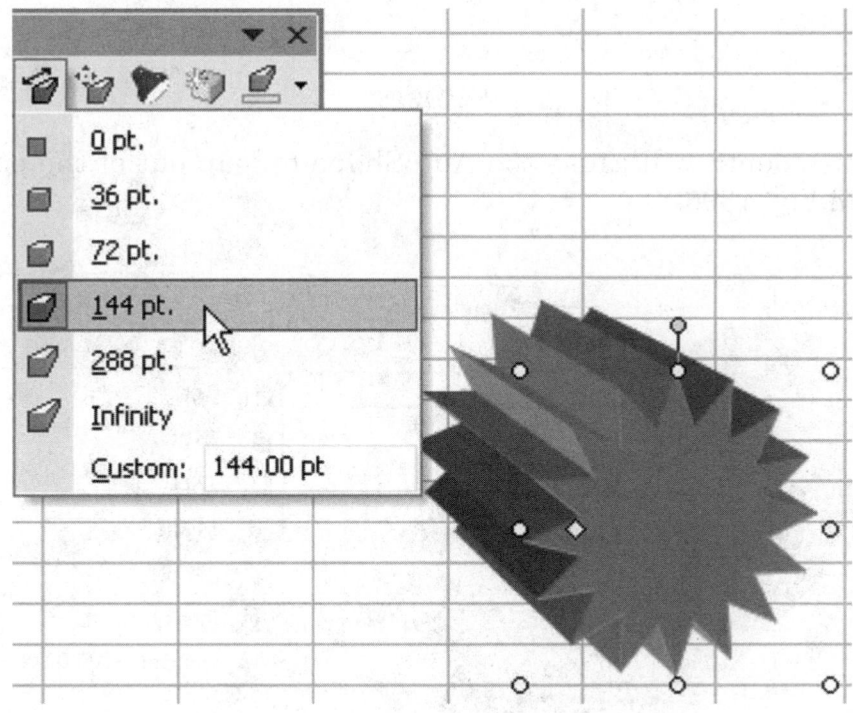

Fig. 1394

As shown in Fig. 1395, a depth setting of 9600 is like choosing Infinity on the dropdown.

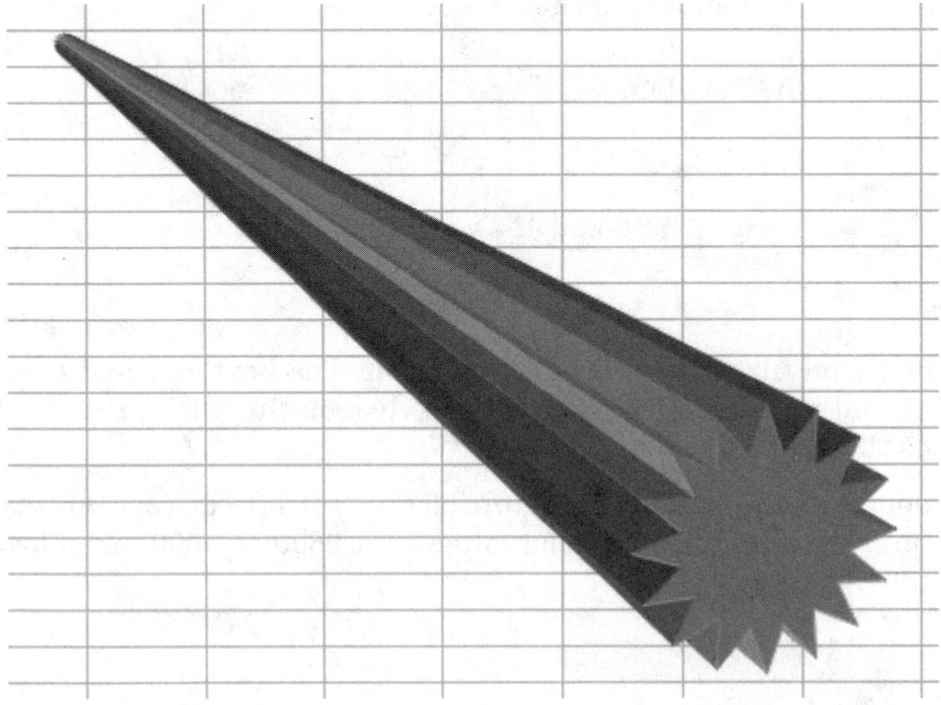

Fig. 1395

A negative depth will cause the AutoShape to leap out of the page, as shown in Fig. 1396.

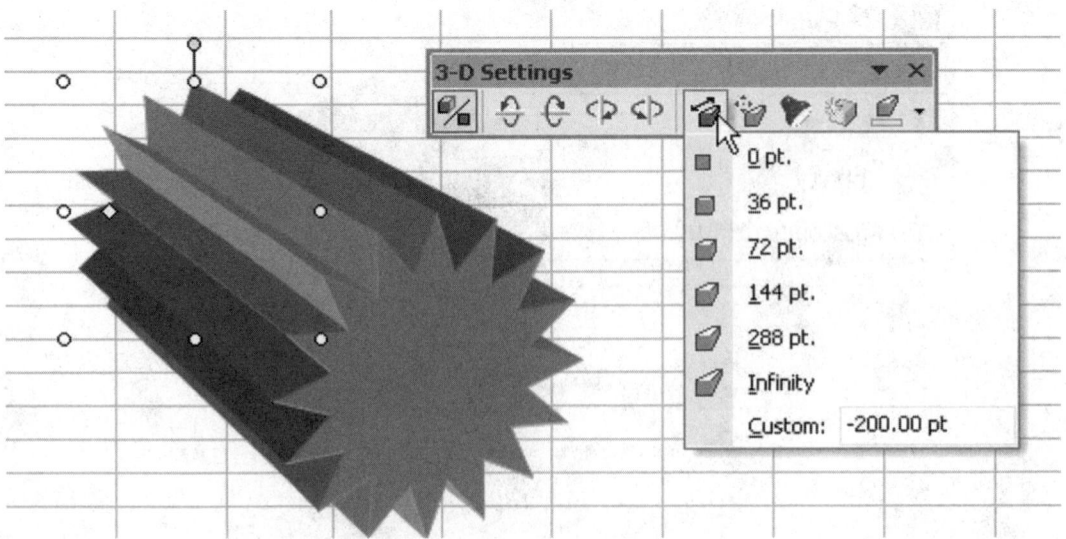

Fig. 1396

As shown in Fig. 1397, there are nine directional choices.

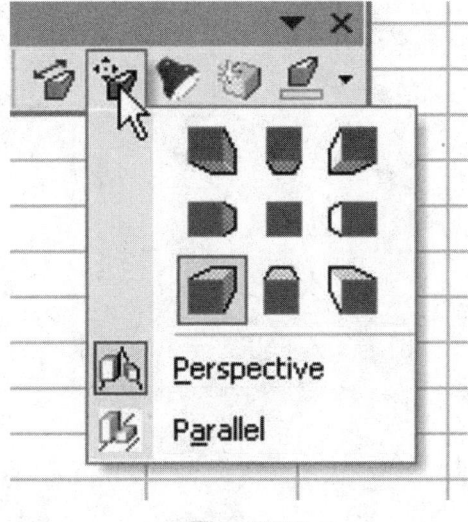

Fig. 1397

For Lighting, you can place one light in one of eight locations, as shown in Fig. 1398. Only the Bright light seems to have a noticeable effect. With the Normal or Dim light, you will barely be able to see the object.

Part IV

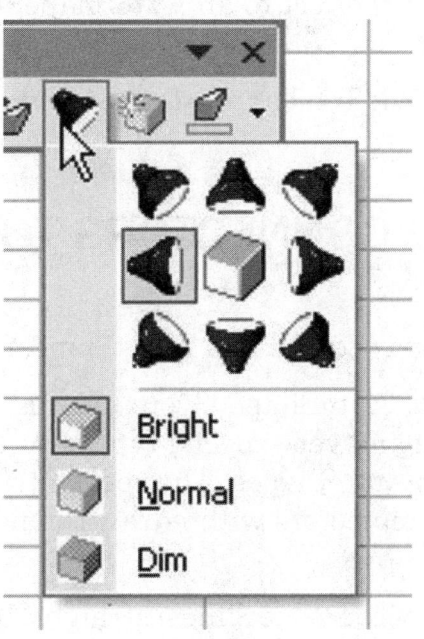

Fig. 1398

As shown in Fig. 1399, the Surface icon offers Matte, Plastic, Metal, or Wire Frame options.

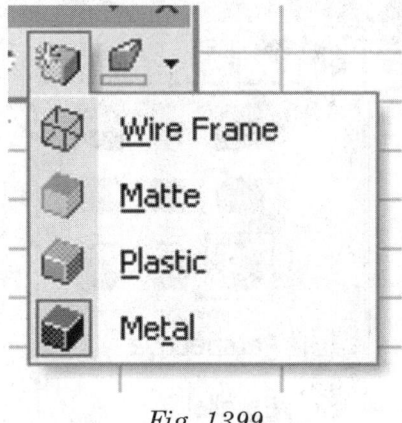

Fig. 1399

The 3-D color changes the color of the 3-D effect. If you have a yellow star and make the 3-D effect orange, then the face of the AutoShape is yellow while the 3-D surface is orange.

Gotcha: Once you select a 3-D effect, the shadow options are removed. You cannot have both a Shadow and 3-D.

Summary: To add a 3-D effect to an AutoShape, use the 3-D dropdown on the Drawing toolbar.

Commands Discussed: Toolbar – 3-D dropdown

ADD CONNECTORS TO JOIN SHAPES

Problem: Is there a way to join two AutoShapes?

Strategy: One of the AutoShape flyout menus is called Connectors. These are an amazing and very special type of AutoShapes. A connector is designed to join two AutoShapes. The special trick is that as you move the AutoShapes, the connectors will redraw themselves to keep the connection intact.

There are three types of connector lines: straight, bent, and curved. Each type is available with no arrows, one arrow, or two arrows.

1)   Draw two AutoShapes on your worksheet. Make sure that neither AutoShape is selected. From the AutoShapes dropdown, select a connector, as shown in Fig. 1400.

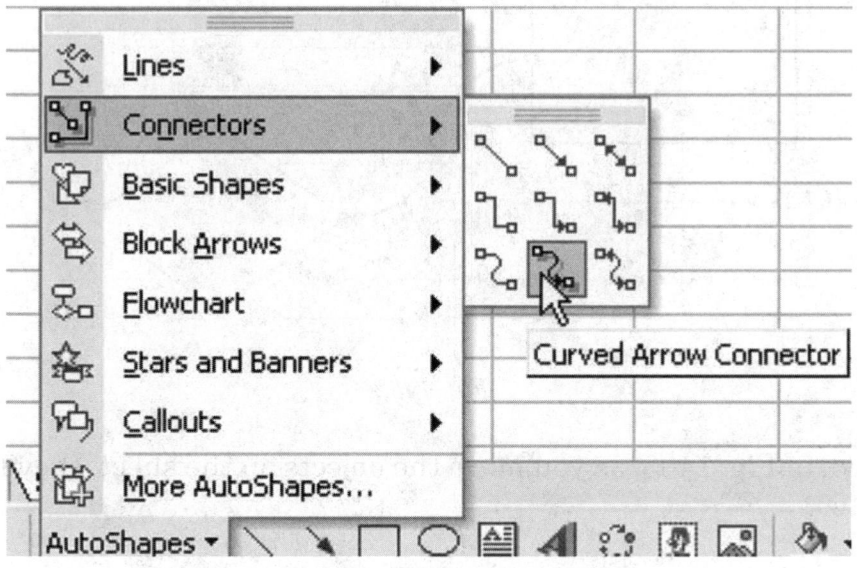

Fig. 1400

2)   You must start at one of four connector points on an AutoShape. Hover the mouse over the AutoShape to show the four connection points, as shown in Fig. 1401.

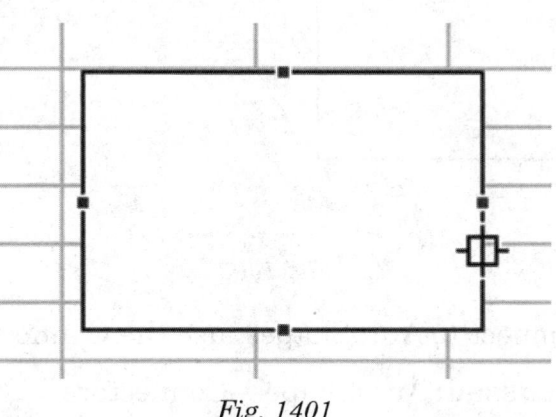

Fig. 1401

3)   Click on one connector point and drag towards another AutoShape.

Part
IV

When you get near another object, the mouse will jump to one of the connector points on the other object, as shown in Fig. 1402.

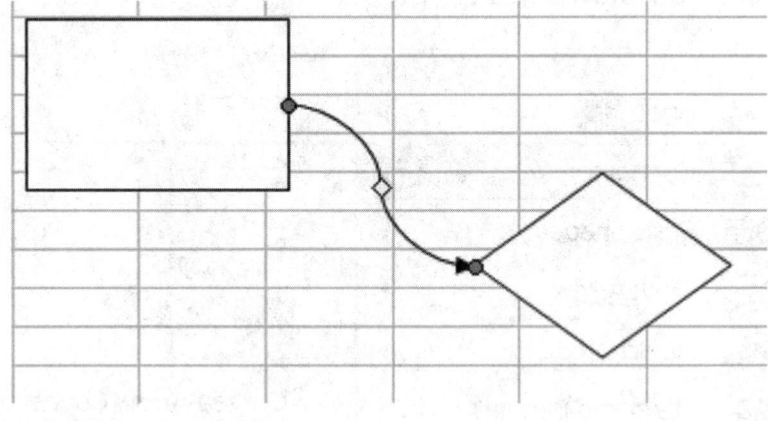

Fig. 1402

As shown in Fig. 1403, as you move the objects on the sheet, they remain connected.

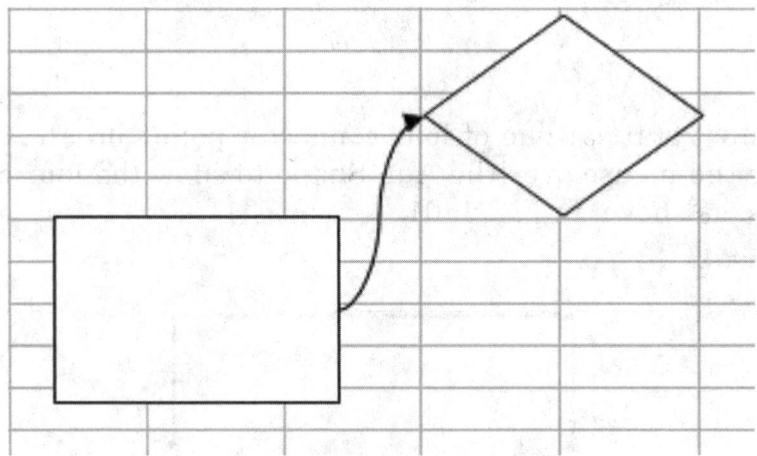

Fig. 1403

Summary: To connect to AutoShapes, use the Connector flyout menu.

Commands Discussed: AutoShape – Connectors

JOIN TWO AUTOSHAPES

Problem: Sometimes, you may want to have a few AutoShapes that are connected as a group. That way, when you move one AutoShape, they will all move together.

Strategy: Group the AutoShapes. Using the mouse, select one AutoShape. Hold down the Ctrl key while you click on additional AutoShapes. Select Draw – Group from the Drawing toolbar, as shown in Fig. 1404.

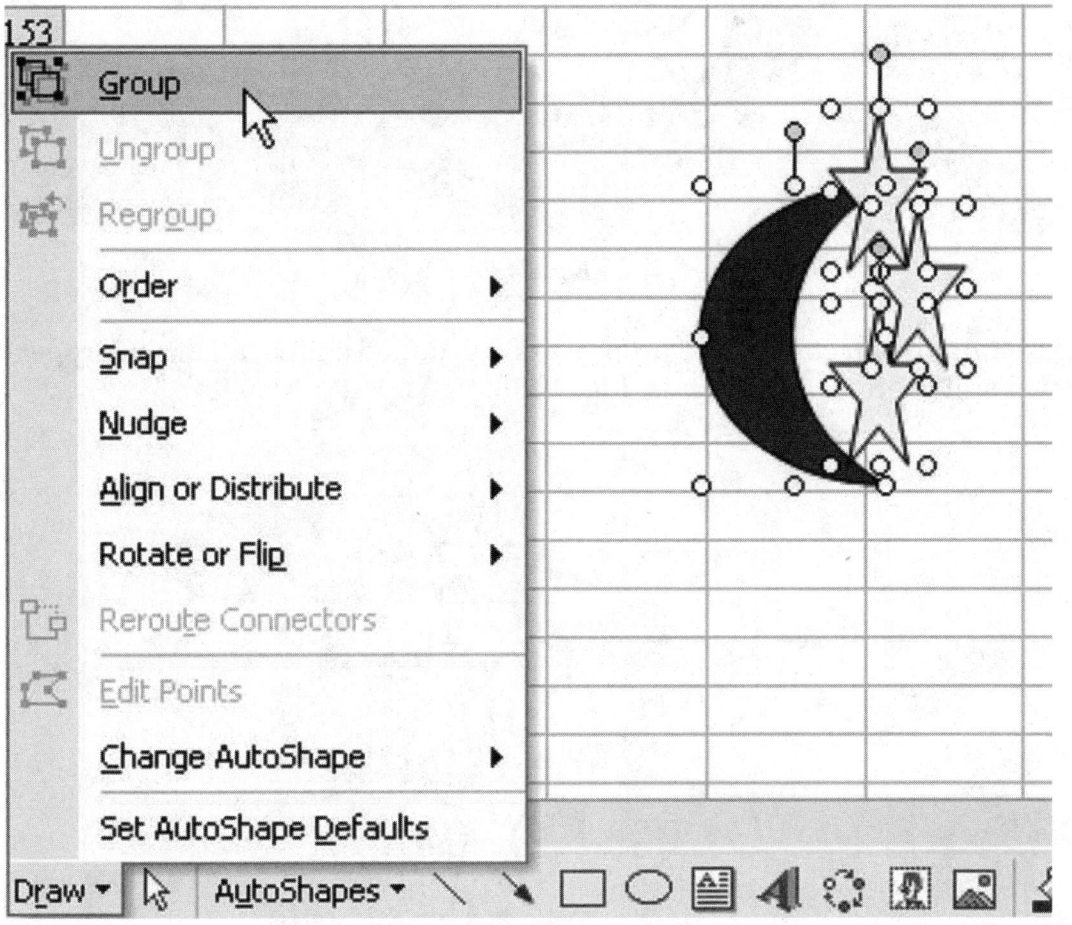

Fig. 1404

Part
IV

Result: When you select the shape and move it, all of the grouped shapes will move, as shown in Fig. 1405.

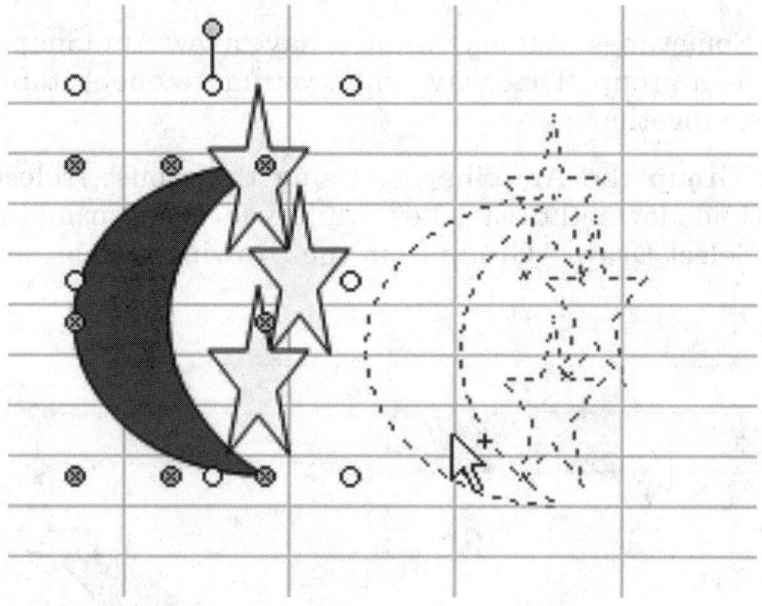

Fig. 1405

Gotcha: If you change the property of a grouped shape, all of the properties will change, as shown in Fig. 1406.

Fig. 1406

Summary: To group AutoShapes together, select an AutoShape and, while holding the Ctrl key down, select the other AutoShapes to be grouped, and then use Draw – Group.

Commands Discussed: Draw – Group

CHANGE PROPERTIES OF
ONLY ONE AUTOSHAPE IN A GROUP

Problem: You've grouped AutoShapes so that they will move together. Now you need to change the properties of only one of the shapes. If you try to change the properties, all of the shapes will inherit the new property, as shown in Fig. 1407.

Fig. 1407

Part
IV

Strategy: Choose the grouped shapes. From the toolbar select Draw–Ungroup, as shown in Fig. 1408.

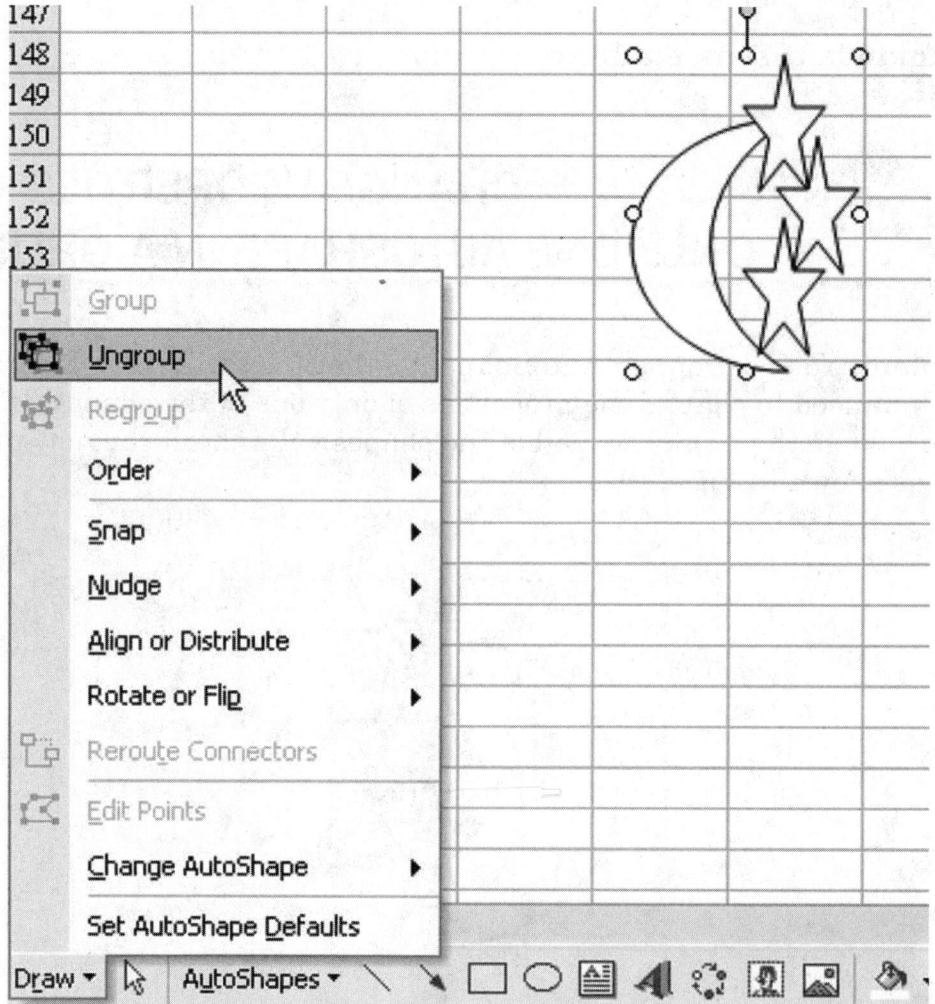

Fig. 1408

Select the one shape to change and change any attributes. With the shapes still selected, choose Draw – Regroup, as shown in Fig. 1409. The original set of shapes will be grouped again.

Fig. 1409

Summary: To change the attributes of only one shape in a group, select Draw – Ungroup, change the desired shape's attributes, and then choose Draw – Regroup.

Commands Discussed: Draw – Ungroup; Draw – Regroup

WHEN TWO AUTOSHAPES OVERLAP, CONTROL WHICH IS ON TOP

Problem: You need one AutoShape to partially overlap another AutoShape. By default, the newer shape will appear on top of the older shape. In Fig. 1410, the starburst was drawn first and then the rectangle was added.

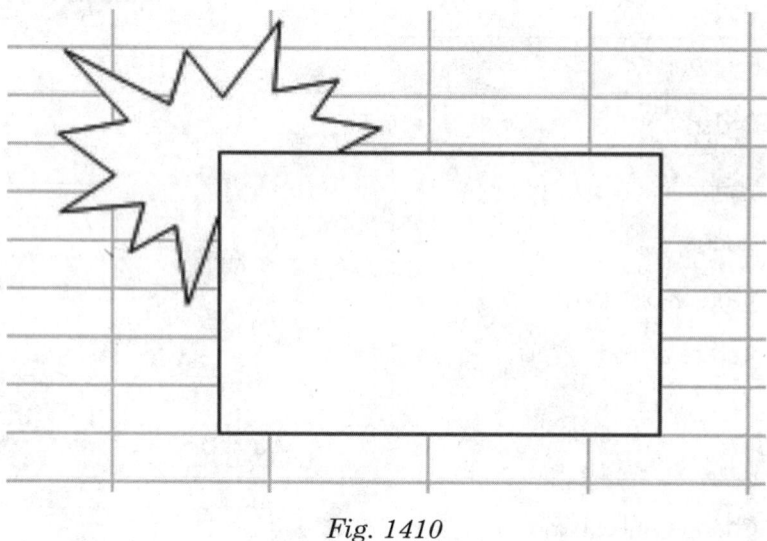

Fig. 1410

Strategy: To bring a shape in front of another shape, follow these steps:

1) Select the shape to move forward.

2) From the Draw menu on the Drawing toolbar, select Order – Bring to Front, as shown in Fig. 1411.

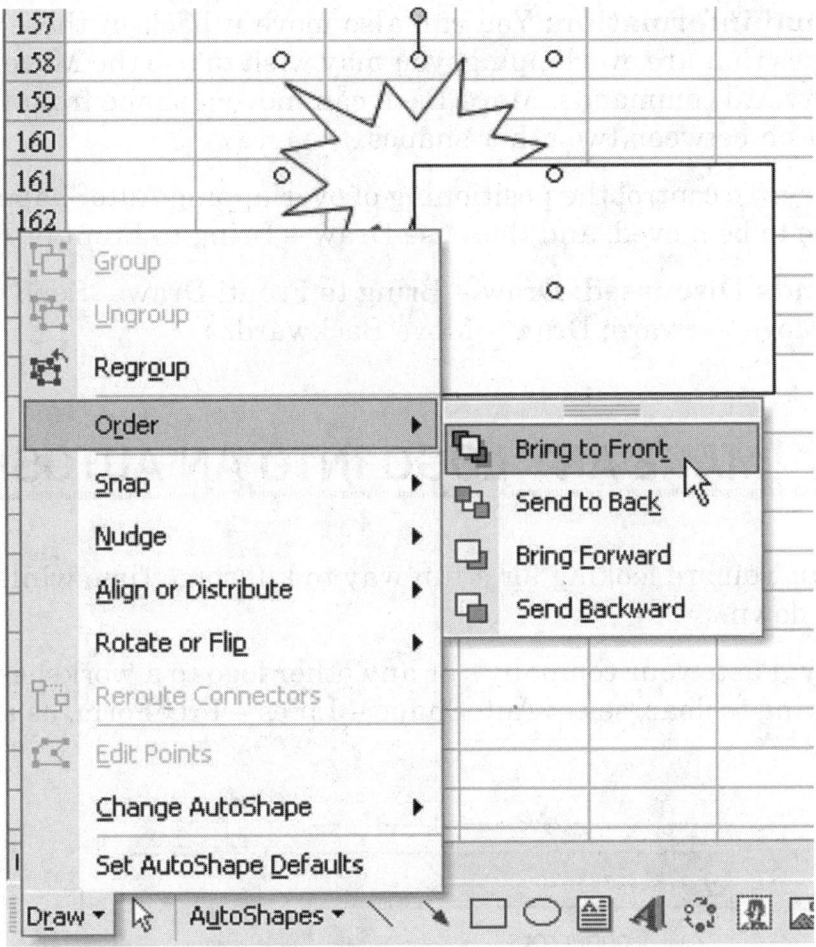

Fig. 1411

Result: As shown in Fig. 1412, the selected shape will appear in front of all other shapes.

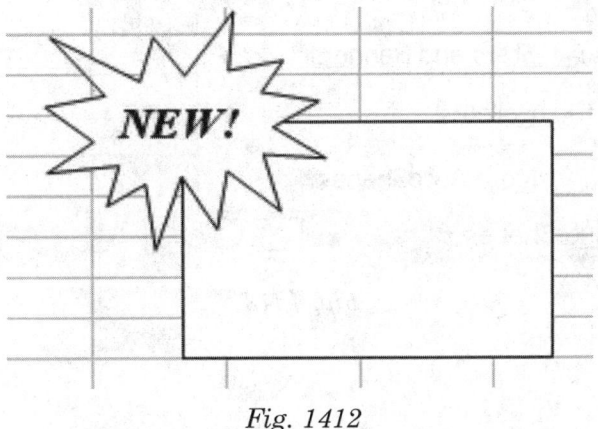

Fig. 1412

Additional information: You can also move it back. If there are several shapes that are overlapping, you may wish to use the Move Back or Move Forward commands. Move Back can move a shape from the front to a position between two other shapes.

Summary: To control the positioning of overlapping AutoShapes, select the shape to be moved, and then use Draw – Bring to Front or Back.

Commands Discussed: Draw – Bring to Front; Draw – Send to Back; Draw – Move Forward; Draw – Move Backward.

MAKE ANY LOGO INTO AN AUTOSHAPE

Problem: You are looking for a fun way to kill some time while the Internet is down.

Strategy: Paste your company's or any other logo to a worksheet. From the Drawing toolbar, select AutoShape – Lines – FreeForm, as shown in Fig. 1413.

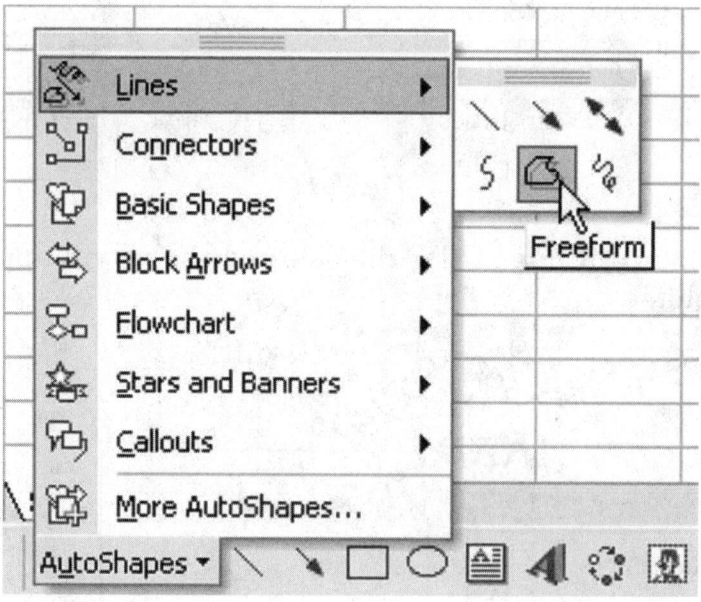

Fig. 1413

This is great for drawing straight lines. Trace your company logo. Start at one corner of the logo. Click on the corner, as shown in Fig. 1414.

Fig. 1414

As shown in Fig. 1415, move the mouse to the next corner and click again.

Fig. 1415

Continue clicking at each corner. When you get back to the original corner of the logo, click again and the AutoShape will appear, as shown in Fig. 1416.

Fig. 1416

You can now move, color, re-size, and rotate the AutoShape. As shown in Fig. 1417, here is Max Cell with a little color and 3-D added in.

Fig. 1417

Result: You will have an AutoShape of your logo that you can resize or shrink to your heart's content.

Summary: Use the Freeform AutoShape tool to draw any angular shape.

Commands Discussed: AutoShape – Lines – FreeForm

USE THE SCRIBBLE TOOL

Problem: Your logo is not an angular logo, like the MrExcel logo. You want to try out the previous technique.

Strategy: As shown in Fig. 1418, there is a Scribble tool in the AutoShape – Lines menu.

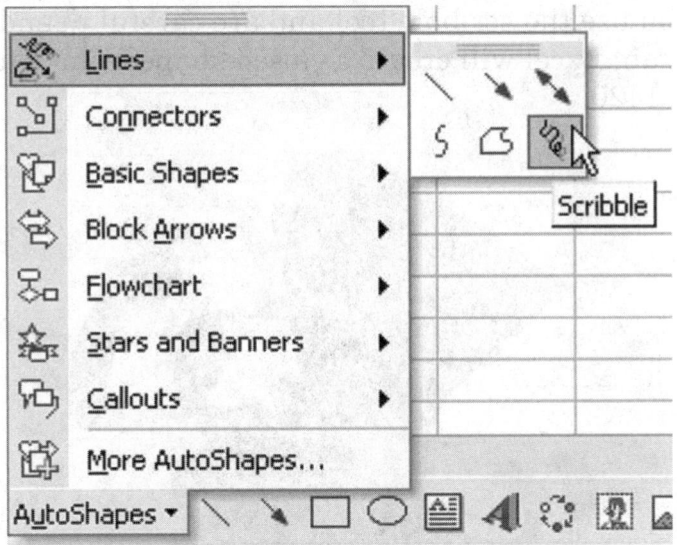

Fig. 1418

With the scribble tool, you can create either a line or a shape. If you scribble and do not close the shape, Excel will create a line, as shown in Fig. 1419.

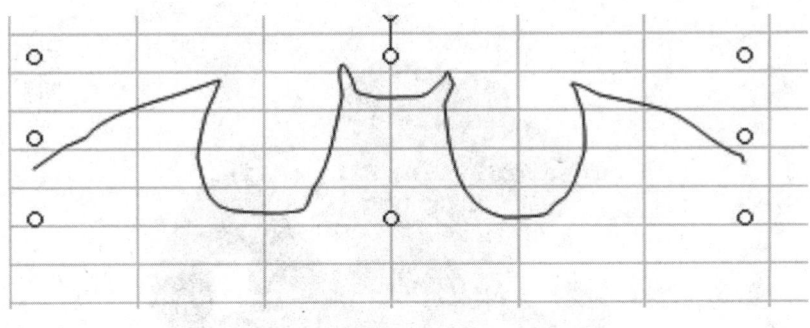

Fig. 1419

Part
IV

However, if you use the scribble tool and are careful to end very near to where you began, Excel will create a closed shape from your scribble, as shown in Fig. 1420.

Fig. 1420

As shown in Fig. 1421, you can then add shadows, color, or 3-D effects to the shape.

Fig. 1421

Summary: Use the Scribble AutoShape tool to draw any shape.

Commands Discussed: AutoShape – Lines – Scribble

PLACE CELL CONTENTS IN AN AUTOSHAPE

Problem: Rather than static text in an AutoShape, you want to display the results of a calculation in the Shape, as shown in Fig. 1422.

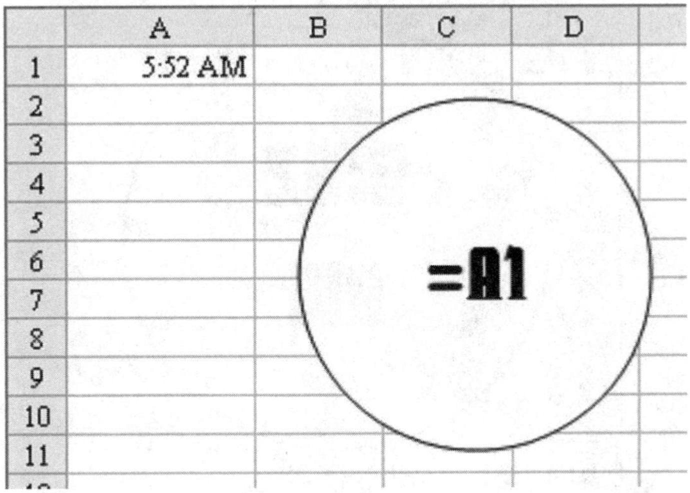

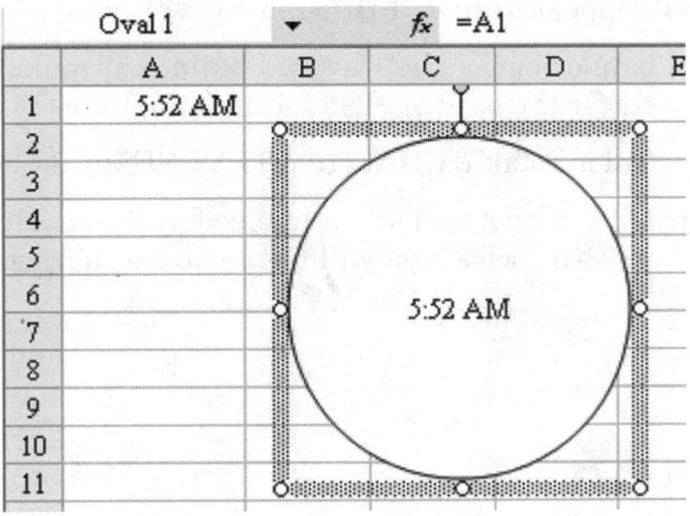

Fig. 1422

Strategy: This is possible, although the method shown in Fig. 1422 is not the way to do it. **Part IV**

1) Select the AutoShape. Click in the formula bar; type =A1, as shown in Fig. 1423. Hit Enter.

Fig. 1423

2)   Format to center and enlarge the text. Right-click the dots sur-
rounding the shape, and then choose Format AutoShape. Use a
large, bold font. Center horizontally and vertically on the Alignment tab, as shown in Fig. 1424.

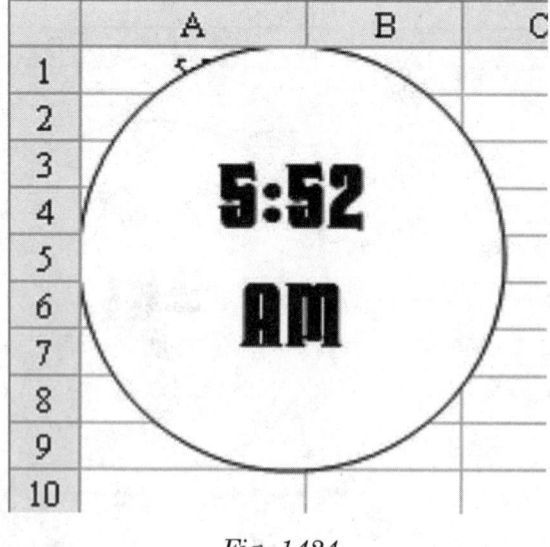

Fig. 1424

Additional Information: The formula in the formula bar can only refer to a single cell. You cannot enter a formula in the formula bar for
an AutoShape. However, there is a workaround. Say that you want to
display today's order total in a banner at the top of an order entry log.
The banner will appear in rows 1 through 4 of the log.

1)   Move the banner out of the way and build a formula in cell D2 to
hold the text for the banner. The formula might be:

="Today's Order Total:"&CHAR(10)&TEXT(SUM(C8:C200),"$#,##0")

The Char(10) function will add a linefeed in the result if Cell wrap
is turned on. Otherwise, you will get a square character, as shown
in Fig. 1425.

	D2	▼		*fx* ="Today's Order Total:"&CHAR(10)&TEXT(SUM(C8:C200),"$#,##0")						
	A	B	C	D	E	F	G	H	I	J
1	XYZ COMPANY									
2	ORDER ENTRY LOG			Today's Order Total:□$2,308						
3	DATE:	12/1/2004								
4										
5										
6										
7	Order #	Rep	Amount							
8	1901	Joe	174							
9	1902	Mary	244							
10	1903	Joe	210							
11	1904	Mary	136							
12	1905	Joe	167							
13	1906	Mary	249							

Fig. 1425

2)   Draw a banner. Select the banner and enter =D2 as the formula for the banner. As shown in Fig. 1426, format the banner to be center-aligned with an interesting font. (This is ParkwayResortHotel from my friends at the Chank! Foundry).

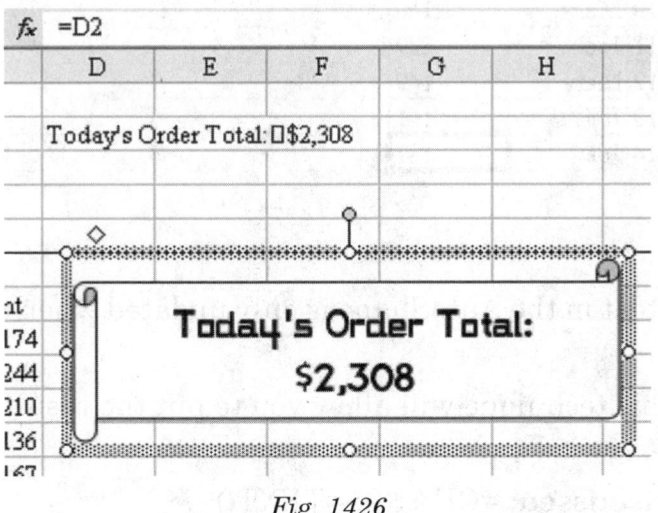

Fig. 1426

3)   Finally, move the banner so that it covers the formula in D2. As new orders are entered in the log, the total will update, as shown in Fig. 1427.

	A	B	C	D	E	F	G	
1	XYZ COMPANY							
2	ORDER ENTRY LOG			Today's Order Total:				
3	DATE:	12/1/2004						
4				$2,495				
5								
6								
7	Order #	Rep	Amount					
8	1901	Joe	174					
9	1902	Mary	244					
10	1903	Joe	210					
11	1904	Mary	136					
12	1905	Joe	167					
13	1906	Mary	249					
14	1907	Joe	215					
15	1908	Mary	137					
16	1909	Joe	117					
17	1910	Mary	140					
18	1911	Joe	229					
19	1912	Mary	149					
20	1913	Joe	141					
21	1914	Joe	187					

Fig. 1427

Gotcha: The text in the AutoShape is only updated when the worksheet is calculated.

Summary: This technique will allow you to put the results of a cell into an AutoShape.

Functions Discussed: =CHAR(); =TEXT()

DRAW BUSINESS DIAGRAMS WITH EXCEL

Problem: Your manager needs you to graphically document the steps in a project plan, as shown in Fig. 1428.

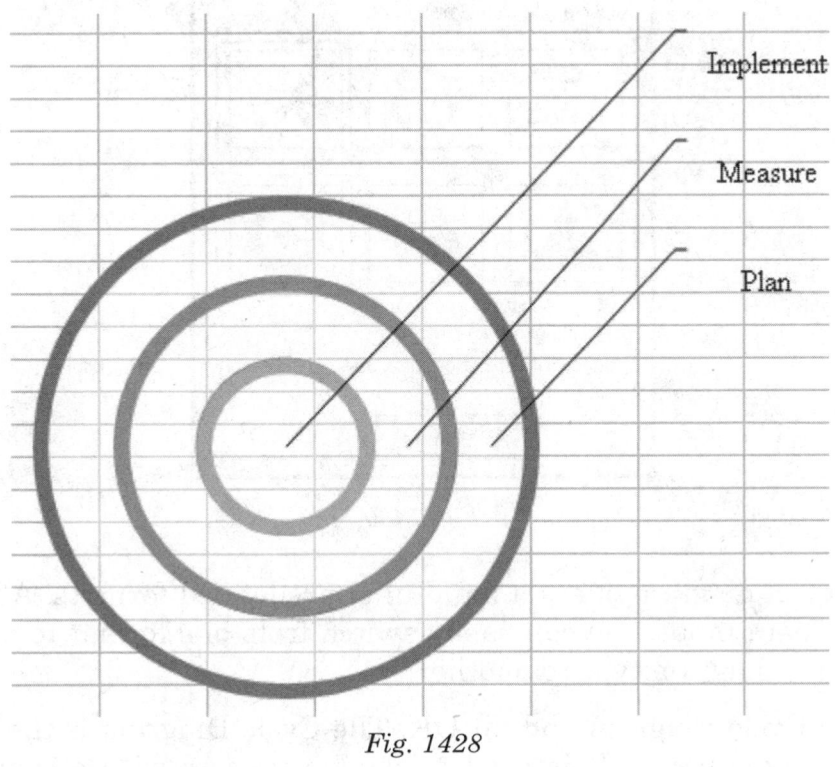

Fig. 1428

Strategy: Excel offers five fairly sophisticated tools for creating certain types of business diagrams. All five types are accessed from either the Insert – Diagram option on the menu or from this icon on the Drawing toolbar, as shown in Fig. 1429.

Fig. 1429

Ignoring the OrgChart option for now, the other five types are all some-what interchangeable. As shown in Fig. 1430, these are the diagram types available: Cycle, Radial, Pyramid, Venn, and Target.

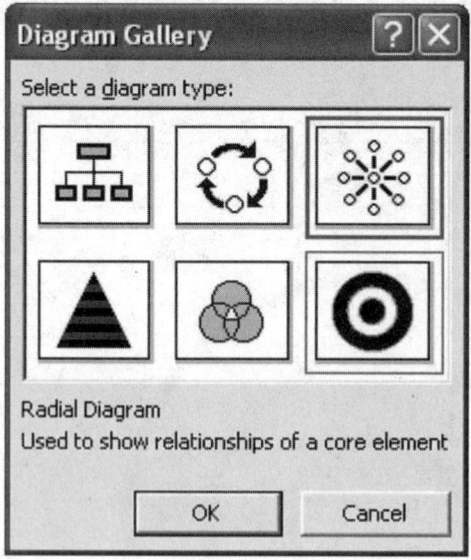

Fig. 1430

Each type of diagram offers a handful of predefined formats. After you have the data input, you can easily switch from one format to another, or from one diagram type to another.

Choose a Cycle Diagram and hit OK. The Cycle Diagram is the middle choice in the top row. It is used to show a process with a continuous cycle.

A default diagram draws with three steps. Each step says "Click to Add Text". Click in the first text box and type "Identify Opportunities for Improvement", as shown in Fig. 1431.

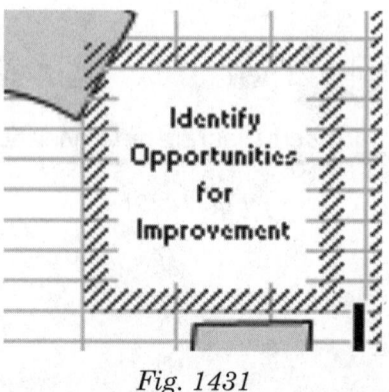

Fig. 1431

The next step is "Identify Root Causes". The third step is "Identify Possible Solutions". At this point, you need to add a fourth and a fifth step. As shown in Fig. 1432, in the Diagram toolbar, choose Insert Shape to add a fourth step. Choose this button a second time to add a fifth option.

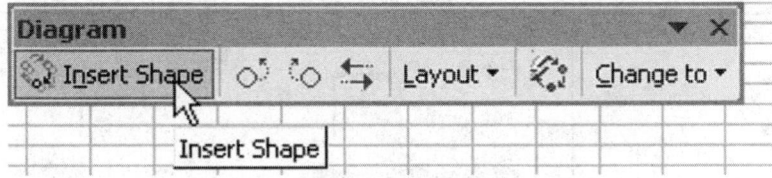

Fig. 1432

Type the text for the fourth and fifth steps. You will have a basic default diagram, as shown in Fig. 1433.

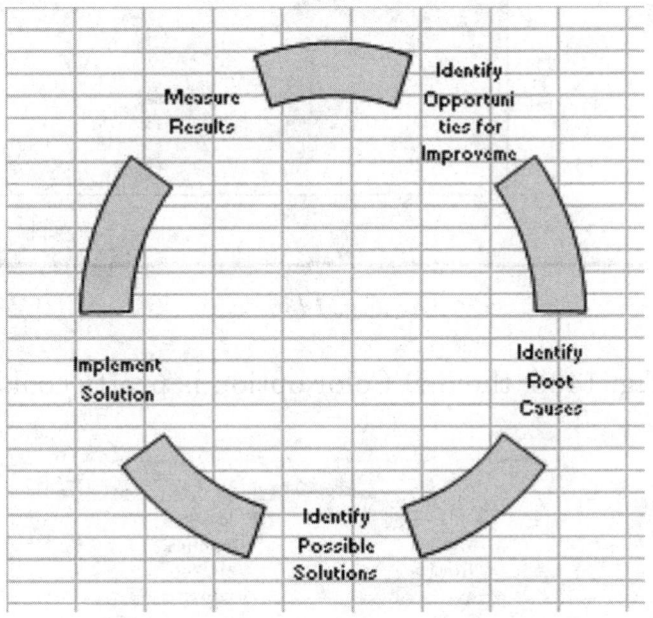

Fig. 1433

As shown in Fig. 1434, choose the AutoFormat button in the Diagram toolbar.

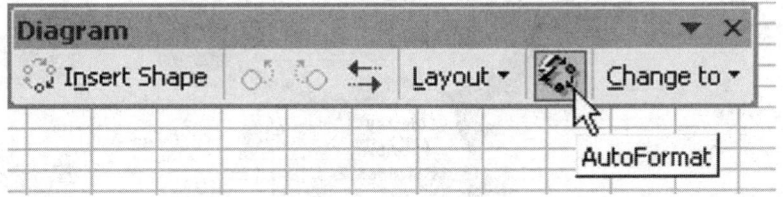

Fig. 1434

You will have ten options to choose from, as shown in Fig. 1435.

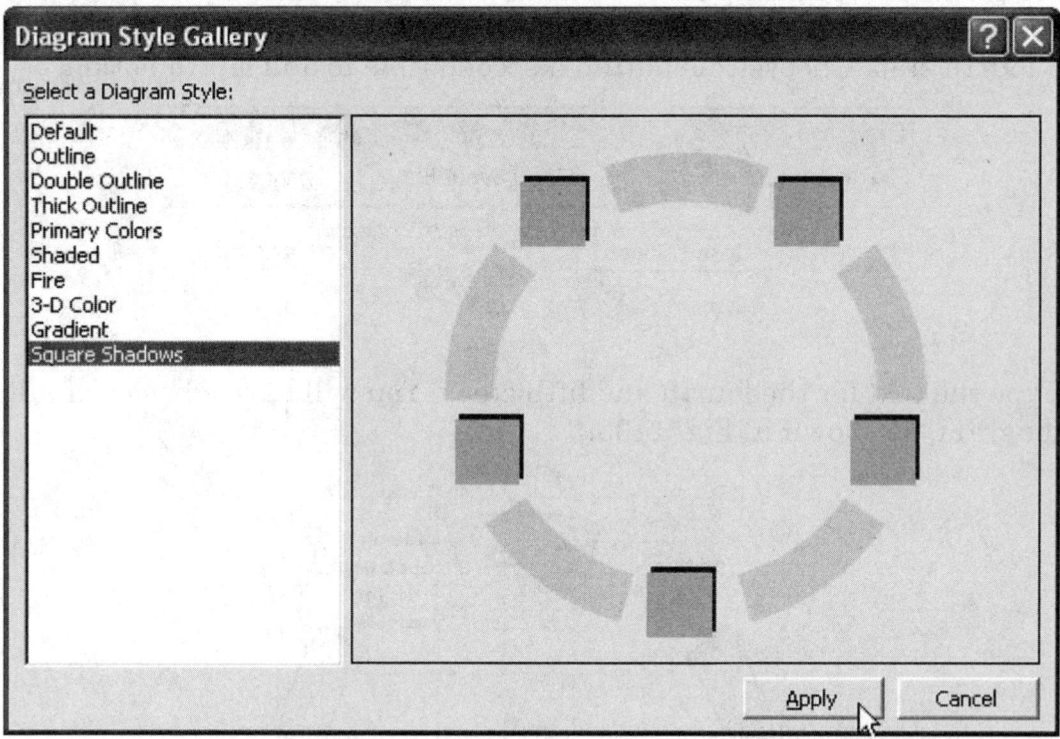

Fig. 1435

As shown in Fig. 1436, the 3-D Color option is pretty cool.

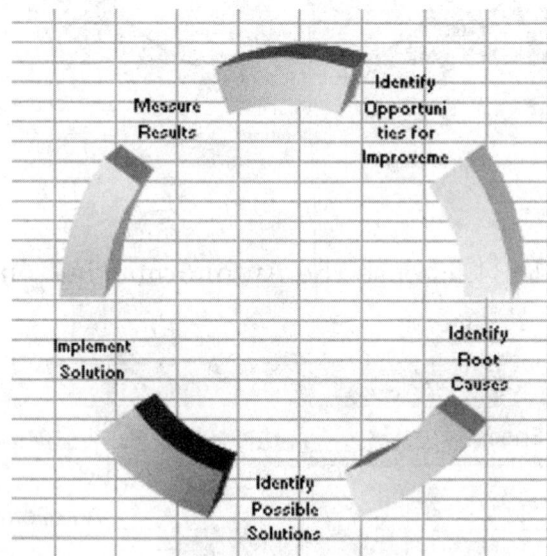

Fig. 1436

After you have a diagram set up, you can see how this data would look in another diagram type. As shown in Fig. 1437, from the Diagram toolbar, select the Change To dropdown to change between the five types.

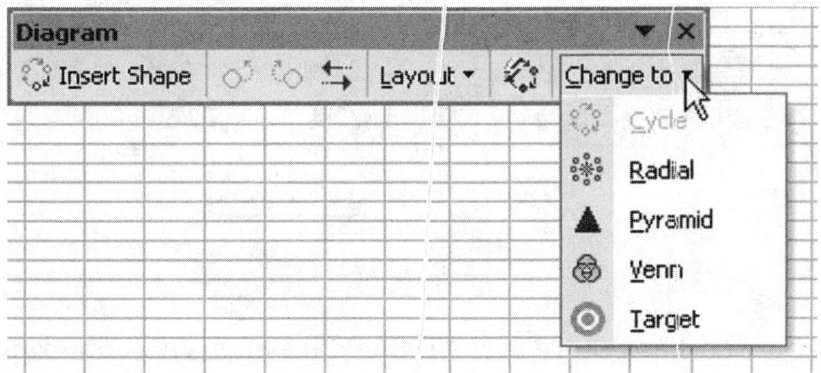

Fig. 1437

As shown in Fig. 1438, here is the same data on a Target chart.

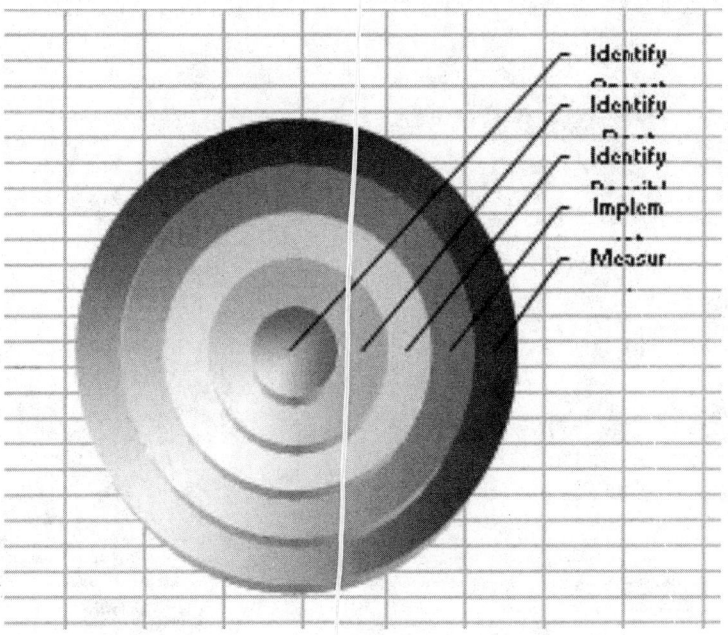

Part IV

Fig. 1438

In a Target chart, the innermost circle is supposed to be the final step in the process. In this case, you need to reverse the order of the rings. Use the Reverse Diagram button on the Diagram toolbar, as shown in Fig. 1439.

Diagram
Insert Shape
Layout
Change to
Reverse Diagram

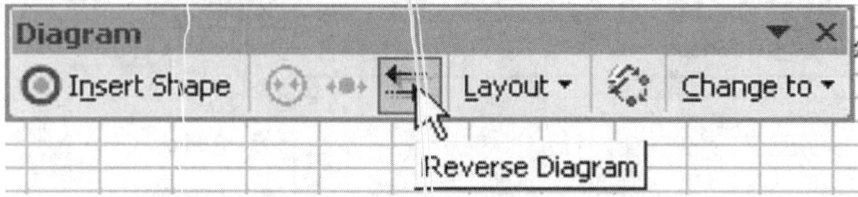

Fig. 1439

As shown in Fig. 1440, here is the same data on a Venn diagram.

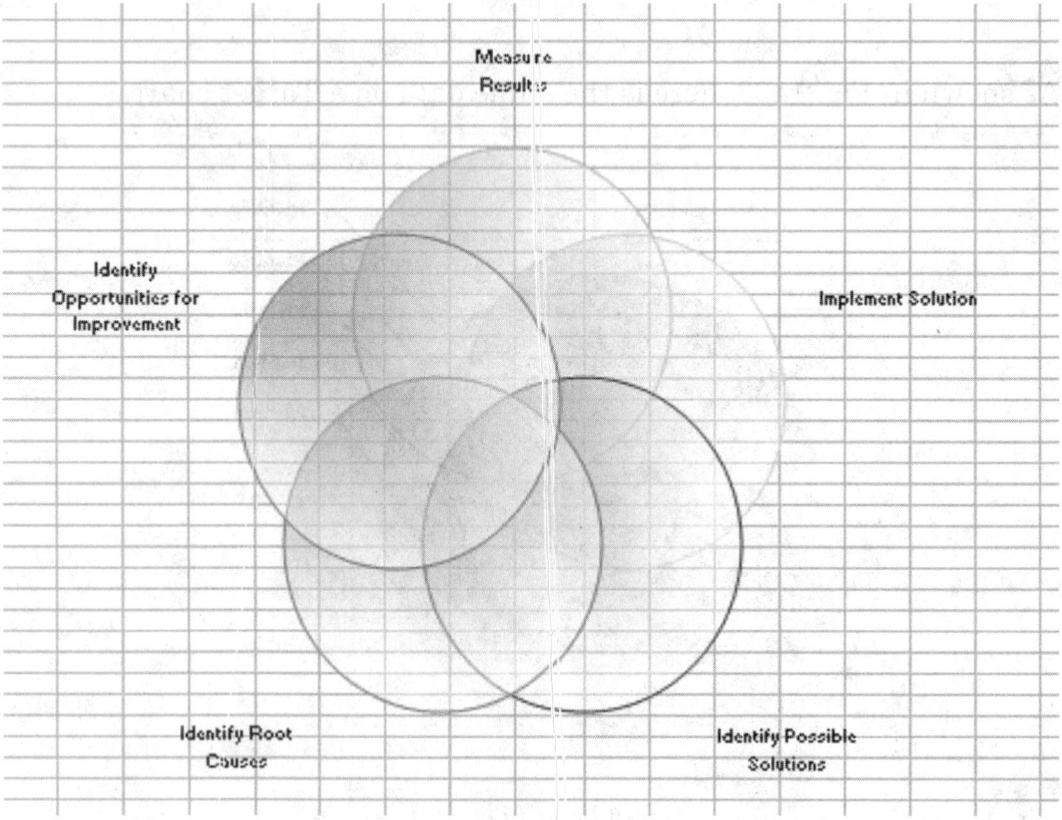

Measure Results
Identify Opportunities for Improvement
Implement Solution
Identify Root Causes
Identify Possible Solutions

Fig. 1440

Here is a Pyramid diagram, as shown in Fig. 1441.

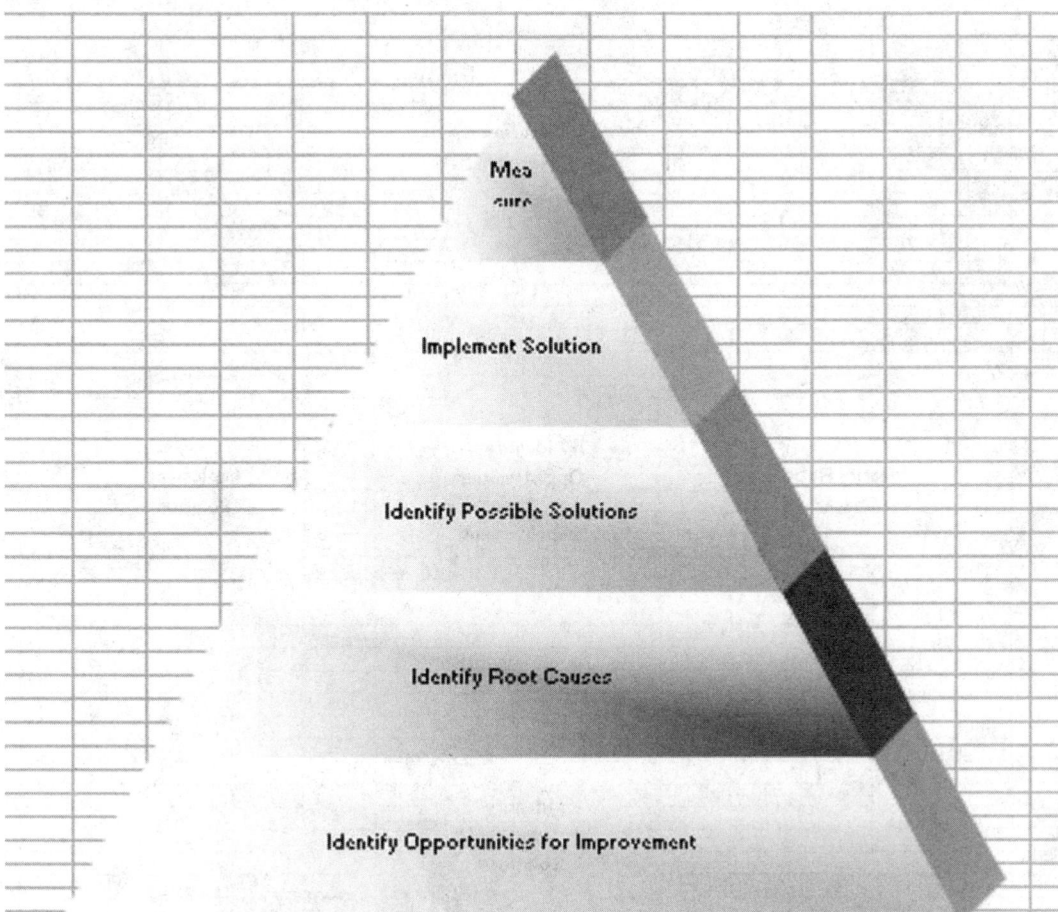

Fig. 1441

And, finally, a Radial diagram, as shown in Fig. 1442.

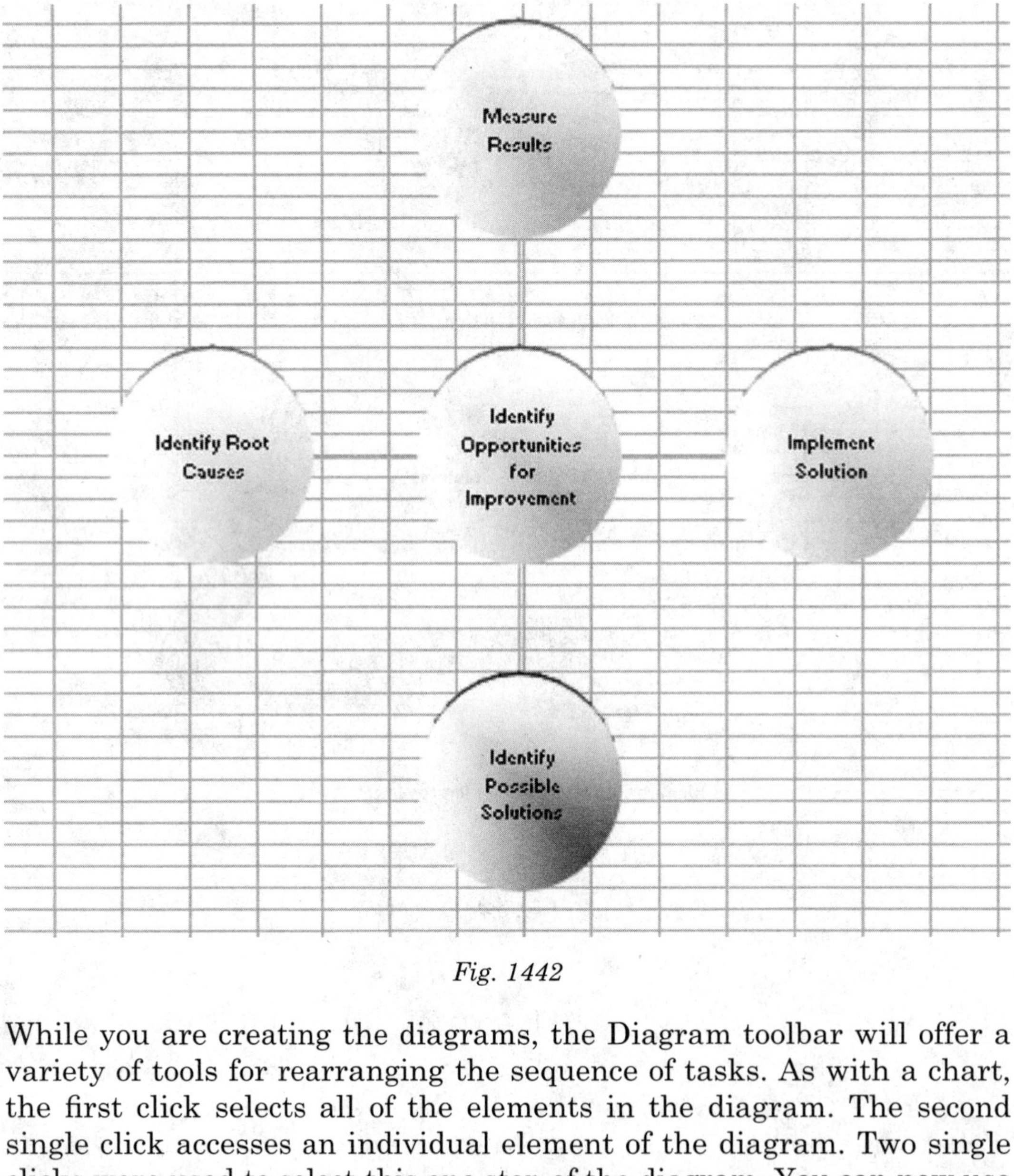

Measure
Results

Identify Root
Causes

Identify
Opportunities
for
Improvement

Implement
Solution

Identify
Possible
Solutions

Fig. 1442

While you are creating the diagrams, the Diagram toolbar will offer a variety of tools for rearranging the sequence of tasks. As with a chart, the first click selects all of the elements in the diagram. The second single click accesses an individual element of the diagram. Two single clicks were used to select this one step of the diagram. You can now use the Move Shape Forward or Move Shape Backward icons on the toolbar, as shown in Fig. 1443.

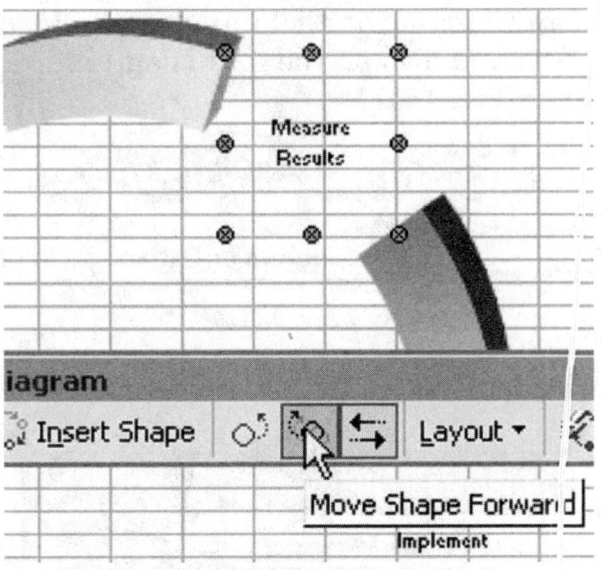

Fig. 1443

Gotcha: Excel will frequently truncate longer text entries in business diagrams. You will have to adjust the font sizes or shorten your words.

Summary: The five business diagrams on the Drawing toolbar are all interchangeable with each other. They each offer ten unique AutoFormats, making for the possibility of 50 different looking diagrams.

Commands Discussed: Insert – Diagram

Part
IV

DRAW ORG CHARTS WITH EXCEL

Problem: As shown in Fig. 1444, Excel offers a nice utility for drawing organizational charts, but you want to know more about it.

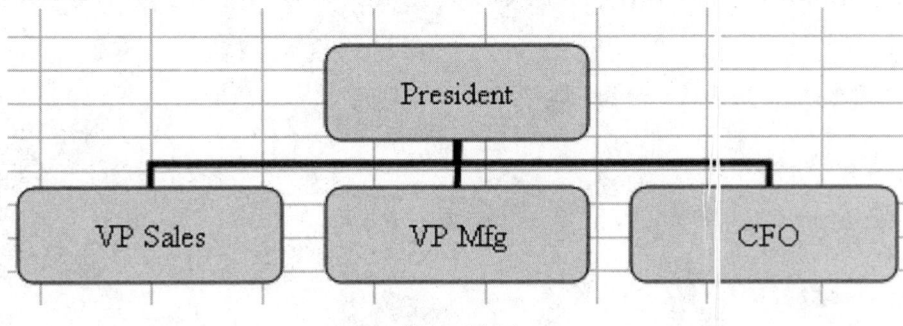

Fig. 1444

Strategy: The Org Chart utility is located in the Insert – Diagram selection on the menu and also on the Add Diagram icon on the Drawing toolbar, as shown in Fig. 1445.

Fig. 1445

In the Diagram Gallery, select Org Chart, as shown in Fig. 1446.

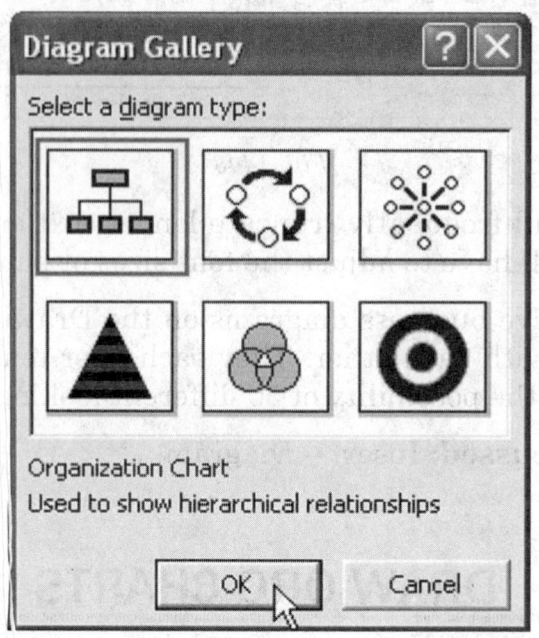

Fig. 1446

As shown in Fig. 1447, Excel will draw a default Org Chart with three branches below a main branch. Click in any box to change the text.

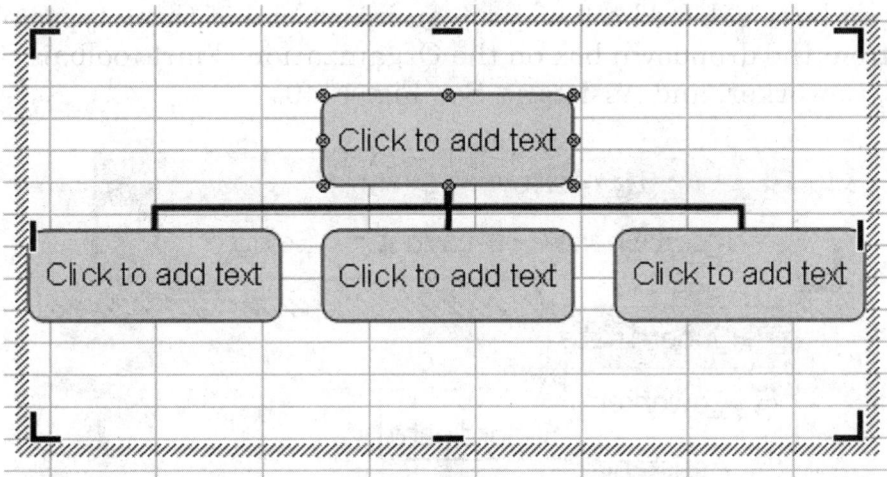

Fig. 1447

The chart can be expanded. Select one of the boxes in the diagram, as shown in Fig. 1448. With the first click, the text box will be selected and it will be surrounded with diagonal lines. With the second click, the box itself will be selected.

Tip *You can replace the two single clicks with a Ctrl+Click.*

Part IV

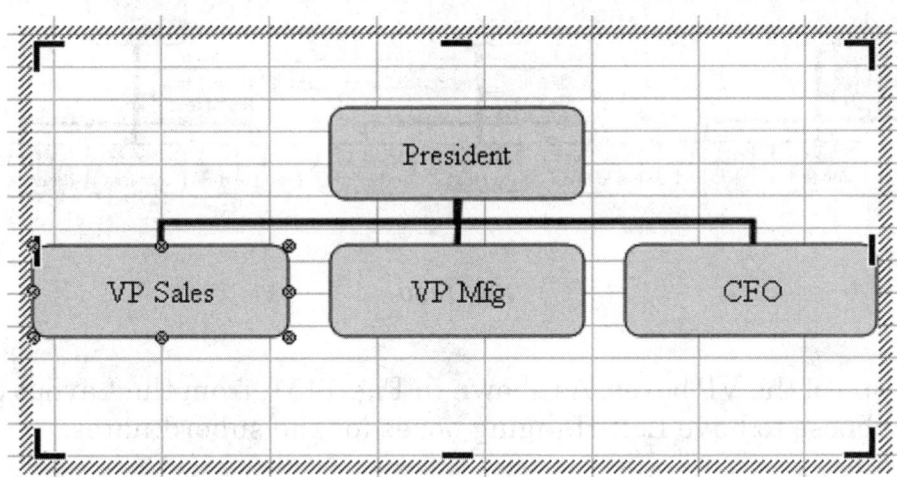

Fig. 1448

After you have selected a box, you can insert one of three types of new boxes from the dropdown box on the Organization Chart toolbar: Subordinate, Coworker, and Assistant. See Fig. 1449.

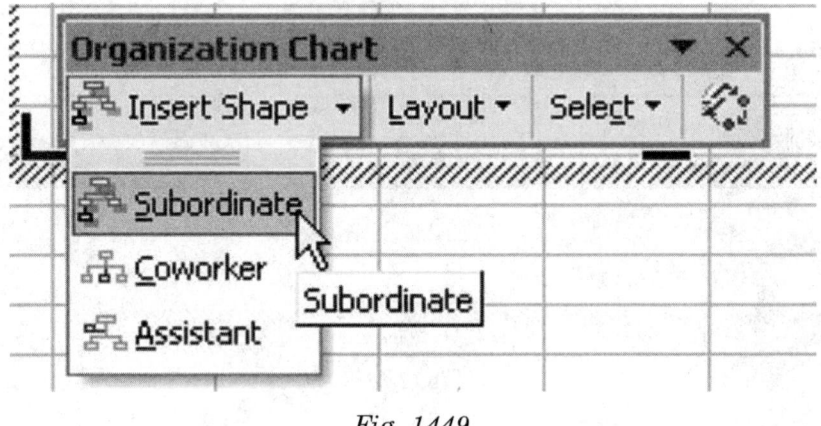

Fig. 1449

This chart has three subordinates and one assistant added to each VP. The chart is starting to get fairly wide, as shown in Fig. 1450.

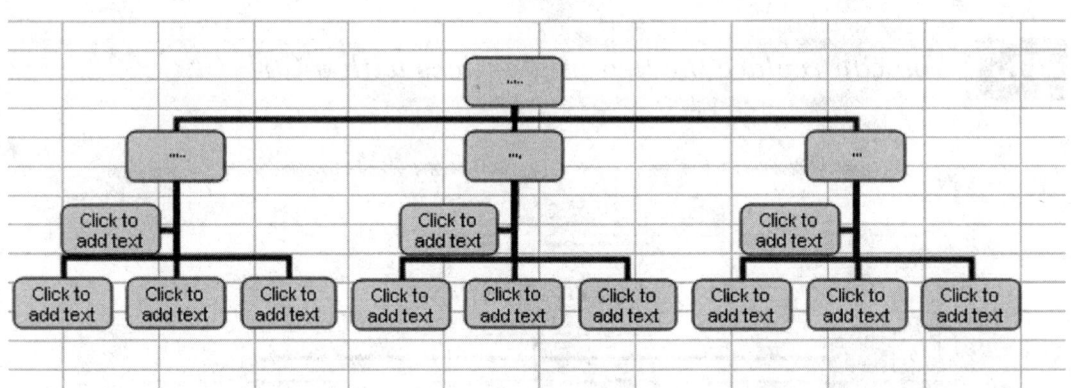

Fig. 1450

Select one of the VP boxes. As shown in Fig. 1451, from the Layout dropdown, choose to have Left Hanging boxes for the subordinates.

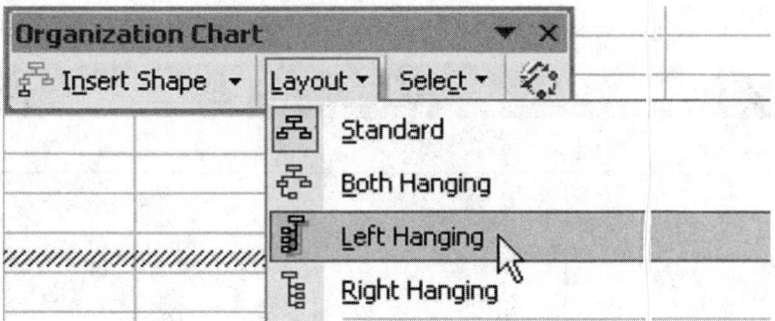

Fig. 1451

The subordinates and assistant for that VP will be arranged vertically, as shown in Fig. 1452.

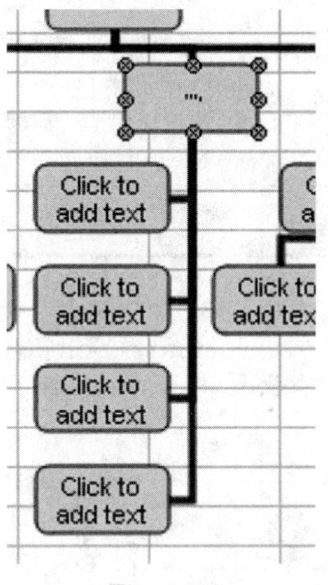

Fig. 1452

Part IV

As shown in Fig. 1453, select the AutoFormat button on the Organization Chart toolbar.

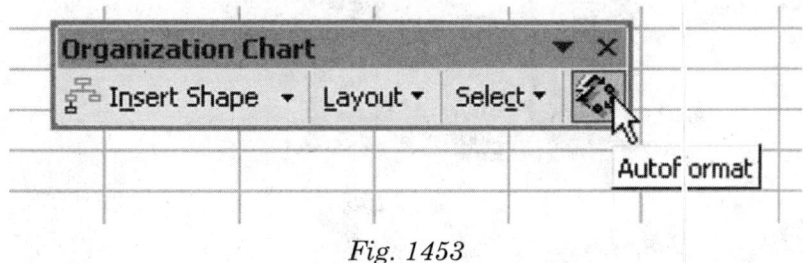

Fig. 1453

You have 16 different formats to choose from, as shown in Fig. 1454.

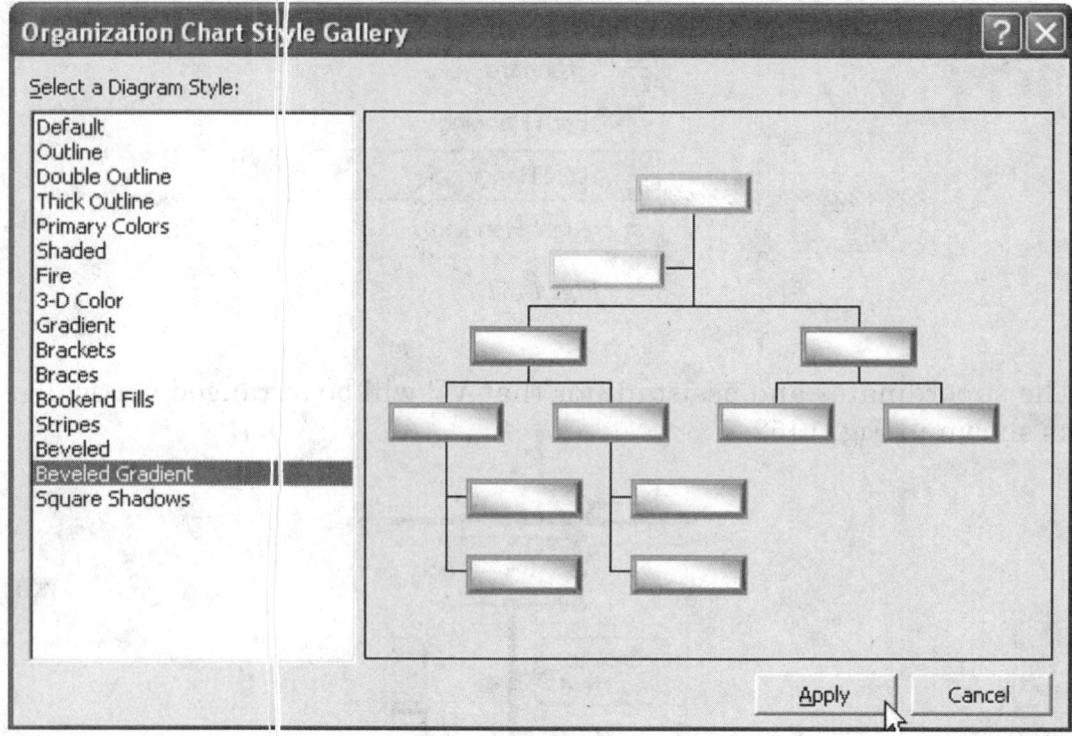

Fig. 1454

You can also create your own formats. Select the VP of Manufacturing. From the toolbar, choose Select – Branch, as shown in Fig. 1455.

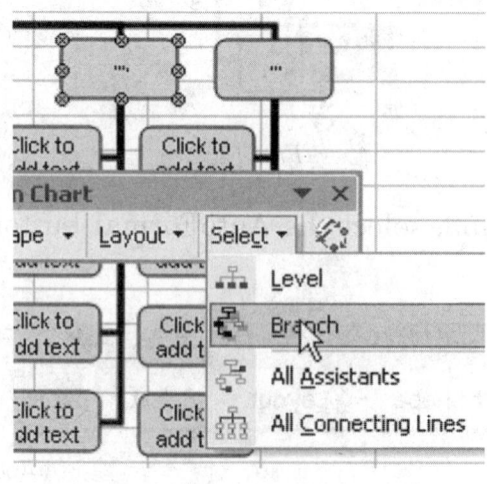

Fig. 1455

This will select the entire Manufacturing branch. You can now use the fill icon on the Drawing toolbar to change the color of that branch, as shown in Fig. 1456.

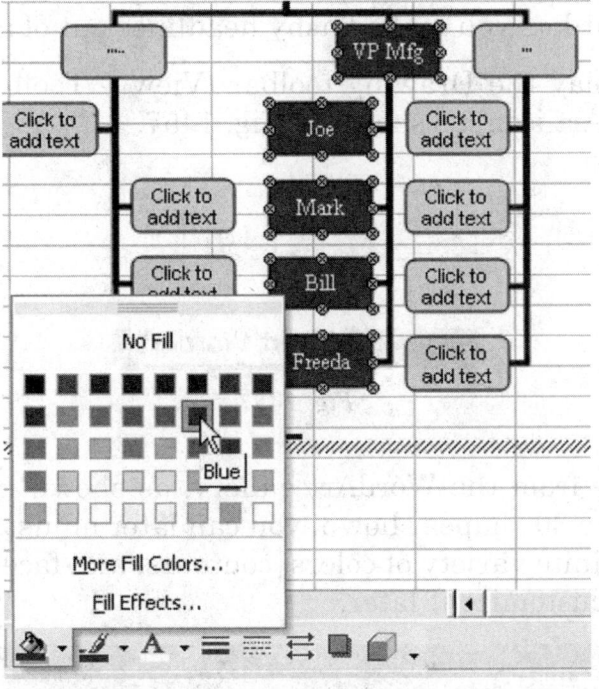

Fig. 1456

While a branch is selected, you can use the Font Size and Name dropdowns on the Formatting toolbar to change the font of the selected boxes.

Summary: You can use Excel to draw fairly complex organizational charts.

Commands Discussed: Insert – Diagram – Org Chart

ADD WORDART TO A CHART OR WORKSHEET

Problem: Create eye-catching spreadsheets by adding WordArt. Word-Art is a tool that lets you make flashy headlines out of any words.

Strategy: Display the Drawing toolbar (View – Toolbars – Drawing). Click the WordArt icon, as shown in Fig. 1457.

Fig. 1457

Choose a shape from the WordArt gallery, as shown in Fig. 1458. Although there are 30 shapes shown, you can later adjust these shapes in a seemingly infinite variety of colors, contours, and faces. Choose something now and customize it later.

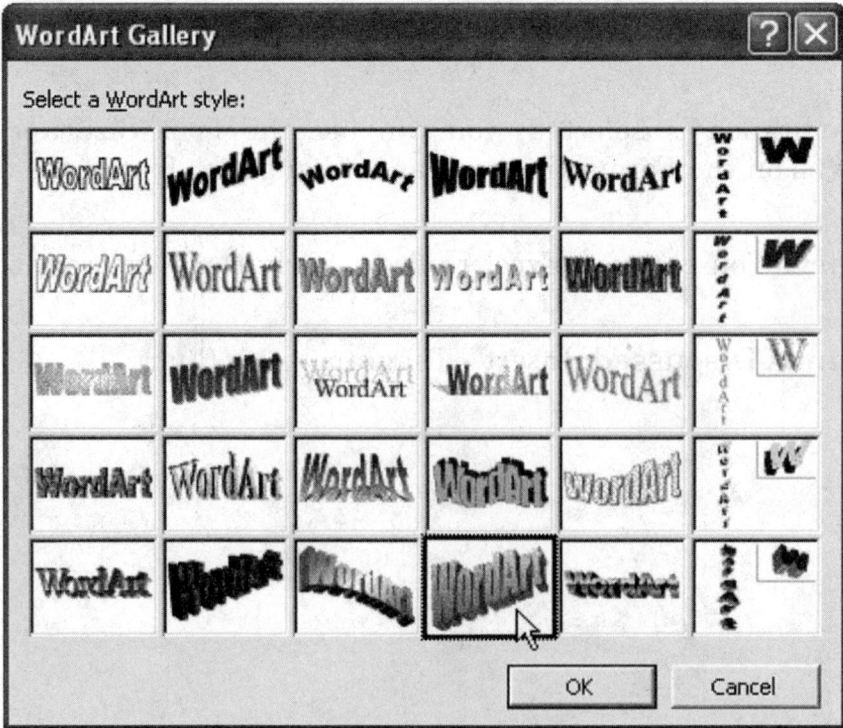

Fig. 1458

Next, you will be asked to enter the text, as shown in Fig. 1459. You can use the Return key to start a new line.

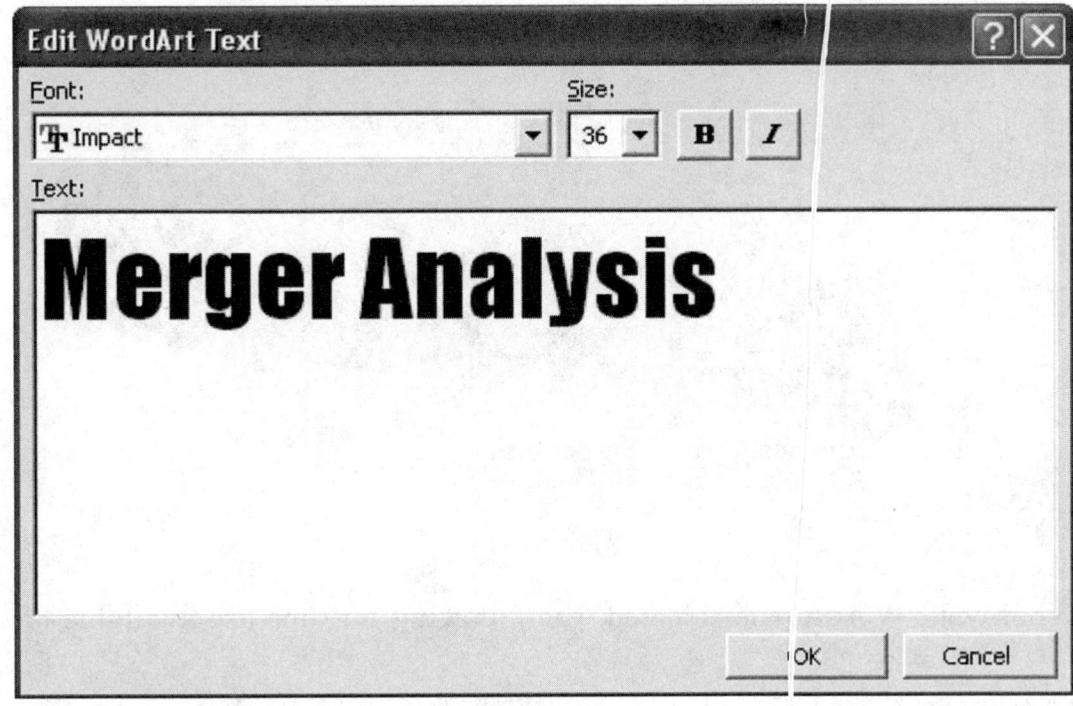

Fig. 1459

Click OK and the WordArt appears, as shown in Fig. 1460.

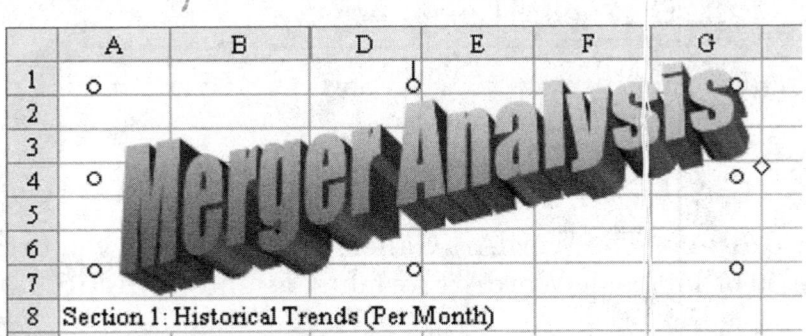

Fig. 1460

You will see handles to stretch or shrink the WordArt. You also will
often have a yellow diamond handle to adjust the amount of tilt of the
WordArt. As shown in Fig. 1461, in the following image, the WordArt
was stretched to the right, and the yellow diamond was moved down-
wards.

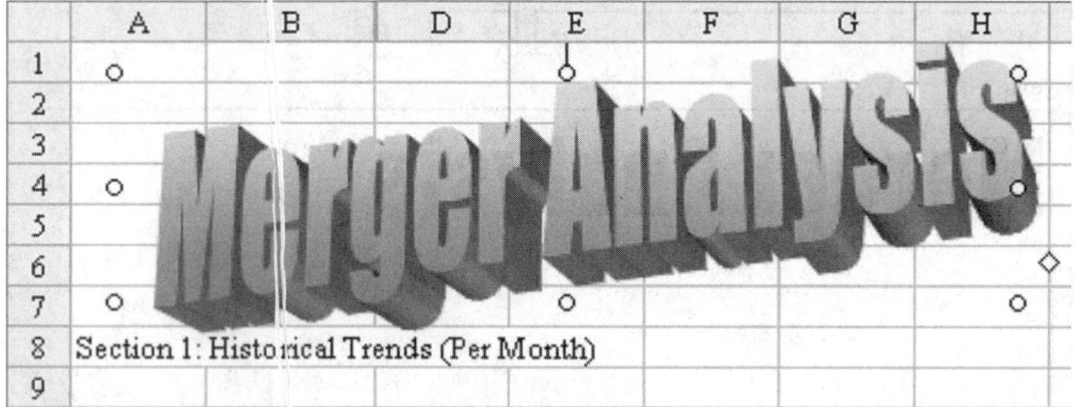

Fig. 1461

When your WordArt is selected, the following buttons are available on
the WordArt toolbar.

Edit Text: As shown in Fig. 1462, this button will allow you to edit the
text that makes up the WordArt.

Fig. 1462

WordArt Gallery: The WordArt Gallery button allows you to change to
one of the 30 other basic WordArt formats, as shown in Fig. 1463.

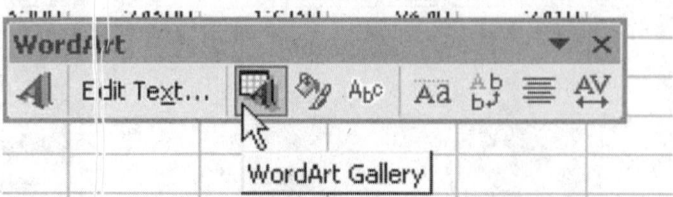

Fig. 1463

Format WordArt: Some of the WordArt shapes have a color for the letters and another color for the outline of the letters. You can change both of these colors in the Format dialog, as shown in Fig. 1464.

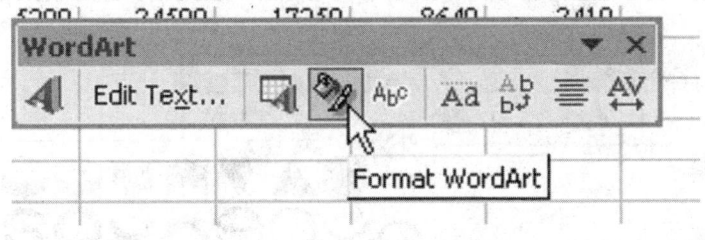

Fig. 1464

As shown in Fig. 1465, the Format dialog gives you options to change the color and, possibly, the line color. You cannot adjust the shadow color here.

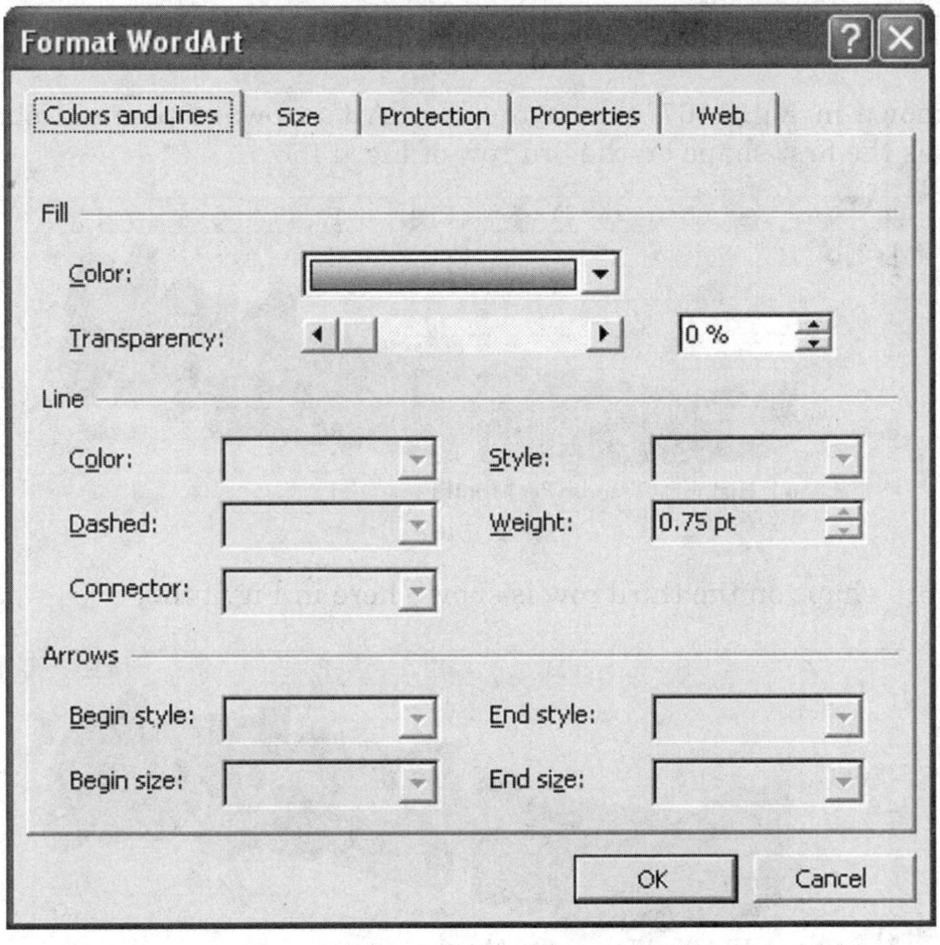

Part
IV

Fig. 1465

WordArt Shape: The WordArt Shape button allows you to choose from 40 different shapes for your WordArt, as shown in Fig. 1466. By choosing one of the 30 basic WordArt formats from the Gallery, you are selecting one particular shape. However, you can change the shape here.

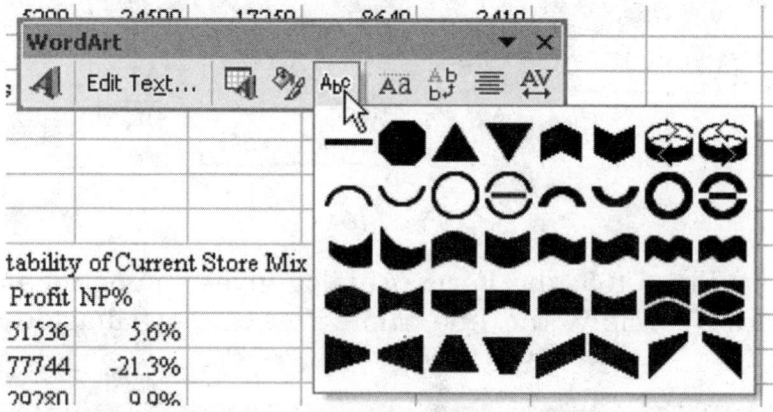

Fig. 1466

As shown in Fig. 1467, this is the WordArt's upward pennant shape. This is the first shape on the 3rd row of Fig. 1466.

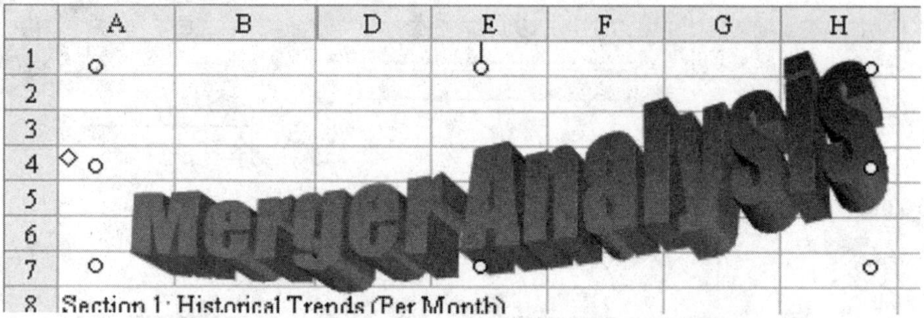

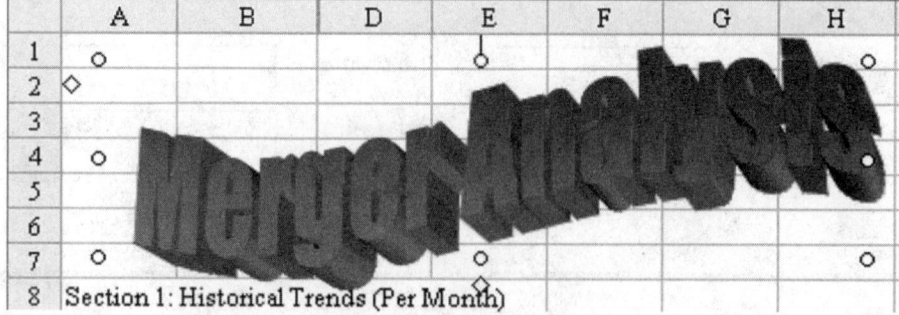

Fig. 1467

The 6th shape on the third row is shown here in Fig. 1468.

Fig. 1468

Same Letter Heights: The next button is to make all of the letters the same height, as shown in Fig. 1469.

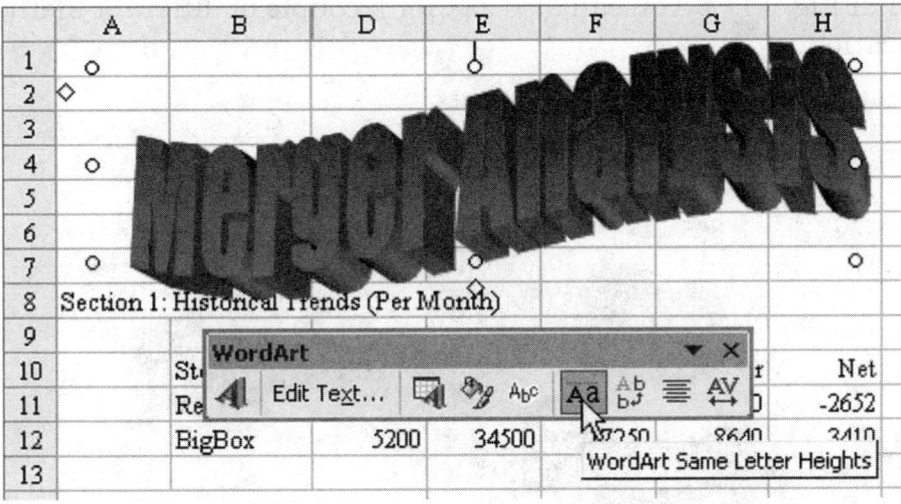

Fig. 1469

Vertical Text: The next button will make the type appear vertical instead of horizontal, as shown in Fig. 1470.

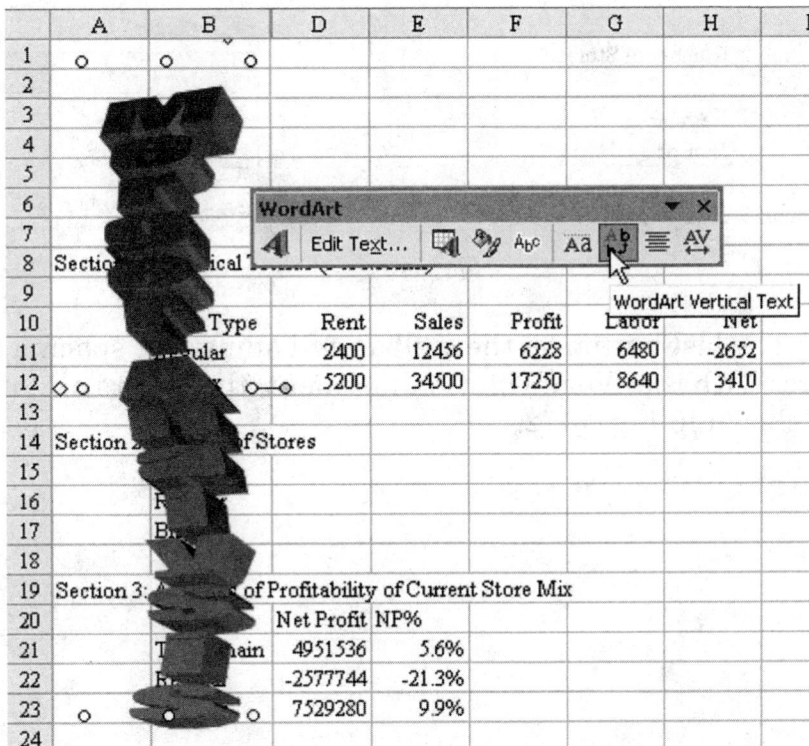

Fig. 1470

Align/Justify: If your WordArt consists of two lines of text, use the next button to indicate whether the lines should be left- or right-aligned, as shown in Fig. 1471. You can also ask for a couple of different methods of justification.

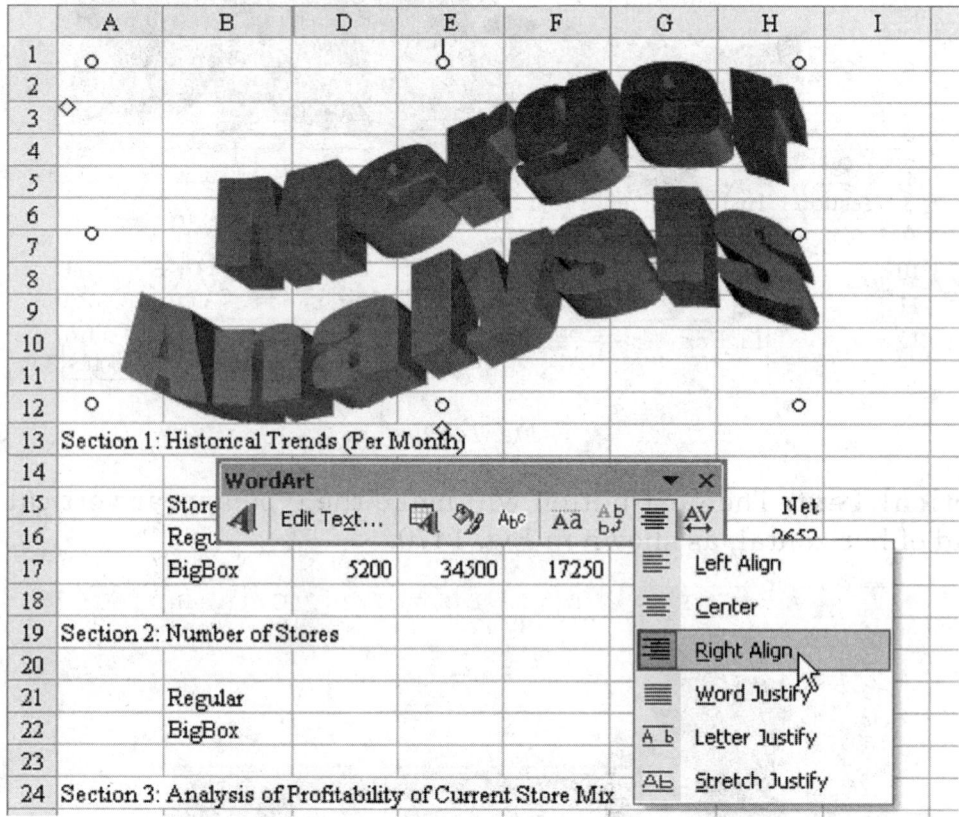

Fig. 1471

Spacing: The last button on the toolbar will adjust the spacing between characters. With the "Very Tight" adjustment, the letters all touch each other, as shown in Fig. 1472.

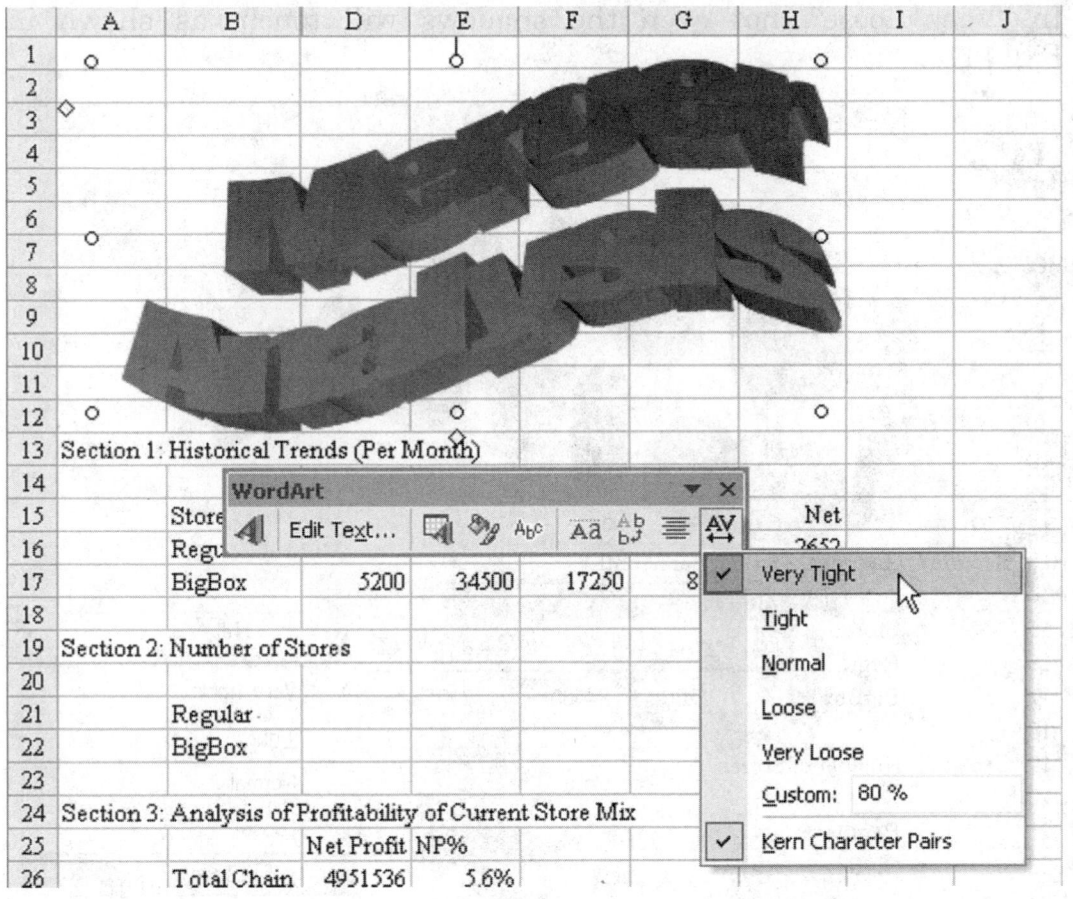

Fig. 1472

In "Very Loose", not even the shadows will touch, as shown in Fig. 1473.

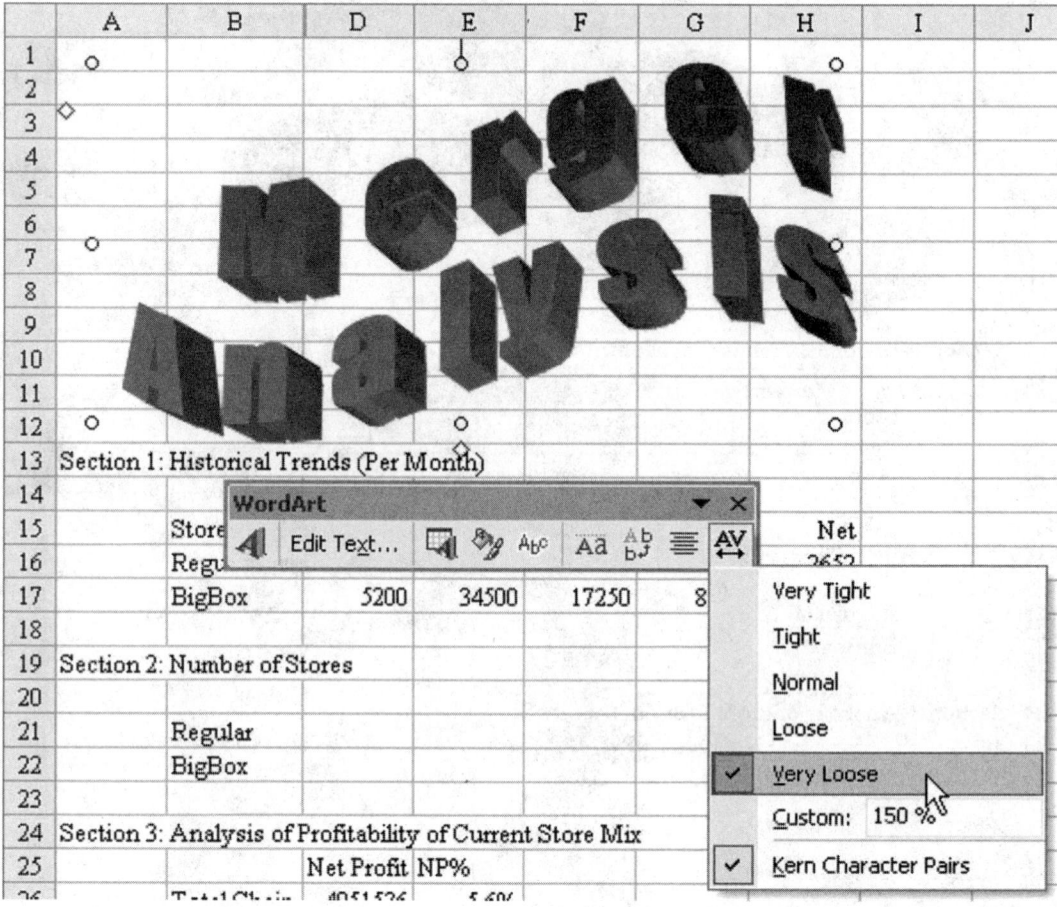

Fig. 1473

Some WordArt adjustments are made on the Drawing toolbar. To adjust the shadow or 3-D settings, use those buttons on the Drawing toolbar. A 3D effect is shown in Fig. 1474.

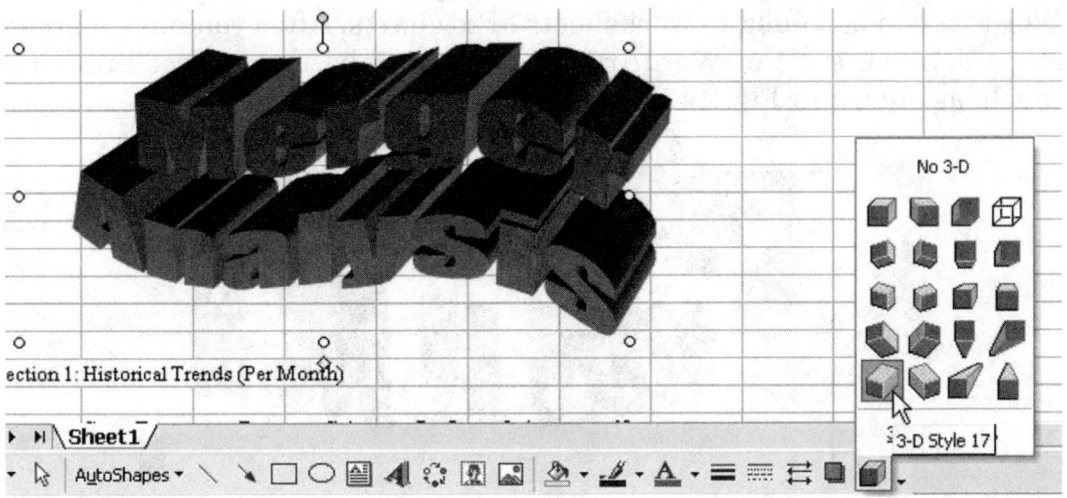

Fig. 1474

A shadow style is shown in Fig. 1475.

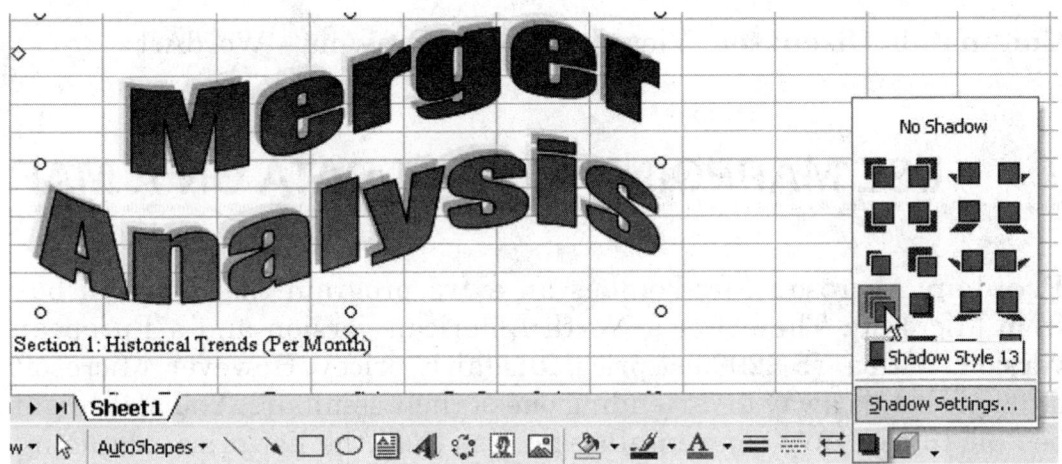

Fig. 1475

So, let's see – you have 30 basic WordArt Formats x 40 Shapes x (20 3-D + 20 Shadow) x 256 colors x 6 spacing. This yields about 73 million different variations of WordArt!

WordArt can be added to worksheets or to charts. After you have a great chart defined, a bit of WordArt for a title can be the perfect finishing touch, as shown in Fig. 1476.

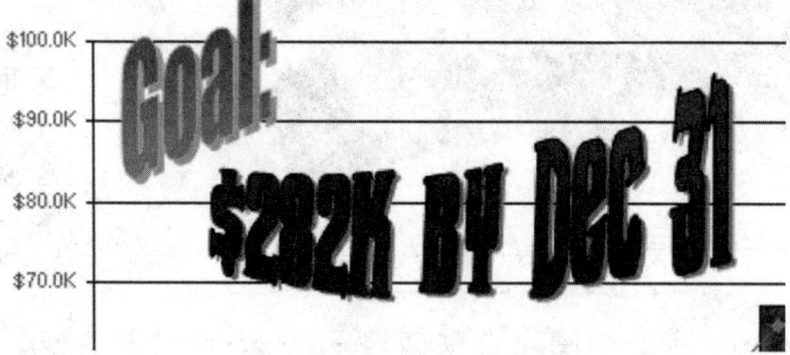

Fig. 1476

Summary: Using WordArt and its various options can make your worksheets and charts really eye-catching.

Commands Discussed: View – Toolbar – Drawing – WordArt

USE MAPPOINT TO PLOT DATA ON A MAP

Problem: Microsoft MapPoint is an extra program that you can buy from Microsoft. They offer a North American version and a European version. With a US $299 list price, it is fairly pricey. However, Microsoft often gives this away for attending one of their seminars. You also might be able to pick up a copy on eBay for less than the list price. MapPoint allows you to do some very cool geographic analysis of data.

Strategy: Let's say that you have a retail store and keep a mailing list of everyone who shops in your store. The data contains street address, city, state, and zip code, as shown in Fig. 1477.

	A	B	C	D
1	Address	CITY	STATE	Zip Code
2		AURORA	OH	44202
3		TWINSBURG	OH	44087
4		MCKEAN	PA	16426
5		AMHERST	OH	44001
6		GATES MILLS	OH	44040

Fig. 1477

Select the data, including the headings, and select the MapPoint symbol, as shown in Fig. 1478.

Fig. 1478

MapPoint will match your addresses to its database. Soon, you will have a map in Excel that shows your customers, as shown in Fig. 1479. This store had one customer from Alaska and several from Florida.

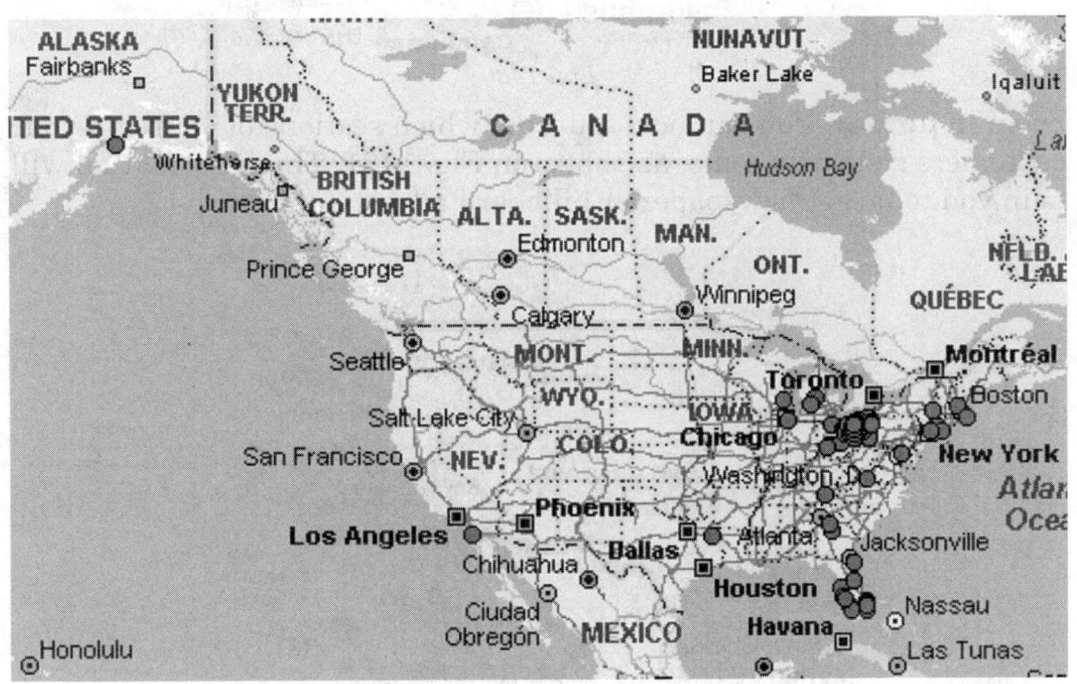

Fig. 1479

Click and drag to zoom in to the region around your store. You can see that you get a lot of customers from the local area, plus also people who travel the interstate. As shown in Fig. 1480, this store in Cleveland gets a fair amount of traffic from people who live along I-90, I-80, or I-76.

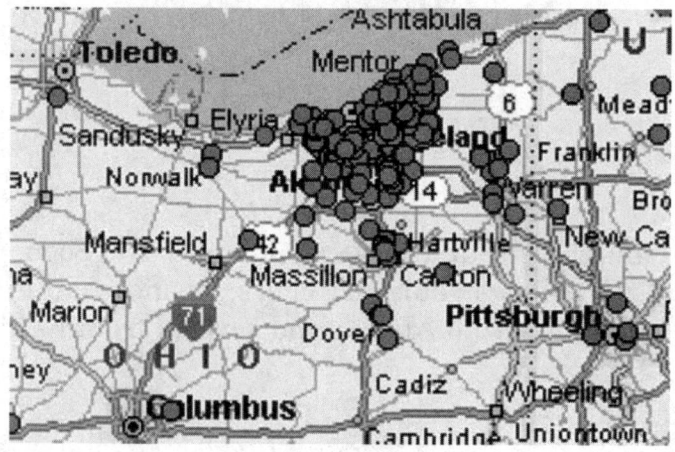

Fig. 1480

Zoom in further. You can now see from which sections of your city your customers generally come, as shown in Fig. 1481. This information will help you to target newspaper or billboard advertising.

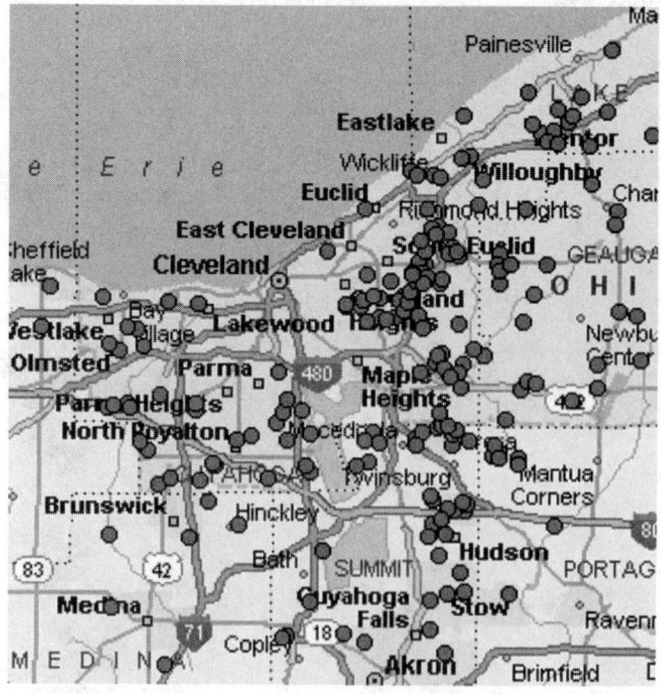

Fig. 1481

Gotcha: In several previous versions of Excel, Microsoft had a license to bundle a MapInfo product called Microsoft Map with Excel. Microsoft Map was taken out of the default install in Excel 2000 and removed from the product entirely in Excel 2002. The MapPoint product offers far more flexibility than Microsoft Map.

Summary: Plotting geographic data in MapPoint is a great way to get a visual of your customer base.

Commands Discussed: MapPoint icon

ADD A DROPDOWN TO A CELL

Problem: You need your sales managers to select a product from your product line. All of the pricing lookups in the worksheet rely on the product being entered correctly. You find that if you allow the manager to type an entry, they will find too many ways to misspell the item. You may be expecting "PDT-960", only to find they entered "PDT 960", "960", and many other variations, as shown in Fig. 1482. If you could offer them a list to select from, they would automatically select the correct spelling of the product.

Part IV

	C8		f_x	=IF(ISBLANK($B8),"",VLOOKUP($B8,$K$2:$M$6,2,FALSE))			
	A	B	C	D	E	F	G
1	XYZ Company Sales Order						
2							
3	Customer:						
4							
5	Qty	Item	Description	Unit Price	Ext. Price		
6	25	PDT-960	Data Entry Terminal with Scanner	795	19,875		
7	10	PDT-710	Data Entry Terminal - 512K	250	2,500		
8	125	PDT 960	#N/A	#N/A	#N/A		

Fig. 1482

Strategy: You can easily allow the manager to select from a list by using the Data – Validation command. It turns out that every cell has a data validation setting to allow any value. You can change this default setting.

1) Select a cell and choose Data – Validation from the menu, as shown in Fig. 1483.

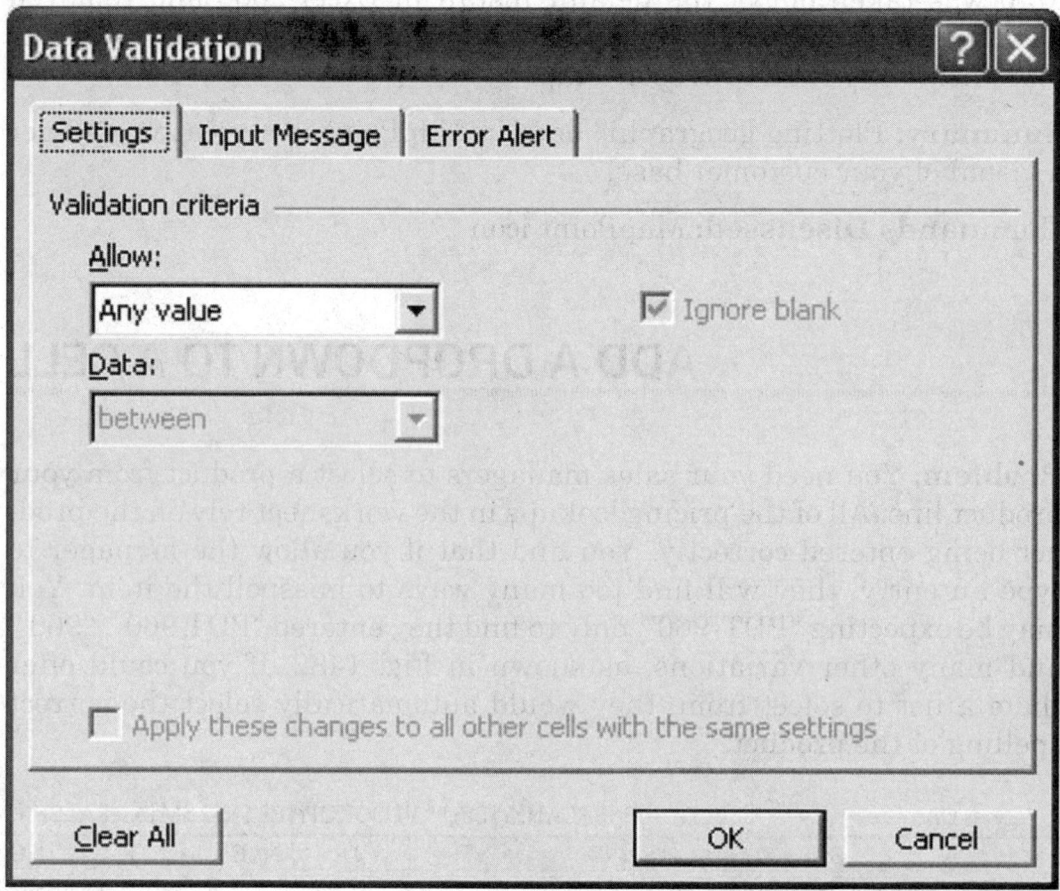

Fig. 1483

2) Choose the Allow dropdown and change "Any value" to "List". The checkbox for In-Cell Dropdown appears and is automatically checked, as shown in Fig. 1484.

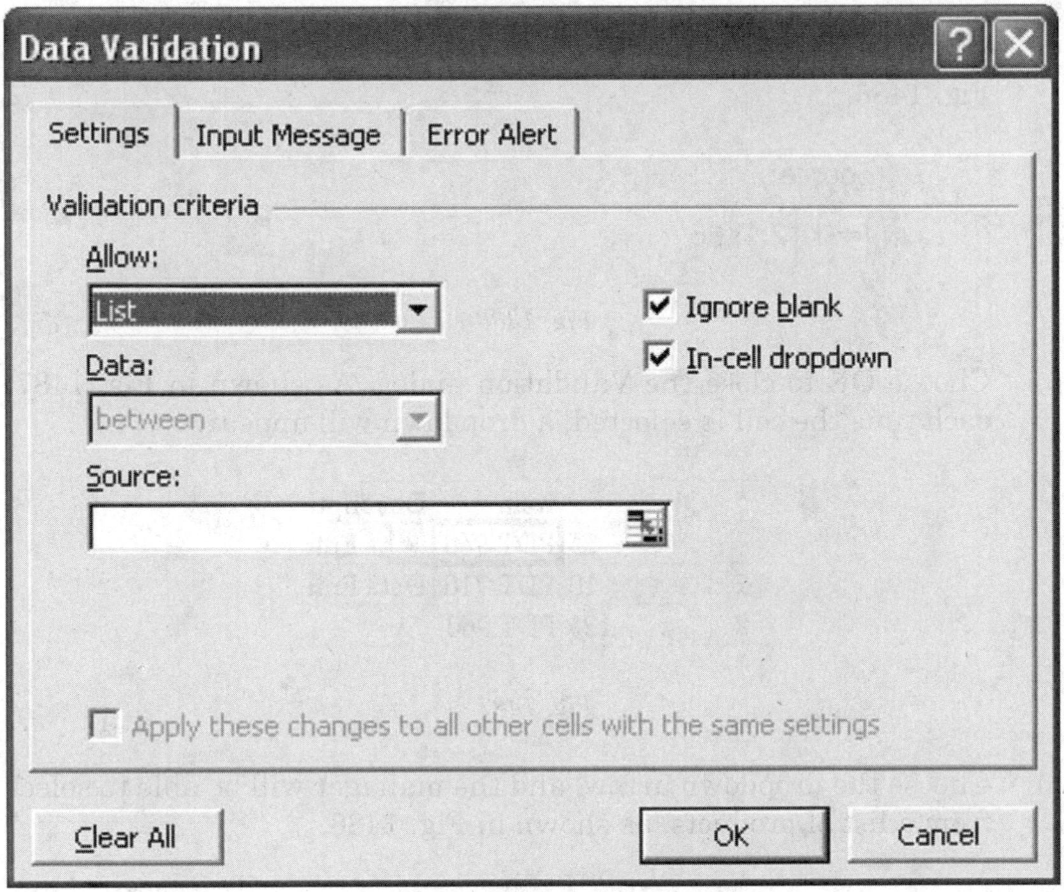

Data Validation ?☒

Settings | Input Message | Error Alert

Validation criteria

Allow:

List ▼   ☑ Ignore blank
          ☑ In-cell dropdown

Data:

between ▼

Source:

[   ]

☐ Apply these changes to all other cells with the same settings

Clear All   OK   Cancel

Fig. 1484

3) You can type your list right in the Source field, as shown in Fig. 1485. Or, if you already have the list of products on the worksheet, you can reference the range containing the list. This particular worksheet already has the valid products as the first column of a lookup table used to get prices.

Source:

PDT-600,PDT-610,PDT-710,PDT-860,PDT·

Fig. 1485

Part
IV

4) Select the Collapse button at the right end of the Source box and highlight the range containing the valid products, as shown in Fig. 1486.

Source:

=$K$2:$K$6

Fig. 1486

5) Choose OK to close the Validation dialog. As shown in Fig. 1487, each time the cell is selected, a dropdown will appear.

5	Qty	Item	Descripti
6	25	PDT-960 ▼	ta Entı
7	10	PDT-710	Data Entı
8	125	PDT 960	
0			

Fig. 1487

6) Choose the dropdown arrow, and the manager will be able to select from a list of products, as shown in Fig. 1488.

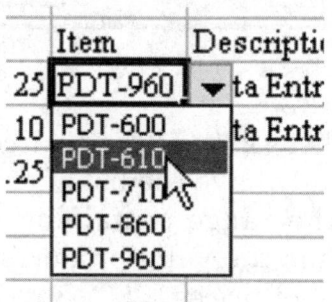

Fig. 1488

Additional Details: After you have set up the validation in one cell, you can copy it to other cells. Select cell B6 and hit Ctrl+C to copy. Select cells B7:B20. Select Edit – Paste Special – Validations.

Gotcha: I am always on the lookout for the sales manager who knows just a little too much about Excel. If the manager were smart enough to delete row 5, he could also delete row 5 of the lookup table off to the right.

Gotcha: In Excel 97, any validation cells that appear above the Freeze Panes area will not work.

Gotcha: If someone copies a bunch of cells from J10:J20 and pastes them over your validated cells in B, the validation will not work. Anyone can get an invalid value in the cell by using copy and paste.

Summary: Use the List option with Data Validation to provide a drop-down in the cell.

Commands Discussed: Data – Validation

STORE LISTS
FOR DROPDOWNS ON A HIDDEN SHEET

Problem: As shown in Fig. 1489, the Validation dropdown will not allow you to specify a list on another worksheet.

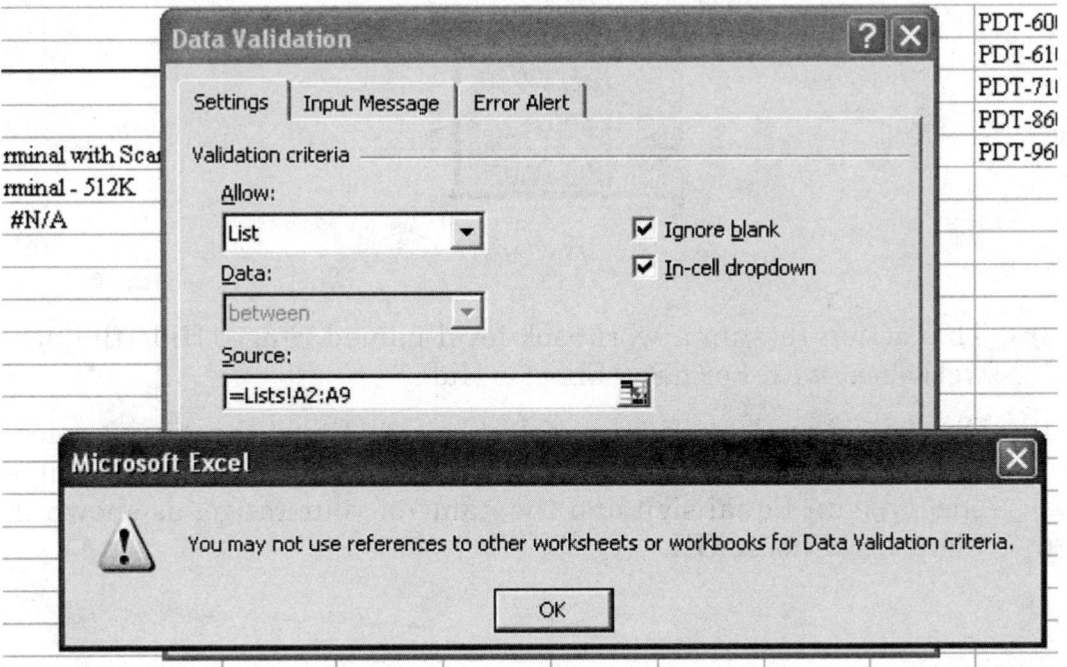

Fig. 1489

This forces you to keep your validation lists in an out-of-the way section of a current worksheet. No matter where you hide the list, someone manages to find a way to inadvertently delete items from it.

Strategy: There seems to be one workaround that works, at least up through Excel 2003. Follow these steps.

1) Insert a blank worksheet in the workbook. Type your list on this worksheet.

2) Highlight the list. Click in the Name box to the left of the formula bar. Type a name, such as ItemList, and hit Enter, as shown in Fig. 1490.

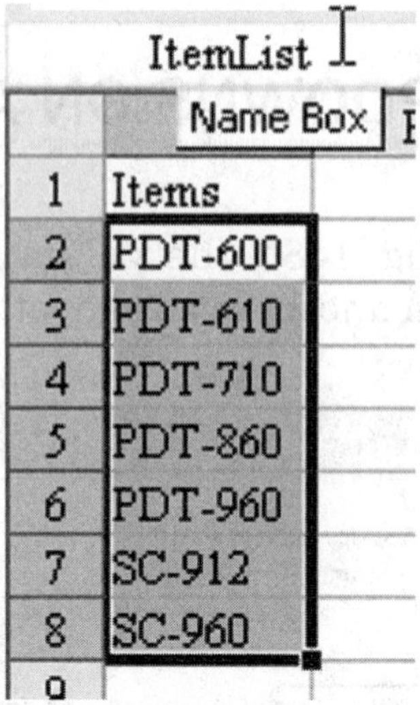

Fig. 1490

3) This action sets up a workbook-level named range. Hide the new worksheet with Format – Sheet – Hide.

4) On the original worksheet, select a cell. From the menu, select Data – Validation. Change the Allow box to List. In the Source box, type an Equal sign and the name of your range, as shown in Fig. 1491. Choose OK.

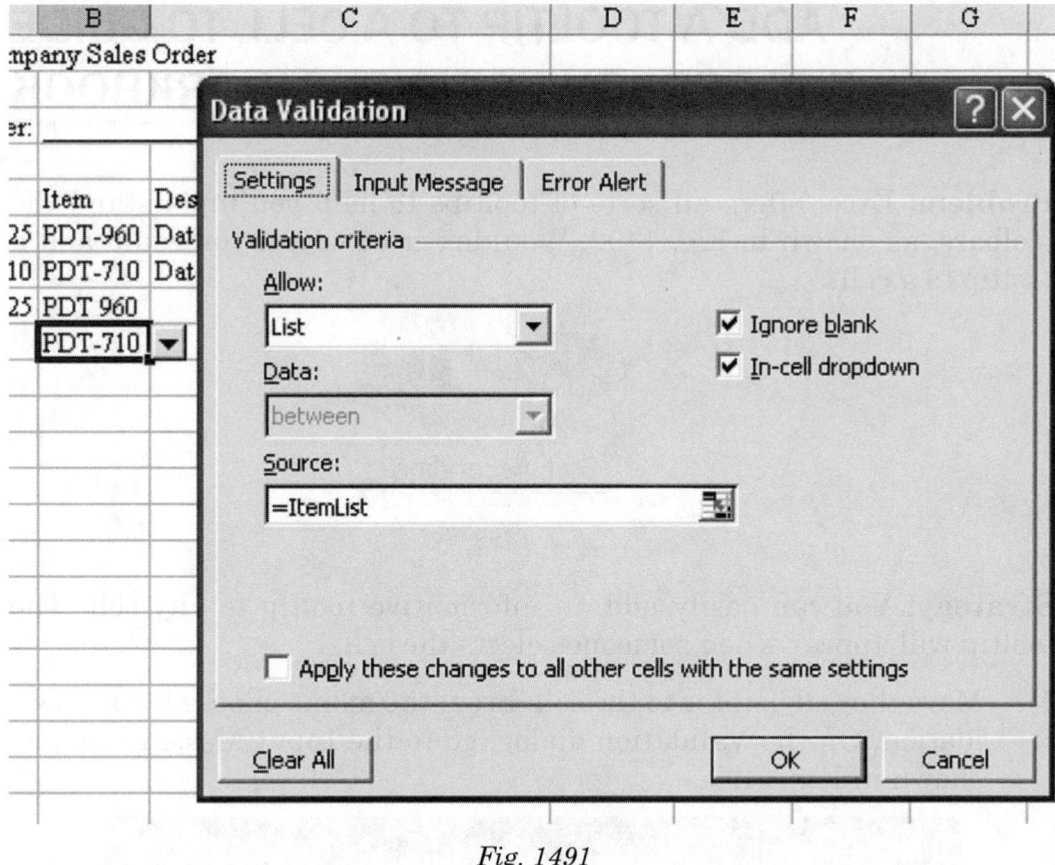

Fig. 1491

Result: The cell will have validation based on a range on another worksheet.

Summary: Although you cannot officially have validation lists on another sheet, by using a workbook-level named range, there is a workaround.

Commands Discussed: Data – Validation

ADD A TOOLTIP TO A CELL TO GUIDE THE PERSON USING THE WORKBOOK

Problem: Excel offers all sorts of tooltips to help you understand the toolbars, as shown in Fig. 1492. Wouldn't it be cool if you could add a tooltip to a cell?

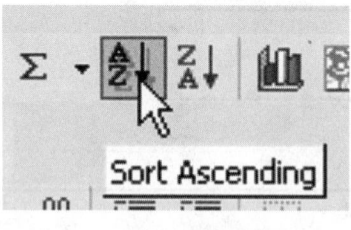

Fig. 1492

Strategy: You can easily add an informative tooltip to any cell. The tooltip will appear when someone selects the cell.

1)　Move the cell pointer to the cell. From the menu, choose Data – Validation. On the Validation dialog, go to the Input Message tab, as shown in Fig. 1493.

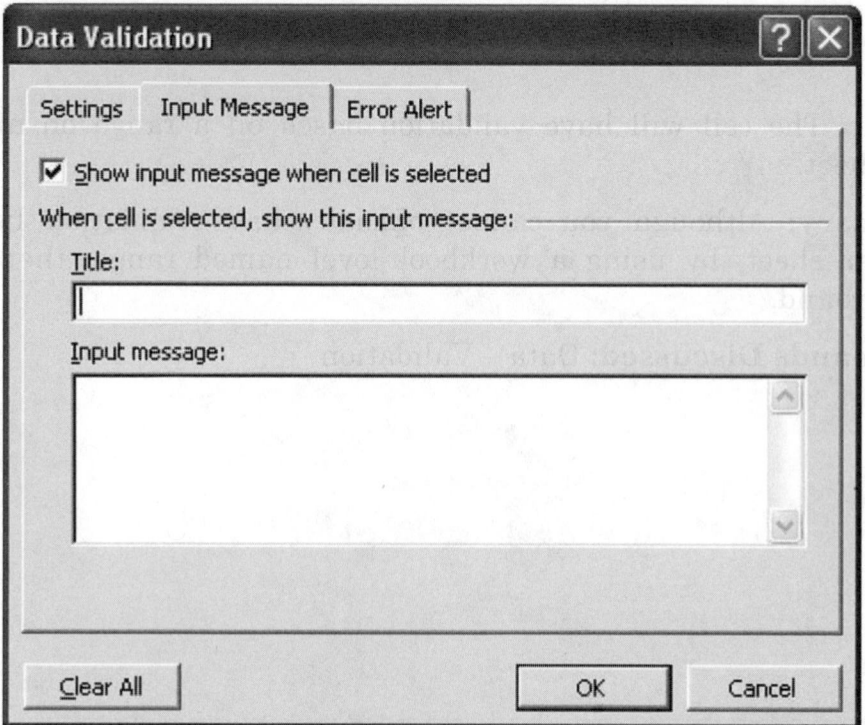

Fig. 1493

2) On the Input Message tab, type a title for the tooltip. In the message area, type instructions for the person filling out the worksheet, as shown in Fig. 1494.

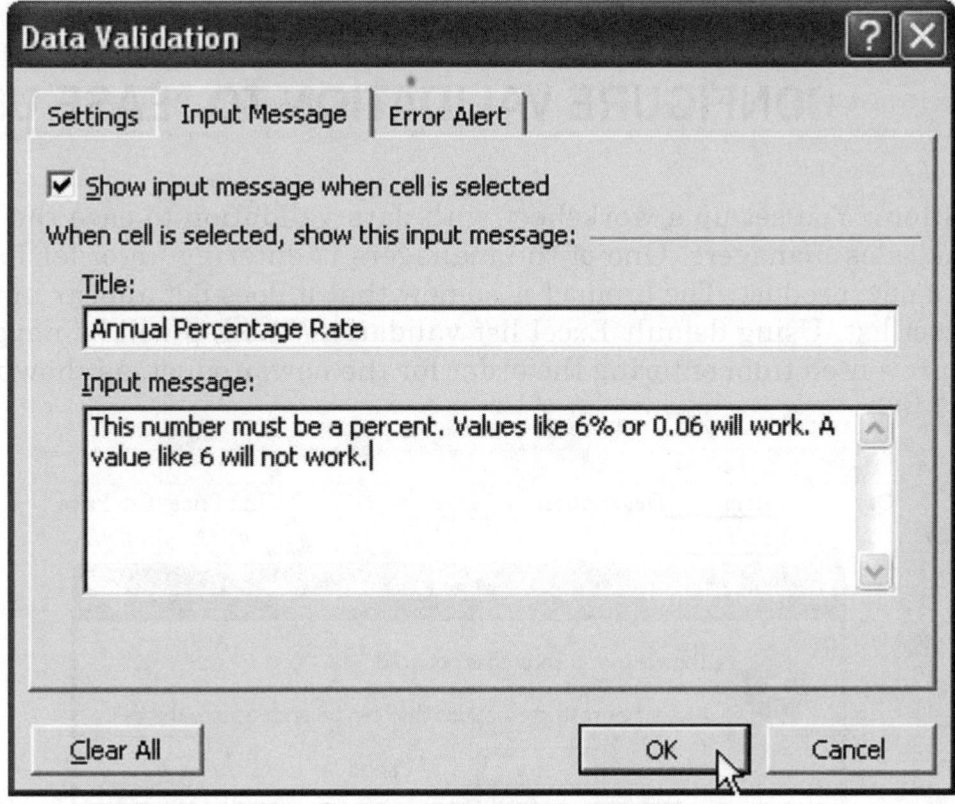

Fig. 1494

Result: When you move the cell pointer to that cell, an informative tooltip will appear, as shown in Fig. 1495.

	A	B	C	D	E
1	Loan Calculator				
2					
3	Amount Borrowed	25000			
4	Annual Interest Rate	5.90%			
5	Number of Months				
6					
7	Monthly Payment	$48			
8					
9					
10					

Annual Percentage Rate
This number must be a percent.
Values like 6% or 0.06 will work.
A value like 6 will not work.

Fig. 1495

Part
IV

Summary: Using the Input Message of the Validation dialog allows you to create helpful tooltips, which can appear in any cell.

Commands Discussed: Data – Validation

CONFIGURE VALIDATION TO "EASE UP"

Problem: You set up a worksheet with data validation to ease the job of the sales managers. One of the managers is entering an order for a brand new product. The product is so new that it does not appear in the product list. Using default Excel list validation, the rep will be nagged and prevented from entering the order for the new product, as shown in Fig. 1496.

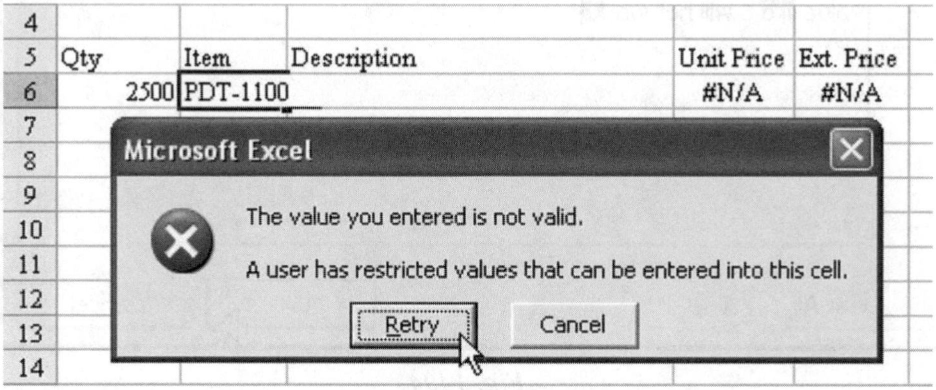

Fig. 1496

You can tell what will happen here. At the next sales conference call, the sales manager will say that he couldn't enter his $4.5 million order because the lousy spreadsheet wouldn't let him. As the spreadsheet designer, you will be demoted to manager of the "revenue prevention" department.

Strategy: There are three different settings on the Error Alert tab for Validation. By default, you get the hard-line version of the message, as shown in Fig. 1496. This is known as the Stop style of Validation.

> **Tip** *If you are ever the victim of a poorly designed spreadsheet that will not let you enter a value that you know is valid (i.e., you are smarter than the spreadsheet), the solution is to enter the value in an out-of-the-way location on the worksheet. Copy the value and paste it to the cell with validation. The validation will be defeated.*

On the Error Alert tab of the Validation dropdown, you can change the Stop to a Warning, as shown in Fig. 1497.

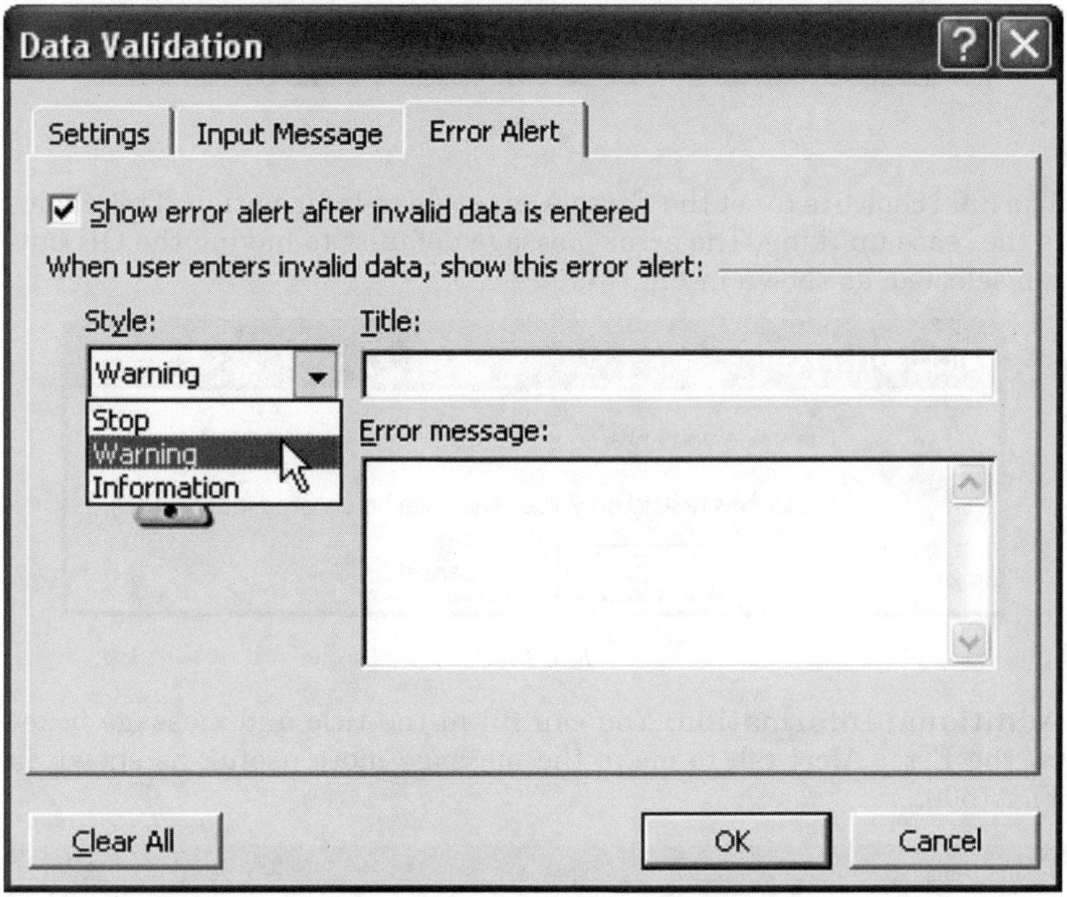

Part IV

Fig. 1497

In this case, the user is greeted with a dialog with three buttons. As shown in Fig. 1498, the Default button is No, but they can override to allow the value if they are absolutely sure.

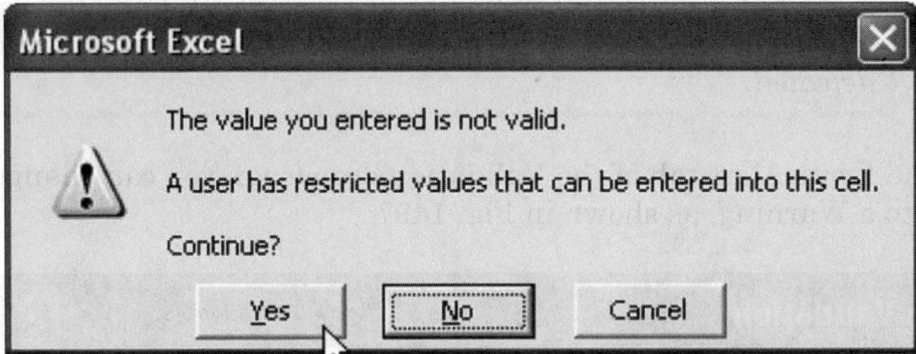

Fig. 1498

The final choice is to set the Error Alert style to Information. This choice is the "ease up" king. The error message defaults to having the OK button selected, as shown in Fig. 1499.

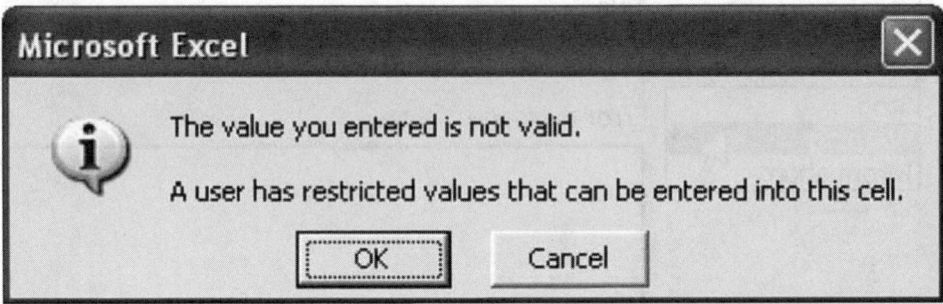

Fig. 1499

Additional Information: You can fill in the title and message boxes on the Error Alert tab to make the message more useful, as shown in Fig. 1500.

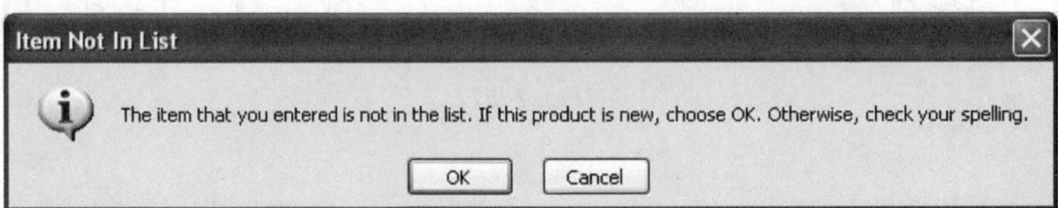

Fig. 1500

Summary: You can decide how strict to make the Validation by using the Error Alert tab on the Data Validation dialog.

Commands Discussed: Data – Validation

USE VALIDATION
TO CREATE DEPENDENT LISTS

Problem: You want to create two dropdown lists. The second list should be dependent on what is selected in the first cell.

Strategy: Use the INDIRECT function as the source of the second list. Follow these steps:

1) On a blank sheet, set up a list of items for the first dropdown: Reading, Science, Math, and Geography. Name the range "Subjects", as shown in Fig. 1501.

Fig. 1501

2) In another column, set up a list of choices available for reading.

3) Name this list Reading, as shown in Fig. 1502.

Fig. 1502

4)   Repeat Step 3 for each item in list 1, as shown in Fig. 1503. In each case, the name of the new range must match the value in column A.

	Math	▼	fx	Patterns		
	A	B	C	D	E	F
1	Reading	Construct Meaning	Physical Science	Patterns	American History	
2	Science	Extends Meaning	Chemistry	Problem Solving	Ohio History	
3	Math	Identifies Main Idea	Biology	Number Relations	Ancient History	
4	Geography	Identify Main Character	Earth Science	Geometry	Politics	
5				Algebra		
6				Estimation		
7						

Fig. 1503

5)   Set up the first dropdown list, where users will pick the subject. Select the cell. From the menu, select Data – Validation. Change the Allow box to be List; in the Source box, type =Subjects, as shown in Fig. 1504.

Fig. 1504

6) When you choose OK, cell D2 will have a dropdown list of subjects, as shown in Fig. 1505.

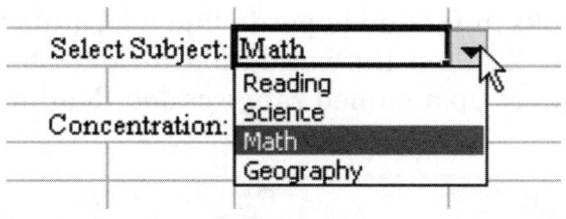

Fig. 1505

7) To set up the second dropdown, select cell D4. From the menu, select Data – Validation. Change the Allow: dropdown under Validation Criteria from Any Value to List. In the Source box, enter this formula: =INDIRECT(D2), as shown in Fig. 1506.

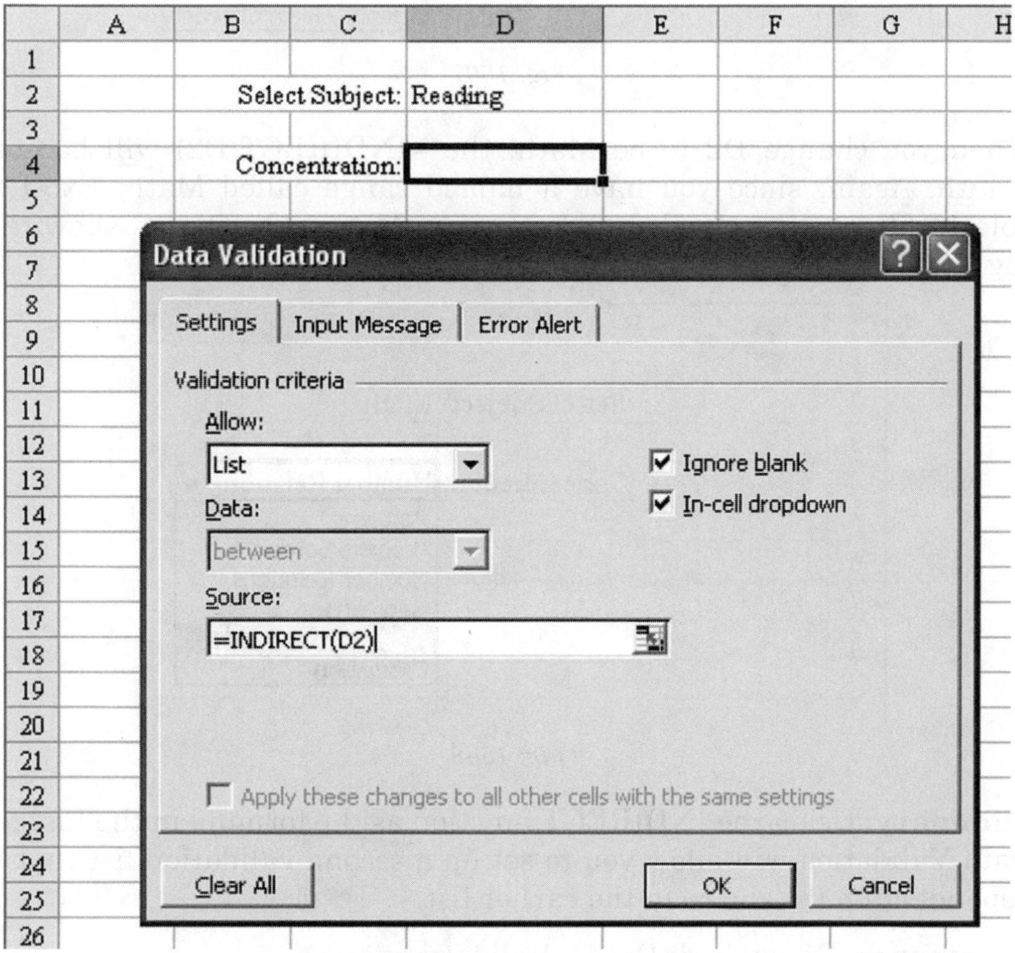

Fig. 1506

Part IV

Result: When you select a value in D2, the formula for the second drop-down list will automatically update, as shown in Fig. 1507. The INDIRECT function looks in D2 and hopes to find a formula there. When they select Reading in D2, then the validation formula becomes =Reading. Since you cleverly set up a named range called Reading, Excel is able to populate the list.

	A	B	C	D	1
1					
2		Select Subject:		Reading	
3					
4		Concentration:		Extends Meaning	
5				Construct Meaning	
6				Extends Meaning	
7				Identifies Main Idea	
				Identify Main Characte	

Fig. 1507

When you change D2 to be Math, the =INDIRECT(D2) will become =Math. Again, since you have a named range called Math, Excel is able to fill in the second dropdown with Math subjects, as shown in Fig. 1508.

	A	B	C	D	E
1					
2		Select Subject:		Math	
3					
4		Concentration:		Number Relations	
5				Patterns	
6				Problem Solving	
7				Number Relations	
				Geometry	
8				Algebra	
9				Estimation	
10					

Fig. 1508

Summary: Using the INDIRECT function as the formula in the List for Data Validation will allow you to set up a second validation list that is dependent on the choice in the earlier list.

Commands Discussed: Data – Validation

Functions Discussed: =INDIRECT()

There you have it – 277 problems and their solutions. Hopefully, you have found many that will make your experience with Excel far more efficient. Undoubtedly, you will still run into problems that are not in this book. Just as when I am teaching the Power Excel class, every new class brings new students with new problems. I invite you to send your problems to NotInTheBook@MrExcel.com. I'll try to get you an answer and your question might end up in the next edition of this book!